Responsibility, Ethics and Legitimacy of Corporations

Jacob Dahl Rendtorff

Responsibility, Ethics and Legitimacy of Corporations

Copenhagen Business School Press

Responsibility, Ethics and Legitimacy of Corporations

© Copenhagen Business School Press, 2009
Printed in Denmark by Narayana Press, Gylling

Book design, typeset and cover design by BUSTO | Graphic Design

1ˢᵗ edition 2009

ISBN 978-87-630-0220-2

Distribution:

Scandinavia
DBK, Mimersvej 4
DK-4600 Køge, Denmark
Tel +45 3269 7788, fax +45 3269 7789

North America
International Specialized Book Services
920 NE 58th Ave., Suite 300
Portland, OR 97213, USA
Tel +1 800 944 6190, fax +1 503 280 8832
Email: orders@isbs.com

Rest of the World
Marston Book Services, P.O. Box 269
Abingdon, Oxfordshire, OX14 4YN, UK
Tel +44 (0) 1235 465500, fax +44 (0) 1235 4656555
E-mail Direct Customers: direct.order@marston.co.uk
E-mail Booksellers: trade.order@marston.co.uk

IN THE MEMORY OF KNUD GUSTAV RENDTORFF

*

Table of Contents

Part 1
Introduction

1. Introduction

The legal and ethical development of values-driven management and corporate responsibility has been tremendous over the past ten to fifteen years. Many modern corporations have introduced ethics and compliance programs and values-driven management, taking not only stockholders but all of the firm's stakeholders into account. In many cases, reporting procedures and accountability programs for corporate and social values have also been introduced. Corporate boards see these measures as a means to ensure not only the responsibility and integrity of their organizations but also as markers of efficient management, competitiveness, and legitimacy in complex democratic societies. We can summarize this as an evolution towards a "new economy of corporate citizenship" that "brings together competencies from civil society, labor organizations, business, government, and international bodies."[1] In short, corporations that implement business ethics and values-driven management contribute to civil governance. In collaboration and dialogue with their stakeholders they become responsible for developing society through long-term social processes. We can say that corporations are changing their role in society, not only through new partnerships with governments, but also by making ethics, social responsibility, and participation in governance processes part of their core strategy. Accordingly, this book analyzes some theoretical and practical aspects of this trend, with the aim of developing a general theory of *corporate citizenship* based on business ethics and values-driven management. It also addresses the fundamental question of the extent to which we can conceive ethics, values, and responsibility as integrated with business strategy for good corporate citizenship in modern democracies.[2]

The impetus for this study arises, in part, from the increasing number of global challenges to corporate legitimacy. A closer integration of ethics and business seems especially necessary after many recent business ethics scandals in the United States and that have persuaded critical stakeholders to require increased social responsibility of corporations. Moreover, public discourse regarding norms, values, and responsibility has changed the social expectations of corporations and challenged basic concepts within business studies, sociology, political science, law, and philosophy. Many corporate executives, state representatives, consumers, members of the general public, and academic scholars call for a renewed emphasis on companies' values, prioritizing values-driven management, and defining good corporate citizenship as fundamental to their social responsibility. This is a tough challenge for management today.[3]

Box 1. Business ethics and corporate citizenship

While morality can be defined as the values, rules, and norms of everyday life, ethics can be defined as the deliberation on and justification of specific norms and values. In this context, business ethics is the theoretical and practical work to develop a well-justified morality for the function of business corporations in society.

Values-driven management is closely linked to business ethics. It represents an effort to formulate correct ethical values to govern the strategy of the firm, which is vital to the vision and mission of management. It is a condition for implementation of ethics in the corporation.

Corporate social responsibility (CSR) must, in this context, be considered as an integrated part of business ethics and values-driven management, because it relates to the fundamental responsibility that a corporation has towards its internal and external stakeholders and constituencies.

Corporate citizenship is the concept that ethical business relations are an essential contribution to the common good. It may, therefore, be understood as the fundamental bridge between business ethics, values-driven management, and corporate social responsibility.

This book integrates values-driven management, business ethics, and good corporate citizenship into a theory with practical consequences. The partial list of current business topics relevant to such theorization includes corruption, stakeholder management, socially responsible investing (SRI), finance ethics, corporate philanthropy, human rights, and public relations and the ethics of branding.

1. Background

The search for corporate citizenship and the effort to forge new relations between public and private bodies has been spurred by globalization (i.e., both the emergence of network society and global risks) and a consequent focus on common human problems, such as poverty, social inequality, and environmental degradation.[4] The evolution of international markets, easy and inexpensive communication structures, increased consumer awareness, wider distribution of risk, environmental awareness, and concern for global equality have put more emphasis on the social responsibility of corporations. In this environment, human rights standards and codes of ethical corporate conduct are being promoted by many business managers, nongovernmental organizations (NGOs), consumer movements, and democratic publics as indispensable for long-term sustainability and good corporate governance.[5] They argue that transparent communication and competitive market conditions require companies to engage in values-driven management in order to meet increasing stakeholder demands for worker security, high quality products, better community relations, and two-way dialogue about complex issues.

Many governments have introduced new policy instruments to incentivize corporate citizenship and corporate social responsibility. For example, the Danish government worked during the 1990s to create social partnerships between corporations and public authorities. Following contemporary international trends, there has since been increasing focus on corporate governance in Denmark.[6] In the United States, the *1991 Federal Sentencing Guidelines for Organizations* (FSGO) made company ethics and compliance programs a mitigating factor when sentencing corporate crime.[7] More recently, in 2002, the European Commission formulated a communication about corporate social responsibility based on an influential green paper on values-driven management. That policy paper, *Promoting a European Framework for Corporate Social Responsibility* (2001), was drafted following the policy proposals of the Lisbon Summit of the member states of the European Union in 2000. Its authors argued that although corporate social responsibility is a voluntary effort for European corporations it is nevertheless an important means to assure Europe's status as "the most competitive and dynamic knowledge economy in the world."[8] The international concern for corporate social responsibility can, furthermore, be seen in Kofi Annan's Global Compact principles, which proposed a United Nations code of conduct for business corporations, and the movement taken by the United Nations Human Rights Commission in 2004 to agree on principles and rules of conduct for multinational corporations regarding human rights.

There are two dominant interpretations of the rise of corporate social engagement, but neither fully captures the radical changes in the economy implied by the notion of corporate citizenship. The first, the so-called neoclassical paradigm of management explains ethics and corporate social responsibility as nothing but a new strategic instrument to ensure long-term shareholder value. As Milton Friedman wrote long ago: "The social responsibility of business is to increase its profits."[9] This position has recently been developed by authors like Porter and Jensen, who articulate arguments to demonstrate the irreconcilability of economic aims with broader social concerns.[10] Michael Porter argues that corporate philanthropy is only meaningful as a part of the economic strategy of a firm, while Michael Jensen maintains that it is logically impossible for a company to serve more than one objective. Although these kinds of arguments can be defended in order to emphasize the economic advantages of corporate social responsibility and the economic duties of corporations, they do not capture the broader role that corporate citizenship plays in society. In this view, increasing corporate emphasis on values and image remains nothing more than a device required by the competitive nature of economic globalization. Any other conception of responsibility is wrong because it violates the rules of fair markets.[11] Although it is important to focus on the economic dimensions of social responsibility, this view is too narrow to handle the political challenges faced by modern corporations.

From the opposite perspective, theorists with critical views on capitalism reduce values and corporate social responsibility to an ideological justification of market economics.[12] According to skeptical critics, the corporation has no responsibility. It is a perfect instrument for individuals and collectives to abstain from any social concern. In his critique of this perceived irresponsibility, Joel Bakan refers to the the collective body of the corporation as a "psychopath."[13] To Bakan, the corporation represents a "dangerous mix of power and unaccountability."[14] While he agrees with Friedman that a corporation is the property of shareholders who have a limited liability for externalities, in his view this leads to the psychopathological state of affairs wherein no one is really responsible in the corporation; it operates simply as an instrument to promote the owner's interests.[15] The doctrine of limited liability implies that, beyond legal strictures, the corporation has no inducement to behave ethically and will, therefore, always act as an immoral economic agent, playing the role of the stranger in civil society. One of this position's shortcomings is its inability to account for the real social concern of companies. It is somewhat ironic that critical theory seemingly works on some of the same presuppositions as the economic theory of corporate social responsibility. Critical authors posit that there is no substance to corporate concern with social goods like employee education, sustainability, and communal social welfare. Ethics becomes reduced to a strategic instrument used by corporations to motivate employees and fool consumers.[16]

This book argues that business ethics, values-driven management, and corporate social responsibility are standards of governance that make it possible to conceive of the corporation as both an economic instrument and a good corporate citizen. The starting point is the republican sentiment of the "good life with and for the other in just institutions," which is realized through the basic ethical principles of autonomy, dignity, integrity, and vulnerability.[17] This approach further argues that clarified values and the integration of corporate social responsibility with good corporate citizenship together provide what could be called a corporate "license to operate."[18] In other words, corporations should not be able to operate without ethical values and social responsibility. This approach frames basic principles for business ethics in sustainable development, here understood as a management strategy based on long-term concerns for the intergenerational, social, environmental, and economic effects of business decisions.[19]

This positive view argues that it is possible and worthwhile to monitor and evaluate a firm's "triple bottom line" of economic, social, and environmental performance.[20] Good corporate citizenship relies on the conception of corporate civic participation as a mutual benefit for the firm, its different partners, stakeholders, and other collaborators.

Box 2. Mintzberg and the need for business ethics and good corporate citizenship

In the aftermath of the attacks on September 11, 2001 and after the business scandals of Enron, WorldCom, and Arthur Andersen, management guru Henry Mintzberg, together with two colleagues, published a paper on his website where he addressed the importance of broadening the role of responsible management beyond self-interest and shareholder value.[21] Mintzberg and his colleagues argue that since the 1930s corporations have been told to be greedy and ignore social responsibility in favor of narrow shareholder value; thus Western society is based on what Mintzberg calls a set of half truths that have led to a syndrome of selfishness. These half-truths, or fabrications, of the selfish society are that: "1) We [westerners] regard ourselves as economic man; 2) Corporations seek to maximize shareholder value; 3) Corporations require heroic leaders; 4) The effective organization is lean and mean; and 5) A rising tide of prosperity lifts all the boats."

These fabrications can be said to constitute the myths of business and organizational theory that promote self-interest rather than business ethics and corporate social responsibility. In a speech to a crowd of European business leaders and academics Mintzberg has recently argued that while these myths are widely accepted, they may prove to be fatal for modern economics and lead to a general depression and crisis of the global business system.[22]

What is wrong with the first premise that each of us is economic man, *Homo Economicus?* It paints a picture of human beings as self-interested and rational decision-making machines who are only interested in utility maximization. This view is characterized by the position that there are no absolutes for economic rationality and that everything is possible to trade-off. According to Mintzberg, this view is incomplete, represents an inferior state of evolution, and ignores the human capacity of judgment.[23]

The second fabrication is premised on the idea that corporations do not serve society but rather exist solely to increase returns for their shareholders, who are viewed as the absolute kings of the corporation and corporate governance. But shareholders are distant owners of stocks who are separated from the daily operations of the firm and this leads to alienation and disengagement.

The third fabrication that corporations require heroic leaders posits the chief executive as the most important person in a firm's hierarchy. Inspirational and brave leadership is considered as essential in order to get good returns while managers are considered as important functionaries who deliberate economic strategies and allocate the human resources of the firm like machines. Heroic leadership is opposed to corporate ethical agents who act slowly, carefully, and collectively. The leader becomes metonymic for the collective unity of the organization.

The fourth fabrication could be considered as a result of the work of economic man. An efficient organization is one that has been downsized and where all unnecessary personnel have been fired, thereby increasing worker productivity. It is premised on the belief that pushing people and machines to their limits is the best way to run the economy.[24]

The fifth fabrication holds that this kind of self-interest maximization, represented by a lean corporation with heroic leadership, has the best promise of providing benefits at all levels of society. But this does not always hold up to empirical observation. As is widely evident in many Western societies, many people are getting richer but still more have to live with greater poverty. It is, therefore, necessary to combine economic growth and prosperity with some form of redistribution of wealth.[25]

While these myths are deeply entrenched, they can be overcome through the theory and practice of corporate citizenship. Instead of capitulating to their inevitability – which Mintzberg seems to have done by envisioning little possibility of escape – the paths of corporate citizenship, business ethics, and corporate social responsibility present viable alternatives.

2. Major theoretical concepts

Political scientists, economists, legal scholars, and ethicists conceive of values in organizations differently. This heterogeneity and complexity necessitates a review of the major research traditions of business ethics, corporate citizenship, and corporate social responsibility. Before doing so, it may be worthwhile to highlight salient aspects of the book's theoretical methodology, which is built on:

a) an interdisciplinary and second-order reflective comparison of different conceptions of and new expectations for value-based organizations;

b) a combination of heterogeneous research traditions in order to explore the particularity of corporate responsibility and the changing nature of corporate personhood, identity and social action;

c) a holistic picture of values in organizations, combining perspectives from both outside and inside the firm;

d) the presumed interdependence of micro- and macro-approaches to corporations in order to fully grasp the changing conditions of business in knowledge society;

e) a hypothesis that organizations and society mutually reflect each other in their mutual expectations of corporate performance.[26]

Here it should be stressed that this investigation combines three major theoretical approaches: 1) organization studies and institutional theory; 2) corporate social and political theory; and 3) business ethics and stakeholder analysis.

Organization studies and institutional theory are used to understand the meaning of values in organizations. They provide the framework for the investigation of values-driven management and business ethics in the organizational context.[27] This analysis examines the limitations and possibilities of dominant theories of business organization in order to understand value-based organizations. At the same time, it also looks at the meaning of individual values, judgments, cognitive processes, and morality as determined by particular organizational structures, life-forms, and cultures. Institutional theory is utilized to investigate how the conditions of economic systems and their interactions with other social systems have changed. This approach will also be applied to clarify the impact of values on corporate performance and organizational efficiency. Different economic, legal, and social values are implicit in decision-making, cognitive learning, and strategic priorities. Special emphasis will be put on the roles of values in theories of economic markets and oppositions between ethical values and economic values. Furthermore, the impact of values-driven management on economic actors and their different positions as consumers, investors, managers, workers et cetera will also be explored.

2) Corporate social and political theory lends valuable crossdisciplinary perspective to this discussion of values in organizations and corporate social responsibility.[28] Corporate political theory has worked with implicit and explicit concepts of corporate responsibility that have an impact on values-driven management. New developments in this area affect corporate politics and concepts of corporate personhood, liability, accountability, and responsibility, and challenge major theories of corporate responsibility in political thought, law, and social systems theory. The social implications of the new policy concept of corporate citizenship will be examined as an example of this process. In this context theoretical interpretations of the interaction between state regulations and corporate actions will also be clarified. Several questions will be posed, for example: How can political and legal systems support instruments for corporate social responsibility and values-driven management? The ascription of responsibility to individuals in corporations is an important issue with political aspects.[29] How does one draw the line between individual and collective responsibility? What are the limits to corporate legal responsibility? Corporate social and political theory will also be used to analyze business policies based on corporate responsibility at the national and international level in Denmark, the European Union, the United States, and the United Nations.

Business ethics and stakeholder analysis are research traditions that can help to clarify the normative dimensions of values in organizations.[30] Business ethics is an interdisciplinary research discipline with philosophical roots from Aristotelian skepticism towards earning money to Weber's Protestant ethics.[31] It differs from economic sociology and corporate social and political theory in its focus on the normative and moral presuppositions of different theories of institutions. While morality is concerned with existing norms and values, ethics is fundamentally normative, meaning that is addresses the rational justification of morality and questions of right or wrong. Business ethics also investigates the conception of values within legal and economic theory and problematizes the legitimacy of basic terms like profit maximization and property. Furthermore, it gives suggestions in order to define good business culture, management, or social justice. Accordingly, different theories of the responsibilities of organizations will be discussed. Normative business ethics helps to focus on ethical dilemmas in an enterprise in relation to stakeholders, corporate culture, or business conduct. The rights of different stakeholders will, therefore, also be examined, including the interests of consumers, managers, workers, and other interested parties.[32] Modern stakeholder analysis has emerged out of the business and society movement, public relations research, basic philosophical research, and different theories about organizational stakeholders or interested parties.[33] An overriding concern of this section is how different ethical theories can be combined in order to better understand how various social structures and values set the conditions for economic action.

The task to produce a systematic theoretical study of how business ethics, values-driven management, and corporate social responsibility are integrated in good corporate citizenship is relevant both to academics and business practitioners. The synthetic and general approach adopted here stands in opposition to many other related studies and articles by considering values and ethics in an integrated and holistic framework. While many business school and universities in Europe and the United States approach one aspect of the topic, there are few research environments producing comprehensive interdisciplinary theoretical research. There is a developed tradition of business ethics and also of institutional theory, but few texts have brought the two into dialogue. The importance of an integrated social scientific approach to business ethics will be underscored by concrete discussions of codes of conduct, mission statements, values-driven management programs, ethical accounting, and the reporting procedures of different companies.[34]

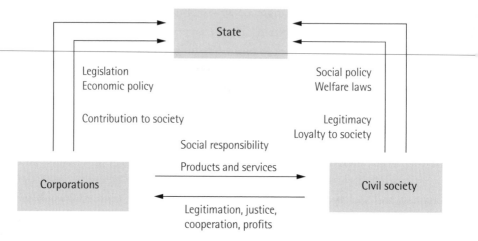

This model illustrates the relation between state, business, and civil society in a welfare state with market economy
Source: (Verstraten 2000, 178)

3. Research methodology: Scope and boundaries

This kind of theoretical social research can generally be described as a form of *social theory* in which the researcher – using argumentation and personal creativity – combines ideas and theories in a systematic way. Following the proposal by W. Laurence Neuman, this kind of social theory can be defined as a collection of approaches that produce "a system of interconnected abstractions or ideas that condense and organize knowledge about the social world."[35] Theoretical social science stands in contrast to empirical qualitative and quantitative research methods, which are based on a methodology that analyzes systems of ideas and specific relationships in order to produce knowledge about the world. This book relies on theoretical analysis and literature review in the relevant fields.

More specifically, the theoretical research informing this analysis can be defined as hermeneutical or interpretative social science. This approach goes back to the sociological theory of Max Weber who was inspired by the tradition of German hermeneutics from Schleiermacher to Dilthey.[36] The hermeneutical method asks fundamental questions about the meaning of social action and of human beings in society. It is an ideographic approach that analyzes meaning from an historical comparative perspective.[37] The approach in this book is based on the critical hermeneutic philosophy of Paul Ricœur.[38] For Ricœur, the process of understanding is a process of *distanciation* where the social theorist interprets the textual conceptualizations of social reality.[39] In this context, the use of critical hermeneutics implies not only interpreting the meaning of different forms of theoretical argumentation about business ethics, but also looking critically at how social reality is conceived in business ethics texts.[40]

Ricœurian critical hermeneutics operates in the space between the precomprehension of belonging to a historical tradition, as expressed in the *Wirkungsgeschichtlichen Bewusstseins* of Hans Georg Gadamer, and Jürgen Habermas's critical theory of emancipation from ideological repression.[41] This position argues – in a critique of Gadamer – that hermeneutics should not only look for meaning, but also be critical towards unjust forms of domination in society. It similarly differs from Habermas by asserting that critical theory cannot abandon meaning.[42] Critical social science does not only operate within the ideographic universe of interpretation of meaning, but it also investigates the limits of proposed concepts by asking "embarrassing questions" and using "the transformative power" of science to create the basis for a new and better social reality.[43] Critical hermeneutics combines insights and elements from different theoretical traditions in order to make a loyal presentation of their views, but also to submit those views to critical investigation and discussion.[44] According to Ricœur critical hermeneutics oscillates between belonging to a tradition and critical distanciation from it through utopian critique of its ideological presuppositions.[45]

This theoretical argument does not contribute to the quantitative or qualitative empirical measure of the long-term impact of corporate social responsibility on the performance of the firm. Though business processes are discussed, there is no comprehensive empirical study of particular corporations, their mission statements, codes, or corporate practices. When case studies from the literature or real life are used, they are proposed as concrete illustrations of the theoretical argument in order to indicate that it is possible to establish close links between theory and practice.[46] The case studies were selected according to how well they illustrate the theoretical argument and how well they clarify or generally typify the problem discussed. They can be further broken down into cases that: *a)* illustrate an *ethical crisis* or scandal in a corporation; *b)* illustrate an *ethical dilemma* or a hard choice faced by the corporation; and *c)* illustrate a strong *ethical effort* by the corporation to build corporate integrity and citizenship.[47] When dealing with company material, the method of critical hermeneutics also uses discourse analysis in order to clarify its strategic intentions.[48] Accordingly, the analysis and presentation of the cases is not based on observation of empirical social reality, but rather on the discussion of ideas and concepts linked to the empirical social reality of the corporations.[49]

The book is structured in five major chapters. Chapter one is this introduction. Chapter two presents the foundations of values-driven management and argues for the need for business ethics and social responsibility in a global postindustrial society. Chapter three elaborates corporate citizenship in relation to the internal and external constituencies of the firm and to the concepts of environmental, social, and economic sustainability. Chapter four presents an analysis of the concrete developments of values-driven management and social responsibility in Europe and the United States, and also with regard to the efforts of corporations to develop codes of conduct and guidelines for business ethics. Finally, as a culmination of the analysis in the different sections, chapter five accomplishes the aim of the book expressed in the idea of strategizing global business ethics by proposing basic ethical principles for a sustainable strategy for business ethics and corporate social responsibly.

Box 3. Expectations and criticisms of corporations

The research importance of the relationship between business ethics, corporate citizenship, and the political legitimacy of corporations has been connected to high public expectations. A 1999 poll by the firm Environics showed very high expectations for corporate social performance and social responsibility among citizens in different countries. Over seventy percent of those participating mentioned the importance of high employee security and protection, the equal treatment of employees, banning corruption and child labor, and environmental protection as very important things that companies should respect. More than sixty percent emphasized paying taxes, job security, and worldwide respect for high standards as high priorities. The following illustrates some of the damages that companies who do not respond to these expectations may expect to face:

The vicious circle of criticism
The actions and symbols of corporations in their social environment→
Interpretations of those actions and symbols→
Critical responses from the social environment→
The companies ignore those criticisms and responses→
Greater mistrust and sceptical attitudes toward corporations→

Interpretations of those actions and symbols→

Negative expectations of corporations and increased scepticism and criticism

**To overcome the vicious circle with help from business
ethics and good citizenship**

The actions and symbols of corporations in their social environment→

Interpretations of those actions and symbols→

Critical responses from the social environment→

Proactive strategy directed towards increased social responsibility from corporations→

Growing recognition from the social environment→

Long-term strategic focus on good corporate citizenship from corporations→

Increased recognition and trust from the social environment of corporations→

Positive interpretations of the actions and symbols of the corporation

Endnotes

1   James D. Wolfensohn, "Foreword" In *Perspectives on the New Economy of Corporate Citizenship*, edited by Simon Zadek, Niels Hojensgard and Peter Paynard (Copenhagen: The Copenhagen Centre, 2001). See also Simon Zadek, *The Civil Corporation. The New Economy of Corporate Citizenship* (London: Earthscan, 2001), 10.

2   In order to focus on the importance for business ethics for strategy, I use the term strategizing to indicate that this investigation ends up with a proposal for a strategy for good integration of business and ethics. The term strategizing can be considered "as the complex, contextual interplay that takes place within firms, outside firms, and between firms". See Claus Nygaard, *A Reader on Strategizing* (Copenhagen: Samfundslitteratur, 2001). See also Malcolm McIntosh, Deborah Leipziger, Keith Jones, Gill Coleman, *Corporate Citizenship, Successful Strategies for responsible companies* (London: Financial Times, Pitman Publishing, 1998).

3   John Hendry, *Between Enterprise and Ethics. Business and Management in a Bimoral Society*, (Oxford: Oxford University Press, Oxford 2003, 32.

4   Simon Zadek, *The Civil Corporation. The New Economy of Corporate Citizenship* (London: Earthscan, 2001), 13.

5   John Elkington, *Cannibals with Forks. The Triple Bottom Line of 21st Century Business* (Oxford: Capstone (1997), 1999). See also Richard Welford, *Environmental Strategy and Sustainable Development. The Corporate Strategy for the 21st Century* (London: Routledge, 1995).

6   Erhvervs- og selskabsstyrelsen, *Nørby udvalgets rapport om Corporate Governance. God selskabsledelse i Danmark* (Copenhagen, 2001). Jørgen Valter Hansen, Thomas Riise Johansen and Teddy Wivel, *Corporate Governance- Et bud på danske bestyrelsers rolle* (Copenhagen: Forlaget Thomson), 26ff.

7   Jeffrey M. Kaplan, Joseph E. Murphy and Winthrop M. Swenson, *Compliance Programs and the Corporate Sentencing Guidelines, Legal Manual* (New York, 1994-2002).

8   European Commission. Directorate-General for Employment and Social Affairs, Industrial Relations and Industrial Change, Unit EMPL/D.1, *Promoting a European Framework for Corporate Social Responsibility, Green Paper* (Luxembourg: Office for Official Publication of the European Communities, 2001).

9   Milton Friedman, "The Social Responsibility of Business is to increase its profits", *New York Times Magazine*, September 3, 1970. Reprinted in Scott B. Rae and Kenman, L Wong, *Beyond Integrity. A Judeo-Christian Approach to Business Ethics* (Grand Rapids Michigan: Zondervan Publishing House, 1996), 241-246.

10 Michael E. Porter and Mark R. Kramer, "The Competitive Advantage of Corporate Philanthropy" in *Harvard Business Review on Corporate Responsibility* (Harvard, Cambridge, Massachusetts: Harvard Business School Press, 2003). Michael C. Jensen, "Value Maximization, Stakeholder Theory and the Corporate Objective Function" in *Unfolding Stakeholder Thinking*, edited by J. Andriof (New York: Greenleaf Publishing, 2002). See also Michael Jensen: "A Theory of the Firm, governance, residual claims and organizational forms", *The Journal of Financial Economics*, 1976.

11 In his treatise on management, Peter Drucker also addresses the issue of responsibility from the point of view of efficiency of management. See Peter Drucker, *Management. Tasks, Responsibilities, Practices* (Oxford: Butterworth, Heinemann, 1974).

12 Naomi Klein, *No Logo. Taking Aim at the Brand Bullies*, (New York: Picador, Saint Martins Press, 2000).

13 Joel Bakan, *The Corporation: The Pathological Pursuit of Profit and Power* (London: Constable 2004), 16.

14 Ibid: 27.

15 Ibid: 79.

16 Alain Etchegoyen, *La valse des ethiques* (Paris : Le Seuil, 1991). Gilles Lipovetsky, "Les noces de l'éthique et du business", *Le Débat*, numéro 67, (1991), novembre-decembre, 145-167.

17 In *Soi-même comme un Autre* (Katheleen Blamey, trans., *One Self as Another* (Chicago: University of Chicago Press, 1992), 172), Paul Ricœur develops this idea as the aim of ethics based on the primacy of ethics over the moral norm. The ethical intention *"aiming at the 'good' life with and for others, in just institutions"* includes three basic components. First is the Aristotelian idea of the "good" life, or the true life, defined as a practice of fulfilling an aim according to the standards of excellence as defined by wise judgment (i.e., phronesis) (Aristotle: *Nichomachean Ethics*, 1.1.1009a1-3). Ricœur understands the aim of the good life as commensurable with the aim of narrative unity in one's lifelong self-interpretation. The second component is that the good life is aimed "with and for others." Ricœur refers to the concept of *solicitude* that is advanced as the horizon of the good life approaches, whereby friendship with "esteem of the other as one self and esteem of one self as the other" becomes a matter of necessity (Ricœur 1992, 194). The third aspect of the ethical aim is "just institutions." Ricæur emphasizes ethical primacy over legal formality in the definition of institutions. To take part in an institution presupposes belonging to a community, people, or nation. In this space of life together, common action, decision-making, justice, and equality are important concerns. Just institutions can distribute roles and merits without equalizing everybody in everything (201-202).

18 Simon Zadek, Niels Hojensgard and Peter Paynard, *Perspectives on the New Economy of Corporate Citizenship* (Copenhagen: The Copenhagen Centre, 2001).

19 Andrew Crane and Dirk Matten, *Business Ethics. A European Perspective*, (Oxford: Oxford University Press, 2004), 22.

20 John Elkington: *Cannibals with Forks. The Triple Bottom Line of 21st Century Business*, (Oxford: Capstone (1997), 1999).

21 Henry Mintzberg, Robert Simons and Kunal Basu, "Beyond Selfishness", *Sloan Management Review*, Vol 44 (2002), No. 1: 67-74.

22 Paper of a speech delivered at the First Meeting of the European Academy of Business in Society at INSEAD, France, 2002.

23 Henry Mintzberg, Robert Simons and Kunal Basu, "Beyond Selfishness", *Sloan Management Review*, Vol 44 (2002), No. 1: 67-74.

24 Ibid.

25 Ibid.

26 These different points of view on the methodology of business ethics, as well as many other elements of the discussion, were developed in conversation with members from the research group on values in organizations at Roskilde University. Some of the points are developed in Susanne Holmström, *Grœnser for ansvar - Den sensitive virksomhed i det refleksive samfund* (Roskilde: Center for værdier i virksomheder, Skriftserie, RUC 5/2004).

27 Powell, Walter W. and Paul J. DiMaggio, *The New Institutionalism in Organizational Analysis*, (Chicago: The University of Chicago Press, 1991).

28 My aim is to situate business ethics within a political theory based on elements of political philosophy and political economics. The conceptual vocabulary of political philosophy (e.g., democracy, justice, fairness, etc.) and the theorization of justice developed by thinkers such as Ricœur, MacIntyre, Rawls, and Habermas have much to give the study of business ethics. As corporate citizens, businesses and states face many similar problems. Of course, there are fundamental differences between states and business organizations, for example that the former are non-voluntary organization while the latter are voluntary, these should be seen as differences in

degree rather than kind. This is indicated by the fact that authors who disagree about whether states and business organizations are fundamentally different seem to agree that the application of political theory in business ethics is very useful. See Robert A. Philips and Joshua D. Margolis, "Toward an Ethics of Organizations", *Business Ethics Quarterly* 9: 619-638; Jeffrey Moriarty, "On the Relevance of Political Philosophy to Business Ethics", *Business Ethics Quarterly* Volume 15, Issue 3.

29 Peter French, *Collective and Corporate Responsibility*, (New York: Columbia University Press, 1984).

30 Archie B Carroll and Ann K. Buchholtz, *Business and Society. Ethics and Stakeholder Management*, (Canada: South Western, 2002), Simon Zadek, Peter Pruzan and Richard Evans, *Building Corporate Accountability*: (London Earthscan, 1997).

31 Thomas Donaldson and Thomas W. Dunfee, *Ties that Bind. A Social Contracts Approach to Business Ethics* (Boston Massachusetts, Harvard Business School Press, 1999).

32 Al Gini, *My Job, My Self, Work and the Creation of the Modern Individual* (Chicago: Routledge, 2000).

33 Edward R. Freeman, *Strategic Management, A Stakeholder Theory of the Modern Corporation* (Boston Massachusetts Pitman Publishing Inc., 1984); Kenneth Goodpaster: "Business Ethics and Stakeholder Analysis", *Business Ethics Quarterly*, 1, 1991. R. Grey, R and D. Owen, *Accounting and Accountability Changes and Challenges in Corporate Social and Environmental Reporting*, (London: Prentice Hall, Europe, 1996).

34 Dawn-Marie Driscoll and W. Michael Hoffman: *Ethics Matters. How to Implement Values-Driven Management*, (Waltham Massachusetts: Center for Business Ethics, Bentley College, 2000).

35 W. Lawrence Neuman: *Social Science Research Methods. Qualitative and Quantitative Approaches*. Fifth Edition, (Boston and New York: Pearson Education, 2003).

36 Ibid: 76.

37 Ibid: 76.

38 Paul Ricœur, *Du texte à l'action. Essais d'herméneutique II* (Paris: Le Seuil, 1986), 345.

39 Paul Ricœur, "La function herméneutique de la distanciation" in Paul Ricœur, *Du texte à l'action. Essais d'herméneutique II* (Paris: Le Seuil, 1986), 95.

40 Some qualitative researchers may be surprised that I define hermeneutics as the pure study of texts and not as a form of qualitative phenomenological field study like grounded theory, ethnomethology, practice studies, field studies, et cetera, which provide tools for a qualitative approach to studying empirical reality. I am sympathetic to these approaches, but while they can help to understand ethics in practice, the object of this study is discursive. There are therefore no qualitative phenomenological or hermeneutic field studies in this book.

41 Paul Ricœur, *Du texte à l'action. Essais d'herméneutique II* (Paris: Le Seuil, 1986), 102.

42 This references the famous debate between Gadamer and Habermas about hermeneutics and the critique of ideology, published in *Hermeneutik und Ideologiekritik*, edited by Jürgen Habermas, (Frankfurt am Main:Suhrkamp Verlag, 1971). In fact, although the opposition between hermeneutics and critique of ideology was very strong at that time, Habermas later acknowledged that he was closer to the position of Gadamer than he had originally argued. In this sense, the concept of critical hermeneutics captures very well the essence of the tension between the two social science methodologies.

43 W. Lawrence Neuman, *Social Science Research Methods. Qualitative and Quantitative Approaches*. Fifth Edition, (Boston and New York: Pearson Education, 2003), 82.

44 Øjvind Larsen, *Den samfundsetiske udfordring*, (Copenhagen: Hans Reitzels forlag, 2005).

45 Paul Ricœur, *Du texte à l'action. Essais d'herméneutique II* (Paris: Le Seuil, 1986), 102.

46 The corporations proposed in these cases have been carefully selected according for their paradigmatic value and theoretical relevance. The cases were drawn from important business ethics textbooks; the membership rosters of international organizations for business ethics and corporate social responsibility such as Global Compact, the European Academy for Business in Society, and CSR Europe; and controversial and scandalous examples from public debates. An effort was made to balance European with some American cases in order to vary the picture of business ethics and corporate social responsibility in practice. Justifying the selection on the basis of qualitative evaluation requires a long discussion. Here, it important to remember that the cases – selected based on inductive aspects of grounded theory – should be read as illustrative of the theoretical argument. For a discussion of the concept of qualitative research see W. Lawrence Neuman, *Social Science Research Methods. Qualitative and Quantitative Approaches*. Fifth Edition, (Boston and New York: Pearson Education, 2003), 143 and 146.

47   I disagree with the common criticism of the case study method that it represents only the author's subjective point of view; rather, the cases can be conceived as a concrete illustration of Ricœur's concept of interpretation. See Paul Ricœur, *Du texte à l'action. Essais d'herméneutique II* (Paris: Le Seuil, 1986). Cases may also be understood as a "matter of principles," using a term from Ronald Dworkin's legal theory, in the sense that they express difficult cases that put business ethics to the test. See Ronald Dworkin: *Law's Empire,* (Cambridge MA: Harvard University Press, 1986). See also Chris Megone and Simon J. Robinson (eds.): *Case Histories in Business Ethics* (London: Routledge, 2002). The cases should be read as narrative illustrations of specific problems in business ethics. This is done in order to show the relevance of the theoretical discussion for the practice of business ethics in organizations. See also Hans Klein (ed.): *Case Method. Research and Application, Selected Papers of the Sixth International Conference on Case Method and Case Method Application,* (Waltham, MA: Bentley College, 1989)

48   Anders Bordum and Jacob Holm Hansen: *Strategisk ledelseskommunikation. Erhvervslivets ledelse med visioner, missioner og værdier* (Copenhagen: Jurist og Økonomforbundets forlag, 2005), 25-63.

49   We may characterize this kind of case material as "secondary data," which is collected by other business ethicists, companies, government, or other sources. The increasing number of cases and amount of empirical research in business ethics in recent years in itself helps to justify the use of such secondary data in business ethics. See Christopher J. Cowton, "The Use of Secondary data in business ethics", *Journal of Business Ethics 17* (1998): 423-434.

Part 2
Globalization, values–driven management, and business ethics

1. Values, markets and global capitalism

Our time has been interpreted as the age of global capitalism. At the end of the cold war and under the blessings of a new *Pax Americana,* multinational corporations can operate safely and maximize profits all over the world. But there are also great cultural challenges to the Western market economy. Beginning with the September 11, 2001 attacks and continuing through the war against Iraq, the waves of terrorism have been interpreted as a desperate reaction on the part of poor people in other cultures against the capitalist Western world. Although it may be difficult to find any coherent political expression in terrorism it can still be considered as a possible consequence of global economic inequality and destabilization.

Critics of globalization argue that cynical corporations with growing power are replacing investments and factories around the world according to maximal returns without any responsibility for the environment or social justice.[1] Because of this, there has been an increased focus on the values and responsibilities of corporations in global society. While globalization has been accompanied by increasing liberalization of world markets and a weakening of the power of nation-states, it has also heralded the emergence of a transnational civil society with its own laws.[2] This new transnational customary law is based on cooperation between private individuals and organizations rather than on explicit agreements among state actors, the United Nations, or other international public institutions. These world legal institutions are based on commercial and maritime historical rules and norms that have been constantly evolving towards a common civil society.[3]

The institutional dimension of this development is the formation of a less formal but also more comprehensive "world law" among different civil society and private actors. It involves not only international law between states, but also international private customary law, based on a plurality of civil norms that have evolved in the process of the globalization of the world economy.[4]

Because these norms are not exclusively a result of the processes of state legislation and authority, the field of world law is determined by the actors' willingness to contribute to the common good. As nation-states promote the liberalization of national and international markets, they lose the power to sanction laws and regulations; transnational companies have, therefore, an important role to play in contributing to the formation of this world law. Business ethics becomes, in turn, an important factor for building and stabilizing national and international market institutions. Because of this power, multinational corporations are being required by civil society and the international community to increase focus on their social responsibility and ethical values.

1.1. Universalization of capitalist market economy

Globalization is a fact of the present world economy. After the duality of the cold war system the new world order is based on market capitalism. The international system might be said to have gone from a bipolar to a multipolar and pluralistic system, though in many ways it resembles the one-system world of the nineteenth century. Some argue that we are moving towards an age of global empire.[5] But the present world system is also qualitatively different from the colonial system. Globalization is a dynamic social phenomenon of global development of the market economy. It is based on science and technology in a way that radically change the human life-world and cultural conditions of existence.[6] The international exchange of goods and services is rapidly increasing. Liberalization means that free trade and market competition are becoming dominant. This situation represents a challenge to nation-states. Because they do not have the same ability to operate at the international and global level as in their national economies, they become evermore dependent on corporate social responsibility.

Motivated by liberal governmental reforms of the world economy to promote free trade, it has become possible for most large companies to operate at a transnational level in the global market. They operate on the basis of computer technology and electronic monetary exchange as they navigate a global network society consisting of new and more flexible organizational forms.[7] At the international economic level, multinational corporations face not only increased freedom but also eonomic competition and global economic responsibility.[8] In this context it becomes a challenge to conceive the international community in terms of institutional interdependence rather than in realist Hobbesian terms, wherein morality is a nothing but a certain form of strategic behavior.[9]

Globalization covers a number of different tendencies in contemporary international development beyond economics. It also indicates a radicalization of the modernization processes (e.g., secularization and rationalization) that began in the West, though this process is far from harmonious or peaceful. Strong values conflicts and confrontations between civilizations inevitably arise, not least due to the charge of Westernization implicit in modernization. Moreover, it points to the breakdown of the nation-state and the establishment of a new international reality that cannot be conceived properly within the conceptual horizon of national policies. Hence, globalization is a broad phenomenon with indefinite political, technological, cultural, and social consequences.

In this globalized era, problems can only be dealt with in a decisive and politically legitimate way at the international level in a truly global community.[10] This is the case for questions such as the legitimacy of producing of nuclear or biological weapons, finding solutions to an increasing number of environmental problems, and finding ways to alleviate world social inequality.[11] In order to solve these problems we have to consider them in a universalistic perspective, which treats all human beings as equal and deserving of dignity and autonomy. The politics of human rights and common environmental agreements like the Kyoto Protocol represent initiatives to develop transnational frameworks for approaching international problems. This is a necessary response to the limitations of nation-states in dealing with problems that transcend national borders and national economic markets. Not only international organizations and NGOs, but also the economic resources and social institutions of civil society – including companies – need to be included in the framework of international decision-making bodies.

The worldwide spread of new developments and innovations in information and communication technology is another important characteristic of globalization, which has significantly increased the possibilities for transnational decisionmaking.[12] The emergence of the "New Economy" was just a further consequence of this technological development. With the advent of nearly instantaneous communication technology, such as fax and email, new forms of industrial organization were facilitated including, for example, the ability of project groups to work together without being physically proximate.[13] A new world community and public space has been created utilizing these new electronic communications; one that is essential for the movement towards a global cosmopolitan political community, wherein individuals can become world citizens with not only human, but civil and political rights in the world community of states.[14]

Computer technology allows the distribution of information and communication cheaply and quickly,[15] which in turn affords business the ability to separate from time and space constraint. This separation is manifest in the fact that production, sales, administration, and so forth can now be distributed freely around the globe.[16] The defining technologies of globalization are computerization and digitalization, including telephones, Internet technologies, and satellites.[17] These technologies make market economics nearly universal and are essential for companies to effectively operate in a transnational context. Many herald the profound effects that e-commerce will have on human existence, which raises many new ethical and legal questions surrounding the right to privacy, the defense of intellectual property rights, et cetera.

Inexpensive telecommunications technology make global financial markets – where it is possible to trade, sell, and invest at the same time all over the world from one single computer – possible. Because computerized investments can instantly be handled all over the world, financial institutions are no longer restricted to the major stock exchanges in New York, Frankfurt, and London.[18] This interlinking of the world's markets also results is global market sensitivity.[19]

In a global system characterized by free market capitalism, international corporations increasingly control money, technology, and markets. This global system unifies the world's citizens in a common consumer culture. Critical voices characterize this as Disneyfication or Hollywoodization, in which we all live according to an increasingly standardized worldview driven by the American entertainment industry.[20] Some speak about McDonaldization or the Coca-Cola effect, meaning that big firms with publicity for their brands are inventing lifestyles that are quickly contributing to a more monodimensional and uniform way of life. These effects can be seen in, for example, the disturbing ways that global cities, with their nearly identical financial centers and consumption cultures, increasingly resemble each other.

Multinational corporations have the capacity to rationalize production across national borders and to use workers from different countries according to efficiency and economic returns. In addition to lucrative trading with bonds and stocks there are great possibilities in the global economy for product development, expansion of production by using cheap labor, and for rationalization of management and organization. The increased number of mass firing and downsizing in many big international organizations can be considered a consequence of these changed conditions of competition.[21] While the international economy during the Cold War was dependent on prevailing political power and ideology, the globalization of free market capitalism has given economically strong companies a competitive advantage.

Indeed, this free market can be conceived as a realization of the neoliberal economic theory of the 1980s, which posited that firms should concentrate on economic profit in a universal situation of *laissez-faire*. Social responsibilities would be left to the state, which at the same time had the responsibility to de-regulate the economy to follow the forces of the free market.[22] The subsequent elimination of all kinds of restrictive and protectionist barriers for economic development provided the opportunity for new economic growth.[23]

Critical voices have argued that this emphasis on freedom for multinational corporations has the potential to undermine feelings of civic and social respon-sibility on the local, regional, and national levels. As long as they follow the rules of the market, corporations have no goal other than profit maximization without regard to other international, national, or local interests. According to critics, no one questions this goal among the neoliberal leadership of inter-national economic institutions. Indeed, even international organizations like the Organization for Economic Cooperation and Development, the North Atlantic Treaty Organization, the World Bank, and the International Mon-etary Fund have sympathies to neoliberal principles and arguably care too little about corporate social responsibility. In general, modern corporate profit seek-ing is approved by international organizations, who support the formation of global markets in order to facilitate efficiency in economic developments.

Box 4. Globalization and the business strategy of the Danish government: The globalization of Denmark

Since 2003, the business strategy of the Danish liberal-conservative government was articulated in a publication entitled *The Globalization of Denmark*. This strategy, which is common among many liberal-conservative European governments, assumes that globalization is a fact of the international economy and can be read as an argu-ment for business ethics. The government wants to strengthen the position of Den-mark and of Danish firms in the process of liberalizing and internationalizing national markets. The values that are promoted as crucial for the Danish economy include higher productivity, growth, and the rights of shareholders, consumers, and corpora-tions. The government emphasizes the need for clear standards in the financial sector in order to attract foreign investment, to encourage liberalization of the public sector and services, to create public-private partnerships, and to spur further education and research. [24]

This strategy of growth is based on economic efficiency and bureaucratic simplification in an effort to avoid protectionist trade barriers both nationally and internationally. The Danish government works to facilitate personal initiative and free choice with regard to innovation and entrepreneurship. This policy promotes transparency, the facilitation of knowledge management and resource development, efficient competition, and a proactive attitude towards globalization.

With this emphasis on growth and liberalization the government can be said to move from rules to values. In its promotion of the possibilities of the free market, the government is following many tenets of classical and neoclassical economics represented by thinkers such as Adam Smith, Friedrich Hayek, and Milton Friedman. This view considers the "invisible hand" of the market and personal wealth maximization as the bases for economic growth in society and prosperity for all. What is important for the government, as stated in *The Globalization of Denmark,* is therefore healthy, dynamic, and fair competition in a global market where actors are committed to the principles and values of the market within the laws and customs of society.[25]

This strategy of growth implicitly relies on the need to strengthen values and social capital in civil society. The strategy of growth of the Danish government is, therefore, not very far from what Amartya Sen emphasizes as the institutional foundation of market economics. In promoting transparency, minimal bureaucracy, the rights of shareholders and creditors, good corporate governance, competition legislation, the inclusion of consumers as citizens with free choice, and the strength of consumer protection, the government goes beyond the strict limits of neoclassical economics and includes political and social frameworks for economic markets. Such promotion of healthy and free markets within the spirit of fair competition emphasizes how better business ethics can facilitate the liberalization and globalization of Danish firms. This strategy expresses the paradox of a neoliberal conception of economic development. On the one hand the government promotes market freedom, while on the other the concern for common affairs and respect for civic virtues renders ethics an important tool to integrate society and ensure that corporations recognize their social obligations.

1.2. Cultural and social consequences of economic globalization

A persistent critical voice in the debate on globalization is the sociologist Zygmunt Bauman.[26] He argues that the increased global possibilities of rational management and marketing can be conceived as a part of the increased modern power of government, as illustrated by Jeremy Bentham's panoptical prison.[27] According to Bauman, globalization has enlarged the possibilities of this form of domination and control, principally through the power of computer technology to transcend time and space.

The breakdown of nation-states has caused the emergence of a new rationality of power and made possible a process of social exclusion by which corporations, with their strong economic power, take over control of the economy. Power in the form of discipline and punishment has similarly not decreased during globalization. For an American example, even though California is the home to important biotechnology and information technology firms, and is one of ten leading economies in the world, prisons account for a larger amount of state spending than universities. At the same time California still uses the death penalty. This illustrates how power is used to guard the economy from irregularities. The technology of the Panopticon helps firms to change the world into a uniform and homogenous global space. The global space of modernity has become a cybernetic system of transparency as a consequence of the desire to dominate through the Panopticon.[28] Internet technology provides nearly comprehensive information about people through the databases that function as instruments for social exclusion and domination.

Bauman also emphasizes that globalization will have large cultural consequences for the world. The process is so comprehensive that nobody can avoid the influences on life and the conditions of production. In a sense, we are all becoming global as our experience of time and space – geographical roots appear to have decreasing importance – changes profoundly. Globalization also carries with it greater social and material inequality. Not to be a part of globalization is a sign of social depravation and degradation.[29] Bauman describes globalization as a process of larger social exclusion and increasing social control. At the same time, postmodern human beings are universal tourists or vagabonds, with loosening natural ties to a particular life-world or local community.[30] In a consumer society, the rich, eternal tourists are endlessly searching for satisfaction of their endless desires.[31] They follow the credo: "I shop therefore I am." In contrast, the poor and the dispossessed are trying to escape from their conditions. Rather than moving repeatedly for pleasure or entertainment, they are forced to move due to the degradation of their local geographical and cultural spaces.

Bauman argues that globalization has given the company less social responsibility. Because it is free to relocate, it is also free to avoid consequences.[32] The mobility of modern capitalism includes the autonomy of the economic system, where capital no longer has to engage with "the otherness of the other" outside the system. According to Bauman, who is inspired by the French philosopher Paul Virilio, we should not talk about the end of history but rather of the end of space.[33] The technological revolution of communication and transportation means that the human body is increasingly liberated from its natural constraints.[34] But these changes in time and space increase the differences between global and localized human beings; the poor are locally bound while the rich travel. For the capitalist elite, social and cultural spaces are no longer constraints on their actions, while the poor are linked to their local computer or television watching the actions and movements of this powerful and global economic minority.

The decreased control of nation-states, coupled with the growing influence of multinational corporations driven by profit, results in increased global disorder.[35] Bauman points to this new world disorder as a symptom of the lack of control of market forces.[36] The liberalization of world trade and investment across borders may imply a lack of rationalized economic planning, which is good for economic speculation but not for sustainable development. Bauman's criticism of globalization is relevant, but it is not the whole truth. Globalization is an ambiguous phenomenon. It has not only resulted in more disorder, but also opened up possibilities for cosmopolitanism and world citizenship.[37]

Even though the British sociologist Anthony Giddens – as a democratic liberal – is more open to the social and cultural consequences of globalization, he also takes a very critical position towards its development.[38] Giddens describes globalization as modernization in terms of risk distribution. Earlier societies conceived risk as part of their natural lives. In modern society risk is "manufactured," or constructed by industrialized and technological society. Giddens argues that manufactured risk is an integrated part of the global capitalist economy and that concerns for values in business and social responsibility are manifest reactions to this increased level of risk.[39] In modern society, states, corporations, and local communities interact in common responsibility for risk management. In opposition to the increased risk taken by actors in the modern market economy, the welfare state can be conceived as a gigantic system for risk management. It compensates for risks by giving citizens insurance and protection.

It is important to emphasize that globalization, which inevitably involves conflict and contest, is a complex process influencing all levels and dimensions of society. In this vein, Samuel Huntington famously argues his thesis of the clash of civilizations and Francis Fukuyama also refers to increased battles of recognition between different groups in society.[40] In his bestseller, *Lexus and the Olive Tree*, Thomas L. Friedman, a writer for the *New York Times,* analyzes the inevitable opposition between movement and resistance in globalization: The Lexus is a metaphor for the global market forces at work in the movement of globalization, while the olive tree refers to the locally embedded traditions and different cultures that determine human life.[41] Many globalization processes have to find the right harmony between these two dimensions in the ongoing process of social change.

One of the challenges of globalization is to create a civil society that can be balanced with the forces of libertarian market economics.[42] Anthony Giddens discusses how the perspective of universal critical reason changes, and poses continuous challenges to, tradition.[43] Many of the forces of globalization (e.g., the information revolution and the increased penetration of critical enlightenment thinking) open up the path for increased democratization and reflexivity among citizens. The emergence of urban subcultures in postindustrial society, the liberation of women in the twentieth century, as well as the changes in the family, are all good examples of resultant changes. Because globalization challenges communities and local identities, it highlights the possibilities and limitations of tolerance as an important ethical value. Hopefully, corporations can also be mobilized to be socially responsible and develop norms and values for global civil society.

1.3. Principles of a global market economy

At a time when there are no strong political and ideological alternatives to capitalism, it appears that the economy of a global market based on liberty and autonomy has conclusively decided the battle between liberalism and socialism.[44] At the end of history, when there is no real debate about possible alternatives to pluralist liberal democracies, we have to face the pragmatic superiority of the market economy as a means for exchanging goods and contributing to social prosperity and wealth. No other economic organization has proved to be as efficient as the free market system.[45] There is, however, great disagreement about the philosophical and political justification of market systems and about how to conceive the market freedom to exchange. Market freedom is arguably not absolute freedom, but should be conceived within some definite social rules and legal norms defining the ends and means of economic organization.

Some claim the emergence of the global market at the end of history as a return to Adam Smith's liberal vision of the eighteenth and nineteenth centuries. In *The Wealth of Nations*, Smith (1776) put forward his theory of economic prosperity, arguing that global prosperity and welfare was conditioned by the freedom of economic actors to exchange goods at the market.[46] He posited that the division of labor and the creation of large markets are essential for the rational pursuit of self-interest by each economic actor in *fair* competition. This competition – in which each actor seeks to minimize cost and maximize profits – would, further-more, lead to more common prosperity in the long term.

According to Smith, the common good is best established through a *laissez-faire* market where the "w" of individual egoistic strategic behavior can oper-ate in an environment of economic liberty with very few restrictions. Smith's vision of the invisible hand working on the market has been considered as an argument for a total libertarian economy. Many interpreters have used Smith's theory as an argument to ban all regulation of economic markets. This is not a perfect application of his theory because Smith did recognize that legal rules and norms should set limit to the market mechanism.[47] Moreover, Smith's ac-count of the wealth of nations did not foresee modern industrial organization where huge corporations are essential in the world economy.

Since Smith's time, economists have tried to demonstrate this efficiency of the free market and contribute with a scientific justification of liberalism. Wilfred Pareto introduced the concept of *Pareto-optimality*. He argued that free markets optimize the total welfare and goods for the community without reducing the goods and welfare for the individual. Those who defend the lib-eralization of international markets argue that Pareto-optimality can be seen as an important consequence of the laissez-faire organization of the international economy, because the laws of competition will establish an equilibrium of optimal welfare for everybody.[48]

Joseph Schumpeter is also one of the major economists that contribute to the understanding of the global market system.[49] He argued that the capitalist system was an expression of "creative destruction."[50] He thought that economic freedom was a condition for increased welfare in society and emphasized the significance of economic and technological innovation in order to understand competitive advantage in an economy. Along the same line, Fredrick Hayek em-phasized the significance of knowledge in order to understand rational action in modern economic markets. Analyzing the concept of information, Hayek con-cluded that there is no way a central government would be able to get sufficient information to be more efficient then liberal economics. In order to be rational and efficient, economics rely on the knowledge and dispositions of individual economic actors.[51] Economic freedom is based on the ability of free individuals to get information about the quality and price of specific products.[52]

The works of Amartya Sen provide a necessary extension of and correction to the insights of neoclassical liberal economists, who do not adequately ad-dress the meaning of competition in the process of globalization. Sen argues convincingly that the particular dynamics of the capitalist system cannot be understood solely on the basis of rational actors pursuing private ownership, self-interest, and greed. In order for the system to really succeed in raising output and generating income, most of the effective transactions of the capitalist system must rely on much more complex behavioral and cultural aspects.[53] The implied norms of competition, contracts, and fairness also presuppose a number of political and social institutions that are not really present in the market system alone, but are necessary to support the stability of institutions in a global market economy.

Thus, contrary to many good arguments of economic science, it is clear that capitalist markets are not self-sufficient and alone and do not meet expectations. Many of the problems of globalization are caused by uncritical belief in the capitalist economy. Without market regulation or other controls, such as environmental protection, it is likely that the laissez-faire economy will lead to greater pollution and inequality, for example: unsustainable development for poor countries where there is already a surfeit of bad sanitary conditions and substandard housing, and an unequal repartition of dangerous waste between developing and industrial countries. The multinational biotechnology corporation, Monsanto, is another case of the effects of inadequate oversight. Monsanto is seeking profits from small poor farmers by selling them patented seeds, effectively making them directly dependant on their products without taking into account sustainable development. In other words, Monsanto's policies have been created without respect for the ecology of the local environments where their seeds are used.[54] There are no conditions in the market mechanism that help to guarantee a good solution to these problems, nor can the market system contribute to its own foundation. The social institutions that determine the market mechanism are essential in this regard.[55]

The dangers of globalization and unchecked corporate power impact a number of issues of social responsibility including, for example, international money transfer to avoid tax burdens. It is also easier to generate profit and to indulge in crude speculation rather than make good investments that respect local markets.[56] Speculative investments cause unstable financial markets and indecent, unhealthy work conditions in the so-called third world. This is the case when Western companies locate factories in developing countries in order to reduce their economic costs. In so-called sweatshops, clothing and shoe factory workers often receive minimal wages and work under inhumane conditions, but there are also many other factories in developing countries where firms provide inadequate salaries without any responsibility for fundamental human rights.

A further problem of globalization of the free market may be sales overseas of products that are not in compliance with legislation in Western countries because of security or health reasons. Developing countries often have difficulty establishing and enforcing laws with rules as strict as those in advanced industrial nations. Moreover, there is a generic risk in technology and capital transfer to countries who don't have any government control of these products or technologies. In addition, globalization makes it easier to violate trade secrets or copy computer software, films and videos.[57]

Despite the arguments for the importance of the market for global economic welfare, a number of critics maintain that globalization should be understood as the final victory of libertarian capitalism over the national sovereignty. They argue that these powerful multinational firms have usurped the power of governments and that they have no concern for the miserable environmental conditions of the world. Neither do they care about social responsibility or the common good in the societies in which they operate.[58]

Some commentators view globalization as a radicalization of neoclassical economics. They argue that corporations are motivated and evaluated primarily by economic growth and that actions are evaluated according to profits, and based on competition rather than cooperation. Michael Hardt and Antonio Negri think – following Foucault – that network society and the global empire of capitalism have intensified the sovereign "biopolitical power" of states and corporations over life and over human bodies.[59] In this view of corporate cannibalism as the reality of globalization, the global market is based on the right to free transactions among firms.[60] This is, indeed, based on the presupposition of a value free and objective economic rationalism. In the concept of the global market, the end of history is characterized by the "universal consumer society" with a pragmatic balance between the forces of government, the market, and civil society.[61] The proposition that the neoliberal paradigm is leading to a world empire of global biopolitical forces with no one to control the endless oppression of humanity produces a dystopic and dark criticism of globalization.[62]

The logic of neoliberalism – that markets promote prosperity better than human rights and respect for ethical norms – can lead to a situation where, for example, it may be justifiable to suspend the human rights of child laborers simply because it contributes to economic development. Corporations are, according to this view, economic players not politically responsible actors.[63] There should be a sharp separation between economics and politics and corporations should not mix with political affairs. The problem with the neoliberal paradigm is that it follows the principle of individual utility maximization and does not conceive the social and cultural impacts of economic development.[64] Moreover, the neoliberal paradigm has not comprehended the cultural and human consequences of globalization and the importance of respecting cultural differences beyond economic concerns.

Because governments have little influence on their activities, international society is very vulnerable to the activities of these global corporations. Consumer choice is weakened. Unions are declawed, because workers have less power to protest. The critics are also skeptical toward international institutions like the Organization for Economic Cooperation and Development, the International Monetary Fund, and the World Bank. These institutions like legal regulation of markets are conceived as dependent on their interests in corporate profit maximization rather than truly prioritizing the social and physical needs of human beings. Corporate libertarianism challenges basic democratic attitudes.

Even though there is no substitution for the market system, the international community needs instruments to regulate transnational corporations at the global level; to regulate the transfer of capital, goods, and technology; and to deal with problems of environmental sustainability and social justice. The successful use of the market system depends on institutional values and norms, but also rules of customary law, to limit economic interactions.[65] The ideal of profit maximization is dependent on a number of complex conditions and rules of behavior based on trust and related to cultural and historical values in particular traditions. According to Amartya Sen, even Adam Smith emphasized that sympathy, humanity, generosity, and public spirit are basic dimensions of our humanity that influence economic interaction.[66] The global market is conditioned by dimensions of culture, which determine the logic of exchange of economic interactions. It is not possible for countries in the global system to take part of the capitalistic system without accepting certain fundamental rules of behavior.

Case 1. Business ethics and globalization: The case of the Coca-Cola Company

One of the symbols of global capitalism is Coca-Cola. This company tries to present itself as a philanthropic contributor to global prosperity. The company's mission is: "To Refresh the World. . . in mind, body, and spirit. To Inspire Moments of Optimism. . . through our brands and actions. To Create Value and Make a Difference. . . everywhere we engage."[67] With this mission, the company presents itself as responsible to the benefit of its customers, suppliers, distributors, and local communities To this end, the corporation has established the Coca-Cola Foundation, which donates money for projects that improve "the quality of life of community and enhance individual opportunity through education." Together with sponsorships from The Coca-Cola Company, this foundation helps to give the corporation a philanthropic image.[68] Moreover, in its self-representation the company emphasizes its global efforts to develop programs of community involvement and community support.

With approximately 867 factories around the world, Coca-Cola is a multinational company with broad social influence. With regard to local business, the company states that it supports retailers and micro-entrepreneurs, for example through its kiosk programs, which sell Coca-Cola products in Africa. Moreover, the company says that it engages in helping their business customers to develop their businesses. In addition, the company engages in dialogue with suppliers about employee rights and corporate social responsibility, including issues regarding child and forced labor, health and safety, and work environment and environmental practices.[69]

In its corporate citizenship reports, Coca-Cola emphasizes its activities aimed at empowering employees in the workplace. In addition, the concepts of human rights, dignity, health and safety, workplace fairness and global diversity, training and development, employee engagement, and respect for employee rights are mentioned as important concerns.[70] Moreover, the company prioritizes environmental stewardship through standards, such as systems for protecting the environment. Coca-Cola wants to ensure good environmental performance, for example through the use of environmental friendly technologies; thus, Coca-Cola has launched a global water initiative in order to increase consciousness of the importance of water.[71] Coca-Cola also takes part in a stakeholder forum concerning the importance of water and global water issues. Coca-Cola argues that it has fundamental roots in communities around the world, and tries to develop active engagement in local community, partly through different kinds of charitable donations.[72]

Looking at Coca-Cola's philanthropic activities, it becomes apparent that capitalism is not always a hindrance to morality; rather, the growth and prosperity of international corporations may serve the disempowered. Corporate philanthropy may give the poor in developing countries hope that it is possible to escape from their misery. When companies like Coca-Cola are no longer exclusively concerned with profit, but rather use their surplus in support of community needs, they can benefit from community engagement as a way to develop their brands. The reputation and respect for corporations is dependant on the sincerity of these forms of engagement. Modern companies like Coca-Cola are searching for a respectable vocation, which will justify their economic profits in terms of community service through economic creativity. Sustainable business based on trust implies the level of social acceptance where the corporation is conceived as a fellow community member.

1.4. Values of the market system: Corporations as key actors

Moving past the ideological debate about alternatives to capitalism, the ethical concern becomes how to conceive the norms of capitalism and how to understand the role of the global market in the broader perspective of the common good in a world community.[73] Strengthening this common good necessitates that the market must address social and political problems, paying attention to global justice and responsibility. More specifically, it indicates that the problems of the developing countries must be taken into account by the rich countries.

Amartya Sen has argued for the importance of conceiving development as freedom.[74] Social development and business ethics similarly depend on the free capabilities of individuals.[75] The most important presupposition of social development is the political and economic freedom of citizens to participate in the development process. The view of Amartya Sen can be said to imply an *integrative* understanding of the market mechanism. The freedom to exchange at the capitalist market is not independent of social development. Business organizations are not neutral economic institutions, but take part in social processes as normative actors who contribute to social development. An integrative approach means that behavioral and institutional reform is needed to condition an efficient global economy.[76] This view of the market mechanism further posits that global economic growth should be conceived as a holistic process, based on close collaboration between both private and public sector institutions. In this collaborative environment, corporations cannot be simply neutral economic devices, but actively contribute to economic, social, and political freedom. This link between development and freedom implies that liberty is more important than utility, but further that the aim of utility and efficiency should be freedom.

Freedom is inextricable from social justice, which is in turn a partial constraint to markets. The formulation of values in business contributes to ensuring that minimal social and political rights are conditions for the function of economic markets. At the same time, Sen emphasizes that markets are essential to economic life as the basic conditions for social exchange. Social justice has to leave room for markets, which would not exist without basic rules of exchange.[77] The markets are limited by values and visions of social justice that determine what should be on the market, including the limits of commodification.

In this context it is important to emphasize that in addition to corporate values and behavioral rules, market freedom is determined by certain external conditions. Recent social science research shows that social capital, which depends on factors of trust, influences the efficiency and utility of market conditions.[78] Certain cultural dimensions are also necessary. There are a number of basic freedoms and securities, including infrastructure and technology access, which condition the liberty to be an economic actor on the market. The freedom and security of market transactions are also governed by external institutions to help guarantee that people act efficiently.[79] These institutions contribute to the formulation of values for the market mechanism. While recognizing the role of exchange in human life, it is also necessary to formulate market limits for exchanging goods.[80] Legal constraints are very important in this regard.

Even though the efficiency of the global market economy in allocating goods and services is undeniable, it should be increasingly obvious that the economic system is considerably more complex than than the doctrine of self-interest allows. Following Sen, the external conditions for the system contribute to rendering the ethics of capitalism as an important factor for the growth of wealth and prosperity.

1.5. Business ethics and values–driven management in global community

It is important for multinational firms to strengthen the internal and external norms of the market by including ethical rationality in formulating their management strategies.[81] At the local and international level corporations can respond to these responsibilities and challenges by formulating values codes for the international community that include prioritizing fair competition, moral and social capital, the public good, just distribution, and environmental sustainability. Values-driven management at a global scale ensures that ethical values are implied in the management strategies of the firm.

Many large European and American companies play an important leadership role in developing programs and policies on values-driven management and business ethics. In Europe the movement for corporate social responsibility was strengthened following the communication from the European Commission on that subject in 2002, which also announced the creation of a European Stakeholder Forum.[82] In the United States the enactment of the FSGO, which afforded corporations with ethics programs more favorable treatment in sentencing, have incentivized American corporations to work with ethics programs and good corporate citizenship.[83] Because the United States is a leading actor in the process of globalization, world democratization depends on the willingness of American companies to contribute to this process.[84] But the need for values-driven management does not only concern European and American companies.[85] It is very important that the process has a global impact, touching companies in countries in all over the world. To this end, international guidelines like the 1994 Caux Round Table and United Nation's Global Compact principles on business ethics have been formulated.

It is important to bear in mind that globalization has largely meant modernization, including a movement toward democratization, which as a product of Western and Enlightenment values is conceived as universally justified. Ergo, globalization is a movement toward democratic institutions.[86] As these democractic values spread, pressure increases on companies to follow basic ethical rules. From this perspective on globalization, business ethics might be conceived as an effort to realize the idea of humanity in the international economic system. Fulfilling this promise requires overcoming the hostility to business ethics that has marked many cultures all over the world. Important ethical principles include respect for human autonomy, dignity, integrity, and vulnerability in the framework of responsibility and justice.[87] The effort to formulate codes of ethics and values-driven management in this manner can be conceived as an advantage to business, because it aims at improving the international ethical legitimacy of the firm, thereby increasing its vitality.

Values codes have, therefore, an important integrative function in the world community. They are the internal moral standards that meet the external requirements of minimal conditions for the global market. Codes might be developed by the business community, but also by international organizations and governments contributing to the external constraints on the market system. Codes can be understood as contracts between business and society that establish minimal international norms and a bottom line for economic actors in the international community.[88]

Values are important alternatives to legal standards because they involve both compliance and virtuous behavior. In a framework with no legal rules – what might be called empty spaces – values are important tools to guide correct behavior. At the same time they can help to back up existing regulatory standards. Moreover, because they are founded in ideals of uncompromising integrity they can complement rules and standards of excellence.[89] Individuals and private groups lay pressure on the market due to globalization; they increasingly require that companies make more information open to the public. Firms take part in the global political public sphere, where they are confronted with NGOs, governmental organizations, pressure groups, and other international organizations, who function as global watch dogs of unethical behavior. In this regard, values-driven management is an instrument to improve the public relations of the firm.

The need to be aware of values is also due to the many cross-cultural dimensions of modern society, which are marked by increased culture clash. Companies are increasingly confronted with cultures different from their own, both inside and outside the firm, which provokes insecurity concerning values. In this context, business ethics contributes to the awareness of cultural conflicts and aims to improve the cross-cultural understanding and communication about cultural differences.

Global ethical issues might be conceived as a problem of risk distribution at the international level. In taking basic values into account, companies might become aware of unjust burdens that are put on specific countries and groups. This can include environmental issues, but also issues about employee or customer protection. Given the increased availability of manufactured risk in modern society, not only states but also private business organizations should be aware of problems of risk and risk distribution.

While it is a very delicate matter of analysis to clarify the relation between embedded cultural values and universal norms, there is a certain "free moral space" inside which each culture, political or organizational community is entitled to determine their particular values and codes.[90] Debates about values take the firm's many stakeholders and interest groups into account. By looking at stakeholders' interests and relations between risks and rights, these debates translate into the practices of the firm, especially addressing basic human rights violations.[91] Human rights are important for values-driven strategies that seek to mediate between local and universal norms in the activities of business organizations. In this way, human rights concerns are as important for the internal organizational activities of the firm as for decision-making about commercial activities in different contexts.

In manifold ways, this analysis of globalization demonstrates the importance of good political, social, and cultural institutions for the promotion of good economic development.[92] In contrast to the focus on individual rights and interests, the concept of citizenship moves in the direction of the republican constitutional state, respecting basic rules of democracy and the rule of law. According to this republican paradigm of international relations, companies must understand themselves as political actors.[93] The republican concept of business emphasizes the importance of the *res publica*, that is, goodness and justice are important aspects of institutional engagement in globalization. Corporations should not only be considered as *global players* in competition but rather as *global citizens*. As discussed above, neoliberals argue that the global market leads to greater prosperity while critics argue that globalization destroys social coherence. Global corporate citizenship, with its focus on business ethics, values-driven management, and corporate social responsibility represents an essential alternative position.[94] Multinational corporations can use codes of conducts to shape their organizations toward this goal.

Case 2. Sweatshops and fair wages in the global supply chain: The case of Nike

The Nike Corporation has already become a classic business studies case of a major multinational dealing with globalization. The case illustrates a multinational firm in an *ethical crisis*.[95] In April 2000, the founder and managing director of Nike, Philip Knight, stopped donating to the University of Oregon. In the previous twenty years, Knight, a former University student, had donated nearly fifty million dollars of his own money. His reason for stopping was that the University had joined the workers' rights consortium (WRC) in order to help assure that sweatshop labor was not used in the manufacture of products branding the university. WCT was an organization that was critical to the Fair Labor Association (FLA) of which Nike was a member. [96]

WCT argued that FLA did not sufficiently help workers in factories in developing countries. Like many other international corporations, Nike had chosen to outsource production to suppliers in developing countries in order to lower production costs. Nike had around 20,000 direct employees with nearly 500,000 contract employees working in more than 565 supplier factories in more than forty-six countries around the world. The earnings of Nike in 1999 were more than nine billion dollars and, at that time, the corporation dominated forty-five percent of the sport shoe market. Philip Knight owned thirty-four percent of the shares making him one of the richest people in the United States.

By this time, Nike had moved the bulk of its production to Southeast Asia to take advantage of lower wages and firms in these countries – particularly in Taiwan and Korea – that specialized in shoe production, which cannot be automated and requires manual labor. Moreover, in Asia there is easy access to raw materials and Asian firms are regarded as efficient.[97]

The incident with the University of Oregon was just one of many leading to increased pressure on the Nike Corporation to take responsibility for the low wages, poor working conditions, and potential use of child labor in the supply factories. In response, Nike argued that they were not responsible for what happened in supply factories and the way these factories were managed. This did nothing to silence the criticism by different organizations that the company was in violation of international human rights.[98] Consequently, Nike has been obliged to work to promote human rights in the international community.[99] Nike introduced a code of conduct implying that local labor and environmental laws should be respected. In 1998, Nike had already established a division for corporate social responsibility and the corporation had started to work with different programs for improving working conditions and education and health among local employees in supplier factories.[100] Despite these efforts, the scandal with the University of Oregon only highlighted the suspicion of the firm's true intentions.

With the creation of these programs, Nike hoped to make its desire to follow international labor standards explicit and even though Nike has done much to promote fair labor standards, the company's story illustrates how difficult it is to restore a damaged corporate image. Despite considerable efforts to support corporate social responsibility and to avoid sweatshop labor, Nike lost credibility with the public. The move by the University of Oregon, among other institutions having close relations to Nike, to join the WRC is a demonstration of how important it has become for multinationals to respect labor standards.

Endnotes

1   Hans-Peter Martin and Harald Schumann, *Die Globalisierungsfälle. Der Aufgriff auf Demokratie und Wohlstand* (Hamburg Rowolt Taschenbuch Verlag, 1998), 71. Ulrich Beck, *Power in the Global Age: A new political economy* (London: Polity Press, 2006). David Held and Anthony McGrew, *The Global Transformation Reader. An introduction to the globalization debate* (London: Polity Press, 2002). Michael Blowfield and Allan Murray, *Corporate Responsibility. A Critical Introduction* (Oxford: Oxford University Press, 2008).

2   Harold Berman, "World Law", *Fordham International Law Journal*, Vol 18, No 5: 1619.

3   Ibid: 1619.

4   Ibid: 1619.

5   Michael Hardt and Antonio Negri, *Empire* (Cambridge Massachusetts: Harvard University Press, 2001), 13.

6   Ulrich Beck, "Living Your Own Life in a Runaway World: Individualism, Globalisation and Politics" in *Global Capitalism*, edited by Will Hutton and Anthony Giddens, (New York: New Press, 2000), 164. Michael Blowfield and Allan Murray, *Corporate Responsibility. A Critical Introduction* (Oxford: Oxford University Press, 2008), 70.

7   Manuel Castells, *The Rise of Network Society, The Information Age, Economics, Society and Culture*, Volume I, (Oxford: Blackwell Publishers), 1996.

8   Hans-Peter Martin and Harald Schumann, *Die Globalisierungsfälle. Der Aufgriff auf Demokratie und Wohlstand*, (Hamburg Rowolt Taschenbuch Verlag, 1998), 89. Michael Blowfield and Allan Murray, *Corporate Responsibility. A Critical Introduction* (Oxford: Oxford University Press, 2008).

9   David Gauthier, *Morals by Agreement* (Oxford: Clarendon Press and University Press, 1986). Thomas Donaldson, *The Ethics of International Business* (Oxford: Oxford University Press, 1991).

10 Richard Falk, "The Making of Global Citizenship" in *Global Visions. Beyond the New World Order*, edited by Brecher et al. (Boston 1993), 40.

11 Will Hutton and Anthony Giddens, *Global Capitalism* (New York: New Press, 2000), 213.

12 Anthony Giddens, *Runaway World. How Globalization is reshaping our lives* (London: Routledge, 1999). Michael Blowfield and Allan Murray, *Corporate Responsibility. A Critical Introduction* (Oxford: Oxford University Press, 2008).

13 Manuel Castells, *The Rise of Network Society, The Information Age, Economics, Society and Culture*, Volume I, (Oxford: Blackwell Publishers, 1996), 52.

14 Anthony Giddens, *Runaway World. How Globalization is reshaping our lives*, (London: Routledge, 1999), 22-23.

15 John Boatright, "Globalization and the Ethics of Business", *Business Ethics Quarterly*, January 2000, Vol 10, no. 1.

16 Manuel Castells, "Information Technology and Global Capitalism" in *Global Capitalism*, edited by Will Hutton and Anthony Giddens, (New York: New Press, 2000), 52.

17 Thomas L. Friedman, *The Lexus and the Olive Tree* (New York: Ferrar, Straus, Giroux, 1999). Michael Blowfield and Allan Murray, *Corporate Responsibility. A Critical Introduction* (Oxford: Oxford University Press, 2008).

18 John Boatright, "Globalization and the Ethics of Business", *Business Ethics Quarterly*, January 2000, Vol. 10, no 1.

19 Thomas L. Friedman, *The Lexus and the Olive Tree* (New York: Ferrar, Straus, Giroux, 1999), xi.

20 Polly Toynbee, "Who's afraid of Global Culture" in *Global Capitalism*, edited by Will Hutton and Anthony Giddens, (New York: New Press, 2000), 191.

21 For example, take the Canadian journalist Naomi Klein's critiques of globalization in her book, Naomi Klein: *No Logo. Taking Aim at the Brand Bullies* (New York Picador, Saint Martins Press, 2000).

22 Hans-Peter Martin and Harald Schumann, *Die Globalisierungsfälle. Der Aufgriff auf Demokratie und Wohlstand* (Hamburg Rowolt Taschenbuch Verlag, 1998), 145. Michael Blowfield and Allan Murray, *Corporate Responsibility. A Critical Introduction* (Oxford: Oxford University Press, 2008).

23 Among European governments, this strategy of globalization as liberalization is also promoted by the Danish government in its business strategy. *Globalization of Denmark* (Copenhagen 2002).

24 Danish Government, *The Globalization of Denmark*, Report (Copenhagen 2003).

25 Ibid.

26 Zygmunt Bauman, *Globalization: The Human Consequences*, (New York: Columbia University Press, 1999).

27 In this archetypal prison, soldiers – from a particular point – have full view and control over the whole society. Bauman also draws on Foucault's conception of the Panopticon as a prison where control and surveillance is possible through transparent cells, metaphorically illustrating the condition of modern life and of the rationality of government in efficient management organizations. Michel Foucault, *Surveiller et punir* (Paris: Gallimard, 1973). Michel Foucault: *Naissance de la biopolitique* (Paris: Gallimard-Seuil, 2004).

28 Zygmunt Bauman, *Globalization: The Human Consequences*, (New York: Columbia University Press, 1999), 49.

29 Ibid: 2.

30 Ibid: 77.

31 Ibid: 83.

32 Ibid: 9.

33 Paul Virilio, *Vitessse et politique* (Paris : Éditions Galilée, 1977).

34 Zygmunt Bauman, *Globalization: The Human Consequences*, (New York: Columbia University Press, 1999), 16.

35 Ibid: 58.

36 Ibid: 118.

37 How should we evaluate Bauman's harsh criticism of globalization? While ruthless capitalism may not yet be the rule of the day, Bauman warns us that we need concern for ethics and values in international society in order to avoid the destruction of international society. The danger of the Panopticon may not be a literal threat, but it

nonetheless serves as a useful metaphor for the contrast of uniform labor discipline to the dreams of enlightenment, democracy, and freedom. Bauman lays too much emphasis on the opportunistic and egoistic aspects of neo-liberalism. Globalization also has potentially positive ramifications, including the role that corporations can play in the development of world citizenry. Internet globalization is not only a sign of the erosion of the nation-state, but also opens new possibilities for networking and democratic discussion. Instead of viewing globalization as necessarily creating a world with greater poverty, it can also be seen as a new means to achieve global unity, furthering the possibility of solving the world's problem together. In line with this more positive outlook, I argue that business ethics and concepts of the good citizen corporation are important ways to avoid the dangers that Bauman presents. See Zygmunt Bauman: *Liquid Modernity, The Individualized Society* (London: Polity Press, 2000).

38   Will Hutton and Anthony Giddens, *Global Capitalism* (New York: New Press, 2000), 49-50.

39   Globalization of financial markets includes increased financial and environmental risk. Anthony Giddens, *Runaway World. How Globalization is reshaping our lives* (London: Routledge, 1999), 44.

40   Samuel P. Huntington, *The Clash of Civilizations and the Remaking of the World Order* (New York: Touchstone Book (1996), 1998). Francis Fukuyama, *The End of History and the Last Man* (New York: The Free Press, 1992).

41   Thomas L. Friedman, *The Lexus and the Olive Tree* (New York: Ferrar, Straus, Giroux, 1999), 29.

42   Ibid: 96.

43   One manifestation of this is the contemporary emergence of fundamentalism. See Giddens (1999).

44   Francis Fukuyama, *The End of History and the Last Man* (New York: The Free Press, 1990).

45   Will Hutton and Anthony Giddens, *Global Capitalism* (New York: New Press, 2000). Michael Blowfield and Allan Murray, *Corporate Responsibility. A Critical Introduction* (Oxford: Oxford University Press, 2008).

46   Adam Smith, *An In Inquiry into the Nature and Causes of The Wealth of Nations* (New York: The Modern Library (1776), 2000). Adam Smith, *The Theory of the Moral Sentiments*, Cambridge: Cambridge Texts in the History of Philosophy, Cambridge University Press, (1759), 2002).

47   Adam Smith is often described as the author who defends a pure *laissez-faire economy* in international community. However, as indicated, if we understand the concept of self-interest as enlightened self-interest, including the virtues of prudence, self-restraint, cooperation and equality of treatment, we get another impression of the concept of the free market in the *Wealth of Nations*. Moral virtues like sympathy and justice are central to moral judgment. In fact it is the virtue of justice and the idea of the impartial spectator that are important in the theory of moral sentiments. In this sense, we have to read the *Wealth of Nations* in the light of the *Theory of Moral Sentiments*. For Smith, human beings are not exclusive self-interested utility maximizers, but concepts of self-restraint and cooperation – as well as equality of treatment – are indeed also important virtues (Patricia Werhane, *Adam Smith and his legacy for modern capitalism*, Oxford: Oxford University Press, 1991, 4-5). This means that there is a double dimension of the norms of the global market and that there is a limit to self-interested action of corporations and nations. Moreover, it is important to remember that as an eighteenth-century thinker, Smith is not a radical liberalist, but recognizes the importance of nation states and constitutional law (Werhane, 13). Thus, with Werhane, we can emphasize that the idea of the invisible hand is not a normative concept of justice or an ultimate ideal. It is simply a description of how some of the market forces seem to work. At the same time, there is a link between the invisible hand, the concepts of justice and cooperation in the sense that the ideas of impartiality and fair play are determined for good market behavior, where it is not allowed to break the rules and hurt the neighbor (Werhane, 14-15). This means that Smith is someone who recognizes sympathy and cooperation in institutions as important aspects of the wealth of nations.

48   We can relate welfare economics to theory of development. See Amartya Sen, *Development as Freedom* (New York: First Anchor Books Edition, 2000).

49   Thomas L. Friedman, *The Lexus and the Olive Tree* (New York: Ferrar, Straus, Giroux, 1999). Michael Blowfield and Allan Murray, *Corporate Responsibility. A Critical Introduction* (Oxford: Oxford University Press, 2008).

50   Joseph Schumpeter, *Capitalism, Socialism and Democracy*, 3rd edition (London and New York: Routlegde, (1950) 1994).

51   F.A. Hayek, *Law, legislation and liberty. A new statement of the liberal principles of justice and political economy*, including Vol 1: *Rules and order*, Vol 2: *The mirage of social justice*, Vol 3: *The political order of a free people*, (London: Routledge, (1983), 1998).

52   Manuel G. Velasquez, *Business Ethics. Concept and Cases*, 5th edition, (New Jersey: Prentice Hall, 2002). Michael Blowfield and Allan Murray, *Corporate Responsibility. A Critical Introduction* (Oxford: Oxford University Press, 2008).

53   Amartya Sen, *Development as Freedom* (New York: First Anchor Books Edition, 2000), 265.

54 Vandana Shiva, "The World on the Edge" in Will Hutton and Anthony Giddens, *Global Capitalism* (New York: New Press, 2000), 126.

55 Amartya Sen, *Development as Freedom* (New York: First Anchor Books Edition, 2000).

56 Hans-Peter Martin and Harald Schumann, *Die Globalisierungsfälle. Der Aufgriff auf Demokratie und Wohlstand* (Hamburg Rowolt Taschenbuch Verlag, 1998), 155.

57 Gerald F. Cavanagh, S.J., "Political Counterbalance and Personal Values: Ethics and Responsibility in a Global Economy", *Business Ethics Quarterly*, January 2000, Vol. 10, no. 1: 43-51.

58 David C. Korton, *When Corporations rule the World* (San Francisco: Kumarian Press, Berrett-Koehler Publishers, 1995).

59 Michael Hardt and Antonio Negri, *Empire* (Cambridge Massachusetts: Harvard University Press, 2001), 27. Michel Foucault, *Surveiller et punir* (Paris: Gallimard, 1973). Michel Foucault, *Naissance de la biopolitique* (Paris : Gallimard-Seuil, 2004).

60 Michael Hardt and Antonio Negri, *Empire* (Cambridge Massachusetts: Harvard University Press, 2001), 207ff.

61 Ibid: 88.

62 Hardt and Negri share the same tradition of left-wing anticapitalist criticisms of globalization as Foucault and Bauman. This theoretical approach points to possible negative consequences of globalization that might result from a completely *laissez-faire* attitude. Antiglobalization theorists in the postmodern and poststructuralist tradition argue that globalization increasingly dominates and destroys individual life possibilities. They also seem to argue that this development is impossible to govern because the biopolitical forces of the empire are so strong that they cannot be avoided. The conception of power is problematic in this approach. It refuses to recognize the possibility of action and possible human intervention to change those processes. I agree that we are sometimes inclined to consider the reality of the modern world as marked by such limited possibilities of intervention; however, behind the forces of globalization we all encounter real human beings who can act as change agents, even though they may be embedded in organizational life. While theories of biopolitics and power describe the dark side of international developments, they cannot refute all theories about the possibilites of human action. To borrow a phrase from Paul Ricœur, these theorists are important "penseurs de soupçon" (Paul Ricœur, *Le conflit des interpretations* (Paris: Le Seuil, 1969) who, through their criticisms and negations of globalization, help to establish the need for ethics and the establishment of international norms for good governance.

63 Andreas G. Scherer and Albert Löhr, "Verantwortungsvolle Unternemensführung im Zeitalter der Globalisierung – Einige kritische Bemerkungen zu den Perspektiven einer liberalen Weltwirtschaft" in *Unternehmensethik und die Transformation des Wettbewerbs*, edited by Brij Nino Kumar, Margit Osterloh and Georg Schreyögg., (Schaffer/Poeschel, 1999), 270.

64 Ibid: 277.

65 Harold Berman, "World Law", *Fordham International Law Journal*, Vol 18, No 5.

66 Adam Smith, *The Theory of the Moral Sentiments*, Cambridge: Cambridge Texts in the History of Philosophy, Cambridge University Press, (1759), 2002). Amartya Sen, *Development as Freedom* (New York: First Anchor Books Edition, 2000), 272.

67 Coca Cola: Corporate Citizenship Report, 2004. www.coca-cola.com

68 www.coca-cola.com

69 For example, when the company faced criticism from Human Rights Watch regarding the use of child labor in a sugar plantation in El Salvador, Coca-Cola made an effort to solve the problem. Coca Cola: Corporate Citizenship Report, 2004. www.coca-cola.com.

70 Ibid: 26.

71 Ibid: 32.

72 Ibid: 37.

73 Robert B. Putnam, *Bowling Alone. The Collapse and Revival of American Community* (New York: Touchstone, 2000).

74 Amartya Sen, *Development as Freedom* (New York: First Anchor Books Edition, 2000), 6.

75 Georges Enderle: "Global competition and corporate responsibilities of small and medium-sized enterprises", *Business Ethics. A European Review*, 2004.

76 Amartya Sen, *Development as Freedom* (New York: First Anchor Books Edition, 2000), 168.

77 Ibid: 113.

78   Francis Fukuyama, *Trust, The Social Virtues and the Creation of Prosperity* (New York: The Free Press, 1995).

79   Amartya Sen, *Development as Freedom* (New York: First Anchor Books Edition, 2000), 116.

80   Ibid: 126.

81   Malcolm McIntosh, Deborah Leipziger, Keith Jonas and Gill Coleman: *Corporate Citizenshp, Successful Strate-gies for Responsible Companies* (London: Financial Times, Pitman Publishing, 1998), 61.

82   European Commission, *Green Book: A European Framework for Corporate Social Responsibility* (Bruxelles, 2001). Also see Communcation 2002 and 2006.

83   US Sentencing Commission, *Proceedings of the Second Symposium on Crime and Punishment in the United States: Corporate Crime in America. Strengthening the "Good Citizen Corporation"*, (Washington D.C.: US Sentencing Commission, September 7-8, 1995).

84   Thomas L. Friedman, *The Lexus and the Olive Tree* (New York: Ferrar, Straus, Giroux, 1999), 304 and 354-355.

85   See reprint of the Caux Principles in *International Business Ethics*, edited by Georges Enderle (Notre Dame: Notre Dame University Press, 1999).

86   Anthony Giddens, *Runaway World. How Globalization is reshaping our lives* (London: Routledge, 1999).

87   Jacob Dahl Rendtorff and Peter Kemp, *Basic Ethical Principles in European Bioethics and Biolaw, Vol I-II* (Barcelona and Copenhagen: Center for Ethics and Law, 2000). In this book there is a definition and exploration of the basic ethical principles.

88   Thomas Donaldson, *The Ethics of International Business*, (Oxford: Oxford University Press, 1991).

89   Lynn Sharp Paine, "Managing for Organizational Integrity", *Harvard Business Review*, 1994.

90   Thomas Donaldson and Tom Dunfee, *Ties That Bind* (Cambridge Massachusetts Harvard Business School Press, 1999).

91   Thomas Donaldson, *The Ethics of International Business* (Oxford: Oxford University Press, 1989), 133.

92   The idea of corporate involvement in community is illustrated by the concept of citizenship solidarity (*staatsbürgerlichen solidarität*). Andreas G. Scherer and Albert Löhr, "Verantwortungsvolle Unternemensführung im Zeitalter der Globalisierung – Einige kritische Bemerkungen zu den Perspektiven einer liberalen Weltwirtschaft" in *Unternehmensethik und die Transformation des Wettbewerbs* , edited by Brij Nino Kumar, Margit Osterloh and Georg Schreyögg (Schaffer/Poeschel, 1999), 278. Jürgen Habermas, "Die Postnationale Konstellation und die Zukunft der Demokratie", in Jürgen Habermas, *Die Postnationale Konstellation* (Frankfurt am Main: Suhrkamp Verlag: 1998, 91-169).

93   Andreas G. Scherer and Albert Löhr: "Verantwortungsvolle Unternemensführung im Zeitalter der Globalisierung – Einige kritische Bemerkungen zu den Perspektiven einer liberalen Weltwirtschaft" in *Unternehmensethik und die Transformation des Wettbewerbs*, edited by Brij Nino Kumar, Margit Osterloh and Georg Schreyögg., (Schaffer/Poeschel, 1999), 262.

94   Ibid: 282. Also see chapter 5 where this concept of global corporate citizenship is discussed in detail.

95   The material for this case is selected from James E. Post, Anne T. Lawrence and James Weber, *Business and Society, Corporate Strategy, Public Policy, Ethics* (New York: McGraw-Hill, Irwin, 2002). Archie B Carroll and Ann K. Buchholtz, *Business and Society. Ethics and Stakeholder Management* (Canada: South Western, 2002, 628-633). See also Scott B. Rae and Kenman L. Wrong: *Beyond Integrity: A Judeo-Christian Approach to Business Ethics* (Michigan: Zondervan Publishing House, 1996, 182): "Nike and Cheap Labor".

96   James E. Post, Anne T. Lawrence and James Weber, *Business and Society, Corporate Strategy, Public Policy, Ethics* (New York: McGraw-Hill, Irwin, 2002), 570-572.

97   Ibid: 570-572. Michael Blowfield and Allan Murray, *Corporate Responsibility. A Critical Introduction* (Oxford: Oxford University Press, 2008).

98   Andreas G. Scherer and Albert Löhr: "Verantwortungsvolle Unternemensführung im Zeitalter der Globalisierung – Einige kritische Bemerkungen zu den Perspektiven einer liberalen Weltwirtschaft" in *Unternehmensethik und die Transformation des Wettbewerbs*, edited by Brij Nino Kumar, Margit Osterloh und Georg Schreyögg., (Schaffer/Poeschel, 1999), 264.

99   George Enderle, *International Business Ethics, Challenges and Approaches* (Notre Dame: University of Notre Dame Press, 1999).

100 Ibid.

2. Values, organizations, and management

Having established the role of corporations in the process of globalization and the importance of ethics and values-driven management, the problem becomes how to define the meaning and function of values in organizations. What status and role do values have in modern corporations and how do they impact people in the organizations? Organizational life seems to be characterized by many different forms of values, but behind these differences some essential shared components can be observed. In private companies, these values are commonly related by a focus on economic incentives, the structure of the market, and the accomplishments that characterize market organizations.

John Dienhart provides the methodological basis for the study of the relation between business institutions and values.[1] He defines institutions as "complexes of norms and behavior that persist over time by serving collectively valued purposes." In this sense, institutions are the basis for individual choices and behaviors that are shaped by the values of the institutions. The concept of the institution is very broad and can include virtually every form of human behavior beyond convention or coincidence. According to Dienhart and the economic institutionalism of Douglass North, the particularity of economic institutions is that they provide a temporal framework for economic transactions by linking past, present, and future, and also that they provide the necessary incentive structure for the economy.[2]

With this in mind economic organizations can be said to consist of norms, rules, and principles of human relationships (i.e., values) that organize economic and human action. These values may be conventional and tacit, but they can also be the result of motivated ethical choices and strategies of values-driven management; however, such values are not the only ones that influence modern organizations because not all values are ethically justified. There may be a tension between some of the original values of the firm and the proposed ethical values.

Values-driven management and business ethics may, therefore, be introduced on the basis of an ethical investigation of fundamental values of the firm.

2.1. The concept of value

Values have been defined in many different ways.[3] Some consider them as subjective perceptions of an objective factual reality. In this sense they are preferences, demands, and expectations. They can also be conceived as dimensions of common realities in institutions or communities. Values are perceived as assumptions or commitments presupposing particular views on the world. They function as evaluative frames or ideals determining blame, recognition, or merit when judging particular relations. Values are what people find important or praise in their existence and social relations.

The impact of conflicts over values is an important aspect of analyzing their function in an organization. Sometimes, values only become noticed and articulated in times of crisis or conflict. This can lead to a search for values that are intrinsically good. Following Ronald Dworkin, intrinsic values are those with a metaphysical quality that exist independently of what people happen to enjoy or want or need, or what is good for them.[4] There are wide array of values (e.g., economic, political, ecological, ethical, and legal) that contribute to shaping the organization. Even though they might not be intrinsically valid (i.e., possess metaphysical properties) these values form the basic structure of an organization.

Values have influence on the historical and cultural position of the firm. Human society might be considered as a value-generating structure; the same holds for the firm. The values of the firm determine its interaction with the environment. Values characterize the place of the firm in time and space, and its whole organizational structure reflects the basic values of the firm. Values may also have an ideological function and significance as the basic legitimizing force of the organizational actions and development. Business leaders and managers are influenced by the values of their particular organizations, which require analysis from different philosophical, sociological, legal, and psychological perspectives.

Max Weber argued for a strong distinction between fact and value, between normative and descriptive statements. This has characterized many theories of modern social science, including much of modern sociology. This distinction is very critical when dealing with organizations and values. Values are a factual part of organizations and descriptive sociology can describe and analyze the meaning of values in specific organizations. Values can also have a normative and ideological function that influences the decision-making of the organization.

The clarification of the descriptive meaning of value is important for understanding its normative impact on the life of the organization. Values can be defined as beliefs of actors that motivate actions toward specific goals. In this definition, values are beliefs that are held in order to realize certain fundamental goods that an agent wants to bring into being. In this way, a value-system in an organization is a cluster of beliefs and normative presuppositions that guide the way people in the organization perceive and understand a number of states of affairs in the world. Values have, therefore, both cognitive and behavioral impacts on the way individuals and organizations act. This may be characterized as a psychological theory of value.[5]

Sociology defines values as the systems of beliefs of a particular group or culture, indicating human relations to the environment. Values are examined as the normative standards that determine the worldview of particular organizational cultures. Sociology might talk about the *shared values* of societies and the possible *values conflicts* between different groups of people. Indeed, values in this context could refer to particular traditional systems of thought.

Values can be considered as the normative bases of people's judgments in business organizations.[6] Accordingly, William C. Frederick refers to John Dewey's concept of values as the criteria for judgments in the process of evaluation. Dewey considers values as the goal of the human search for the whole self; indeed, they are the imaginary inventions and constitutive experiences of the self.[7] As the normative background for organizational methods, goals, and aims, values are instrumental criteria for judging the success or failure of a particular operation of the organization.[8]

The place of values in modern corporations cannot be understood without reference to the concept of organizational culture. In *Organizational Culture and Leadership,* Edgar Schein conceptualizes culture as a cluster of values, and organizational culture as the incarnation of particular values in a given corporation.[9] He develops an empirical analysis of the formation of values in organizations, and how different organizational cultures represent different orders of values and different values systems. Schein argues that organizational culture is based on certain artifacts and creations. These visible aspects of culture represent more basic assumptions and mutual understandings that determine the meaning of the organization.[10] Organizational values constitute the cultural make-up of the organization. In this context, congruence between the values of managers, workers, and other members of the organization is necessary in order to maintain the systemic integrity of the organization. It is also necessary to have congruence between individual and organizational values in order to make the organization work.

Geert Hofstede has emphasized the values in the workplace of power, distance, uncertainty, avoidance, individualism-collectivism, and masculinity-femininity.[11] These values might also be conceived from an intercultural perspective. Organizations and individuals in organizations embody values that reflect other external cultural and national traditions. Values are generally accepted standards of rationality, and support the norms that shape organizations. Moreover, they shape the personality of individuals and the identity of organizations. One could even say that human beings live for values.[12] Values have ideal normative impacts that form existence and in this way they can be said to signify what is considered important. Values are, therefore, linked to the human search for the good and to striving for the "good life".[13]

Intrinsic values can be endowed with meaning in relation to human culture and history. They do not have to be perceived as something mysterious and totally apart. A popular argument for the existence of intrinsic values presupposes that not all values can be instrumental. Basic values are intrinsic values with objective and universal status, which is established after they emerge in a particular historical and cultural setting. Consequently, some values have intrinsic and objective cultural significance, but are nevertheless dependent on the historical and cultural setting in which they emerge. In this way we may search for the original or basic values that affect modern corporations and business organizations.

Business ethics is considered by many as the descriptive mapping of managerial values and of the beliefs and codes in the organization. This research is important and necessary in order to clarify normative presuppositions of the function of business organizations, but it is not enough. The research must also involve normative evaluations of the status of particular organizational values. In addition it might include proposals of how to structure values-driven management in a particular organization. The search for values-driven management as the basis for corporate citizenship involves a double task: 1) identification of basic, major, or original values influencing business corporations, and at the same time 2) examination of these values in order to propose justified ethical values (or principles) to guide judgments, decision-making, and strategies for business organizations.

Case 3. The Ford Pinto case: Ethical versus economic values

The case of the Ford Pinto, a small car introduced in the 1970s, illustrates that economic decision-making cannot be made without considering ethics, in this case respecting the dignity and inviolability of human beings.[14] The Pinto was involved in an unsually large number of fires during rear-end accidents and was plagued by doubts about its security almost as soon as it was released. In 1977, a newspaper magazine claimed that Ford was selling a car that they knew was dangerous simply because it helped to lower costs and increase profits. The article suggested that the Ford Corporation was arguing that the car was safe even though company engineers had discovered that the placement of the gas tank in the rear of the vehicle rendered it unusually susceptible to the risk of catching fire. The writers further argued that Ford refused to accept this fact, and instead lobbied to change security regulations of gas tanks in small cars.

In the course of the public debate after the accidents, an indication of the economic cost-benefit calculations behind the strategy of the Ford Corporation came to light. This published analysis estimated that it would have cost Ford eleven dollars per car to shift the tank to the front during assembly and reach acceptable security standards. According to Ford's calculations, however, these expenses would not be profitable, because they would be much higher than the official economic worth of a human life, which had been proposed by highway authorities on the basis of suggestions from the car industry.

There was much debate about the actual calculations of the number of dead and wounded per car accident. From the point of view of pure cost-benefit considerations, fire accidents would only cost about five dollars for each car. This was one of the major economic reasons that Ford did not change the construction. In one particularly notorious case in 1978, the gas tank of a Ford Pinto exploded after a minor crash.[15] Three teenagers in the car were burned to death. After the accident, a legal investigation was started to find out whether Ford was responsible for selling a defective product. In the legal proceedings, Ford was charged with criminal homicide, because of the crude cost-benefit considerations behind the company's strategy. The corporation was found not guilty of homicide, but it had lost face in major public debates.

The case of the Ford Pinto illustrates the tension between ethics and economics, and the possibly absurd consequences of basing business decision solely on economic calculations. The critical issue in this example is that the corporation did not reflect on its responsibilities to particular human beings, viewing its decisions from a broader ethical perspective. If the respect for human dignity had been taken seriously, the corporation may have done more to make the car safer. Ironically, this strategy may also have been the most economically rational considering the substantial financial loss stemming from the company's diminished public reputation, brand value, and factoring in costs associated with the law suits brought against the company.

2.2. The Place of values in corporations

From an historical perspective, values have always been an essential aspect of business life. When Weber wanted to show the particular link between capitalism and the Protestant ethos, he looked to the roots of capitalism in American Puritanism.[16] Weber's views on capitalist values – as can be seen in the previous discussion of corporate legitimacy – prevailed in business ethics through the end of the twentieth century.[17] He emphasized the rational and bureaucratic nature of modern business corporations as a characteristic feature of the modern capitalist economy.[18] Weber described the bureaucratic individual, "the organization man" who only acts according to his place in the instrumental rationality of the organization.[19] Moreover, the organization man can be conceived as the hard working individual who lives and belongs to the organization. As such, his formulations describe the central aspects of a modern rationalized organization.

In their work on American organizational culture, Scott and Hart define values as explicit or implicit conceptions of the desirable ends for action. They state that managers seldomly speculate over the moral or ethical principles behind their actions.[20] Scott and Hart consider modern organizations as managerial systems using individuals, groups, and technologies in order to achieve given goals in the most efficient manner; thus, they describe the culture of these organizations as driven by an *organizational imperative,* or the search for organizational economic efficiency, maintenance, and growth.[21] Because this organizational imperative is the basis of the values structuring managerial action, collective organizational values determine the actions of individual managers. When acting in organizations, managers are evaluated according to their loyalty and service to the organization. The principles of modern American organization represent a synchronization between the individual and organization in which the happiness and desires of the individual are considered insignificant.[22]

This phenomenon of synchronization is not limited solely to organizations in the United States; indeed, the fusion between the rationality of organizations and individual actions characterizes managerial and technological society at large. This aspect of the relations between individuals and organizations has a rather totalitarian quality.[23] In order to prevent this totalitarian development of the organizational imperative, Scott and Hart look for other ethics and values in order to improve management. They can be said to propose an existentialist improvement of management based on genuine moral leadership, in the sense that business leadership is not only about technical bureaucracy but also concerns the fundamental values of the corporation.

Accordingly, William C. Frederick has argued that the original values of an organization might be conceived as the outcome of the intersection between economization, power aggrandizement, and ecologization.[24] Frederick states that these are the original values that have influenced the development of the modern American business organization. He wants to show how a certain number of beliefs, relationships, and judgmental presuppositions are the determining characteristics of American firms. Frederick argues that these values are embedded in natural evolution and that they are archetypal of the business system. As the background for the function of business organizations in society, these values enjoy a great amount of social legitimacy and acceptance.[25]

Economization refers to the organization's activity as an entity acting on the economic market and seeking economic growth. At this level, the firm seeks systemic integrity and flourishing as an economic organization. Economization is based on using cost-benefit calculations to determine the success or failure of the activities of the firm. The values of economization are based on the significance of the bottom line for the survival of the firm.

With C.P. Snow, Frederick wants to overcome the gap between the natural sciences and humanities, and in this case business culture, too. To this end, he argues that research into the laws of thermodynamics offers great insight into the development of organizations.[26] While the first law of thermodynamics tells us that the energy in the universe is constant, the second law holds that energy and matter move toward a condition of maximum integration, disorder, and degradation.[27] These laws are interrelated through two possible interpretations. The first states that the result is energy degradation, or *entropy*. The second interpretation holds that while entropy represents a maximum of disorder, it is simultaneously a development towards a new level of equilibrium. According to this interpretation, the creative self-organization of the system moves it towards a new more developed position, thereby overcoming the dangers of disintegration.

Using this as a metaphor for the business organization, Frederick argues that the values of growth and striving for systemic integrity are central to the values of economization and are original values of the system.[28] This insight is also present in system theory. According to this conception, systems are characterized by processes of growth as they search for identity, integrity, and stability in order to survive.[29] The concrete formation and strategic structure of a business organization might be considered as ways of improving this *autopoetic* development of the system.

On this basis Frederick discusses whether profit maximization may be an original value of the business organization. He argues that profit is not an essential part of economizing, but rather a consequence and outcome of the development of the organization.[30] This argument is important because it shows that profit maximization is not the productive reason for the development of a business system. There are other factors of production causing organizational growth and energy that cannot be conceived purely in terms of profit maximization.

Power aggrandizement concerns a firm's goals to increase its power and position in the world. These aggrandizing values indicate the presence of power in an organization and they indicate both the internal and external search for power. Power is both a fact and a representation in people's minds. It indicates the hierarchical structure of business organizations based on economic power and ownership.

Frederick emphasizes that dominance over others is an archetypal feature of a business organization.[31] This dominance includes many symbolized meanings and ritualized structures backing up power formations in business organizations. The decision-making power of managers depends of these structures. Internal and external relations of the organization can be seen as an effort to establish and maintain a maximized power equilibrium according to the organization's capacities. Frederick emphasizes that the quest for power determines the economizing activities of organizations and that the functions of the organization are determined by the coercive powers of leading managers, who form organizational strategies, policies, and other developments.

Frederick further includes ecologization as a basic value of the firm. The notion of ecology should be understood from a very broad perspective, in this context referring to the interaction of companies with the environment. The firm seeks a favorable relation with the social and ecological environment in order to survive as an organizational structure. In its nature the firm seeks to accomplish these values. In the interaction with the environment as an organization the firm functions as a life-form seeking to be an integral part of community.[32] In this way there is a close connection between the economization of the firm and its participation in an ecological system of natural and social processes.

Being in interaction with the environment, the firm is confronted with the carrying capacity and ecological position of the Earth. The firm is an entity taking part in an ecological process in confrontation with human society. Natural conditions, products of nature, material conditions and life cycles of the earth might be conceived as basic conditions for the survival of the firm and its interaction with a sustainable environment. Survival of the firm depends on its capacity to cope with the ecological significance of the environment.

It is important to emphasize the dynamic nature of interactions between different values within the process of exchange with the environment. Frederick points to the concept of technology as a way to overcome conflicts between different original values of the firm.[33] Technological innovation might improve the growth, systemic integrity, power equilibrium, and environmental stability of organizations. In this sense, technological values help to establish new links between values of the organization. Technology and technological development lead towards higher systemic integrity of the organization.

Values-driven management can also be proposed according to basic ethical principles and values as a way to improve the systemic integrity of an organization. Like technological innovations, improvements in ethical management might be a way to overcome conflict between the organization in relation to external and internal environments. But these improvements also imply that unethical values have an impact on the firm. Business ethics is a more fundamental attempt to reconcile organizations with society, because the normative systems of the organization open it up to stakeholder demands to introduce general social principles that improve accountability of organizations. Moreover, ethical values do not emerge as unified clear-cut concepts. Organizations are blends of many egoistic, duty-based (i.e., deontological), utilitarian, or virtue-oriented values. At the same time, business and ethical values are mutually dependent. Managers might primarily have economic motives in making money while this activity might at the same time have indirect ethical impacts on people's lives in society; therefore, even if the managers pretend to be neutral, there cannot be business without ethical values. [34]

2.3. Values–driven management and organizational systems

With this description of organizations as system that are based on fundamental values, but also in constant interaction with their environments, values-driven management can be conceived as a strategic response to the fact that corporations are open systems in society. In fact, it is possible to combine system-based conceptions of organization within organization theory with philosophical conceptions of ethics and practices in order to define the role of values-driven management as the basis for ethics in organizations. By being explicit about ethical norms and values, communication and information about the organization can be improved. In this context, systems theory conceives organizations as systems based on communication as generalized media for interaction.[35] Ethical communication opens the organization to the environment and it contributes to making the aim of organizational development more explicit. Ethics becomes a reflective mechanism of governance and acts as an important supplement to the instruments of power and domination that are most commonly used in organizations (e.g., economic management and instrumental goal rationality). In fact, because of the dominance of such systemic rationality, the spheres of economics, law, and politics are often strangers, alienated from moral reflection.

Even though such a strong distinction between ethics, power, and economics has been criticized – some point to the fact that no social system can totally exclude ethics, for example, in the case of power, which also expresses an ethics – it is important from the point of view of organization theory. This distinction allows an investigation into how individuals in organizational systems become absorbed by their roles, effectively by forms of domination, which accordingly limit ethical communication. In many organizations as the general demands for growth and profit increase, so do the requirements of individuals.[36] According to systems theory this kind of power has consequences on the individual level. Individualization and isolation in mass society makes people feel lost when they do not take part of the functional systems and organizations in society. This need to belong to organizations and systems, combined with the increased pressure of the system on individuals in modern organizations, implies that systems and structures cannot avoid challenging the humanity of modern organizations.

Ethics in organizational systems concerns, therefore, the search for solutions in order to avoid the human vulnerability and the loss of individual autonomy, dignity, and integrity in modern organizations. Ethics and values-driven management express efforts to deal with organizations as well-ordered systems of action producing outputs and reducing complexity. The difficulty of implementing values-driven management in organizational systems arises in cases of limited resources and in situations where choices are determined by necessity.[37] With values-driven management, concepts of ethics are integrated into the logic of the organization's information systems. When problems and dilemmas arising between different stakeholders in the organization are confronted, this logic of immanent rationality – that is, restricted to the norms of instrumental rationality within the economic, legal, and political systems of the organizational bureaucracy – becomes insufficient. Ethics can be conceived as a new instrument in the communicative process that deals with the solution of different types of conflict between organizational stakeholders.

Moreover, they also help with organizational development and create a strategic vision for how to conceive "the good life" with respect for employees in the organization. Ethics in values-driven management is an important instrument to improve: *a)* decision-making processes, *b)* argumentation (broadening the values foundation), *c)* the legitimation of decisions (including a broader groups of stakeholders), and *d)* the basis of decision-making (transparency about decision-making processes). With these different concerns, management can ensure a broader ethical basis for decision-making.

Values-driven management may contribute to the democratization of organizations. Management contributes by recognizing the importance of employees in the decision-making process. Referring to Habermas's views of communicative action, values-driven management must be based on the force of the better argument and dialogical communication, where one is open to different points of view.[38] Such democratic communication between employees and managers may be conceived as an unconventional form of management: one that limits traditional hierarchical structures of power and is based on the personal conceptions of managers. This form or deliberative decision-making has much in common with democratic politics.

The concept of values-driven management arguably makes ethical values an important supplement to management based on the traditional systems and structures of the corporation. As an aspect of managerial decision-making, ethics are introduced at the local level of organizational systems. Values-driven management should aim at a complex integration of issues: foundations, premises, distinguishing between systemic and ethical values, and also accounting for differing general conceptions of values in the organization. Accordingly, values-driven management can be conceived as a kind of rational negotiation of decisions, which integrates ethics and concern for the common good into systems and structures of organizations as institutional totalities.

The necessity of values-driven management as an instrument for ethics may, in particular, be motivated by the fact that it is impossible to know the degree to which a firm conceives of its own good as being tied to the larger social good and how this is implied in organizational decision-making. Values are expressed in multiple ways at different levels of the organization, directed both internally and externally. It is the task of values-driven management to ensure clarification of the function of values in the organization, and also to clarify what values are important for its future. Values-driven management is an important instrument to ensure communication between individuals with many differing conceptions of values. Values-driven management integrates ethics into general conceptions of management, thereby rendering them central to organizational development.

This is illustrated in the role that values-driven management plays in change management.[39] Theorists of change management consider values as very important for organizational development. Change processes are much more likely to succeed when they governed by a strong vision, based on efforts to alter the collective consciousness and identity of the organization. A vision of change management must be honest and convincing. This is possible when it appeals to ethics, concepts of the common good, and the mission of the organization. Moreover, change management implies values that posit the world as open and indeterminable; no standard bureaucratic picture of organizational reality is able to communicate these new values and to deal with the complexity of changing the organization. In this sense, the soft vocabulary of values has replaced the bureaucratic vocabulary of instrumental rationality of efficiency and organizational imperative. In change processes, values-driven management implies transcendence of the system, radicality, and creatively proposing ethics and social responsibility as an alternative to traditional organizational governance.

Box 5: Organizations, values, and ethics

In the famous book *Images of Organization*, Gareth Morgan describes some of the most common theoretical metaphors of organizations.[40] The metaphors presented in the book can also be conceived from the perspective of values-driven management and business ethics. These different conceptions of organizations all have a relation to values and ethics. Moreover, ethics and values can be used as critical instruments for normative evaluation of the different organizational forms:

Organizations as machines: In the conception of the organization as a machine, ethics is replaced by functional systems. Ethics becomes, however, important as an instrument to ensure that the machine organization is not captured by functional logic and efficiency rationality.

Organizations as organisms: In an organization that is conceived as an organism, ethics centrally contributes to its environmental adaptation. Values function as the basis for communication with the environment.

Organizations as brains: An organization that is based on knowledge management needs ethics and values in order to make it easier to share knowledge and communicate with the different knowledge centers in the organization.

Organizations as cultures: When one conceives an organization as a culture, ethics and values emerge as the founding elements of this culture. If one goes deeply into cultural development, it is necessary to include the ethics and values of the corporation.

Organizations as political systems: The political organization functions on the basis of a confrontation between different conceptions of values and ethics that form the organization in mutual conflict and cooperation.

Organizations as psychic prisons: Here values and ethics function as oppressing mechanisms that capture the employees in the organization and determine its valid norms.

Organizations as flux and transformation: Here values-driven management becomes an instrument to support and develop organizational change processes. Values are used as instruments to teach the employee to operate within ambiguity and to act in turbulent environments.

Organizations as instruments of domination: In the organization conceived as an instrument of domination values-driven management can be considered as an instrument of control in order to discipline the employees. Or it can be used as a critical measure to change the power structures of the organization through corporate democracy.

2.4. The ideology of management: The case against values-driven management

The call for values-driven management has been received in many different ways. Alain Etchegoyen states that we live in a crisis of ethics where universal morality has been replaced by many particular orders of ethics. He conceives the emergence of ethics programs as an attempt to reconstruct ethics after its deconstruction.[41] Modern organizations are marked by interest in money and power and they have no moral initiative. From this point of view, the new ethics movement is not a re-establishment of good morals, but rather a sort of Taylorism of moral reflection, a new ideology of management using ethical principles to improve the efficiency of the firm.

In modern firms, ethics is no longer based on moral imperatives, but functions as publicity and communication of the firm in order to improve its image. Etchegoyen conceives of the new ethics as local cultures forming morals, which constitute the ideology of a particular group, without any concern for universality. According to Etchegoyen, values-driven management is not seeking universal moral value, but it is rather an arbitrary choice of principle in order to improve the performance of the firm. Ethics has become a market for consultancy groups proposing different ethical models in order to legitimize the firm and to bypass traditional skepticism towards business. The slogan that "ethics pays" has replaced traditional concern for morals. Integration of ethics language into the mission and purpose statements of firms aims to make employees feel committed to their organizations. But this is ideology; it makes the poor workers think that they are building a cathedral.[42]

Critics have conceived many forms of values-driven management as myths.[43] Initiatives to portray firms as responsible have been used by management as a new form of manipulation. Modern management wants to engage individuals in work by envisioning the company as a common culture where individuals are directly involved, thereby rendering a new form of collective consciousness.[44] This new management utilizes many different symbols to achieve this aim, even invoking religion in order to integrate workers in a common value-culture. This is particularly noticeable when noting the impact of Eastern mysticism and New Age culture on management theory and practice.

The danger of this approach is that ethics, instead of creating an opening for free and autonomous reflection, becomes simply another utility of management, modeling the movements of the firm.[45] Management moves from necessity to virtue and is considered a place for creative and imaginary individuals. Change management becomes conceived in terms of community and common solidarity, rather than being solely based on economic contracts. This new kind of management depends upon worker participation and their identification with the firm. The enterprise is conceived as an entity of common imagination in order to realize the individual in the workplace. These efforts to create a common identity of the enterprise stand in strong opposition to the problem of the lack of democracy in the firm. It seems that values-driven management remains an ideology as long as this problem is not addressed. The challenge is how to integrate the firm in society and in culture without forgetting its particular economic and social characteristics, and confounding it with church.[46]

Modern managers could even be accused of attempting to reintroduce a kind of utopian socialism. Like the utopian philosopher Claude Henri Saint-Simon, they want to unite human beings in the company. By mobilizing individuals for common production they want to establish a common culture, where production serves the common good.[47] As mentioned previously, this position bears similarity to religious ideas of common realization, in this instance applied to human beings in the workplace. This position encourages individuals to view their personal work in the corporation as a part of building a community.

Ethics communication functions as both an external and internal ideological justification. Values-driven management becomes an instrument to endow words like solidarity, responsibility, loyalty, integrity, respect, courage, tolerance, transparency, autonomy, personal development, and perfection with meaning.[48] This ethics is local because it aims to reinforce the particular mission of the firm, which is to gain economic power. Values-driven management creates the illusion that management has a conscience and that the firm should have a kind of collective "soul" and that it serves the common good of the many.

From this perspective, the ethical manager is a social monster, perpetuating the fiction that economics and morality can be combined.[49] Market values in particular companies cannot be moral values but, instead, are ethics principles used crudely to reinforce management goals; thus, the distinction between market values and social values must be maintained. According to Etchegoyen, it is not the job of the manager to fix ethics. It remains an issue for the responsible political legislator to determine the universal moral content of the law. Firms should not be the primary conveyors of meaning in our lives.

Accepting Etchegoyen's critique of values-driven management as ideology, ethics must not be reduced to a new marketing or human resource device. But this is not an argument against all kinds of business ethics and values-driven management. In fact, by focusing on its morality, some possibility of business ethics can be seen as implicit in the argument of Etchegoyen. He tries to base ethics on the philosophies of Kant and Lévinas, who emphasized sympathy and compassion with the other. This ethics is, therefore, defined by responsibility for the other and emphasizes the social solidarity of firms. Moreover, inspired of Habermas, he wants to base morals and moral development on a comunicative ethics, highlighting universal truth claims rather than strategic action. True morality – with universal principles of generosity, solidarity, and respect for the other as other – replaces the ideology of different particular ethics.[50]

Box 6. Arguments against values-driven management

The general criticism of values-driven management shares the implication that business ethics and corporate social responsibility cannot be critical to capitalist organization, but rather are based on internal rational organization. With this in mind, the general criticism can be broken down into seven important anticapitalist arguments.[51]

1. Values are economic instruments

According to this criticism, values and ethics are nothing but a new and more sophisticated form of stakeholders manipulation. They do not imply emancipation or a better society, but rather are a new form of Weber's "iron cage." Values and ethics only reflect the new conditions of capitalism, where corporations are confronted with individualistic employees and customers who need to be respected and motivated. Values-driven management and business ethics are seen as simply providing tools to meet these new conditions.

2. Values are management ideology

According to this criticism, values are ideological instruments to reintroduce lost meaning and coherence into work life. Ethics and codes of conduct have to fill the empty space of secularization after the death of Protestant ethics. Values and ethics in corporations give employees the false impressions that they serve the common good, but in reality they are nothing other than a reinforcement of the bottom line. As long as more fundamental issues of democracy and global inequality are not addressed, business ethics and values-driven management remain ideology.

3. Values and the ethics of sensitivity

According to this criticism, "soft values" are becoming "hard values" that are used as disciplinary measures and instruments to ensure employee loyalty. Values that emphasize morality and ethics encourage employees to internalize their duties and devotion to the company based on a personal morality and consciousness.

4. Values and the search for flexible employees

According to this criticism, the ongoing moralization of business implies a response to the fact that modern workers must be flexible, ready for changing projects, work areas, and work fields. In this context, employees must have feelings of initiative, responsibility, and engagement, as well as personal values. Given these new work conditions, values-driven management aims to ensure that employees identify with the firm; however, fundamental relations of power and oppression remain unidentified.

5. Deconstruction of morality

Deconstructive positions emphasize that the current age is an era of ethical crisis where many particular forms of values are replacing universal morality.[52] Values-driven management is viewed as a desperate attempt to reconstruct ethics where it is no longer possible. This position is not really treating values as ethics, but rather as a form of ideology of power and domination.

6. Values as the instrument of corporate power

Values-driven management is used as an instrument of power, where individuals are subsumed by community values and ethics. Accordingly, values-driven management becomes an instrument to ensure power over employees. Management forms its own codes of conduct and governing rules, which employees come to perceive as their own, and uses them as an instrument of discipline.

7. From bureaucracy to project capitalism

Luc Boltanski and Eve Chiappelo describe the development from traditional forms of organization to project capitalism. This development, which has involved many changes, is based on the transition from traditional forms and structures of organization to contemporary forms of unstable project organization.[53] The new forms of management and business ethics appear as the current ideology, where soft forms of leadership are replacing hierarchical theories of management. The organization of employees by projects is an expression of this new management and reinforces the power of the corporation over its employees.

2.5. Values, moral development, and organizational learning

The following vision for values-driven management attempts to overcome the ideology of management that conceives values only as tools for improving economic efficiency. The essential message is that establishing a code of ethics or business principles can, in the long run, promote better ethical business of the organization. Managers are needed who are able to understand and work with the values of corporations in an easy and reflective manner. One of the difficulties with the concept of values is that it may be conceived differently by people or organizational cultures, depending on the level of experience. It is necessary that moral imagination and reflective conceptions of values are the basis for organizational learning and improving business ethics. This analytical approach to moral development was originally developed in relation to individual psychology, but the subsequent discussion will evaluate its application to organizational learning and cognitive development.

In *Business Ethics and Values*, Colin Fisher and Alan Lovell distinguish between a number of different approaches to value experience. They refer to, among others, a traditional scheme of shared values, which is opposed to a pragmatist or postmodernist perspective on value experience.[54] Moreover, they consider values-driven management as a kind of institutional and organizational learning by referring to Lawrence Kohlberg's theory of cognitive moral development.[55] What is important about Kohlberg's theory is the ability to explain differences in value judgments and value experiences from the perspective of psychological development of the capacity for ethical decision-making.

In fact Kohlberg's theory of moral development can help conceive values-driven management in a reflective way that encompasses the criticism of ethics in business as ideology.[56] It provides a means to reconcile the clash and potential tension between the original incentive values of the corporation: economizing, power aggrandizing, and ecologizing one the one hand, and the pursuit of a personal vision of the good life, belief in the reciprocity of community, search for the greatest happiness for the greatest number, and respect for universal rights and human dignity on the other. In his analysis of Kohlberg's framework, John Dienhart provides the basis for a reflective conception of values-driven management. [57]

The distinction between pre-conventional, conventional, and post-conventional levels of development of cognitive moral development is essential to Kohlberg's scheme.[58] These three categories can be applied to institutions and express the levels of reasoning about values of different members of organizations. This schematization of values as moral beliefs can be said to determine and direct behavior and cognitive perceptions of members of different organizations.[59]

At the pre-conventional level of moral reflection it is likely, using Dienhart's application of Kohlberg to values in organizations, that the workers in the organization will only have limited understanding and loyalty to the values of the organization. At this level, they are likely to follow self-interest and are only able to evaluate decision-making in these terms. This level includes two major stages.[60] At the first stage, values are sanctioned in terms of authority and punishment, and value-orientation is formed according to those values and actions that are not punished. At the second stage of this level, individuals are capable of relating to others by promoting self-interest in terms of a future-oriented value selection.

At the conventional level, individuals bind themselves to rules that function in groups, organizations, or communities. Moral behavior is developed in terms of conventional rule following and individuals bind themselves to the values of collective institutions, without any reflection about the legitimacy of these values.[61] Here resides the third and forth stages of moral development. At level three, the individual considers reciprocity as valuable because it contributes to holding the group together. The fourth stage may be considered a "law and order" orientation, according to which the individual follows the norms, values, and legal rules of not only the local group, but also a larger group – for example, loyalty to the organization or to national values.

At the post-conventional level, members of an organization have developed the capacity to reflect over universal ethical standards. Now they reject the partiality of self-interest and group interest, and they refer to universal values by asserting that all human beings have equal and intrinsic value. It is only on this level that individuals require the capacity to interpret their participation in institutions from a universal and reflective perspective.[62] The post-conventional level encompasses the fifth stage, whereby individuals develop an orientation towards rights and social contracts and, at the same time, acquire a utilitarian attitude promoting the well-being of the human beings involved. It is only at the sixth stage of moral behavior that individuals acquire the truly universalist capacity to consider respect for human dignity as the ultimate principle of moral reflection.

When we argue against the criticism of values-driven management as ideology, it is important to emphasize that it is only at the post-conventional level of moral reflection that this kind of activity is really valuable. Even though Kohlberg thought that not very many people had reached this level, it still plays an important function to facilitate competent ethical decision-making. It is also at this level that the different values of the firm can be evaluated in comparison to each other. Moreover, Kohlberg puts forth a compelling feminist argument against a formalist interpretation of the post-conventional level. In her famous book, *In a Different Voice,* Carol Gilligan promoted this view by arguing that women's moral development includes a relational component, which is not inferior to post-conventional morality. According to this view, the reflective capacity to reason about values also implies care and compassion for other human beings.[63]

At the level of reflective morality, Kantian universalism combines focus on the abstract other and the intrinsic value of human dignity one the one hand, and the feminist relational perspective, taking into account the particularity of the situation of action, on the other. This is another version of Etchegoyen's discussion of Kant and Lévinas, which was proposed as the basis for morality.[64] Personal self-interest and utilitarian search for welfare are perspectives that are inferior with regard to the universalist approach to moral reflection.[65] It is this post-conventional level of reflection that provides the necessary ability to evaluate values and norms in institutions. It is the basis for creating an ability of moral imagination and sensitivity in order to detect conflicts of values in organizations. It is from this level that the criticism of business ethics and values-driven management as ideology can be overcome.

Box 7. Aim of ethics and values–driven management programs

Values-driven management can be defined as an important step of practical realization of business ethics. It is a characteristic aspect of values-driven management that ethics is developed and implemented through the formulation of corporate vision, mission, and foundational values. This realization is indeed a question of communication and it is important to involve internal and external stakeholders in the formulation of values, as well as in the formulation of company strategy and its practical implementation. The following aspects of business ethics are topics that can be addressed through values-driven management. Business ethics:

1. Contributes to solving management problems in the corporation
2. Develops common values and vision
3. Solves internal ethical problems in the company
4. Treats ethical problems in relation to external stakeholders
5. Provides an environmental focus: treating environmental ethical issues
6. Addresses finance and investment ethics – ethics of corporate economics
7. Deals with the ethics of marketing in postmodern society
8. Includes consumers in management and decision-making
9. Concerns problems of discrimination and affirmative action
10. Protects employee rights to privacy (autonomy)
11. Addresses ethical issues regarding corruption and bribery
12. Helps efforts to deal with transparency and openness in company activities
13. Develops criteria for product safety
14. Improves employee satisfaction and autonomy
15. Improves work environment and health at work
16. Emphasizes a proactive attitude to crisis situations

2.6. Strategies for values–driven management

This discussion of values-driven management from the point of view of the post-conventional moral reflection addresses the difficult question of integrating ethics and business, and provides a way to conceive values-driven management such that it does not end up as ideology. Despite the apparently permanent tension and opposition between the traditional values of economizing, power, ecologizing and the ethical values of a business organization, it is still possible to imagine a complementary coexistence within business organizations.

Indeed, a social reality where corporations have to express and signal their political attitudes can be described as an illustration of *polycentric* conditions of decision-making in complex societies. In times were politics is no longer restricted to the sphere of the formal, the role of companies in society is no longer considered to be value-neutral. Firms should document, promote, and develop their political and ethical values in public debates and in society, as such. Following Ulrich Beck, the new corporate values represent one of many examples of a subpolitical process between politics and nonpolitics.[66] The polycentric condition of decision-making about ethics and politics assures that values and business ethics play a central part in debates about the future of the corporation.

A further aspect of the polycentric conception of policy-making, where corporations are integrated in society as actors who are expected to contribute to the common good, is the emergence of business ethics and ethics codes as corporate self-regulation, and as a source of legal regulation for the problems of society. Despite the fact that ethics based on philosophical conceptions of the good life and what is morally right have been considered as subjective and relative compared to the objectivity and universality of parliamentary legislation or regulation, ethics rules are becoming more and more widespread and important for law, regulation, and legal decision-making.[67]

As indicators of custom, habit, virtue, and good values and norms, ethics rules are becoming important supplements to existing legislation. In fact, they function as regulations that are not directly initiated by state laws but nevertheless have legal significance. That these "soft law" standards are attributed to ethics codes is very clear in the case studies. Ethical rules contribute to autonomous regulation of different businesses and industries. In contrast to legal rules that may be based on pure power considerations, ethics and codes of conduct are supposed to be based on universal ethical rationality. Ethics and codes of conduct are, as indicated by case studies, founded on inner motivation and not only as a response to outside pressure. In this sense, the content of ethical principles transcends a positivistic conception of law. They are not always formulated according to the legal norms of government; rather, these principles are ethical concepts of the good proposed by business and industry for autonomous self-regulation.

Turning to the insights of Mette Morsing, four ideal types of strategy for values-driven management can be defined: religious, democractic, controlled, and illusory.[68]

According to the religious strategy, values are based on faith. The aim of the values is to create a community of faith in the corporation.[69] The key actor of values-driven management is corporate management and the expected outcome is commitment of employees and customers to the corporation. The danger of this strategy is loss of faith and the realization that the values are nothing but illusions.

According to the democratic strategy, values are process tools in order to create a democratic company.[70] The aim of values is to ensure dialogue and discussion about the future of the firm. Values are used to mediate between management and employees, and the democratic dialogue should determine the most important values of the firm. The expected outcome of this dialogue is self-determination, but the danger is that it can introduce too much complexity.

According to the strategy of control, values are rational management tools to ensure transparency and dominance over employees.[71] In this context, values-driven management is considered as an efficient tool for normative control over the company. The potential danger of the strategy is that employees loose motivation and commitment to their work.

According to the strategy of illusion, it is the aim of values in organizations to maintain and develop the brand value of the corporation.[72] In this strategy, the aim of values is to be a good instrument of marketing. The focus of values-driven management is the customer, who should be influenced by the branding strategy of the organization. At the same time, the danger of this strategy is that the customer will become aware that there is nothing beyond the illusion.

In addition to these four strategies, values can also be an organizational tool or concept for handling criticism; Hanne Knudsen has defined the concept of values-driven management by referring to this "license to criticism."[73] According to this strategy, which is close to the democratic strategy, it is the aim of values-driven management to ensure critical evaluations and legitimacy of the corporation among its stakeholders.

It is possible to say that there are six critical and practical challenges to values-driven management in practice in organizations. The dangers of practical strategies for values-driven management, as something essentially different from good business ethics, include:

1) Codes of conduct and vision statements can be overly general and banal. This challenge emerges out of the previous discussion and analysis of strategies for corporate values-driven management. It may be argued that these strategies do not represent anything more than a clever marketing tactic. If codes of

conduct and proposals for values in corporate strategies are too quotidian and generic, they cannot realistically be the basis for an elaborate strategy of triple bottom-line management or corporate ethics programs.

2) The use of clichéd language by corporations when they present their values and business ethics. This challenge is linked to the challenge of banality. People who are very skeptical towards business ethics cannot see why the concept should not be an oxymoron. They feel offended by the corporate approach to ethics, because they have the strong opinion that corporations are only concerned with maintaining a good reputation and really do nothing to be ethical. Corporate value charts and codes of conduct become offensive because they are simultaneously pragmatic, meaningless, and idealistic.

3) The challenge of hypocrisy is also very severe. It is argued that corporations are not honest and that any kind of corporation with strong integrity would not promote itself by using banal and clichéd values; in fact, they undermine corporate credibility precisely because they appear so far removed from the complexity and profundity of real moral dilemmas. Moreover, values used as strategies represent a very mean cynicism that is remote from real moral sensitivity. The truth of ethics, it is argued, is much more complex than can be accommodated by facile values statements and smart codes of conduct.

4) This argument may be considered as another version of the theory-practice problem. While values-driven management looks very nice in theory, as it emerges in the codes of conduct of corporations, it is something different. The real practice of corporations does not seem to correspond to the ideal theorization of values and ethics. From this perspective, values-driven management in practice remains an ideology, which can at best be considered as a discourse, or an effort to establish an ideal narrative about the virtues of the corporation.

5) Indeed, there may be huge differences between the efforts of corporations to promote themselves as ethical, with the use of particular codes of conduct and instruments for values-driven management, and the reality of intepreting the actions of these corporations in their social environment. The values of corporations are nothing other than buzzwords that have no deeper significance than all the other methods of marketing and publicity that the corporation uses to promote its activities.

6) The final problem involves the conceptualization of human beings in values-driven management. Even though corporations are doing a great deal to present their values as good ethical values that are respectful of human beings, some argue that, in the end, they are based on strategic and instrumental concepts, which have no basis in true philosophical ethical concepts of humanity.

Again, there seems to be a strong divide between the theory and practice of business ethics. Ethics in practice seems to be a cliché rather than a real accomplishment of the philosophical ideals.

Box. 8. Different theoretical conceptions of values-driven management

The different conceptions and theories of values-driven management, as a concrete instrument for corporate change and development, diverge on important points. The following are characteristic approaches that seek to overcome the criticism of values-driven management as ideology:

Values instead of rules. According to this conception, values are conceived in fundamental contrast to rules and laws. Values come from within and are motivating and inspiring, while rules come from without and are authoritarian and limiting. According to this approach, rules belong to an earlier paradigm of management, which was founded on the concept of the hierarchical organization and the strong boss, while values instead of rules presuppose a dialogical conception of management focused on meaning.[74] In particular, this approach focuses on situation-based leadership.

Values as dialogical democratization. According to this approach, values are first and foremost expressions of democratization of the corporation. They allow a growing number of stakeholders to be heard in the process of management.[75] Values-driven management must be used for democratization and development of the organization in close collaboration with stakeholders.

Values as an ethical framework for leadership. This conception combines elements of the other two but makes the concern for ethics the central focus point for developing values in businesses and organizations.[76] This ethical approach conceives values and rules as basically complementary, and it agrees with the importance of democratization, but integrates the concern for particular stakeholders into a general focus on ethical principles and of the vision of the good life.

Values as a part of a strategy for organizational integrity. This conception tries to formulate a closer link between values and corporate business strategy. Values-driven management is supposed to be combined with business ethics, corporate social responsibility, and corporate governance in order to express a holistic concern for good ethical management of the organization. Accordingly, it creates organizational integrity.

2.7. Ethical values-driven management: From rules to values

Ethical values must be integrated into the values of the business organization. Put differently, business values are incarnations of specific conceptions of ethics. Values-driven management is often introduced in situations of moral crisis for an organization, where there has been a threat to its systemic integrity. The following is a preliminary definition of ethics and values-driven management as the basis for the subsequent analysis of the major ethical perspectives that play a role as the foundation of institutions in free economic markets. This concept of values-driven management should, indeed, be able to overcome the danger of the ideology of management previously described.

Values-driven management can be considered as a way to ensure that the organization and individuals in the organization act ethically.[77] The actions of individuals must be considered in a larger systemic perspective. Driscoll and Hoffman emphasize that values-driven management should be analyzed at the organizational level. They agree that there is a close connection between legal rules and values, but values-driven management and compliance may not be mixed. Compliance to the law is only the most basic level. Values indicate a broader and more idealistic approach to organizational ethics. There is a close connection between ethics and values, even though values-driven management and ethics are not the same.

Although values-driven management aims at a fundamental bottom line and compliance with regulations, it basically seeks to make a more human and engaged relation between individuals and organizations. Values-driven management aims to make people see the good and gives them capacities to act rightly and justly in difficult situations. The capacity of the ideals of values-driven management to improve the systemic integrity of organizations through genuine individual engagement is very high.

It is important to emphasize that well-working programs of values-driven management integrate values in the culture of an organization and that the embodiment of these values in the behavior of individuals in an organizational structure is not based solely on external compliance.[78] Values may be described as internal virtues, as personal standards of excellence in order to guide the behavior of individuals. From an historical perspective, many companies have started values-driven management with a compliance approach, but in the long run they have understood that values depend on virtues rather than on strict adherence to rules.[79] This does not mean that values can work without rules. On the contrary, experience show that ethics are much stronger when they are backed up by legal rules.

The establishment of values-driven management in an organization aims to reinforce systemic integrity by developing programs of ethical rules, codes of conducts, or ethical principles. At the same time that these values should reflect the particularity of the ethical situation of specific companies, they should also be in accordance with universal ethical standards. There may be a considerable amount of free moral space and ethical particularity in a given company (e.g., not all companies have the same work values or conception of privacy); however, an organization's values cannot be in total opposition to universal ethical concepts. It is a very difficult task to find the right balance between universal moral rules and particular substantial ethical visions.

Values-driven management may have many different structures. It may be only a very simple credo, but it can also have a complex structure consisting of statements, rules, and reporting and accounting procedures. Different firms of different size and with different types of employees may choose a particular program of values-driven management according to their needs and corporate culture.

Given these differences in concrete structure of values-driven management, it is important to notice that an organization without values-driven management assumes great risk.[80] Such an organization does not have principles on external and internal relations, including relations to society, consumers, investors, employees, et cetera. The company is simply leaving these relations to develop randomly. Instead of a strategy exlusively targeting economic considerations, values-driven management aims at formulating principles for conceiving the culture of the organization.

Such initiative to implement values-driven management may be considered as an effort to formulate the collective identity and mission of the organization. In this sense, it is a form of reflective self-awareness on the part of the corporate culture. The organization is oriented toward knowledge of internal and external aspects of its corporate culture and behavior in relation to its goals and aims, and with regard to the law. In this context, the organization begins by describing the ethical problems and dilemmas that it faces, which makes it possible for management to address the core of critical issues.

Values-driven management cannot work without commitment from the top.[81] The executive board of the organization and the larger board of directors should be involved in order to implement values-driven management. The board should be aware of the importance of ethics. At the same time, their full commitment is necessary in order to make the values program efficient. A commitment from the top is also necessary in order to overcome the ethical and moral blindness, muteness, or incoherence in the organization. This commitment to the values of the organization on the part of the morally aware manager is not only a question of personal character, but it also involves the manager's understanding of the need to work with values at the level of the ethical culture and systemic interaction in the organization.

As standards for legal and ethical conduct, ethics programs have a strong connection to a firm's economic prospects and should be taken seriously. Ethics programs and the status of values in the organization should be discussed at board meetings. The board should be communicating a clear profile of its commitment to ethics throughout the organization.[82]

Values-driven management may be conceived as an attempt to increase the employee's awareness of ethical issues, by prompting self-reflection on the part of an employee having to do something that appears ethically controversial. The employee may ask him or herself if the action makes them feel bad or if they are ashamed by doing it. Moreover, they may reflect on how it would look if the public knew about the action. As an additional benefit, this space for reflection is also independent of the opinions of supervisors and executive managers.

Ethics programs in organizations may take many different forms. The formulation of basic ideals of commitment should indeed be written, but it is not necessary to create a long and complicated statement of principles. The basic values should be easy for the members of the organization to understand. It should not be empty words, but should include clear objectives. The code of value, of business practice, or code of ethics should not be written in difficult legal language, but should involve relevant information that is user-friendly for the people in the organization.[83]

It is important to remember that an effective ethics program cannot be made solely by the board of directors and institutionalized from the top. Effective ethics programs are based on democratic and open communication about values throughout the organization. They involve communication with key internal and external stakeholders. In the development of ethics programs, it is necessary that the employees take part of the process in order to make their awareness and understanding of the process more complete. This communication of values could be formed as a process of value development involving all members of the organization.

The involvement of the whole organization in the creation of ethics programs helps to increase the commitment of the employees to the values of the organization. Effective values-driven management must be based on the internal embodiment of values in the culture of the organization. Values are, in this sense, developed out of dialogue between stakeholders, and this dialogue is essential to secure the right commitment to values in the organization. It does not work unless these values are integrated into the culture of the organization.

It must be emphasized that values-driven management cannot be understood as a fait accompli, but is rather an ongoing process involving the whole organization. The introduction of values should, therefore, be followed up in ways that enhance organizational ethical awareness, reasoning, concrete action, and moral development. This might be accomplished by training programs that enhance the ethical capacities and competencies of the organization's members.

An important outcome of values-driven management is the improvement of individual capacities for ethical reasoning on the part of employees and other members of the organization. Beginning an ethical training process is, therefore, very important for the process of values-driven management.[84] This serves the process, whereby a culture of ethics is realized through the collective process of organizational learning and self-reflection.[85]

Though this institutionalization of a culture of common values makes individuals much more engaged in an organization's activities, aims, and goals, a process of learning might not be enough. An efficient program of values-driven management should be controlled by efficient methods of evaluation and auditing. These evaluations may be considered as important as the economic audits of the organization. Audits may be more or less formal according to the character of the organization, but they are nonetheless essential in order to measure its ethical culture. They are also a condition for the acceptance of the sincerity of ethics programs by individuals in organizations.

This preliminary definition of values-driven management as the foundation of corporate citizenship seeks to overcome the danger of management ideology and to conceive ethics as an integrating force in business life. It is motivated by concern for the common good, surpassing individual and ideological notions of values. In this way, values-driven management might be a way to resolve the problem of totalitarian organizations with *a)* social responsibilities or *b)* an impact on ethical problems in society. Values-driven management should find the right balance between individuals and organizations, and between organizations, society, and political democracy.

Box 9. Ten steps of an efficient ethics and compliance program

Understanding the difference between compliance and ethics programs is essential for integrating ethics into organizational culture. Compliance programs are based on institutional authority rather than individual autonomy.[86] Motivation for obeying compliance programs is based on the force of law and sanctions of the law, as well as the internal desire of individuals to obey the law. Proponents of compliance programs think that value-led ethics programs and values-driven management may be too vague in comparison with clear legal programs.[87] Those who prefer value-based programs argue, to the contrary, that such programs promote individual autonomy and responsibility; they allow for individual engagement and motivation, as well as a larger space for personal decision-making.

Given these differences between rules and values, a good program of values-driven management may be one that preserves the tension between rules and values, thereby allowing for individual autonomy and responsibility while keeping the advantages of institutional authority. This was the intent of Michael Hoffman when he formulated ten steps of an effective ethics and compliance program as a part of the ethics officer's course at the Center for Business Ethics, Bentley College, Waltham, Massachusetts. These ten steps represent a very convincing illustration of the elements of a good and efficient ethics and compliance program combining values and rules.

This proposal to integrate ethics into compliance programs, in order to establish an ethical culture, consisted of the following steps:

1) *Self-assessment.* An evaluation and examination of the ethical climate of the organization is necessary as the basis for decision-making. This survey of beliefs and attitudes of employees and other stakeholders may be done with the help of an external consultancy.

2) *Commitment from the top.* An ethics and compliance program cannot succeed without commitment and consensus among leading board directors and management. In addition, it may be useful to appoint a board member or senior staff person as ethics officer.

3) *Codes of business conduct.* It is important that the corporation formulates a written code of ethics that presents the values and policies of the organization. Such codes of conduct may vary, but should be concrete and easily accessible to all members of the organization.

4) *Communication vehicle.* The code of conduct and ethics program is useless if it is not communicated to the members of the organization. There should be an ethics communication policy. This is facilitated by modern means of communication, such as the Internet.[88]

5) *Training.* Employees must learn how to act ethically. Training in ethical values is important for communicating and creating an ethical organizational culture. Training must be based on critical and constructive examination of organizational structures, strategies, policies, and goals.

6) *Resources for assistance.* When instituting an ethics program, it is important that the organization create resources (e.g., hotlines or help lines, offices, and people) that employees can turn to for help, guidelines, comfort, and protection when they report ethical dilemmas or violations of the law.

7) *Organizational ownership.* It is important that the ethics program is not considered as an isolated element of the organization. Moreover, ethical visions and compliance issues must be integrated at all levels of the organization, and with individual concern for ethical responsibility.

8) *Consistent response and enforcement.* This involves systems of incentives, evaluations, and measures for improvement in order to promote the ethics and compliance program. Enforcement should be just and coherent.

9) *Audits and measurements.* Ethics and compliance programs should be continuously evaluated and unnecessary bureaucracy should be avoided. Ethics programs should be audited as an integrated part of auditing the immaterial values of the firm.

10) *Revision and refinements.* Ethics and compliance programs should be continuously revised and refined in light of new ethical experiences, corporate policies, and strategies.

Endnotes

1   John W. Dienhart, *Business, Institutions and Ethics. A Text with Cases and Readings* (Oxford: Oxford University Press, 2000), 62. Dienhart quotes Douglass North article "Institutions" in *Journal of Economic Perspectives* 5: 1, 1998.

2   Ibid: 63.

3   Brenda Almond and Bryan Wilson, *Values. A Symposium* (Atlantic Highlands, Humanities Press International, 1988).

4   Ronald Dworkin, "Intrinsic Value. A false Foundation" in Tara Smith, *Viable Values, A Study of Life as the Root and Reward of Vitality* (New York: Rowman and Littlefield Publishers, 2000), 62.

5   William C. Frederick, *Values, Nature and Culture in the American Corporation*, (New York: Oxford University Press, 1995), 16-17.

6   Ibid: 17.

7   Hans Joas, *The Genesis of Values* (Chicago University of Chicago Press, 2000), 102.

8   William C. Frederick, *Values, Nature and Culture in the American Corporation* (New York: Oxford University Press, 1995), 18-19.

9   Edgar H. Schein, *Organizational culture and leadership*, Second Edition (San Francisco Jossey-Bass Publishers, 1992). This book might indicate an analysis of the connection between values and organizational culture.

10   William C. Frederick, *Values, Nature and Culture in the American Corporation* (New York: Oxford University Press, 1995), 99.

11   Geert Hofstede, *Cultures and Organizations: Software of the Mind* (New York: McGraw-Hill, 1997). William C. Frederick, *Values, Nature and Culture in the American Corporation*, (New York: Oxford University Press, 1995), 107.

12   See for example Jean-Paul Sartre, "l'Être pour la valeur" in *L'Etre et le Néant* (Paris: Gallimard, 1943). We might also mention the work of Max Scheler on the notion of value, in order to understand the position of value in human existence. From the existentialist and phenomenological point of view, values are closely linked to human existence as expressions of the existential projects and conceptions of life of particular people.

13   Tara Smith, *Viable Values, A Study of Life as the Root and Reward of Vitality* (New York: Rowman and Littlefield Publishers, 2000), 85.

14   Laura Pincus Hartman "The Ford Pinto Case", *Perspectives in business ethics* (Chicago: Irwin McGraw-Hill, 1998), 169.

15   Ibid.

16   Donald E. Frey, "Individual Economic Values and Self-Interest: The Problem in Puritan Ethics", *Journal of Business Ethics*, Oct. 1998.

17   Max Weber, *The Protestant Ethics and the Spirit of Capitalism*, translated by Talcott Parsons from: Max Weber: *Die Protestantische Ethik und der Geist des Kapitalismus* (Allan and Unwin 1930). Reprinted with an introduction by Anthony Giddens (London: Unwin Paperbacks, 1987).

18   Weber analyzed the particularity of the economic organization of the firm in an unfinished major work about economy and society. Max Weber (1903-1972), *Wirtschaft und Gesellschaft. Grundriss einer verstehende Soziologie*, Mohr 5 auflage, Edition 1972, Tübingen 1976. English translation: *Economy and Society* (Berkeley: University of California Press, 1978).

19   William H. Write, Jr., *The Organization Man* (New York: A Clarion Book (1956), 1972).

20   Scott and Hart, *Organizational America* (Boston: Houghton, Mifflin Company Paper Back, 1979), 4.

21   Ibid: 36 ff.

22   Ibid: 101.

23   Ibid: 211.

24   William C. Frederick, *Values, Nature and Culture in the American Corporation* (New York: Oxford University Press, 1995), 7 ff.

25   We might mention the French School of Conventions as an example of a theoretical school of thought that is very close to the developments of Frederick. This school proposes an empirically based investigation of values having an impact on organizational development and activity.

26   William C. Frederick, *Values, Nature and Culture in the American Corporation* (New York: Oxford University Press, 1995), 36.

27   Ibid: 37.

28   Ibid: 48.

29   In this context, we find congruence between the theory of William Frederick and the theories of systems by Maturana and Luhmann who have tried to characterize the general characteristics of social systems. In this context we might conceive autopoesis and systemic differentiation as basic features of the social organization of business systems.

30   William C. Frederick, *Values, Nature and Culture in the American Corporation* (New York: Oxford University Press, 1995), 51.

31   Ibid: 61. With this in mind, it is interesting to note the military origins of many business organizations.

32   Ibid: 146.

33   Ibid: 206.

34   William C. Frederick, "Anchoring Values in Nature: Towards a Theory of Business Values", *Business Ethics Quarterly*, Volume 2, 1992.

35   Ole Thyssen, *Værdiledelse, Om organisationer og etik*, 2. reviderede udgave (Copenhagen: Gyldendal, 1999), 20.

36   Ibid: 54.

37   Ibid: 95.

38   Jürgen Habermas, *Theorie des kommunikativen Handelns I-II* (Frankfurt: Suhrkamp Verlag, 1981).

39   Peter Beyer, *Værdibaseret ledelse. Den ældste vin på nye flasker*, 2 udgave (Copenhagen: Forlaget Thomson, 2006).

40 Gareth Morgan, *Images of organization* (London: Sage publications, 1997).

41 Alain Etchegoyen, *La valse des ethiques* (Paris, Le Seuil, 1991), 36ff.

42 Ibid: 121.

43 Jean-Pierre le Goff: *Le mythe de l'entreprise* (Paris: La Decouverte, 1995). A similar criticism of values-driven management can be found in postmodern organization theory, for example in Hugh Willmott: "Towards a New Ethics? The contributions of Poststructuralism and Posthumanism" and Hugo Letiche: "Business Ethics: (In) Justice and Anti-Law – Reflections on Derrida, Bauman and Lipovetsky" in *Ethics in Organizations*, edited by Martin Parker (London: Sage Publications, 1998). For more discussion of critical organization theories see also Christopher Grey and Hugh Willmott, *Critical Management Studies* (Oxford: Oxford University Press, 2005).

44 Jean-Pierre le Goff : *Le mythe de l'entreprise* (Paris: La Decouverte, 1995), 49.

45 Ibid: 72.

46 Ibid: 153.

47 Ibid: 218.

48 Alain Etchegoyen, *La valse des ethiques* (Paris: Le Seuil, 1991), 123.

49 Ibid: 135.

50 Ibid: 237.

51 Peter Hagedorn-Rasmussen, Søren Jagd and Jacob Dahl Rendtorff, *Fra værdiledelse til værdier i arbejdslivet*. (From values-driven management to values in the worklife). Rapport til LO projekt støttet af EUs Socialfond, Institut for samfundsvidenskab og erhvervsøkonomi (RUC 2006), 42-50.

52 Alain Etchegoyen, *La valse des ethiques*, (Paris: Le Seuil, 1991).

53 Luc Boltanski and Eve Chapello, *Le nouvel esprit du capitalisme*, (Paris: Gallimard, 1995).

54 Colin Fisher and Alan Lovell, *Business ethics and Values* (London: Prentice Hall, 2003)

55 Ibid: 174-175.

56 B. Kjonstad and H. Willmott, "Business Ethics: Restrictive or Empowering", *Journal of Business Ethics*, 1995, Vol 14. The authors discuss Kohlberg's theory and they help to show how business ethics contributes to moral and cognitive development of the firm.

57 John W. Dienhart, *Business, Institutions and Ethics. A Text with Cases and Readings*, (Oxford: Oxford University Press, 2000), 65.

58 Lawrence Kohlberg, *Stages in the Development of Moral Thought and Action*, (New York Holt Rinehart and Winston, 1969) and Lawrence Kohlberg, *Essays in Moral Development, Volume 2, The Psychology of Moral Action*, (New York: Free Press, 1994).

59 John W. Dienhart, *Business, Institutions and Ethics. A Text with Cases and Readings*, (Oxford: Oxford University Press, 2000, 66).

60 Ibid: 67.

61 Ibid: 67.

62 Ibid: 67.

63 Carol Gilligan, *In a Different Voice*, (Cambridge Massachusetts: Harvard University Press, 1982).

64 With reference to our discussion of the good life in the previous chapters, we can emphasize that this approach to deontology and morality must be viewed in the light of the aim of the good life in just institutions.

65 With John Dienhart, I agree on the importance of this perspective as a basis for understanding conflict between values in organizations. John W. Dienhart, *Business, Institutions and Ethics. A Text with Cases and Readings*, (Oxford: Oxford University Press), 82.

66 Ibid: 16.

67 Henrik Zahle, *Praktisk retsfilosofi*, (Copenhagen: Carl Ejlers forlag, 2005), 93.

68 Mette Morsing, "Værdier i danske virksomheder – skitse af et fænomen", Copenhagen Business School, 2003. Mette Morsing and Peter Pruzan, "Values-based Leadership" in *Ethics in the Economy. Handbook of business ethics* edited by L. Zsolnai, (Oxford: Peter Lang, 2002), 253-293. See also Peter Hagedorn Rasmussen, Søren Jagd and Jacob Dahl Rendtorff, *Fra værdiledelse til værdier i arbejdslivet*. Rapport til LO projekt støttet af EUs Socialfond, Institut for samfundsvidenskab og erhvervsøkonomi (RUC 2006), 22-23.

69 Mette Morsing, "Værdier i danske virksomheder – skitse af et fænomen", Copenhagen Business School, 2003. Mette Morsing and Peter Pruzan, "Values-based Leadership" in *Ethics in the Economy. Handbook of business ethics* edited by L. Zsolnai, (Oxford: Peter Lang, 2002), 253-293.

70 Ibid.

71 Ibid.

72 Ibid.

73 Hanne Knudsen, "Licens til kritik – og andre måder at bruge værdier på i organisationer" in *Offentlig ledelse i managementstaten*, edited by D. Pedersen (Copenhagen: Samfundslitteratur, 2004). See also Peter Hagedorn-Rasmussen, Søren Jagd and Jacob Dahl Rendtorff, *Fra værdiledelse til værdier i arbejdslivet*. Rapport til LO projekt støttet af EUs Socialfond, Institut for samfundsvidenskab og erhvervsøkonomi, (RUC 2006), 23.

74 Lynn Sharp Paine, "Managing for Organizational Integrity" in *Harvard Business Review*, 1994.

75 Edward R. Freeman, *Strategic Management. A Stakeholder Approach* (Boston Massachusetts: Pitman Publishing Inc., 1984).

76 Dawn-Marie Driscoll and W. Michael Hoffman, *Ethics Matters. How to Implement Values-Driven Management*, Centre for Business Ethics, (Waltham Massachusetts: Centre for Business Ethics, Bentley College, 2000).

77 Ibid: 1 ff.

78 W. Michael Hoffman, Dawn-Marie Driscoll and Mollie Painter Morland, "Integrating Ethics into organizational Cultures" in *Business Ethics: Facing up the Issues* (London: The Economist books, 2001), 38

79 Dawn-Marie Driscoll and W. Michael Hoffman, *Ethics Matters. How to Implement Values-Driven Management*, (Waltham Massachusetts: Centre for Business Ethics, Bentley College, 2000), 21.

80 Ibid: 33.

81 Ibid: 59-69.

82 W. Michael Hoffman, Dawn-Marie Driscoll and Mollie Painter Morland: "Integrating Ethics into organizational Cultures" in *Business Ethics: Facing up the Issues* (London: The Economist books, 2001).

83 Dawn-Marie Driscoll and W. Michael Hoffman, *Ethics Matters. How to Implement Values-Driven Management*, (Waltham Massachusetts: Centre for Business Ethics, Bentley College, 2000), 89.

84 Ibid: 135.

85 Driscoll and Hoffman emphasize the significance of the consultant for developing such a program. I agree about the importance of institutionalizing ethics in this way. External consultancy might be a way to be aware of the ethical blind spots of the organization. These spots might be so hidden that they cannot be detected by members of the organization; however, we have to emphasize the critical function of such ethics consultancy in relation to the firm, in the sense that it should help to liberate democratic dialogue in corporate interactions.

86 W. Michael Hoffman, Dawn-Marie Driscoll and Mollie Painter Morland, "Integrating Ethics into organizational Cultures" in *Business Ethics: Facing up the Issues* (London: The Economist books, 2001), 38.

87 Ibid: 39.

88 Ibid: 43.

3. From values–driven management to business ethics

This analysis is predicated on the importance of values-driven management for corporate citizenship, which must be closely integrated with business ethics. The previous investigation of globalization and definitions of values will now be related to particular definitions of business ethics. This chapter will develop the concept of organization and of values in relation to the major theories of business ethics. It will demonstrate values-driven management with regard to these conceptions in order to define the theoretical basis for values in business. The analysis is based on the assumption that values have fundamental significance in each of the particular theories of business ethics. The overall aim is to give a definition of the concept of corporate citizenship. From the institutional perspective, different theories of business ethics represent different conceptions of value rationality in institutions.

Business institutions confront different values of self-interest, utility maximization, the common good, universal principles, and contractual justice. Ethical theories relate these values and specify what is good and right with regard to organizational procedures and outcomes.[1] Theories of business ethics contain, on the one hand, an interpretation of the values that are important in business institutions. On the other, they propose at normative point of view of the values to be promoted. The normative viewpoint of the corporation as a "good citizen" relies on the conception of the corporate ontology. In this context, business ethics is defined as the tradition of ethical evaluation of business practices and of managerial decisions in relation to business institutions.

This definition will be the impetus for the following investigation of the relation between values and theories in business ethics. These theories represent different values conceptions that have an impact on the incentive structure of the firm. The most important theories of business ethics that will be analyzed are: 1) liberal property right theories of business ethics, 2) concern for the stakeholders, 3) communitarian values-driven management, 4) social contract theories of business ethics, 5) Kantian and universalistic perspectives on business ethics, and 6) republican business ethics. This approach is based on the view that there is a progression of scope and application of the theories such that each subsequent theory assumes elements from the preceding ones. The goal of the analysis is, therefore, to show how a republican theory of business ethics based on the preceding theories might be the most comprehensive concept in a complex modern society.

Case 4. Liberal theory and search for market dominance: The case of Microsoft

According to traditional economic theory, monopolization is one of the most important evils because it destroys the market and fair competition. Accordingly, many economists speak of monopolies in moral rather than scientific terms. The actions of Microsoft are a good illustration of how ethics – in this case creating fairness and respect among competitors – are required as the basis of economics.[2]

The case of Microsoft has been selected because it is an important and powerful global corporation, which has several times been accused of acting as a monopoly. The story of Microsoft has become a classic case of a corporation facing an *ethical crisis*, in the sense that it prioritizes market share over respect for acting fairly.

During the 1990s, Microsoft conquered most of the market for software and at certain moments it nearly had total dominance. Recently there have been many controversies about the behavior of Microsoft in relation to their competitors. Microsoft tried to dissuade Intel and other companies from entering the market and they wanted IBM to discontinue producing their own software system. When Netscape Navigator was becoming more popular, Microsoft developed their own web browser, Internet Explorer, which was bundled into all Microsoft software systems. Because of Microsoft's market power, this effectively made it impossible for Netscape Navigator to compete.

The Department of Justice charged Microsoft with violating competition laws because of these actions.[3] With their market strength, Microsoft had the opportunity to raise the price on their software systems. As a consequence of this unfair price competition, the Department of Justice wanted the firm to be separated into to sub-firms. The court case resulted in a settlement where other software and hardware producers were given better opportunities to install software products on computers.

The case of Microsoft raises the ethical issue of establishing fair competition in sound markets. Since competition requires a multitude of actors, state authorities are required to intervene in order to create such competitive conditions. In the United States, several authorities monitor that companies are respecting competition law and the rules of fair markets. In Europe, after the liberalization of free market competition, state authorities have also become very important for dealing with fair business practices in economic markets. Thus, we can observe increased awareness of the rules of good competition in order to create healthy global markets.

3.1. Liberal property rights theory of business ethics

This approach to business ethics can be defined as a neoclassical and utilitarian approach to the problems of business ethics and managerial ethics. It is based on classical individualist philosophy and it emphasizes the rights of the individual to self-development and self-perfection.[4] The foundation for ethics is the rational choice of personal interest maximization. This is linked to a utilitarian theory of preference maximization, based on the idea that the pursuit of self-interest in will, in the end, promote the common good. This egoistic and hedonistic ethics regards human beings as economic individuals who act according to their self-interest. The goals of this approach to business ethics are to ensure the values of efficiency, profitability, nondiscrimination, economic stability, and fair competition in order to ensure that the needs and interests of the rational economic actors are met. Legal regulation to support this economic approach to business ethics should be based on a "law and economics" approach, rendering law a result of economic theories of efficiency.

The theoretical justification for a free market society with very little restraints on the rights of individuals to act as they wish in an economic market is found in John Locke's philosophy of the natural law doctrine of the social contract. The social contract is supposed to protect national and inalienable rights to liberty and property.[5] Robert Nozick's defense of a minimal, liberal state is a modern version of such a libertarian philosophy.[6] Rights are grounded in nature before the constitution of society. Within this view, every individual has the right to live without being violated by others.[7] This approach implies a rights-based critique of utilitarianism, arguing for the protection of rights as being the primary function of a minimal state. Nozick's approach has often been put forward as a defense of a liberal "night watchman state" of classical liberalism, because it implies a strong defense of individual property rights as fundamental to a free society. This approach can, therefore, be viewed as the philosophical justification of a liberal market economy.

According to this liberal conception of business ethics, economic action is based in utility maximizing individuals acting rationally in an economic market in order to secure the most effective allocation of resources and goods in society. From this view, the responsibility of corporations is restricted to the production of goods and services based on a purely economic definition of rationality, utility, and efficiency. In general, neoliberals have been skeptical of the doctrine of corporate social responsibility, which they consider as too vague and dismissive of the real objectives of the firm: serving stockholders, and contributing to economic efficiency. Furthermore, they consider it a trivial responsibility of the firm to follow the rule of law, be decent, and do some charity. Any social engagement beyond that would be damaging to the free market economy.[8] As Friedrich Hayek put it, "nobody would seriously contend that. . . corporations should be run in. . . (management's). . . interests."[9] The manager should not have any other responsibility apart from being an agent for the interests of the owners and the shareholders.[10] According to the liberal approach, social responsibility is only useful when it is integrated in the objective of getting profits for the owners and shareholders of the corporation.

Milton Friedman has proposed one of the most consequential statements of this approach to business ethics. He defined the social responsibility of corporations in *Capitalism and Freedom* (1962) and in the infamous article, "The Social Responsibility of Business is to Increase its Profits" (1970)".[11] According to Friedman, the only ethical behavior of business is to get as much profit as possible in an economically rational manner. Friedman wants to make the rules of the market economy the most important regulation of business behavior. He does not refuse to admit some external norms governing economic activity, but these norms are nothing other than the rules of fair competition of a liberal market economy. Friedman mentions the following constraints on the principles of profit maximization: "That responsibility is to conduct the business in accordance with their desires [the desires of the employers], which generally is to make as much money as possible while conforming to the basic rules of society, both those embodied in law and those embodied in ethical custom."[12] Furthermore, "there is one and only one social responsibility of business – to use its resources and engage in activities designed to increase its profits so as it stays within the rules of the game, which is to say engage in open and free competition without deception or fraud."[13]

Friedman views the concept of corporate social responsibility as socialism and a threat to the free market system in a liberal society. The corporation should exclusively serve the interests of its shareholders, while staying within the rules of the game; in other words, legal requirements and other rules within the market economy. Friedman attacks the rationale of the values-based organization, and his views represent a challenge to conditioning a firm's actions on embedded economic values.

Friedman attacks the idea that responsibility can be attributed to companies. Companies do not represent anything other than the sum of individual actions.[14] Indeed, an organization has legal responsibilities as an artificial, judicial entity, but this is nothing more than a legal fiction, because it is never the organization, as such, but specific individuals who are attributed vicarious responsibility for the actions of the organization. Accordingly, from Friedman's perspective, the concept of social responsibility of business organizations is meaningless, because organizations are nothing but collections of individuals. Only human individuals, with consciousness and intention, and with a free will, can be attributed moral responsibility.

Friedman also points out that at another possible significance of thinking that a firm has social responsibility is that the chief executive officer (CEO) is seen to assume part of this burden on behalf of the organization. Some maintain that the manager has a responsibility to ensure the social standing of the company by, for example, avoiding discrimination and encouraging environmental concern.

In responding to this view, Friedman states that the CEO of the organization legally and economically only has responsibility towards his or her employers. If it is a market-driven organization, it is natural to presuppose that the owners and shareholders primarily are interested in earning money. The manager does not have any other responsibility apart from being an agent for the interests of the owners and the shareholders.[15] Friedman admits that the personal responsibility of the CEO may be oriented towards society, but this does not coincide with his responsibility as an employee in the company; furthermore, if the CEO wants to serve social goals, he is misusing his position instead of doing his job and providing more profit to the owners and shareholders of the company.

Friedman argues that the idea that the firm should take a stance on social issues at the limits of neutral economic markets is not only illegal, but also not very democratic. The reason is that the CEO and the board have no political support to use the money of the firm for social purposes. In this case, which Friedman finds unacceptable, the firm is no longer an economic actor but also functions as a political agent, in much the same way as the state takes taxes and reallocates resources between shareholders, customers, consumers, and the weakest in society. Only the state should be responsible for environmental protection, protecting the local community, fighting unemployment, and keeping prices low in order to combat and avoid inflation.[16]

Friedman does not exclude that individual citizens have the right to work for social issues. In this case, they only work as normal citizens following their political rights and duties as members of democratic societies. When an individual takes on the responsibilities of a CEO or individual shareholder, and acts for social purposes in order to make the company pursue political purposes, they go beyond what is acceptable for corporate action in a democratic liberal society with a sharp distinction between economics and politics.

Friedman posits that 'social responsibility' is, in many cases, not really social responsibility at all, but rather the firm's interest in getting stability is a cover to secure long-term value. This is in some cases acceptable, but it can also be problematic. When a corporation hides its profit-maximizing motives, it consequently destroys the possibilities of fair competition, because society is given the false impression that the company works with social motives for social values.[17]

At the same time, the free market system requires property and contract law on an institutional basis to assure the rules of fair competition.[18] This principle is an ideal formal principle and in concrete situations it is dependent on conditions for legitimate action, social custom, consequences of actions, and implied stakeholders. It is the task of the firm to produce the best products at the lowest prices and this should be done in harmony with the market rules for the correct regulation of economic activity. An important justification of this ethics of the market is the economic efficiency of capitalist economic systems. Only markets can allocate resources efficiently and private property is useful to ensure motivation for action.

Milton Friedman's position continues to haunt business ethics. Today is is difficult not to be confronted with the seemingly oxymoronic relationship of social responsibility and profit maximization, which Friedman pointed out. It is, however, still possible to ask the critical question: What really is left when Friedman's position is examined more deeply? Thomas Carson has argued that Friedman's position is internally inconsistent when submitted to further scrutiny.[19]

Carson analyzes how the idea that the "obligation of business [is] to maximize its profits while engaging in open and free competition without deception or fraud" is cited differently in *Capitalism and Freedom* than in "The Social Responsibility of Business is to Increase its Profits." In the latter publication, Friedman's position, according to Carson, is that "business executives are obligated to follow the wishes of shareholders (which will generally be to make as much money as possible while obeying the laws and the 'ethical customs' of the society)." In the former statement, emphasis is put on "open and free competition," while in the latter it is emphasized that the corporation should maximize profits following the laws and respecting the ethical customs of society. Carson argues that avoiding fraud and deception does not amount to the same thing as respecting ethical and legal norms. In *Capitalism and Freedom,* Friedman does not integrate his concept of profit maximization into respect for ethics and law. In fact, this difference leads Carson to argue that Friedman's position in *Capitalism and Freedom* is inconsistent with the position of the article, because the first statement says nothing about ethical custom while the second position integrates ethical custom in the limits of profit maximization, such that it explicitly states that profit maximization cannot happen contrary to ethical custom.[20]

The inconsistency in the second formulation, regarding the early libertarian position, implies an opening in Friedman's concept. It allows for some integration of ethics and economics, because Friedman says that legitimate profit maximization respects the laws and ethical custom of society. Consequently, it may be argued that the change in his position moves the liberal concept of business ethics away from a purely libertarian conception to one that implies an openness towards ethical and legal market constraints. From this point of view, Friedman can be seen as saying only that corporations have obligations to their stockholders and that corporate social responsibility – if not conducted strategically for the benefit of the firm – may be considered to be illegitimate. This limitation on corporate social responsibility in the second formulation does not, however, exclude respect for business ethics and legal rules. In contrast to the libertarian position in *Capitalism and Freedom,* the idea that "the social responsibility of business is to increase its profits" is based on a fundamental ethical and moral conception of business, because open and free competition not only shall refrain from fraud and deception, but also always respect ethical custom and laws in society. When Friedman argues that business executives should not give money to social objectives because it would violate the basic economic aim of the corporation, this is still respecting the laws and ethical custom of society. Seen from this angle, it becomes possible to argue that there is an ethical core in Friedman's article that is very close to the Protestant work ethic. Friedman can easily agree to basic ethical principles and duties while proposing the economic argument that the goal of corporate social responsibility is to increase profits.[21]

This ethical limitation of the economic activities of the firm does not support the argument that Friedman is a principalist in business ethics; rather, he uses liberal and utilitarian arguments inspired by Adam Smith and neoclassical concepts of economic action.[22] However, this is a shortcoming of the theory. By presupposing that the consequences of profit maximization are exclusively good, he neglects to discuss its negative potentiality. This premise of the argument requires further justification and a more developed ethical framework.

The obsession with profit maximization as the major economic responsibility of business haunts the followers of Friedman's conception of social or moral responsibility of business. More recently, authors like Michael Porter, Mike Kramer, Michael Jensen, and William Meckling have defended positions that are somewhat similar to the views of business ethics proposed by Friedman.[23] Jensen, for one, has persistently argued that corporate social responsibility is not compatible with the concept of the firm as an agent for the shareholders. He thinks that this idea destroys the original purpose of the firm and makes market economics inefficient.[24]

Porter, the "grand old man" of strategy, has tried to use Friedman's approach to integrate corporate social responsibility and strategic management. Porter started his approach to this debate with an argument about better economic use of corporate philanthropy.[25] With Kramer, his colleague, Porter argues that corporate philanthropy is in decline and that it is necessary to justify charitable expenditures in terms of bottom-line profits. As an example of this unreflective attitude to corporate philanthropy, the American tobacco company Philip Morris once used seventy-five million dollars on charitable contributions and hundreds of millions on an advertising campaign for their charitable contributions.[26]

Quoting Friedman, Porter and Kramer argue that the corporation is an instrument of the stockholders who own it, and that its social responsibility is to increase profits. They discuss whether Friedman is right in saying that corporate philanthropy is a waste of money. They also argue that Friedman distinguishes between social and economic objectives, and they assume that corporations are better than individual donors at addressing social objectives.[27] They argue that corporations can use charitable giving to improve their competitive context and, contrary to Friedman, that charitable donations can improve long-term business prospects. This could be called *context-focused* philanthropy. Porter and Kramer abandon the separation between the company and society, and consider companies operating as a part of society. Competitiveness depends on productivity, which depends on good workers, good information and infrastructure, and the size of the local market.[28] Operating within Friedman's perspective of profit maximization, but taking a critical stance toward his separation of economics and society, Porter and Kramer argue that there may be a convergence of interest between pure business and pure philanthropy.[29] Competitive context has become more critical. Corporations are, therefore, dependent on local partnerships and more collaboration between suppliers and customers is needed.

Porter and Kramer refer to the four elements of competitive context that are described in Porter's earlier work. According to the theory of competitive advantage, there is a cluster of elements that influences competitive advantage: local context of strategy and rivalry; demand conditions of customers and market segments; factor conditions of human resources, capital resources, and physical infrastructure; and related and supporting industries, local suppliers, and companies.[30] Through corporate philanthropy, the company can purportedly improve its competitive context and long-term prospects by creating better physical infrastructure, improving the sophistication of local customers, helping local societies with policies for more transparent and fair competition, and by helping suppliers perform better. In this context, Porter and Kramer emphasize that corporate philanthropy is more than public relations. In order to be efficient, corporate philanthropy should be much more focused on "the right causes in the right way."[31] They should adopt a context-focused approach of collaboration with local partners. Porter and Kramer argue for the need to focus strategies of giving based on an examination of competitive context, and evaluation of philanthropic activities, potential new initiatives, partners, and results. Only in this way can companies, following Friedman, add significantly more value than individual donors.[32]

In fact, this concept of philanthropy considers it from a purely economic and strategic perspective, which implies that Porter and Kramer do not really have a view on right and wrong in terms of principled business ethics. Along with Friedman, they are concerned with value creation and profit maximization; however, while Friedman rests within a somewhat skeptical liberal position regarding corporate social responsibility or corporate philanthropy as win-win situations for both business and society, the evocation of partnerships and mutual interdependence between business and society in corporate philanthropy prompts Porter and Kramer to consider this position with concern for welfare economics (i.e., common value creation of the greatest good to the greatest number). Even though they do not agree with Friedman that corporate philanthropy is a waste of money, they rely on a utilitarian ethics based on the idea of profit maximization as the motive for corporate philanthropy. A fundamental problem with this position is that Porter and Kramer consider philanthropy and corporate social responsibility from a limited perspective of profit maximization. Consequently, they, like Friedman, end up dismissing fundamental ethical problems with the aims of corporations in society. The question is whether Porter and Kramer refuse business ethics or simply do not see it as an important topic for this discussion. In fact, this view does not exclude a deeper foundation of corporate social responsibility in business ethics and the need for republican business ethics in order really to understand the role of corporations in society.[33]

Further application of the concept of corporate social responsibility as CSR is found in another article by Porter and Kramer, in which the authors seem to be hostile towards business ethics as the moralization of a firm's CSR activities.[34] The authors acknowledge that CSR has become an inevitable element of business and that companies are pressured to think of CSR as a generic element of corporate strategy; however, the authors also argue that prevailing concepts of corporate social responsibility are fragmented and not very strategy oriented. The authors want to conceive the relation between business and society in CSR as one of mutual benefit. The authors acknowledge that CSR has moved into corporate boardrooms and that companies are compelled to make reports on ethical, social, and environmental risks.[35] Not many corporations seem, however, to have a focused CSR strategy, which necessitates re-evaluating its prevailing justifications. They mention the *moral* appeal and imperative as something that is predominant in the CSR field. Moral calculus is considered as a method to weigh social and financial benefits against each other.[36]

According to Porter and Kramer this ends up rendering many terms meaningless, for example, the term *sustainability*, which seems to lose its significance in this moral confusion of the CSR debate. Porter and Kramer recognize pragmatic elements in the concept of corporate citizenship as "license to operate." The stakeholder view is considered important, but also as a dangerous opening of the firm's interests to pressure groups. Finally, Porter and Kramer mention the *reputation school* as an approach to CSR that is also confused. They go on to argue that it is a cliché that corporations should be integrated in society and that there is a close relation between good societies and successful corporations.[37] What is needed, rather, is focus on *shared value*, which corporations are required to integrate into their core activities. Porter and Kramer emphasize focus on generic social issues, value-chain social impacts, and interest in the social dimensions of competitive context.[38] CSR activities should be integrated in the value chain (i.e., activities that create economic value) of the company as described by the concepts of strategy and competitive advantage, for example by mitigating harm in this value chain.[39] Strategic CSR also moves beyond good corporate citizenship and mitigation of harm in the value chain, because it works for a symbiotic relation between strategy, social responsiveness, and creation of value by integrating inside and outside perspectives on strategy and CSR, and because it acknowledges that there is a social dimension to the value chain.[40] The authors end the article by saying that companies should stop thinking about corporate social responsibility, but rather focuse on corporate social integration.[41]

What is the ethics in this conception of CSR? It seems confusing that somebody like Porter, who has been so focused on competitive strategy from the economic perspective, is so open to integration between business and society while being still very critical towards moralization of the firm. In fact, this concept of strategic CSR is not so far from Friedman's position in the sense that Porter and Kramer now seem to agree that business – in order to be socially integrated – should operate within the legal and ethical customs of society. Nonetheless, this concept still combines self-interest and economic welfare arguments that CSR has mutual benefits for corporations and society. As the rhetorical criticism of corporate citizenship shows, Porter and Kramer still seem to work within a single objective conception of the firm, where profit maximization is the most fundamental aim of corporate activities. In this sense they still represent liberal and utilitarian business ethics.

This view of business ethics can be put to a number of critical points.[42] One could argue that individual self-interest and profit maximization cannot be the ultimate aims of business. While free market theory relies on the assumption that individuals will respect the rules of the free market, in reality many violations of the principles of fair competition occur. An ethics of the market is, therefore, needed to restrict egoistic action. Indeed, business ethics should fight against opportunism and discrimination, and ensure fair competition. This should be a requirement of free market justice.[43] As a social practice being integrated in society, business has definite internal and external boundaries. Rights to profits are exclusively defined in terms of property rights, which, referring to Marxist criticism, are inequally distributed in a capitalist economy. Furthermore, through property right theory may define the firm in terms of formal and informal contracts, it does not overcome the difference between owners and employees.

Profit maximization must be viewed from the perspective that business is a part of a social and cultural reality with specific norms in particular societies, because the view that "business is business," and that morality is internal to the market, is not aware of these structural conditions of legitimate business activities.[44] Indeed, it can be argued that no theory of profit maximization can escape external constraints, or that profit maximization is only meaningful as a moral duty within social legitimacy. When isolating the idea of profit maximization without content, the concept becomes empty. It is always important to ask: Profit for what? For whom? At what time? None of these questions can be answered within objective economic theory, but instead depend on definitions of human nature, society, and on values and ethical principles; thus, arguments for profit maximization as a metaphysical virtue and life-form of Protestant "economic man" presuppose the external view of the common good.

These external factors require that profit maximization must be justified from the perspective of general social welfare. Consequently, Pareto-optimality and utilitarian welfare policy might deliver the sufficient conditions for coherence of the doctrine of profit maximization. This approach to social welfare seems to undergird the arguments of Porter and Kramer. It could be argued that concern for short-term shareholder profits should be replaced by long-term profits for the general welfare of consumers and community. This is not, however, possible on a purely formal basis, or solely on the conditions of the market. Principles for maximizing community welfare are dependent on social legitimation. Moreover, shareholder value can only be defined as a means of exposing the other stakeholders to long-term profit maximization. This is very far from the original individualist definition of shareholder value.

Such external limitations of profit maximization signify that even if this principle is constitutive for the economic market, it should always be considered as integrated in other social life-forms and practices. Real profit maximization can only be morally legitimate profit maximization.[45] It is dependent – from the perspective of the theory of corporate citizenship – on socially defined conceptions of the common good in a republican state.[46]

This view of business ethics should not be confused with an instrumental ethics or the tautological – some would say oxymoronic – reduction of business ethics to nothing other than a moral investment in good business, where "good ethics is good business" only in order to improve the company's strategic position, image, or public relations.[47] The strategic improvement of external and internal relations might be an important consequence of ethical behavior, but is not the whole and exclusive meaning of the term "business ethics," which is further constituted through reference to external critical reflections on market conditions and conceptions of economic justice. The following analysis is, therefore, based on the assumption that ethical principles and theories regulating economic behavior cannot be found exclusively inside the rational choice and profit maximization conception. In order to justify a specific structure of economic markets, a broader discussion in the light of different theories of the aims, character, and functions of business within political democracy is needed.

3.2. Extension of values: Stakeholder theory

Stakeholder theory helps to overcome the limitations of the liberal property right approach to business ethics. In stakeholder theory, ethical principles and values emerge as important values in the dialogue between organizations and their stakeholders. Stakeholder business ethics considers communication with stakeholders analogously to the dialogue that goes on in a political democracy. Such an ideal conception of communication among interested parties in the firm is based on the reasoned political deliberation in the critical public sphere. Deliberation contributes to a communicative foundation of business ethics by imbuing it with universal validity, which stems from the rational critical examination of arguments in a space of open dialogue.[48]

The stakeholder theory of the firm begins with a critique of the free market view of the firm. It states that the firm can create value by taking into account concerns other than mere planning analysis, and by integrating them into strategic management. In fact, this view of value is necessary for the firm to survive in a modern society where efficiency, concern for rational self-interest, and strategy on the basis of competitive advantage cannot secure the growth of the corporation. The stakeholder view argues that a pure market economy does not, in fact, exist. Moreover, it is critical towards market domination of corporations.

Stakeholder theory implies that there has never really been an economy of free trade and fair competition, as supposed by the rational utilitarian view of the firm; rather, competition tends to be aggressive and only the most dominant and powerful corporations usually survive. Contrary to Milton Friedman, adherents of this argument posit that large corporations have an ability and tendency to abuse their economic power.[49] Moreover, large corporations tend to assume power over the economy, thereby diminishing the power of shareholders or employees over corporate actions. There has, indeed, been an increase in the power of the executives, which is evident by examining the size of their salaries.[50] The result can be a negative impact on the situation of the employees and customers, and society at large, though the situation is changing due to the rise of different groups in society who increasingly put pressure on corporations. Because of these changes, business and industry can no longer ignore these different stakeholders. It is necessary to listen and go into dialogue with the stakeholders of the firm, if the firm wants to survive in an environment of increased global competition. The need for stakeholder theory results from pressure outside the firm.

As a consequence, traditional theories of management like Porter's concept of competitive strategy for industrial analysis are becoming insufficient in order to account for the necessary values of the organization. These concepts are mostly based on an internal view of efficiency in order to make a strong organization. Porter generally focuses on the rational structure of the division of labor. His views on organizations might be assumed to support a "survival of the fittest" mentality.[51] When he discusses the social integration of companies, and even when he appears open to CSR, he does not really look at society from the point of view of the stakeholders, but always from the strategic view of the benefits to the corporation. A similar critique is put forward against the human resource view of the corporation, which focuses on the needs and relations of employees, by trying to integrate individuals in the organization. This human resource approach to organizations does not work in a time where individual employees and customers are becoming more conscious of their rights. In this situation, a more complex view of the organization is needed. Stakeholder theory might rely on the cybernetic systems theory of organizations, where systems and organizations are conceived as constantly interacting with the environment. The cybernetic theory assumes that an organization's survival depends on taking into account information delivered by the environment in order to sense or monitor its place in the world. This can help the organization to take action when it discovers problems or discrepancies with the surrounding world.[52]

The stakeholder corporation might be considered as a kind of organizational ecology, where the organization, instead of being a bureaucratic military entity, is considered as an inclusive company in constant interaction with the environment. This interaction contributes to the self-perception of the company in order to secure its growth and survival. Dialogue with stakeholders is conceived as a process of communication and learning in order to improve the reflectivity of the organization. The inclusion of the stakeholders in a learning process becomes a basic condition for the organization to "learn how to learn."[53] By developing formalized dialogue with stakeholders as a part of the activity of the firm, it is possible to engage in a closer and more productive dialogue with the environment of the firm.

Stakeholder theory arguably represents a complex view on strategic management. In fact, R. Edward Freeman argues that stakeholder theory ensures managers are responsive in times of turbulence and change. As the concept of stakeholder indicates, it goes beyond the concept of the stockholder and searches for a broader concern for management. The term came from the Stanford Institute (SRI international) in the 1960s.[54] The concept was initially developed from a basis in strategic planning, but is now used in relation to systems theory and organization theory, as well. Stakeholder theory is an instrument to identify critical stakeholders in the environment of the corporation in order to define developments for strategy. In system theory and organization theory, and also in institutional theory, organizations are conceived as open systems. In this context, stakeholder analysis can clarify network relations. Moreover, in the contexts of business ethics and corporate social responsibility, stakeholder analysis has been used to identify important areas of concern.[55]

Stakeholder analysis can be considered as a method to identify new strategic management approaches to changing environments and corporate problems. In the strategic context, the object of stakeholder management is achieving the strategic objectives of the firm efficiently, but it is important to emphasize that stakeholder theory refuses to give single economic concern prevalence over other concerns.[56] In contrast to stakeholder theory, strict economic concepts of strategic management do not presuppose the possibility of including broader social and ethical concerns. Stakeholder management is, therefore, also important for values-based management and normative theories of business ethics. Indeed, it is important to emphasize that stakeholders do not necessarily have to be groups, but can also be concrete people with names and faces.[57] As a strategic and normative approach to leadership, stakeholder management represents an integrated approach to management that implies the impossibility of managing different stakeholder claims in the same direction.

As a result, stakeholder theory goes beyond mere pragmatist consequentialism, which defines stakeholders exclusively as subjects and causes of possible benefit or harm for the company. The claims of different stakeholders are, rather, evaluated from the perspective of the vision of the good life, implied in the values of the firm.[58] There is also a universal and Kantian dimension of stakeholder theory, in that it combines the subfields of business ethics, corporate social responsibility, corporate social performance, and corporate governance and organization theory within a concept of strategic development of the firm.[59] Including business ethics and values, stakeholder theory implies a strategic perspective on the values and norms of the corporation.[60]

Edward Freeman's definition of a stakeholder can illustrate this position: "A stakeholder in an organization is (by definition) any group or individual who can affect or is affected by the achievements of the organization's objectives."[61] Everyone, even those who are silent, have a right to be heard and included in strategic decision-making. In other words, stakeholders are every group or individual, regardless of whether they are a victim or a beneficiary of corporate actions.[62]

Although it is common to talk about the rights of stakeholders, defining stakeholder status is actually extremely complicated.[63] Three different stakeholder relationships must be clarified: 1) voluntary and involuntary stakeholders, such as owners and non-owners, 2) primary and secondary stakeholders, such as owners and customers, and 3) external and internal stakeholders (e.g., employees and customers). When selecting between stakeholders, it is important to be aware of their position in these different categories because these criteria contribute to the correct and fair relation to particular stakeholders.[64]

If this definition of stakeholder status seems too broad, one can also take into consideration a more narrow theory of the organization's stakeholders. This theory breaks status into three categories. A stakeholder is any group or individual that 1) is vital to the survival, success, or well-being of the corporation; 2) helps to define the organization, its mission, purpose, or goals: and/ or 3) is most affected by the organization and its activities. Stakeholders may take different organizational roles and positions within or outside the firm. Stakeholder management is based on the active inclusion of the different participants in the organization.

This definition is symmetric and strategic, not only because it takes into account future changes in the strategy of the firm (including duties towards new individuals or groups of stakeholders), but because it relates to broader issues of policy. From this perspective, stakeholders are viewed as participants in a communicative process aimed at increasing the legitimacy of the organization. As such, they should be treated as ends and not only as means. Today, it is unacceptable that the property rights of the firm should allow the owner to do whatever he or she wants. The firm is not an isolated abstract economic entity, but it is situated in a social context of duties and responsibilities. Property rights cannot, therefore, be a license to ignore respect for persons.[65] This business ethics aims at institutionalizing concern and respect for stakeholder rights as a part of the culture of responsibility in business.

A further discussion is required concerning the relationship between instrumental, normative, descriptive, and managerial theories of stakeholder identification.[66] *Descriptive* theory aims at describing the factual stakeholders of the firm. *Instrumental* theory integrates stakeholder concerns in corporate strategy.

Normative theory is about why certain peoples or groups should be taken into account by managers, and descriptive theory is about who really counts as a firm's stakeholder.[67]

An important approach to stakeholder theory has been to rely on "stakeholder salience," or the degree to which managers give priority to competing stakeholder claims. Proponents of this approach argue that this effort is not only normative but also descriptive, and that it goes beyond mere stakeholder identification. Ronald Mittchell, Bradley Agle, and Donna Wood try to provide a very profound analysis of the problems of stakeholder theory. They argue that three views of salience are predominant in stakeholder theory: 1) the stakeholder's power to influence the firm, 2) legitimacy of the stakeholder's relationship with the firm, and 3) urgency of the stakeholder's claim on the firm. In their view, stakeholder theory is about which stakeholder should care for running the firm in daily life. To this end, stakeholder salience is an important way to describe how to select between stakeholders. It should, however, become apparent in the following discussion that these criteria need to be integrated into the perspective of the principles and virtues of theories of business ethics, corporate citizenship, and corporate social responsibility.

In elaborating the state of the art of stakeholder theory, Mitchell, Agle, and Wood emphasize that there is not much disagreement about the broad view of a firm's possible stakeholders. Many different persons, groups and institutions may count as stakeholders.[68] The stakeholder inclusive company works to define its stakeholders in order to improve its activities in the relations with the environment. Stakeholder theory should be seen from the perspective of the governance structures of the organization. More concretely, the following stakeholders have been mentioned as groups or individuals that should be taken into account in stakeholder dialogue: 1) investors and shareholders, 2) managers, 3) employees, 4) business partners, 5) customers, 6) the local community, 7) civil society, including NGOs and political organizations in the community, and 8) the natural environment, including human future generations, nature, and animals, and their representatives among different pressure groups and organizations.

One might critically argue that there cannot be such a broad range of responsibility for the firm. Moreover, the different stakes of the different groups or individuals might be in conflict, rendering it impossible to secure agreement among the different groups that represent such divergent interests. As a reply, it should be clarified that stakeholder management is, first of all, based on dialogue with the different groups to be included in the governance of the company. Stakeholder dialogue is an attempt to increase the self-awareness of the company, but this does not necessarily include respecting all the interests of the possible stakeholder groups. Stakeholder dialogue is an unfinished process improving gradually towards the inclusion of all the interests represented among the different groups.

The difficult question about what is really important to take into account when managers have to choose between different stakeholder claims has still not be sufficiently answered. Looking at initial definitions, that there is certain vagueness in the concept of the stakeholder, Freeman's broad definition of a stakeholder leaves many things to individual corporations. According to Mitchell, Agle, and Wood, this may not have been the case with the initial Stanford definition from 1963, which counted stakeholders as those groups or individuals on whom the "organization is dependant for its continued survival."[69] So here again, the dilemma of the relation between broad or narrow views of corporate stakeholders arises, through this distinction betweent broad and primary provides an opportunity to further distinguish between primary and secondary stakeholders, thereby contributing to possibly making Freeman's definition instrumental for management.[70] When discussing narrow stakeholders, one can argue for the importance of their relationship with the firm. In addition, relationships between the basic interests of the firm (economic, social, political legitimacy, et cetera) have been proposed in order to define who should count as the most important stakeholders. The distinction between claimants and influentials is another important distinction in order to define stakeholder salience.

To be claimant does not necessarily imply that you have an important influence in the firm. One may, therefore, focus on stakeholders with power rather than all those who have a claim in the firm. Moreover, the distinction between actual and potential stakeholders should be taken into account. The importance of "sleeping stakeholders" should not be forgotten.[71] Actual stakeholders may be less important than potential stakeholders, because potential stakeholders may have much more power and influence over the firm. In this context, both mutual power and mutual dependence of stakeholders should be mentioned as possible aspects of stakeholder status. Choosing among these different criteria, power and legitimacy may legitimately be considered as the most important criteria for defining stakeholder salience.[72]

In the view of transaction cost and agency theories, power is considered as very important for stakeholder identification. Behavioral theory also emphasizes the function of stakeholders for the political power of a firm. Mitchell,

Agle, and Wood argue that institutional theories of the organization, for example Richard W. Scott,[73] who considers organizations as open systems, take the view that "legitimate stakeholders are the ones that really count" because managers live in a socially constructed world where "illegitimacy" results in "isomorphic pressures" of becoming like the others (that is, in organizations that operate outside accepted norms).[74] From this point of view, stakeholders are related to the organizational ecology of the firm and urgency becomes an important element for stakeholder identification.

The concern for power in the literature is based on traditional conceptualizations, where power is an important utilitarian and survival-oriented means to cope with coercion. Legitimacy is also related to power, but is considered as a broader category referring to the groups and people that are considered important for society at large. Legitimate stakeholders are considered important for authority. Mitchell, Agle, and Wood define legitimacy it as "a generalized perception or assumption that the actions of an entity are desirable, proper, or appropriate within some socially constructed system of norms, values, beliefs, and definitions."[75] Legitimacy is difficult to determine and it refers to multiple levels of analysis at the individual, social, and organizational levels, and it may indeed even include actors that are very critical to the organization.[76] Urgency is defined as "immediately pressing" or "pressing." This criteria refers to time intensity regarding particular stakeholders, meaning that time may change the degree to which particular stakeholders are considered important. Indeed, it is important to notice that stakeholders are variable, evolving, and change with degree according to social development and context. This may be the reason for changing relationships between different notions of stakeholder salience.

Different stakeholder claims may change over time, but they constitute an important systematization of relevant stakeholder concerns for managers who have to decide who and what really counts. This is both corporate social responsibility in a moral sense, but also as the capacity of corporations to respond to social issues. There is also a normative core to this concept of stakeholder theory, which stipulates that "power and urgency must be attended to if managers are to serve the legal and moral interests of legitimate stakeholders."[77]

Stakeholder management is principally a way to improve the scope of values-driven management, because it broadens the concept's relevance to larger groups of interested parties. Stakeholder management is indeed paradoxical, because it says that managerial responsibilities go beyond, and may sometimes even contradict, contractual obligations or fiduciary duties to shareholders.[78] With an approach to stakeholder management that factors in power, legitimacy, and urgency, it becomes possible to integrate business ethics into the stakeholder approach to strategic management. Stakeholder management is open to proactive communication and partnerships with the environment of the corporation.[79] Moreover, stakeholder management implies that political and social issues are integrated in strategic management. Normative justifications of stakeholder theory may indeed be found in business ethics theories that use stakeholder management to contextualize their value claims; however, stakeholder theory is not, in itself, a comprehensive moral doctrine. It is true that stakeholder theory is not primarily concerned with financial and economic objectives, but this does not imply that it is pure socialism, or that it requires enormous legal changes in order to be operational.[80] While it combines democratic concerns for principles and fairness with strategic concerns for integration with the environment, this does not a priori define the implied stakes for governance. After having identified relevant stakes, it is the job for management to make the correct decision among these implied interests.[81] A theory of stakeholder interests is, therefore, insufficient without some view of the good life – including "the other" – as the general aim for all stakeholders. The basis of stakeholder theory should be the idea of the corporation as a responsible citizen searching for the common good.[82] An important guide in this process is the normative justification of stakeholder management within different theories of business ethics. The discussion will start, after the case presentation, by considering virtue ethics and the communitarian theory of values-driven management.

Case 5. The stakeholder firm as a social activist: The case of Body Shop International

A firm that has been typically conceived as a real stakeholder firm is The Body Shop International. The case of Body Shop has been selected because it is a company that has been very closely associated with the idea of stakeholder management. In this sense, the story of Body has become a classic example of a political firm dealing with stakeholder management. This particular case is also an example of an *ethical crisis* because the company has had problems of living up to its announced image as a socially responsible corporation.

Anita Roddick founded the Body Shop in Brighton, England in 1976. She initially opened a shop for natural cosmetic products on the basis of natural recipes collected from different parts of the world. As the company grew, she continued to focus on natural products, recycling of bottles, and other cost-saving techniques. The company did not use marketing, but it was made clear that this was an activist company supporting community service, human rights, and environmental protection. Roddick also refused animal testing in the devlopment of its cosmetics.[83]

The concept of Body Shop was totally new in the cosmetic industry, which mostly used animal testing and did not rely on old and already used natural recipes. Animal testing was considered as important to comply with different kinds of regulations. Body Shop argued that such testing was cruel and unnecessary and refused to collaborate with any suppliers that had used such testing during the five years preceeding their negotiations. With its new approach, the firm very soon found a market and grew very quickly from 1976 until the firm went public in 1984. It grew to become a firm with 1600 shops and more than 5000 employees in forty-seven countries.[84]

With its environmental profile and image as a social activist firm, including its ecological approach to cosmetics, observers in the early 1990s estimated the compnay to have a very strong potential for growth. The firm had grown on the basis of combining good products with a very strong political message, and it was the declared vision of Anita Roddick that that firm should not only earn money but also contribute to social change. As a part of this vision, the company actively worked with NGOs and organizations like Greenpeace and Amnesty International.[85]

However, with all its success the company was also vulnerable to criticism, especially when journalists in the 1990s wrote that Body Shop's products did contain artificial products and that the firm did not treat its franchising shops in the same way as shops that were company owned. Moreover, there were doubts about the efficiency of the refusal to use animal testing among suppliers. The firm's fair trade practices were also questioned. The firm tried to fight such accusations by lawsuits and efforts to avoid negative press. This strategy backfired and raised even more doubts about the integrity of the company.

As a response to such criticism, Body Shop started making detailed reporting about social and environmental progress of the company. In 1997, the report mentions policies in areas of protection of human rights, environmental sustainability, and animal protection. The performance of the firm with regard to these issues is carefully evaluated and measured with regard to the objectives of the firm. These reports were continued the following years and based on interviews and dialogues with all important internal and external stakeholders of the firm.[86]

Body Shop was a market innovator as a political firm creating an image of social activism. The firm is still considered a leader in this area, but now it encounters much more competition and criticism with regard to the sincerity of its visions of natural products and animal protection.

3.3. Communitarian values–driven management

The communitarian approach to values-driven management goes deeper than both property right and stakeholder theories. Its main assumption is that these theories are not sufficiently aware of the importance for business of social practices and concerns for the common good.[87] The communitarian vision of the good life and excellence includes virtues like friendship, honor, integrity, and loyalty as basic to the successful business. Furthermore, business is seen as a matter of common social practices and good organizational culture rather than individual competition and greed. Corporations are viewed as human communities of people working together in social practices in order to achieve common social goals. Excellence and virtue, rather than rational choice and self-interest, are the main sources of social responsibility in corporations.

Robert Solomon has developed such a view of the corporation as a community of excellence.[88] His is an Aristotelian approach to business ethics.[89] Solomon begins by showing how the liberal view of business endorsed by Adam Smith, Milton Friedman, and representative game theorists is too superficial to capture the reality of business life. These theories cannot explain the sense of community and the need for virtues and trust which are necessary in order to conduct good business. Profit maximization and competition come second only to social interaction and cooperation in social context as the function of business. Aristotelian ethics is used as a criticism of Homo Economicus and the view that business is only about making money.[90]

Free market capitalism is based on a number of metaphors that are very misleading. Neither abstract greed, the "will to power," nor egoistic self-interest can explain business interactions and productivity. The view that business only has responsibility to shareholders is in deep opposition with the bounded character of markets and business organizations. The idea of a *moral market*, described in abstract terms of economic models and game theory, is very dangerous when this view is supposed to describe human social rationality.

The practices of daily business life cannot be understood in terms of mutual rational self-interest and greed.[91] Business interaction cannot work without presupposing some common goals between the actors, and markets should not be considered as closed rational games of utility and profit maximization. They are, rather, interactions governed by practices facilitating the pursual of the common good for the implied actors and stakeholders. In this sense, business life should rather be considered as a life-form, a community of practice, a kind of practical rationality with its own rules, goals, and role models for actors.

The communitarian approach further implies a criticism of prevailing views of the capitalist economic system. It accepts the importance of competition for economics, but it refuses to view it in terms of rational choice theory. Competition is not primary, but is based on more fundamental virtues of cooperation, trust, and durable commitment.[92] Moreover, the emphasis on individualism in economics is also construed as a myth of liberalism. In modern corporations, individuals are embedded in social arrangements and communities where cooperation is essential to common achievements; indeed, individuals are shaped in terms of the common values and cultures of the organizations.[93] Individuals act within larger moral frameworks where the business organization, as a whole, is not isolated. An institution within society acting as a whole acquires something like citizenship, because it is embedded as an actor with responsibilities in common social practices.[94]

This communitarian criticism of liberalism does not reject all aspects of Adam Smith's market capitalism. As has been discussed at previous points in the book, Smith's theory of moral sentiments was concerned with the common good and the interpersonal virtues of society. In fact, rational self-interest can be understood on communitarian grounds. According to Solomon, self-interest should not primarily be understood as competition, but rather as a genuine engagement in cooperation. Looking more closely on Smith's definition of self-interest, which was the concept leading to his theory of "the invisible hand," it becomes apparent that selfishness cannot be separated from interpersonal interest in social recognition.[95] A similar argument can be made with regard to John Stuart Mill's utilitarianism, by saying that utility calculations presuppose an interest in the common good and a sense of community among participants in society.[96]

Alternatively, the Aristotelian and communitarian approach to business ethics considers business as a human practice in order to achieve excellence and the common good in community. [97] Aristotle was, indeed, very critical to business. He considerered profit making to be undignified, and businessmen as parasites.[98] This critical view of business activity as inferior has had a long history in the Western tradition.

The communitarian perspective, with its view of the corporation as a human practice, may contribute to a more positive view, by framing the business community as a political human community. As a member of a society, it is the task of the individual to contribute to the common good.[99] At the same time, there is a link between individual virtue and integrity, and the community. Following this logic, each individual could be said to work for the common good in the practice of business.

The individual also receives personal fulfillment in business activities. For Aristotle, the aim of business is not only the maximization of profits. Business activity improves the self-respect and life achievements of the individual, as a member of the group. Greed or egoistic self-interest are secondary to the individual's belonging to a community of practice aiming at the common good.[100]

The ultimate aim of business as a social practice would, therefore, be happiness and the common good. The good has a teleological structure. Every action of the individual contributes to their personal character and virtue, and further contributes to the constitution of the role of the individual in business as a good social practice. Their roles are defined in relation to their responsibilities to other members of the organization. Corporate responsibility is not solely directed towards shareholders but involves all the stakeholders of the organization.[101]

Viewing the organization as a social practice, its members see themselves as part of a community, and are oriented towards its traditions and culture. Corporate culture is viewed as unifying the organization through common values, aims, and goals, which precede the interests of various stakeholders. In this way, the communitarian understanding of business life may defend the conception of the organization as a moral agent, where every individual is bound to its moral unity.[102] The members of the organization have a strong sense of commitment to the organization and they identify themselves with the mission and values of the corporation. The common identification with the organization constitutes the unity of the corporation as a moral agent.

The most important virtues are integrity, justice, and good judgment. Individual character is formed by the exercise of these virtues in concrete situations, rather than by following formal principles.[103] The exercise of virtues is based on an individual's sense of membership in the corporation as a moral community. The virtues of trust, integrity, friendship, honor, loyalty, compassion, and caring are in strict opposition to the vices of greed and resentment.[104]

In business, as indicated, the exercise of good judgment is considered to be the capacity to take into consideration all the relevant factors of the situation. On this basis, a good and considerate judgment is made.[105] This is grounded in the teleological structure of the specific values and interests of the practice of the corporation from the perspective of the common good. The virtue of judgment is not only about including all stakeholders, but also to do so in light of the common good that constitutes the corporation. Judgment is the capacity to make the right decisions in order to secure the integrity of the corporation, and contribute to the good life of the individual members of the organization.

Solomon emphasizes that justice is the ultimate aim of corporate life. Without fairness and justice, the good life in the corporation cannot persist. In the communitarian view, justice primarily signifies that "equals should be treated equally and unequals should be treated unequally."[106] Justice is closely linked with the concepts of virtue and excellence, though this should not be taken to exclude the basis of justice as the universal idea that all human beings are equally deserving of dignity and integrity. It does mean that justice is dependent on the particularity of situations and specific social practices in the firm. A number of factors to be included in the communitarian vision of justice include equality, merit, ability, need, risk and uncertainty, rights, the public good, duties and responsibilities, market value, loyalty, tradition, moral virtue.[107] It is important to stress that justice, in this view, is based on the commitment and belonging of responsible individuals to a community of excellence and the ethical style of the organization.

The communitarian approach to business ethics redefines the corporation as a community of practice and contributes to solving the flaws of rational choice theory. Moreover, it goes a bit deeper than the stakeholder theory, because it shows how stakeholder considerations must presuppose the common good of the organization. While the idea that organizations and corporations are moral communities implying visions of the good and common values of excellence seems compelling, this view is not sufficient in a world of increasing globalization in search of universal norms. Even though it may seem very attractive, there are some intrinsic difficulties in maintaining a pure communitarian position as the foundation of business ethics. How can one be assured that the values and tradition of the firm are good values that can function as the basis for morality? The fact that a corporation has adopted certain values as a way of life does not justify those values. Moreover, to ground business ethics in the common values of the organization may be a rather weak way to justify values, because tradition and common virtues do not imply a universal justification of ethics. There is also the danger of the organization serving the power of authoritarian and aristocratic leaders who decide on their own how to define the values of the firm. Communitarianism has understood the role of excellence and virtues, but needs a better protection of individual rights.

It is important that the communitarian approach serves the promotion of the good life, but this must never lead to destruction of individual autonomy. The life in the organization should generate individual happiness, not lead to the destruction of personal life in organizations.[108] Promoting the individual's freedom and autonomy in the organization, while at the same building an organizational culture linking individuals closer together, must, therefore, be an important part of the communitarian approach to organizational ethics. Corporate culture is important to give meaning to life and make people happy, but the fact remains that corporate culture can pose a great danger to individual autonomy.[109] The potential exists for corporate culture to make people into brainwashed soldiers who act without any personal ethical reflection. It is the aim of the corporation as a good community to ensure that no singular ideological conception of the good life dominates.

The communitarian approach is in danger of absorbing individuals in the values of the community without giving them any possibility of external evaluation of the values of the firm as a community. Totalitarian organizations use corporate culture to encourage uniformity and destroy individuality.[110] In addition, the corporation is never an isolated community, as in ancient times, but an actor in the world community; therefore, there should be a universal dimension to the defintion of the corporate good. The communitarian view must be put in relation to a Kantian theory of business, meaning moving beyond the concrete morality of the firm as a community towards a possible universal foundation of business ethics.

Case 6. Ethics, culture, and the virtuous firm: The case of Wetherill Associates, Inc.

Wetherill Associates, founded in 1978, is an American firm that delivers electronic parts for car repairs. They serve as an illustration of a firm that partially followed the communitarian ideals of virtue ethics.[111] Wetherill Associates is not a case that is well-known; however, it is a very good illustration of a company searching to make an *ethical effort* and it may become a classic Harvard Business School case of the problems with and possibilities of communitarian values-driven management.

Wetherill Associates expanded during the 1990s and in 1992 it had 300 employees, 6.9 million dollars in revenues, and more than eighty-one million dollars in product turnover. The firm started in Royersford, Pennsylvania, but now has centers of distribution in Los Angeles, Atlanta, Chicago, and Dallas. The firm's exports account for more than seven million dollars to customers in Mexico, Europe, Canada, Australia, Taiwan, and South America. Most of the employees work in Royersford and there is an equal distribution of age and sex.

What is special about this firm is that it is founded on the basis of the philosophy of Richard W. Wetherill, a management consultant who can be said to be a devoted believer in the virtue of "right action" as the key to corporate success. The idea behind this philosophy is that the virtue of right action is like a national law; therefore, company policy that encourages honesty, integrity, and quality is considered to be the fundamental constitution of its action: "Whenever an action is known or felt to be right, the action is to be taken. Whenever an action is known or suspected to be wrong, the action is not to be taken."[112]

The philosophy of right action is distributed to all primary stakeholders of the firm. According to Wetherill's philosophy, uncompromising integrity of right action eliminates doubt about doing wrong things for profit, and strengthens the firm and its relations to stakeholders. The firm tries very seriously to be principled with regard to its applications of core ideas. The outcome of this virtue ethics is that employees are trained to fulfill the demands of right action to the best of their ability rather than to make profit or avoid losses. In other words, employees have to follow what they estimate to be the right action and avoid what is suspected to be wrong. This is the gist of Wetherill Associates' Quality Assurance Manual.

The right action principles are reflected in the corporation's treatment of employees, customers, and other stakeholders. Employees are treated equally according to the principle of right action: therefore, the firm works with a high degree in equality in salary. Salary is not based on enticement but on concern for the welfare of the employees. Moreover, the employees share profits. What is important among employees is good fellowship and commitment to community. With regard to customers, the firm is committed to quality. It is stated that right action is much more important than making money.

Wetherill Associates illustrates the virtue ethics conception of the firm because economic profits of self-interested individuals are regarded as secondary to the community of right action, which constitutes the firm. What may be considered as problematic in this conception is the potential for right action ethics to turn into some kind of corporate religion and ideology, where employees have no freedom with regard to the commitments to community. On the other hand, the firm represents an important emphasis on the need for community as the basis for ethical commitment in a corporation. Here, is a firm where values, vision, and virtues constitute a common consciousness and identity of the organization.

3.4. Kantian and universalistic perspectives on business ethics

While communitarian approaches to business ethics focus on the corporation as a moral community, Kantian business ethics is based on a universalistic conception of morality. This deontological understanding of morality lays the foundation of morality in duty rather than virtue. Moreover, the moral law is universal and individuals have the duty to follow the moral law.[113] Even though Immanuel Kant wrote very little about capitalism and economics, it is possible to apply his philosophy to modern business systems. The Kantians would agree with the communitarians about the necessity to conceive the firm as a moral community, but this idea of business ethics would also go beyond the community and conceive morals from a global and cosmopolitan perspective. The Kantian theorist would be open to the communicative concept of stakeholder theory.

Norman E. Bowie (1999) tries to draw the consequences of Kantian theory for modern capitalism.[114] While stakeholder theorists sometimes do not make their foundations explicit, Bowie argues for a stakeholder theory of the modern corporation based on Kantian capitalism. This is the challenge to the conception of stakeholder theory as a strategic and utilitarian instrument, which has been proposed by many scholars of the rational choice tradition. It is possible to combine stakeholder theory and the Kantian approach to business ethics, but stakeholder theory must be evaluated according to the rules of practical reason. Moreover, the Kantian approach implies a strong criticism and limitation of the communitarian view of the good. Only a vision of the good that is compatible with universal principles of morality may be accepted as valid for values-driven management.

According to Bowie, Kantian business ethics is about how to conceive, manage, and structure a business firm in a capitalist economy according to the principles of Kant's ethics. In this context, Kant's categorical imperative becomes essential to ethics. Kant formulated three versions of the categorical imperative, which is the foundation of morality: 1) an action is moral if is can be a universal law; 2) never treat human beings only as a means, but also always as ends in themselves; and 3) the ideal of the moral law is the Kingdom of Ends of individuals who respect each other in their autonomy and dignity.[115] If business were based on these principles, one might say that this approach represents an international perspective on the business corporation. The moral law of the categorical imperative is meant to deal universally with all moral situations; however, this is the reason why good will is needed at the level of the ethical aim to support the

Kantian vision.[116] It has been argued by many critical voices that the Kantian approach is purely formal, though it justifies the need for communitarian morals. As indicated, the norms that establish the firm as a virtuous community have to be universally validated. The norms and virtues of the corporation should also be related to those of other stakeholders.

The Kantian approach to the corporation is closely linked to the communicative concept of stakeholder capitalism. Structuring the firm according to the principles of the categorical imperative means that actions should be based on duty and that the moral law provides the basis for decision-making. This is indicated by the first formulation of the categorical imperative. From this perspective, business corporations are obligated to treat stakeholders with as much honesty as possible.[117] In opposition to the strategic arguments of utilitarian stakeholder theory, Kantian stakeholder theory does not only consider stakeholders as devices for increased profit making, but seeks to respect stakeholders as agents with independent and intrinsic preferences. This is indicated by the second formulation of the categorical imperative. As the third formulation indicates, the notion that the firm should be treated as a moral community of beings with independent dignity is an end in itself. The idea of the moral community as Kingdom of Ends provides the foundation for understanding the morality of the business organization.

On the basis of these different perspectives, it is possible to discuss a Kantian view of the firm. Naturally, Kantian theory provides the formal framework for concrete developments of ethics in the firm. Moreover, it provides a universal justification for values-driven management in concrete situations. In theories of management and organizational behavior, Kantian approaches to business ethics help to justify the protection of rights of individual members of the firm, as well as other stakeholders. In opposition to the utilitarian concept of ethics and standard economic theory based on transaction cost economics, the Kantian approach to business ethics provides another understanding of economic actors. Kantian moral philosophy is not based on the idea of egoistic well-maximizing agent. According to Kant a rational economic agent has to follow the moral law, which is essentially the "golden rule" of do-unto-others-as-you-will-have-done-unto-you. Following this maxim, it seems difficult to justify cheating and lying in business life. Accordingly, it would be unethical, or even a contradiction in terms, to break a contract or make an immoral business transaction, which effectively renders universal moral reason as a limit to economic rationality.

On the basis of this interpretation of economic rationality, Bowie provides a Kantian analysis of the concept of trust. While trust in mainstream economic literature is viewed as an instrumental concept based on mutual calculation, a Kantian approach to trust conceives it as a moral condition of good business transactions.[118] Instead of being viewed as a dimension of strategic interaction, trust is a positive condition for good business in a well-functioning economy. It is significant that of the little he knew about Adam Smith's economic philosophy, Kant admired his work on moral sentiments.

The second categorical imperative establishes the necessity of respecting the dignity and integrity of human beings as rational persons with intrinsic value. The requirement to treat human beings not only as means, but also always as ends in themselves, indicates the importance of mutual respect, dignity, and self-respect for business life. In particular, the Kantian approach focuses on respect for the employees of the corporation and the members of the firm as a moral community.[119] The ideas of equal respect and impartiality follow from the idea of moral reason and rationality; therefore, Kantian business ethics puts strong emphasis on giving employees meaningful work without reducing them to slaves.[120] Employees should not be coerced and their dignity should be highly safeguarded, for example with job security, long-term employment, protection of workers' rights, and initiatives for their empowerment at work. Furthermore, concepts like employee democracy and profit sharing cannot be excluded from the Kantian view on ethics.

Because employees cannot be viewed as machines or instruments, they have to be respected as equal participants in the corporation. Kantianism is the opposite of Taylor's scientific management, based on specialization and the division of labor.[121] The Kantian concept of meaningful work implies, rather, that the autonomy and independence of workers are respected. Meaningful work should support the rationality and development of the individual employee, including recognizing the continuity between the private self and working life.[122] This indicates that values-driven management should be very seriously concerned with respecting the humanity of employees, and further, that the firm as a moral community should be viewed from this perspective.

Kantian business ethics would agree with the communitarian concept of the firm as a social community, and not only as a nexus of contracts, or the sum of stakeholder preferences. Bowie mentions John Rawls's concept of a *social union* as an appropriate way to describe the concern for the common good in corporations. This is a way to conceptualize social ties in organizations on a universal foundation. An organization is a unity of rational beings who follow the categorical imperative and see themselves as members of the Kingdom of Ends.[123] Every rational being must participate in deliberation and make a free decision. An organizational democracy where all stakeholders contribute to the policies and values, as well as daily practice of the organization, is, therefore, very important. This perspective is obviously in opposition to organizational structures that are overly authoritarian and hierarchical. Moreover, Kantianism views work as a cooperative effort to solve problems and promote common humanity.

The Kantian approach favors corporate citizenship and social responsibility as expressions of the moral debt of corporations to society. Deliberative democracy and collaborative work efforts are built on a procedural concept of justice where concerns for fairness imply that all people are respected as ends in themselves. This is based on duty to the moral law, meaning that one must do certain things because "they are right, rather than because they have good consequences."[124] Kantian business ethicists are skeptical towards business leaders and managers who see profit maximization as the sole goal of business, to the exclusion of the welfare of their corporations and their stakeholders. While Kant does not exclude the possibility that moral behavior can have good consequences – in many cases, he would assume so – these actions should be undertaken because they represent the morally right thing to do. In opposition to Friedman, Kantians would argue that the moral motive is prior to the profit motive, and that profit maximization, as such, cannot be a moral action.[125]

Norman Bowie stresses the universalistic and cosmopolitan dimensions of Kantian business ethics, where it is important to establish universal norms and rules that support moral reason and build a culture of trust. In opposition to communitarian and cultural relativism, this approach suggests the achievement of international standards for trade as a way to build global community. In order to avoid bribery, discrimination, and global inequality, it is necessary to develop universal norms for the business community. Human rights are especially important for democratic development. Moreover, this universalistic approach to business ethics and values-driven management agrees with the emphasis on the democratic potentiality of capitalist economies.[126]

Kantian business ethics is right to introduce a universal concept of organization that promotes human dignity and formal rights, because it is needed; however, it is important to safeguard concrete values and norms. A communitarian criticism of Kantian business ethics is that it is too formalistic, and that it cannot connect with the concrete ethical horizon of the culture of the organization. As a response to the communitarian criticism, it is important to avoid a separation between formal and correct rules on the one hand, and concrete ideals of the good life on the other. The concepts of universal rights and the categorical imperative are important for business ethics, but it must never be forgotten that the aim of universal principles should be the good life, and that ethical principles have to be contextualized to concrete communities in organizations in order to be realized.

3.5. Values and social contract theory

Thomas Donaldson and Thomas Dunfee attempt to conceive the universal conception of business ethics taking the aim of the good life into account.[127] They propose social contract theory – working, as well, with stakeholder theory and the contractual concept of business – as their normative framework. Social contract theory is less formal than Kantianism, because it is founded on social contracts in concrete community rather than on the abstract language of the categorical imperative. At the same time, this approach maintains the universalism that is lacking in the communitarian take on business ethics. While still compatible with a communitarian vision of the unity of the firm in a common culture, and the view of business as a social practice, social contract theory promotes the values of fairness and integrity as the basis of ethical norms.

From this perspective, the values of an organization are not primarily considered as functions of a biological process, as proposed by Frederick, but rather as the result of these normative social contracts. These contracts are not primarily formalist, impartial, and universalistic, but can be said to emerge out of the institutional practices of business life.[128] Social contract theory starts with the assumptions that these values, institutions, and practices, as well as their corresponding obligations and norms, should be considered as the result of "fair agreements," or contracts, between different groups and communities in society. In the contract theory, it is supposed that the normative basis of these institutions can be viewed as a hypothetical contract. The clarification of these contracts is the basis for determining the ethical relations between the firm and its stakeholders.

Donaldson and Dunfee's social contract theory contributes to the debate between universalism and communitarianism, in the sense that it is not only based on universalistic *macro-contracts*, but also recognizes that the social practices of the firm, the existing *micro-contracts*, are constitutive for business relations. In fact, this social contract theory can be said to combine micro-contracts in community life with those macro-contracts of global business life. Along with communitarianism, integrated social contract theory begins with the pluralism of many communities and cultures; however, viewed with reference to universal norms, some communitarian arrangements may be judged invalid.[129] Thus, comprehensive social contract theory can be seen to mediate between communitarianism and universalism.

In comparison with Rawls's theory of justice, social contract view may be considered as a less idealistic formulation of the basis of agreements. In contrast to an idealized situation of deliberation "behind the veil of ignorance," business actors are supposed to know their preferences and how they act in real life.[130] They are also supposed to have an elaborated understanding of right and wrong, thereby implying certain universal normative assumptions, though, of course, the formulators of the theory are supposed to be ignorant of particular preferences of specific actors.[131] Moreover, the communitarian idea that there is a common core morality preceding economic arrangements seems to be a necessary presupposition so that the social contracts are related to concrete norms of society.

The starting point for social contracts is "bounded moral rationality," an idea holding that there are implicit moral principles in economic practice, which cannot be considered exclusively in terms of either a Hobbesian *state of nature* or of Friedman's view of economics as rational choice and maximization of self-interest. Contractors (i.e., the individuals that take part in social contracts) are, on the basis of a certain cultural environment, determined by specific values and religious understanding of their culture and society, and seek to reduce uncertainty and to maximize economic efficiency. On the basis of these microsocial arrangements that are determined by specific norms and cultural understandings of particular societies, they hold certain universalistic claims that make them participate in macrosocial arrangements of universal norms and standards.

Organizations and individuals within specific business practices are, therefore, supposed to live within certain local cultural and social communities possessing their own substantial norms. Because these norms are culturally variable, they are in a "moral free space," which is recognized as a primary element in the formation of social contracts.[132] A free moral space is defined as a room for self-determination of the values and norms that should guide a specific culture and society. Membership in a specific community is supposed to be the basis for specific contractual agreements. Without recourse to global or universal norms, members of a community may define practical norms. Organizations live with "bounded rationality" and diversity within specific norms in moral free space. Each business organization has its own traditions, culture, and behavioral rules, along with different ethical codes, credos, and values.

In contrast to a strong communitarian view, social contract theory now argues that these norms in local communities must be tested against universal standards. These "global contracts" are called *hyper-norms*. They express a thin universal morality, which is essential as the foundation of economic activity.[133] Hyper-norms may indicate the limits of certain communitarian arrangements in specific areas of moral free space. They are the universal limits on community consent inside local organizational practices.

Hyper-norms are defined as the norms that are shared among different cultures and communities. They constitute very fundamental, second order principles of morality, which are universal principles for business behavior, in the same way as there are universal legal rules for the world. Hyper-norms can be considered as procedural rules or, following thinkers like Habermas and Alexy, as rules of argumentation, communication, and validity that function as sources for evaluating community-generated norms.[134]

Hyper-norms express the boundaries of moral free space. They imply the imposition of ethical norms within given micro-social communities. The violation of hyper-norms, which are authentic and legitimate as defined by norms emerging in local communities, is not permitted. The global macro-social contract for business can be summarized as the permission of local communities to have diversity and free moral space, but these norms are only legitimate when they are compatible with hyper-norms. In cases of conflict between microsocial and macrosocial contractual arrangements, priority must be given to hyper-norms.[135]

As a result of macrosocial contractual agreements, hyper-norms can simultaneously be structural, procedural, and substantive. Their articulation may be the result of overlapping consensus between specific cultural microsocial worldviews.[136] Extreme universalism is impossible when based on principles founded in specific communities. Business principles or values may have the status of hyper-norms when they are well known and there is consensus about their universality. These are principles endorsed by a plurality of international firms, governments, nongovernmental and other organizations or supported by major religions and/or philosophical worldviews. An example of a substantive hyper-norm may be the Caux Round Table business principles or the United Nations Universal Declaration of Human Rights.[137]

The foundation of hyper-norms should not be viewed as either a pre-established consensus, or as a natural process towards agreement. They are the result of an open process of recognition among cultures moving towards consensus. In this way, social contract theory embraces cultural particularity, but also creates an opening for ethical universality by seeking common norms for different cultures as the basis for coexistence in a global economic system. Donaldson and Dunfee argue, with Rawls and Sen, that the requirements of fairness, economic efficiency, prosperity, and justice in a well-ordered society constitute hyper-norms. Fairness and aggregative welfare are supposed to be necessary for a good and happy life in any society.[138]

Rawls's theory in *Political Liberalism* (1992) may add that respect for basic civil liberties and social cooperation for mutual benefit are necessary goods in order to achieve procedural justice within a society structured according to the principles of efficiency and justice in economic institutions. Shaping these institutions will happen with respect to diverse ethical norms and is a task for particular communities and business organizations according to their specific traditions, professional codes, and conceptions of values-driven management.

In this way, social contract theory implies an important universalist perspective on communitarian business ethics, but it also includes a useful reformulation of stakeholder theory. Social contract theory does not exclusively follow Anglo-American liberalism by prioritizing the community shareholders; rather, it acknowledges European and Japanese inclusion of a wider account of the stakeholders of the firm.[139] Social contract theory is not only grounded strategically in the narrow economic interests of the firm, but provides a normative foundation for stakeholder theory and stakeholder management. Stakeholder management, in this sense, is based on a normative evaluation of particular stakes. The validity of these norms is, in turn, established through the tension between authentic community norms and legitimate hyper-norms. This is not a formalist and universalist justification of stakeholder theory. Locally determined obligations of the firm, in accordance with legitimate norms in free moral space, come first. Global and universal norms requiring that the firm should take into account more remote stakeholders come later.

Authentic community norms define stakeholder status and are limited and shaped by the hyper-norms of the community.[140] Diverse local values may, therefore, be said to play an important role in the character of relevant stakeholder obligations of the company. As the foundation for relevant stakeholders, local community norms have priority, though they do not exclude stakeholder obligations, which are based on universalistic considerations. In comparison with a strict universalist and formalist Kantian view on relevant stakeholders, this approach avoids imposing stakeholder status from the outside. As long as they do not conflict with hyper-norms, a firm's community values are the primary determinants of stakeholder status.[141]

3.6. A republican concept of business ethics

In order to establish a normative foundation of business ethics, the analysis of property right theories, stakeholder management, communitarian, universalist, and social contract theories must be accompanied by conceptualizing business ethics within a republican theory of liberal democracy. The German business ethicist Peter Ulrich has put forward a theory of integrative business ethics, which argues that it is the aim of economic markets to contribute to the realization of the good life in political community among free and responsible citizens. Viewing business in the light of social development towards a free and justice society means that it should contribute to the promotion of the rights of individuals and corporate citizenship in political community.[142]

Contracts and agreements within a business community are only really legitimate insofar as they contribute to the development of political and social structures. Business should respond to the quest for legitimacy in a public political debate among members of a deliberative democracy by acting in a continuing dialogue with community. Business ethics and values-driven management could even be seens as an emancipatory, ideally contributing to more liberty in society.[143] The concrete development of rights to economic citizenship occurs within the framework of the political structures of deliberative democracy.

In the republican conception, economic action should – in order to acquire legitimacy – be based on recognizing critical public reason as the basis for defining the responsibilities and stakeholders of the firm. Economic actors should strive to behave according to republican virtues in order to constitute a just economic market. The social ideal of democratic business ethics is republican liberalism with a critical democratic public sphere as the basis for decision-making.[144] In order to be legally acceptable, private economic actions must accord with public reason, based on deliberate reflection, communication, and argumentation on the part of rational participants in a community.

From the republican perspective, it is the task of public debates in a political community to contribute to the formation of the normative structures of legitimate business activity. In such a "civilizing of civil society," the legitimacy of the economic system depends on the critical public sphere of society. The logic of the market is dependent on the public opinion about how to structure the norms of the economic system.[145] This conception goes further than the liberal tradition, which bases economics on negative rights of freedom and ownership, by viewing it as an aspect of a society's political structure.

Economics is used as an active instrument for achieving collective social and political goals aimed at the common good.[146] Such a constitutional conception of economics views business ethics as a part of the deliberative politics of liberal democracy. Within this framework, the rights of citizens are formulated in accordance with critical public reason; indeed, stakeholder dialogue based on integrated social contract theory is an important way of ensuring the integration of economic behavior in a political community. In particular, the privileges of ownership and power within free economic markets are subject to critical debates. If economic inequality is permitted on account of liberal requests for economic freedom and efficiency, democratic structures of governance may neutralize such social differences by facilitating public debates and individual access to common goods. Thus, corporate citizenship defines the participation of the corporation in the political community as a responsible actor with rights and duties. Constitutive elements of corporate citizenship are, therefore, concepts like business ethics, corporate social responsibility, corporate responsiveness, corporate accountability, corporate philanthropy, and corporate governance.[147] In developing policies on these issues, the corporation actively fulfills its duty towards society as a part of its license to operate. The goal of corporate citizenship to contribute to sustainable development based on respect for the triple bottom line of economic, social, and environmental dimensions of the strategy of the firm becomes important.

The idea of good corporate citizenship implies that not only individuals, but also firms as collective units, are ascribed a political and ethical responsibility for the common good in the social and political institutions of society. A republican concept of the firm implies that a company should be responsive to social demands for good corporate governance and social responsiveness, simultaneously caring for economic profits and a good political reputation in society. The ethical and political conception of the firm, which is developed out of this discussion of the major theories of business ethics, implies an ethical concept of politics. The prudent firm does not only understand politics as power, but follows the democratic view of the firm as a participant in community. The emergence of the concept of good corporate citizenship implies that social responsibility and responsiveness are at the forefront of the firm's license to operate.[148] As a good corporate citizen, a corporation works actively to bridge the tension between ethics and economics by formulating economic strategies that include conceptions of the common good.

This conception of corporate citizenship implies an idealization of politics, where politics is defined as a concern for common values in society. From this point of view, corporations contribute to the allocation of values in society by defining politically legitimate goals for economic action. Stakeholder involvement is an indication of this emergence of "political corporations." When consumers choose products according to the values of the corporation, its suppliers, shareholders, employees, and investors are also marked by large democratic political requirements to respect human rights and ecological sustainability. Hence, democratic welfare society has begun to consider corporations as important actors who can help to realize common political and social goals.

Requirements of alternative reporting, social and ethical accountability, and different types of values-driven management are expressions of this search for good corporate citizens. Values-driven management is an important factor in the realization of the ecological, social, and ethical sustainability of the firm; therefore, corporate citizenship includes international responsibility for product development and protecting the rights and welfare of employees, as well as external engagement in environmental and social issues, such as the protection of human rights of vulnerable groups. To this end, corporate transparency and the communication of a firm's attitudes and policies in these areas have become important for the development of corporate citizenship based on sustainable development; hence, corporate citizenship is developed in open stakeholder dialogue.

Deliberative public communication with stakeholders may help a good corporate citizen to identify relevant stakeholders.[149] Public relations dialogue is a very important vehicle through which the firm, in a deliberative political democracy, can internalize stakeholder concerns and stakeholder rights as part of its values. In this sense, republican business ethics aims at making democratic values the core of values-driven management by responsible corporations.

Case 7. Urgent ethical action: The Johnson and Johnson Tylenol crisis

The Tylenol crisis has been selected because it has become a classic, nearly trivialized, business ethics case. It is an example of a company putting forth an *ethical effort*. While not so commonly used as an illustration of Kantianism, this case represents an action based on ethical duty rather than utility. In this sense, it can be said to represent a sense of corporate citizenship.

Johnson and Johnson is a health and medical supplies company that was put through a huge crisis on September 30, 1982. There was a rumor that several deaths in Chicago were due to one the company's products, the pain reliever Tylenol, which was one of its main products and widely available without a prescription. There was a suspicion that the people had died from taking "cyanide-laced capsules of extra-strength Tylenol."[150]

Tylenol was very important for the earnings of Johnson and Johnson and the company had improved its market share due to the popularity of the product. The contamination scandal was very damaging for the reputation and trustworthiness of the company, despite the fact that the contamination was done at a production facility. Nevertheless, the name of the company was still associated with the contamination. The management of the corporation was faced with the difficult problem of how to restore the reputation of the company. The question was whether the corporation should withdraw all Tylenol products from the market, assuming a loss of more than one hundred million US dollars.[151] The managers of Johnson and Johnson not only faced the problem of salvaging the reputation of their company's brand name, but also of saving the credibility of future pharmaceutical products.

Their decision has become famous in the history of business ethics. In order to keep the trust of the public and to maintain the integrity of the organization, while also demonstrating the reliability and accountability of Johnson and Johnson, the firm decided to withdraw all Tylenol products from the market to assure the public that no one else would be poisoned.

One of the reasons for this decision may be found in the ethical culture of the firm, which is partly expressed in their corporate credo:

We believe our first responsibility is to the doctors, nurses, and patients, to mothers and fathers and all others who use our products and services. In meeting their needs, everything we do must be of high quality. We must constantly strive to reduce our costs in order to maintain reasonable prices. Customers' orders must be serviced promptly and accurately. Our suppliers and distributors must have an opportunity to make a fair profit.

We are responsible to our employees, the men and women who work with us throughout the world. Everyone must respect their dignity and recognize their merit. They must have a sense of security in their jobs. Compensation must be fair and adequate, and working conditions clean, orderly, and safe. We must be mindful of ways to help our employees fulfill their family responsibilities. Employees must feel free to make suggestions and complaints. There must be equal opportunity for employment, development, and advancement for those qualified. We must provide competent management, and their actions must be just and ethical.

We are responsible to the community in which we live and work and to the world community, as well. We must be good citizens – support good works and charities, and bear our fair share of taxes. We must encourage civic improvement

*and better health and education. We must maintain in good order the property
we are privileged to use, protecting the environment and natural resources.
Our final responsibility is to our stockholders. Business must make a sound
profit. We must experiment with new ideas. Research must be carried on, innovative programs developed and new products launched. Reserves must be
created to provide for adverse times. When we operate according to these principles, the stockholders should realize a fair return.[152]*

The Tylenol case can be interpreted as an effort to follow the virtues and duty of good
citizenship. Of course, there were also very prudent and utilitarian arguments for
stopping the release of the product; more deaths that could be related to the product would have led to distrust of the company. It is interesting to observe that this
initial event became important for the subsequent development of ethics programs
in Johnson and Johnson related to a realization of the importance of good corporate
citizenship for corporate success.

Endnotes

1   John Dienhart, *Business, Institutions and Ethics, A Text with Cases and Readings* (Oxford: Oxford University Press, 2000), 97.
2   The material for this case is selected from Joseph W. Weiss, *Business Ethics. A Stakeholder and Issues Manage-ment Approach*, Third Edition (Canada: Thompson, SouthWestern, 2003). O.C. Ferrell, John Fraedrich and Linda Ferrell, *Business Ethics. Ethical Decision Making and Cases* (Boston and New York: Houthton Mifflin Company, 2005), 335-343. Manuel G. Velasquez, *Business Ethics. Concepts and Cases*, Fifth Edition (New Jersey: Prentice Hall, 2002), 153-159.
3   James E. Post, Anne T. Lawrence and James Weber, *Business and Society, Corporate Strategy, Public Policy, Ethics* (New York: McGraw-Hill, Irwin, 2002), 548-558.
4   Tibor R. Machan, "Business Ethics in a Free Society" in *A Companion to Business Ethics* edited by Robert E. Frederick (Oxford: Blackwell Publishing (1999), 2002), 89.
5   Ibid: 177. See also F.A. Hayek, *Law, legislation and liberty. A new statement of the liberal principles of justice and political economy*, including Vol 1: *Rules and order*, Vol 2: *The mirage of social justice*, Vol 3: *The political order of a free people*, (London: Routledge, (1983), 1998).
6   Robert Nozick, *Anarchy, State and Utopia*, (New York: Basic Books, Incs Publishers, 1974).
7   Ibid: 52.
8   F.A. Hayek, "The Corporation in a Democratic Society: In Whose Interest Ought It and Will It Be Run" (1960), Reprinted in H. Igor Ansoff (ed.): *Business Strategy* (London: Penquin Modern Management Readings, 1969), 225.
9   Ibid: 227.
10 Ibid: 232.
11 Milton Friedman, "The Social Responsibility of Business is to increase its profits", *New York Times Magazine* (September 13), 1970. Reprinted in Scott, B Rae and Kenman, L. Wong, *Beyond Integrity. A Judeo-Christian Approach to Business Ethics* (Grand Rapids Michigan: Zondervan Publishing House, 1996), 241-246.
12 Ibid: 242
13 Ibid: 245

14 Ibid: 243
15 Ibid: 244
16 Ibid: 245
17 Ibid: 245
18 Manuel G. Velasquez, *Business Ethics. Concepts and Cases*, Fifth Edition (New Jersey: Prentice Hall, 2002), 173.
19 Thomas Carson, "Friedman's theory of Corporate Social Responsibility", *Business and Professional Ethics Journal*, Vol 12 (1993), no 1.
20 Ibid: 11.
21 Ibid: 16.
22 Ibid: 13
23 Milton Friedman, "The Social Responsibility of Business is to increase its profits", *New York Times Magazine* (September 13), 1970. Reprinted in Scott, B Rae and Kenman, L. Wong, *Beyond Integrity. A Judeo-Christian Approach to Business Ethics* (Grand Rapids Michigan: Zondervan Publishing House, 1996), 241-246.
24 Michael Jensen: "A Theory of the Firm, governance, residual claims and organizational forms", *The Journal of Financial Economics*, 1976.
25 Michael E. Porter and Mark R. Kramer, "The Competitive Advantage of Corporate Philanthropy" in Harvard Business Review, December 2002, Reprinted in *Harvard Business Review on Corporate Social Responsibility*, (Cambridge Massachusetts: Harvard University Press, 2003).
26 Ibid: 29.
27 Ibid: 31.
28 Ibid: 33.
29 Ibid: 33-34.
30 Ibid: 36.
31 Ibid: 52.
32 Ibid: 59.
33 Porter and Kramer mention the donations of the Grand Circle travel company, which organizes cultural and historical travel for older American (p. 44). This company has given generously to historical preservation projects, including protection of the State Museum of Auswitch-Birkenau in Poland, so that the museum could be improved. This donation was a direct consequence of the interest of the travel company in having good sites for their customers to visit. Porter and Kramer mention this example as a kind of win-win situation of corporate philanthropy, because both company and museum get advantages out of the donations. This is, however, a perfect example of the limitations of crude utilitarianism because the ethically concerned Kantian may ask whether it is moral to be so focused on earning money from the Auschwitz tragedy. Accordingly, this example shows intuitively how the economic concept of corporate philanthropy cannot stand alone, but must be evaluated in terms of basic ethical principles in business ethics.
34 Michael E. Porter and Mark R. Kramer: "Strategy and Society. The Link between Competitive Advantage and Corporate Social Responsibility", *Harvard Business Review*, December 2006.
35 Ibid: 80.
36 Ibid: 82.
37 Ibid: 83.
38 Ibid: 85.
39 Ibid: 88.
40 Ibid: 89.
41 Ibid: 92.
42 Peter Ulrich, *Integrative Wirtschaftsethik,. Grundlagen einer lebensdienlichen Ökonomie*, 2 Auflage (Stuttgart, Wien: Haupt, 1998).
43 Manuel G. Velasquez, *Business Ethics. Concepts and Cases*, Fifth Edition, (New Jersey: Prentice Hall, 2002), 228.
44 Peter Ulrich, *Integrative Wirtschaftsethik. Grundlagen einer lebensdienlichen Ökonomie*, 2 Auflage (Stuttgart, Wien: Haupt, 1998).
45 Ibid: 415.
46 Ibid: 416.
47 Ibid: 421.

48 This view of stakeholder theory puts it in the perspective of good corporate citizenship. I think that the literature on stakeholder management is characterized by the tension between strategic and dialogical approaches to stakeholder management. In the strategic approach, it might be the instrumental concern for corporate survival that is the most important, while the dialogical approach integrates strategic concerns into broader work for stakeholder democracy. Although stakeholder democracy is a controversial term, I think that this might be the most important outcome of good stakeholder management. See Dirk Matten and Andrew Crane, "What is stakeholder democracy? Perspectives and Issues", *European Journal of Business Ethics*, Volume 14, (2005), Number 1, 6-13. Brenda O'Dwyer: "Stakeholder Democracy: Challenges from social accounting", *European Journal of Business Ethics*, Volume 14, (2005), Number 1, January, 28-38.

49 David Wheeler and Maria Sillanpää, *The Stakeholder Corporation. The Body Shop Blue Print for Maximizing Stakeholder Value* (London: Pitman Publishing, 1997), 33.

50 Ibid: 58.

51 Ibid: 114.

52 Ibid: 126.

53 Ibid: 133.

54 R. Edward Freeman and John McVea, "A stakeholder approach to strategic management" in *The Blackwell Handbook of Strategic Management*, edited by Michael A. Hitt, R. Edward Freeman and Jeffrey S. Harrison (New York: Blackwell Business, 2004), 190.

55 Ibid: 192.

56 See Michael Jensen's discussion of stakeholder theory and the necessity of a single objective for the firm. Jensen argues that efficiency requires a single objective, which does not seem evident to me. In fact, the triple bottom line approach requires that corporations are much more open to different management concerns. With this approach, it seems that it is exactly the ability to integrate different concerns that should be the essential aim of good management. Jensen is too focused on the idea of a single value to understand that management instruments, such as "balanced scorecard" and stakeholder management, can increase general economic efficiency precisely because of their ability to include multilevel objectives in the management of the firm. Moreover, I would argue that although stakeholders may have different interests from the start, good stakeholder management tends to work for the integration of these functions in the same direction so that stakeholder management does not have to be as confused as Jensen seems to suppose. See Michael C. Jensen, "Value Maximization, stakeholder theory and the corporate objective function", *Business Ethics Quarterly*, Volume 12, (2002), Issue 2. See also Oliver Williamson's defence of the primacy of shareholder approach from the point of view of transaction cost economics. Oliver Williamson, *The Economic Institutions of Capitalism* (New York: The Free Press, 1984).

57 R. Edward Freeman and John McVea, "A stakeholder approach to strategic management" in *The Blackwell Handbook of Strategic Management*, edited by Michael A. Hitt, R. Edward Freeman and Jeffrey S. Harrison, (New York: Blackwell Business, 2005), 195.

58 Antonio Argandona, "The Stakeholder Theory and the Common Good", *Journal of Business Ethics*, (1998), Vol. 17).

59 R. Edward Freeman and John McVea, "A stakeholder approach to strategic management" in *The Blackwell Handbook of Strategic Management*, edited by Michael A. Hitt, R. Edward Freeman and Jeffrey S. Harrison, (New York: Blackwell Business, 2005), 195.

60 This was the case when Freeman and Evan developed their principled and Kantian approach to stakeholder management, where stakeholders should be treated as an end in themselves. See R. Edward Freeman and W. Evan, "A stakeholder theory of the Modern corporation: Kantian Capitalism" in *Ethical Theory and Business*, edited by Thomas L. Beauchamp and Norman Bowie, 5th Edition, (Englewood Cliffs, N.J., Prentice Hall, 1993), 75-84.

61 Edward R. Freeman, *Strategic Management, A Stakeholder Approach* (Boston, Massachusetts: Pitman Publishing Inc, 1984).

62 Edward R. Freeman, "The Stakeholder Corporation" in Laura Pincus Hartman: *Perspectives in business ethics*, (Chicago: Irwin McGraw-Hill, 1998), 250. William M. Evan and Edward R. Freeman: "A stakeholder theory of the Modern corporation: Kantian Capitalism" in *Ethical Theory and Business*, edited by Thomas L. Beauchamp and Norman Bowie, 5th Edition, (Englewood Cliffs, N.J., Prentice Hall, 1993), 75-84.

63 The evolution of the stakeholder concept implies different levels of relations to power, legitimacy, and urgency that affect, or are affected by, groups or individuals. This definition of stakeholder management implies a reinterpretation of the role the stakeholder in strategic management. A stakeholder is not only someone who can be used instrumentally to manipulate the interests of the firm, but is rather a group or an individual who has any kind of relation to the firm or organization. This stakeholder might be someone who participates in a common process or is engaged in some kind of interaction with the firm, or it can be a person or a group of persons who are more distantly related to or affected by the corporation. If we go back to the early definitions of stakeholders within strategic management in the early 1960s, a stakeholder is someone who has vital influence over the survival of the corporation. A stakeholder can, according to this point of view, be a person or a group who decides whether the firm shall have the right to survive, but a stakeholder can also be a powerful person or group within the company whose power includes the ability to decide everything about the future of that person (Ronald K. Mittchell, Bradley R. Agle and Donna S. Wood, "Toward a Theory of Stakeholder Identification and Salience: Defining the Principle of Who and What really counts", *Academy of Management Review* Vol 22, (1997), 860). Others argue that stakeholders are implied in a common power relation with the firm, and that stakeholders have importance as an integrated part of the company. This definition is close to the definition according to which the stakeholder is related to the firm in a symbiosis, and where the stakeholder qua stakeholder should have legitimate demands that influence the activities of the firm. This is connected with the idea that a stakeholder also has legitimate moral claims on the company, which may imply that the firm is required to have specific moral concerns for selected stakeholders. On the basis of these definitions, we can clarify the concept of a stakeholder as proposed by Mitchell et al., and by Freeman, as someone who affects or is affected by the firm, including stakeholders who have relations of power, legitimacy, or urgency to the firm. In addition to these two levels, we can mention the dialogical level in which the firm's stakeholders are included in communication and dialogue about the future of the firm's strategy and other activities.

64 When we discuss stakeholder management from the perspective of corporate citizenship and corporate social responsibility in part 3, where further criteria for the selection of stakeholders are developed.

65 Edward R. Freeman, *Strategic Management, A Stakeholder Approach*, (Boston, Massachusetts: Pitman Publishing Inc., 1984).

66 Thomas Donaldson and Lee E. Preston, "The Stakeholder Theory of the Corporation: Concepts, Evidence and Implications", *Academy of Management Review*, Vol. 20, (1995), 1.

67 Ronald K. Mittchell, Bradley R. Agle and Donna S. Wood, "Toward a Theory of Stakeholder Identification and Salience: Defining the Principle of Who and What really counts", *Academy of Management Review*, Vol 22, (1997), No 4, 853 –886.

68 Ibid: 855.

69 Ibid: 856.

70 Thomas M. Jones, "Instrumental Stakeholder Theory: A Synthesis of Ethics and Economics", *Academy of Management Review*, Vol. 20, (1995), No 2.

71 A striking example is a case from the Netherlands. The local government wanted to build a brigde for a highway through a natural resource area, where a small endangered species lives. Critical environmentalists started to defend the right to survival of the small animal that was threatened with extinction. Suddenly, the animal became a powerful stakeholder and the building project had to be abandoned.

72 Ronald K. Mittchell, Bradley R. Agle and Donna S. Wood, "Toward a Theory of Stakeholder Identification and Salience: Defining the Principle of Who and What really counts" in *Academy of Management Review* 1997, Vol 22, No 4, 862.

73 Richard W. Scott, *Institutions and Organizations*, London: Sage Publications, 1995.

74 Ronald K. Mittchell, Bradley R. Agle and Donna S. Wood, "Toward a Theory of Stakeholder Identification and Salience: Defining the Principle of Who and What really counts" in *Academy of Management Review* 1997, Vol 22, No 4, 864. The article refers to the work about institutional theory of Dimaggio and Powell in 1983.

75 Ibid: 866.

76 Robert Philips, "Stakeholder Legitimacy", *Business Ethics Quarterly*, Volume 13, (2003), Issue 1.

77 Ronald K. Mittchell, Bradley R. Agle and Donna S. Wood, "Toward a Theory of Stakeholder Identification and Salience: Defining the Principle of Who and What really counts" in *Academy of Management Review* 1997, Vol 22, No 4, 882.

78 Kenneth Goodpaster, "Business ethics and Stakeholder Analysis", *Business Ethics Quarterly*, Number 1: 53-73. Kenneth Goodpaster and T. Holloran, "In defense of a Paradox", *Business Ethics Quarterly*, Number 4: 423-30.

79 R. Edward Freeman and John McVea, "A stakeholder approach to strategic management" in *The Blackwell Handbook of Strategic Management*, edited by Michael A. Hitt, R. Edward Freeman and Jeffrey S. Harrison, (New York: Blackwell Business, 2005), 199.

80 Robert Philips, R. Edward Freeman and Andrew C. Wicks, "What stakeholder theory is not", *Business Ethics Quarterly*, Volume 13, Issue 4: 479-502.

81 Thomas M. Jones, Andrew C. Wicks and R. Edward Freeman, "Stakeholder Theory: The State of the Art" in *The Blackwell Guide to Business Ethics*, edited by Norman Bowie, (Oxford: Blackwell Publishers, 2002), 19-38.

82 Antonio Argandona, "The Stakeholder Theory and the Common Good", *Journal of Business Ethics*, (1998) Vol. 17.

83 Material for this case is selected from the comprehensive descriptions in Laura Pincus Hartman, *Perspectives in business ethics* (Chicago: Irwin McGraw-Hill, 1998), 528-566. See also Archie B. Caroll and Ann K. Buchholtz, *Business and Society. Ethics and Stakeholder Management*, (United Kingdom: Thomson, South-Western, 2003), 601.

84 Ibid: 609.

85 Ibid: 602.

86 Ibid: 610.

87 Antonio Argandona, "The Stakeholder Theory and the Common Good", *Journal of Business Ethics*, (1998), Vol. 17.

88 Robert C. Solomon: *Ethics and Excellence, Cooperation and Integrity in Business* (New York: Oxford University Press, 1992). See also Robert C. Solomon, "Business Ethics and Virtue" *A Companion to Business Ethics*, edited by Robert E. Frederick (Oxford: Blackwell Publishing, (1999), 2002).

89 In this sense it represents a modern interpretation of Aristotelian ethics for business ethics. We may say that it is an application of the Aristotelian framework for business ethics, based on the original ethics. See Aristotle, *Ethics* in *The Complete Works of Aristotle*, edited by W.D. Ross in The Revised Oxford Translation, vol. 2, revised by J.O. Urmson and edited by Jonathan Barnes (Princeton: Princeton University Press, 1984).

90 Robert C. Solomon, "Business Ethics and Virtue" in *A Companion to Business Ethics*, edited by Robert E. Frederick (Oxford: Blackwell Publishing (1999), 2002), 19. See also Aristotle, *Ethics* in *The Complete Works of Aristotle*, edited by W.D. Ross in The Revised Oxford Translation, vol. 2, revised by J.O. Urmson and edited by Jonathan Barnes (Princeton: Princeton University Press, 1984).

91 Robert C. Solomon, "Business Ethics and Virtue" in *A Companion to Business Ethics* edited by Robert E. Frederick (Oxford: Blackwell Publishing (1999), 2002), 59.

92 Ibid: 30-38.

93 Robert C. Solomon: *Ethics and Excellence, Cooperation and Integrity in Business* (New York: Oxford University Press, 1992), 81.

94 Ibid: 84.

95 Ibid: 89.

96 Ibid: 92.

97 The communitarian approach is an important way to integrate economics with virtue and practice. Business is viewed as a human practice of excellence rather than as a mere game of individual choices. In business, human beings act together in order to achieve human excellence. We may say that action in the organization is generated by virtues and that these virtues are constitutive of organizational practices that acquire a collective element of common action. In the practice of excellence of an organization, there is a close relation between the "right" and the "good." Egoism is not the starting point because individual action only requires meaning on the basis of a collective practice. Such practices are rather tacit and intutitive, and given in community. They can be explained through storytelling and case studies. Accordingly, there may be a link between communitarianism and practice theory.

98 Aristotle, *Ethics* in *The Complete Works of Aristotle*, edited by W.D. Ross in The Revised Oxford Translation, vol. 2, revised by J.O. Urmson and edited by Jonathan Barnes (Princeton: Princeton University Press, 1984). Robert C. Solomon: *Ethics and Excellence, Cooperation and Integrity in Business* (New York: Oxford University Press, 1992), 101.

99 Aristotle, *Ethics* in *The Complete Works of Aristotle*, edited by W.D. Ross in The Revised Oxford Translation, vol. 2, revised by J.O. Urmson and edited by Jonathan Barnes (Princeton: Princeton University Press, 1984).

100 Ibid: 104. See Robert C. Solomon, "Business Ethics and Virtue" in *A Companion to Business Ethics* edited by Robert E. Frederick (Oxford: Blackwell Publishing (1999), 2002), 30-38

101 Robert C. Solomon: *Ethics and Excellence, Cooperation and Integrity in Business* (New York: Oxford University Press, 1992), 111.

102 Ibid: 133.

103 Aristotle, *Ethics* in *The Complete Works of Aristotle*, edited by W.D. Ross in The Revised Oxford Translation, vol. 2, revised by J.O. Urmson and edited by Jonathan Barnes (Princeton: Princeton University Press, 1984).

104 Robert C. Solomon: *Ethics and Excellence, Cooperation and Integrity in Business* (New York: Oxford University Press, 1992), 26.

105 What is missing in the pure communitarian concept of judgment is the Kantian emphasis on universal elements of reflective judgment.

106 Robert C. Solomon: *Ethics and Excellence, Cooperation and Integrity in Business* (New York: Oxford University Press, 1992), 234.

107 Ibid: 241. See Robert C. Solomon, "Business Ethics and Virtue" in *A Companion to Business Ethics* edited by Robert E. Frederick (Oxford: Blackwell Publishing (1999), 2002), 30-38.

108 Erwin M. Hartman, *Organizational ethics and the good life* (Oxford: Oxford University Press, 1995), 121.

109 Ibid: 152.

110 Erwin M. Hartman mentions the infamous Zimbardo prison experiments conducted at Stanford University in 1971 as an example of the possible totalitarian aspects of corporate culture. Among highly qualified students, a special number were selected for Zimbardo's psychological experiment to recreate the conditions of imprisonment. Half of the students were supposed to be prisoners and the other half guards. After only two or three days, the guards started quickly enjoying their roles and the prisoners demonstrated deep psychological problems. The guards liked the experiment while the prisoners felt more and more inferior and wanted the experiment to stop. Afterwards, the guards were deeply embarrassed by their sadistic behaviour. The lesson for corporations is that culture in a particular organization may shape individual roles and destroy personal autonomy. Erwin M. Hartman, *Organizational ethics and the good life*, (Oxford: Oxford University Press, 1995), 152.

111 The case is Harvard Business School case 394-113. Material for the case is selected from Lynn Sharp Paine, *Cases in Leadership, Ethics and Organizational Integrity. A Strategic Perspective* (Chicago: Irwin, 1997), 171.

112 Ibid: 177.

113 Relevant works for business ethics from the Kantian perspective include Immanuel Kant, *Kritik der praktischen Vernuft* (1784) (Hamburg: Felix Meiner Verlag, 1985). Immanuel Kant, *Grundlegung zur Metaphysik der Sitten* (1785) (Hamburg: Felix Meiner Verlag, 1999). Immanuel Kant, *Metaphysik der Sitten* (1797) in Immanuel Kant, *Werke*, Band IV (Darmstadt, 1983). Immanuel Kant, *Kritik der Urteilskraft* (1794) (Frankfurt: Suhrkamp Werkausgabe, 2004). See also Kant, Immanuel: *Gesammelte Werke*, (Frankfurt: Suhrkamp Verlag, 1972).

114 Norman E. Bowie, *Business Ethics. A Kantian Perspective*, (Cambridge, Massachusetts: Basil Blackwell Publishers, 1999). See also Norman E. Bowie, "A Kantian Approach to Business Ethics" in *A Companion to Business Ethics*, edited by Robert E. Frederick, (Oxford: Blackwell Publishing (1999) 2002), 3-17.

115 Immanuel Kant, *Grundlegung zur Metaphysik der Sitten* (1785), (Hamburg: Felix Meiner Verlag, 1999).

116 Immanuel Kant, *Kritik der praktischen Vernuft* (1784), (Hamburg: Felix Meiner Verlag, 1985).

117 Norman E. Bowie, "A Kantian Approach to Business Ethics" in *A Companion to Business Ethics*, edited by Robert E. Frederick, (Oxford: Blackwell Publishing, (1999) Oxford 2002, 2).

118 Ibid: 32.

119 Ibid: 57.

120 Ibid: 63.

121 Ibid: 109. See also Norman E. Bowie: "A Kantian Approach to Business Ethics" in *A Companion to Business Ethics*, edited by Robert E. Frederick (Oxford: Blackwell Publishing (1999), 2002), 3-17.

122 Norman E. Bowie, *Business Ethics. A Kantian Perspective* (Cambridge, Massachusetts: Basil Blackwell Publishers, 1999), 74.

123 Ibid: 87.

124 Ibid: 115.

125 Ibid: 142.

126 Ibid: 165.

127 Thomas Donaldson and Thomas W. Dunfee, *Ties that Bind. A Social Contracts Approach to Business Ethics* (Boston Massachusetts; Harvard Business School Press, 1999), 11. See also Thomas Donaldson and Thomas W. Dunfee: "Towards a Unified Conception of Business Ethics: Integrative Social Contract Theory" in *Academy of Management Review,* Vol. 19 (1994), no 2. Further see Thomas W. Dunfee and Thomas Donaldson, "Social Contract Approaches to Business Ethics: Bridging the "is-ought" gap" in *A Companion to Business Ethics*, edited by Robert E. Frederick, (Oxford: Blackwell Publishing (1999) 2002), 38-56.

128 Thomas Donaldson and Thomas W. Dunfee, *Ties that Bind. A Social Contracts Approach to Business Ethics* (Boston Massachusetts: Harvard Business School Press, 1999), 14.

129 Ibid: 23.

130 Integrated social contract theory follows Rawls's contextualization of the principles of justice, moving from metaphysical foundations in the "veil of ignorance" in *A Theory of Justice* (Cambridge Massachusetts: Harvard University Press 1971) to more pragmatic and political foundations in "overlapping consensus" in *Political Liberalism* (Cambridge Massachusetts: Harvard University Press 1992).

131 Thomas Donaldson and Thomas W. Dunfee, *Ties that Bind. A Social Contracts Approach to Business Ethics* (Boston Massachusetts: Harvard Business School Press, 1999), 27.

132 Ibid: 39.

133 Ibid: 44. See also Thomas Donaldson and Thomas W. Dunfee, "Towards a Unified Conception of Business Ethics: Integrative Social Contract Theory" in Academy of Management Review, Vol. 19 (1994), no 2. Further see Thomas W. Dunfee and Thomas Donaldson, "Social Contract Approaches to Business Ethics: Bridging the 'is-ought' gap" in *A Companion to Business Ethics*, edited by Robert E. Frederick (Oxford: Blackwell Publishing, 2002), 38-56.

134 Thomas Donaldson and Thomas W. Dunfee, *Ties that Bind. A Social Contracts Approach to Business Ethics* (Boston Massachusetts: Harvard Business School Press, 1999), 51.

135 Ibid: 46.

136 Ibid: 57.

137 Ibid: 68.

138 Ibid: 121.

139 Ibid: 235.

140 Ibid: 245.

141 Ibid: 261.

142 Peter Ulrich, *Integrative Wirtschaftsethik. Grundlagen einer lebensdienlichen Ökonomie*, 2 Auflage (Stuttgart, Wien: Haupt, 1998), 235.

143 Ibid: 283.

144 Ibid: 304.

145 Ibid: 346. This has been called "New Constitutional Economics." See James Buchanan's view on the subject: "The domain of constitutional economics" in *Constitutional Political Economy*, Vol 1.

146 This is a concrete formulation of the "ethical aim of the good life with and for the other in just institutions" as discussed earlier.

147 Andrew Crane and Dirk Matten, *Business Ethics. A European Perspective*, (Oxford: Oxford University Press, 2004), 61-69.

148 Ibid: 41-49.

149 Peter Ulrich, *Integrative Wirtschaftsethik,. Grundlagen einer lebensdienlichen Ökonomie*, 2 Auflage, (Stuttgart, Wien: Haupt, 1998), 443.

150 Material for this case is taken from John R. Boatright, *Ethics and the Conduct of Business*, Third Edition (New Jersey: Prentice Hall, 2003), 1. Ronald M. Green, *The Ethical Manager: A new Method for Business Ethics*, New York: Macmillan, 1994, 208-19 where the case is presented.

151 John R. Boatright, *Ethics and the Conduct of Business*, Third Edition, (New Jersey: Prentice Hall 2003), 2.

152 Patrick E. Murphy, *Eighthy Exemplary Ethics Statements* (Notre Dame: University of Notre Dame Press, 1998), 123-124.

Part 3
Business ethics and corporate social responsibility in different fields of business

1. Corporate social responsibility and principles of stakeholder justice

The principles of responsibility and justice can be defined as the framework for concrete applications in different fields of business ethics. These concepts are related to the protection of the human person as an important aspect of business ethics. The strategy of sustainability and corporate social responsibility can be considered as a practical application of the concept of the good citizen corporation in business ethics. Moreover, on the basis of these concepts, the idea of "justice-as-fairness" can be related to stakeholder theory as a framework for inclusion of stakeholders in corporate decision-making. With regard to the protection of human rights, four ethical principles of protection of autonomy, dignity, integrity, and vulnerability are important expressions of justice-as-fairness.

The basic structure of this argument is to analyze the ideas of sustainability and corporate social responsibility as the foundation and framework of organizational justice within the horizon of corporate citizenship. From this point of view, ethical principles should be considered as the bases for applying business ethics in strategic management and in concrete fields of business ethics. While sustainable development and corporate social responsibility are of primary importance for organizational policies and strategies at the collective level, the ideas of autonomy, dignity, integrity, and vulnerability primarily concern protection of individual stakeholders; thus, the ethical principles of sustainability, responsibility, justice, and protection of the human person are developed in order to propose an ethical framework for values-driven management in organizations.

The following discussion of the idea of corporate social responsibility as an expression of corporate citizenship in business ethics is divided into six sections: 1) corporate social responsibility between ethics, law, and economics; 2) towards an integrated view of ethics and corporate social responsibility; 3) corporate social responsibility and strategic management; 4) CSR, corporate governance, and stakeholder justice; 5) basic ethical principles in stakeholder management: autonomy, dignity, integrity, vulnerability; and 6) from responsibility, fairness, and ethical principles to social responsiveness and issues management.

1.1. Corporate social responsibility between ethics, law, and economics

The concept of corporate social responsibility for sustainable development can be defined as the broad goal of ethical business, which emerges out of good corporate citizenship.[1] Sustainable development has been proposed by the World Commission on the Environment, in the 1987 Brundtland Commission, as common goal for the international community.[2] It is defined as respectful use of natural resources in order to leave possibilities for future generations to live on Earth with the same, or better conditions, as present generations. Environmental sustainability has, at least since 1987, been a fashionable term for the international community.[3]

The term "sustainability" does not, however, only apply directly to the field of environmental relations. For a long time, it was better known to designate the long-term maintenance and development of the firm.[4] In the framework of the idea of corporate citizenship, and with the emergence of the United Nation's concept of sustainability, this term has become broadened to include not only economic, but social and environmental concerns in the definition of corporate sustainability.

This idea of sustainability has further been developed in the idea of the triple bottom line, according to which the firm does not only account for its economic returns but includes its impact on the environment and social relations with employees, the local community, or governments in its evaluation of the economic success and prosperity of the firm.[5] Using this concept, a firm's sustainability is supposed to be integrated into the global initiatives of public policies of sustainable development. It can be seen as an application of the idea of corporate citizenship in business ethics.

It is important to see this work on the triple bottom line as a part of the development of applied business ethics, as a sustainability response to the traditional values of economizing, ecologizing, and power aggrandizing of the firm. The concern for the firm's interaction with its environment requires a temporal dimension or, in other words, integrating relations with consideration to future generations. Moreover, the perspective of republican business ethics developed above amends Ricœur's idea of "the good life with and for the other in just institutions" so that it becomes "the good life *within nature.*"

The concept of sustainability should be considered from the perspective of corporate social responsibility, which is the other important concept for applied business ethics in relation to internal and external constituencies of the firm. The concept of responsibility is implied in the concept of the firm as a political and moral actor, which is the result of the idea of corporate citizenship. Lynn Sharp Paine argues that there is value-shift in the economy, which entails no longer conceiving the firm as an amoral instrument for profit maximization or a fictive legal person, but as a morally responsible actor with values and ethical princi- ples.[6] This is the basis for the republican conception of the corporation as a good citizen. This concept of responsibility implies that the firm should not only obey the law, but engage constructively in social betterment of society.

The German philosopher Hans Jonas has defined the concept of responsi- bility in the technological age. He argues that technological and scientific de- velopment has lead to a much greater responsibility for humanity, because we now have so much power to destroy the Earth.[7] According to Jonas, the ethics of responsibility is not only about respecting present human beings, but is an absolute categorical principle for individuals to ensure the sustainability of the earth in perpetuity.

This ontological and categorical concept of responsibility can be said to be the foundation for corporate social responsibility. This concept defines moral action as not only an individual but an institutional responsibility, as well. Corporate social responsibility relies on the capacity of the firm to be ethically accountable for its actions, strategies, and policies. The strategies of values-driven manage- ment can be defined as the basis for a corporate decision-making structure that installs a culture of responsibility in the organization. In this sense, corporate social responsibility is not only conceived as an "enlightened self-interest,"[8] based on economic concerns for higher returns, but on the view of the corporation as a good citizen with rights and duties towards society.[9]

In this moral sense, responsibility is linked to the power and capacity of the corporation to respond to its own actions. The argument for taking respon- sibility into account is based on the realization that corporations have strong capacity for action. The institutional responsibility of the firm, the responsibil- ity of executive directors and managers, and the responsibility of the employees of the organization need to be distinguished. Such fundamental concepts as the moral responsibility of the firm go beyond mere legal responsibility and include a broader array of ethically defined responsibilities to the different stakeholders. In this connotation, corporate social responsibility is based on a "moral view of the economy," which implies a link between good corporate citizenship and a firm's duty to contribute to the protection of the vulnerable and weak in society.[10]

The concept of corporate social responsibility can be said to emerge as a consequence of this fundamental morally responsible view of corporate citizenship. This idea is promoted in opposition to those who argue against corporate social responsibility by saying that morality and CSR have nothing to do with each other, and furthermore, that it has not been proven that corporations can be held accountable; only shareholders have legitimate interests in corporations, and corporate social responsibility takes away the freedom of the corporation to act according to its own wishes on the economic market. Beyond the economic and morale benefits of CSR, a rebuttal to these criticisms might add further that *a)* because corporations really do have so much power to make substantial contributions to solving problems and *b)* because they have such a strong social impact on many different stakeholders, their moral and political responsibility is increasing.

Corporate social responsibility is in the interest of business because, by contributing to social change, it can create a better environment for its own transactions, thereby developing business while being socially responsibly.[11] Moreover, corporate social responsibility may improve the public image of business. If business is proactive with regard to promoting its engagement with society, this may also help to avoid government regulation. Socially responsible businesses can meet the expectations of society and can help to solve its problems, even if they turn social problems into business opportunities in the process.

Remaining conscious of moral responsibility and good corporate citizenship, and following the work of Archie B. Caroll,[12] CSR can be distinguished between economic, legal, ethical, philanthropic, or discretionary responsibility.[13] The different dimensions of corporate social responsibility can be visualized either as a pyramid, or in the perspective of a Venn diagram (see fig. 3.1).[14]

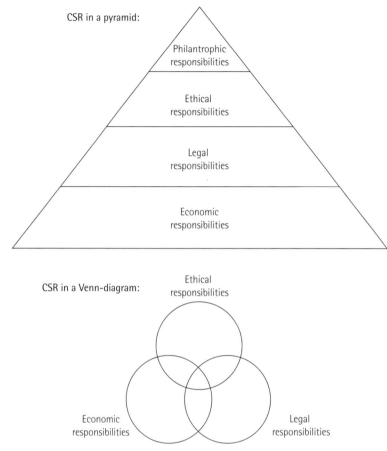

Figure 3.1 The two images of CSR

Economic responsibility can be defined by the Friedman quote discussed earlier: "The social responsibility of business is to increase its profits."[15] Here, economic responsibility means that the firm must manage economic resources with prudence and efficiency, but this responsibility also implies good corporate governance and fair treatment of shareholders. Compliance and formulations of codes of corporate governance can be considered as a contribution to such economic responsibility. Moreover, the conscious and prudent use of resources includes management and employees. It also includes the technical and professional duties of management and production to see and exploit market opportunities. In this sense, economic responsibility is different from moral responsibility, because it is about following self-interest and exchanging goods at the market according to capitalist principles.[16]

Legal responsibilities are about the obligation to follow the law and to play "within the rules of the game." This also means doing everything to operate within the limit of the law and to make an effort to comply with the intentions of the legislator with regard to specific laws. In fact, efforts to formulate internal compliance programs and programs for values-driven management can be seen as a means to operate in accordance with the laws of society. Legal compliance should not only be at the national level, but also locally and internationally.

In the debates about corporate social responsibility, ethical responsibilities are defined not only by efforts to do what is right in economic and legal terms, but also as the pursuit of voluntary measures to be virtuous and excellent. Ethics is this arena is about finding the right balance in the gray zone where corporate actions may be considered economically valid, but not legally justified. Ethical duties may override economic and legal concerns in cases of conflict. Ethical responsibility is about formulating values and norms for the corporation that contribute to its performance as a good corporate citizen, and imply wider concerns for corporate and social justice, and sustainability. In this way, the level of ethical responsibility encompasses the other two economic and legal responsibilities, and is defined by the respect for justice and fair treatment of all stakeholders. Ethical responsibility ultimately contributes to the democratic legitimacy of the firm in its community.

Philanthropic responsibilities are not inherently virtuous, but entail actions that really benefit society. There is a long tradition of corporate philanthropy in which corporations give grand donations to society as a demonstration of power, wealth, and because they want to do some good for the local community. In many cases, corporate philanthropy is directly linked with efforts to obtain at better public image in society. To reiterate, it is important to link the philanthropic activities with other strategic and economic initiatives of the firm.[17] There should be more strategic reflection over how philanthropic money is spent to ensure the greatest benefit for society.

Carroll's definition has been one of the most persistent and widely used definitions of corporate social responsibility, though it has also be the subject of criticism.[18] Some have argued that Carroll's conception of the relations between philanthropic and other kinds of responsibilities is unclear. Would it be more logical to include philanthropic responsibility within the general ethical responsibility of the corporation? Moreover, it is not clear why it should be a pyramid. The ethical responsibilities are somewhat restricted to a specific area, instead of being considered as the most fundamental. Indeed, the pyramid does not really integrate economic, ethical, and legal responsibilities.

As a response to these criticisms, Carroll and Schwartz (2003) published an article attempting to define the relationship between business and society.[19] This new formulation was an effort to make the definition of CSR more clear and useful for business. In the article, Carroll and Schwartz argue that the pyramid formulation, with economic and legal responsibilities as required responsibilities at the bottom, and ethical and philanthropic responsibilities at the top as expected and desired responsibilities, had a danger of leading to a misunderstanding of the content of corporate social responsibility.[20] Consequently, they propose a new model, where a Venn digram replaces the pyramid, and the concept of philanthropic responsibilities is conceived as included in the other kinds of responsibilities.

This perspective addresses the fact that it is misleading to conceive of philanthropy as a responsibility in itself, when it can be subsumed under ethical responsibilities. Carroll and Schwarz emphasize that it is important to conceive CSR, not as a discrete concept, but as a one that has overlaps in the ethical, economic, and legal domains.[21] They point out that the concept of corporate social responsibility has its foundations in business ethics. CSR cannot be conceived solely from a strategic or utilitarian perspective, but must rely on considerations of Kantian deontological morality as well as moral management (i.e., an integrity strategy for organizational leadership and governance).[22] Ethics should be the driving force in an organization, even though economic and legal responsibilities are still important. But in the ideal unity of the three kinds of responsibilities, it is the ethical responsibility that is the pivotal point in relation to the two other kinds of economic and legel responsibility. With this three-dimensional perspective on corporate social responsibility, the most important challenge is to conceive how the corporation can act responsibly when it engages in multiple domains at the same time. Carroll's presentation of the possible responsibilities implies purely economic, legal, and ethical responsibilities, but also mixed and multiple responsibilities.

In the tension between the economic domain and the others, the problem is how to perform economically while still respecting legal and ethical responsibilities. This tension is manifest in corporate conversations about how to balance legal compliance with ethical and economical priorities. When something is permitted by the law, but may be considered unethical, there is a tension between ethics and law; and when something is economical but possibly unethical, there is a tension between ethics and economics. In fact, when dealing with these sorts of tensions, the important problem is to find moral standards of management that can satisfy the rights of the corporation's different stakeholders.[23]

There are, of course, limitations with this three-domain model. There may be responsibilities at the borderline between the three kinds of responsibilities, and the model does not necessarily include all possible scenarios of corporate social responsibility. Despite these cautions, it is important as a model that considers CSR in a general strategic framework for organizational integrity and moral responsibility. As an approach to CSR that confirms the close relation between business ethics, corporate citizenship, and corporate social responsibility, this perspective corroborates the points that have been repeatedly emphasized throughout the previous discussion. CSR is built on basic ethical obligations to stakeholders and to society.

Case 8. Vestas Wind Systems: Social responsibility and sustainable energy

The Danish firm, Vestas Wind Systems, promotes itself through a discursive self-representation with a strategy linking sustainability, ethics, and social responsibility. This case has been selected because it is an example of a company dealing proactively with CSR, sustainability, and corporate citizenship. It is a case of a company making an *ethical effort* to formulate a policy on business ethics.[24]

The core business of Vestas is developing, producing, marketing, and maintaining energy systems using wind to produce electricity.[25] Through these systems, the corporation contributes to reducing worldwide CO_2 emissions. Since it began producing windmills in 1979, the corporation has become a global player in high technology business. By 2005, they had more than 10,600 employees.

The corporation emphasizes the importance of environmental responsibility, and works to integrate environmental concerns and fair labor practices in the development of its products. With regard to windmills, this approach includes examining the raw materials used in production, as well as the mills' visual, aesthetic, and noise-related impacts. For example, the wind systems contribute to sustainable development but may also have a negative effect on visual impressions of landscapes. The effects of the mills on animals, for example birds, are also an important aspect of the environmental policy of the company. The company considers all of theses things when it constructs its windmill parks throughout the world.

On its website, with its rhetorical self-representation, the company emphasizes that social responsibility is considered as an integrated part of its values and management philosophy. The concepts of sustainability, and external and internal social responsibility, are taken seriously. The company addresses the improvement of working conditions by offering employees education and skills training. Moreover, many of the company's efforts with environmental and social responsibility are done in collaborations with business partners,

Vestas mentions that it subscribes to international codes of conduct as layed out in the materials of organizations like the UN, the International Labor Organization (ILO,) and the Organization for Economic Co-operation and Development (OECD). Of particular importance are The World Declaration on Human Rights from 1948 and the Covenants on political, as well as social and economic, rights and different ILO conventions related to working conditions and free labor.

The corporation seeks an integrated management system for the two aspects of production – environmental impacts and labor conditions – in order to ensure sustainable production. In this context, important priorities include, respect for legislation, concern for global cultural differences, open communication, and efficient use of resources. Moreover, the company stresses the importance of compliance with international standards of environmental protection and work policy, such as ISO 14001 and OHSAS 18001.

1.2. Business ethics and the many faces of corporate social responsibility

The concept of corporate social responsibility has been developed and used in many different ways by different authors since Carroll's influential formulation.[26] Elisabeth Garriga and Domènic Melé argue that the territory of the concept can be organized around four categories: 1) economic, or the need to meet objectives that produce long-term profits; 2) political, or using business power in a responsible way; 3) integrative, particularly of social demands; and 4) ethical, or evaluating a company's contribution to the good society by doing what is ethically correct.[27]

This categorization captures important elements of the CSR concept. The corporation functions as an instrument to create social wealth, and it has power and and political responsibility. Moreover, it is dependent on integration and adaptation with society. It works for the common good in order to bring society together. From this point of view, instrumental theorists include authors like Friedman, Jensen, and Meckling (who refer to CSR's single objective as "enlightened value maximization"), Porter, and Kramer. Instrumental theories include resource-based views of the firm, which emphasize CSR as an instrument to improve the dynamic capabilities of the corporation, and strategies (such as cause-related marketing) to work for social issues in order to improve the economic conditions and the company brand.[28] As has already been argued, this economic concept of CSR is too weak to capture the whole dynamic of the concept.

Political theories of CSR emphasize that corporations have political power and responsibility to act as a good corporate citizens. These theories emphasize the link between CSR and the contract between business and society. Moreover, they go beyond corporate philanthropy and conceive citizenship as related to ethical, economic, and legal responsibility. Integrative theories, based on the interaction between business and society, establish legitimacy through compliance with societal expectations regarding management issues and stakeholder dialogue. The concept of CSR in corporate citizenship cannot do without these integrative theories.

Economic, political, and integrative theories of corporate social responsibility must be accomplished with the ethical theories of CSR, including Kantian and Rawlsian normative stakeholder theory. Indeed, ethical theories propose universal principles and codes of conduct, and they emphasize the importance of the relation between CSR and sustainable development.[29] Theories that centralize business ethics as the basis of CSR emphasize that a view of the common good is the foundation of CSR. Such a common good approach may be said to refer to the ideal of *primum non nocere* (first, do no harm). Organizational integrity is the framework of a strategy for CSR.[30]

While this mapping of the concept of CSR make its complexity apparent, the view of CSR propsed in this text captures its core. This view sees CSR as a fundamental integration of ethical (political), legal, and economic responsibility with the strategy of organizational integrity, which is expressed in the multiple dimensions of instrumental, political, integrative and ethical aspects of CSR's theoretical development.

Recent European developments in the use of the concept illustrate this complexity. The European and Scandinavian debates around CSR have, in particular, been linked to labor market policies. Denmark, for example, developed the idea of social responsibility as an effort to work for labor market inclusion as a part of active labor market policy.[31] During the 1990s, the government of the Social Democratic Party changed social policy from being based on passive support to a policy based on activation of the poor and unemployed. CSR became a key component in this redefinition of social welfare policy into an active employment policy. They talked about the "inclusive labor market." where corporations contribute to social policy by taking responsibility for the integration of new employees in the labor market. According to this point of view, the core of social responsibility is the active support of corporations to develop labour market policies. The key concept is the idea of partnerships between government and corporations. Governments contribute with support to create jobs for poor and unemployed people, and corporations employ those people and help to create open and inclusive labor markets.[32]

Corporate social responsibility should not, however, be exclusively defined as a new kind of social welfare policy. Although corporate social responsibility in the labor market is one of the key components of the concept, social responsibility is central as an umbrella concept. It is based on the ethical framework of business ethics and corporate citizenship, which is very present in the link between sustainability and corporate social responsibility. The approach to CSR in this book is that the notion of corporate citizenship and the ideas of political philosophy represent the foundations of the concept, which is further based on the idea of the corporation as a good corporate citizen who is morally responsible. Taken from this approach corporate social responsibility is a rather comprehensive concept that includes a variety of ethically based engagements of the corporation with its environment. Corporate social responsibility is about the concrete existence of the firm as a responsible organization in society.[33]

Consequently, corporate social responsibility must be considered from the perspective of business ethics and values-driven management. This definition should not be interepreted as something extra, in addition to the efforts a company may already be making to live up to the standards of good citizenship. Moreover, from the ethical perspective, CSR should not be restricted to "social relations" but rather extended to express a fundamental "responsibility for society," which cannot be limited to "social responsibilities." Instead, this responsibility expresses more general relations to society. On the other hand, it could be argued that this definition is less focused. This is why some argued that CSR is a more concise term. A possible solution to this dilemma would be to use the concept of CSR as "social responsibility," but at the same time still emphasize that the concept should be understood broadly, and always considered in close relation with the fundamental ethical responsibility of business corporations.[34]

The distinction between fundamental (moral) responsibility for society and specific social responsibilities (CSR) may be based on the reemergence of the concept of social responsibility in the European Union during the 1990s. The European Union defined the concept as a "voluntary action" that goes beyond the already established legal and economic duties of the corporation.[35] In fact, it may be argued that the ethical dimension of CSR is particularly present in this definition, which means that social responsibility is based on ethics and is, therefore, more fundamental than the ordinary legal and economic responsibilities of corporations. The argument for voluntariness that has become implicit in the debate on corporate social responsibility also reflects the focus on inner motivation that characterizes the value-based approach to organization and management. This supports the argument that corporate social responsibility is closely related to ethics and values-driven management; it concerns the effort to compel the corporation to extraordinary responsibility beyond its economic and legal responsibilities. This ethical approach to voluntary social responsibility is, however, also subject to criticism. As long as this responsibility is voluntary – without legal or political constraints – there is no guarantee that the corporation will not simply refuse it. This argument seems reasonable and this is why it is necessary to consider CSR from the point of view of the fundamental ethical responsibility of the corporation. Social responsibility is always an expression of this basic ethical responsibility, which cannot be reduced to relatively insignificant "voluntary" or "arbitrary" measures that are easily adopted.

As founded on the ethical idea of moral responsibility, and closely linked to the concept of the corporate good citizen, corporate social responsibility can be defined as an umbrella concept combining elements from the most predominant schools of corporate social responsibility, which are present in the theory and practice of management. Inspired by Helene Djursø and Peter Neergaard, the five most important approaches to corporate social responsibility are:

1) the "dogmatic school," which focuses on the utility and economic benefits of CSR. This perspective is represented by the economic and strategic approaches by Milton Friedman and Michael Porter.

2) The international school is oriented towards the protection of human rights and engagement of corporations in human rights and improving the economies in developing countries. Donaldson and Dunfee and Georges Endele are representatives of this school.

3) The dialogical school focuses on the importance of stakeholder communication as an integrated element of corporate social responsibility. It is repre-

sented by David Wheler and Maria Silanpää and theories of corporate social responsibility, as inspired by stakeholder theory.

4) The social policy school, which has been dominant in Denmark – among other countries – marks a focus on corporate social responsibility as an element in creating a good and inclusive labor market, integrating society through social partnerships and social policy.

5) In addition to those approaches, the ethical school argues, from the point of view of corporate citizenship, that corporate social responsibility represents the license to operate in society, because it is the right thing to do, and because it generally contributes to good social development of the political and social community.[36]

In this sense, corporate social responsibility can be conceived as an element of the strategic realization of good corporate citizenship through the idea of organizational integrity. It is important that a strategy for corporate social responsibility is integrated into a firm's overall strategy for corporate citizenship, business ethics, and values-driven management. On the foundation of the framework of corporate citizenship, the firm defines corporate social responsibility in relation to its values and conceptualization of business ethics. This can be integrated into a strategy of stakeholder management, which aims to define ethics and responsibility as integrated in the other aspects of corporate strategy. Moreover, performance of corporate social responsibility is reported in the annual report so that CSR is regarded as integrated in the policy and strategy of the corporation.

The arguments for this integrated concept of corporate social responsibility in the framework of business ethics and corporate citizenship are that social responsibility contributes to better and more sustainable development. In this sense CSR gives the corporation a better position in society. Moreover, with corporate social responsibility the corporation realizes its aim to be a good corporate citizen by self-regulation and by contributing to the coherence of society. Accordingly, social responsibility represents advanced risk and reputation management that gives the corporation a good reputation in society that contributes with social legitimacy and recognition by society as a contributor to the common good. Moreover, by being socially responsible, the firm can retain and attract motivated employees who are committed to the values of good corporate citizenship.

By focusing on corporate social responsibility, the firm is viewed as a part of society and can, therefore, be held collectively responsible in front of society. Managers do not only have to be responsible to the shareholders and investors in their decision-making, but also to the different stakeholders of the corporation. There is a close connection between social responsibility, stable investment, and economic gain. Corporate social responsibility is, in a sense, a sophisticated form of "long-term shareholder value."[37] Moreover, corporate social responsibility acknowledges that a company cannot avoid being political. To be socially responsible is to acknowledge that business also has political aspects and that corporations are forced to behave self-reflectively with regard to their own values and ethics. Accordingly, social responsibility expresses a necessary burden for companies in coherent democratic societies that fight exclusion and give the weakest in society good living and working conditions.

Case 9. The good corporate citizen in global community: The case of Merck and Co.

Biotechnology firms, such as Novo Nordisk and Lundbaek in Denmark, have refused to give better access to their drug patents, so that AIDS patients in the developing world could get affordable medical treatment. Several American drug companies went so far as to take legal action against the South African government to protect their economic interests, though in April 2001 the case was dropped, due to intense international criticism of their actions.[38]

In opposition to this protective attitude, business ethicists often refer to the generous actions of Merck and Co. who developed, distributed, and donated their medicine, Mectizan, to millions of Africans in order to protect them from river blindness.[39] The case of Merck has been selected as a classic business case of how an *ethical dilemma* can promote good corporate citizenship.

Merck invented Mectizan in 1978 to treat river blindness (onchocerciasis), an illness caused by a water-bourne parasite that creates painful itching in the eyes and, if left untreated, can lead to total blindness. It is a widespread problem outside of highly developed countries and has large economic and human impacts. At that time, it was estimated that more than eighty-five million people were at risk of acquiring the illness, and more than 340,000 people were already sick.[40]

During the 1970s, Merck had become one of the largest pharmaceutical companies in the world. Much of the company's brand was driven by the mission of Merck's founder, who said that the company should try "never to forget that medicine is for the people."[41] While the company had created a drug with the potential to have a profound impact on those suffering from river blindness, it was going to cost upwards of a million US dollars to properly test and develop the product according to market standards. This cost could not be passed on to poor residents in underdeveloped countries, who could not afford to pay for expensive medications. Putting the drug on the market would probably have implied great financial losses for the corporation.

Despite having produced a promising treatment, Merck researchers and management soon found themselves in a dilemma. The advocates for great intentions and corporate profits were at odds.

With the values and visions of the company in mind, Merck finally decided to facilitate donations of the medicine free of charge to the poor. From the perspective of republican business ethics, this was a very noble and generous idea that considered business from the framework of viewing society as a community of ends. By donating the drug, Merck had a possibility to confirm its basic commitments and licence to operate in community. As such, the corporation emerged as a very responsible and good corporate citizen. Furthermore, the willingness to give the drug away has had a very important impact on the image of the corporation. This is a very fine example of an action where a corporation takes responsibility for its position as a good corporate citizen in global community.

Some critical voices have urged that Merck's philanthropic donation was not entirely altruistic because there was nothing else to do in the face of the poverty of the drug's intended users, other than donate it to the people with the disease. But this was not an easy decision, for the reasons discussed above, but also because the firm had to consider other consequences, such as the drug's possible side effects. Despite the criticism, the positive effect of Merck's action should be emphasized. This action has given the firm a great reputation for philanthropy and generous contributions to solving problems in the developing world.

1.3. Corporate social responsibility in sustainability management

The question remains whether the combination of ethics and corporate social responsibility is possible in practice. The issue is how to formulate a strategy combining business and corporate social responsibility. Michel Capron and Françoise Quairel-Lanoizeelée argue for such a practical application of corporate social responsibility by connecting CSR with the concept of sustainable development.[42] They claim that the United Nations has asserted that corporations have a role to play in sustainable development by managing their operations and stimulating economic growth, while simultaneously protecting the environment and promoting social responsibility. The idea is that the firm should be considered as a part of society, and that environmental and social issues should be integrated in strategic management of the firm. At the international level, as a good corporate citizen of the world, the corporation is obliged to contribute to solving all the important problems of world politics regarding the environment (e.g., the destruction of the biosphere through poor use of resources and environmental degradation), the fight against poverty, the prevention of war and conflict, as well as the promotion of human rights, good working conditions, and social stability. Corporate social responsibility implies the conscious contribution of the firm to engage with the problems of the world community as revealed by the different declarations and statements of intent by international bodies of the United Nations.[43]

The European Commission follows the UN initiatives when it argues that corporate social responsibility not only indicates compliance with legal obligations, but is a voluntary effort to do something more for human rights, the environment, or for the relations with other stakeholders.[44] The commission formulates an explicit link between corporate social responsibility and sustainable development.[45] The concept of the triple bottom line is central in reporting and evaluating the success of a firm that is not only accountable for economic growth but for social development and environmental protection, as well.

This view of corporate social responsibility implies a general strategy for strategic values-driven management in the age of globalization. Corporate social responsibility is based on an institutional view of the firm, but also of other public private and third-sector organizations, as a part of society with duties and obligations. Corporate social responsibility is the basic principle of values-driven management in an era where social expectations to the firm are increasing. As good corporate citizens, firms cannot ignore problems of human rights, environmental degradation and world conflict. Sustainable development requires rethinking corporate strategy in this light.

Sustainability is, in this sense, an important concept of corporate citizenship. It is linked to the idea of the triple bottom line for corporate strategy, as developed by Simon Zadek. The metaphor of the triple bottom line indicates that there somehow is an important relation between social, environmental, and economic dimensions of corporate citizenship. The concern for how the environmental, social, and economic dimensions of corporate behavior are closely connected is an essential element in good corporate citizenship.[46] The triple bottom line might even be said to express the human condition, where natural resources, social welfare, and satisfaction of human needs form the basis for human interactions.[47] From a basic ontological level "economic activity is no more and less than the process through which humans create social and environmental outcomes."[48] The concept of the triple bottom line can, in this sense, be linked to the original values of the corporation, which refer ontologically to the values expressed in the concepts of economizing, power aggrandizing, and ecologizing.[49]

Certainly, new expectations of the firm also emphasize corporate social responsibility as a matter of enlightened self-interest. When international opinion becomes more focused on the values of human rights and protection of the environment, corporations run great risk when they chose not to comply with the norms of sustainable development. Corporate social responsibility is, therefore, closely linked to prudent risk management in order to protect the image and reputation of the firm. According to Capron and Quairel-Lanoizeelée, the pressure on organizations for corporate social responsibility has increased because of the emergence of many active NGOs, such as the World Council of Sustainable Development, Transparency International, and many others.[50]

International declarations like the Rio Declaration on Environment and Development of the 1992 United Nations Conference on Environment and Development (UNCED) or the 1997 United Nations Educational, Scientific, and Cultural Organizaton's (UNESCO's) Universal Declaration on the Genome and Human Rights are important guidelines for the responsible contributions of corporations to enforcement of the common heritage of humankind. Other important international guidelines for multinational corporations include the 1994 Caux Round Table Principles for Business, which resulted from talks between Eastern and Western business leaders who met to constitute principles of better business behavior in order to improve the economic and social conditions of the world. Here the Japanese concept of *kyosei*[51] (i.e., living and working together for the common good) is combined with the Western European concept of "human dignity" as the basis for a code of conduct of responsible business behavior.[52]

Recently, the United Nations has agreed to the Global Compact principles, which promote values of corporate social responsibility based on UN Human rights declarations of principles for protection of the environment.[53] Further there are the guidelines for corporate social responsibility of the ILO[54] and the OECD Guidelines for Multinational Enterprises.[55] These guidelines and codes of conduct for values-driven management are considered as contributions to healthy and fair competition in order to promote growth and social change, as well as fair treatment of all major stakeholders of the firm (including, but not limited to, customers, employees, owners, investors, suppliers, competitors, and local communities).

This international process of formulating principles for sustainable development implies the development of global civil society in which the firm is considered as a responsible participant. Pressure of civil society organizations like NGOs and workers' unions contribute to the establishment of international soft law guidelines for corporate social responsibility, but also ethically, ecologically, and politically conscious consumers in Europe and the United States have advocated principles of fair trade and respect for the environment as important criteria for responsible business. Consumer organizations have promoted the idea of environmental or ethical labeling which has been important for the "fair trade movement", for example in the Max Havelaar products, which are guaranteed to have been produced ecologically under acceptable working conditions.[56] Moreover, the movement for socially responsible investments is growing. There is increased concern for principles of responsible business, including nonfinancial criteria for investments, among shareholders and institutional investors. The need for protection of a firm's brand and good reputation, as discussed previously, is often mentioned as an important reason for integrating corporate social responsibility in strategic management.

From the managerial perspective, it is argued that corporate social responsibility is not only a confirmation of the status of the firm as a moral agent, but also an important argument for the economic growth of the firm. Corporate citizenship through CSR does not only grant the real license for the firm to operate, but it is gives also the basis for economic sustainability. The argument for this relationship between responsibility and economic performance is basically an argument from the theory of corporate legitimacy. When the firm is an actor that is integrated in the norms and values of society, and when economic markets cannot be separated from social context, it is necessary for good corporate management strategy to conform or comply with the values of society, otherwise the firm would be excluded from spheres of social legitimacy. It is likely that stakeholders would be indifferent or reluctant to deal with such a firm, or might even turn away from it and boycott its products and services.[57]

Although this legitimacy argument is very strong, it has not been possible to determine a direct casual link between economic growth and corporate social performance. There have been many empirical studies, but they show both positive and negative correlation between economic and ethical performance.[58] Indeed, there are many problems of how to measure such performance, including evaluating situations where everyone chooses to be a free rider regarding promoting social responsibility and the values of the common good. Free rider actions are difficult to repeat over time because other actors will be aware of the irresponsible behavior, and stakeholders may turn away from the company in question. Moreover, there are not only microeconomic arguments of short-term profit for corporate social responsibility, but also arguments for long-term profits in terms of sustainability and promotion of the common good. These arguments are founded on broader considerations of justice and republican business ethics, situating the firm in the broader context of social legitimacy where the ethical values of doing good and respect for the human person are important.

From the strategic perspective, economic arguments can be combined with normative arguments of business ethics and sociological arguments about corporate social responsibility to increase the legitimacy of corporations in society. In the light of institutional theory, strategies of corporate social responsibility in combination with stakeholder analysis contribute to the understanding of how direct and indirect stakeholders influence the firm. Corporate social responsibility does not only include stakeholders with power or explicit contracts with the firm, but also other stakeholders who have an interest in the firm from the point of view of social legitimacy.[59] Moreover, corporate social responsibility implies a concern for the common good as important in legitimate relations with stakeholders.[60] This concern, echoing Capron and Quairel-Lanoizeelée, includes the Kantian perspective of the firm as a world citizen.[61] What is important about corporate social responsibility for stakeholders is the promotion of the common good of humanity in order to increase sustainability and enhance the world citizenship of corporations, which includes the commitment to engage in the problems of globalization.

In this sense, strategic management of corporate social responsibility combines concern for economic performance with the search for the social legitimacy of the corporation. From the institutional perspective, the corporation is an integrated part of society and the values of the organization are shaped by the perceptions of internal and external actors and stakeholders.[62] Social responsibility is necessary for strategic management because it ensures the legitimacy of the corporation as a good corporate citizen. In the light of institutional theory, and again refering to Capron and Quairel-Lanoizeelée, it can be argued that legitimacy is determined by the institutional environment of the organization. This environment represents social and cultural expectations about a corporation's appearance and behavior. In order to cope with these social expectations, the organization is required to construct its image and social appearance in accordance with values and norms of the institutional environment. This institutional legitimacy is not always directly visible. It may also be a tacit and presupposed structure of norms and habits as the basis for legitimate rational action.[63]

From the perspective of institutional theory, stakeholders hold a number of different, and maybe even contradictory, economic, social, and environmental expectations that corporations will embody.[64] These expectations are ideals, but are often reflected in factual claims. Shareholders want returns on their money, good risk management, economic transparency, and ethical social and environmental management. States and international bodies want corporations to contribute to the wealth of society, respect the laws and the environment, and they want corporations to be good citizens. Banks and creditors want risk management and economic security, but also respect for social and environmental issues. Employees and trade unions want corporations to ensure equality and give good social conditions, and they want the firm to have ethical values and ensure motivation, learning, and development at work. Customers and clients want just price, quality of products, respect for the environment, and respect for ethics and law. Suppliers want stable relations, acceptable payments, respect for contracts, and control of production so that they themselves won't have to violate law and ethics. Competitors expect corporations to be fair and respect the rules of the game, for example by abstaining from environmental and social dumping. Local communities want engagement and companies to contribute to the community development. International organizations and NGOs want transparency, respect for human rights, and sustainability, and they want corporations to abstain from bribery and follow the legal rules of countries where they operate.

According to institutional theory, the firm can more or less consciously choose different strategies to cope with such social expectations for corporate performance. An organization can ignore, or try to avoid, such claims of legitimacy. This reactive strategy can be combined with symbolic manipulation of expectations or dramaturgy, in order to be a free rider in regard to legitimacy claims. Another strategy would be proactively conforming to social expectations. The strategic management of values and corporate social responsibility arguably correspond to such a proactive search for legitimacy. Corporate social responsibility further contributes to the maintenance of legitimacy, once established.[65] The strategies of values-driven management and business ethics can be considered as conscious and rational initiatives to align the firm to societal expectations for best practice and virtuous behavior. From the strategic perspective, corporate social responsibility can be considered as a symbolic reaction to social expectations in order to protect and develop the brand, image, and reputation of the firm.[66]

Despite the importance of legitimacy for corporate performance, there is a business case for corporate social responsibility. This approach has been developed by John Elkington (1997)[67] who discusses how the triple bottom line metaphor allows the possibility of increased long-term economic performance.[68] Even though there is a tension between ethics and economics, the ideal situation is convergence between corporate social responsibility and economic performance. The ideal of good corporate citizenship is a firm that produces values for shareholders, employees, and customers, and also contributes considerably to the common good of society. This firm does not only consider corporate social responsibility and values-driven management as a matter of risk or reputation management, but it views legitimacy as a license to operate. Moreover, it regards stakeholders as resources who contribute to improve the firm's innovation, learning, and competitiveness.

In order to integrate corporate social responsibility in the global strategy of the firm, the concern for the triple bottom line and sustainability can be linked with the concept of the *balanced scorecard* as developed by Robert Kaplan and David Norton.[69] The balanced scorecard was originally created as an instrument to measure financial, social, and intellectual capital when integrating employee performance and customer relations to financial accounts, but it can easily be extended to apply to performance among a wider number of stakeholders. These approaches constitute an effort to make instrumental values-driven management and corporate social responsibility an integrated part of corporate strategy. The Danish firm Novo Nordisk, among others, has tried to integrate sustainability management and the balanced scorecard. Capron and Quairel-Lanoizeelée propose a *sustainability scorecard* that includes social stakeholder orientation and environmental dimensions of performance when measuring and developing competitiveness and corporate strategic behavior. In this sense, corporate social responsibility is not only risk management but aims at developing proactive operational procedures for values-driven management and stakeholder inclusion, in order to improve social acceptance of the firm.

Case 10. Royal Ahold: A sustainable food provider company

The Dutch-based international food provider, Royal Ahold, has integrated concepts of responsibility and sustainability into their core strategy. This company is a member of CSR Europe, which is a lobby group of European corporations, and has been selected as a case study because it is a company that tries to make an *ethical effort* in dealing with issues of corporate citizenship and sustainability.

The company's approach to sustainability is combined with a vision of charity and corporate philanthropy. In this sense, the company tries to express its responsible profile by charitable giving. This implies local initiatives to assist area food banks, schools, youth groups, and health-related organizations.[70] It involves different kinds of support and sponsorships.

The company is working for a strategy of healthy living where sustainability is linked to a vision of health and quality of life for customers and other stakeholders. The company is committed to the UN Brundtland Commission's definition of sustainability as development and growth with respect for the quality of life of current and future generations. The corporation defines sustainability as follows:

"– Managing our business in a responsible, ethical, and transparent way.
– Giving customers the best value, unique, and innovative products and services, and fresh, healthy foods produced under responsible conditions.
– Being "a great place to work." We will be a company reflective and supportive of the communities we serve, where people are treated fairly and experience a fulfilling career through our business growth.
– Minimizing the negative and maximizing the positive social and environmental impact of our supermarket and logistics operations.
– Being a proactive corporate citizen through dialogue with key stakeholders and building strong relationships in the communities where we do business."

Ahold works for a close strategy between sustainability and competitive advantage. Sustainability is linked to developing innovative categories and products, for example with regard to environmental protection and concerns in the food and retail industry. The corporation has developed a vision and value-statement based on this approach to sustainability. The protection of labor rights and development of a social profile is integrated in the company's concept of sustainability. Other stakeholder engagements include efforts to develop customer-oriented approaches. In the food industry, the corporation deals with high labor costs and low profit margins. The effort to develop distinctive Ahold brands is based on assuring food quality, implying focus on food safety, consumer health, and production with care for the environment, animals, and human beings. The corporation defines sustainability as fresh, safe, and high quality products. This includes efforts to develop sustainability in the supply chain and in local production, for example through sustainable fisheries.

The firm's website provides a case example from the company's 1997 effort to develop a program of independent and credible systems for producing fair trade coffee called Utz Kapeh. What is important here is the ethical traceability of food products. This program seeks to establish a system for defining good practices of coffee production. The Ahold coffee company works with other companies in order to provide good practices for production with regard to origin and traceability. The Utz Kapeh foundation was developed in order to establish a system for supplying coffee according to international sustainability standards with regard to use of pesticides, protection of labor rights, and access to education and health care.[71] The program involved independent control of farms and a system tracking the coffee's origins.

1.4. CSR, Corporate governance, and stakeholder justice

Formulated as a general aim of corporate citizenship, CSR makes it possible to integrate values-driven management and business ethics with good governance of the firm. Conceiving corporate governance from the perspective of the good corporate citizen means integrating the idea of corporate governance into the larger framework of theories of corporate citizenship and good governance.[72] This general and more profound conception of corporate governance should be conceived as the foundation of the dominant technical and formal conceptualization of corporate governance. It indicates the rules and guidelines for good and professional governance of the corporate board, in order to protect the interests of shareholders and investors, which has become an important application of the concept of corporate governance.[73] Since it is closely linked to CSR, corporate governance cannot be reduced to the legal aspects of corporate management, but it may include a perspective of governance informed by political philosophy and political theory (see previous discussion of the framework for business ethics). In fact, sustainability management and the triple bottom line are essential elements of this approach to corporate governance. The technical legal aspects of corporate governance have to be conceived within the framework of good corporate citizenship.

Utilizing the theory of corporate citizenship, the following conception of corporate governance is situated within the framework of corporate social responsibility and stakeholder management. Conceiving corporate governance within the theory of corporate citizenship means understanding it as part of the theory of governance proposed in the tradition of political philosophy.[74] Corporate governance cannot ignore the foundations of theory of government as the one proposed in the framework of the idea of the good life with and for the other in just institutions. In a firm, the shareholders, management, and the board may be conceived as those who govern, while the stakeholders are those who are governed. It is important to extend discussions of corporate governance beyond the legal and technical framework towards a general perspective of good governance, like the one found in political philosophy and social theory.[75] This concept of governance originates in classical theories from the idea of the Republic to the modern state, from Bodin to Hegel. Governance was related to the public thing (*res publica*). In this tradition, the focus was government of the state, and this led to the foundations of modern nation-states and later democratic governments. With a renewed focus on governance within political theory and political philosophy, the democratic function is emphasized.

The focus on governance means that there is no other government behind the process of governance than this process itself: there is no essence of governance, only concrete actions. To govern means to search for legitimacy, and this is the commonality of stakeholder management and new theories of political governance. Both approaches focus on standards of legitimate governance. To situate corporate governance within this framework means to make the legal principles of governance dependent on the larger framework of good governance. The functionalist aspects of governance that are expressed in the legal dimensions of the concept, but also in a "pure efficiency" concept of management (understood as technical governance), are situated within the larger framework of governance, which can be defined as deliberations about the totality of a firm's decisions, principles, and management decisions. From the point of view of republican business ethics, corporate governance is not only a functionalist term but relates more generally to concepts of the common good in society and the legitimacy of the corporation (in addition to issues regarding good governance in daily activities of the firm). Within this overall framework of corporate governance, concern for fair principles of dealing with shareholders and stakeholders is the general aim of good corporate governance.

Accordingly, the concept of corporate governance may be said to include elements of stakeholder management and concerns for ethics codes and programs within the firm. Managers and directors have to inform the board about such issues, and the board should compel managers to be concerned with such issues, because managers are those who know about the important stakeholder relations of the firm. It should not be forgotten that "the principles of who and what really counts depend on the interests and perceptions of managers."[76]

In order to formulate this link between corporate governance and stakeholder theory, Mitchell, Agle, and Wood's understanding of how the ideas of power, legitimacy, and urgency contribute to a stakeholder typology is useful. They have identified nine important stakeholder categories: 1) dormant stakeholders, 2) discretionary stakeholders, 3) demanding stakeholders, 4) dominant stakeholders, 5) dangerous stakeholders, 6) dependent stakeholders, and 7) definitive stakeholders. The last two, 8) latent stakeholders and 9) nonstakeholders, are not perceived to be important for management of the firm.[77]

These stakeholders are groups and individuals that affect the corporation and that should not be neglected in corporate governance. Among the latent stakeholders there are the dormant stakeholders with strong power, who may suddenly attack and require that the corporation act urgently and legitimately. Discretionary stakeholders demand legitimate action, but they have no power or influence on the firm. Such stakeholders may be candidates for corporate philanthropy, in order to make the image of the firm more legitimate. Demanding stakeholders are groups who have neither power nor legitimacy, but who have some claim on the firm and make a lot of noise, "like mosquitoes in the air."[78]

Dormant stakeholders include expectant stakeholders, who are both powerful and legitimate in the corporation and who form a dominant coalition in the enterprise.[79] They have some mechanisms in place in the boardroom, public affairs office, and so forth, in order to maintain their position. Management has, of course, to be very respectful to these stakeholders. Dependant stakeholders are stakeholders who lack power but have an urgent and legitimate claim on the firm, for example in connection with the firm's responsibility for damaging action upon these stakeholders. The natural environment is the most salient dependent stakeholder.

Dangerous stakeholders are groups who have claims of power and urgency. They may, for example, use coercive means to advance stakeholder claims. Definitive stakeholders combine the categories of power, legitimacy, and urgency. Those stakeholders are very important and they can also be dormant or dangerous stakeholders.

It is the task of corporate governance as stakeholder management to confront these different individuals and groups of stakeholders, and be aware of their different claims.[80] Stakeholder management may, however, face some obstacles which typicfy stakeholder relations. It can be very time consuming to include all individuals and stakeholder groups. Moreover, there may be a culture clash between different groups, stakeholders, and management, and there may be strong problems in uniting the different views of the action of the firm. This is related to the problems of conflict between different stakeholders, which may be so strong that it is difficult to find a possible solution that will satisfy all the different individuals and groups.[81] The corporation also runs the risk of controlling the different stakeholder claims in a way that means that stakeholder dialogue leads to a conclusion that cannot be accepted by the firm. There are also problems within stakeholder groups, for example, they may not want to engage in close dialogue with the corporation because they fear being absorbed by it. There are, furthermore, problems of accountability, and with legitimizing their own actions as an NGO or firm.[82]

On this foundation, and with close relations between stakeholder management and corporate governance, the link between corporate social responsibility and our concept of the good corporate citizen can be developed by using the principle of fairness as the basis for just relations to stakeholders. This concept of justice is very important for a normative concept of CSR. Fairness can be conceived as a concrete realization of the idea of corporate social responsibility in regard to the stakeholders of the corporation. In this sense, fairness is an essential aim in corporate governance and stakeholder management. Robert Philips's (2003) work helps to define the principle of fairness as the basis for stakeholder relations.[83] Philips tries to combine stakeholder theory with the moral and political theory of John Rawls as the basis for a theory of organizational ethics.[84] This concept of fairness provides the link between the argument for republican business ethics and the development of the concept of corporate social responsibility. From the republican perspective, it is possible to transfer the principle of fairness from political philosophy and democratic theory to organizational ethics. Fairness provides the basis for responsibility to important stakeholders. In conjunction with responsibility, fairness is the basis for legitimate treatment of stakeholders. As an ideal of organizational justice, fairness helps to select among normative constitutive stakeholders on one hand, and derivative stakeholders or nonstakeholders on the other.[85]

Viewing corporate social responsibility from the theoretical perspective of organizational integrity and good corporate citizenship, stakeholder theory should be viewed as a manner of maximizing the search for the common good of stakeholders, which is expressed in the idea of sustainable development. To argue for stakeholder fairness in the light of corporate social responsibility and corporate governance does not mean that all stakeholders should be treated equally, but that there at least should be some fairness in a firm's procedures of decision-making. Philips emphasizes that a simple egalitarian interpretation of stakeholder fairness would be wrong.[86] Fairness for stakeholders would be procedural and distributive. While Philips is correct when he argues that radical changes in business laws are unnecessary in order to introduce stakeholder management, however, the term "stakeholder" can be widely interpreted. Take politics, for example when Tony Blair, inspired by Anthony Giddens, introduced the concept of a *stakeholder economy*.[87] Contrary to Philips, the concept of a stakeholder management can be seen as a basis for good corporate citizenship and is not clearly an abuse of the concept, with too wide an application.

Stakeholder theory should not, as has been argued several times, be interpreted as a comprehensive moral doctrine, but as a procedure for the firm to deal with different forms of legitimate claims by different actors with different levels of power and urgency. Stakeholder theory is a way to account for the obligations of organizations to different agents and constituencies in society. From a Rawlsian perspective, an organization is a voluntary association and not, as such, a part of the basic structure of society. This perspective implies that the whole society cannot be a stakeholder, although corporations have obligations to social actors that go beyond obligations to shareholders.[88] In the discussion of the theories of business ethics in the preceding chapter, we have already examined how political philosophy can be used in business ethics. When applying these insights to developing the concept of fairness from a Rawlsian perspective, it can be argued that it is possible to apply his concepts of "the original position," "the veil of ignorance", and "the difference principle" to the levels of the organization.[89]

Following Freeman and Rawls, the moral core of stakeholder theory, which follows from the difference principle, is that justice-as-fairness in the organization implies that constitutive stakeholders like shareholders, customers, suppliers, employees, and local community are to be treated equally, and that inequalities can only be justified insofar as they improve the conditions of the least well-off.[90] Philips argues against Freeman, who does not make a distinction between "organizational membership" and "citizenship," that more intraorganizational inequality is justified than was the case with regard to political community.[91] Against this position, and siding with Freeman, the Rawlsian concept of fairness, when applied to organizations, only justifies major inequality insofar as it is justified on the basis of the difference principle. This is the result of the application of the agenda of corporate citizenship as corporate social responsibility onto the corporation as a moral agent. Freeman is right when he argues that Rawls's principle of difference can have direct implications for fairness regaring core stakeholders of the corporation. This is certainly the case with economic markets.

This means that the constitutive stakeholders of the organization can be said to take part in an original position, which indicates their attitude regarding basic liberties and establishes the principle of difference as the foundation for organizational justice-as-fairness. Such a view implies that the issues of political and moral rights are introduced as the basis for understanding the constituencies of the corporation. In this sense, a difficult question emerges of how to justify the lack of political democracy in corporations. Such inequality may be justified on the basis of the principle of difference, which indicates the need for economic efficiency in order to increase wealth in society. This is, however, also an argument against the *stakeholder paradox*, which states that an organization cannot have fiduciary duties to constituencies other than shareholders because this would eliminate the meaning of the concept of fiduciary duty.[92] Viewing the corporation from the perspective of the original position means that it is possible to argue for a multitude of fiduciary duties in order to accomplish the duty of responsibility and of justice-as-fairness, which requires us to respect not only shareholders, but all of the firm's stakeholders.

Applying the principle of fairness as the basis for just actions of organizations in economic markets can be conceived as concern for *fair play*. Philips retraces the concept of fair play back to John Stuart Mill, who defined it as as cooperative conduct with other persons that creates new obligations of cooperative conduct and moral responsibility.[93] This concept emerges as an ethical response to the danger of opportunism. According to Philips, the concept of fair play was already present in Rawls' early articles where he argued that fair play is a requirement in a mutually beneficial and just scheme of cooperation, where people participate with restrictions on their liberty. Under these conditions there is a duty to cooperate for the benefits of all.[94] Justice-as-fairness, expressed in the duty of fair play, implies the responsibility of cooperating towards mutual benefit and equality when dealing with the claims of different stakeholders.[95] Justice-as-fairness includes a reciprocal obligation to work for mutual benefit, and this obligation supports stakeholder management as the basis for business ethics and corporate social responsibility.

On this basis, corporate governance as stakeholder management can be conceived as a response to society's expectations of corporate citizenship and corporate contribution to the common good. Stakeholder management is also legitimate from the perspective of strategic management, because stakeholders have legitimate claims to just treatment by their organizations. Different groups of stakeholders are legitimate stakeholders, to the extent they have justified claims of being treated with fairness by the organization. From the perspective of corporate citizenship, the principles of responsibility and sustainability must be included in this account of fair treatment of stakeholders. While stakeholders who do not directly cooperate with the corporation do not, as a consequence, have a direct normative claim as a core constituency, they may have a derivative claim. Accordingly, following Philips, civil society organizations or social activists can have legitimate claims insofar as they are representatives of core constituencies of the corporations, for example, employees or local communities.

Box 10. R. Edward Freeman's principles of stakeholder responsibility

Stakeholder management is a strategy for increasing self-perception as the basis for decision-making. This is the essence of Freeman's principles of stakeholder management. In relation to the debate on corporate social responsibility and corporate governance, Freeman argues for "corporate stakeholder responsibility" as a much more pragmatic and honest way to defend a social approach to corporate responsibility. These principles can be considered as a way to work for fairness in stakeholder relations.[96] This implies the following principles of corporate stakeholder responsibility, which Freeman has defended on numerous occasions:

1) Stakeholder interests go together over time.
2) Stakeholders consist of real people with names and faces and children. People are complex.
3) We need solutions to issues that satisfy multiple stakeholders simultaneously.
4) We need intensive communication and dialogue with stakeholders, not just those who are friendly.
5) We need to have a philosophy of voluntarism, to manage stakeholder relationships ourselves rather than third parties, such as governments.
6) We need to generalize the marketing approach.
7) Everything that we do serves stakeholders. We never trade off the interests of one versus the other over time.
8) We negotiate with primary and secondary stakeholders.
9) We constantly monitor and redesign processes to make them better serve our stakeholders.
10) We act with purpose that fulfills our commitment to stakeholders. We act with aspiration towards fulfilling our dreams.

In fact, Freeman's principles of stakeholder management can be used to formulate a fundamental revision of stakeholder theory, in comparison with traditional concepts that would place the corporation in the center of the stakeholder diagram with the different stakeholders of the corporation placed around it. A more progressive way to express the idea of corporate citizenship within stakeholder management would be not to situate the corporation in the center of the diagram, but rather conceive it as one stakeholder among others contributing to the common good of society. In this perspective, the firm is no long in the center of stakeholders but rather one among other stakeholders who work together to improve the good of all individuals in community. This revised version of stakeholder theory can be formulated in this way:

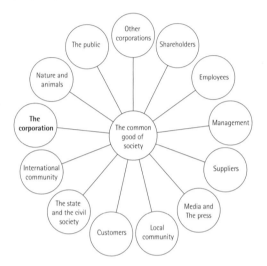

1.5. Basic Ethical Principles in Responsible Stakeholder Management

The kinds of inequality that are permissible remain fairly abstract. Put another way, what are the core constituencies of human stakeholders that may absolutely not be violated? In order to answer this question, four ethical principles of autonomy, dignity, integrity, and vulnerability are proposed as the basis for treating stakeholders fairly.[97]

From the point of view of stakeholder management, these principles have significance for organizations as the basis for human rights.[98] In the framework of corporate citizenship, organizational integrity, sustainability, responsibility, and justice-as-fairness, the ethical principles provide guidance for important concerns in stakeholder dialogue founded on a "wide reflective equilibrium" or "domination-free communication."[99] The principles are protected in stakeholder dialogue, which follows discursive ethics by recognizing the power of the best argument and by listening to all parties.[100] The ethical principles represent the rights and concerns for all core constituencies of the firm, shareholders, customers, suppliers, employees, and local communities.

These principles can be defined in the following manner:[101]

1) Autonomy should not only be interpreted in the liberal sense of "permission," but instead five aspects of autonomy should be put forward:

i. the capacity to create ideas and goals for life;

ii. the capacity of moral insight, self-legislation, and privacy;

iii. the capacity for rational decision-making and action without coercion;

iv. the capacity of political involvement and personal responsibility;

v. and the capacity of informed consent.

Autonomy remains, however, merely an ideal, because of the structural limitations imposed by human weakness and dependence on biological, material, and social conditions, lack of information for reasoning, et cetera.

2) Dignity should not be reduced to autonomy. Although originally a virtue of outstanding persons and of self-control – qualities that can be lost, for instance, by lack of responsibility or in cases of extreme illness – it has been universalized to include all humanity. It now refers to both the intrinsic value of the individual and the intersubjective value of every human being in its encounter with the other. Dignity concerns both oneself and the other: I must not give up civilized and responsible behavior, and the other should not be commercialized and enslaved. Human rights are based on this principle of dignity.

3) Integrity accounts for the inviolability of the human being. Although originally a virtue of uncorrupted character, expressing uprightness, honesty and good intentions, it has, like dignity, been universalized. It refers to the coherence of life that should not be molested and destroyed. It is a way of cohering life through memory and can, therefore, be expressed in narrative. Respect for integrity is respect for privacy and, in particular, for the employee's right to self-determination and noninterference in personal life projects. Integrity is the most important principle for the creation of trust between people, because it also indicates the moral virtue of commitment and engagement in a personal vision of the good life.

4) Vulnerability concerns integrity as a basic principle for respect and protection of human and nonhuman life. It expresses the condition thàt all life is vulnerable to being hurt, wounded, and killed. It is not integrity as completeness in any sense, but the integrity of life that must be respected and protected as vulnerable. Vulnerability concerns animals and all self-organizing life in the environment, and must be considered as a universal expression of the human condition. The idea of protecting the vulnerable can, therefore, create a bridge between moral strangers in a pluralistic society. Inculcating respect for vulner-

ability should be essential to strategic decisions in corporations and policy-making in the modern welfare state. Respect for vulnerability is not a demand for perfection or immortality, but a recognition of the suffering and finitude of human life.

1.5.1. Autonomy

Applying these principles in stakeholder management, it should not be forgotten that the word autonomy consists of two roots *auto* and *nomos*, which translates literally as "self-government."[102] In the Western philosophical tradition, this concept refers to the freedom of individual human beings. It points to the right of every person to live an independent life according to their capacities and to make personal choices for their future lives. Immanuel Kant stressed that every person is an end-in-themselves, participating in a community of the Kingdom of Ends, due to human reason, judgment, and moral responsibility.[103] To be autonomous means not to let oneself be governed by measures other than reason and moral law. Even though this concept has been viewed mostly within the context of principles of democratic autonomy in political systems, the Kantian concept of autonomy might indeed be very important in liberal market economics. In fact, autonomy might be the central value to economic markets, indicating freedom to exchange.[104] People want to be free to work, produce, trade, buy, sell, and make profits.

This liberty of the market is not something external to autonomous moral reason, but is a very basic part of human nature; indeed, liberals view property rights and economic freedom as central to humanity. Even more socially and egalitarian philosophers emphasize economic freedom as a part of equal opportunity.[105] The ideal of autonomy justifies the activities of the firm on the market in order to make profits within the "rules of the game." With regard to the Kantian concept of autonomy, this also means that the firm should act in an economically responsible fashion. Accordingly, the firm is not only considered as an economic actor, but as a responsible legal person, moving away from the law and economics approach toward accepting the notions of organizational culpability and responsibility. This legal view of the firm confirms our ethical ideas of giving autonomy a meaning at the organizational and institutional level.

The principle of autonomy does not, however, apply exclusively on the company as a legal, social and economic entity, but also concerns individual actors within the company and relations between the company and its stakeholders. This should manifest in the rights and freedoms of employees within the workplace. One example of this is the freedom of employees to join unions, which is being institutionalized in most countries with liberal market economies. Moreover, participation in economic contracts is based on free will and workers should be free to accept different types of work. Particularly important applications of autonomy with regard to employees are issues of nondiscrimination, affirmative action, and the establishment of equal opportunities for all employees at the workplace. The value of autonomy also reminds us to consider our fellow employees as free human beings who see their working environments as fulfilling parts of their their personal lives. From this perspective, respect for autonomy motivates organizations to act as dynamic institutions consisting of individuals in creative and learning environments.

The ideal of autonomy can also lead to problems. First of all, autonomy has lead to severe social inequalities due to individual differences in luck, opportunity, and economic capacity. All kinds of economic, social, and organizational constraints indicate that decision-making at the market is far from free. And at the business market, autonomy is only understood as the rule of market liberalism, or the unhindered right to pursue your own interest and to maximize profits. The moral dimensions of autonomy have been totally forgotten. Autonomy has been understood as the right to egoism rather than as the Kantian ideal.[106]

This understanding of autonomy at the institutional level supports the position that the firm should focus on its own interest and refuse to take ethical responsibility for the social environment and people that do not have a strategic interest for the firm. Organizational autonomy of the firm has been defined as the right of the firm to be independent and autonomous in relation to society, though this consideration of autonomy is challenged by the shareholder-stakeholder controversy.[107] This stakeholder view of the firm does not define the firm as an independent entity, rather it argues that the firm should take into account the social context – not only its own autonomy, but also the autonomy of all stakeholders that have an interest in the firm. The whole idea of social responsibility of the firm indicates such a communitarian critique of the abstract idea of autonomy, arguing for seeing the firm as situated in local community.

Another example of this change of the notion of organizational autonomy has been the recent development of values-driven management from a perspective of democratic communication.[108] Such a theory emphasizes the interests and autonomy of all participants in the dialogue with regard to the formulation of goals and accountabilities of the firm. According to a communicative view on business ethics, to respect autonomy means being aware of the interests of all the stakeholders, who all have a perspective that includes the respect for their autonomy. Such a relational concept of autonomy of the firm is in accordance with the democratic theory of the stakeholder society. Ethical accountability of the firm is a reflective way, from the perspective of dialogue free from domination, to measure all types of interests and stakeholders.

1.5.2. Dignity

In a similar way the concept of dignity can be borrowed from political philosophy and applied to the field of business ethics. There is a close link between dignity and autonomy. Sometimes dignity is even equated with autonomy. Human dignity is a very powerful concept in the western tradition.[109] It states that human beings have a very special position, in dominion over the natural and biological world. As moral beings, humans have freedom and autonomy, implying a capacity of moral reasoning and responsibility. Human beings are assigned dignity (*dignitas*), which determines their value and position in the world. In the beginning, dignity related to intersubjective relations between individuals. The idea of individual human life possessing intrinsic value and dignity was developed in Christianity and was a byproduct of the freedom to choose between good and evil. A life lived with dignity, or spent securing the dignity of others, was a manifestation of the good. In antiquity, and certainly from early Christianity through the Renaissance, the concept of dignity expressed the moral superiority and responsibility of human beings in relation to themselves, animals, nature, and the whole universe.

These aspects of human dignity found a new synthesis in Kant's conception of the human being as an end-in-itself, and in the ideas of the moral law and the categorical imperative. Kant proposed treating every human being as a person of intrinsic value, because of his or her autonomy and self-governance. Every human being possesses dignity and sovereignty because of her will and inner intrinsic value. In Kant's philosophy, human dignity is a basic moral principle. Because of the human capacity for losing and acquiring dignity, its protection becomes a great moral requirement and closely linked to the concept of personal autonomy. [110]

The close connection between dignity and autonomy is very important in existentialist philosophies. In fact, Jean-Paul Sartre's defense of existentialism as a humanistic philosophy connects human dignity, freedom, and autonomy.[111]

Because of the intrinsic capacity for choosing the meaning and significance of one's own life, the value of human life can be lost or destroyed. Human dignity applies to the intrinsic human capacities of engaged existence in passion, or action in the world. What is essential in this kind of humanism is the protection of what is human and how to develop the characteristics of human dignity in a future social life.

In order to apply this concept of dignity at the organizational level concerning actions and behaviors of private companies, the essential significance of human rights (as in the concept of human dignity) needs to be emphasized. This concept of dignity is essential at the workplace. It applies to the treatment of workers and the relation between employees and managers of the firm. Concerning weak individuals, dignity indicates the respect for each human being as an end-in-herself. This is the foundation of human rights declarations. The respect for the right to work is a strong corollary, since dignity in working life is widely held to be essential to individual well-being. While these concepts should apply in business life, practically it can be difficult because people essentially sell themselves and their bodies to employers. Self-respect is related to how one is treated by others in the workplace. Dignity is important to indicate limits of the rights of business to corporeal exploitation and workplace discrimination. Because degradation in the workplace occurs within an organizational hierarchy, respect for dignity also means limiting the rights of superior officers to reduce their employees to mere things.[112]

Dignity also finds an interesting application concerning powerful individuals. How responsibly they treat their employees is a matter of dignity for a firm's directors and board. They lose moral dignity if they do not respect the people who work for them. Similar things can be said about criminal behavior of the firm, such cases where the firm is uncooperative with law enforcement. Moreover, the dignity of the company is dependent on the dignity of its high level directors, who should behave in a way that is good for the moral and social image of the company in society. It follow that a firm's public relations can be analyzed with concern for dignity. Thus, it is a matter of dignity how high officials cope with success and failure. Some leaders are not able to handle success and they lose dignity while experiencing success or failure. To act with dignity is evidently a question of moral virtue in the experience of happiness or tragic loss.

As with autonomy, the extent to which dignity applies to organizations is a large discussion. The problem of dignity of organizations relates to the question of whether they can be held responsible for their actions, and it concerns the relations of organizations to the environment. The initiatives of organizations that have had success contributing to social success and welfare illustrate how organizational dignity can be demonstrated through superior generosity.

1.5.3. Integrity

Organizational integrity has already been emphasized several times as an important element for the concept of corporate citizenship in republican business ethics. In the following discussion of the concept as an important ethical principle, there will be some overlap with the description of organizational integrity within the framework of corporate citizenship.[113] Integrity is, however, also important as a virtue of the individual. As a philosophical concept, integrity is closely connected with autonomy and dignity. As a virtue, it concerns the wholeness of the human person, and the personality.[114] The sphere of integrity is both physical and moral, and is a concept that has been quite popular among scholars of business ethics.[115] Integrity has mostly been defined as coherence or completeness, indicating the purity of a totality that has not been destroyed. The notion is associated with true identity, honesty, respect and trust. In short, business ethics has been working with personal integrity as a moral ideal.

There is a close connection between integrity, personal identity, and character. Integrity has, since Platonic times, meant basic moral virtue and human character. In the history of philosophy, integrity was related to the human character and identity as an expression of the moral personality of the individual. The physical and psychic aspects of integrity confirmed this comprehensive definition, and related it to privacy rights and to the concepts of autonomy and dignity.

In a legal sense, integrity originates in Roman law. It is etymologically derived from the Latin *integritas*. It also related to the notion of something being "intact," and signifies the Latin expression, *noli me tangere*, which translates as "the untouchable, undisturbed, and what should not be touched." This notion of integrity of the person plays an important role in the declarations of human rights and different European constitutions. It is, therefore, essential to legal protection of the human person. Furthermore, the concept of integrity indicates protections for the social and economic integrity of the person.

But this notion of integrity has, in modern legal theory, been extended to institutional structures and legal entities.[116] Ronald Dworkin uses the concept of integrity to describe the political morality of a just legal order. In this understanding of integrity, judges and agents in the legal order are said to have integrity when building their decisions on impartiality and fairness. They can be said to confer to each person "equal concern and respect." This might be the basis for an organizational definition of integrity.

Focusing on integrity in organizations rather than individuals, the efficiency of legal standards and compliance programs is encouraged if accompanied by integrity principles, but a values-driven model of management would be preferable. When viewing integrity as the close relation between ethics and law in the formulation of ethics programs, the evaluation of the company as a good citizen is very important for the "wholeness" of the organization. We can say that organizational integrity expresses the moral accountability and trustworthiness of a corporation.

Such a notion of organizational integrity implies a collective perspective on values-driven management that considers individual decision-making within the framework of the structural characteristics of the organization. Moral and legal responsibility is not only individual responsibility, but also dependent on the structure and culture of the firm as a "nexus of formal and informal contracts." The focus should not exclusively be on the moral manager but also on the organization's interaction with the environment (e.g., the moral market).[117]

Many researchers have stated that management by values, where corporate values are taken into account by all stakeholders of the firm, is an important way to ensure sound and just decision-making, The programs of values-driven management indicate that ethics is not merely a personal issue, but is influenced by the culture of the organization. The demand for an effective ethics program as a prevention of wrongdoing implies the possibility of becoming more conscious of the ideals and values of the organization. An ethics program can help the corporation to improve its social legitimacy and participation in the life of the community. Such procedures "will not prevent all illegalities or improprieties, but they can help to influence the character of an organization and its employees."[118] An institutional account of integrity moves the perspective from individual morality toward the analysis of the "ethical logic" of basic concepts of modern economies (i.e., organizations, markets, property, information, et cetera).

1.5.4. Vulnerability

The concept of vulnerability is closely linked to the idea of the social responsibility of the firm, because responsible business managers are particularly concerned with the firm's relations with the vulnerable in society. Emmanuel Lévinas defined the concept of vulnerability as the foundation for understanding the human condition and morality. Morality is compensation for humankind's vulnerability.[119] Care for the other is a moral imperative and involves an ethical responsibility for the other. In this way, vulnerability can be said to imply an immanent normativity in which vulnerability is expressed in the corporeal incarnation of the other (e.g., the face of the other). Lévinas formulates the imperative "though shall not kill" as the most basic concept of vulnerable existence.[120] From this perspective, the deepest point of morality is revealed in the vulnerable situation of human beings in the world. Vulnerability manifests an asymmetrical imbalance between the weak and the powerful, and in this context, it demands an ethical engagement of the powerful to protect the weak. It is our vulnerability that makes us receptive to the responsibility emanating from the other as a vulnerable being. This ethical receptivity is a fundamental point of the human condition. The same concern for vulnerability as a fundamental concept can also be shown in the philosophy of Jürgen Habermas.[121] His argument for a communicative understanding in a dialogue free from domination also situates vulnerability at the center of ethical concern. This is an openness towards the vulnerable other that is necessitated by the demands of true dialogue.

Vulnerability, defined as an ontological concept, seems to be contradictory to the idea of competitive market relations, which involves a struggle for success but also survival. In this struggle, vulnerability can have little significance or it can have paramount importance because it leads to destruction. Social Darwinism indicates the vulnerability of the weakest to destruction in the competition at the market. The market conditions for free competition mean that the search for profit is only submitted to some minimal restrictions.

The dark side of business is that each participant in market competition has vulnerabilities.[122] Vulnerability expresses the exposure or disadvantaged position of an entity (a person, or an organization) to another who is able to do harm. This vulnerability points to some special characteristic(s) of the entity, which can lead to the possibility of its destruction under certain conditions. In this way, vulnerability is a part of the condition of business, because no one is invincible.

On the basis of this rather metaphysical notion of vulnerability, it is possible to identify some particularly vulnerable groups. Although some overlap exists among these groups, they cannot be totally identified with the disadvantaged, but must be considered as a distinct group.[123] Particular vulnerabilities possess psychological, physical, and social dimensions. Especially in marketing, concern for the vulnerable means that firms should be specifically aware of vulnerable groups of consumers, such as children, elderly, the poor, and people from developing countries. But it could also mean responsibility toward employees with particular vulnerabilities. It must be the aim of the firm or society to avoid irresponsible action leading to destruction of these particularly vulnerable groups.

The meaning of vulnerability in business ethics leads, therefore, to a principle of fair treatment; not exploiting the vulnerable, but rather caring for and being aware of their dispositions. Responsible managers and salespeople would not exploit vulnerable populations, but rather support them in a responsible business relation built on dignity, integrity, and trust.

Box 11. Workplace ethics: Respect for human dignity

The concept of respect for human dignity, in the context of integrity and individual vulnerability, is central for workplace ethics. Different corporations have tried to include the concept of human dignity in their ethics statements, codes of conduct, and corporate credos. Here are some examples:

We believe in the dignity of the individual. However large and complex a business may be, its work is still done by people dealing with people. Each person involved is a unique human being, with pride, needs, values, and innate personal worth. For Borg-Warner to succeed we must operate in a climate of openness and trust, in which each of us freely grants others the same respect, cooperation, and decency we seek for ourselves.[124]

– Borg-Warner, a consumer and business services corporation

Principles for Business. These Principles are rooted in two basic ideals: *kyosei* and human dignity. The Japanese concept of *kyosei* means living and working together for the common good – enabling cooperation and mutual prosperity to coexist with healthy and fair competition. "Human dignity" refers to the sacredness or value of each person as an end, not simply as a means to the fulfillment of other's purposes or even majority prescription.[125]

– The Caux Round Table

Our creed. We believe in the free enterprise system. We shall consistently treat our customers, employees, shareholders, suppliers, and the community with honesty, dignity, fairness, and respect. We will conduct our business with the highest ethical standards.[126]

– Johnson Controls, Inc., a business service company

Treat all associates fairly with dignity and with respect. All associates are entitled to a work environment without verbal, physical, and sexual harassment. The Company is committed to the principles and procedures described in its Guarantee of Fair Treatment. The Company is also committed to providing equal opportunities for minorities, women, veterans, and persons with disabilities. The Company believes promotion of work force diversity is an important objective in its own right, a source of competitive advantage, and a requirement of Equal Employment Opportunity laws.[127]

– Marriott, a company in the hospitality industry

Respect for the individual. We respect the dignity of each individual, whether an employee, shareholder, client, or member of the general public. We strive to be a lean, decisive, and aggressive organization, but on a personal level to treat each individual with dignity, consideration, and respect. This means sharing the credit when credit is due, avoiding public criticism of one another, and encouraging an atmosphere in which openness, cooperation, and mutual consultation are the norms. It means following the Golden Rule.[128]

– Merrill Lynch, an investment company

We respect human rights and dignity. We believe that people should work because they want or need to, but not because they are forced to do so. We believe that people have the right to freely associate with whichever organizations or individuals they choose. We believe that children should not be unlawfully employed as laborers.[129]

– Starbucks, beverages and retailing business

1.6. From principles of ethics to corporate social performance and responsiveness

When applying basic ethical principles in corporate governance as stakeholder management, they are integrated with corporate social responsibility and with concern for justice-as-fairness. Liberal economic markets depend on justice and responsibility as outer constraints determined by economic morality, legal rules, and ethical principles. On this basis, the ideas of autonomy, dignity, integrity, and vulnerability constitute important guidelines for fair business and market interaction. The task is to see them as normative standards for institutions and organizations so that the legitimacy of the economic markets can be justified. This is the significance of the institutional application of the basic ethical principles.

The basic ethical principles in this framework of justice provide the necessary framing of corporate social responsibility to become real corporate responsiveness. In fact, this is important because the debate about corporate social responsibility has turned away from searching for definitions towards concrete response to social pressure.[130] This means that the focus has become a problem of how to apply corporate social responsibility to the concrete reality of the corporation. In this sense, corporate responsiveness is defined as the capacity of the corporation to go into stakeholder dialogue and really do something about corporate social responsibility as a good corporate citizen. I think that the basic ethical principles, as a contribution to protecting human rights and professional business ethics, provides the necessary frame for concrete corporate social responsibility, which has been desired by the proponents of corporate social responsiveness.

Such a turn towards a case-oriented focus on corporate social responsiveness may, therefore, not only be considered as an effort to escape theoretical problems.[131] It is also an effort to be more concrete and apply ethical principles within the institutional context of business, so that business ethics can have an impact on the corporation. The good citizen corporation, with its emphasis on basic ethical principles and stakeholder dialogue, can be considered as a reenactment of a closer link between corporate social responsibility and corporate social responsiveness.

Frederick has described this development from corporate social responsibility (CSR1) to corporate social responsiveness (CSR2).[132] Corporate social responsiveness lays emphasis on the company's practical contribution to social management rather than on its capacity to talk about it. Corporate social responsiveness is not only about government initiatives to incentivize social responsibility, but also proposals from corporations to make concrete contributions to social betterment.[133]

Joseph W. Weiss provides an important clarification of the relation between corporate responsiveness by considering stakeholder theory from an issues management approach.[134] Principles of justice can be applied to management of different organizational issues, and contribute to establishing legitimacy in terms of organizational crises. Like issues management, stakeholder analysis considers the justice and fairness of stakeholder inclusion with regard to particular business issues. It seeks to respond with values in an adequate and strategic way.[135] Combining social responsiveness and issues management also signifies organizational preparedness for crises management and the ability to react to problems of legitimacy, and respond to emergencies.[136]

Corporate social performance is arguably closely linked to corporate social responsibility as an expression of the interactions between business and society. By emphasizing the ethical dimensions of CSR, ethical responsibility becomes a constitutive normative restraint on corporate responsiveness. Corporate social performance based on corporate responsiveness concerns the capacity of the corporation to serve the social good. Responsibilities and values-driven management, based on ethical principles, are important for corporate social responsiveness. They work as foundations for corporate social performance.[137]

Within the framework of stakeholder justice, autonomy, dignity, integrity, and vulnerability can have a powerful significance and application in business ethics. Moreover, the ideas of corporate citizenship, sustainability, responsibility, and fairness, but also concerns for community, universal principles, and utility become important, not only as theoretical ideas, but as practical guidelines for corporate social responsiveness in stakeholder and issues management. There is much further work to do concerning the particular applications of principles and values in the light of reflective judgment. In the following section, the great importance that these ethical principles have in particular fields of business ethics and in the practical definition of values-driven management as foundational for good citizenship will become clear.

··

Endnotes

1   Andrew Crane and Dirk Matten, *Business Ethics. A European Perspective* (Oxford: Oxford University Press, 2004), 21. The concept of corporate social responsibility has a long history and only recently has there been this close relation between sustainability, corporate social responsibility, and corporate social citizenship. Earlier usages are discussed in three widely cited publications: H.R. Bowen, *The Social Responsibilities of Business Men* (1953), Keith Davis: "What does businessmen owe society?" (1967) and "Can business afford to ignore its social responsibilities" (1960). See Mark S. Schwartz and Archie B. Carroll, "Corporate social responsibility: A Three domain approach", *Business Ethics Quarterly*, Volume 13, (2003), 503-530.

2   World Commission on Environment and Development, *Our Common Future*, (New York: Oxford University Press, 1987).

3   I will later discuss the concept of sustainability in detail with regard to environmental protection and the triple bottom line. This is, therefore, a relatively short introduction to the term as closely linked with corporate social responsibility.

4   Andrew Crane and Dirk Matten, *Business Ethics. A European Perspective* (Oxford: Oxford University Press, 2004), 24.

5   John Elkington, *Cannibals with Forks, The Triple Bottom Line of 21st Century Business* (Oxford: Capstone (1997), 1999).

6   Lynn Sharp Paine, *Valueshift. Why Companies Must Merge Social and Financial Imperative to Achieve Superior Performance* (New York: McGraw-Hill, 2003).

7   Hans Jonas, *Das Prinzip Verantwortung* (Frankfurt am Main: Insel Verlag, 1979).

8   Andrew Crane and Dirk Matten, *Business Ethics. A European Perspective* (Oxford: Oxford University Press, 2004), 41.

9   As already discussed, I argue that there is always a link between business ethics, CSR, and the concept of good corporate citizenship. This implies a criticism of Michael Porter's attempt to conceive CSR exclusively in purely strategic terms, reducing the internal link between CSR and business ethics. See Michael E. Porter and Mark R. Kramer, "Strategy and Society. The Link between Competitive Advantage and Corporate Social Responsibility", *Harvard Business Review*, December 2006.

10 Amartya Etizioni, *The Moral Dimension. Towards a New Economics* (New York: Collier Macmillan, 1988).

11 Rogene A. Buchholz and Sandra B. Rosenthal, "Social Responsibility and Business Ethics" in *A Companion to Business Ethics*, edited by Robert E. Frederick (Oxford: Blackwell publishing (1999), 2002), 304.

12 Archie B. Caroll, "A Three Dimensional Conceptual Model of Corporate Performance", *Academy of Management Review*, Vol 4, (1979), no. 4,. See also Michel Capron and Françoise Quairel-Lanoizeelée, *Mythes et réalités de l'entreprise responsable. Acteurs, Enjeux, Stratégies* (Paris: La Decouverte, 2004), 105.

13 Andrew Crane and Dirk Matten, *Business Ethics. A European Perspective* (Oxford: Oxford University Press, 2004), 44

14 This figure illustrates the contrast between two fundamental conceptions of CSR: as a pyramid and from the perspective of a Venn diagram. As will become apparent, the Venn diagram conception is much more compatible with the idea of the moral agency of the corporation that is implied in the concept of corporate citizenship. This is because the pyramid seems to suggest that there is no overlap between the different kinds of responsibility, while the Venn diagram, on the other hand, is much more open to interactions between the different dimensions of responsibility. See Archie B. Carroll, "A Three Dimensional Model of Corporate Social Performance", *Academy of Management Review*, 4. 497-505. See also Archie B. Carrol and A. K. Buchholtz, *Business and Society: Ethics and Stakeholder Management*, 4th edn. (Cincinnati: South Western College, 2000).

15 Milton Friedman, "The Social Responsibility of Business is to increase its profits", *New York Times Magazine* (September 13), 1970. Reprinted in Scott, B Rae and Kenman, L. Wong, *Beyond Integrity. A Judeo-Christian Approach to Business Ethics* (Grand Rapids Michigan: Zondervan Publishing House, 1996), 241-246.

16 André Comte-Sponville, *Le Capitalisme est-il moral? Sur Quelques ridicules et tyrannies de notre temps* (Paris: Albin Michel, 2004). Comte-Sponville defends a strict separation of the spheres of rationality and responsibility. He argues that there is an ethical sphere, a legal sphere, a moral sphere, an economic sphere, and a religious sphere that should not be confounded. He is, therefore, very critical towards "la mode de l'éthique des affaires," where the firm is made into a moral subject. This distinction may have some resemblance between the present distinctions of social responsibility within different spheres of the company, although I would not agree with a too strict separation between economic and ethical rationality, nor with the statement that economic rationality is amoral. This is a very old-fashioned view of scientific rationality.

17 Michael E. Porter and Mark R. Kramer, "The Competitive Advantage of Corporate Philanthropy" in *Harvard Business Review on Corporate Responsibility* (Harvard, Cambridge, Massachusetts: Harvard Business School Press, 2003). Michael E. Porter and Mark R. Kramer: "Strategy and Society. The Link between Competitive Advantage and Corporate Social Responsibility", *Harvard Business Review*, December 2006.

18 In their article "Corporate social responsibility: A Three domain approach", *Business Ethics Quarterly*, Volume 13, (2003), 503-530, Carroll and Schwartz refer to many important authors on corporate social responsibility who have used the four dimension pyramid (p. 504). This shows that Carroll's definition has had widespread influence and impact on the discussions of CSR. Some notable work that is mentioned in that article as work that has been influenced by Carroll's definition include: Donna Wood, "Corporate social performance revisited", *Academy of Management Review* 16 (4) (1991): 691-718. Diana Swanson, "Addressing a Theoretical Problem by Reorienting the Corporate Social Performance Model", *Academy of Management Review*, 20 (1) (1995): 43-64 and Diana Swanson, "Toward an Integrative Theory of Business and Society: A Research Strategy for Corporate Social Performance", *Academy of Management Review* 24 (3) (1999): 521-596. M.B.E. Clarkson, "Defining, Evaluating, and Managing Corporate Social Performance: The Stakeholder Management Model" in *Research in Corporate Social Performance and Policy*, edited by W.F. Frederick (Greenwich, Conn.: JAI Press, 1995), 331-358. John Boatright, *Ethics and the conduct of business*, (Englewood Cliffs, H:J: Prentice Hall). R.A. Buchholz, *Business, environement and Public Policy*, 5th ed. (Englewood Cliffs, N.J.: Prentice Hall, 1995). Joseph Weiss, *Business Ethics, A managerial Stakeholder Approach*, (Belmont, California: Wasworth Publishing Co, 1995). Donna Wood and R.E. Jones, "Research in Corporate Social Performance: What have we learned?", in *Corporate Philanthropy at the Crossroads*, edited by D.R Burlinggame and D.R. Young (Bloomington, Indiana: Indiana University Press, 1995), 41-85.

19 Mark S. Schwartz and Archie B. Carroll, "Corporate social responsibility: A Three domain approach", *Business Ethics Quarterly*, Volume 13, (2003), 503-530.

20 Archie B. Carroll: "The pyramid of corporate social responsibility. Toward the moral management of organizational stakeholders", *Business Horizons* (July-August 1991), 39-48.

21 Mark S. Schwartz and Archie B. Carroll: "Corporate social responsibility: A Three domain approach", *Business Ethics Quarterly*, Volume 13 (2003): 503-530, 505.

22 Ibid: 518.

23 Ibid: 508.

24 This case is inspired by the presentation of the Vestas Wind Systems in Anders Bordum and Jacob Holm Hansen, *Strategisk ledelseskommunikation. Erhvervslivets ledelse med visioner, missioner og værdier* (Copenhagen: Jurist og Økonomforbundets forlag, 2005), 144-148. They present an outline of a discursive analysis of the strategic elements of corporate communication in connection with values-driven management. Analysis of the discursive elements in this case is also based on their methodology.

25 www.vestas.com.

26 Esben Rahbek Pedersen, *Between Hopes and Realities: Reflections on the Promises and Practices of Corporate Social Responsibility (CSR)* (Copenhagen: Copenhagen Business School PhD Series 17 2006), 22. Here, we find a list with multiple definitions of CSR, showing how this umbrella concept is used in different ways. Despite this variation, it seems to be one of the core elements of the concept is that it integrates stakeholder management (30-32).

27 Elisabeth Garriga and Domènec Melé, "Social Responsibility: Mapping the Territory", *Journal of Business Ethics*, 53 (2004), 51-71, in particular 52-53 and 65.

28 Ibid: 54-55.

29 Ibid: 60.

30 Wim Dubbink, "The fragile structure of free market society. The radical implications of corporate social responsibility", *Business Ethics Quarterly*, Volume 14, (2004), Issue 1: 23-46, 27. Dubbink refers to Peter Drucker as the one who formulated the principle of minimizing harm to the greatest possible extent as the basic principle of CSR.

31 Helene Tølbøll Djursø and Peter Neergaard, *Social ansvarlighed: Fra idealisme til forretningsprincip*, (Copenhagen: Gyldendal Academica, 2006).

32 Kjeld Mølvadgaard and Ove Nielson, "Social ansvarlighed i danske virksomheder" in *Social ansvarlighed. Fra idealisme til forretningsprincip* edited by Helene Tølbøll Djursø og Peter Neergaard (Copenhagen: Academica, 2006). Mølvadgaard, Kjeld og Ove Nielsen, "Det sociale ansvar og det rummelige arbejdsmarked" in *Social ansvarlighed. Fra idealisme til forretningsprincip* edited by Helene Tølbøll Djursø og Peter Neergaard (Copenhagen: Academica, 2006).

33 André Boyer, editor, *L'impossible éthique des enterprises*, (Paris: Éditions d'organisations, 2001).

34 Although there may be disagreement about this concept of corporate social responsibility as closely related to corporate citizenship and business ethics, those of us in the French tradition of discussion of the concept refer to a number of authors who agree that this link is important. See for example: Fréderic Le Roy et Michel Marchesnay, editors, *La responsabilité sociale de l'entreprise. Mélanges en l'honneur du professeur Roland Pérez* (Paris Management et scoiété, éditions EMS, 2005), Charles Maccio, *Exercer une responsabilité* (Lyon: Savoir communiquer, Chronique sociale, 2001). Alain Chauvenau et Jean-Jacques Rosé, *L'entreprise responsable, Développement durable, responsabilité sociale de l'entreprise, éthique* (Paris: Editions Organisations, 2003). From the Danish context we can mention: Mette Morsing and Christina Thyssen (editors), *Corporate Values and Responsibility. The Case of Denmark*, (Copenhagen: Samfundslitteratur, 2003).

35 European Commission. Directorate-General for Employment and Social Affairs, Industrial Relations and Industrial Change, Unit EMPL/D.1: *Promoting a European Framework for Corporate Social Responsibility, Green Paper*, July, (Luxembourg: Office for Official Publication of the European Communities, 2001)

36 Helene Tølbøll Djursø og Peter Neergaard, *Social ansvarlighed: Fra idealisme til forretningsprincip* (Copenhagen: Gyldendal Academica, 2006). The approach of Djursø and Neergaard emphasizes different important dimensions of CSR, similar to those proposed by Elisabeth Garriga and Domènic Melé. There is some overlap between the two attempts as the categories seem to be very close to one another. As I have proposed, it is important to argue that the concept of corporate citizenship, based on organizational integrity and accountability, is the foundation of a useful approach to CSR.

37 In fact, the implied concept of competition, which relates to this approach, does not have to be seen as purely instrumental. It may be possible to compete ethically, which has been one of the key aspects of fairness in good institutions of the market economy. It may actually be possible to develop strategies for fair and responsible competition. This kind of moral competition can produce and improve the moral legitimacy of the corporation. See Bert van de Ben and Ronald Jeurissen, "Competing Responsibly", *Business Ethics Quarterly*, Volume 15, Issue 2: 299-317.

38 This case is selected from Thomas Donaldson, Patricia H. Werhane and Margaret Cording: *Ethical Issues in Business. A philosophical Approach* (Upper Saddle River, New Jersey: Prentice Hall, 2002). See also John R. Boatright: *Ethics and the Conduct of Business*, Third Edition (New Jersey, Prentice Hall 2003), 97.

39 See Richard De George: "International Business Ethics" in *A Companion to Business Ethics* edited by Robert E. Frederick (Oxford: Blackwell Companions to Philosophy, Blackwell Publishing, 1999), 237.

40 Thomas Donaldson, Patricia H. Werhane and Margaret Cording, *Ethical Issues in Business. A philosophical Approach* (Upper Saddle River, New Jersey: Prentice Hall, 2002), 240.

41 Ibid: 240.

42 Michel Capron and Françoise Quairel-Lanoizeelée, *Mythes et réalités de l'entreprise responsable. Acteurs, Enjeux, Stratégies* (Paris: La Decouverte, 2004), 5.

43 Ibid: 6.

44 Ibid: 9.

45 European Commission. Directorate-General for Employment and Social Affairs, Industrial Relations and Industrial Change, Unit EMPL/D.1: *Promoting a European Framework for Corporate Social Responsibility, Green Paper*, July, (Luxembourg: Office for Official Publication of the European Communities, 2001).

46 Simon Zadek, *The Civil Corporation, The New Economy of Corporate Citizenship* (London: Earth Scan, 2001), 110.

47 Ibid: 113.

48 Ibid: 114.

49 See discussion in chapter 5.2.

50 Michel Capron and Françoise Quairel-Lanoizeelée, *Mythes et réalités de l'entreprise responsable. Acteurs, Enjeux, Stratégies* (Paris: La Decouverte, 2004), 31.

51 Calvin M. Boardman and Hideaki Kiyoshi Kato, "The Confucian Roots of Business Kyosei", *Journal of Business Ethics*, Volume 48, (2003), Number 4, 317-333. The article analyzes the roots of the concept of kyosei in ancient Confucian thought. Kyosei has been important for Japaneese codes of ethics in business and for development of concepts of corporate social responsibility and stakeholder dialogue.

52 George Enderle, *International Business Ethics, Challenges and Approaches* (Notre Dame: University of Notre Dame Press, Notre Dame 1999), 43.

53 United Nations, *The Global Compact. Report in Progress and Activities. July 2002-July 2003*, (New York: United Nations Global Compact Office, June 2003).

54 International Labour Organization, *A Guide to Tripartite Declaration of Principles Concerning Multinational Entreprises programme* (Geneva: ILO, 2002).

55 OECD, Les *Principes Directeurs à l'intention des entreprises multinationals* (Paris : OECD, Rapport Annuel, 2002).

56 Michel Capron and Françoise Quairel-Lanoizeelée, *Mythes et réalités de l'entreprise responsable. Acteurs, Enjeux, Stratégies* (Paris: La Decouverte, 2004), 66.

57 Ibid: 93.

58 Ibid: 95. Capron and Quairel-Lanoizeelée refer to the study of J.J. Griffin and J.F. Mahon in which they investigated fifty-one studies from the last twenty-five years. Their study demonstated that twenty studies showed a positive correlation, twenty-two showed a negative correlation, and nine were inconclusive. See J. J. Griffin and J.F. Mahon: "The Corporate Social Performance and Corporate Financial Performance Debate: Twenty Five Years of Incomparable Research", *Business and Society*, Vol. 36. n. 1. 1997, 1-31.

59 Ronald K. Mittchell, Bradley R. Agle and Donna S. Wood, "Toward a Theory of Stakeholder Identification and Salience: Defining the Principle of Who and What really counts", *Academy of Management Review* Vol. 22, (1997), No 4, 853 –886.

60 Antonio Argandona: "The Stakeholder Theory and the Common Good", *Journal of Business Ethics*, (1998) Vol. 17.

61 Michel Capron and Françoise Quairel-Lanoizeelée, *Mythes et réalités de l'entreprise responsable. Acteurs, Enjeux, Stratégies* (Paris: La Decouverte, 2004), 101.

62 Ibid: 105. They refer to the important article of M.C. Suchman: "Managing Legitimacy: Strategic and Institutional Approaches", *Academy of Management Review*, Vol. 20. (1995), no. 3, 572.

63 Capron and Quairel-Lanoizeelée mentions very important articles from institutional theory that help to understand this normative basis for institutional legitimacy of corporate behavior. See for example C. Oliver: "Strategic Response to Institutional Processes", *Academy of Management Review*, Vol 16. (1991), no. 1, 145-179., J. W. Meyer and B. Rowan: "Institutionalized Organizations: Formal Structure as Myth and Ceremony", *American Journal of Sociology*, Vol. 83, (1997), no. 2, 340-363., P. J. Di Maggio and W.W. Powell: "The Iron Cage Revisited: Functional Isomorphism and Collective Rationality in Organizational Fields", *American Journal of Sociology*, no. 48, (1983), 147-160.

64 Michel Capron and Françoise Quairel-Lanoizeelée, *Mythes et réalités de l'entreprise responsable. Acteurs, Enjeux, Stratégies* (Paris: La Decouverte, 2004), 156-157.

65 Ibid: 107.

66 Ibid: 108.

67 John Elkington, *Cannibals with Forks, The Triple Bottom Line of 21st Century Business* (Oxford: Capstone (1997), 1999).

68 Is the metaphor of the triple bottom line really adequate? As mentioned by Norman Wayne and Chris MacDonald, it has become nearly synonymous with CSR linked to sustainable development. To measure the success of CSR on its environmental and social/ethical performance is considered essential for good stakeholder management. In fact, it is interesting that the term was not really used much before the publication of Elkington's book but now has become a triviality. With their critical questions, Wayne and MacDonald help us to be aware of the fundamental problems of measuring CSR. They argue that the metaphor of the triple bottom line cannot really be understood as real measurement, aggregation of value, or maximization of social/environmental profit of performance. Firms cannot really measure their social and environmental bottom line in the same way as they measure economic returns. However, arguments for linking the triple bottom line to CSR are not only economic arguments, but also about convergence, strong social obligation, and transparency. Although it is important to be aware about the fundamental problems with the metaphor, I would not go so far as to argue that the concept is fundamentally misunderstood. It is a concept that allows for a concrete realization of CSR according to the language of business economics. The term is, therefore, not only rhetorical, but important for giving CSR concrete content in corporate practice. It only needs to be explained through the formulation of concrete indicators. For the criticism of the concept of the triple bottom line see Norman Wayne and Chris MacDonald: "Getting to the bottom of the triple bottom line!", *Business Ethics Quarterly*, Volume 14, Issue 2, (2004), 243-262.

69 Michel Capron and Françoise Quairel-Lanoizeelée, *Mythes et réalités de l'entreprise responsable. Acteurs, Enjeux, Stratégies* (Paris: La Decouverte, 2004), 134.

70 Material for this case is mostly selected from the website: Ahold Sustainability Report. www.Ahold.com.. For more case material see: Ray A Goldberg and James M Beagle, "Royal Ahold NV: A Global Food Provider", Harvard Business School Case 902-416. Analysis of the discursive elements of this material is based on Anders Bordum and Jacob Holm Hansen, *Strategisk ledelseskommunikation. Erhvervslivets ledelse med visioner, missioner og værdier*, (Copenhagen: Jurist og Økonomforbundets forlag, 2005).

71 www.Ahold.com

72 Mana Bonnafous-Bocher, "Quelques enjeux philosophiques de la corporate governance: Le propriétisme et la théorie des parties prenantes" (Paris 2004).

73 We will later discuss this more restricted concept of corporate governance as closely linked to improving the business ethics of the different constituencies of the firm. For elaboration of this idea of corporate governance see Robert A. G. Monks and Nell Minow, *Corporate Governance*, Third Edition (Oxford: Blackwell Publishing, 2004).

74 This is explained in earlier chapters.

75 See J. Rosenau and E-O Net Czempiel, *Governance without government, Order and change in world politics*, (Cambrigde: Cambridge University Press, 1992).

76 Ronald K. Mittchell, Bradley R. Agle and Donna S. Wood, "Toward a Theory of Stakeholder Identification and Salience: Defining the Principle of Who and What really counts", *Academy of Management Review*, Vol 22, (1997), No 4, 853 –886, 872.

77 See also our earlier discussion of stakeholder theory.

78 Ronald K. Mittchell, Bradley R. Agle and Donna S. Wood, "Toward a Theory of Stakeholder Identification and Salience: Defining the Principle of Who and What really counts", *Academy of Management Review*, Vol 22, (1997), No 4, 853 –886.

79 Ibid: 876.

80 Andrew Crane and Dirk Matten, *Business Ethics. A European Perspective* (Oxford: Oxford University Press, 2004, 161.

81 Ibid: 161.

82 Ibid: 162.

83 Robert Philips, *Stakeholder Theory and Organizational Ethics*, (San Francisco: Berrett-Koehler, Inc., 2003).

84 The political theory of John Rawls provides an important basis for our view of a just society founded on an ideal theory of justification. Primarily developed and defended in *A Theory of Justice* (Cambridge, Massachusetts: Harvard University Press, 1971), Rawls's conception of justice as fairness is based on two principles as the basic structure of society: 1) the political freedom of all citizens; and 2) the principle of difference, stating that social inequality can only be justified insofar as it is for the benefit of the least advantaged in society. This second principle is Rawls's justification of the freedom and equality of free markets economies, because they contribute to increasing the wealth and income of the least advantaged. I share this view although it may be a very difficult task to decide in concrete circumstances what inequality can be justified as of substantial benefit for the poorest in society. In addition, my emphasis on the need for a communitarian foundation of ethical reflection joins the communitarian criticism of John Rawls as proposed by Michael Sandel. In *Liberalism and the Limits of Justice*, Sandel argues that Rawls cannot work with atomized free floating subjects, but is required to have a theory of the common good and of the self as a participant in society in order to justify his principles of justice. This was the reason why Rawls, in *Political Liberalism* (Cambridge, Massachusetts: Harvard University Press, 1992), restated his view in terms of an "overlapping consensus" between "comprehensive doctrines" as a political view on justice, which does not exclusively rest on a rational metaphysics. In arguing for justice as fairness as the basis of stakeholder dialogue, I rely on this late reinterpretation of the concept of justice, which Rawls develops explicitly in *Justice as fairness. A Restatement* (Cambridge Massachusetts: Harvard University Press, 2001). In this work, Rawls defines justice as fairness as a political conception for a democratic society (p. 21), which develops a system of fair cooperation founded in a reasonably overlapping consensus (p. 33). The two principles of justice are defined as principles for background institutions of a well-ordered society.

85 Robert Philips, *Stakeholder Theory and Organizational Ethics* (San Francisco: Berrett-Koehler, Inc., 2003).

86 Ibid: 28.

87 Ibid: 32.

88 Ibid: 38.

89 Ibid: 49.

90 R. Edward Freeman, "The Politics of Stakeholder Theory: Some Future Directions" in *Business Ethics Quarterly*, (4) 4, 1994, 409-422.

91 Robert Philips, *Stakeholder Theory and Organizational Ethics* (San Francisco: Berrett-Koehler, Inc., 2003), 51.

92 K. E. Goodpaster, "Business Ethics and Stakeholder Analysis", *Business Ethics Quarterly 1* (1), 53-73. Robert Philips, *Stakeholder Theory and Organizational Ethics*, (San Francisco: Berrett-Koehler, Inc., 2003), 69f.

93 Ibid: 86.

94 Ibid: 86. Philips cites an early article of John Rawls, "Legal Obligation and the Duty of Fair Play" in *Law and Philosophy* edited by S. Hook, (New York: New York University Press, 1964).

95 Robert Philips, *Stakeholder Theory and Organizational Ethics* (San Francisco: Berrett-Koehler, Inc., 2003), 116.

96 R. Edward Freeman, "Managing For Stakeholders: An Argument, Ten Principles, and Eight Techniques", Lecture (Copenhagen Business School, November 2004). Also printed in R. Edward and S. R. Velamuri, "A New Approach to CSR: Company Stakeholder Responsibility" in A. Kakabadse and M. Morsing *Corporate Social Responsibility: Reconciling Managerial Strategies Towards the 21st Century* (London: Palgrave MacMillan 2006).

97 Jacob Dahl Rendtorff and Peter Kemp, *Basic Ethical Principles in European Bioethics and Biolaw*, Vol I-II, (Copenhagen and Barcelona: Center for Ethics and Law: 2000). The book was the result of a research project with 22 partners from different European countries. The book was delivered as a report to the European Commission. Kemp and I argued that these concepts should be considered as guiding ideas for a European ethical and legal culture. Even though this book was primarily about protection of the human person in medical and biotech-

nological development, the principles do not apply exclusively to this field and can be used as the basis for stakeholder justice in republican business ethics.

98 Jacob Dahl Rendtorff and Peter Kemp, *Basic Ethical Principles in European Bioethics and Biolaw*, Vol I-II, (Copenhagen and Barcelona: Center for Ethics and Law: 2000), 14.

99 See John Rawls, *A Theory of Justice* (Oxford: Oxford University Press, 1971) and Jürgen Habermas: *Theorie des kommunikativen Handels* I-II, (Frankfurt: Suhrkamp Verlag, 1982). See also R. Edward Freeman: *Strategic Management. A Stakeholder Approach*, (Boston Massachusetts: Pitman Publishing, 1984).

100 Jürgen Habermas: *Faktizität und Geltung* (Frankfurt am Main: Suhrkamp Verlag, 1992).

101 Jacob Dahl Rendtorff and Peter Kemp, *Basic Ethical Principles in European Bioethics and Biolaw*, Vol I-II, (Copenhagen and Barcelona: Center for Ethics and Law: 2000).

102 Ibid.

103 Immanel Kant, *Grundlegung zur Metaphysik der Sitten* (1785) (Hamburg: Felix Meiner Verlag, 1999). Immanuel Kant, *Kritik der praktischen Vernuft* (1784), (Hamburg: Felix Meiner Verlag, 1985).

104 Amartya Sen, *Development as Freedom*, (New York: First Anchor Books Edition, 2000).

105 Ronald Dworkin, *Sovereign Virtue: The Theory and Practice of Equality* (Cambridge Massachusetts: Harvard University Press, 2000).

106 Immanuel Kant, *Grundlegung zur Metaphysik der Sitten* (1785) (Hamburg: Felix Meiner Verlag, 1999). Immanuel Kant, *Kritik der praktischen Vernuft* (1784) (Hamburg: Felix Meiner Verlag, 1985).

107 Kenneth Goodpaster, "Business Ethics and Stakeholder Analysis", *Business Ethics Quarterly*, 1991.

108 Ole Thyssen, *Værdiledelse*, 2. reviderede udgave (Copenhagen: Gyldendal, 1999).

109 Jacob Dahl Rendtorff and Peter Kemp, *Basic Ethical Principles in European Bioethics and Biolaw*, Vol I-II, (Copenhagen and Barcelona: Center for Ethics and Law: 2000).

110 Immanuel Kant, *Grundlegung zur Metaphysik der Sitten* (1785) (Hamburg: Felix Meiner Verlag, 1999).

111 Jean-Paul Sartre, *L'existentialisme est un humanisme* (Paris, Nagel, 1946).

112 Jacob Dahl Rendtorff and Peter Kemp, *Basic Ethical Principles in European Bioethics and Biolaw*, Vol I-II, (Copenhagen and Barcelona: Center for Ethics and Law: 2000).

113 I would like to emphasize that integrity in the cluster of the basic ethical principles is used as a principle guiding stakeholder management, while integrity as a part of a strategy of values-driven management expresses an overall concern for developing corporate citizenship, rather than protecting individuals or groups of stakeholders. The basic ethical principles in conjunction with other ethical principles constitutes, in this way, an integrated part of the overall strategy for organizational integrity and corporate citizenship.

114 Jacob Dahl Rendtorff and Peter Kemp, *Basic Ethical Principles in European Bioethics and Biolaw*, Vol I-II, (Copenhagen and Barcelona: Center for Ethics and Law: 2000).

115 Joseph F. Badaracco and Richard F. Ellsworth, *Leadership and the Quest for Integrity* (Cambridge, Massachusetts: Harvard Business School Press, 1991).

116 Ronald Dworkin, *Law's Empire* (Cambridge, Massachusetts: Harvard University Press, 1986).

117 John R. Boatright, "Does Business Ethics Rests on a Mistake", Presidential Address to the Society of Business Ethics, 1998, reprinted in *Business Ethics Quarterly*, 1999.

118 Dawn-Marie Driscoll and Michael W. Hoffman, *Ethics Matters. How to Implement Values-Driven Management*, Center for Business Ethics (Waltham, Boston: Bentley College 2000).

119 Jacob Dahl Rendtorff and Peter Kemp, *Basic Ethical Principles in European Bioethics and Biolaw*, Vol I-II, (Copenhagen and Barcelona: Center for Ethics and Law: 2000).

120 Emmanuel Lévinas, *Totalité et infini, Essai sur l'extéorité* (La Haye: M. Nijhoff, 1961).

121 Jürgen Habermas, *Theorie des Kommunikativen Handelns I-II* (Frankfurt am Main: Suhrkamp Verlag, 1981).

122 Georges Brenkert, "Marketing for the vulnerable" in *Perspectives in business ethics*, edited by Laura Pincus Hartman, (Chicago: Irwin McGraw-Hill, 1998).

123 Ibid: 517.

124 Patrick E. Murphy, *Eighthy Exemplary Ethics Statements*, Notre Dame: University of Notre Dame Press, 1998, 27. As mentioned, Murphy has done good work in collecting ethics statements from different companies.

125 Patrick E. Murphy, *Eighthy Exemplary Ethics Statements*, Notre Dame: University of Notre Dame Press, 1998, 46. The general principles seek to clarify the spirit of kyosei and human dignity, while the specific stakeholder principles are concerned with their practical application.

126 Ibid: 125

127 Ibid: 141.

128 Ibid: 145.

129 Ibid: 184.

130 Andrew Crane and Dirk Matten, *Business Ethics. A European Perspective* (Oxford: Oxford University Press, 2004), 49.

131 Rogene A. Buchholz and Sandra B. Rosenthal, "Social Responsibility and Business Ethics" in *A Companion to Business Ethics*, edited by Robert E. Frederick, (Oxford: Blackwell Publishing (1999), 2002), 306.

132 William C. Frederick, "From CSR1 to CSR2: The Maturing of Business and Society Thought", *Business and Society, Vol. 33*, August 1994, 155.

133 Ibid: 160.

134 Joseph W. Weiss, *Business Ethics. A Stakeholder and Issues Management Approach,* 3rd Edition (Canada: Thompson, SouthWestern, 2003), 61.

135 Ibid: 54.

136 Ibid: 67.

137 Diane L. Swanson, "Toward an integrative theory of business and society: A research strategy for corporate social performance", *Academy of Management Review* Vol 24 (1999), No 3, 506-521.

2. Ethics of the internal constituencies of the corporation

Based on the previous discussion of corporate citizenship, corporate social responsibility, corporate governance, and basic ethical principles, we are now able to look more closely at the internal constituencies of the firm. In this context, it is mostly values of economizing and power-aggrandizing which are relevant. These values must, however, be related to the ethical values of the firm. The problem becomes how to conceive the ethics of the firm in relation to the internal constituencies and stakeholders of the organization. There are roughly the following categories of internal constituencies, which are important for the development of the firm: managers, shareholders and owners, and the employees at the workplace.

The relationships between these different internal constituencies will be analyzed from the perspective of basic ethical principles and in framework of sustainability, responsibility, solidarity, and justice (fairness), and addressing the theory of corporate citizenship as corporate responsiveness. These ethical principles, located between community virtues and universal principles, will be related to the original power-aggrandizing, economizing, and ecologizing values of the firm. The tension between economic rationality and ethical rationality, which is often present regarding the ethics of the internal constituencies of the firm, will be investigated.

The internal constituencies of corporate executives, owners and shareholders, and managers and employees hold primary interest in the firm, and they are important for the development and conceptualization of values-driven management. The stakeholders will be related to the theory of the firm and some of the concrete fields of business ethics. It is the aim of the following chapter to analyze values-driven management from the perspective of internal stakeholders. The chapter has five subheadings: 1) internal constituencies and the theory of the firm; 2) corporate governance between shareholders and stakeholders; 3) ownership and shareholders: the ethics of finance; 4) shareholder ethics: socially responsible investments; and 5) ethics in the workplace: management and employees.

2.1. Internal constituencies and the theory of the firm

In this context, autonomy may be considered to be the dominant value in the theory of the firm, which is based on the idea of autonomous rational action. An ethical vision of corporate citizenship is proposed that is based on stakeholder theory, integrated contract theory, and the four ethical principles. This discussion begins by examing the extent to which this theory may be compatible with the prevailing economic contract theory of the firm. It concludes by asserting that though they can be combined in principle, there is a fundamental tension between contract theory and the ethical vision of the firm.

From the perspective of the dominant theory of finance, business is understood as the game of wealth maximizing individuals. One theory of the firm is the finance paradigm.[1] The dominant rationality in finance is an instrumental rationality based on individual maximization of interests and profits. In this finance paradigm, the firm is based on property rights and contractual agreements. The shareholders are considered as primary stakeholders because they take economic risk and put money into the corporation. The aim of the corporation is to maximize shareholder wealth. Management has to be fiduciary to stakeholders. Both European and American law support the property right theory of the corporation. The famous 1919 American Supreme Court decision, Dodge vs. Ford Motor Company, stated that Ford had a duty to pay dividends to its shareholders.[2] The premise was that the shareholders were the owners of the corporation that had decision-making rights.

It may be argued that shareholders cannot have absolute power over the corporation. Today, shareholders are a heterogeneous group with, in many cases, very little involvement in the corporation. Moreover, separation between ownership and management challenges the idea of absolute ownership. Indeed, it could be argued that the fiduciary duties of management should be broader.[3] In many cases, the risks to shareholders are very low and this seems to be a weak argument for their primary influence. Moreover, long-term profit maximization may exclude short-term shareholder value. It is the objective of the firm to contribute to economic efficiency at the market, but this may imply concerns other than total shareholder loyalty.

The concept of rationality in the dominant financial paradigm is questionable, and is susceptible to a communitarian criticism of the ideal of rational profit maximization of individual agents.[4] According to this critique, the market should fundamentally be conceived as a social system. Individuals act in a social context determined by bounded rationality. The market is structured by fundamental social ties. These intersubjective dimensions are not limitations of economic competition, but rather basic conditions for good economic systems. The economic system cannot be separated from other political and social aspects of society.[5] Individual autonomy cannot be totally separated from the idea of moral sentiment based on a broader concept of rationality. The firm should be considered as a social institution based in a historical and cultural context.

Economic rationality may be linked with the concept of virtue in such a way that it cannot be separated from the idea of financial rationality.[6] This implies a challenge to the rationality of the traditional economic theory of the firm, which considers the firm as the consequence of economic actions on markets. Basing a counter argument on this challenge to economic rationality, we might say that the firm cannot be consistently considered as a tool for opportunistic wealth maximization. This implies a criticism of the idea that the firm is a "black box" with no relation to the environment that can be used as an instrumental tool for profit maximization in a perfect economic market. The effects of culture and bounded rationality on the formation of the structure of the firm must be taken into account.

In fact, the classical theory of the firm took this into consideration, which led to the *transactions cost theory* of the firm. This led to a different form of the traditional property rights financial paradigm. Many economic thinkers have struggled with the problem of why firms exist in imperfect markets. Ronald Coase came up with the definition of the firm as a "contractual nexus" in his famous article from 1937 about why firms exist.[7] Coase presented an economic approach to social institutions and organizations. If the market had been perfect, there would have been no need for firms to do transactions, but since the market is not perfect agents use firms in order to minimize transactions costs. The transaction costs necessary for producing, buying, and selling at actual markets have made firms the most effective way for individuals to act on actual economic markets.

Michael Jensen presents a theory of the firm, which follows-up on Coase's definition. Jensen defines firms as "legal fictions," which serve as a nexus for a set of contracting relations among atomistic individuals that acts at markets.[8] This theory tends, however, to abstract from the conception of the firm as a meeting point of conflicts of interest. The firm should be viewed rather as a contractual nexus among different interests. In this context, overlapping interest, claims, and objectives between different stakeholders, customers, employees, management, shareholders meet in the firm.[9] In order to really promote a contractual understanding of the firm, it must be seen as a nexus of both informal and formal contractual relations. There may be explicit legal enforcement of contracts, but implicit enforcement may also be encoutered.

John Boatright has proposed a modified version of Coase's theory of the firm, which tries to promote a broader concept of relevant contractors.[10] Boatright is also critical of the definition of the firm as a device for obtaining individual profit maximization. Boatright gives a pluralistic interpretation of the idea of the firm as an institution where different contractors meet. According to this view, the firm is a nexus of contracts between not only shareholders, but includes a broader amount of corporate constituencies. Different groups, investors, suppliers, customers, managers are all considered as contractors of the firm and actors who seek economic benefits of their relations to the firm.

From this perspective, it is not a priori certain that the firm has primary obligations to shareholders. The other constituencies of the firm may have greater contractual ties to the corporation and it is not certain that shareholders are the most important residual risk takers. This contractual conception of the firm is critical towards the idea that the corporation is the property of shareholders. Shareholders are nothing other than people who have put money in the corporation, but this does not entitle them to anything beyond what people holding contractual rights receive. They are not owners in any strict sense of the word.[11] The contractual theory of the firm sits uneasily with the idea that the corporation is, first and foremost, a social institution that serves the good of society. Society is simply one of the important contractors of the firm.

Even if a number of cases have supported the idea that companies have prior responsibility to shareholders, the legal definition of the firm helps to challenge the monistic concept of fiduciary responsibility to shareholders, because the firm is considered as an independent legal subject with specific rights and responsibilities. From the perspective of bounded rationality, shareholders may have an interest in respecting other stakeholders as management and employees. Therefore, it seems possible to overcome a sharp opposition between stakeholder theory and shareholder theory in the definition of the firm, because stakeholder interests in many cases can be considered as long-term shareholder interests. Defending stakeholder management, an extended version of contract theory, which includes stakeholder relations, may be formulated. In this inclusive perspective of integration of stakeholder theory in contract theory, it is argued that, in principle, an opposition between shareholders, management, and other internal stakeholders does not have to exist. This perspective not only recognizes property rights as contracts, but posits a contract theory that is able to include contractors other than owners.[12]

Contract theory can include both explicit and implicit contracts as a part of transaction costs. Moreover, the firm can be said to engage in implicit contracts with the local community, customers, employees, and so forth, which also implies specific transaction costs. Even though these contracts are not perfect, it cannot be denied that stakeholder relations may be conceived as a form of extended contract relations. Such a marriage between stakeholder theory and contract theory is not always without tensions, because different contractors have different interest in the development of the firm. It is important to be aware of the ethical problems of contract theory. It may focus too much on internal efficiency of the firm.[13] Nevertheless, this is also an advantage of contract theory, because it can extend the traditional concept of the firm without totally abandoning the economic perspective. Contract theory may be the bridge between the narrow property-based conception of the firm, and a more comprehensive stakeholder theoretical perspective.

The important question is whether it is possible to unite contract and stakeholder perspectives on the firm. In the argument for ethical principles and corporate citizenship this is very important. It is clear that stakeholder theory goes beyond the property view of the corporation because it defines stakeholders as "any group or individual who can affect or is affected by the corporation"; however, stakeholder theory also proposes a strategic and utilitarian perspective on corporate governance.[14] This more narrow definition of stakeholders of the corporation includes those groups who are vital to the survival and success of the corporation, and is very close to the contractual approach to corporate governance.

Without a balanced account of stakeholders, the survival of the corporation will be at risk. Instead of exclusive focus on shareholder interest, stakeholder theory is focused on fair management and equilibrium among the stakeholders. From the perspective of this understanding of internal stakeholders, it seems possible to create a bridge between stakeholder theory and the contractual view of the firm. Contract theory aims at integrating different stakeholders in the contractual conception of the firm; however, the problem is whether such a theoretical move will imply abandoning the idea of transaction cost theory. It may be argued that integrating contract theory and stakeholder theory overcomes a strict utilitarian understanding of the firm, and changes the traditional financial paradigm. Even though it seems possible to give stakeholder theory meaning from the perspective of integrated social contract theory, there is a potential conflict between pluralistic and monistic concepts of the firm. This potential conflic expresses the confrontation between an economic and moral view of the firm.[15]

The financial paradigm of contractual relations does not leave room for much ethics in its conception of the individual action of wealth maximization. The financial agency theory argues that ethical principles and the idea of trust have no value in themselves but should be considered from the perspective of economic strategic behavior.[16] Agency theory operates with two basic kinds of strategic behavior: *adverse selection* (i.e., bad results due to information asymmetry) and the concept of *opportunistic* behavior. These problems of adverse selection and moral hazards are often dependent on lack of information and the encounter of new trade partners. It is argued that contracts depend on these kinds of behavior. Individuals calculate trust and contracts on the basis of earlier experiences and bounded rationality. In game theory, agents may chose a "tit for tat" strategy where cooperation depends on the counterparts cooperation. This is the strategy envisioned by David Gauthier, based on "morals by agreement."[17] When trust is founded on this strategic choice, reputation becomes a major basis for the success of cooperation. A good reputation or company brand would enforce the willingness of other agents and firms to engage with the firm in contractual relations.

The question to ask is whether reputation is enough to avoid moral hazards and if a firm's success in financial markets can exclusively be based on a strategic concept of reputation. I argue that the concern for ethics at financial markets comes from the fact that reputation cannot be understood solely on the basis of strategic behavior. Reputation seems to be based on internal ethical culture. This culture could be founded on a code of ethics, and a conception of fairness and good judgments at financial markets. In order to overcome the vulnerabilities of strategic behavior, it is necessary to establish internal standards of ethics that improve the basis for the reputation of the firm. Establishing a firm's ethical behavior constitutes an effort to create virtuous agents that are acting beyond motives of strategic rationality and utility. This is done in order to create an atmosphere of accountability in the firm, whereby the establishment of trust on an international scale is seen as a value intrinsic in the corporation.[18] Put differently, the firm is considered as a community that builds an atmosphere of trust and excellence through virtue. [19]

Case 11. From Protestant Ethics to Social Responsibility: The Case of Maersk

The Danish shipping firm, Maersk Line, may be said to have relied on the traditional Protestant values and ethics that are the foundation of liberal economics. The philosophy of the firm – which has become one of the world's largest shipping companies – was defined with the words of the founder A.P. Møller, who wrote to his son during the Second World War: "No loss should hit us, which could be avoided with constant care".[20]

These words express the concern that the worker should be devoted to the company and act dutifully in accomplishing her life's vocation. The image of vocation, dutifulness, and devotion (which Weber emphasized as essential to Protestant ethics) have been a part of the myth of the company and of the present owner, Maersk McKinney Møller, who has proved to be a paternalistic, conservative leader, devoted to the traditional values of Danish society: God, kingdom, and patrimony. Møller's donation of 2.5 billion Danish crowns toward building a new opera house in Copenhagen could also be seen as an expression of these Protestant virtues, in the sense that Møller's donation appeared to be an expression of his devotion and respect to God and country, and the desire to be remembered as a good and generous citizen.

It is arguable that recent ideas of corporate social responsibility, corporate governance, sustainability, and business ethics express a revival of some of these themes. The renewed focus on values and ethics in this age of increased liberalization, globalization, and privatization might be defined as a "new spirit of capitalism," replacing but also revitalizing the spirit of the Protestant ethics. It was the concept of "constant care" that characterized the classic paternalistic corporate director and manager who was determined by a deep sense of duty and conscience about his (and it was almost always a 'he') responsibility for his dependents (e.g., employees, customers, and suppliers). This was an ideal of virtue based on strong integrity, which was supposed to limit personal greed and place concern for integrity and responsibility in the center of corporate strategy and mission.

In fact, looking at the self-representation of Maersk Line it is clear that the concept of constant care has been reinterpreted. In 2006, the company stated that constant care implies a strong dedication to promote the health and safety of employees and others in the industry and in the world around us.[21] Moreover, constant care is considered as central to the company's environmental policy, as in this example for the firm's website: "Maersk Line is committed to the protection and conservation of the environment and places high priority on environmental considerations in managing its business. . . .", "We aim to ensure that all our global operations are managed responsibly with respect for the world around us. Our education and training programmes include environmental sensitivity and awareness. We engage in many initiatives to protect the environment; whether it is onboard a ship or on land."[22]

Accordingly, in times of sustainability and corporate social responsibility, constant care is reinterpreted from the perspective of the corporation as a good citizen. In this sense, constant care is closely linked to integrity and the conception of the firm as a contributor to the common good in community.

2.2. Corporate Governance: Between shareholders and stakeholders

As previously described, there is a close relationship between good corporate citizenship, corporate social responsibility, and corporate governance. Corporate governance based on CSR implies that that the board and central management acknowledge their responsiblility for good corporate governance, based on concern for fairness as stakeholder justice and respect for the ethical principles of autonomy, dignity, integrity, and vulnerability. Good corporate governance implies a program for values-driven management, ethics, or compliance that relates to the stakeholders of the corporation. However, there are also important economic arguments for improving corporate governance. In light of economic theory, corporate governance is first of all about creating efficient structures of governance for the firm. It is argued that the system of modern capitalism and the economic institutions of market economies are, in order to encourage efficiency, providing necessary reductions of transaction cost for economic actions. There are firms with governance structures and shareholders, simply because it is the most efficient way to provide the basis for economic progress in society. This is the position of Boatright, who wants to justify the exclusive and decisive role of the shareholder from this economic perspective.[23]

Inspired by the transaction cost theories, both Coase and Boatright argue that the firm is a hierarchy of contracts and a structured system of authority relations. Shareholders are in a principal-agent situation, in which the corporate board makes decisions for the shareholders. Shareholders take risks because they have asymmetric and incomplete information.[24] In modern society, shareholders are not to be conceived directly as owners, but rather as important contractors with certain rights. Corporate governance and fiduciary duties to shareholders are justified from this perspective, and corporate law provides the necessary justification for shareholders within the framework of economic contracts.

Boatright defends this form of governance, even though a system where ownership and influence are based on economic investment may seem undemocratic from a strictly political perspective. The economic argument for the efficiency of governance structures is based on the evolution of corporate law, which has implied a trial-and-error process of searching for the most efficient form of corporate governance.[25]

Even though I have defended the importance of stakeholder theory and a broader view of economic rationality, within the present economic system, it is important to protect the role of the shareholder regarding corporate governance. Transparency and stability of corporate governance is a condition for healthy economic markets, because shareholders should have clear knowledge about risk behavior, but this also necessitates that shareholders take their roles as stakeholders seriously and are conscious about their rights and possibilities of control.[26]

Many of the recent debates in European countries are due to the perceived separation of shareholders as owners and the executive managers and boards of many corporations. The potential conflict between shareholders and managers concerning returns and aims of the corporations has, after the collapse of companies like Enron and WorldCom, become an even hotter topic in business debates.

The ethics of corporate governance is about defining and following the duties of the corporate board and directors towards the shareholders. The duties of managers to shareholders are fiduciary, and to work for their interest; however, given the importance of corporate citizenship and of other stakeholders, it is important to argue that the ethics of corporate governance is not restricted to shareholders, but should be included in the broader perspective of stakeholder management.

Corporate governance, in a restricted organizational sense, is the process by which the board and shareholders formulate the goals and strategies of the firm, and in which shareholders can participate by sanctioning and supervising the decisions of the board. In a broader sense, this would include decision-making regarding stakeholder claims.[27] The principal-agent problem is one of the major reasons for the need for an ethics of corporate governance. Shareholders need some measures for controlling the corporate board and securing that managers do not follow their own interests with regard to company salaries, strategies, and goals. There may, for example, be strong conflicts of interest between managers and shareholders, but also with other stakeholders.

In order to create such an ethics, which primarily protects shareholders but also ensures efficient management and openness to stakeholder interests, the United States and many European countries have worked with formulating codes of corporate governance. These codes reflect different national cultures regarding corporate law and organizational ownership structures. There are, for example, differences between companies that are primarily owned by a number of different and dispersed shareholders and companies that are owned by few very strong shareholders who, in close networks, have for many years decided over the strategy of the firm. In firms with changing ownership there may be more focus on immediate returns, but management may also be rather free to decide over the policies of the firm, while family-owned companies with a few strong shareholders may have long-term strategies for financing the firm.

In this context, the ethics of corporate governance is about creating structures of transparency and control, which ensure that management delivers a competent contribution to leadership. The ethical aspect of corporate governance is the debate about how to deliver governance structures that contribute to controlling the shareholder's board. It is important to formulate some kind of structure, whereby external bodies can supervise the activities of the board. This task may involve setting up nonexecutive boards or directors who can control managers and board members.[28] Members of such external bodies should have some degree of neutrality with regard to the corporation in order to be objective in evaluating corporate decision-making.

Such a program for integrating business ethics and corporate governance may be based on international guidelines and rules about CSR and the triple bottom line.[29] These are based on the principles of sustainability, respect for human rights, and concern for people, the planet, and profit (the "three Ps"). Concrete strategies and policies for corporate governance emerge from these principles. The following issues may be addressed as a part of good corporate governance:

- What are the rights of shareholders and will they be respected?
- How high are the salaries of corporate directors and managers? Are they too high?
- What is the constituency of the board? Is the board professional and without conflict of interest? How does accounting function and who is in control of accounts? Is it done on an objective and independent basis?
- How are top managers elected? Is it done professionally?
- Are accounting practices and reporting accountable?

- Do the stakeholders of the firm participate in financial decision-making? Are they informed about it? Does the corporation have the relevant compliance and ethics programs?
- Are external and internal investors professional and does the corporation follow their recommendations?
- Does the corporation regularly communicate its reports and accounts?
- Does the leadership have a strategy of triple bottom line management?
- Does the corporation discuss the relation between shareholders and other stakeholders?

The international preoccupation with formulating codes of corporate governance is based on combining ethical concerns for shareholders, but also more broadly for other stakeholders of the firm, with economic concerns for efficiency and economic excellence. Although this formulation has not been primarily on the legislative level, but rather at the level of interest organizations and of corporate self-regulation, it is an important contribution to the institutionalization of ethical values in economic markets.

These values codes and principles also express combined procedural and substantial principles for corporate conduct. Procedural recommendations for good corporate governance include issues such as the regulation of the size and structure of the board, proposing boards of independent supervisors and non-executive directors who meet regularly, advocating for the rights and influence of employees in corporate governance, disclosing executive payments, ensuring meeting participation and voting, and retaining independent supervising and auditing bodies in order to ensure transparency of corporate action.

As mentioned previously, it is important to extend reflections on corporate governance and the formulation of future codes of corporate governance beyond shareholders to include relations to other stakeholders. These other stakeholders cannot be excluded when dealing with political issues of the firm. Active shareholders might be interested in substantial ethical aspects of corporate governance such as employee human rights, the strategies of suppliers, and contributing to protecting the environment. Codes of best practices cannot exclude such issues in a global liberal market where ethics has become an element of competition and investment.

Accordingly, good corporate governance is about finding ethical and legal structures that contribute to the professionalization of the board and that ensure a sustainable long-term strategy. We can conceive a convergence between a general political notion of governance and corporate governance in a more technical sense.[30] This might include oversight of a firm's strategy and development. This oversight of top management should not be reduced to risk management, but should be built on broader concerns for good governance. There is a close link between the general concept of corporate governance based on good corporate citizenship and CSR, and the implementation of corporate governance in the daily practice of the firm. In this practice, it is important to solidify the operation of a professional and responsible board. This may include:

- strategies for ensuring the independence of board members, such as including directors from both outside and inside the firm as members of the board;
- encouraging close communication between board members and senior management;
- promoting close relations between board members and other important authorities of the corporation, such as audit and other review committees;
- controlling the compensation and salaries of high level managers;
- actively contributing to the formulation of corporate strategy and policies;
- actively preparing for board meetings and regular meetings with senior management;
- working on formulating long-term strategies, including corporate vision, mission, and values;
- periodical review of performance and work by board members and senior management;
- efforts to avoid engaging board members who do not actively participate; and integrating business ethics and corporate social responsibility in board activities.

In this context, the function of corporate governance may be summarized as a general effort to empower the board.[31] A firm's work for corporate governance should empower it to develop with a focus on ethics and corporate social responsibility. Business managers have, however, different attitudes regarding the development of corporate governance.[32] Although business leaders generally approve of good morality and ethics in board management, they are somewhat sceptical of the many rules and bureaucratic procedures that may have the opposite effect of making management less efficient. Consequently, some board members and managers worry about more legislation on the management relations of the firm. They insist that legislation and rules are not enough to improve the relations of governance.[33] Critical voices also argue that international reports on corporate governance, like the British Cadbury report from 1992, are too bureaucratic and do not adequately capture the problem of good governance.

Of course, these worries are not shared by all managers and board members. Others argue that corporations need professional boards due to the globalization of business activities. They emphasize that there is a close relation between ethics, CSR, and good corporate governance. From this perspective, it is wrong to limit corporate governance to the issue of the relationship between owners and management, because increasing focus on the social legitimacy of the corporation indicates a close relationship between corporate governance, corporate citizenship, and corporate social responsibility in the future. The development of new external and internal forms of governance is important to improve the competitive ability of the corporation. Good ownership is important and this may be improved with the rules of corporate governance. In this context, the values of transparency, openness, integrity, and fairness should be emphasized as important for good corporate governance. Moreover, the communication of such standards of good corporate governance is important in order to create relations of trust in the corporation.[34] This applies also to relations with society. It is, thus, an essential element of corporate communication with external and internal stakeholders.

Two concrete recommendations for linking corporate governance with ethics and social responsibility include 1) efforts of the board and top management to work for good corporate citizenship and 2) stakeholder management. Stakeholder management can be implemented through a program for values-driven management ethics or one of compliance that includes different stakeholders of the firm. Such programs must be formulated in accordance with international guidelines and rules about corporate social responsibility and triple bottom-line management, based on concern for the three Ps. On this basis, the firm formulates concrete strategy and policy plans for further development of the firm. Good corporate governance implies fair concern and respect for the important principles of stakeholder management and organizational fairness.

Case 12. Norsk Hydro: Oil and global corporate governance

Norsk Hydro is one of Norway's largest companies and one of the world's largest producers of gas and oil from the sea. The company is a member of CSR Europe and the case of Norsk Hydro is an illustration of a company making an *ethical effort* to promote good corporate citizenship.

In 2002, Norsk Hydro had a turnover of more than twenty billion euros. The company had more than 50,000 employees worldwide. For over thirty years, the company has been producing oil in the North Sea. More recently it has engaged in developing wind power and producing hydrogen for energy purposes. In addition, the company is a large producer of aluminium for the car industry and other purposes. Working with natural resources means a responsibility for their effective and environmentally conscious use.

Contrary to the Shell Corporation, Norsk Hydro has managed to avoid great scandals in the North Sea or in other parts of the world. This may be a byproduct of the firm's close collaboration with the Norwegian state, which has, since its inception, promoted the link between the creation of economic and social responsibility. The firm promotes its activities as concentrated on value for customers and local community.[35]

In the company's value statement, it proposes a discursive self-representation with the vision of "creating a better and more vital society through innovative development of natural resources and products." The basic values of the company are courage, respect, collaboration, and the ability to look forward.[36] The company agrees with the idea that real value-creation includes the creation of values for all "its stakeholders and society as a whole." The company wants to protect the environment, improve quality of life and economic stability, find new ways to make resources useful, and respect safety and the value of human life in order to create a more "vital society." In this context, the company stresses its efforts to work for a responsible use of natural resource with respect for nature and the environment.

In the company's statement of its social responsibility principles, the purpose of the firm is described as "sustainable value-creation for our shareholders, other stakeholders, and the communities where we operate."[37] The pursuit of opportunities should be combined with risk management, taking into account social impact of the operations of the company. As basic principles of corporate social responsibility, Norsk Hydro mentions: respect for human rights, contributing to sustainability, diversity, dialogue, and integrity. The policies on corporate social responsibility are carried out by reporting of social impact, developing knowledge of corporate social responsibility, anticipating issues, assessing social impacts, and investing in the community.

Moreover, the company developed a program of ethics and compliance.[38] The ethics principles include making management responsible to the organization's ethics rules, requiring mutual respect among employees, prohibiting drugs, optimizing equal opportunities, stressing integrity in conflicts of interest, prohibiting bribery (although donations are accepted in accordance with local traditions), promoting responsible investment in other companies by employees, disallowing donations of money to political organizations, and protecting confidential information.

In addition, Norsk Hydro has developed policies on biodiversity, health, and values-driven management. The company represents an effort to appear as a responsible corporate citizen in the international community.

2.3. Ownership and shareholders: Ethics of finance

The ethics of finance covers the field of corporate finance – including financial markets, financial services, and financial management[39] – and is one of the basic aspects of the theory of the firm. It is concerned with central issues of ownership, shareholders, and economic control over money and corporations. Indeed, ethics of finance can be considered as a kind of integrated social contract theory. Finance ethics is a good example of the tension between shareholders and stakeholders in relation to the firm and clearly shows the need to use corporate governance in order to find a bridge between the shareholder contract conception and stakeholder view of the firm. Financial professions have fiduciary duties towards their clients and firms may have implicit contracts with different stakeholders. The market is structured according to the gain and efficiency for shareholders, but at the same time a number of other stakeholders must be respected. Furthermore, financial transactions must be based on basic rules of fairness and equity. Financial markets are characterized by a fundamental tension between economic efficiency, respect for different contractors, and the need to accept basic ethical principles.

Worldwide, financial markets do not have reputations for ethical behavior. There is constantly news about financial scandals due to fraud, manipulation, or unreliable investment behavior. Some brokers have acted in ways that threaten the whole market and the existence of good companies. Moreover, the workings of financial markets appear to render business ethics an oxymoron. This may also be seen as one of the reasons why ethics in financial markets is necessary. These ethical problems include issues of legal compliance, fairness in contractual obligations, rules of confidentiality in making contracts, and general issues of codes of ethics for the finance profession. Finance ethics can be viewed as the basis for self-regulation and development of proper values-driven management for the finance industry. Values and ethics for finance are, indeed, very important since this industry constitutes the basis of the development of a capitalist economy.

Finance ethics concerns the most fundamental ethical principles of buying and selling corporations, money, and other financial products at financial markets. In this context, financial ethics is first and foremost about developing fair and just trading practices when acting on financial markets. This includes clarification of fiduciary duties and obligations of traders due to implicit or explicit contracts with different stakeholders. The ethics of contracts includes revealing all relevant information on the parties to the contract and defining possible sanctions in the future when one of the parties in the contract fails to keep its obligations. As a nexus of contracts, financial firms have to balance the interests of competing stakeholders and determine specific obligations when making financial contracts with specific individuals and institutions.

Accordingly, finance ethics covers a wide range of contractual arrangements and deals. It addresses the ethical activities of investment firms, banks, institutional investors, and the behavior of individual shareholders in the firm. The financial services industry gives capital to different firms to develop their activities, but finance also includes all the activities of investors in financial markets and the professional services offered by financial companies to individual clients. In this context, broker firms often have the reputation for misleading individual investors and withholding information about stocks. They might even lie or perform deceptive practices to their own advantage. An important dimension of fairness in financial markets is, therefore, the demand for full disclosure of information. Moreover, brokers should avoid other kinds of excessive practices, for example trading that does not benefit the client, multiple changes in order to get higher commissions, or concealing the risks involved with specific financial operations.[40] These requirements for fair trading practices and client interactions act as a general standard for the integrity of financial products, so that they are fairly priced and meet the general standards of the market.[41]

Finance ethics is a central part of business ethics because it concerns the most fundamental issues of corporate governance. Financial management is the legal key to corporate ownership in situations where different shareholders have power relative to their share holdings. Finance ethics is, therefore, about the relation between shareholders and firms. In modern economies, institutional investors are becoming increasingly influential in financial markets. Moreover, employees and managers may have shares and investments in their companies. Individual shareholders sometimes want to take part of the management of corporations. In all these cases, the tensions between shareholders, trading, and investment may include ethical dilemmas of fair transactions, conflicts of interest, and deceptive actions or practices for personal gain by financial companies. In addition, the availability of money for personal loans and investments is also a condition for survival in modern society. Abuse of individuals, for example through racial and social discrimination with regard to access to bank loans, may be considered as an example of lack of fairness in financial systems.

The problem of finance and corporate governance is becoming more important because of the increasing power of institutional investors. In many cases, these investors want to have direct influence on management decisions. They also want to promote certain values and policies for the company. While individual shareholders have tended to be more passive, institutional investors assume a much more active role in corporate governance. However, finance ethics also includes the ethical behavior of investments firms in financial markets.[42] Many ethical issues emerge among different actors on financial markets, which have important consequences for the structure of the market and the possibility to develop a more just, stable, and ethical economy.

It is a good approach to the theoretical basis of finance ethics to conceive it in tension between issues of fairness, integrity, and equity on the one hand and problems of market efficiency and necessary cost-benefits on the other. From this perspective, it is the aim of the basic ethical principles in finance to establish a framework for conceiving fairness in financial markets. This implies clarification of the interests, rights, and duties of actors in financial relations.[43] These dimensions should be based on the concept of integrated social contract theory, combined with relevant concerns and fiduciary duties for stakeholders of the finance industry and corporations in financial markets.

The relationship of finance, ethics and corporate governance is important in situations of bankruptcy, mergers, or hostile takeovers. Here, financial decisions influence the very existence of the firm, and they have strong impact on the different stakeholders of the corporation. Bankruptcy involves many ethical and legal problems. In economics, the concept of bankruptcy is a natural feature of economic markets. The corporate financial failure is considered as a necessary byproduct of market social Darwinism (i.e., survival of the fittest). This utilitarian perspective is, in many cases, accompanied by blaming the moral failure of management and employees. In many countries bankruptcy legislation has been enacted to protect the corporation from total destruction by the demands of creditors. In this way, bankruptcy has been proposed as a vision for restructuring of the corporation.

When creative managers use bankruptcy as a strategic tool for overcoming organizational crises, this poses an ethical problem. Instead of helping good companies to reorganize, in some situations, management may use bankruptcy to increase profits or empty the company of money. In other situations, corporations may consider bankruptcy as one of many strategic choices to overcome bad situations.[44] In such cases, management may also use the law to avoid a problematic legal situation. For example, take the case of the Johns-Manville Corporation. Although not insolvent, in 1982 the company declared bankruptcy in order to avoid a large number of legal suits from people who became ill from the company's main product, asbestos. Even though many people view the strategic use of bankruptcy legislation skeptically, it should be emphasized that the declaration of bankruptcy implies serious economic consequences for a corporation. The ethics of bankruptcy can be seen as a very good example of the need to find the necessary balance between efficiency and fairness, which is very important in business ethics.[45]

This should also be the case with the ethics of mergers, or hostile takeovers. A hostile takeover is defined as the acquisition of a company that is opposed by the management of the target corporation.[46] Although they are not the only kind of restructuring, which includes friendly mergers, liquidations, or other restructuring, hostile takeovers reveal very sharply the dilemmas of relations between shareholders and other stakeholders. Hostile takeovers challenge the relation to existing management and employees because the majority of shares are sold to new shareholders that represent a potential threat to other stakeholder interests. There have been waves of hostile takeovers in many countries oer the last twenty years, and while many consider them unfair and unjust some economists defend hostile takeovers as necessary for dynamic markets.[47] Hostile takeovers show the limits of a property-based view of the firm, because there is no possibility of arguing against any efforts by new management to destroy the company.

From the perspective of a contract-based, stakeholder-inclusive view of the company there is, however, a limit to the ethical acceptability of such takeovers. In many cases, it would be required that takeovers involve fairness to stakeholders and management approval. Many countries have established securities regulations, which determine some of the basic legal issues of the relation between fairness and efficiency in financial markets. Echoing John Boatright, fairness can be defined as the external regulation of efficiency in order to create just and moral markets. In order for this definition to work, the potential conflict between efficiency and fairness must be acknowledged.

It may be argued that the basic ethical principles and justice-as-fairness are necessary in financial markets in order to secure their ethical functioning.[48] In this context, fairness is introduced to protect the interests of the common good and the state in situations where economic speculation goes beyond a society's reasonable capital development. The best example of this need for finance ethics based on fairness is the crash of the American stock market in 1929 and the subsequent world depression. The ultimate aim of finance ethics is to avoid unjust speculation and corruption in financial markets. Although fairness is a very general term, three important dimensions of fairness in financial markets give general directions for the application of ethical principles in finance: 1) fraud and manipulation, 2) inequalities in information and bargaining power, and 3) inefficient pricing.

With regard to fraud and manipulation, it may be evident that deceptive practices do not respect the rules of market economics. It is clear that stock trading should not be based on manipulation of the customer. Moreover, it is often emphasized that equal access to information is a necessary condition for equal trading in markets. Asymmetrical market information makes financial transactions unfair. This is the reason why insider trading could be considered as wrongful not only from a legal, but also from an ethical standpoint. Still, access to information is different from the ability to use such information. Finance markets allow differences in the ability of investors to use and make decisions on the basis of acquired information. This is considered as an element of fair competition. Indeed, competition is also present in the process of bargaining for economic contracts and deals. Even though access to information and voluntary agreements without coercion are necessary conditions for fairness of negotiation, unequal bargaining power remains an aspect of the idea of fairness in stock trading and financial services.

The inequality of resources, processing abilities, and other differences between securities firms and individual shareholders are realities in the transactions of economic markets. Even though the finance job, as a part of the free market, has historically been conceived as a task for the common investor, financial markets are so specialized today that the job has become a professional activity. Indeed, the professionalization of knowledge accentuates these differences, while simultaneously increasing the responsibilities of the finance profession. In this context, an important part of professional fairness would be to refrain from inefficient pricing and to stick to the profession's fiduciary duties to customers. The need for values-driven management in the finance profession may be considered as a part of professional ethics, as in the case of other professional groups like lawyers or doctors, where specialized knowledge leads to the establishment of a high degree of organization and self-regulation.[49] Certainly, professions are thought to follow specific codes of conduct and to be aware of their general responsibility to society. In this context, the need for a code of conduct securing fairness in financial markets is very important.

In financial services, such a code of conduct should ensure fair sales practices. It is also important that financial agents do not deceive customers. The rationality of sales is that both buyer and seller are able to make a fair choice in the transaction process. This is an argument against abusive practices where the seller engages in unjust pricing, takes too large a fee from the client, or keeps offering evermore expensive services to the client without giving him or her any benefits of the transaction. This also includes systematic malpractice, such as the case of brokerage firms who get increased economic advantages on behalf of their clients. Moreover, a code of ethics for the finance profession should propose fair regulation of the difficult problem of personal trading among employees of financial services firms. Some argue that an employee will unavoidably abuse their knowledge and position in their own interests and that a ban on personal trading for employees of huge mutual funds or investment firms would, therefore, be reasonable. On the contrary, it is also argued that regulation is difficult to implement, and that many investors are still able to distinguish between personal and professional trading of stocks and securities.

A code of conduct for finance should further address insider trading, which is closely linked to personal trading by employees in financial services firms. Insider trading is defined as trading that is made on the basis of nonpublic, or insider, information. In this context, the trader violates both legal and ethical principles. The trader has misused the fiduciary trust; thus, insider trading is unfair because nonpublic information is used to gain economic advantage in the trading process.[50] Insider trading is banned in most legislation, because of this violation of the rules of the market. Some have argued that it is unclear why the use of inside information to make good deals should be seen, in principle, as unfair. Why does the company, or its shareholders, have priority rights to this information? In response, it is argued that in instances of insider trading, the relation of trust with the company has been violated.

A code of conduct for financial markets should include respect for the interests of customers and shareholders as a basic requirement, but this should not lead to securities speculation, which implies great risk for society and local communities. Moreover, personal trading should not interfere with the professional duty of the investment manager. Codes of ethics in the securities industry should strengthen the professional consciousness of securities firms, leading to ethical rules that deter bribery, insider trading, or fraud.

Due to recent changes in the character of financial markets, the need for codes of ethics and values-driven management in capital markets is becoming more important. The separation of the constituencies of the firm into individual shareholders on the one hand, and corporate management on the other has, in many cases, resulted in passive shareholders with little active political interest in the firm, other than increased dividends. The contemporary emergence of the movement of socially responsible investing has, however, changed this situation. As the stock market becomes increasingly constituted by individual investors and groups of large institutional investors, the separation between passive shareholders and autonomous management, with regard to daily corporate governance, has been challenged.

How should we conceive good corporate citizenship in the finance industry? The theoretical foundations of values-driven management and ethical companies represent a challenge to a limited conception of corporate ownership. Business ethics focuses on the responsibilities of corporations to include social obligations and engage in society in decisions about finance. Accordingly, there may be some possible tensions between business ethics and mainstream finance theory. It is a challenge for corporate citizenship in finance to deal responsibly with these tensions. This includes the fact that republican business ethics is based on a community oriented conception of economic life that is critical towards the conception of the isolated actor who maximizes her utility (this individual is normally supposed as foundational to finance theory). In business ethics, the market is not conceived as a pure economic system, but as a subsystem of other social systems where economic actors are placed in a social context in connection with culture and civil society. In addition, the power of shareholders is not conceived as absolute, but it is limited by concerns for external and internal stakeholders. This challenges predominant conceptions of the relation between management, owners, and other stakeholders of the firm. Moreover, the obligations of the firm towards other stakeholders mean that the legal subjectivity of the firm – that is, the duties and rights of the company – cannot be identical with the interests of the owners. There are a number of interests in relation to third parties that the company must take into account, for example concerning the environment, social relations, and local community. Applying corporate citizenship in finance means that the relationship between a company and its shareholders can no longer be conceived as exclusively monistic, but must be seen rather as dualistic, because there is always the possibility of divergent interests, for example concerning the problems of long-term versus short-term profits. Finally, the application of the concept of corporate citizenship in finance ethics implies that conceptions of finance must be based on a stakeholder theory that places corporations in a broader social context.

Case 13. The work ethics of corporate mergers: The case of Fleet Boston Bank

This case of Fleet Boston Bank is an illustration of an *ethical dilemma* of a merger between two corporations with different cultures. It is a case of how to deal with the differences between different cultural values and economic values during a process of organizational change.

Fleet Bank and Bank of Boston were submitted to a merger into Fleet Boston Bank. They were two rather large banks that were mediated into a very large bank, Bank of Boston, valued at 170 billion dollars, with more than 55,000 employees and twenty million customers worldwide.[51] At the time of the merger, the two banks were characterized by very different local cultures.

The different cultures of Fleet Bank and Bank of Boston created conflicts after the merger. The two organizations had very different concepts of the banking business and the aims of their respective organizations. Bank of Boston had a culture of value-creation for the benefit of customers and employees.[52] Fleet Bank was much more oriented towards shareholder values even at the expense of employees and customers. These differences were reflected in the management styles of the top leaders of the two banks. Bank of Boston was rather universalistic and based on respect for human individuals, while Fleet Bank was much more utilitarian.[53] Fleet Bank was oriented towards cost-benefit considerations with regard to increasing corporate returns.

After the merger Fleet Boston's business was, to a larger degree, directed towards business customers. Many employees from the old Bank of Boston and, to some extent, from Fleet Bank were rather dissatisfied with the new working conditions. They felt that they had not been treated fairly and that the new bank was much more profit-oriented. The employees felt that the merger had not respected them and that it was only the CEOs, in particular Terry Murray who came from Fleet bank and became the CEO of the new Fleet Boston Bank, who benefited from the merger (from which Murray gained millions of dollars).

This merger illustrates the difficulties of uniting organizations with very different cultures and the fact that mergers are often driven by concerns for profit maximization as the major goal of business. In the merger of the two banks, concern for values and stakeholder demands became less important than the effort to make the bank a larger and more competitive organization. Only the managers and the shareholders received real benefits from this merger and the management of the merger was not very open to ethical values of stakeholder inclusion and creating a common culture of integrity, respect and concern.

2.4. Shareholder ethics: Socially responsible investments (SRI)

In recent years many investors, for example individual people with certain ethical values, religious group, foundations, public organizations, and nonprofit institutions have proposed socially responsible investing. This desire to control the production of the firm in which one invests is not new. As early as the 1920s, many people in the United States did not want to own the "sin stocks" of tobacco or alcohol and, as a result, the Pioneer Fund for ethical investments was established. Since the 1960s this movement has become stronger. Investors have proposed criteria beyond economic concerns for their investments, including issues such as environmental protection, nondiscrimination, human rights, customer support, and ecological production. Investors want to make ethical investments and invest with their values. Indeed, these requirements have made ethics reemerge as a major theme in finance.

It is, however, a point of discussion whether socially responsible investment strategies can give sufficient returns to be competitive or change the market. From the standpoint of financial theory (i.e., the efficient market concept) it may be argued that socially responsible investing cannot give better economic output because it is required to assume higher risks in order to get higher economic output.[54] But this may not be the case in making socially responsible investments and it may also not be true that the market ignores information about the level of social responsibility of the company. It is possible that the interest on the part of some investors in socially responsible companies may have made social responsibility more important in the financial market. In some cases investors may even pay higher prices for socially responsible companies. Mainstream companies may have made an effort to integrate strategies of social responsibility in order to get a better image on the market. Moreover, external influence of the structure of markets may also come from the willingness of investors to support new companies that are socially responsible but that are not likely to get support from professional investors.[55] Even though socially responsible investing may not internally change the market structure, it certainly has an impact on the market valuation of corporations.[56]

These developments are reinforced by changes in capital market and possible investors. Today, the most important shareholders are institutional investors, mutual funds, pension funds, et cetera. Such investors are much more powerful than individual investors and they are often determined by certain ethical rules and codes of conduct that influences their investment decisions. Institutional investors also have the power to lay pressure on corporations. They are increasingly beginning to use that power to control critical decisions of corporate governance. Many people have been skeptical of the development towards more political decision-making in organizations and the powers of large institutional investors are growing.

Institutions have the power to employ people with the skills necessary to analyze a firm's strategies in order to become more active in corporate management. Indeed, institutional investors are changing the role of finance and power relations in companies such that there is now a closer link between management and shareholders. They have diversified portfolios and are more dependent on general economic health than the success of individual firms. In this way, institutional investors represent an important aspect of the movement from individual ownership of corporations towards the idea of corporate citizenship, where investment decisions and corporate governance decisions are made in order to take care of a diversified number of demands and interests.

Russel Sparkes argues that there is a close link between ethical investing and corporate socially responsible investing. He goes so far as to state that socially responsible investing is close to becoming a principle of modern trust law.[57] In regard to institutional investors, ethical investing is defined as the construction of portfolios that combine ethical and financial goals in order to obtain returns on the stock market.

The main concerns for the institutional investor interested in ethical investing are respect for the environment, corporate governance, and human rights. It is important to include financial performance in the concerns for ethical investment and emphasize that economic sustainability is also is an important criteria.

Pressures on institutional investors come not so much from shareholder activism as from NGOs, for example Greenpeace and Amnesty International, or representatives from the antiglobalization movement who act as advocates for stakeholders. In some countries it is, however, possible to find increasing activism from people who want their pension funds to be appropriately invested.

It is important to remember that the movement for ethical investing is one of practical social responsiveness, where individuals and institutions share a combined concern with both the nonfinancial with financial criteria of investments. Four major kinds of ethical investors can be distinguished. First is the religious investor. This was probably the first ethical investor, who emerged in critical reaction to the perceived immorality of alcohol, tobacco, and gambling. Stocks representing these vices were simply taken out of the portfolio. Today, there are many churches that still practice this kind of negative investment strategy by avoiding controversial companies in their portfolios; however, to achieve their aims more effectively, this reactive approach should be combined with a more proactive attitude to the economic market. Churches should care not only about excluding some companies, but also look at the performance of the companies positively selected for investments.

The second kind of ethical investor is the political investor who combines negative criteria of avoidance with positive criteria by selecting companies who promote certain products and practices. Of course, there are some political investors who mainly use the negative criteria of avoiding companies who trade with oppressive regimes, damage the environment, or produce arms, but there are increasingly positive selection criteria among political investors focusing on company engagement in community, fair trade practices, animal rights, and efforts to fight environmental pollution. Important landmarks in the political investor movement include shareholder activism in the United States against companies selling weapons for the Vietnam War and the international boycott of South Africa.[58] This last boycott was eventually so efficient that it caused serious economic problems for South Africa.

As a slightly different type, the third kind of ethical investor is not so focused on single political issues, but is rather broadly occupied with not investing in companies with morally problematic profiles. This ethical investor does not stop with single issues but wants to go further and have a positive impact on society. They include a broader evaluation of best practices, and look for good to excellent performance in their evaluation of a corporation. They want a positive return on their money without having a bad conscience.[59] These ethical investors may even be joined by a fourth kind of ethical investor, who chooses to invest in ethical companies, not because of his or her own ethical convictions, but because of the belief that ethical companies will give the best return.

In addition to the different strategies of these investors, ethical investment also includes shareholder activism and investment decisions based on consulting different indeces of socially or environmentally responsible performance. As mentioned previously, this landscape also includes large pension funds, which prefer socially responsible investments because they are held accountable with regard to their ethical performance, and because they have a particular responsibility towards society as a whole.[60]

The difficulties regarding ethical investing include not only assessing whether positive or negative ethical investment can actually make a difference on the market, but also insufficient capacity of companies to reliably screen for procedures and practices that are either negative or positive in regard to investment decisions. In addition, ethical investments must also combine financial and economic sustainability with concerns for values and norms that satisfy respect for the common good in society.

Different international investment funds have developed different criteria for screening. As an example of the negative side, the screening criteria for Friends Provident Stewardship, a British fund, illustrates a common list of things to be avoided: 1) environmental damage and pollution, 2) unnecessary animal exploitation, 3) oppressive regimes, 4) exploitation of the third world, 5) manufacture and sales of weapons, 6) nuclear power, 7) tobacco and alcohol production, 8) gambling, 9) pornography, and 10) offensive and misleading advertising.[61] On the positive side the fund mentions: 1) supplying basic necessities, 2) products and services for the benefit of community, 3) conservation of energy or natural resources, 4) good employment practices, 5) community involvement, 6) equal opportunities, 7) environmental improvement, 8) stakeholding, and 9) training and education.[62]

This strategy of favoring companies with good products, practices, and markets reflects a convergence between ethics and economics; thus, ethical investment strategies promote those companies that place a high priority on stakeholder management, social and environmental responsibility, as well as good corporate social responsiveness. Consequently, ethical investment strategies are important because they motivate companies to be socially responsible and to care about their ethics and values.

How can corporate citizenship be applied with regard to ethical investing? Corporate citizenship must be defined as the effort to apply the ethical strategy of negative or positive screening in order to ensure socially reponsible investment.[63] When dealing with corporate citizenship in investing, ethical investment is based on the emergence of the political corporation, where shareholders and owners are required to engage more actively in order to ensure corporate sustainability and respect for the fundamental values of society by working for the values of the three Ps. Owners and investors are not only refusing particular products, but they work to integrate an ethical strategy into the core of the organization.

Case 14. Ethical investments: From Banco to Etik Invest

The case of Banco and Etik Invest has been selected to illustrate the *ethical dilemmas* of ethical investing. The Danish company Alfred Berg, owned by the European Bank ABN-AMRO, was started in 2000 to develop an ethical investment group with an ethical and social profile in the security business. This investment group was called Banco. They had ambitious plans to quickly develop a base of 60,000 customers. The company's director, Kirsten Fjord, was hired to engage actively with NGOs and other organizations to promote the field of ethical investing. Their proposed screening for investing included negative criteria, such as excluding the weapons and the tobacco industries, as well as companies that did not respect UN conventions on human rights, child labor, nondiscrimination, and protection of the environment.[64] Banco also tried to make active involvement with stakeholders a criterion.

Kirsten Fjord was supposed to promote the investment group actively among possible customers. When companies were judged to be acting unethically, Banco was to consider withdrawing investments in these firms. Banco did not want to invest in unethical firms and the organization consulted its ethical investment council before making the decision to invest in specific firms. Contacts with NGOs were considered particularly important for deciding about negative or positive criteria for investments.[65]

In addition to its ethical investment policy, Banco wanted to enter into close dialogue with humanitarian organizations, for example by supporting projects helping children in the developing world. The idea was that investors would donate money to poor people in developing countries, for example by supporting organizations like the Red Cross, Caritas Denmark, UNICEF, Aid for children, Amnesty International, et cetera; however, the board and the director had difficulties finding customers to support this initiative. Consequently, Kirsten Fjord was fired in autumn 2005 and the company discussed dissolving the investment group, though this did not happen. It wasn't until March 3, 2006 that Alfred Berg refused to be the administrator of the group because it was too little and didn't earn enough money, meaning that the board, which had little professional investment experience, was left with eighty million Danish crowns to administer. However, the board resisted the temptation to dissolve the group and recreated it with the name Etik Invest.

Stories of Banco's bad and unethical management and individual greed appeared in the press, even though the new firm had positive expectations for 2006. Humanitarian associations would receive part of the money that the investment club would earn from the investments. As a result, Banco was associated with many humanitarian organizations, which indirectly contributed to the group's publicity. The firm was considered as a humanitarian organization rather than a professional investment company. It seemed difficult to convince people about the possibilities of ethical investments.

The lack of success of establishing an ethical investment business in Denmark is rather astonishing compared to other countries. In Sweden, ethical investing has become big business with more than 150,000 investors who invest more than fifteen billion Danish crowns.

As a further example, the Co-Operative Bank, based in the United Kingdom, has defined extensive criteria for its ethical investment policy. The Bank developed its ethics statement in 1992 and it was updated in 1995. This ethics statement was based on a consumer research review and the bank formulated an ethical investment policy that also dealt with several controversial issues.

The bank states in its ethics policy that it : will not invest or supply financial service to any regime that violates political human rights or that engages in torture; will not invest in the manufacture of weapons; supports fair trade initiatives; encourages a proactive stance on environmental issues; tries to avoid the exploitation of its financial services for criminal purposes like drug trafficking and tax evasion; refuses to invest in tobacco manufacturing, armaments and weapons, fur trade, animal experimentation, and blood sports involving animals (e.g., fox hunting and hare coursing).[66]

2.5. Ethics in the workplace: Management and employees

Analyzing ethics in finance and investment demonstrates the potential conflict between the internal constituencies of the firm: shareholders, management, and employees. In this context, shareholders – as owners – are often not directly engaged in the daily management of the firm and are represented by employed managers. These managers are therefore in a double bind: On the one hand, they belong to the owners of the firm and represent their interests. On the other, they are employed like other workers in the firm and could, therefore, be counted as employees. However, in most cases management seems to foster the interests of shareholders, because this is their job according to the law and because managers often have significant shares in the company. The interests of shareholders and the interests of employees do not often go together. Shareholders are in many cases largely focused on economic returns and profit maximization, while employees by and large work in order to make a living. Moreover, while shareholders do not use much of their time in the corporations, employees spend much of the lives at their work. In many cases, for the employees, the corporation is much more than a device for profit making; it is the place where they find meaning and significance in their lives.

Because of its responsibility, it is important that management at all levels is acting ethically. Management of business ethics represents the attempt to integrate ethics at all levels of the organization.[67] It can also be understood as a contribution to corporate social responsibility. Managers at all levels of the organization can set an example for employees by acting ethically. It involves the formal introduction of ethics codes and policies of values-driven management, but it also implies the capacity of situational decision-making and the informal capacity to make the right decisions. Management should work with mission statements, codes of ethics, and introduce measures for ethical, social, and environmental reporting. From the institutional economic perspective, such ethical behavior has an impact on the bottom line, since ethics builds trust and confidence, and because an environment where people rely on each other contributes to organizational efficiency.[68] Moreover, ethical leadership contributes to stakeholder dialogue and loyalty. Ethics functions as an alternative to authoritarian domination in management.

Managers at all levels have, therefore, an important responsibility for realizing the ideals of stakeholder fairness and values-driven management. Leadership with integrity contributes to developing trust and building the core values of the organization. Joseph Weiss characterizes this process as the *creative destruction* and *creative reconstruction* of values in the organizational culture.[69] Stakeholder management aims at implementing values that include ethics and compliance in the fundamental processes of the organization. Managers can be aware of this when they plan the strategy of the firm, and by reviewing and developing values and values-driven stakeholder criteria that contribute to formulating "best practice" policies of the firm. These efforts help to create an atmosphere that might lead to a "genuine spirituality" at work.

The danger of moral blindness exists with regard to management. In her famous book, *Eichmann in Jerusalem: An Essay on the Banality of Evil* (1964), Hannah Arendt contributes to the understanding of such ignorance of morality.[70] Arendt discusses the case of Adolf Eichmann, who was considered as the bureaucratic brain behind the logistical organization of the Holocaust. Reporting from his war crimes trial in Jerusalem in 1961, Arendt argued that Eichmann did not represent radical evil because of his demonic mind, but instead because of his total lack of moral reasoning and critical judgment. As a bureaucrat, Eichmann defended his action by saying that he was just "following orders" from Hitler when he eagerly planned the transportation of Jews to the extermination camps. Eichmann's behavior characterizes blind subordination to ones' superiors, a diabolic management "by objective," which in this case meant organizing the extermination of European Jewry as efficiently as possible. According to Arendt's concept of the "banality of evil," Eichmann's case is a clear example of blind obedience to authority, where individuals act without moral awareness or the ability to take an ethical perspective on the consequences of their actions. Eichmann's actions stand as a reminder of the critical necessity of managerial ethics and the importance of the ability to take moral responsibility.

It is important to be aware of certain specific dimensions of human activity in organizations that are capable of great harm. The danger of the banality of evil in organizations is the fact that individuals in organizations do not have any capacity for ethical judgment. This was, indeed, the case with Eichmann.[71] He did not have the capacity to think critically. He had no moral imagination or reflective judgment. He did not have any ethical sensitivity and conceived himself as the dutiful employee with ambitions of being promoted. Eichmann was basically a kind of "organization man," who became identical with his role as a bureaucrat in the system. What we learn from this example, however, has also a wider impact. In 1974, the social psychologist Stanley Milgram tested the so-called Eichmann personality. What he discovered is that ordinary people, as members of a hierarchical system of order under pressure, are capable of committing immoral actions.[72] The subjects who were participating in his experiments were so eager to fulfill their obligations in their work that they, without question, were willing to expose others to great pain and suffering.[73] According to business ethics, Milgram's approach can be described as a *cybernetic-organizational* conception of obedience that focuses on the dependence of employees on the structures and systems of the organization. The lesson to be learned is that it is necessary to develop organizational and institutional ethics that can deal with the system-based banality of bureaucratic evil.

From the point of view of organization theory, such distantiation from ethical issues can take different forms. Weiss speaks about *ethical blindness* and *ethical muteness*, which indicate the lack of ability to understand, or talk about, ethical issues. There are also cases of fundamental *ethical incoherence, ethical inconsistency* among values, *ethical paralysis, ethical hypocrisy*, and *ethical schizophrenia* where values do not apply, do not correspond with practice, or are so contradictory that there is no coherence in the management of the organization.[74] Finally, there is the case of *ethical compliancy* where managers believe that they are so strong and perfect that ethics does not apply to their decisions. Instead of embodying the organization's best practices and just ethics codes, or programs of values-driven management, the manager becomes an expression of the banality of evil: the bureaucratic figure who defends the system against the people who are its key components.

This highlights the need for values-driven management and respect for the basic ethical principles of autonomy, dignity, integrity, and vulnerability as the core of corporate citizenship. They should be considered as important with regard to the structure and organization of the workplace. It is an important dimension of organizational integrity and leadership in relation to corporate decision-making that companies have structures promoting ethics within the organization. In large corporations these structures are necessary to ensure ethical responsibilities throughout the organization, but in mid-sized and small companies they are also important because they make concrete individuals responsible for ethical actions. Following international pieces of legislation, such as the FSGO, many organizations have started to employ staff in an office of ethics. The ethics officer acts in collaboration with other staff and serves as a kind of reporter who is responsible for initiatives in relation to ethical questions regarding management. Such a role may be defined as a kind of "corporate secretary for ethics."[75]

This employee is most likely a person who feels especially responsible for the corporation and is someone who knows the corporation very well. Because of her position in the firm (i.e., in close collaboration with the board and management) she will be considered to have very experienced judgment, to be motivated for ethics and organizational integrity, and have the necessary power to implement her decisions. This ethics officer and her staff will also take initiatives to develop ethics, codes of values, and values-driven management throughout the organization.

Such an effort aims to solve internal ethical problems, such as ethical issues with regard to management and leadership, but also issues regarding the full range of stakeholders. Of course to be effective, the contributions of the ethics office should be sanctioned. Accordingly, an ethics officer in an organization would represent the collective consciousness of the organization, conceived as a kind of consciousness of corporate integrity.

There has been a lot of criticism of the idea of an ethics officer as the basis for ensuring corporate integrity. Critics conceive the ethics officer as a kind of police person of thought whose purview includes unacceptable monitoring and control of the company. Therefore, a number of specific conditions must be fulfilled to make sure that the person chosen to be the ethics officer will be responsible for corporate ethics and integrity:

- It must be clear whether the individual has enough integrity and influence within the corporation.

- It must be discussed whether this person is respected and trusted both by colleagues and top managers.
- The person unders consideration for this role has to reflect on whether they have enough resources to conduct internal and external investigations and implement procedural change in the corporation.
- This person must also think about whether they will have access to information and support mechanisms that will have a positive impact on organizational integrity (e.g., issues concerning early warning or codes of conducts with regard to ethical issues).
- The question of how employees might feel about the function of such an ethical ombudsman should also be taken into consideration.

Following our discussion, it is possible to surmise that the ethics officer's judgment must be based on the basic ethical principles of respect for autonomy, dignity, integrity, and vulnerability.

When applying the basic ethical principles and corporate citizenship in the work environment, the identification of ethical problems is of utmost importance. In this context, several problems can be mentioned, including different forms of stress behavior based on feelings of inferiority and lack of dignity, lack of equal recognition, or because of disease, age, work level, inhuman practices in relation to rationalizations of production, and restructuring in the firm. Moreover, it is necessary to deal with ethical problems in relation to change, organizational development, and multicultural relations in the firm. Accordingly, in the daily work environment of the firm a central problem is the ability of the manager, but also of all employees, to focus on integrity and, as has been discussed, to develop the capacity of moral thought and judgment.[76]

This need for judgment can also be called the need for *ethical formulation competency*. This competency consists in the identification of the capacity of ethical formulation, which consists of identifying, analyzing, reflecting on, and understanding ethical problems and questions. By putting *ethical dilemmas* into words and formulating notions about the ethical, it is possible to create an operational framework for conceiving ethical issues that are not necessarily conceptualized as a part of daily practice. At all levels of ethics a manager or an employee should be capable of evaluating and formulating ethical problems and dilemmas. This is the case for all the dimensions of corporate activities (including investment and ownership) and for all stakeholders (including consumers, employees, and other stakeholders in relation to internal and external relations of the firm). Accordingly, a manager or an employee must be aware of and able to incorporate ethical concerns in their daily work activities. If they develop the capacity of ethical competency, they will be able to 1) identify ethical aspects that are important for the corporation; 2) find and justify ethical aspects of their decision-making; and 3) use ethics in their daily work and development of the corporation. The importance of such a capacity of ethical formulation can quickly be conceived in 1) the work of implementing (cultural) values; 2) the capacity to understand ethical dimensions of daily work and management: and 3) the capacity to more broadly legitimate and justfy decisions. Another dimension of ethical competency is expressed in the capacity to enter in a dialogical process with the different stakeholders of the corporation.

In this context, workplace ethics also concerns employee rights and the duties of management as organizers of work and corporate production. Indeed, work is characterized by many fundamental paradoxes.[77] Today people spend nearly more of their adult life at work than on free time or with their families. Work is basic to the structure of the self and there is a close connection between work and the formation of personal identity. To put it bluntly: you are what you do at work.[78]

From an historical perspective, this has not always been the case.[79] In ancient Greece it was not considered dignified to work. Aristotle emphasized the aristocratic virtues of the free man who did not work, but devoted himself to politics. The Greeks considered work as a slavish activity. Money was to be used for exchange and not for investment.[80] One constant is that most people do not want to work all the time. Academics may think that they are fortunate to be paid to read and write books, until writing and reading consume all their free time. Very few people, indeed, see the beauty in this kind of life.

A critical look on the history of management describes a very sorry development: increasing corporate demands require total commitment from more and more people.[81] At the same time that corporations and other organizations increasingly shape peoples' lives, employees have become less motivated, to such a degree that management has had to invent all sorts of techniques in order to improve corporate culture. Some of the earliest European inducements to work included the efforts of Calvin and Luther. As discussed previously, the Protestant work ethic promoted work as a religious and moral obligation.[82] Work was considered as a moral justification of human existence and people who did not work were considered to be morally corrupt. Joanne B. Ciulla argues that this concept has developed to combine principles of fairness and obligation: the idea that one should work in accordance with one's best abilities, and that one's work obligation is a moral and spiritual calling from God.[83]

With the emergence of modern economics, another idea enjoined these visions. This was the utilitarian concept of work as a self-interested instrument to ensure material wealth; a concept which, as introduced by Benjamin Franklin, may be considered as a secularization of the Calvinist and Lutheran concepts of the calling.[84]

According to Ciulla, the work ethic of the calling, and even perhaps the materialist work ethic of self-interest, have been replaced by a "work ethic of fear." In other words, in modern corporations, people work because they are afraid of being fired, not because they follow a calling or seek salvation.[85] In this world, where corporations are taking over peoples' lives, the social contract between the corporation and its workers might be expressed as: "if you do your job, you will keep it." Even this minimal contract is, in many ways, not even respected anymore. The laws of finance and the market imply that corporations are gaining absolute power over people.

More precisely, the decision-making structure between shareholders, management, and employees, through which shareholders have absolute property over corporations, implies that workers have little influence on their own life. One might go so far as to say that private market society, with corporations excercising total power over working life, has never really treated people as adults. What is at stake in the working relationships of corporations is no less than the dignity and self-respect of human beings. It could be argued that the ethics of the workplace implies the development of the possibility of good and honest work, where people can develop their personality without losing their self-respect. Halcyon visions about a future information society, where boring and hard work has been abolished, may contribute to this.

The idea that work can be overcome definitely seems romantic. The state of being busy, of playing and enjoying work, is a condition of the human species. Instead of pursuing the unrealistic goal of totally abandoning work, it might be better to focus on eliminating its bad aspects. Since labor in modern society is primarily organized around organizations, it would be a good strategy to improve working conditions in corporations. This could help people to develop their identities in the social realm. As Marx argued, working for others in big corporations represents human alienation. In this context, it is important to be aware that money is a symbolic medium and cannot be the sole basis of satisfaction with work. Working for money may contribute to alienation if it becomes the only measure of identity.

When evaluating the relationship between managers and employees, regarding the search for values-driven management that will lead to good working conditions where people are treated as adults, the importance of workers' unions cannot be excluded.[86] In a sense, industrialization forced most working class people to fight for better job conditions in their organizations. In this context, ethics in the workplace concerns the basic rights of workers, such as dignity and autonomy, but also implies respect for equality and nondiscrimination.[87] Historically, the general effort to improve working conditions can be seen as a contractual negotiation between business and employees. In free market economies, independent unions have traditionally played an important role in promoting employee interests. Union strength inevitably opens the question about the justification of strikes. Some have argued that the right to strike must be respected in a liberal society. Although management has many ways to damage it, the right to strike – within strict guidelines – is likely to be accepted as a part of the tension between management and employees. In fact, this form of *contractual bargaining* is now an important means to protect human rights and civil liberties in the workplace.

The problem of how to protect civil liberties in the workplace covers a wide range of issues.[88] The background for this concern is the fear of corporate domination and power over individuals in the workplace. Different strategies of management, like scientific management, Taylorism, or Fordism, but also newer concepts of management like the human relations school, have problems integrating basic human rights like free speech and privacy in management practice. Protecting human rights can be considered as a part of the required concern for human dignity and autonomy in order to develop personal self-respect and identity. Issues where respect for human dignity and autonomy are germane include decisions regarding hiring, policies about screening, testing, and interviewing new employees. The duties and responsibilities of workers on the job and the working conditions under which they operate are also relevant. Moreover, decisions about promotions, and eventual nepotism and discrimination in such decisions, may be elaborated. In addition, decisions to fire or lay off employees can be mentioned as situations where workers' rights are at stake.

Even problems such as the size of just salaries and wages, or fairness in the formation of pensions and retirement programs, challenge our views of human dignity and inherent worth. The complexity of such determination may involve respecting the law and being aware of the general standards of wages in the industry. Moreover, the nature of the job and the required qualification may be taken into account. It is also a problem whether the job is secure or can represent a threat to the health of the employee. In this context, the idea of fairness may, in line with John Rawls's argument, require us to accept some sort of equality with regard to proper contribution from the employee, based on the idea that this would be for the benefit of the worst off.[89] The idea of respect for human dignity may justify some relation between job performance and salary. In addition, the contributions of the employees to the general wealth of the corporation could be taken into account when calculating a fair and just salary.

Since the Universal Declaration of Human Rights in 1948, efforts have been made to promote universal standards for the human rights for employees. It is argued that international and national human rights regulations lay the foundations for such basic freedoms. A possible "bill of rights" for employees might include the right to free speech and the right to have free views on cultural, religious, economic or political matters, including views on the policies of the corporation, which might differ from management.[90] The right of employee privacy is also paramount to organizational life. This right implies that the employee should have the right to keep his or her things in privacy at work, and that the employer – without authorization – has no right to intervene in this privacy. Protection of employee rights may also limit the rights of management to communicate with future employers about the earlier performance of the employee. In addition, employees should be given good reasons in cases of discharge or transference to another job.[91]

Furthermore, rights of nondiscrimination because of sex, race, sexual orientation, or other differences may be mentioned as very important human rights in the workplace. Ethical management includes critically examining the dangers of discrimination in the workplace in order to protect vulnerable individuals. Affirmative action and nondiscrimination are based on the promotion of human dignity in the working environment.

Since the workplace can be conceived as unity of management and employees, creating a common culture based on a contractual relation, certain rights of management over employees must be acknoweldged. Indeed, the right of an emplyer to employ and dismiss whomever and whenever they wish is considered a cornerstone of the free market economy. The employer has the right to decide over the time and place of the work contract, while respecting the worker's fundamental rights. Workers also commit themselves to certain contractual responsibilities and duties when they engage in the work. In general, employers argue that they are entitled to keep their rights to corporate governance and that too much regulation of the economy would represent a threat to the efficiency and success of the corporation. This confrontation between management and employees indicates that the status of business ethics lies somewhere between concerns for economic efficiency one the one hand, and respect for basic ethical principles of human autonomy, dignity, integrity, and vulnerability on the other.

In many cases, conflicts of interests in the workplace represent a confrontation between management and employees. It is often a problem about the extent of a company's ownership of the information an employee has acquired during her work for the company. In finance, insider trading and personal trading are examples of such employee use of company information. Another problem is the degree to which employees are allowed to receive gift or bribes as a part of their job.[92] In United States government offices in Washington, D.C., a rule was made whereby a federal employee could only be taken by external parties to a lunch valued at twenty dollars or less and could not receive gifts valued at more than twenty-five dollars. Soon after, a restaurant in the Washington area poked fun at the rules in its advertising by prompting patrons to: "Invite your favorite government employee for an ethical lunch." Obviously there are difficulties in determining precisely when a gift is acceptable or not. In general, companies require their employees to be aware of the value, purpose, and circumstances of the gift, as well as the reason why the gift has been given.[93] Moreover, many ethics and compliance programs ask employees to be aware of the company's gift policy and general legislation about bribery and gifts. In many cases, employees have been accepting gifts without knowing that they are at the limits of the law and industry practice.

An equally important issue of conflict between the interests of employee duty and loyalty to their company versus their duties and responsibilities to third parties is the problem of "whistle blowing." A whistle blower is an employee of an organization who has obtained knowledge that their organization is engaged in activities that may cause harm to third parties or that may be legally or morally wrong. The employee is said to blow the whistle when taking this information to the public.[94] An employee has a duty to blow the whistle when it is in the public interest. As Richard De George has suggested, this is the case when considerable evidence identifies a serious threat, when the employee has good reason to believe that the firm is committing serious and considerable harm to the public, when the immediate supervisors do not take action, and the employee has good reasons to expect that whistle blowing will be worth the risk and provoke a mitigation of harm and danger.[95]

The whistle blower should arguably discuss matters with management beforehand, to the extent it is possible. However, whistle blowing is not an easy matter. In major cases, such as the McDonnell Douglas production of DC-10 planes with insecure cargo doors, or in the case of Ford's production of the Pinto model that included defects, when employees tried to inform management this resulted in claims of ignorance and persecution.[96] Indeed, whistle blowing is a challenge to employee integrity where the employee has to stay committed to personal ideals in situations that risk personal well-being and where the protection of innocent people is at stake. It is therefore important to establish some kind of protection for whistle blowers in the corporation, such as creating an anonymous telephone hotline or employing an ombudsman.

In cases of bribery and whistle blowing, it is the loyalty of individuals to their corporation that is at stake. The contractual relationship to the corporation is the basis of certain loyalties, responsibilities, and duties; however, the virtue of loyalty to the employer depends on the specific context of the corporation. Employee loyalty cannot be of the same degree as political loyalty or the loyalty required of family and friends. No one is required to demonstrate unlimited devotion by dying for their corporation. The underlying argument supporting this distinction is that business corporations and other institutions do not have the inherent worth to qualify for such great devotion.[97] Although organizations with values-driven management and common norms may require loyalty as a part of the values of the organization, this loyalty does not imply blind acceptance of the organizational policies. Still, acceptance of organizational values may include some willingness to universalize these values as the basis of what is considered to be ethical. This implies that a minimal requirement of loyalty may be considered as "reasonable expectation of trust."[98]

It remains, however, important that management rights do not dominate employee concerns. The concept of privacy is closely linked to the basic ethical principles. Privacy is important for personal autonomy and it protects human vulnerability and dignity. In the age of information and digitalization, with increased possibilities of surveillance in the workplace, the need for protecting privacy is more urgent. People are not able to exercise their autonomy when they are subject to external control in the work environment.[99] Self-determination and decision-making over personal life plans justify that management cannot interfere in the private life of employees. Employees would be much more vulnerable if they were subject to constant supervision.[100] In this way employee vulnerability places a challenge to the contractual relationship between management and employees. As mentioned previously, the employment relation is always marked by an asymmetrical power imbalance. In order to protect vulnerable employees from management interventions into their privacy, management and shareholder property rights must be limited regarding control over the private lives of employees.

Today, privacy protection is becoming even more challenging. Different kinds of psychological tests of personality, genetic and other physical tests, information technology, health tests, drug tests, dress codes, and so on confront the standards of legitimate versus illegitimate interventions in employee privacy at work. The argument for different kinds of testing often states that it is in the interests of employee health or safety that it is necessary to test individual workers. A good example of this argument is the problem of whether management has a right to require obligatory drug testing of their employees. Does such testing violate the contractual relationship between management and employees by invading the privacy rights of employees?[101] The arguments for such drug testing are that employees who take drugs are at greater risk of lower job performance, that they increase the company's healthcare costs, decrease productivity, and that they pose a risk of possible self-injury, harm, or danger to others while on the job. It is possible that knowledge of employee drug abuse helps the firm avoid these dangers; therefore, the corporation has the right to intervene in the privacy of an employee in order to prevent harm.[102] The corporation may, in specific cases, have a responsibility to avoid such harm, danger, or risk to itself, its customers, or the product.

Employee welfare at work is an important concern for values-driven management. Welfare is important both from the point of view of fairness and from the point of view of efficiency. Welfare implies a good working environment without corruption and the struggle with despotic management. New management styles that focus on employee quality of life in order to overcome dissatisfaction among workers have proven to be very effective. It is important for increased worker motivation, and decreases stress by making workers feel in control of their environment. This, in turn, increases employees' feelings of dignity and self-respect. There are many different management strategies and programs for improving worker satisfaction and participation. This book has proposed values-driven management as a central strategy in order to fulfill this aim. Values-driven management may be seen as a good strategy to increase productivity and efficiency, while at the same time improving employee satisfaction. Employee participation in values-driven management through organizational democracy represents one of the most important strategies for achieving this aim.

Respect for the basic ethical principle of dignity helps to promote some very important moral reasons for respecting employee participation. Employee participation in the development and implementation of values is very important for increased efficiency and worker welfare in organizations. While persisting theories that base the firm on property rights and shareholder ownership are very skeptical towards employee participation, stakeholder and contract theories of the firm do not exclude the moral relevance of some degree of employee participation.

Employee representation and democracy represent a challenge to the traditional view of corporate decision-making structure, which is justified by the rights of owners to exert full control over their property in cases of management disloyalty. Moreover, employees have no right to contradict owners' decisions.[103] Because they are not owners, it is argued that nonmanagement and employees have neither the abilities nor interests to make good policy decisions. The result is the traditional hierarchical structure of organizations with ground floor personnel, middle management, and executive management reporting to the board and the shareholders.

In this context, it is the shareholders who have final control over corporate decision-making. Employee participation is threatening to the power of management and constitutes a subversion of shareholders rights to profit maximization. This is not, however, a necessary consequence of employee participation. Encouraging worker participation and extending rights to qualified personnel may improve the earnings of the company. Moreover, society can limit the rights of owners over their property and corporations should be concerned with employee welfare. So it might be argued that very important goods are at stake, goods that limit the absolute right to decision-making to owners.[104] In addition, it can be argued that the contractual relationship with stakeholders alters the property concept of the firm so that it must conceive of employee participation in decision-making as part of treating workers fairly.

The proponents of total or partial corporate democracy argue that employee participation, contrary to paternalistic management governance, increases productivity and general corporate welfare. Corporate democracy and systems that represent worker interests increase fairness in business and secure equitable treatment of workers. In order to make the corporation aware of their interests and demands, no one beside workers, or their union representatives, should be able to speak for their concerns.

Another argument, which references the principle of respect for inherent human worth, states that the right to political participation is a necessary requirement for human self-respect and dignity.[105] Both the Kantian and Rawlsian positions grant that the dignity of human beings is dependent on their capacity to have an autonomous life based on self-determination and participation in community with fellow human beings. Following this logic, one must agree to participatory rights in the workplace and respecting workers' adult decision-making abilities.

Without self-confidence and respect from management, workers will lose their self-respect and this loss of their own sense of dignity will have influence on their well-being, motivation, and productivity.[106] If they are excluded from decision-making, workers will be alienated and feel unimportant, which will have long-range effects on the performance and culture of the company. Lack of participation and repetitive work without control damages the mental and psychological health of employees.[107]

On the contrary, promoting participatory rights helps to create a better working environment, though this may require overcoming traditional hierarchical and authoritarian structures in the firm. Such structures often decrease productivity. Moreover, worker participation may help to make the larger society more democratic by making people feel closer to their communities. Participation in work decisions not only creates a better work environment, but it may also make people more apt for being citizens in a democratic society.[108]

Summing up, we have emphasized ethical management and leadership as a response to the dangers of moral blindness in the workplace. Corporate citizenship in the workplace must ensure the capacity of autonomous decision-making and the critical judgment of employees. Moreover, corporate citizenship must be about the effort to create the framework for the realization of the good life in organizations. The good life is – as demonstrated – not exclusively about the collective good, but also about the rights of individuals to be respected for their personal conceptions of the good life. Responsibility and respect for employee rights, ethical principles, and fairness are, of course, very important to ensure the right balance between employer and employee power in the workplace; employers keep their rights to property while respecting the integrity and dignity of their employees.[109] In order to cope with the modern work ethic of fear, it is important that fair workplaces protect constitutional rights and of the right of workers to unionize. It should go without saying that the right to self-determinations, protection against discrimination, harassment, and invasions of privacy are important parts of the constitutional rights of workers. Finally, workplace democracy is justified according to ethical principles and justice-as-fairness, and this kind of democracy can be promoted through stakeholder dialogue and values-driven management in the good citizen corporation.

Endnotes

1   John Dobson, *Finance Ethics* (New York: Rowman and Littlefield Publishers, 1997), 14
2   John R. Boatright, *Ethics in Finance (Foundations of Business Ethics)* (Oxford: Basil Blackwell Publishers, 1999), 172.
3   Ibid: 181.
4   Amartya Etizioni, *The Moral Dimension. Towards a New Economics* (New York: Collier Macmillan, 1988).
5   Ibid: 257.
6   John Dobson, *Finance Ethics* (New York: Rowman and Littlefield Publishers, 1997).
7   Ronald Coase, "The Nature of the Firm" (1937) in *The Nature of the Firm: Origins, Evolution and Development* edited by Oliver E. Williamson and Sidney G. Winter (Oxford: Oxford University Press, 1991), 18-34.
8   John Dobson, *Finance Ethics* (New York: Rowman and Littlefield Publishers, 1997), xiv.
9   Ibid: 7.
10 John R. Boatright, *Ethics in Finance (Foundations of Business Ethics)* (Oxford: Basil Blackwell Publishers, 1999), 170.
11 Ibid: 171.
12 John R. Boatright, "Business Ethics and the Theory of the Firm", *American Business Law Journal*, Volume 34/2, (1996), Winter.
13 Ibid: 234.
14 R. Edward Freeman: *Strategic Management, A Stakeholder Approach* (Boston, Massachusetts: Pitman Publishing Inc., 1984).
15 Atle Midttum: "Business Ethics and the Logic of Competition: Is there a Scope for the Moral Firm". Unpublished Paper (EBEN conference, 1999).
16 John Dobson, *Finance Ethics* (New York: Rowman and Littlefield Publishers, 1997), 14.
17 David Gauthier: *Morals by Agreement*, (Oxford: Clarendon Press and Oxford University Press, 1986).
18 John Dobson, *Finance Ethics* (New York: Rowman and Littlefield Publishers, 1997), 21.
19 Ibid: 146.
20 A.P. Møller in a letter to his son Mærsk Mc-Kinney Møller December 2. 1946.
21 www.maerskline.com
22 Ibid.
23 John Boatright, "Justifying the role of the Shareholder" in *The Blackwell Guide to Business Ethics edited by* Norman Bowie (Oxford: Basil Blackwell, 2002).
24 Ibid: 41.
25 Ibid: 58.
26 Andrew Crane and Dirk Matten, *Business Ethics. A European Perspective* (Oxford: Oxford University Press 2004), 185.
27 Ibid: 186.
28 Ibid: 190.
29 See *Harvard Business Review on Corporate Governance* (Cambridge, Massachusetss: Harvard Business School Press, 2000).
30 Robert A. G. Monks and Nell Minow, *Corporate Governance*, Third Edition (Oxford: Blackwell Publishing, 2004). Christina A. Mallin, *Corporate Governance* (Oxford: Oxford University Press, 2004).
31 Jay W. Lorsch, "Empowering the Board", *Harvard Business Review on Corporate Governance*, 2000: 22-23
32 Steen Thomsen, "Holdninger til corporate governance i dansk erhvervsliv", in *Corporate Governance i Danmark. Om god selskabsledelse i dansk og internationalt perspektiv*, edited by Jens Valdemar Krenchel and Steen Thomsen (Copenhagen: Dansk Industri, 2004), 81.
33 Ibid: 4.
34 Eva Parum, *Strategisk kommunikation om ledelse. Et corporate og public governance perspektiv* (Copenhagen: handelshøjskolens forlag, 2006).
35 This case is selected from company material and company reports. See www.hydro.no. Material for analysis of discoursive self-representation of the company has been selected from Anders Bordum and Jacob Holm Hansen, *Strategisk ledelseskommunikation. Erhvervslivets ledelse med visioner, missioner og værdier* (Copenhagen: Jurist og Økonomforbundets forlag, 2005), 25-63.

36 Norsk Hydro: *The Hydro Way*, www.hydro.no
37 Norsk Hydro: "Hydro's Social Responsibility Principles", www.hydro.no
38 Norsk Hydro: "Vårt etiske ansvar", www.hydro.no
39 John R. Boatright, *Ethics in Finance (Foundations of Business Ethics)* (Oxford: Basil Blackwell Publishers, 1999).
40 Ibid: 16.
41 Ibid: 17-18.
42 Ibid: 26.
43 Ibid: 30.
44 Ibid: 149.
45 Ibid: 152.
46 Ibid: 153.
47 Among others: Michael C. Jensen: See John R. Boatright, *Ethics in Finance (Foundations of Business Ethics)* (Oxford: Basil Blackwell Publishers, 1999), 153. Boatright also mentions the example of the hostile takeover of Pacific Lumber Company in the 1980s. John R. Boatright: *Ethics and the Conduct of Business*, Third Edition (New Jersey: Prentice Hall, 2003), 339. Pacific Lumber was known for its sustainable use of California redwood forests and good pension policies with huge benefits for their employees. The majority of the shares in the company were bought by a Houston firm owned by a person who wanted to gain exceptional profit on the use of the forest and the annihilation of the pension policies. The result was much conflict with workers and environmentalists and the State of California had to intervene in 1991.
48 John R. Boatright, *Ethics in Finance (Foundations of Business Ethics)* (Oxford: Basil Blackwell Publishers, 1999), 31.
49 Ibid: 44.
50 Ibid: 135.
51 The material for this case is selected from Joseph W. Weiss, *Business Ethics. A Stakeholder and Issues Management Approach* (3rd Edition) (Canada: Thompson, SouthWestern, 2003), 386-402. At page 402 in Weiss's book, there is comprehensive documentation of newspaper sources, reports, and other sources that helps to establish the content of the different elements of the case. In my analysis of the case I have tried to lay emphasis of the different elements of the case and how the case relates to different elements of the connection between culture and ethics.
52 Joseph W. Weiss, *Business Ethics. A Stakeholder and Issues Management Approach* (3rd Edition), (Canada: Thompson, SouthWestern, 2003), 394.
53 Ibid: 398.
54 John R. Boatright, *Ethics in Finance (Foundations of Business Ethics)* (Oxford: Basil Blackwell Publishers, 1999), 111.
55 Ibid: 114.
56 The Dow Jones Sustainability Index and the Boston based KLAD organization for measurement of social responsibility are very good examples of this new investment situation.
57 Russell Sparkes, *Socially Responsible Investments. A Global Revolution* (London: John Wiley and Sons, 2002), 40.
58 Ibid: 52.
59 Ibid: 74.
60 Steen Vallentin, "Socially responsible investing: Approaches and Perspectives" in *Værdier, etik og socialt ansvar i virksomheder. Brudflader og konvergens*, edited by Jacob Dahl Rendtorff. (RUC: Center for Værdier i virksomheder, 2003), 114.
61 Russell Sparkes, *Socially Responsible Investments. A Global Revolution*, (London: John Wiley and Sons, 2002), 98-99.
62 Ibid: 100.
63 Steen Vallentin, "Socially responsible investing: Approaches and Perspectives" in *Værdier, etik og socialt ansvar i virksomheder. Brudflader og konvergens*, edited by Jacob Dahl Rendtorff. (RUC: Center for Værdier i virksomheder, 2003), 117.
64 This case has been selected from the Danish newspaper, *Politiken*. The method of discursive analysis is inspired by Anders Bordum and Jacob Holm Hansen, *Strategisk ledelseskommunikation. Erhvervslivets ledelse med visioner, missioner og værdier* (Copenhagen: Jurist og Økonomforbundets forlag, 2005), 25-63
65 Politiken, April 19, 2006, 12.

66 The case of the cooperative bank is selected from Patrick E. Murphy, *Eighthy Exemplary Ethics Statements*, (Notre Dame: University of Notre Dame Press, 1998), 60-61.

67 Andrew Crane and Dirk Matten, *Business Ethics. A European Perspective*, (Oxford: Oxford University Press, 2003), 144.

68 Archie B. Carroll, "Ethics in Management" in *A Companion to Business Ethics, Blackwell Publishing*, edited by Robert E. Frederick (Oxford: Blackwell Publishing (1999), 2002), 142.

69 Joseph W. Weiss, *Business Ethics. A Stakeholder and Issues Management Approach* (3rd Edition) (Canada: Thompson, SouthWestern, 2003), 104.

70 See Hannah Arendt: *Eichmann in Jerusalem - A Report on the Banality of Evil* (New York: Penguin Books, 1964).

71 Ibid. See also *Ondskabens banalitet. Om Hannah Arendts Eichmann i Jerusalem* edited by Carsten Bagge Laustsen og Jacob Dahl Rendtorff (Copenhagen: Museum Tusculanums Forlag, 2002).

72 Stanley Milgram, *Obedience to Authority: An Experimental View*, (New York: Harpercollins, 1974).

73 *Ondskabens banalitet. Om Hannah Arendts Eichmann i Jerusalem* edited by Carsten Bagge Laustsen og Jacob Dahl Rendtorff (Copenhagen: Museum Tusculanums Forlag, 2002).

74 Joseph W. Weiss, *Business Ethics. A Stakeholder and Issues Management Approach* (3rd Edition) (Canada: Thompson, SouthWestern, 2003), 124.

75 US Sentencing Commission, *Proceedings of the Second Symposium on Crime and Punishment in the United States: Corporate Crime in America. Strengthening the "Good Citizen Corporation"* (Washington D.C. September 7-8, 1995). Robert J. Rafalko, "Remaking the Corporation: The 1991 US Sentencing Guidelines" *Journal of Business Ethics*, 13 (1994): 625-636.

76 Lynn Sharp Paine, "Law, Ethics and Managerial Judgment", *The Journal of Legal Studies Education*, vol. 12, (1994) no 2.

77 Joanne B. Ciulla, *The Working Life, The Promise and Betrayal of Modern Work* (New York: Three Rivers Press, 2000).

78 Al Gini, *My Job, My Self, Work and the Creation of the Modern Individual* (Chicago: Routledge, 2000).

79 Joanne B. Ciulla, *The Working Life, The Promise and Betrayal of Modern Work* (New York: Three Rivers Press, 2000).

80 Ibid: 36

81 Joanne B. Ciulla, *The Working Life, The Promise and Betrayal of Modern Work* (New York: Three Rivers Press, 2000). Joanne B. Ciulla, Clancy Martin and Robert C. Solomon, *Honest Work, A Business Ethics Reader* (Oxford: Oxford University Press, 2007).

82 Joanne B. Ciulla, *The Working Life, The Promise and Betrayal of Modern Work* (New York: Three Rivers Press, 2000), 49.

83 Ibid: 54.

84 Ibid: 56.

85 Ibid: 162.

86 Ibid: 166.

87 John R. Boatright, *Ethics and the Conduct of Business*, Third Edition (New Jersey: Prentice Hall, 2003), 184. "Discrimination and Affirmative Action".

88 William H. Shaw and Vincent Barry, *Moral Issues in Business*, 7th edition, (Belmont, California: Wadsworth Publishing Company, 1998), 252.

89 John Rawls, *A Theory of Justice*, (Cambridge, Massachusetts: Harvard University Press, 1971).

90 William H. Shaw and Vincent Barry, *Moral Issues in Business*, 7th edition, (Belmont, California: Wadsworth Publishing Company, 1998), 278.

91 Ibid: 279.

92 The 1977, the United States Foreign Corrupt Practices Act regulated American companys' use of bribes in foreign countries. This practice had become very widespread in the United States and it was necessary to stop it; however, the problem of gifts and bribery is more complicated as a intercultural question, where different cultures have differing habits of giving and receiving. This problem will be discussed extensively in the chapter on international business ethics.

93 William H. Shaw and Vincent Barry, *Moral Issues in Business*, 7th edition, (Belmont, California: Wadsworth Publishing Company, 1998), 357.

94 Ibid: 360.

95   Joseph W. Weiss, *Business Ethics. A Stakeholder and Issues Management Approach* (3rd Edition) (Canada: Thompson, SouthWestern, 2003), 247.

96   Mike W. Martin, "Whistleblowing: "Professionalism and Personal Life", *Business and Professional Ethics Journal vol 11*, no. 2 (1992) reprinted in William H. Shaw and Vincent Barry, *Moral Issues in Business*, 7th edition, (Belmont, California: Wadsworth Publishing Company, 1998), 401-402.

97   Ibid: 377.

98   David E. Soles, "Four Concepts of Loyalty", *The International Journal of Applied Philosophy 8* (Summer 1993) reprinted in William H. Shaw and Vincent Barry, *Moral Issues in Business*, 7th edition, (Belmont, California: Wadsworth Publishing Company, 1998), 380.

99   Richard L. Lippke: "Work, Privacy and Autonomy", *Public Affairs Quarterly 3* (April 1989) reprinted in William H. Shaw and Vincent Barry, *Moral Issues in Business*, 7th edition, (Belmont, California: Wadsworth Publishing Company, 1998), 331.

100 Ibid: 333.

101 Joseph R. Desjardins and Ronald Duska: "Drug Testing in Employment in *Contemporary Issues in Business Ethics*, 3ed, Belmont, Calif, Wadsworth 1996, reprinted in William H. Shaw and Vincent Barry, *Moral Issues in Business*, 7th edition, (Belmont, California: Wadsworth Publishing Company, 1998), 326.

102 Ibid: 327.

103 John J. McCall: "Participation in Employment" in Joseph R. Desjardins and John J. McCall: *Contemporary Issues in Business Ethics*, 3ed, Belmont, Calif, Wadsworth 1996, reprinted in William H. Shaw and Vincent Barry, *Moral Issues in Business*, 7th edition, (Belmont, California: Wadsworth Publishing Company, 1998), 339.

104 Ibid: 345.

105 Ibid: 341.

106 Ibid: 342.

107 Ibid: 343.

108 Ibid: 343.

109 Joseph W. Weiss, *Business Ethics. A Stakeholder and Issues Management Approach* (3rd Edition) (Canada: Thompson, SouthWestern, 2003), 219.

3. Ethics of the external constituencies of the corporation

From internal constituencies we now move to the analysis of the ethics of corporate citizenship and values-driven management in relation to the external constituencies of the firm. Having defined shareholders, management, and employees, as well as other business partners, as internal stakeholders, it is clear that the firm has strong responsibilities towards these different constituencies; however, these are not the only important constituencies of the firm. The corporation is situated in an external environment, with different agents who help the firm economize and gain power, which is central to the life and business activities of the organization.

Consumers, business suppliers, customers, government, and civil society can all be considered as external agents. Though the external environment of the firm clearly also includes the ecology of the natural world, the following discussion focuses on these various social constituencies.

This section attempts to show how basic ethical principles and values relate to the external constituencies of the firm. The discussion of external constituencies is structured in relation to following dimensions: 1) the ethics of business to business relations; 2) responsibilities and ethical relations to consumers; 2) the ethics of marketing and advertising; 4) the ethics of public relations to government, local community, and civil society; and 5) accounting for ethics and values: towards a multiple bottom line for accounting ethics.

Case 15: Coop ethical trading initiative

The case of the firm Coop Nordic has been selected as an example of a corporation dealing proactively with *ethical efforts* to work for sustainability and respect for ethical consumers. Coop is supported by the Danish association of distributors (FDB), which has worked to promote ecological products and fair trade. Ecological products are sometimes more easily accepted than fair trade products because the consumer can see their direct benefits. The ethics policy of Coop Nordic was initiated by FDB in 1996, and later became FDB's own policy. This ethical profile combines ecological products with fair trade initiatives.

At its website, the organization states that Coop Nordic's ethical trade initiative implies respect for the UN and ILO codes of conduct, basic human rights, and labor rights in different codes of conduct.[1] An important principle in this effort to build ethical trade is to establish an active relationship with suppliers, in order to foster respect for basic human rights in production and development. Coop Nordic commits the Nordic part of the corporation to ensuring respect for basic human rights and rights of workers in developing countries, and other places where the organization is operating. The organization also works to establish production in accordance with the official ethics policy and codes of ethics. It is important to have instruments to verify and document this strategy.

Moreover, Coop Nordic is committed to improving their suppliers' production conditions in order to comply with ethical guidelines. According to its self-representation as a green supermarket business, they work systematically with ethics and utilize the fair trade label for appropriate products, where it is required and demanded by governments and consumers. The organization works with a yearly ethical report and it will try to develop a dialogue on ethics with consumers, public authorities and other stakeholders.

In this sense ethics is not only reflected holistically in fundamental values of the organization. It is also reflected in different products with a specific importance for sustainability. Ethics is promoted as a part of the identity of the organization in its self-representation as conscious of ecology and nature. It could also be argued that it is represented by the democratic ideals of the company. The values of democracy and social equality are fundamental values of the FDB, which are transmitted to Coop. The FDB can be described as a kind of "consumer's association" based on the values of the Danish agricultural communities' movement.

3.1. The ethics of business-to-business relations

The ethical problems that emerge in interaction with business partners and in competition with other businesses can also be considered as external stakeholder relations issues. Both business partners and competitors can be accounted for as stakeholders according to the definition of a stakeholder as anyone who affects or is affected by the corporation.[2] There are many ethical problems related to suppliers, competitors, and other businesses with which the corporation interacts. Relations between businesses are becoming increasingly important in the context of globalization and network economy.[3] There has been a penchant to regard business competition as dependent on economics and not as a subject for ethical analysis; however, as has been previously discussed, there is an ethics of competition, which corporations should follow in interaction with each other. Moreover, in the global environment, suppliers may sometimes be considered as equivalent to employees. A corporation may have increased responsibility towards its suppliers, who are very dependent on its treatment of them. In the competitive environment of business-to-business relations, there are also a great many ethical questions related to problems of trust in dealing with trading partners and in formulating contracts. In international business, the question of bribery and gift giving is also important and emerges not only in relation to governments, but also in business-to-business situations. There may, furthermore, be an ethics of negotiation with possible business partners and suppliers, which sets limit to possible aggressiveness and deceptive practices.

Certainly, there are many ways in which a corporation can hurt and violate the rights of suppliers and competitors, but there is also a great deal of mutual dependence between the corporation and the other corporations in the business environment. Some complain about an environment of negative dependence on competitors, in the way that businesses in mutual competition shape the social field of their industry and its developments and innovations, but it is often possible to learn a lot about business developments by looking at the actions of competitors. The same sort of dialectics between competition and dependence may to lesser extent be the case with supplier relations, where a different kind of dependency may exist. Sometimes a corporation cannot live without its suppliers and they totally determine its existence, for example, in the case of suppliers of very sophisticated software for televisions or computers. In other cases, it may be that the corporation is so strong, and there may be so many suppliers on the market, that the corporation can do anything it wants with suppliers. This raises provocative questions about multinational companies and their relations to some suppliers in developing countries. In both cases, corporations have to respect basic ethical principles and comply with the laws and values of competition and values-driven management.

Surely corporations are not isolated entities, but are mutually dependant on other companies in modern network economies. The general ambience of ethics in different industries is very significant for the integration of values-driven management. It is routinely argued that a corporation cannot, and will not, establish an ethics program because it is not common in the industry and, further, that the expense of an ethics program will raise overall costs and have a determinant influence of the corporation's competitiveness. Consequently, in order to succeed with ethics policies, it is necessary to convince all corporations in the industry to make an effort to comply with ethics and advance ethics programs. This was the case when the United States defense industry, pushed by the government, formulated its business ethics program and codes of compliance in 1986.[4]

Ethic issues related to suppliers concern questions of loyalty and partnership. These issues are particularly complicated when people from different countries collaborate in a global economy. Issues of correct behavior and different cultural norms, as well as different conceptions of a contract and loyalty, may complicate the issue of partnership. The power differentials that exist between business partners, for instance in meetings between Western and non-Western partners, or big and small firms, may define the pressure of ethical behavior. Large European or American firms have quite extensive responsibilities towards their eventual suppliers from poor and small third world countries. Powerful corporations can use their force in regard to self-interested profit maximization in order to dominate suppliers in a negative way that has a damaging impact on their mutual relationship.[5] Suppliers can play with their loyalty in order to deal with the best buyer, but they can also go into stable business relations with one business partner, which may benefit both corporations. Loyalty may likewise be broken because of better business opportunities with different suppliers.

The ethics of business negotiations between different corporations presents comparable issues. As Albert Carr has argued, there is a close link between the ethics of business competition and negotiation, but there is a wider degree of latitude to the game of negotiation.[6] Most would agree that there is nothing wrong with being rude, as long as one plays by the "rules of the game." However, there are also practices of negotiation that are at the borderline. What about lying, deception, misleading nondisclosure, exploitation, or simply running away from previous agreements?[7] How many of such practices are part of rules of the game? And what about the cultural differences in concepts of negotiation, such as cases where one party may view the aggressive style of American negotiation as a kind of war? With a bias toward the basic ethical principles of autonomy, dignity, integrity and vulnerability, it is possible to conceive of negotiation as consensual openness searching for solutions that will be an advantage for all. Such a conception of negotiation is based on Kantian concepts of honesty, sincerity, and confidentiality, and may shape negotiation as a cooperative rather than a conflictual game.

As economists emphasize, competition is necessary for business innovation, but it can also be destructive insofar as businesses use aggressive measures to obtain market share or destroy other competitors.[8] In addition to the issue of aggressive competition, the ethics of oligarchic and monopolistic practices are of concern in free markets. State intervention in such practices by firms with dominant market share is occurring in many countries in order to protect the ethics of free markets. In the context of liberalization and globalization of international markets, this issue of the legal and ethical limitations of market behavior is becoming more important.

Corporations may not only have to be aware of their own relations with competitors and suppliers, but also to investigate the ethical dimensions of their supply chain.[9] Ethical supply chain management involves investigating the ethical issues pertaining to all the members of the business network. In relation to developing countries, the firm would probably have to deal with questionable working practices of business partners in these countries. A widespread practice of supply chain ethics management is represented by the fair trade movement, which was discussed previously.[10] To provide proof of supply chain ethics, firms are often requested to give a transparent description of the production history of their goods.

Case 16. McDonald's: The parody of corporate social responsibility?

The controversial case of McDonald's has been selected as a illustration of an *ethical dilemma,* where a company produces a very criticized product while at the same time being obliged to appear ethical in the public. For the skeptical critics of the so-called brand bullies, the effort of MacDonald's to appear as socially responsible seems to indicate that business ethics and corporate social responsibility have become meaningless concepts, totally subsumed under corporate branding and publicity. How can a company that has become such a cliché of modern American capitalism and whose products are widely considered to be damaging to people, be considered socially responsible? These are important questions, but from a more positive perspective, the fact that McDonald's has a position in relation to corporate social responsibility can be seen as an illustration of how mainstream CSR has become. It signifies CSR's total integration into the values of the modern economic systems of global capitalism.

In fact, the appearance of corporate social responsibility on the McDonald's website may, in this sense, represent a proactive strategy to do something with the problems and challenges to the corporation. This is indicated by the company's presentation of its mission of corporate social responsibility: "At McDonald's, responsibility means striving to do what is right, being a good neighbor in the community, and integrating social and environmental priorities into our restaurants and our relationships with suppliers and business partners."[11] That the company tries to be proactive and aware of its many critics is further indicated: "We are working hard to understand the complex issues that confront our business and our industry and we can make a significant difference."

The effort to be socially responsible is expressed in the company's concern with creating products that contribute to "balanced, active lifestyles" based on the saying: "it's what I eat and what I do." We might say "you are what you eat"! Therefore, the corporation has started an international "nutrition information initiative" where a consumer gets nutrition information on product packaging. This initiative is supported by continuous improvement of its products.

McDonald's mentions efforts to be responsible towards workers not only in McDonald's, but also with regard to suppliers. The corporation argues for respect and recognition as basic principles of management, for example by offering training programs and by ensuring respect for diversity in the work environment. This is promoted through concrete collaboration and development of long-term solutions for poor workers. In order to ensure corporate social responsibility among suppliers, McDonald's has established programs regarding the treatment of animals, the use of antibiotics, product safety, health at restaurants, employment practices, and so forth.

With regard to communities, the organization indicates that it contributes to helping families and children achieve a "balanced, active lifestyle," for example by offering healthier items on its restaurant menus. Other community programs include help for the handicapped, youth sports, community programs, and house charities. Moreover, McDonald's has worked for the creation of a sustainable profile of environmental protection with programs of recycling and resource conservation, including respect for sustainable development and the needs of future generations.

Those who refute corporate social responsibility as a cynical parody should take a closer look at McDonalds. The fact that corporate social responsibility is central to their self-presentation indicates an ongoing moralization of business and corporations, which situates responsibility at the collective institutional level. Even McDonalds, the symbol of capitalism, is now forced, if only nominally in its rhetorical self-representation, to appear as socially responsible.

3.2. Responsibilities and ethical relations to consumers

Consumers and customers are, of course, very important external constituencies of the corporation. Without consumers the corporation would not survive on the market, though possible consumers or customers constitute a very different group, ranging from government offices to other businesses and individual citizens who act as buyers of corporate products on the market.[12] From the perspective of the different theories of the firm, the relation of the firm to consumers can be analyzed at three different levels. Firstly, the relationship between the firm and the buyer of the corporation's products can been seen as strictly contractual, according to which the firm or the consumer has no extra-contractual liabilities and responsibilities. Contractual responsibility is viewed as a purely legal responsibility. This concept of consumer responsibility may be considered as compatible with the property-based view of the firm as a device for increasing shareholder profits. However, when the firm is seen as a nexus of both informal and formal contracts, the formal contractual view appears to be too limited. Understanding the relationship between a firm and its consumers required considering many informal understandings and presuppositions.[13]

These contractual norms embedded in social relations closely link consumers and firms. It may even be appropriate to consider the consumers as stakeholders of the firm with preferences and demands. Moreover, consumers may be considered not only as external stakeholders, but also as internal stakeholders. This means that the desires and preferences of stakeholders should not only be accounted for in terms of the firm's instrumental self-interest in profit maximization and power aggrandizement, but also as part of the constituencies of the firm that have intrinsic value. It is with this view of the firm that ethical principles can be integrated in relation to consumers. Consumer ethics should be based on the respect for the autonomy, dignity, integrity, and vulnerability of consumers in the asymmetrical dynamic between the firm as producer and consumers as buyers. This means conceiving of consumer ethics as the possibility and right of consumers to engage in the exchange relation with the corporation on a fair basis, with access to the right information and without being mislead or deceived by the corporation.

The general development towards a *hyper-complex society, knowledge society,* or a society of second order consumption (*la société d'hyperconsommation,* as the French sociologist and philosopher Gilles Lipovetsky defines it), implies new conditions of consumption and marketing.[14] Lately, the term *experience society* has come into use. It describes these new social conditions, building on the concept of the *experience economy,* where the economy of industrial society and consumer society is transformed by a focus on experience.[15] What is important in modern society is not to sell and buy products, but instead to sell and buy emotions, feelings, experiences, and attitudes.

Critics argue that this is an expression of the absolute dominance of the market economy over the subjective reality of human experience. Following Karl Marx, they argue that the whole world has become a place for marketing, where even our most intimate and subjective experiences can now be bought and sold. The concept of the experience economy corresponds very well to what may be called the cult of personal self-realization in postmodern society. We now have a relation to ourselves and our values, where we conceive our experiences as something that can be constructed and selected through strategic sales and purchase. While experience was earlier defined as something that just happens to you, the economization of experience has changed it into a selective choice of consumption, into something that can be acquired through the market.

This economic trend is conceived by many as the aestheticization of society, where art, creativity, and innovation replace the old industrial conception of companies as machines of production. The question becomes, what does this move from moral values and production to reputation, style, branding, appearance, emotion, experiences, and sensations mean for the ethics of consumption? In fact, contrary to what some may think, the new trends of branding and reputation makes ethics even more important as a part of self-realization in the experience economy. As society becomes increasingly complex, the aesthetic value of experience and personal self-realization is increasingly combined with other values. Because of increased focus on experiences, brand, and reputation as a part of products, ethics becomes more integrated in consumption. The increased focus on ethics by consumers is compatible with the emergence of the new experience economy, because ethical values are an important part of human experience.

It is in this framework that the issues of consumer ethics should be addressed. The concept of the *political consumer* represents a challenge to corporations.[16] Political consumers require good products and fair treatment of stakeholders by the corporations, and react critically towards unethical and irresponsible actions among firms. This means that the external and public pressure on corporations to make good products has increased. Increasing activism and commitment among more educated and enlightened consumers in the Western world imply that corporate management has to be aware of critical attitudes among consumers with regard to environmental issues, product responsibility, human rights, and employee policy, including issues of the public image of the corporation. Since the 1990s, consumers have become more active and interested in the values, ethics, and social responsibility of corporations. Consumers ask for economic actions where corporations respect moral standards and are concerned about their stakeholders. Political consumers also focus on ethical investments of corporations and they select companies who have a good record of safety, environmental or social issues. In this way political consumers have lead to an important actualization of moral issues in business.

Events like the international boycott of South Africa and of French wine and other products because of French testing of atomic weapons in the Pacific Ocean contributed to the emergence of the concept of the political consumer in the 1980s and 1990s. The ethics of the political consumer can be defined as choosing products from the perspective of production conditions and decent treatment of employees, with an understanding of the political conditions in the country of origin, taking note of the character of the product, the influence of the product on the environment, or the use of animal testing for making the product.[17] From the point of view of the market, political consumption represents a criticism of unethical corporate behavior. From the perspective of the individual political consumer, it can be characterized as the conscious use of values that are directed towards the community and the common good.[18] These community-oriented choices can, as is the case with socially responsible investments, be based on both positive and negative criteria representing the political and ethical preferences of the consumer. In this sense, the political consumer expresses an active effort to pressure the firm to act as a good citizen corporation. The negative strategy is based on boycotting specific products while the positive strategy is based on the choice of "politically correct products," such as ecological or fair trade products.[19]

The concept of the political consumer is closely connected to the idea of the *green consumer*. In 1988, John Elkington and Julia Hailes wrote *The Green Consumer Guide*, in which green consumption is defined as an effort to avoid products that represent a threat to health, the environment, are largely energy absorbing, contain unnecessary waste, contain material from endangered animals or rare plants, or that have been produced with cruel treatment of animals. Elkington and Hailes connect green consumption with the protection of human rights, sustainability, and animal welfare.[20] From the point of view of republican business ethics, political and green consumption strategies represent a criticism of the liberal concept of individual self-interested utility maximization, because consumption is directed towards common values and integrate the consumer in the political debate of society.[21] Political consumption implies that criteria apart from purely economic concerns are the basis of product selection. Political consumption represents an individual political choice, or simply letting a value-preference be decisive for consumption, while acting on the economic market. As such, political consumption can be understood as a reaction to the organization of markets where firms take no ethical point of view in producing and selling products. It also represents a reaction against a strong separation between business and politics, implying that the economic market is characterized by fairness and respect for basic ethical principles.

Mads Sørensen examines the extent to which the concept of the political consumer can be integrated into a liberal market economy. He relates the concept of political consumers to the marginal theory of utility by William Stanley Jevons, who argued that it is not trade or work but the utility, feelings, or beliefs in the product that are value-creating. According to marginal utility theory, the utility of a product diminishes as the quantity of a product grows. In some sense, the idea of the political consumer is compatible with the concept of marginal utility because value is not considered as an objective notion, but as dependent on the preferences of the consumer; however, Jevons's notion of utility was rather materialistic and at the borderline of the kind of values that are prioritized by political consumers. Moreover, critical sociologists like Ulrich Beck have expressed their skepticism towards this unification of politics and business. The problem is that political consumers may be rather unstable and consumer choices are not a result of a legitimate political process.[22] From the perspective of integrative business ethics and according to the concept of the good citizen corporation, this criticism of the potential subversive function of political consumers does not hold up. Rather, political consumers in the age of branding and brand value represent a conscious demand of corporate social responsibility and strong ethical engagement of firms in issues of human rights and sustainability. Moreover, with regard to large buyers, like public organizations or institutions, political and ethical concerns seem very important as justification of legitimate action.

In addition to investigating this synthesis between politics and business, consumer ethics also concerns all other moral dimensions of the sales relationship. Fairness and justice in the sales relationship means that it must be voluntary. To be voluntary it must be based on a framework of information, rationality, and non-coercion. These criteria are general measures for evaluating the sales practices by corporations.[23] It is presupposed that fair sales practices are based on the autonomy of the consumers and their freedom to choose products, which implies that consumers have the best knowledge about their own interests and preferences. However, in order to secure that decision-making is free, it must be ensured that both buyer and seller understand, and have full information, about the exchange relation. They must be independent and have enough knowledge to make a rational decision about the exchange of the product. Although this fairness requirement may seem very idealistic, given the number of deceptive practices in the marketplace, it is arguable that this condition is necessary in order to ensure just development of the market.

First and foremost among the ethical responsibilities that companies face with regard to consumers is the responsibility of product safety. The firm has a basic obligation to produce a product that is safe and that does no unintentional harm to the consumer. The presence of questionable goods like so-called sin products (e.g., alcohol and cigarettes, different kinds of medicines or drugs, or even defense industry products like weapons or car industry products) shows how difficult it is to determine the limits of products and to what extent dangerous products should be allowed in society.

Closely related to product safety is the responsibility of the firm to sell products with at least a minimum standard of product quality relative to the price. This is also related to the duty of companies to secure that the buyer has correct information about the product from the seller. This is the case when the buyer is deceived by misleading advertising or marketing, incorrect information about what the product is, or wrong labeling and packaging. Indeed, the problem of consumer choice is how to give them correct and full information about the product so that they can exercise autonomous choices with informed consent. In this process of decision-making, it is again the basic ethical principles of autonomy, dignity, integrity, and vulnerability of the consumer that are at stake. In modern society, it is necessary to care for these aspects of the identity of the consumer, because it is becoming increasingly difficult to judge the content of products, particularly new technologies, without honesty and help from the manufacturers. Consumers do not have the technical knowledge and expertise to evaluate products themselves without assistance from corporations or consumer protection laws and agencies.[24]

This situation represents a criticism of the idea of an equal relationship between buyer and seller in which the buyer has as much responsibility for reasonable behavior as the seller. Today, consumer law and ethics starts from the idea that there is an asymmetrical relation between consumers and the corporation. This means that consumer law has moved away from the concept of *caveat emptor* (let the buyer beware), which has historically played a large role in determining whether an economic exchange transaction can be considered to be fair and just. Although it is not totally insignificant the principle of consumer responsibility has been rendered less important by the power of corporations on the modern market and the complexity of consumer choice.

Recent legal developments signify that consumers are considered very vulnerable and in need of having their ability to exercise autonomous choices protected. The realization of consumer vulnerability implies a broader concern for their integrity and vulnerability beyond exclusive reference to their preferences. It is no longer the consumers who are exclusively responsible for demonstrating that the manufacturer has made a mistake when there is something wrong with a product, rather the doctrine of strict corporate liability has come to dominate the legal doctrines of consumer law.[25] This means that it is the corporation's burden to prove that it did not do anything wrong in cases where it is sued by buyers of its products. In a number of legal cases in Europe and the United States, corporations have been held responsible to prove that their products are not dangerous and that they were made in accordance with relevant quality control procedures.[26] The argument for extending a corporation's responsibility for its products is that this is the most effective way to ensure product safety. The corporation is considered to be in a much better position than the consumer to take effective responsibility for product safety, which also implies a burden on the corporation to bear the costs for damage or defects to its product.[27]

Legislation on product liability is the general basis for the ethical responsibilities of corporations towards consumers. Governments in Europe and the United States have made consumer protection laws in order to enforce these responsibilities. In 1972, the United States consumer product safety act went into practice, which also established the consumer safety commission. Similarly action has been taken in many European countries, where consumer protection regulation has been established.[28] It is the task of these regulations to set standards to protect and ensure a decent and fair promotion and sales of products. In many countries, consumer protection agencies have both enforcement and education functions in order to research and gather information about products, advertising, and sales practices.

Even though these regulations are designed to protect free consumer choice, skeptics consider them as excessively paternalistic. They argue that many interventions to protect consumer safety actually challenge the rights of consumers to decide for themselves over the use of products and imply a restriction of the free market. Moreover, the question is to which extent regulation can change the attitudes of corporations, though regulation and consumer protection arguably demonstrate how concerns for consumer safety and corporate profits may, at the end of the day, work together. There are many examples in different industries, for example in the automobile and airline industries, where lack of concern for consumer safety ended up being very expensive for the corporations, due to costly court cases brought by consumers and the subsequent attacks on their reputations.

Because of these concerns, businesses should prioritize their responsibility to protect consumers and guarantee the safety of their products. This implies that corporations should avoid thinking that consumer accidents are solely a result of the misbehavior of consumers, but rather businesses should take prime responsibility for product deficiency and try to improve their products on the basis of consumer complaints. Moreover, among the requirements for product safety should be the intensified efforts of businesses to monitor their manufacturing processes.[29] This is an important part of the required efforts of business to contribute with self-regulation on the market. Internal efforts to test products and product safety are very important in order to ensure good customer relations; therefore, internal monitoring activities should be an integrated part of values-driven management's efforts to work with the values of customer and consumer protection. This could imply that companies have product safety staff to review new products when they are ready to go on the market.[30] Efforts to ensure good and honest market information about the products should be among the priorities of a corporation. This institutional responsibility is a requisite precondition in order for consumers to exercise autonomous choice and to get necessary information about the products.

Instead of being hostile to consumer complaints, companies could make an effort to work in a proactive fashion with consumers, so that complaints are carefully examined as a source of information to improve the company's reputation and product. In this way, communication with consumers about products is considered as a useful way to improve the interaction of the company with the environment. Instead of deceptive practices, sales should be related to respect and an understanding of consumer vulnerability, so that companies work to give consumers fair information about their products. Indeed, the emergence of increased consumer awareness, as indicated by the movement of political and conscious consumers, may be considered as an indication of the need for such a proactive dialogue with consumers as stakeholders.

In this context, the responsibility of a company for its product includes concern for high quality. In fact, this might be in the interest of a business to improve its reputation and goodwill among consumers.[31]It is also important to work for clear labeling and packaging to respect consumer autonomy. Conscious consumers have asked for environmental and other information on the labels and packages of products, but in many cases companies have used this information as a tool to improve their reputations without really improving the products. Product quality is indeed related to pricing, yet this is a very sensitive issue. There are many cases where companies manipulate the prices of their products in order to increase market shares or profits. However, it is an important task for values-driven management, business ethics, and good citizenship to address the issue of fair and just pricing and to determine "reasonable profits." One way to promote this would be to make sure that consumer choices are based on informed consent.[32]

Case 17. Product responsibility: The case of the Dow Corning Corporation

Dow Corning Corporation is a classic business school case that deals with product responsibility. The case has been selected to illustrate the *ethical crisis* that can appear without good product responsibility.[33]

Dow Corning Corporation has produced silicone for, among other things, female breast implants since the 1960s. Although the product was conceived as relatively safe in the first few decades of production, and was accepted as a means for various health and cosmetic breast improvements, women begain reporting increasing numbers of health problems during the 1990s. Many women who had had implants started issuing legal suits against the compnay, charging that Dow had long been aware of the possible risks of their silicone implants.

Dow Corning Corporation was founded in 1943 as a merger between Dow Chemical Company and Corning Glass Works. The two firms benefited by combining their knowledge about chemical processes and production on the one hand and knowledge about manufacturing of silicone on the other, in order to produce different kinds of silicone products in many different branches like airplanes, cars, electronics, medical products, et cetera.[34] Silicone for breast implants has always been a small part of the firm's business. In 1991, the sales of breast implants were only one percent of the company's total income.

Dow Corning had been considered an innovative and modern organization. In the 1960s, it introduced a division-based matrix organization with teamwork and informal culture. The firm had also developed a code of conduct and ethical guidelines of social responsibility for employees and local communities in the countries where the firm was operating. Dow Corning tried to formulate rules of product stewardship, ensuring that the products of the corporation would be "safe, efficacious, and accurately represented in literature, advertising, and package identification."[35]

During the 1950s and 1960s, Dow Corning started to work with the development of silicone implants for plastic surgery in order help women who had had their breast removed due to breast cancer or for other cosmetic reasons. Though they had discovered some negative health-related consequences from the effects of silicone, the firm took no action to stop the production of silicone for plastic surgery. This early knowledge of the potentially damaging effects of silicone meant that the company lost many of the legal suits brought by dissatisfied customers in the 1980s and 1990s, even though there has been disagreement about the causal link between silicone and the damage claimed.

Some argue that the firm should continue to manufacture the produce because it helps women, but others argue that ther risk of potential damage from silicone implants is so high that they should never have been introduced on the market. When the firm lost a legal suit against a woman named Mariann Hopkins it was held responsible for many damages, which was very expensive for the firm. However, the firm did not stop producing silicone, because many women still find the product very important.

In order to avoid further legal prosecution, Dow Corning collaborates with government institutions. However, the corporation did not really commit itself to its ethical values and it can be argued that ethics from the beginning were not really integrated in the effort to develop silicone products, because the risks of the product were heavily underestimated. This was to a large extent damaging for the corporation, considering that such a small proportion of its income came from breast silicone products. In order to be more aware of ethical aspects of their products, Dow Corning should have had a greater commitment to its ethical program.

3.3. The ethics of advertising and marketing

Issues of marketing and advertising are closely related to consumer ethics protection. Marketing ethics is about how advertising and marketing influence people and the ethical problems that emerge in this context.[36] In marketing ethics, four important themes emerge that may be subjected to ethical analysis:

1) The ethics of the product deals with how to market products and what means companies are allowed to use in order to publicize them. In particular, it is important that there is a reasonable relation between the image of the product that is used for marketing and the product itself.

2) The ethics of price deals with the relation between pricing and quality of the product, but also in relation to the bargaining and manipulation of the price in economic markets. Issues of integrity and accountability arise in relation to determining the price of the product.

3) The ethics of distribution deals with the justice in this distribution, or how different communities are targeted based income and other variables.

4) The ethics of communication deals with the way in which the sales and marketing of products are communicated to the public.[37]

The whole problematic can be conceived by referencing Hermes from Greek mythology. Hermes was, at the same time, god of thieves and merchants, and the messenger of the gods. Selling and buying are very important kinds of communication, operating as social glue that keeps society together. Lack of respect for the norms of the market may lead to stealing, which to some extent has the power to destroy the market. The figure of Hermes is interesting because he represents this tripartite relation and tension between stealing, selling, and marketing, which further explains the ambiguous attitude to the market in Western culture. The figure of Hermes reminds us that there is certain cohesion in this communication, which is a matter of mutual exchange and, accordingly, an expression of the logic of the gift between generosity and economic exchange.

Advertising and media marketing are integrated parts of product information in modern society. Advertising is thought to be a necessary component of modern sales practices because it is an efficient way to use mass communication to deliver information about different products. Moreover, it contributes to developing a prosperous economy.[38] It is important to define a modern communicative concept of marketing that is related to basic ethical principles. One issue is the extent to which marketing professionals are allowed to use deceptive techniques and conceal objective facts in order to promote specific products. Traditionally, there has been much criticism of the manipulative powers of advertising and marketing, though today people in highly industrialized countries are daily exposed so many advertisements that they barely notice. With regard to the consumer's rights to exercise autonomy, concealment of information or misinformation is ethically problematic. There are rhetorical strategies used to sell products that many people find totally acceptable because they do not misinform, but only translate the promotion of the product into the language of marketing and advertisement.

Today, branding and the symbolic promotion of products is really important for progress in sales and market development. Large campaigns of advertisement and publicity represent symbolic and rhetorical ways of communicating information about products to consumers. In the modern emotional branding economy, advertising and marketing create symbols and illusions that are useful in order to give correct information about products. The rhetoric of marketing is not considered as an assault on reason and objectivity because reason in itself has rhetoric dimensions. Therefore, advertising is rather a creative art based on illusions and symbols, and it can barely be conceived as manipulating or distorting the life and autonomy of the consumer. From this point of view it is contested that advertising represents a threat to the autonomy and the free will of the consumer, and that consumers – even though advertisements function as works of art – are not necessarily misled by the creative message of advertising symbolism.[39]

It is, however, important to protect consumers in marketing. The basic ethical principles of respect for autonomy, dignity, integrity, and vulnerability are very important in order to develop good marketing practices. To respect consumer autonomy in marketing means to present and promote products in a way that allows consumers to make qualified and informed choices about products. An example of this is the practice of extending product labels to give information about the history of the product and about how the company deals with ethical issues and ethical problems. To respect autonomy also means to respect the wishes and freedom of the consumer in the promotion of specific products. Accordingly, it is important that the consumer has a free choice in deciding what products he or she wants to buy. In this sense, it is important that advertising in mass society does not subvert this respect for the autonomy and freedom of human beings.[40] Advertising should respect the capacity of rational choice and the freedom of consumers.[41]

To respect human dignity in advertising and marketing implies that product promotions do not present human beings in a nondignified manner. This is relevant, for example, with issues of discrimination or oppression in marketing products. Commercials are required to respect human rights and human dignity, and it is important that they do not oppress specific individuals in their presentation of the products. It is important that commercials respect the capacity of human beings to make rational decisions independently of the promotion of the commercials. The advertising industry should also try to respect the integrity of human beings in the sense that commercials should be respectful of personal privacy, for example spam or marketing materials should not be distributed to households without consent.

There are justifiable legal and ethical limitations on marketing practices.

Following George Brenkert when he cites management Peter Drucker, this position is supported by the idea that marketing professionals should respect no other ethical codes and customs than those of society.[42] Marketing ethics is fundamentally based on the recognition of the vulnerability of consumers in cases where they are not able to resist. It is also directed at improving the social responsibility and ethical citizenship of companies. Responsible marketing practices involve ethical marketing statements and values-driven management in market organizations, as well as ethical audits of marketing practices. This approach to marketing includes a broader view on the stakeholders of marketing, taking into account both consumer privacy, social issues in marketing, and environmental marketing. The challenges to marketing ethics focus on the development of adequate normative standards for marketing behavior in order to avoid bad consequences of consumer society. The ideas of social and environmental marketing have, in this context, been proposed as international responses to the demand for fair marketing practices.

In response to the pressure of political, green, and ethical consumers, marketers are realizing that they can use their ability to influence consumer behavior in a constructive ethical manner. The idea in social marketing is that commercial marketing strategies can be used to achieve social aims. Practitioners of social marketing construct ethical advertisements for their customer corporations in a way that helps to influence the public understanding of their client's corporate ethics. Social marketing moves beyond a consumption oriented definition of marketing and regards marketing ethics as synonymous with corporate social responsibility.[43] From this perspective, ethical marketing is about creating openness and transparency in corporate communication, where the firm contributes with proactive strategies to achieve social and environmental aims, for example by highlighting the firm's work to protect human rights in developing countries or promote environmental protection. Recently, issues such as protecting online privacy and customer security around e-marketing strategies have become increasingly important.[44]

Social marketing also implies inventing marketing strategies based on dialogical relations with consumers and customers: however, this raises the difficult question about the responsibility of corporations for their involvement with customers, in the sense that dialogical marketing is very personal. To what degree do the ends justify the means in marketing and advertising? Especially vulnerable groups in advertising are young children who become even more vulnerable, when exposed to different deceptive techniques.[45] Children are very vulnerable because they don't have the capacity of being a "reasonable consumer," and they don't have the ability to make critical judgments of the contents of different kinds of publicity.

With regard to the problem of how marketing companies and agencies view their moral obligations to consumers, recent research shows that advertising agencies can be conceived as moral communities.[46] Marketing agencies understand the need for ethics. In fact, marketing may be conceived as one of the most ethical areas of business. The marketing profession is highly regulated and interviews show that the marketing profession is aware of the need for ethical values. The industry is characterized by general recognition of possible ethical problems within controversial product areas such as cigarettes, alcohol, firearms, or video games. Many agencies simply refuse to create campaigns for products that they consider too dangerous. Moreover, there is recognition of possible ethical failures in messages dealing with minorities, race, disabled people, the elderly, et cetera. The agencies are also aware of the problems of deception in advertising, although most agencies do not go as far as considering advertising threatening to society. On the contrary, many members of advertising agencies consider their work to reflect people's desires and wants rather than constructing new ones.

On the basis of this recognition of ethics in marketing, the attitudes toward ethics among senior employees in marketing agencies can be put into the following categories: severely myopic, modestly myopic, and open.[47] Marketing employees with *severe myopia* consider ethics as irrelevant to marketing. They typically argue that consumers are smart and can make their own decisions. Even children, they say, have become more critical consumers. Moreover, they argue that it is not the marketing employee's job to care about ethics. They considered themselves simply as employees working on a company's campaign, but without final culpability. Marketers could be said to have legal responsibility, but they cannot be said to have a more comprehensive social and environmental responsibility. They argue that marketing does not create values but rather is a mirror to those that already exist in society. When an advertisement shows a thin person eating ice cream, it is not reinforcing the value of thinness, but rather reflects a desire prevalent in society: to indulge in fatty ice cream without gaining weight. It is also a fundamental aspect of democratic societies that marketing agencies have freedom of speech so that they can make whatever campaign they want. This concept of advertising does not see any problems with highly persuasive campaigns and argues that corporations, as the clients, have the right to decide what kind of campaign they want the agency to run.

The attitude of *modest myopia* is more open towards ethics in the marketing business. This position recognizes that there is a certain implicit creativity in the marketing and advertising business. Looking more closely at the business, different kinds of ethical problems and conflicts of interest related to the different spheres of marketing begin to emerge. While some care is taken to mind the social consequences of different marketing practices, a certain compartmentalization takes place whereby ethical issues get ignored in the daily work. The marketing profession is characterized by a kind of Pandora's Box, where the controversial ethical issues remain hidden away without discussion or explanation. Upon closer examination of these issues, it is clear that the marketing profession is marked by many problematic issues.

The positive and *open attitude* towards ethics is characterized by a recognition of the profession's ethical responsibility. In many cases, agencies with this attitude refuse to accept corporations with proposals for ethically controversial campaigns or products. They argue that agencies should not undertake a certain campaign if they have ethical doubts. It is, for example, problematic to run a political campaign for a person or a party that espouses values that you cannot share. An understanding of the multitude of ethical issues is present in this openness to ethics in marketing, which renders it necessary for the marketing agency to clarify its basic values through daily communication about values and ethical issues. In addition, the agency should be willing to have transparency in decision-making processes and values, both internally and externally, in relation to clients. Indeed, there should be an emphasis on actions in order to improve the profile of the organization.

Because of these differences, marketing agencies are aware of the need for values statements and clarification of values for their potential clients. It is considered important that the agency clarify its values so corporations can get clear information about their particular values. In this context, it is important that the advertising profession is more open to communicating basic values. Accordingly, marketing agencies are becoming increasingly open towards ethics, and social and environmental issues as a fundamental part of marketing, even though there still is abundant skepticism towards ethics and values-driven management as a useful part of marketing.[48]

An essential conception of marketing ethics might state that lying, deception, or withholding information implies a violation of the commercial exchange relationship and social contract between buyer and seller. Thomas Aquinas reflected this sentiment when he wrote that a "sale was rendered unlawful by a defect in the thing sold about which the seller failed to inform the buyer. If the seller did not know about the defect, he had not committed a sin, but had to recompense the seller."[49]

To protect the consumer, the truth in advertising movement – as developed by the American jurist and Supreme Court Justice, Oliver Wendell Holmes, in the nineteenth century – devised the so-called ten commandments of good advertising, which are classic elements of a good code of conduct:

1) Thou shalt have no other gods in advertising but Truth.
2) Thou shalt not make any graven image of wealth, or power, or station and thou shalt not bow down thyself to them nor serve them except with honor.
3) Thou shalt not use the power of advertising in an unworthy cause or in behalf of unworthy goods.
4) Remember the working day to keep it holy.
5) Honor thy business and thy advertising that they may honor thee, and thy days of usefulness may be long upon the land.
6) Thou shalt not kill fair competition from without, nor ambition from within, thine organization.
7) Thou shalt not lie, misstate, exaggerate, misrepresent, nor conceal; thou shalt not bear false witness to the public, but thou shalt be fair to thy merchandise.
8) Thou shalt not steal by false pretense in statements, spoken, written, or printed.
9) Thou shalt not permit adulteration or substitution in advertised goods.
10) Thou shalt not covet, nor imitate, nor run down thy neighbor's name, nor his fame, nor his wares, nor his trade, nor anything that is thy neighbor's.[50]

From a Kantian perspective, deception in marketing cannot be justified, not even in situations where the firm has severe economic problems. According to Thomas Carson, respect for the categorical imperative (i.e, always tell the truth) should be the guiding principle of the marketing profession.[51] In order to create a fair and just exchange relationship, responsible marketing professionals have, even when using rhetorical devices in publicity, a duty to be transparent and reveal all aspects of the product, so that reasonable consumers can make clear and argued choices in the exchange relationship.

Case 18: Privacy and marketing in the digital age: The case of Double-Click

The case of Double-Click has been selected to illustrate an *ethical crisis* following corporations that do not respect the right of privacy in marketing. In the digital network society, the problem of privacy protection is becoming more urgent. In marketing, for example, collecting information about customers is very important in order to understand their wants and needs. This makes it easier to respond to their preferences, shopping, and buying behavior. But there is a fine line between legitimate data collection and violations of privacy, and questions about to what degree corporations are required to protect the privacy of customers and consumers.

Double-Click is a firm that is confronted with these issues because it sells and distributes cookies on the Internet.[52] In 1999, the firm decided to buy Abacus Direct (a database with personal identification about online buying behavior) and combine the databases of the companies, leading to a very powerful storage bank of personalized knowledge about buying behavior on the Internet. The new knowledge would make it possible for Double-Click to make their cookie-based publicity much more focused on particular customer segments.

Double-Click had a privacy policy that stated that it was not allowed to collect personal information about customers. The agreement under which personal information was given to Abacus did not explicitly allow its transfer to another organization. Consumer organizations were very critical of this information sharing because it would give Double-Click much stronger sales power and violate the privacy of the consumers. After strong criticism, Double-Click decided that customers were free to decide if they wanted their personal information to appear in the database.

The Double-Click case also led the United States Government to make legislation about the responsibilities of online marketing and publicity firms. Double-Click was pressured by the criticism of consumer organizations and their falling shares, so they decided to postpone setting up the new database.

This case highlights the need to protect online consumer protection from "big brother" in the information society. The ethics of information technology includes a necessary protection of privacy and informed consent among consumers. Double-Click had a privacy policy but they were unable to analyze the consequences of this policy with regard to the new possibilities of efficient registration of consumers. However, this was necessary in order to avoid violation of the autonomy and integrity of consumers.

3.4. The ethics of public relations

The ethics of public relations does not deal with advertising or marketing, but with the legitimate relations of the firm to the public. This sharp distinction between public relations and advertising is, however, blurred by emerging concepts like branding, storytelling, and corporate identity in which there is convergence between the search for legitimacy and the search for publicity. Corporations are using values and values-driven management not only for internal purposes, but in order to improve sales and market share. Some are very critical of this development, arguing that comingling ethics with branding, environmental profiles, or storytelling about the good values of the firm, has turned ethics into business. They argue that business ethics is nothing but a new commercial stunt of the corporate world. Others conceive this evolution as an indication that public relations and the quest for legitimacy are becoming even more important in business. The convergence of public relations and advertising is considered as an extension of the sphere where legitimate public relations are needed.[53] From this perspective, it is important to emphasize that public relations is not only about instrumental communications, but concerns the totality of the values, ethics, and identity of the corporation as a whole.

The concept of legitimacy is, therefore, very important for understanding the ethics and practice of public relations in order to promote accountability, integrity, and corporate citizenship. While organizations in the classical theories were conceived as closed rational systems, the increased focus on the ethics of corporations implies a new conception of the corporation in close interaction with its external environment. Corporations are conceived as open systems, where it is not the material or technological relations, but ethical values, cultural norms, as well as symbols and epistemological conceptions in its surroundings that are decisive for its development.[54] The concept of legitimacy is important for this conception of organizations. As we know from Weber, in contrast to traditional, charismatic, authoritarian, and rational forms of legitimation, modern organizations are supposed to be based on rational strategic planning. But as we have discussed, legitimacy is no longer only based on rationality. Modern society requires a broader conception of legitimacy that includes ethics and democratic values. According to Mark C. Suchman, the distinction between strategic and institutional conceptions of legitimacy can be seen from different pragmatic, normative, and cognitive perspectives. However, the commonality remains that legitimacy emerges as the process by which an organization justifies it rights to exist in relation to other organizations and in relation to society.[55] Organizational legitimacy is based on values and cultural norms that constitute the right of this particular organization to exist. From the point of view of public relations, acquiring legitimacy means creating the presuppositions (e.g., a number of pre-given values and norms) by which to conceive and judge an organization. In this sense, legitimacy may be conceived as a cultural construction that is more or less integrated in fundamental conceptions of society. Organizations that use a purely administrative and technological concept of management, and do not reflect consciously about these relations of legitimacy as relations of public relations, are very vulnerable in relation to their external environment. Therefore, there is increased focus on both pragmatic moral and cognitive legitimation of the activities of the corporation. As a part of public relations, ethics is used as an important instrument to develop and influence this process of legitimation and values-driven management. This ethics contains elements of practical, moral, and cognitive legitimation of the activities of the corporation in order to "naturalize" it as a solid element of society.

Public relations should, therefore, be defined as a matter of management and an important part of corporate leadership. What is needed is a public relations office that is part of the executive office of the firm. This office would not only deal with formulating values as a part of the identity of the corporation, and with communicating these values, but it would also be concerned with stakeholder relations and with protecting the firm's brand and image in crisis situations. Moreover, public relations offices should work proactively in order to promote the ethical image of the corporation to the general public, government, the local community, the civil society, and to a variety of stakeholders, in particular consumers and NGOs. Public relations has been defined in the academic literature as a "continuant systematic management function by which corporations, private, and public organizations and institutions are searching to require perception, sympathy, and support in those parts of the public, with whom they are or will be in contact."[56]

As a firm communicates its image, profile, and identity to the general public, it can act defensively, trying to avoid being a part of the public debate, or it can act proactively trying to construct a public dialogue about its values and product. Conceiving the role of the firm as a political actor in society and defining the firm as an ethical actor searching for socially responsible relations to the public are important for sustainability of the corporation. Public relations is about sustaining and enforcing the social legitimacy of the firm as a good corporate citizen.

Habermas described the function of the public in modern society.[57] The ideal of a public sphere is a place where different actors meet for open-minded and serious discussion of political issues in society. Each moral person is considered, as such, a citizen of the public sphere. This vision of the public sphere is inspired by the idea of the Greek Agora, where citizens gathered to discuss the future of the city-state. In the age of the Enlightenment, "public spaces of discussion" emerged where citizens gathered to discuss issues of public interest.[58] In modernity, this ideal of citizenship in the public sphere has become problematized by the immense pressure because of the economic and technical progress and the increasing dominance of the private sphere as the realm of civic discussion. Habermas fears that citizens in late modernity are reduced to consumers and that the public sphere is so commercialized that there is no room for genuine political discussion.[59] In mass society, there is the danger that public discussion is replaced by one-way manipulation of citizens by mass media.

Given this danger, the maintenance of dialogue in a free public sphere is of primary importance in modern societies in order to protect democratic citizenship. The public space institutionalizes the possibility of critical discourse, and this requires obligations of legitimacy for actors in a community.[60] In public relations, legitimacy is defined as the institutional dimension of the honest search for truth and action based on practical rationality. Habermas argues for the ideal of communicative reason based on respect for the better argument and willingness to listen to all voices in the debate.[61] This view of the public sphere is opposed to an instrumental and strategic use of communication in the public sphere, where it is used exclusively to promote self-interest and commercial gain. This view of the public defends the possibility of argumentative communication as central to public debate.[62]

It is an important charge of the ethics of public relations that corporations contribute to maintaining and evolving this public sphere. There is no real opposition between having a strategy for public relations and respecting basic principles of argumentative communication. The ethics of public relations insists on the deontological values of republican business ethics. This signifies respect for truth and honesty, and strong moral integrity of the firm. Respect and dignity imply that the corporation is faithful to its values and that it follows the virtues of good communication when entering in to the public sphere. The rhetorical devices of *ethos* (moral habitus), *pathos* (emotional expression), and *logos* (rational argument) contribute to trustful communication in which the corporation searches to establish legitimate relations to the environment and to important stakeholders.

The public sphere is the place where business life intersects with civil society and governmental policy. Corporations encounter actors from civil society and from the political system in this public sphere, and it is the place where different actors are promoting their general social legitimacy. There are many miscellaneous civil society organizations that advocate themselves as stakeholders of the firm, for instance trade unions, consumer groups, or NGOs, semi-academic institutions like Accountability (a London-based NGO), and other kinds of public organizations.[63] They are of very different type and scope, with different activities and focus. Some of them, like the antiglobalization movement organization ATTACK, may be very critical towards corporations, constantly challenging the legitimacy of capitalist economies.

Trade unions are stakeholders with strong claims and they are traditionally very well-organized in solid structures. Interest organizations usually select some narrow scope of focus, like the environmental protection, workers' rights, or fair trade practices, and they confront corporations with these interests. Often they have alternative and loosely coupled organization structures based on networks and voluntary engagement by participants.

According to the urgency, power, and legitimacy of civil society organizations, they often challenge corporations in the public sphere, particularly in cases of crisis and when corporations do not respect legal rules or the ethical customs of the society. In these cases, aggressive stakeholders can be quite painful for the corporation, which has to respond to their criticisms. In general, civil society organizations argue against the corporations in the name of society or the public, though in fact it is not always clear who these organization represent. They are also confronted with problems of legitimacy and accountability, and sometimes these organizations have difficulties determining their own legitimate stakeholders.[64] Moreover, in cases where civil society organizations work too closely with corporations in stakeholder dialogue there is the danger that they will loose their independence and function as kind of privileged consultants for the corporations.

The ethical field of the public sphere of civil society is very fluid and difficult to manage. New issues suddenly arise and the firm cannot control its image in the public debate. Indeed, there is a temptation to try to manipulate the public and follow the rhetoric of mediatization of the public by all kinds of commercial means. Although a strategy of deception can, in some cases, be economically beneficial, it is difficult to justify from the point of view of the ethics of stakeholder dialogue and respect for good arguments. Moreover, in cases where it goes wrong, there are strong risks to the firm's image. Issues of perceived unaccountability, lack of credibility, and untrustworthiness can stay with the organization for ages. From the perspective of good Kantianism, it is – as has already been stated – a moral requirement always to tell the truth.

Case 19. Philip Morrris and the selling and marketing of tobacco

In an era of increasing awareness of the need to protect consumers from products with health risks, the tobacco industry has encountered problems of legitimacy. The case of Philip Morris has been selected as example of an *ethical crisis,* where a corporation sells controversial products without wanting to modify them in order to solve their problems.

In the Western world, political consumers have acted very critically towards the cigarette and tobacco industry. Corporations like Philip Morris have difficulties enlarging their markets in the Western world. Therefore, the industry has chosen to diversify products and invest in other branches, like clothing, while at the same time focusing on marketing cigarettes to people in the postcommunist countries and the developing world.[65]

While trying to minimize the health risks of tobacco products, Philip Morris maintains its core activity of selling and marketing tobacco. In the Western world, and particularly in the United, States Philip Morris and the tobacco industry represented very lucrative business. In 1997, Philip Morris's tobacco business had nearly half of the market share in the United States. Philip Morris owned one of the world's most valuable brands, Marlboro. Still, Philip Morris has increasingly enlarged its business into breweries, food, et cetera. While nearly half of the adult American population smoked in the 1950s, by the 1990s that number had been cut nearly in half. [66]

In 1996, the tobacco industry employed more than 700,000 Americans and contributed with more than fifty-five billions dollars to the national product. At the same time, the American Centers for Disease Control and Prevention estimated in 1996 that the cost of smoking related diseases like lung cancer and heart failure was more than fifty billion dollars. The health risks of tobacco have been known since the 1950s. Smokers have much greater risk of getting lung cancer and they may be more susceptible to other diseases. It has been estimated that more than 420,000 die annually because of smoking, while 53,000 die of passive smoking.[67]

The causal link established between smoking and disease has meant that many court cases have been brought against the tobacco industry in the United States. In the 1990s, the tobacco industry had still not lost a case against smokers, but when whistle-blowers in the industry released documents from a tobacco company, Brown and Williamson, which indicated the industry's awareness of the damaging effects of cigarettes on smoker's health, this situation changed. Subsequent to the release of the documents, a large amount of private litigation was initiated against the tobacco industry and, in order to avoid more expenses, it accepted a class action settlement with state and government authorities. Under the terms of the settlement, the industry was obligated to pay 200 billions dollars in damages with the promise that no further litigation could be brought against the industry.[68] This settlement was an advantage for the industry because it avoided further private litigation and expenditures; however, part of the terms of agreement included forbidding the industry from marketing and advertising cigarettes. In addition, the settlement money helped to finance campaings against smoking. Due to these restrictions, the industry could more easily keep new firms out of the market while raising prices and redirecting production towards overseas markets.

Ethical issues of tobacco production imply difficult tensions between the corporate manipulation of consumers with unhealthy and dangerous products and a consumer's free choice to lead an unhealthy lifestyle. Increasing state awareness of corporate social responsibility in the tobacco industry has raised expectations of tobacco firms in the global marketplace.

3.5. The inclusive corporation and the social and ethical audit

An important part of including external stakeholders is the effort to integrate them into the performance of the firm. The inclusive company may be defined as one with a wide range of stakeholders actively involved in decision-making, reporting, and accounting.[69] This company is aware of its impact on the community and the external environment, and is at the same time concerned with its own profits and community wealth. Moreover, ethics and values can only be efficiently integrated in the activities of the firm if they are mapped on the accounts of its annual performance. It is therefore necessary to include the ethical performance of the firm in accounting. This also includes efforts to measure the degree of business involvement in the local community and how partnerships are created with this local community.

The inclusive company is interested in having a positive impact on the local community, which is considered a part of being socially responsible. This commitment can have many forms. It may involve activities for supporting and protecting employees or their families, and educational, health, or other kinds of initiatives. It can also involve helping local organizations; however, it is important that these activities in local communities are not considered exclusively as charity or philanthropy.[70] Real commitment to local community should, rather, be seen as active engagement in a society built on mutuality with partners. Community engagement involves partnerships with local people and organizations. This should be done in order to integrate the firm into the local community so it can achieve legitimacy and support by this society. Naturally, in an age of globalization, local community may be defined rather broadly, involving relevant particular cultures in specific countries, regions, or areas where the firm has an impact. Being integrated in local activities, the firm can "give back" and express thanks and gratitude in return for what is has received from these communities.

In order to engage in local community, a corporation must be able to identify the problems that affect its community. The important issues may vary from community to community, and can include serious problems of crime, homelessness, poverty, unemployment, and racism. When the issues have been identified, it is the task of the corporation to define a procedure for engaging in order to help and improve the local community. The company could work to improve education and health conditions, or to fight unemployment. Moreover, it may investigate the extent to which it contributes to bad conditions in its local surroundings. If this negative contribution is identitifed, it can partner with local groups or NGOs in order to strategize on how to improve the situation. This engagement in local community can lead to active involvement of the community, which is often an advantage for the corporation, because it will get a better reputation and greater trust among local people.

Governments in Europe, in Denmark and the United Kingdom among others, have recently worked for stronger partnerships between government, businesses, NGOs, and local communities. It was realized that governments are no longer strong enough to deal with the problems alone, and that support from local businesses could have a great impact on community development. Businesses have been encouraged to build partnerships in their local communities, establishing common agendas for collaboration between local government, the private sector, and NGOs. These partnerships can be considered as important for the development of a broader commitment of the corporation, including measures for stakeholder dialogue and reporting.

The inclusion of the local community and other stakeholders in strategic management must be reflected in accounting. The difficulty is how to measure the autonomy, dignity, integrity, and vulnerability of stakeholders. Different stakeholders may have very different demands, which can be difficult to recognize; however, it is generally accepted that stakeholder accounting helps businesses to not only care for the economic bottom line, but to include a wide range of issues in the accounting. This is not only necessary in order to improve the corporation, but it will also increase its profits and the brand reputation in the long run. The inclusion of stakeholders in accounting will also help to improve the general transparency and accountability of the firm in relation to the public.[71] Stakeholder mapping is a very good approach to show that a corporation cares about the groups that affect or are affected by the firm.

There is a distinction between old and new accounting ethics. Traditionally, accounting ethics has involved the ethics of financial accounting, whereby the accounting profession is supposed to follow its own ethical rules, based on honesty, objectivity, and compliance with the law.[72] From this perspective, the accounting profession is conceived as a homogenous group who formulate ethical guidelines for practicing with integrity and responsibility.[73] This process might be conceived as more of an art than a science, because it involves judgment and the ethical principles of competence, confidentiality, and objectivity, but also integrity, due care, and concern for the public interest.[74] After accounting scandals linked to American companies like Enron and World Com, the ethics of the accounting profession have received more scrutiny. There has been increased focus on self-regulation and respect for the public interest. Indeed, accounting has been conceived as the key to transparency and public legitimacy of corporations.

This is even more the case with the new accounting ethics. While the accounting profession was exposed to some criticism due to recent scandals, its introduction of alternative reporting mechanisms, including issuing statements of social and environmental performance, have received kudos. The accountant has even become as sort of hero of transparency and corporate social responsibility. It is the accountant who can report about the problems or positive performance of the firm. The new accounting ethics is broader than the ordinary concept of accounting insofar as it involves including external and internal stakeholders as relevant for measurement in the accounting scheme. Financial, ethical, social, and environmental accounting describe new ways of measuring the performance of the firm. These forms of accounting should be linked to international and global standards for measurement and reporting, related to issues of human rights, social and environmental business responsibility.

In opposition to traditional accounting ethics, ethical, social, and environmental reporting aim to include both internal and external stakeholders in the accountancy process. During the 1990s governments in both Europe and the United States made efforts to facilitate corporate participation in community. Inclusive management strategies were introduced in order to make business more responsible and to establish a closer relationship between individuals, business, and society.[75] The new position of business in society and global culture makes stakeholder reporting and stakeholder mapping necessary tools for corporate survival. These new kinds of reporting and accounting are based on dialogue with stakeholders in order to measure the performance of the corporation relative to the rights and responsibilities of stakeholders. The inclusion of external and internal stakeholders in the accounting is based on an effort to be aware of different stakeholder claims in decision-making. New accounting is still based on the idea that good business is profitable business, but at the same time the corporation is viewed as a social institution with obligations to the community, transcending the possible gains on the stock market. Stakeholder accounting is based on the view that corporations, in order to achieve success, have to better understand their relationships with employees, contractors, suppliers, and customers.[76]

In this context, all kinds of human and nonhuman (i.e., environmental and animal) stakeholders may be included in the accounts and the reports. A distinction can be drawn between stakeholders who are supportive or critical, marginal or sleeping, as well as mixed stakeholders who both support and challenge the corporation. Moreover, it is important to be aware of both quantitative and qualitative aspects of stakeholder relations. This implies different kinds of bench marking of performance in relation to the level of stakeholder mapping of the company. An important aim of ethical and social auditing and accounting is the attempt to obtain goodwill and trust in relation to the environment of the corporation. By evaluating its relations to its stakeholders, the firm can identify bad relations and make the necessary changes. In this way, the function of stakeholder mapping and reporting is good communication with the external environment and to identify the different stakeholder claims, but this is also a kind of risk management, because stakeholder mapping and reporting give the corporation stronger ties with stakeholders.

The requirements for stakeholder reporting and accounting may, in fact, represent a great challenge to the measures of the accounting business. The international measures of economic welfare have already been intensively disputed. For example, some argue that the concept of gross domestic product (GDP) is an inadequate measure of the qualitative aspects of human economic and social performance.[77] These indicators only measure quantitative data without taking qualitative dimensions of human existence into account. Many people (including the economist Herman Daly) have, therefore, argued for another kind of measure like the index of sustainable economic welfare (ISEW). While the GDP measures growth in economic activity without including quality of life, people's desires and experiences, or sustainability, an ISEW is supposed to take these issues into account. Moreover, an index of sustainability could also account for durable goods that cannot be commercialized, such as nature, air, or animal life. Measuring sustainability would include long-term provisions for measuring how quality of life and emotional well-being are affected by economic progress.[78] A sustainability index might be said to measure economic impact on human autonomy, dignity, integrity, and vulnerability.

It is a very important challenge to develop broader and alternative models of accounting to embrace measurements of quality of life as well as social and environmental sustainability. The increasing complexity of the impact and consequences of corporate actions emphasizes the need for accounting and reporting instruments that do not exclusively measure financial performance. The many alternative parameters by which business performance can be measured include company policies, regulations, professional standards, and programs of values-driven management. Moreover, a financial audit may not be so simple, because it has to be interpreted according to expectations of different stakeholders.[79] In order to measure the many dimensions of company performance, financial audits that include environmental, social, or ethical audits are a great improvement. As with financial audits these other kinds of measurements must be taken seriously as important indications of company performance. This measurement of values-driven management would have to be verified by external, independent sources in order to achieve credibility. The alternative models of auditing also require strong management commitment, if they are to increase employee and stakeholder acceptance. Since environmental, social, and ethical auditing go beyond economics and include stakeholder relations they are very different from financial audits. They require new methods to report and communicate results.

Measuring economic performance need not be in opposition to accounting for social, ethical, and environmental performance. Measuring progress in terms of bottom-line achievements may give a false picture of the corporation, not indicating the connection between economic and types of performance. If you increase financial performance on the basis of extensive ethical, social, or environmental costs, the performance could turn out to be rather problematic in the long run; therefore, it is necessary to have an integrated view these measure of the company's performance.[80] The advantage of alternative models of accounting is that they can help to stabilize the corporation in many ways, by being used as risk and insurance management and helping to avoid legal problems, because ethical and social accounting makes it aware of eventually sensitive issues. Moreover, using these alternative models improves brand image and consumer confidence, if the company can demonstrate a good social, ethical, or environmental record.

Environmental audits are based on the ability of the organization to contribute to sustainable development. These so-called green audits need to follow a number of technical measures and there has been some progress in defining global standards for environmental audits. Environmental audits may look at the company performance in relation to legal requirements in society, the existing policies of environmental values-driven management in the company, and the efficiency of the concrete efforts to improve environmental sustainability.

Social auditing measures the social performance of the company. This includes the treatment of employees, for example if the company does not give good salaries or abuses human rights. In a wider sense the relationship to the local community is also measured. In the social audit, an objective platform of measures and standards is constructed in order to determine a company's effort to contribute to social responsibility. In this context, social auditing implies a close dialogue with external stakeholders about the social profile of the organization. Social audits try to measure social costs, which cannot be measured financially. Full disclosure and openness in an honest dialogue with stakeholders about the social actions and reputation of the corporation is an important part of social audits.

Ethical auditing is closely related to social auditing; however, it is more focused on the effects of internal standards of values-driven management.[81] The ethical audit reports on the function of internal policies and strategies with regard to the values of the organization. It investigates the extent to which an organization's behavior is consistent with its values as well as conceptions of its employees, management, and other stakeholders. An important aim of ethical auditing is to discover the ethical vulnerabilities of the organization.[82] In this context, the audits of ethical behavior in the firm can be seen as an "integrity thermometer,"[83] which seeks to uncover the dangers of unethical behavior and measure the performance of the company in light of virtues such as integrity, unity, openness, commitment, honesty, and identity.

Ethical and social auditing can equally be of benefit to the corporation. The alternative auditing schemes give new information about what happens inside the company, and how the company is perceived by the external world. In both ways of accounting there is a possibility of achieving increased knowledge about stakeholder views on the company. Alternative accounting also represents a new form of risk management and a way to enhance knowledge as the basis of decision-making. Increased self-knowledge brings a competitive advantage while simultaneously improving a company's public image. Moreover, there may be legal, strategic, and financial benefits because the corporation has more possible measures of company performance. In general, reports and accounting measures indicate the possibility of increased legitimacy in society. In order to ensure this achievement it is important that both social and ethical audits are performed accurately, including external statements from independent auditors about the performance of the company with reference to values, policies, and the different stakeholders. Audits should be done in a clear and honest manner, so that they address real problems and represent a constructive analysis of the company's problems and achievements. Indeed, the development of audits is done in cyclical dialogue with relevant stakeholders in order to ensure the transparency of company policies.

Even though social auditing is fairly new, efforts have been made to establish global standards for its practice, including a focus on social and environmental sustainability and transparency. Through transparency a company can improve its public image and legitimacy, and perhaps also its global performance. In 2001, France enacted a law requiring reporting on social and environmental performance by large companies. Since 1995, Denmark has had a law on reporting with environmental compliance.[84] Similar laws exist in other European countries, for example in Belgium. In the United Kingdom, the SA8000 standards represent an initiative to develop social reporting. SA8000 focuses particularly on human rights and issues of health and safety.[85] As mentioned earlier, in the United States the Enron scandal led to efforts to develop general standards for ethical accounting. At the international level, the Global Compact principles and triple bottom-line reporting represent initiatives for formulating standards of alternative reporting. CERES (the Coalition for Environmentally Responsible Economies) has tried to formulate a set of international standards for reporting and auditing including descriptions of the governance, values, and performance indicators of the firm regarding environmental and social issues.[86] The work of globalizing accounting standards must, however, still be develop. This will be discussed later in the section that elaborates on international codes of conducts and the principles of business ethics.

Case 20. Ethical accounting in a Danish bank: The case of Spar Nord

The concept of ethical accounting was developed in Denmark in the late 1980s and the beginning of the 1990s.[87] This case has been selected to illustrate the difficulties of a corporation that wanted to use ethical accounting to contribute to an *ethical effort.*

Researchers from Copenhagen Business School, Peter Pruzan and Ole Thyssen, had received a grant from the Danish National Research Council to investigate the process of ethical accounting. In this research they collaborated very closely with Sparekassen Nordjylland, which later became known as Spar Nord. Ethical accounting was, in this context, understood of a process of developing and accounting for the values of the corporation in a broad sense, and a process during which management was to remain open and responsive to the thoughts, wishes, and ideas of employees and other stakeholders.

Later, many organizations in Denmark implemented different kind of ethical accounting, understood as a dialogical value-based instrument to develop and account for values of the organization. These organizations included other small banks, like Middelfart Sparekasse, local public administration units, public libraries, hospitals, schools, and other public and private organizations that tried to use dialogical values-driven management.[88]

The starting point of the approach by Thyssen and Pruzan was Habermas's philosophy of communicative dialogue combined with aspects of Freeman's theory of stakeholder management. Their concept of ethical accounting included a dialogue with major stakeholders about how to define and develop the values of the corporation, and afterwards the accounting process would determine the extent to which the corporation could be held accountable for those values. This was based on interviews, questionnaires, or meetings with employees and other stakeholders about the values that they found important in the corporation.[89]

The project of Sparekassen Nordjylland utilized these qualitative methods, including organizing a project group, formulating questionnaires and interview forms for dialogue with stakeholders. After analyzing the results, they pursued further dialogue and finally formulated of strategy with the stakeholders. A public statement of the results, including a description of the strategy and problems encountered, was published.

Sparekassen Nordjylland considered ethical accounting as necessary to get a true image of the organization. Ethical accounting was not exclusively considered as an idealistic approach, but also as a reinforcement of the economic sustainability of the organization. However, later the organization changed the name of the accounting to "quality accounting." In 2000, organizational accounting was based on storytelling and values-driven management. At Spar Nord the concern for values remains, but without a direct concern for ethical accounting as a thoroughgoing process of stakeholder dialogue.[90]

Endnotes

1   Selection of case material for this case is inspired by the analysis of the concept of ethical traceability, indicating that it is an important feature of modern products that it is possible to trace their production history. This analysis is proposed by Christian Coff, Lise Christiansen Walbom and Eva Mikkelsen, "Forbrugere, etik og sporbarhed: om forbrugernes holdninger og handlinger på fødevareområdet" (Copenhagen: Center for ethics and law: 2005). See also www.coop.dk. Method for discursive analysis of the text is inspired by Anders Bordum and Jacob Holm Hansen, *Strategisk ledelseskommunikation. Erhvervslivets ledelse med visioner, missioner og værdier* (Copenhagen: Jurist og Økonomforbundets forlag, 2005), 25-63.

2   Andrew Crane and Dirk Matten, *Business Ethics: A European Perspective* (Oxford: Oxford University Press, 2004), 303 and 305.

3   Ibid: 303.

4   See Lynn Sharp Paine, *Cases in Leadership, Ethics and Organizational Integrity. A Strategic perspective* (Chicago: Irwin, 1997).

5   Andrew Crane and Dirk Matten, *Business Ethics: A European Perspective* (Oxford: Oxford University Press, 2004), 309.

6   Albert Carr, "Is Business Bluffing Ethical?", *Harvard Business Review*, 1968.

7   Andrew Crane and Dirk Matten, *Business Ethics: A European Perspective* (Oxford: Oxford University Press, 2004), 317.

8   Ibid: 318. This has been accurately described by Naomi Klein in her book *No Logo: Taking Aim at the Brand Bullies* (New York: Picador, Saint Martins Press, 2000).

9   Ibid: 329.

10   Ibid: 335.

11   This case is mainly selected from Jesper Kunde, *Corporate Religion* (Copenhagen: Børsens forlag, 1997). English Edition: Jesper Kunde, *Corporate Religion. Building a strong company through personality and corporate soul*, Prentice Hall (London: Pearson Education, 2000), 173. Kunde analyzes McDonald's as an example of corporate religion and he shows how systematization to the "last onion ring" creates a brand. Now, the question is whether McDonald's succeeds in integrating this in relation to corporate social responsibility. Therefore, the case takes source material from McDonald's website, www.mcdonalds.com. In particular, it looks at McDonald's social responsibility reports. The method for discursive analysis used was inspired by Anders Bordum and Jacob Holm Hansen, *Strategisk ledelseskommunikation. Erhvervslivets ledelse med visioner, missioner og værdier* (Copenhagen: Jurist og Økonomforbundets forlag, 2005), 25-63.

12   Joseph R. DesJardins and John J. McCall, *Contemporary Issues in Business Ethics*, Fourth Edition (California: Wadsworth, Thomson Learning, 2000), 305-404.

13   Here, we can refer to our discussions of institutional theory in chapter 2.

14   Gilles Lipovetsky, *Le bonheur paradoxal. Essai sur la société d'hyperconsommation* (Paris: Gallimard, 2005), 35.

15   Joseph B. Pine and James H. Gilmore, *The Experience Economy. Work is Theatre and every Business is a Stage*. (Boston, Massachusetts: Harvard Business School Press 2005).

16   Mads P. Sørensen, *Den Politiske forbruger* (Copenhagen: Hans Reitzels Forlag, 2004).

17   Ibid.

18   Ibid: 14.

19   Ibid.

20   John Elkington and Julia Hailes, *The green consumer guide: From shampoo to champagne: high-street shopping for a better environment* (London: Gollancz paperback, 1989).

21   Mads P. Sørensen, *Den Politiske forbruger* (Copenhagen: Hans Reitzels Forlag, 2004), 36.

22   Ibid.

23   David M. Holley: "A Moral Evaluation of Sales Practices", *Business Ethics and Professional Ethics Journal 5* (1987), reprinted in William H. Shaw and Vincent Barry, *Moral Issues in Business*, 7th edition (Belmont, California: Wadsworth Publishing Company, 1998), 496.

24   William H. Shaw and Vincent Barry, *Moral Issues in Business*, 7th edition, Wadsworth Publishing Company, (Belmont, California, 1998), 461.

25   Ibid: 462.

26   Ibid: 463.

27 Ibid: 463.

28 Ibid: 463.

29 Ibid: 467.

30 Ibid: 467.

31 Joseph W. Weiss, *Business Ethics. A Stakeholder and Issues Management Approach* (3rd Edition) (Canada: Thompson, SouthWestern, 2003), 166-167.

32 William H. Shaw and Vincent Barry, *Moral Issues in Business*, 7th edition (Belmont, California: Wadsworth Publishing Company, 1998), 472.

33 This case is selected from Scott B. Rae and Kenman L.Wrong, *Beyond Integrity: A Judeo-Christian Approach to Business Ethics* (Michigan: Zondervan Publishing House, 1996), 461. Manuel G. Velasquez, *Business Ethics. Concepts and Cases,* Fifth Edition (New Jersey: Prentice Hall, 2002), 355-360. See also James E. Post, Anne T. Lawrence and James Weber, *Business and Society, Corporate Strategy, Public Policy, Ethics* (New York: McGraw-Hill, Irwin, 2002), 558-570.

34 Joseph W. Weiss, *Business Ethics. A Stakeholder and Issues Management Approach* (Canada: Thomson, South-Western, 2003), 351.

35 Lynn Sharp Paine, Cases in *Leadership, Ethics and Organizational Integrity. A Strategic Perspective* (Chicago: Irwin, 1997), 301-302.

36 Georges Brenkert, "Marketing Ethics" in *A Companion to Business Ethics* edited by Robert E. Frederick (Oxford: Blackwell Publishing (1999), 2002), 178-194.

37 André Boyer, *L'impossible éthique des enterprises* (Paris: Éditions d'organisations, 2001).

38 Joseph W. Weiss, *Business Ethics. A Stakeholder and Issues Management Approach*, 3rd Edition (Canada: Thompson, SouthWestern, 2003), 174-175.

39 Theodor Levitt, "The Morality of Advertising", *Harvard Business Review 48* (1970) July-August,84-92) reprinted in William H. Shaw and Vincent Barry, *Moral Issues in Business*, 7th edition (Belmont, California: Wadsworth Publishing Company, 1998).

40 Richard L. Lippke, "Advertising and the Social Conditions of Autonomy", *Business and Professional Ethics Journal* 8 (1989), reprinted in William H. Shaw and Vincent Barry: *Moral Issues in Business*, 7th edition (Belmont, California Wadsworth Publishing Company, 1998), 510.

41 Robert L. Arrington, "Advertising and Behavior Control", *Journal of Business Ethics 1* (1982): 3-12, reprinted in William H. Shaw and Vincent Barry: *Moral Issues in Business*, 7th edition (Belmont California: Wadsworth Publishing Company, 1998), 503.

42 Georges Brenkert, "Marketing Ethics" in *A Companion to Business Ethics* edited by Robert E. Frederick (Oxford: Blackwell Publishing (1999), 2002), 189.

43 Patrick E. Murphy, "Marketing Ethics at the Millenium: Review, Reflections, and Recommendations" in *The Blackwell Guide to Business Ethics,* edited by Norman E. Bowie (Oxford: Basil Blackwell, 2002), 174.

44 Ibid: 181.

45 Georges Brenkert, "Marketing for the vulnerable" in *Perspectives in business ethics* edited by Laura Pincus Hartman (Chicago: Irwin McGraw-Hill, 1998).

46 Patrick E. Murphy, "Ethics in Advertising", (University of Santa Clara: Unpublished paper, 2001).

47 These categories have been developed of Professor Patrick E. Murphy. See also the famous article by Theodore Levitt: "Marketing Myopia", reprinted in Ben M. Enis and Keith K. Cox, *Marketing Classics. A selection of influential articles* (Boston: Allyn and Bacon, 1991), 3-22.

48 The concern for ethical public relations is, indeed, very important; however, I will not treat it in the same category as marketing, but rather see the problem of public relations as a problem of the general legitimacy of corporations in society. Public relations, then, depends on the success of programs of values-driven management on the whole. It also relates to the discussion of economics and corporate legitimacy. But, indeed, it must be a task to develop the ethical aspects of public relations.

49 George C.S Benson, *Business Ethics in America* (Lexington, Massachusetts, Toronto Lexington Books, D.C Heath and Company, 1982).

50 Ibid: 210.

51 Thomas L. Carson, "Ethical Issues in Selling and Advertising" in *The Blackwell Guide to Business Ethics* edited by Norman E. Bowie (Oxford: Basil Blackwell, 2002), 194.

52 Elements of the case are selected from the following sources: Joseph W. Weiss, *Business Ethics. A Stakeholder and Issues Management Approach*, 3rd Edition (Canada: Thompson, SouthWestern, 2003), 446-449. See also Debbie Thorne McAlister, O.C. Ferrell and Linda Ferrell, *Business and Society, A Strategic Approach to corporate social responsibility* (Boston: Houghton Mifflin Company, Boston 2005), 442-447.

53 James E. Grunig and Todd Hunt, *Managing Public Relations* (Orlando: Harcourt Brace Janovich College Publishers, 1984). Here we find the description of authentic public relations as a symmetrical dialogue, which should be proposed as the basis for legitimate corporate relations with the public.

54 M.C. Suchman, "Managing Legitimacy: Strategic and Institutional Approaches", *Academy of Management Review*, vol. 20, (1995), no. 3.

55 Ibid: 575.

56 Mie Femø Nielsen, *Profil i offentligheden. En introduktion til Public Relations* (Copenhagen: Samfundslitteratur, 2001).

57 Jürgen Habermas, *Strukturwandel der Öffentlichkeit* (Frankfurt am Main: Suhrkamp Verlag, 1990).

58 Mie Femø Nielsen, *Profil i offentligheden. En introduktion til Public Relations* (Copenhagen: Samfundslitteratur, 2001), 60-61.

59 Jürgen Habermas, *Strukturwandel der Öffentlichkeit* (Frankfurt am Main: Suhrkamp Verlag, 1990). Jürgen Habermas, *Strukturwandel der Ôffentlichkeit* (1963) (Frankfurt am Main: Suhrkamp Verlag, 1990). Jürgen Habermas, *Theorie des Kommunikativen Handelns I-II* (Frankfurt am Main: Suhrkamp Verlag, 1981).

60 Mie Femø Nielsen, *Profil i offentligheden. En introduktion til Public Relations* (Copenhagen: Samfundslitteratur, 2001), 70.

61 Jürgen Habermas, *Strukturwandel der Öffentlichkeit* (Frankfurt am Main: Suhrkamp Verlag, 1990). Jürgen Habermas, *Strukturwandel der Ôffentlichkeit* (1963) (Frankfurt am Main: Suhrkamp Verlag, 1990). Jürgen Habermas, *Theorie des Kommunikativen Handelns I-II* (Frankfurt am Main: Suhrkamp Verlag, 1981).

62 Mie Femø Nielsen, *Profil i offentligheden. En introduktion til Public Relations* (Copenhagen: Samfundslitteratur, 2001), 71.

63 Andrew Crane and Dirk Matten, *Business Ethics: A European Perspective* (Oxford: Oxford University Press, 2004), 345.

64 James E. Post, Anne T. Lawrence and James Weber, *Business and Society, Corporate Strategy, Public Policy, Ethics*, (New York: McGraw-Hill, Irwin, 2002), 553.

65 Material for this case has been selected from O.C. Ferrell, John Fraedrich and Linda Ferrell, *Business Ethics. Ethical Decision Making and Cases* (Boston and New York: Boston and New York Houthton Mifflin Company, 2005), 329-335. See also James E. Post, Anne T. Lawrence and James Weber, *Business and Society, Corporate Strategy, Public Policy, Ethics* (New York: McGraw-Hill, Irwin, 2002).

66 Ibid: 538.

67 Ibid: 539.

68 Ibid: 542.

69 Malcolm McIntosh, Deborah Leipziger, Keith Jones and Gill Coleman, *Corporate Citizenship, Successful Strategies for responsible companies* (London: Financial Times, Pitman Publishing, 1998), 206.

70 Ibid: 210.

71 Ibid: 197.

72 Jack Maurice, *Accounting Ethics* (London Pearson, Professional Limited, Pitman Publishing, 1996).

73 Mohammad J. Abdolmohammadi and Mark R. Nixon, "Ethics in the Public Accounting Profession" in *A Companion to Business Ethics* edited by Robert E. Frederick (Oxford: Blackwell Publishing (1999), 2002).

74 Mary Beth Armstrong, "Ethical Issues in Accounting" in Norman E. Bowie (ed.): *The Blackwell Guide to Business Ethics*, Basil Blackwell, Oxford 2002. p 153.

75 Malcolm McIntosh, Deborah Leipziger, Keith Jones, Gill Coleman, *Corporate Citizenship, Successful Strategies for responsible companies* (London: Financial Times, Pitman Publishing,1998), 193.

76 Ibid: 196.

77 Ibid: 227.

78 Ibid: 228.

79 Ibid: 232.

80 Ibid: 233. In particular Kirk Hanson, of the Markkula Center for Applied Ethics, has contributed to this point of view. We find a deeper analysis of the relationship between the different kinds of audits in Simon Zadek, Peter Pruzan and Richard Evans: *Building Corporate Accountability* (London: Earthscan, 1997).

81 An important example of ethical accounting is the work of Danish scholars, Ole Thyssen and Peter Pruzan. They have developed ethical accounting as a registered trademark. Their theory is based on Habermas's philosophy of communicative action. The idea is that ethical accounting is based on extensive stakeholder dialogue. This dialogue makes it possible for the firm to view their social and ethical performance. Moreover, it represents an instrument for reform and values-driven management of the organization. When we defined values-driven management as based on fairness and stakeholder dialogue, we were not very far from this concept of ethical accounting. See Ole Thyssen, *Værdiledelse*, (Copenhagen: Gyldendal, 1999).

82 Malcolm McIntosh, Deborah Leipziger, Keith Jones and Gill Coleman, *Corporate Citizenship, Successful Strategies for responsible companies* (London: Financial Times, Pitman Publishing, 1998), 239.

83 This is, for example, the strategy of the Swiss accounting firm KPMG, which works with integrity consulting. This company has developed an integrity-based approach to ethics helping to develop values-driven management. See Malcolm McIntosh, Deborah Leipziger, Keith Jones and Gill Coleman, *Corporate Citizenship, Successful Strategies for responsible companies* (London: Financial Times, Pitman Publishing, 1998), 245.

84 Michel Capron and Françoise Quairel-Lanoizeelée, *Mythes et réalités de l'entreprise responsable. Acteurs, Enjeux, Stratégies* (Paris: La Decouverte, 2004), 196.

85 Malcolm McIntosh, Deborah Leipziger, Keith Jones and Gill Coleman, *Corporate Citizenship, Successful Strategies for responsible companies* (London: Financial Times, Pitman Publishing, 1998), 247.

86 Michel Capron and Françoise Quairel-Lanoizeelée, *Mythes et réalités de l'entreprise responsable. Acteurs, Enjeux, Stratégies* (Paris: La Decouverte, 2004), 202.

87 Elements of this case have been selected from Mette Morsing, *Den etiske praksis - En introduktion til det etiske regnskab* (Copenhagen: HandelsHøjskolens forlag, 1991). See also Anders Bordum: *Det Etiske Regnskab - principper for ledelse mellem magt og konsensus* (Copenhagen: CBS-Ph.D. series: 1998-4; Copenhagen: Samfundslitteratur, 1998). This is indeed a very throughgoing analysis of ethical accounting.

88 Christian Bak, *Det etiske regnskab: Introduktion, erfaringer, praksis* (Copenhagen: Handelshøjskolens forlag,1996)

89 Villy Dyhr, "De nye regnskaber", *Tidsskrift for arbejdsliv*, nr. 2 (1999):73-93.

90 www.spardnord.dk

4. Sustainability, corporate social responsibility, and ethical principles: Environmental dimensions of business ethics

Building on the foundation of the conception of values, stakeholder theory, and basic ethical principles put forward in this book, it is now time to address the issue of sustainability and the values that should guide interactions between organizations and the environment.[1] The problem is the extent to which the basic ethical principles can be considered as foundations of environmental business ethics. The environmental challenge signifies that it is necessary to view ethics from the perspective of organizations as the foundation for the discussion of values in relation to animals and nature. In particular, the threats of global warming and climate change are a challenge to corporate legitimacy.[2] Environmental ethics not only concerns individuals, but is also about the relations between different kinds of organizations and nature. Reflections on bioethics, environmental ethics, and business ethics need to be integrated.[3]

In this presentation of environmental business ethics, autonomy, dignity, integrity, and vulnerability can help make sense of the idea of sustainable development, which today is central to international environmental policy. The problem can be framed around understanding what obligations business may have to respect environmental ethics and what kind of philosophical theory should justify protection of the environment.[4]

The argument in this section begins by examining the changed economic situation of many businesses in relation to questions of environmental ethics. It moves on to clarify how environmental ethics for organizations cannot be understood uniquely at the basis of utility and enlightened self-interest, but must be considered as a challenge to anthropocentric ethics. Moreover, precise and concrete applications of ethical principles are presented in relation to values-driven management in environmental ethics. In this fashion, the connection between sustainability and ethical principles is promoted as the essence of the ethics of organizational behavior in the environment. Finally, this leads to the difficult problem of going from ethics to law. Here, the legal regulation of environmental crime and the function of law as a pragmatic tool to improve the ethical behavior of companies will be discussed briefly.

4.1. Ecology, sustainability, and capitalism

Since the industrial revolution businesses have had to deal with environmental problems, but it wasn't until the late 1960s that these problems came to be commonly understood as severe and requiring thoughtful and efficient solutions on a global scale. There are not only problems of global warming, ozone depletion, acid rain, depletion of air quality, but also problems of water pollution, (e.g., toxic oil spills), temperature increase, the destructive use of ocean fishery resources, and further problems of land pollution (e.g., destruction of forests, chemical or toxic substance deposits, radioactive and nuclear wastes) and deteriorating ecological conditions, including the destruction of animal habitats.[5] Environmental problems have characterized all major cities during the development of modernity. The criticism of industrial civilization has focused on damage to biodiversity due to exploitation of the natural world's resources. As a reaction towards the depletion of natural resources, the environment has been a perenially important issue in global politics. In the words of the ecological ethicist Aldo Leopold, society has been in search of a land ethic of "integrity, stability and beauty" in order to protect the intrinsic value and self-organization of the natural world.[6]

To deal with the increasing concern for global environmental problems, in 1972 the United Nations held its first conference on the environment in Stockholm, leading to the creation of the United Nations Development Programme.[7] In 1983, the World Commission on Environment (WCED) and Development was established. In 1987, the WCED published *Our Common Future: Sustainable Development in International Politics*, which put the concept of sustainable development into the center of international politics. Sustainable development later became pivotal in the global summit on the environment in Rio in 1992.[8] These developments were decisive for international environmental policy. The global nature of environmental problems requires a sustainable use of resources in order to assure the survival of the Earth for future generations. The concept of sustainability had an enormous impact on UN policy, and has been extensively debated and discussed all over the world.

International development policy, based on the idea of sustainability, has also had an impact on economic markets. Until quite recently, economic markets functioned according to the idea that unlimited resources were at hummankind's disposals. It was only during the second half of the twentieth century that an increasing awareness of the impossibility of naturally regulated markets began to emerge. Still, it has been extremely difficult, if not impossible, to find the correct balance between economic growth and the environment. In the last thirty years the view that corporations should focus on gaining economic profit without concern for the environment has been strenuously challenged. Today, there is even more awareness of the fact that environmental concerns in business might contribute to good business and that good environmental policy pays.[9] The problem of global climate change may, because of its serious impact on global life, be one of the drivers for increased awareness of the need for action relating to environmental degradation.[10] Corporations facing this problem start to be aware that they need to take environmental problems seriously in order to obtain social respect and appear as good corporate citizens.

Joseph R. Desjardin emphasizes that the idea of sustainable development implies a new kind of environmental business responsibility.[11] Environmental issues represent a challenge to the concept of growth that is central to neoclassical mainstream economics. When dealing with corporate social responsibility to the environment, business ethics has to rely on the development of a theory of sustainable economics. In this way, the concept of sustainability implies a redefinition of the concept of economics that moves away from the concept of the possibility of endless growth regardless of limited natural resources. Hermann Daly has tried to reformulate economic theory by focusing on environmental concerns, not only as a side constraint, but as essential to all kinds of economic action.[12] Daly argues that there are ecological limits to economic growth, and that the economic system of the world is dependant on the natural world, which functions as the basis for economic resources and energy.[13] In order to deal effectively with the environmental problems of the world, we would have to develop a "steady-state" (i.e., sustainable economics) using renewable resources that do not damage the carrying capacity of the natural system or destroy the planet's life-conditions for future generations.[14] Natural resources should be treated as capital for developing sustainable economic relations, rather than as goods for unlimited use.

Sustainable economics expresses the effort to develop a framework for economic theory that not only searches for regulations in terms of pragmatic utility, but that also recognizes deontological concerns for rights and duties to the living world of animals and nature. Sustainability implies that issues of biodiversity, ecology, and global warming are included in economic considerations.

In such a holistic approach to economics, nature is viewed from the perspective of many different historical, aesthetic, or spiritual values. These values are integrated in an economic business strategy that respects nature and animals as expressions of intrinsic value and the search for the common good of humanity. It is the task of an alternative ecologically oriented economic model to make these concerns explicit and concrete. Daly's 1996 book, *Beyond Growth,* has contributed to this framework for economics by emphasizing that the economy is just a subsystem of the Earth's biosphere.[15] With its abstract concept of growth, neoclassical economics ignores this dependence on the biosphere and is not able to develop an economic system that is based on recycling its limited resources. It is the task of business strategy and values-driven management to comply with the recognition of such biophysical limits to growth and provide models for sustainable development within the firm. This is particularly so for the world's industrial, agricultural, and service-oriented corporations, who have their fair share of responsibility for global environmental problems.

In his capacity as the founder of the London-based consultancy group SustainAbility, John Elkington uses sustainability as a basic tool of values-driven management for modern companies.[16] Elkington suggests that corporations face important challenges of learning how to achieve economic growth on an environmental and social basis. In order to meet this challenge, he argues that corporations should begin an open dialogue with stakeholders, NGOs, governments, consumers, and so on, about the concept of sustainable development.[17] Elkington emphasizes the new responsibilities of businesses at the moment of victory of the ideology of market economy: at the so-called end of history.[18]

The common understanding of the legitimate responsibility of the firm has definitely been changing. All the stakeholders in environmental issues, not only owners and shareholders, but other groups such as consumers, employees, the local community, should be consulted when determining the values and strategic goals of the company. It may be worth reiterating R. Edward Freeman's definition of a stakeholder as "any group or individual who can affect or is affected by the corporation."[19] In a stakeholder economy, the firm is open to these groups and, most importantly, has learned to listen. This search for a moral dimension to the economy is based on the idea that companies, in order to be successful, must have good relations with the community and the social environment.[20] Social capital and good will are considered as conditions for economic success.

These arguments for stakeholder inclusion and for environmental policies based on sustainability are relatively new for many corporations. Despite increasing ecological awareness, being environmentally conscientious was considered romantic "green activism." Very few companies realized that concern for the environment could be a part of the necessary hardcore economic considerations of the firm. They would never have thought that the environment would be among necessary bottom-line measures. They considered ecological problems as political questions, which should not be a part of a firm's strategic actions based on strict economic, market-oriented considerations. At most, they would admit that environmental profiles might strengthen public relations and the firm's image, but it was difficult to see how environmental problems could be essentially damaging for the company and that good environmental policies are as important as economic budgets.

There are many examples of environmental disasters due to wrong or careless actions of companies, for example the 1979 Three Mile Island nuclear accident in the United States, the 1986 reactor meltdown in Tjernobyl, Ukraine, or the catastrophe of the Union Carbide Fertilizer operations in Bhopal, India in 1984, where more than two thousand people died from gas explosions.[21] These are just a few cases demonstrating that ecologically responsible action is necessary, if corporations want to survive in the long run. This action should involve, among other things, examining new technological possibilities of waste management, recycling, and good use of resources. It may also involve principles of environmental auditing, green marketing, and public relations, as well as policies of values for environmental investments, such as establishing environmental mutual funds that have criteria for screening environmentally sound investment objects. The strategy of respect for the biophysical limits of economics and corporate activities, for biodiversity, and for environmental protection must be based on the triple bottom line if companies want to have good relations with stakeholders in the social and economic development of the twenty-first century.[22]

Case 21. The Bhopal disaster and the responsibilities of Union Carbide

Union Carbide is one of the most classic examples of how an international corporation can create an *ethical crisis* by not providing the necessary protection for people and not having the necessary security in relation to its factories. This case illustrates the need to be very careful about international projects in non-Western factories. Moreover, it is a case that helps us to understand the potential destruction that can be caused by careless management on the part of international corporations.

The 1984 disaster of the Union Carbide chemical plant in Bhopal, India is one of the dark symbols of global risk distribution and the environment hazards faced by international business organizations.[23] The Bhopal plant produced sevin, which is a pesticide used in agriculture. The Indian government supported the activities and was part owner of the plant although Union Carbide, an American company, had the majority of the shares.[24] The plant gave jobs to many people and it contributed to the exportation of pesticides abroad. It was a financially successful business.

The disaster was the explosion of the Bhopal chemical plant, which resulted in more than 3000 deaths and more than 20,000 injuries. The explosion was triggered when the chemical methyl isocyanate, which was usually kept liquid in tanks, changed into gas.

After the explosion, Union Carbide was held ethically, socially, and legally responsible for the disaster by the Indian Government. The company offered some money to victims, but this was refused as being too low. The director of the company was temporarily imprisoned and Union Carbide was required to pay billions of dollars in compensation by the government, which it did more or less openly.[25]

The case of Union Carbide in India is often mentioned as one of the most characteristic cases of global risk distribution and the impact of the Western world's irresponsible exploitation and pollution of third world countries. The company was accused of being less strict with safety rules when operating in developing countries and the Indian government was also accused of not being able to handle interactions with international corporations.

4.2. Ethical principles as the basis for sustainability

What are the ethical implications of the search for a concept of sustainable economics as the basis for the triple bottom line? The ethical ideas of autonomy, dignity, integrity, and vulnerability may be values for understanding sustainability as a bridge between the human and nonhuman. This implies that the ethical principles may not only function as the foundation for ethics between human beings in organizations, but also constitute basic values for the interaction between organizations and corporations with animals, plants, and our biosphere as a whole.[26]

In this sense, principles need to be viewed in a broader fashion than usual, but their possible applications must also be critical investigated.

The concept of autonomy (see section 1.5.1) is usually defined as the capacity of self-legislation, freedom to act, and self-realization. Based on the capacity of moral reflection, autonomy seems to be restricted to rational human beings.

Respect for autonomy signifies that no one has the right to interfere in the life of a human being without permission and consent. Defined in this way, it seems difficult to apply autonomy to interactions between organizations with nature, plants, and animals; however, it is arguable that their capacity to feel pain and pleasure as self-organizing organisms means that nonhuman beings are not machines, but are endowed with autonomous instincts. This might be a sufficient reason to say that they have some kind of autonomy. They are independent beings that have developed on their own in a long natural evolution, but, admittedly, this has hardly been relevant to the Kantian concept of moral autonomy.

Dignity originally indicates the moral status of human beings in intersubjective relations. Later it signified the intrinsic value of each human being, but also that human beings – due to their capacity to choose between good and evil; to rise above their nature and fall below animality – can be violated in their dignity. The question is, therefore, whether the principle of respect for dignity can meaningfully be applied to nonhuman living beings. Human dignity could be said to be dependent on the treatment of animals. To complicate matters, even animals living in their natural environments can be said to have a certain dignity, as opposed to instrumental value. This concept of dignity, however, differs qualitatively from our understanding of human dignity.

The question is: To what extent is it meaningful to talk about the *würde der kreatur* (dignity of nature) and loss of dignity in the biosphere.[27] The dignity of nature can never be the same as human dignity; however, the concept has been used in the constitution of Switzerland to denote "the dignity of creation." This conception expresses the intrinsic value of nature, the moral respect due to animals and nature, and also refers to the responsibility of human beings for the Earth and other living creatures.

The principle of integrity relates to a unity or coherence of life that must not be touched or destroyed.[28] It may be argued that this principle refers to nonhuman nature and that it can have significance for different life forms (e.g., plants, animals, and the whole biosphere), which also developed out of natural history. This wider application of the notion of integrity is important to justify, or to argue against, interventions into the environment of nonhuman living nature.

Recognizing the integrity of animals would, for example, refer to their natural evolutionary history, based on their natural teleology as self-organizing beings. Animal integrity could include demands of nonintervention and human respect for their genetic and biological totality, so that there would be limits to the manipulation and instrumentalization of animals for specific human purposes.[29]

Integrity helps to define respect for biodiversity. It refers to the totality and health of living systems in their actual and future ecological stability, potentials, and teleological structure. Integrity expresses the possibilities of natural systems to develop according to their own harmonies. Ecological integrity expresses the development of life as a natural unity with its own purpose and aim as self-organizing system.

The ethical principle of the vulnerability of the whole nonhuman living world, can, even though it sometimes is not explicitly analyzed, be viewed as a basic principle in the ethical debate about the protection of animals, nature, and the environment. The ethical idea of vulnerability is both descriptive and normative. The statement of ethical vulnerability immediately implies the demand for care and protection. The ultimate project of modern industrial society is endless demand for technological progress, the abolition of vulnerability, and the mastery of human nature and its environment. There may be unforeseen limits to progress, due to the vulnerable nature of the living world. The challenge is also the extent to which vulnerability has any meaning in itself. The elimination of vulnerability may imply the elimination of humanity.

The principle of respect for vulnerability applies to animals in the sense that they are very vulnerable in their natural ecosystems. They are threatened by human intervention and destruction. A strong argument for respecting vulnerability is also our incapacity to foresee all the consequences of our actions in the natural world. Respect for vulnerability includes care for finite and fragile ecosystems.

The basic ethical principles may be considered within the framework of socially and environmentally responsible business. Responsibility signifies that there is somebody, an agent with intentional actions, who takes, or is attributed, responsibility for something or someone. Traditionally, this responsibility has been attributed to people; however, power over the whole living world has changed the extension and scope of human responsibility.[30] Corporations may be subject to responsibility to natural entities. What is needed is a meaningful concept of organizational responsibility for animals, nature, and the whole biosphere. This is necessary because humanity, with the help of biotechnology, can change agriculture and food production in a way that would lead to profound social change and possibilities for life on earth. Due to modern technology and science, industrial society takes more and more risks. This requires business organizations, among others, to be responsible for the distribution of the dangers and disadvantages of these risks.

The basic ethical principles are essential to the idea of sustainable development. Even though they are not explicitly discussed in *Our Common Future*, they can be considered as the ethical foundation of the message of the WCED's report. The starting point, according to this view, is the reality of humanity's global responsibility for the survival of future generations. We borrow the environment from future generations and it is the common future of humanity that is at stake, if we do not manage to solve global warming, stop the destruction of rain forests, halt over population, et cetera.

The report emphasizes the close connection between global problems of poverty and environmental problems. It is important to remember that environmental problems are also social problems. Sustainable development implies a close connection between social development and environmental protection.[31] Sustainability is a common ideal for society and nature, in which both human rights and ecological stability must be secured. Sustainability is only possible when it is based on ethical, cultural, and aesthetic concerns.[32]

Our Common Future argues, therefore, for the need to integrate the economy and ecology in the institutional implementation of sustainability.[33] It is important to establish a symbiosis between humanity and nature. Sustainability strategies do not imply hostility to growth. They aim to change the quality of growth in accordance with ecological measures for the basic human needs such as work, food, energy, water, and health. The report addresses all types of businesses, formal and informal, and private and public organizations and institutions. Sustainability is realized through legislation, but indeed, it also implies the willingness of civil societies and private business to make the ethical value of environmental protection central to economic markets.[34]

Even though it is not directly analyzed in the report, one might say that the concept of humanity's political and moral autonomy is very important. Sustainability, it is argued, is not really possible without democracy and human rights. Moreover, the report explicitly states that sustainability strategies imply securing human beings a dignified life.[35] In particular, problems of population density and poverty manifest the need to protect human dignity. The result is that basic education and health are central aspects of sustainability, because of the close link between ecosystem stability and social carrying capacity in establishing social stability and sustainability. [36]

The notion of integrity is very present in the concept of sustainability. In *Our Common Future*, the integrity of ecosystems is given major importance.[37] The report is concerned with protecting forests from destruction, water pollution, or other types of destruction, such as nuclear disaster, which are based on the need to save the ecosystem for future generations. The problem of increased destruction of species is an indication of the international responsibility to preserve the integrity of ecosystems.[38] This implies that the production of foods and other goods should aim to be in harmony with the ecosystem, by, for example, using fewer chemicals (e.g., DDT, pesticides, and other substances) that destroy ecosystems. Society and corporations should contribute to the preservation of the general integrity of ecosystems, not only for future generations but also because of the aesthetic, ethical and cultural concerns, which should precede strict economic market calculations.

In addition, the notion of vulnerability can be mentioned as an important presupposition of the notion of sustainable development. It is often stated in the report that economic development should not lead to increased critical vulnerability.[39] Agriculture should, for example, avoid exploiting resources. Agricultural production should be based on long-term security and quality rather than quantity. Moreover, *Our Common Future* speaks about the need to protect vulnerable populations. Sustainable developments include the important work of "empowering vulnerable groups."[40] This means that local communities should gradually be integrated into larger communities in a way that protects their traditional culture and lifestyle. Put another way, the marginalization of vulnerable groups is a symptom of unsustainable development.

Finally, the concepts of responsibility and solidarity can be said to have great significance for the principle of sustainable development.[41] The notion that we have a responsibility to future generations, which is implicit in sustainability, also draws a close connection between responsibility and solidarity, implying an equitable distribution of risks among all nations.[42] The aim of sustainable world politics is to provide equality among countries in order to provide a decent standard of living for all with integrity and dignity, and in harmony with the ecosystem.

Case 22. Sustainable tourism: Accor Group

The Accor Group originated in France and is a worldwide hotel and tourism business that is committed to a strategy of sustainable development. The Accor Group, which is a member of CSR Europe, has been selected as a case that can illustrate how corporations can make an *ethical effort* to deal proactively with environmental issues.[43]

Accor has more than 500 hotels worldwide with 120 million customers.[44] In 2004, the corporation had 168,500 employees. Accor is mainly owned by institutional investors and has implemented a strategy of good corporate governance and corporate social responsibility. This corporation seeks to present itself in its policies and ethical values as a responsible corporate citizen with concern for the environment.

Accor has established a sustainable development committee to work on the implementation a strategy of sustainable development. Sustainable development management includes agents and networks worldwide in the businesses of the organization. Accor Group has, for a number of years, contributed to the greening of tourism and the development of more sustainable principles in hotel management.

In connection with the strategy of sustainable development, Accor subscribes to the principles of Global Compact of the United Nations, as proposed by the World Economic Forum at Davos in 1999. Accor has signed on to the compact's ten principles, which relate to, among other issues, human rights and the environment, shareholders, local community, suppliers, employees, and customers. Among its sustainable development and corporate social responsibility efforts the corporation mentions that it signed a diversity charter in order to develop its skills and ensure social dialogue.[45]

The corporation requires documents from suppliers in different countries ensuring that they respect human rights and principles of fair trade, as well as principles of sustainablilty in relation to the environment. With a large market share in the hotel industry, the corporation has tried to make its environmental strategy very visible and has signed an environmental charter in addition to contributing to the development of an environmental management and reporting system.

Accor has, in connection with its strategy for sustainable development, tried to come up with ideas for sustainable tourism. The corporation has worked together with UN agencies in order to facilitate this approach to corporate social responsibility and sustainability. This approach has been presented at different international tourism fairs and meetings with other organizations in the tourism business.

Recently, Accor has also tried to stress its engagement in local communities in order to help actions in favor of children, including training employees to combat child prostitution and child sexual abuse in the tourism industry. This effort is an indication of how a corporation can be socially responsible with regard to issues affecting its area of business concern, in this case addressing the problem of sex tourism in many developing countries.[46]

Among good corporate governance standards, Accor has made an effort to be listed on different ethical ratings and sustainability indices, including the Advanced Sustainability Index, the Ethical Sustainability Index, and the Dow Jones Sustainability Index. The corporation has, in addition, subscribed to a number of other index measurements in order to appear on different tables and accounts.

4.3. Beyond anthropocentric environmental ethics

The basic ethical principles imply skepticism towards the anthropocentric perspective on ethics. This is a response to the many people who have criticized the notion of sustainable development for being anthropocentric, but it is also a critique of those who think that the basic ethical principles imply a holistic conception of ethics, which cannot be valid in a post-metaphysical worldview. Some philosophers argue that every non-anthropocentric ethics is meaningless, because neither nature nor animals are able to feel or act on moral responsibility. Others argue for a *trans-anthropocentric-relational* or *anthropocentrifugal* conception of ethics, which would not go totally beyond the anthropocentric approach, but still extends ethics to include the environment.[47]

Among the many conceptions that attempt to go beyond anthropocentric ethics, a general theme is the threat of the destruction of living conditions on Earth. Moreover, this kind of thought is marked by strong criticism of technological culture and capitalist economics. Such critical philosophical movements argue for a new understanding of the relationship between humankind and nature. Other positions go further, and argue for a from of universalism, endowing nature and animals with the same moral status as humans. This is often combined with the *deep ecology* approach, which posits a unique moral status for nature. These arguments propose to overcome the anthropocentric limits of ethics, so that ethics is no longer based on rational individual subjects. Non-anthropocentric positions point to a close relation between nature and the human life-world. This is also the case in *Our Common Future*, when it emphasizes the close connection between nature and culture. These propositions for alternatives to anthropocentric ethics are based on a bridge between person, body, and nature.

Non-anthropocentric positions often rely on a phenomenological conception of human being seeking to overcome a contradictory conception of the relationship between subject and object, between internal experience and external material.[48] What matters is the intrinsic value, richness, and diversity of nature.[49] Moreover, these movements of thought want to avoid oppositions between mechanical and teleological conceptions of nature. Humans are simultaneously considered to be living organisms taking part in an ecosystem, and spiritual beings with the freedom and autonomy to transcend this bond. We experience nature through our bodily incarnation in time and space in our everyday life-world.

The perspective can be taken as the basis of an ethical position bridging the gap between humans and ecosystems. Ethics is, in this context, based on human rationality, a vision of the good life, and reflective judgment. Concrete action and the capacity to practically judge ethical principles are the driving forces in this process. The ethical principles may, therefore, be founded on the presupposition that human beings participate in nature, but at the same time that we can transcend this participation and manifest ourselves as different from nature.

Even though environmental ethics starts from anthropocentrism, it transcends a conception of nature only viewed from the perspective of human relations. Illustrating this from the perspective of deep communication theory, it might be argued that "nature speaks to us."[50] But such a communicative relation is rather problematic because we can never communicate totally with nature, even if some animals have simple rules of language. We can open ourselves to nature, but communication is determined by human reality. Although only human beings can communicate, it might be possible for animals and nature to be a part of this communicative community as objects that we talk about. In such a communicative perspective, human beings and their actions and responsibilities determine ethics, but this does not mean that animals and nature cannot be included in ethical reflections. In this sense, the foundation of ethics is anthropo-original and anthropo-referential, even if the scope of ethics is extended to the totality of the biosphere.[51]

This privileged participation of human beings in nature might therefore be considered as the theoretical and meta-ethical foundation of a non-anthropocentric normative ethics.[52] Kant considered human beings as moral agents with an intrinsic inviolable moral status. Through participation in the categorical imperative and the moral law, we come to recognize other human beings as ends-in-themselves. Animals and nature are not directly seen as moral entities, but this does not imply that Kant should not recognize the need for the ethical protection of nature and animals.

In Kant's philosophy, the ideas of purpose and of teleological self-organization of living systems are central aspects of the foundational contribution of moral status to animals and nonhuman nature.[53] Moreover, this is based on the human capacity of moral reasoning and not primarily on the independent moral status of nature. In this weak anthropocentric foundation, the status of human beings as moral depends on how we treat animals and nature. There is a close connection between the beauty of society and of nature. At the same time, the particular position of nature as a system of self-organizing, autopoetic organisms, as well as its position as an object of human aesthetic enjoyment, might be emphasized; however, in general, the Kantian argument represents ethical justification on the basis of human reality, even though it clearly attributes important independent moral significance to animals and nature. It is this "bio-humanism," or the idea of human and civilization's concern for nature, that is the basis of the proposed relation between sustainability and ethical principles.

~~In short, the basic ethical principles are founded in human bodily partici-~~ pation in nature. Our whole life-world is interconnected with nature. This means that environmental ethics is anthropocentrifugal (i.e., opening from the human sphere towards the natural world), because human moral capacity allows us to be open to other ethical concerns than those belonging strictly to the human sphere.[54] Establishing interests and stakeholders can clarify such an anthropocentrifugal foundation of environmental ethics, but the problem is to what extent it can be meaningfully stated that nonhuman life has legitimate interests, when every moral concern comes from human beings.

In this context, consequentialist ethicists (like Peter Singer) emphasize the significance of suffering.[55] Many living beings can feel pain, and it would basically be wrong to do them harm; however, the concern for suffering should not be primarily based on utilitarian rationality, but rather on advocatory ethics, where concern for the nonspeaking is rationally justified through domination-free dialogue.[56]

The animal ethicist Tom Regan has argued for contributing rights to all bigger animals.[57] He does not only talk about "interests," but uses the concept of intrinsic value of every living being as the foundation of rights. This does not, however, have to follow from the theory of the relation between sustainability and ethical principles. The notion of rights should not be confused with the notion of interests. To use rights language would presuppose moral responsibility, duties, and the capacity for action. This does not apply to animals and other living beings. They are included as interested parties, because they can suffer, because they live on their own, and because they are important in the lives with human beings, but this cannot justify rights in the same sense as human rights.

The problem arises of whether the notion of "interests" can also be attributed to plants as well as other natural beings and objects. Indeed, it seems absurd to contribute interests to rocks and plants. One possibility is to try Aristotelian arguments about the intrinsic teleological nature of things as parts of teleological self-organizing systems striving towards higher spheres of realization. From a more modern perspective it could be argued that every organism follows a teleological movement towards the good in itself in close interaction with the environment. Biosphere and ecosystems could therefore be contributed interests due to the continuing strife for self-maintenance and life. From such an *ecofunctionalist* perspective, nature is considered as a number of ecosystems that have purposes or goals, even though they do not have rationality in the same sense as human beings. This means that we can give meaning to a teleological goal of ecosystems. It is this ecological self-realization that is the foundation of these "interests." They are not based in rationality or the capacity of sense awareness.

An ecofunctional hierarchy might be introduced, where different ecosystems contribute different interests, and where their values are not absolute, but always judged from the perspective of considerate human judgment. The most important argument for ascribing interests to living organisms is their role as self-sustaining, self-organizing cybernetic systems. In their creative self-development, these systems move towards greater and higher situations. This creative development defines their stability and integrity, which should be morally protected. Such a point of view is very different from a deep ecology position, because it does not suspend the primacy of human beings as moral beings, while at the same time striving towards harmony between self-organizing natural processes with the social and economic activities of mankind.

It is the task of ethics to carefully relate and compare the different interests of different kinds of beings. This is the true meaning of Kantian ethical injunction to put "oneself in the place of the other."[58] A non-anthropocentric ethics is concerned with judging the right place between different interests in order to find the difficult balance between self-consciousness, pain, or merely (as in case with ecosystems) the widest interest in the autopoetic self-organization of life. Such an approach is following the golden Kantian rule, whereby pursuing one's own interests is wrong if they violate other involved interests, and possibly extends universal moral judgment to include relations of human beings to self-organizing living systems.

Determining the relationship between ethical principles, sustainable development, and different interests by different stakeholders, including environmental stakeholders, can be proposed as the basis for understanding organizational behavior in relation to the environment.[59] It can be considered as an argument for stakeholder management (i.e., including the environment as a stakeholder). Nature and the environment must be included among the stakeholders of the firm, even though it is not easy to identify these interests. It must be admitted that they are an important part of the future actions of organizations.[60] Being aware of the environment as a stakeholder encourages corporations to extend their perspective on deliberation. Such an intensified ethical sensibility can be illustrated by four basic concerns: 1) *panoramization* (extending the perspective of analysis), 2) *prioritization* (including environ-

mental complexity in decision-making), 3) *politization* (including the environment in formulating the organization's political priorities, and 4) *particularization* (which aims to make the organization increasingly aware of dimensions of
environmental ethical concerns).[61]

Case 23. The Exxon Valdez oil spill pollution disaster

The Exxon Valdez oil spill is one of the largest environmental disasters caused by a modern corporation.[62] This classic business studies case deals with the *ethical crisis* of pollution. It is an illustration of the choices and sanctions that determine decision-making in relation to environmental crises.

In March 1989, an Exxon oil tanker called the Valdez was sailing in the region around Alaska when it had an accident and spilled eleven million gallons of oil. The disaster was caused by a human error and resulted in major ecological damage to the living conditions of both animals and the local people. Apparently, the ship's captain and his crew wanted to avoid a seemingly inevitable collision with a fleet of trawlers, but the decision to change course led the tanker into risky waters. These environmental crimes evoked intensive political debate and ended with improved environmental legislation. In evaluating the case, many people considered Exxon's fine of twenty-five million dollars to be disproportionately small in relation to the 2.2 billion dollar profit earned by the company that year.[63] It should, however be taken into account that Exxon was sentenced to pay for a very expensive "clean-up" procedure, which cost billions of dollars.

The company accepted its responsibility and it contributed three billion dollars for compensation to victims and restoration of the region. Although Exxon had a good international reputation with many oil, coal, and mineral products, the result of the disaster was very damaging to the company's image. Despite this damage, the company still continued to earn a lot of money, which increased the scepticism of environmental groups and local people, whose livelihoods were severly impacted. As well, the government came under criticism for not reacting quickly enough.

Moreover, it seemed like Exxon had done very little to keep up with industry and government security requirements and special regulations. In addition to the legal fees that Exxon had to pay, the government started to enact legislation to punish the company, in effect to make an example of it in hopes of avoiding similar disasters in the future. The corporation was estimated to be responsible for the spill and for the damage to the ecosystem. Accordingly, the Exxon Valdez incident has become a very strong example of how corporations damage the environment and emphasizes the need for responsible policies to protect the environment and foster sustainable development.

Although this case seems to represent one of the important wake-up calls for international business to pay attention to environmental issues, it also represents the tragedy and indeterminacy of possible pollution and environmental damage, because the damage was due to the failure of security and monitoring systems rather than intentional action. However, due to the institutional responsibility of the firm, it can be argued that it is exactly this carelessness with regard to fundamental responsibility that constitutes the failure and irresponsibility of the corporation. It was also this lack of environmental responsibility that later led to heavy public criticism of the business principles of the organisation as well as further innovation and personnel development.

4.4. Towards environmental values-driven management

This argument about organization and sustainability cannot be completed before more concretely addressing environmental values in business. How is sustainability a central value for strategic management in modern business organizations? Sustainability is viewed as a bridge between human and nonhuman, but also as a way to realize a triple bottom line of economy, ecology, and social responsibility. Implicit in this argument is that sustainability strategies are crucial for the long-term survival of the firm because of globalization, increased competition, and public pressure on firms.

In stakeholder capitalism the capacity of companies to listen to the demands of different stakeholders is a central dimension to legitimizing firms in society. As well, different programs of improving environmental awareness in business organizations need to be discussed. There is a need for applying existing business programs to the environmental performance of the organization. This could be, for example, a program of *total quality management* (TQM) or *benchmarking* to assess excellence in an organization, but it could also include the development of new types of values-driven management. Indeed, alternative technologies for fighting pollution, recycling, and making waste management should be explored in order to secure the ecologically efficient use of resources.

The need for values in business can be seen in the fact that many companies in the agriculture and fishing industries are involved in the undignified treatment of animals and of the destruction of natural resources. The basic ethical principles could be regarded as important aspects of codes of values for the firm. Respect for autonomy could be seen as the basis for the demand to include all stakeholders in making sustainable decisions. Surely, animals and nature should be considered as possible stakeholders. Respect for dignity would be present in reference to human rights as central aspects of a firm's social responsibility. Respect for integrity is present in the concern for the integrity of ecosystems and the demand to respect nature as a unity. Finally, the idea of respect for the vulnerability of nature and natural systems can be said to be essential to sustainable development.

The idea of the triple bottom line based on sustainability and basic ethical principles is a powerful basis for a program of values-driven management in modern business. A special feature of such a program is sustainable auditing, where shareholders, management, consumers, environmental activists, and other stakeholders participate in the evaluation of the activities of the company. This audit is based on defining the sustainable economic development of the firm as being in harmony with social and environmental conditions. In the future global market economy, respect for the economic and ecological triple bottom line will be necessary in order to secure the survival of the firm. Respect for sustainable development by companies should, therefore, include an understanding of the importance of different forms of social, cultural, physical, and psychic capital in the formulation of future environmental strategies.[64]

It is necessary that sustainable audits, which evaluate the capacities of corporations to respect the ideals of sustainable development, measure environmental progress along with a certain number of social and cultural indicators.[65] In this context, respect for and integration of minorities, compliance with human rights, dialogue with consumers, dialogue with local communities, and so forth, should be considered in addition to ecological concerns for the integrity of ecosystems and for energy use (e.g. changing from oil and coal to nuclear energy, or concerns for animal well-being and integrity). New forms of evaluations, audits, and social reporting from companies like Shell, Novo Nordic, and The Body Shop are examples of such an effort to concretely measure the capacity of companies to realize sustainability in its activities.

Due to increased public awareness and pressure on companies from stakeholders and consumers, it is not possible to keep sustainability auditing a secret from consumers and the general public. In the global information economy the general population has easier access to all kinds of information about the actions of corporations; therefore, companies must disclose their activities. This is an important part of stakeholder dialogue, and full disclosure includes firms directly collaborating with stakeholders and other parties about important issues. Today, more and more corporations are becoming aware of this necessity of disclosure. Corporations like Monsanto, Novo Nordic, or Shell maintain continuous dialogue with stakeholders in order to secure communication and give the company increased knowledge about the environment.[66] The new model for environmental management seeks consensus among stakeholders about respect for animals, plants, and the biosphere in its totality.

The concrete realization of sustainability and environmental values is, therefore, based on dialogue with important stakeholders (including those who represent the interests of animals and nature). In some cases, stakeholders even participate in management decision processes. Values-driven management for the environment involves, in this context, formulating strategic plans for the company that aim to achieve ecologically efficient management and are based on stakeholder dialogue. These could be based on close analyses of life cycles in relation to interactions between the firm and its environment, in order to establish a harmony between ecological and economic management.

Central to such a vision of environmental management is the development and formulation of ecological technology to foster new forms of interaction between organizations and their environments. Ecological technology focuses on the need to avoid unintended consequences. Six basic dimensions of such an "eco-compass" may be mentioned: 1) understanding health and environmental risks, 2) concern for the conservation of resources, 3) concern for the sustainable use of energy, 4) prudent use of materials, 5) recycling of used materials, and 6) concern for long-term use of materials.[67] These should be integrated in the discourse of general management principles.

An example are the so-called Valdez Principles that were developed after the oil spill (see case 22). In the aftermath of the catastrophe, many businesses were concerned about environmental problems. They agreed to the formulation of the Valdez Principles, which were proposed to guide business organizations in coping with environmental values in the organization.[68] Briefly, the Valdez Principles contain the following dimensions of ethical values for environmental business policy: protection of the biosphere, sustainable use of natural resources, reduction and disposal of waste, the wise use of energy, risk reduction, marketing safe products and services, damage compensation, disclosure, employing environmental directors and managers, and assessment and annual audit.[69]

These principles relate very well to the notion of sustainable development. They promote the elimination of environmental damage to air, water, or earth and its inhabitants in order to protect the biosphere.[70] To safeguard the environment, the principles suggest minimizing the greenhouse effect, destruction of the ozone layer, and acid rain or smog. In proposing sustainable uses for natural resources, the principles concern efforts to conserve nonrenewable resources through efficient use and careful planning.[71] The principles propose to preserve biodiversity, by protecting wildlife habitat, open spaces, and wilderness. Moreover, it is implied that it is necessary to minimize the creation of waste, especially hazardous waste. Safe methods of waste disposal should also be developed.[72] Wise use of energy includes efforts to employ sustainable energy sources in order to invest in improved energy efficiency and conservation. Risk reduction concerns the minimization of environmental, health, and safety risks to employees and communities by employing safe technologies and necessary emergency procedures. Marketing safe products and services implies an awareness of consumer need for such products as well as an investigation into, or awareness of, the environmental consequences of specific products.[73]

Damage compensation signifies that firms will compensate persons who are injured by their products or actions. The principle of disclosure implies that the company will be open and honest about its environmental policies, and actual problems and difficulties in living up to environmental demands.[74] Indeed, the involvement of responsible directors and managers at high levels of the organization is important. At least one member of the board of directors should have environmental responsibilities in the organization and be qualified to represent environmental interests.[75] This responsible person should report directly to high-level officers. Accordingly, the demand for assessment and annual auditing means that there should be self-evaluation of the environmental programs and activities of the firm. These procedures should be independent and made available to the public.[76]

Such an overall environmental business strategy should focus on employees and on the organization by changing knowledge and attitudes, but it should also focus on technology in framing new methods for overcoming environmental problems. Finally, the company should work with its external relations in promoting green marketing and public relations.

The Valdez Principles are not only for good environmental investment by shareholders, but they also indicate an awareness of the status of the environment as an independent stakeholder to be respected. There might even be good economic bottom-line arguments for introducing this kind of environmental policy. Investigations show that proactive environmental compliance can save money.[77] If a company constructs good processes of respect for eco-spheres and the elimination of waste at all levels of the organization, it reduces costs at many levels:

- Being more critical towards environmentally unsound businesses may stabilize the firm's shares on the stock market.
- It can get rid of costs associated with hazardous waste management.
- It can avoid different kinds of green taxes.
- It minimizes the risk of future criminal actions and environmental fines.
- It not only prevents damage to the firm's reputation, but also builds the company's reputation and goodwill with consumers.
- It creates better conditions of health and safety for their employees.

So, in an optimistic light, pollution prevention and waste minimization programs might even be considered as classic win-win situations.[78]

Values-driven strategic management of environmental concern should do more to integrate these concerns into actions to improve the environment. An important issue is long-term strategic planning and change of production, in a way that includes understanding and respect for the interests of future generations and other future stakeholders. Environmental programs should lead to a new green economy based on green strategies in every aspect in economic life. This implies companies seeking market share in accordance with environmental strategies, for example by using recycling and waste management as basic strategies for product development.[79]

The ultimate concern of sustainability strategies for environmental management is – echoing Hans Jonas's ethical language of responsibility – that in the future there will also be human beings on Earth.[80] The triple bottom line also implies concerns for distributive justice and equality between generations in order to secure effective and responsible use of resources in the daily practices of the firm. It is important to emphasize that these concern for environmental values are only relieved when a code of values is accomplished with effective structures of decision-making, including dialogue with stakeholders and open environmental audits, that integrate ethical principles, sustainability, and transparency. These codes should be forward looking in order to make environmental issues, protecting nature, and action to deal with climate change and global warming an integrated part of long-term strategic planning.

Case 24. ABB: A sustainable power and electricity company

The case of AAB has been selected as an illustration of a company that, as a member of CSR Europe, combines *ethical efforts* to improve both corporate citizenship and sustainability. This is accomplished by integrating CSR into the core strategy of the firm.[81] The official discourse of the corporation seeks to define principles of sustainability as the basis for corporate citizenship.

In contrast to the lack of focus on corporate governance at Enron, Swiss-based ABB, an electricity and engineering company with Swedish origins, illustrates an firm's efforts to integrate a general sustainability and triple bottom-line strategy into the heart of the company. ABB is an international technological power firm that is nearly 120 years old. The company has developed many technological innovations with regard to its core business. It contributes to building, developing, and maintaining the power and electricity infrastructures in many countries. In 2004, the company announced that it would build the "world's longest underwater HVDC power transmission link, connecting Norway and the Netherlands." A few years earlier, the core activities were defined as power and automation technologies, and the oil and gas division was sold.[82]

On its website, the firm presents itself as one of the world's leading engineering companies seeking to invent ways to produce and use electrical power as efficiently and sustainably as possible. The firm defines its sustainability strategy in the following way: "Sustainability is integral to all aspects of our business. We strive to balance economic, environmental and social objectives and integrate them into our daily business decisions to create value for all our stakeholders." This implies that the firm works to produce systems and solutions that are efficient for customers, while minimizing the environmental impacts. The corporation works actively to ensure that its business is environmentally friendly and energy-efficient. This includes, for example, factories that are certified by international environmental measures. Eco-efficiency and value for local stakeholders are considered very important because their core business is energy-efficient systems, product, and services. The company also shares the United Nation's concerns about global warming; the company is committed to reducing its emissions of carbon dioxide (CO_2) and has started different global projects to reduce green house gas emissions.[83]

The firm's sustainability policy includes: environmental management systems; taking environmental responsibility for suppliers and the value-chain; manufacturing with a focus on energy efficiency; auditing and measuring environmental performance (including when dealing with other companies); transferring environmental technologies to developing countries; product declarations on the basis of life-cycle analysis; analyzing the environmental aspects of risk assessment of major projects; transparency in annual sustainability reports; and honest accounts of environmental performance in company reports, for example, with detailed environmental product declarations and certification of environmentally acceptable life-cycle analysis.

This environmental policy is accompanied by a social policy that emphasizes ABB's intention to be an active participant in society through its business. According to information on its website, ABB subscribes to respect for human rights, as formulated in the declarations of the UN, the ILO principles, the OECD Guidelines for Multinational Enterprises, the Sullivan Principles, and the SA8000 standards. This implies stakeholder dialogue, respect for the basic freedoms of workers, banning child labor, discrimination, and harassment, supporting workers' health and safety, and employee consultation, communication, and community involvement, for example programs of facilitating access to electricity in Africa and Asia.[84]

ABB includes business ethics in its formulation of business principles with an emphasis on integrity and supporting national and international authorities. In the firm's corporate rhetoric, responsibility and respect are defined as core principles that combine with integrity to build the firm's reputation. ABB has developed internal "zero tolerance" guidelines on business ethics to ensure compliance with legal regulations. These guidelines apply to issues of bribery and corruption, conflicts of interest, insider trading, political contributions, disclosure, violations of regulations, et cetera. Finally, ABB has developed policies on corporate governance to ensure transparency and integrity in accordance with the Swiss Code of Best Practices in Corporate Governance.

4.5. From ethics to law: How to sentence environmental crime?

The discussion about ethical principles and sustainability now moves from ethics to law.[85] Issues of environmental protection not only focus on utility and efficiency, but also on distributive justice and fairness towards future generations.[86] The immediate legal problem is, nevertheless, how to judge or sentence corporations who have been found guilty of committing environmental crime. Today, legislation about environmental issues has become more efficient in many countries; however, there still remain problems regarding just sentencing, how to prevent further environmental crime, or make corporations proactive in their activities in order to prevent environmental crime.

Firstly, can a corporation be forced to be environmentally responsible? It could be argued that if corporations could meaningfully be considered as persons, they could then be held morally responsible. Moral responsibility would, thus, be the basis for legal punishment. The liberal tradition, on the contrary, has – since John Locke – argued that one cannot be responsible for one's own waste since it is no longer one's property. This tradition also does not recognize individual responsibility beyond death. Moreover, corporations are considered as legal fictions: artificial unities of individuals, which cannot have a particular moral responsibility.[87] It is a difficulty for environmental law that it is necessary to consider the corporation as a responsible person in order to attribute moral responsibility to it. The solution may be found in a corporation as a collectively responsible entity that can be considered responsible for its actions, also in relation to future generation. This is not impossible, according to Peter French, who argues that a corporation, like a person, is capable of rational agency.[88]

If we look at the predominant legal traditions in the West, there has been a judicial tendency to exclude the environment as an entity for human concern. In the classical natural law tradition, the relations between human beings, the cosmos, justice, and the nature of things have played an important role in the view that human beings are integrated in a natural teleology of goodness and harmony with the world.[89] When modern theories of the social contract separated the subject and object, wrenching humankind from nature, they neglected to define "nature." It is practically non-existent among the subjects constituting legal and political community. This omission had a powerful effect on the modern conception of the relation between human beings and nature and had an important impact on our willingness to respect the envionment. For Jean-Jacques Rousseau, the social contract is a result of the general will among free human subjects.[90] Rawls's theory of justice also seems to have little room for nature or animals as participants in the community of the original position, who have to decide the structure of future society behind the veil of ignorance.[91]

This might be the reason why the French philosopher Michel Serres has argued for a new natural contract, with a more just contractual relation between humankind and nature. Serres considers the natural contract as an alternative to the dominance of the current warlike conditions, which presently typify the relationship between humankind and nature.[92] Serres can be said to try to extend the idea of corporate citizenship to include corporate relations with the environment. A symbiotic, communicative relation should replace this conflictual situation, wherein human beings interact in close organic connection with the teleology of nature. The new natural contract would replace a situation of instability and constant confrontation with harmonious coexistence.

Along similar lines, the California law professor Christopher Stone has discussed whether natural objects can have a specific legal standing on their own. Stone argues that the consequence of giving such entities legal rights would not granting them the same rights as human beings (which was previously criticized), but only that natural objects would be given some kind of standing on their own. The previous analysis of nature and animals as stakeholders, to which sustainability applies, delivers an outline of such a standing.

Many scholars, among others the neo-Kantian French philosopher Luc Ferry, have criticized Serres and Stone for their tendency to end up in deep ecology. Ferry argues that replacing human beings as the center of the cosmos is very difficult in the modern world, where humanity has become separated from the biosphere and ecosystem. He thinks that the distinction must be maintained between human beings and nature. Rather than deep ecology, the legal regulation of nature should be based on a "humanistic position" that, while recognizing the basic differences between human beings, animals, and nature, is aware of the necessity of a human sensibility towards nature. Ferry defends the dependence of law on human rationality and sensibility, while arguing for overcoming the anthropocentric perspective in order to establish a sustainable relation to nature.

The modified anthropocentric position might also be proposed as the basis for judicial regulation. It is open to the biocentric perspective, without the metaphysical implications of the deep ecology position. Michael Hoffman provides an illustrative example: "If you were the last human being on earth after a nuclear disaster and there only was one tree left. . . [assuming that] you would not be harmed by the existence of the tree, you would be likely to agree that it would be wrong to destroy the tree, that it had its own right to live, and that its existence would make a difference on Earth independent of you."[93] This position might be viewed as a biocentric position, which is compatible with the proposed anthropocentrifugal perspective, and results in corporations having an obligation to work for the improvement of the environment independently of their own interest in economic benefit.

Environmental sentencing is values-driven management's most regulative and preventative function, but the goal of holding corporations legally responsible for the future environmental consequences of their actions cannot be accomplished exclusively through sentencing. How can legislation and legal regulation be used in order to prevent future wrongdoing by corporations? From the point of view of government, the use of law should help to create a civil society, which is capable of acting responsibly regarding the environment and coping with environmental risk. Moreover, government policy should function as an opening for new environmental initiatives. In Europe, this has been accomplished by putting environmental taxes on the actions of companies found guilty of environmental wrongdoing.[94] Tax policy aims to avoid environmental damage by putting substantial costs on using natural resources or polluting ecosystems. Moreover, legislation on environmental issues has, in many European countries, led to laws on the necessity of green auditing, implying both rewards and help to companies that include environmental concerns in their productivity.

The United States has also proposed different kinds of green taxes on environmentally damaging production, for example ozone taxes and other regulations addressing the problems of global climate change. In this context, tax policy was designed to reward companies that invest in sound environmental policies (e.g., life-cycle planning or recycling). As another example, in 1995, Denmark passed legislation on corporate environmental compliance that represented an important effort to integrate environmental responsibility in values-driven management.

Programs of environmental values-driven management are important for creating new ways of securing that companies will self-regulate to demonstrate strict compliance with the law. In order to avoid legal problems, environmental liability is very important for organizations. The internal compliance programs and their evaluations contribute to this detection of environmental problems in the organization. If they have programs of values-driven management, including environmental audits, companies are much better able to comply with governmental regulations, especially when they disclose important information and knowledge in their self-evaluations. Environmental values-driven management functions as a kind of self-policing in cases where there can be hidden environmental problems in the organization.

An important model for new legal thinking in this regard can be found in the FSGO.[95] These mandatory guidelines (which were touched on briefly in previous discussions of sentencing and ethics, and will be covered in more detail in the following chapter) unified American sentencing of criminals by incorporating guidelines on fines and determining the culpability of organizations found guilty of committing crimes. Unfortunately, in the beginning, the guidelines did not include environmental crimes, even though it was understood that their potential social harm could be much greater than individual offenses. Still, the principle behind the guidelines may be the right one. Indeed, a stick-and-carrot approach to environmental self-regulation may be very useful for securing environmental compliance and perhaps improving corporate citizenship in the field of corporate environmental action.

A number of substantial and technical problems kept the FSGO commission from accepting a proposal for guidelines for environmental crimes prior to their enactment in 1991.[96] It was discussed whether it is at all possible to make organizations culpable of organizational crime when it is difficult to identify the agents, the victims, and the consequences of environmental crimes. Some critical voices argued that it is absurd to attribute environmental conscience to corporations. Sometimes, environmental cases are much more difficult to judge clearly than other cases of organizational crime. Indeed, it is often difficult to place direct culpability. There were also concerns that strict guidelines would lead to huge fines that would hurt corporate performance on the economic market.[97] So it was argued that civil law rather than criminal law would be appropriate in order to judge environmental crime.

It is possible that mandatory guidelines for sentencing environmental crimes might improve corporate environmental awareness. To this end, guidelines have been proposed in the context of the discussion of general principles of sentencing of organizations. They are based on the idea that the installation of environmental compliance programs should be considered as a mitigating factor in sentencing of the organization. This would improve the environmental activities of the firm and is indicated by the "minimum factors demonstrating commitment to environmental compliance." They determine that such a program should include: "1) Line management attention and substantial involvement in execution of compliance programs; 2) integration of environmental policies throughout the organization; 3) frequent auditing and continuous on-site monitoring; 4) employee training in regulatory requirements; 5) cash incentives or other types of rewards to employees who have demonstrated commitment to environmental compliance; 6) consistent and visible disciplinary procedures for compliance program violations including reporting individual conduct to law enforcement; 7) organizational self-evaluation procedures to ensure progress toward environmental excellence; and 8) incorporation of innovative approaches to environmental compliance."[98]

Such criteria for compliance could improve the environmental awareness of companies. Looking at the general impact of the FSGO with regard to installing compliance programs and programs of values-driven management, this would have a preventive and pragmatic function by giving organizations a basis for self-regulation and self-improvement. It may even lead to proactive engagement of corporations in environmental efforts. Moreover, such guidelines seem to propose a new concept of corporate culpability that is based on "reactive fault" rather than direct culpability, because organizations are judged

according to their efforts and willingness to work for avoiding the offense.[99]
This pragmatic approach does not, however, exclude Kantian retribuvism.[100]
~~The fact that such sentencing guidelines would be placed under criminal law~~
represents an effort to measure the correct punishment according to the need
for retribution. Indeed, the symbolic nature of criminal law may respond to
public demands for correct and just punishment of organizations perpetrating
criminal damage against the environment.

Endnotes

1   This research is a development of my earlier work on bioethics and law. I argued that the basic ethical principles of respect for human autonomy, dignity, integrity, and vulnerability should be proposed as central values for bi-omedical and biotechnological developments. I have also showed how basic ethical principles can play a role in business ethics. Peter Kemp, Mette Lebech and Jacob Rendtorff, *Den bioetiske vending* (Copenhagen: Spektrum, 1997). Jacob Dahl Rendtorff, *Bioetik og Ret, Kroppen mellem person og ting* (Copenhagen: Gyldendal, 1999). Jacob Dahl Rendtorff and Peter Kemp, *Basic Ethical Principles in European Bioethics and Biolaw*n (Copenhagen and Barcelona: Center for Ethics and Law, 2000). Peter Kemp, "Bæredygtighedens etik" in *Dansk naturpolitik i bæredygtighedens perspektiv* (Copenhagen: Naturrådet, 2000).

2   David L. Levy and Peter J. Newell, *The Business of Global Environmental Governance* (Cambridge MA: MIT Press, 2005), 75. We can even talk about climate change as threat to corporate hegemony.

3   In this context, we may mention the work of environmental scholar Bjørn Lomborg. In his book, *The Skeptical Environmentalist* (Cambridge: Cambridge University Press, 2001), he proposed a close link between ethics and economics. Lomborg's argument seems to be based on the vision that there can be good economic solutions to the most serious problems of humanity. This argument does not exclude basic ethical principles as the foundation of sustainable development; rather, the argument represents a proposal for economic efficiency with regard to the solution of global problems.

4   W. Michael Hoffman, "Business and Environmental Ethics", *Business Ethics Quarterly* 1991.

5   Manuel G. Velasquez, *Business Ethics. Concept and Cases*, fifth Edition (New Jersey: Prentice Hall 2002), 269ff.

6   Ibid: 290.

7   This is described by former high-level UN official Maurice Strong in his book: *Where on Earth are We going?* (New York and London: Texere, 2000).

8   World Commission on Environment and Development, *Our Common Future* (Oxford: Oxford University Press, 1987).

9   W. Michael Hoffman, "Business and Environmental Ethics", *Business Ethics Quarterly* 1991.

10   David L. Levy and Peter J. Newell, *The Business of Global Environmental Governance* (Cambridge MA: MIT Press, 2005), 85.

11   Joseph R. Desjardins, "Business' Environmental Responsibility" in *A Companion to Business Ethics*, Blackwell Companions to Philosophy edited Robert E. Frederick (Oxford: Blackwell Publishers (1999), 2002), 280.

12   Ibid: 286.

13   Herman Daly, *Beyond Growth* (Boston: Beacon Press, 1996).

14   Joseph R. Desjardins, "Business' Environmental Responsibility" in Robert E. Frederick: *A Companion to Business Ethics*, Blackwell Companions to Philosophy, Blackwell Publishers, Oxford (1999), 2002., 288.

15   Joseph R. Desjardins, "Environmental Responsibility" in Norman E. Bowie: *The Blackwell Guide to Business Ethics*, (Oxford: Blackwell Publishers, 2002), 258.

16   John Elkington, *Cannibals with Forks. The Triple Bottom Line of 21st Century Business* (Oxford: Capstone (1997), 1999).

17   Ibid: 229.

18 This is inspired of Francis Fukuyama, *The End of History and the Last Man* (New York: The Free Press, 1990) and Francis Fukuyama, *Trust, The Social Virtues and the Creation of Prosperity* (New York: The Free Press, 1995). We may recall the definition of our new economic system as "stakeholder capitalism that we have earlier discussed."

19 R. Edward Freeman, *Strategic Management: A Stakeholder Approach* (Boston, Massachusetts: Pitman Publishing Inc., 1984). John Elkington, *Cannibals with Forks. The Triple Bottom Line of 21st Century Business* (Oxford-Capstone, Oxford 1997, 1999, 298.

20 Ibid: 234.

21 For further presentation and analysis of these different cases see: W. Michael Hoffman, Robert Frederick and Edward S. Petry (editors), *The Corporation, Ethics and the Environment* (Westpoint, Connecticut, London: Quorum Books, New Port, 1990). See also Colin Fisher and Allan Lovell, *Business Ethics and Values. Individual, Corporate and International Perspectives* (Pearson Education, Essex, UK: Prentice Hall, Finansial Times, 2006), 469-473.

22 John Elkington, *Cannibals with Forks. The Triple Bottom Line of 21st Century Business* (Oxford: Capstone (1997), 1999), 20.

23 See Richard De George, "International Business Ethics" in *A Companion to Business Ethics. Blackwell Companions to Philosophy* edited by Robert E. Frederick (Oxford: Blackwell Publishing, 1999), 240.

24 Richard De George, *Business Ethics* (Upper Saddle River, New Jersey: Prentice Hall, 1999).

25 Ibid: 510.

26 Jacob Dahl Rendtorff and Peter Kemp, *Basic Ethical Principles in European Bioethics and Biolaw* (Barcelona and Copenhagen: Center for Ethics and Law, 2000). Peter Kemp: "Bæredygtighedens etik" in *Dansk naturpolitik i bæredygtighedens perspektiv* (Copenhagen: Naturrådet, 2000).

27 In Switzerland, there has been an interesting discussion about the place of this principle in the constitution: See *Experten Bericht* von Philipp Balzer, Klaus Peter Rippe, Peter Schaber, "Was heisst Würde der Kreatur?" (Bern: Bundesamt für Umwelt, Wald und Landwirtschaft (BUWAL), 1997).

28 Jacob Dahl Rendtorff and Peter Kemp, *Basic Ethical Principles in European Bioethics and Biolaw* (Barcelona and Copenhagen: Center for Ethics and Law, 2000). See also *Genteknologi og etik: konventioner ved Peter Kemp og Kjersti Lunde,* Biotik-litteratur (Copenhagen: 2001). Peter Kemp, "Bæredygtighedens etik" in *Dansk naturpolitik i bæredygtighedens perspektiv* (Copenhagen: Naturrådet, 2000).

29 Jacob Dahl Rendtorff and Peter Kemp, *Basic Ethical Principles in European Bioethics and Biolaw* (Barcelona and Copenhagen: Center for Ethics and Law, 2000). Peter Kemp, "Bæredygtighedens etik" in *Dansk naturpolitik i bæredygtighedens perspektiv* (Copenhagen: Naturrådet, 2000).

30 Hans Jonas, *Das Prinzip Verantwortung* (Frankfurt: Insel Verlag, 1979).

31 World Commission on Environment and Development, *Our Common Future* (Oxford: Oxford University Press, 1987), 9. Peter Kemp, "Bæredygtighedens etik" in *Dansk naturpolitik i bæredygtighedens perspektiv* (Copenhagen: Naturrådet, 2000).

32 World Commission on Environment and Development, *Our Common Future* (Oxford: Oxford University Press, 1987), 13.

33 Ibid: 62.

34 Ibid: 262.

35 Ibid: 97.

36 Ibid: 98.

37 Ibid: 34.

38 Ibid: 67.

39 Ibid: 61.

40 Ibid: 114.

41 Ibid: 114.

42 Ibid: 61-62.

43 The discursive method of analyzing this text is inspired by Anders Bordum and Jacob Holm Hansen, *Strategisk ledelseskommunikation. Erhvervslivets ledelse med visioner, missioner og værdier* (Copenhagen: Jurist og Økonomforbundets forlag, 2005), 25-63.

44 This company is a member of CSR Europe. The case is an important example of sustainable tourism. The case is selected from the website of the company, www.accor.com.

45 Ibid.

46 Ibid.

47 Peter Kemp, "Bæredygtighedens etik" in *Dansk naturpolitik i bæredygtighedens perspektiv* (Copenhagen: Natur-rådet, 2000).

48 See Peter Kemp, Mette Lebech and Jacob Rendtorff, *Den bioetiske vending: The bioethical Turn* (Copenhagen: Spektrum, 1997), where we discuss this phenomenological position of the relation between man and nature. Peter Kemp, "Bæredygtighedens etik" in *Dansk naturpolitik i bæredygtighedens perspektiv* (Copenhagen: Natur-rådet, 2000).

49 Manuel G. Velasquez, *Business Ethics. Concept and Cases*, fifth Edition (New Jersey: Prentice Hall 2002), 289.

50 Dietmar vd. Pfordten, *Ökologische Ethik* (Hamburg: Rowolt Taschenbuch Verlag, 1986).

51 Ibid: 40.

52 Kant's *Critique of Judgment* and *Foundations of Metaphysics of Morals* may here be mentioned as important references for foundation of the ethical principles as basis for the idea of sustainability. See Immanuel Kant: *Grundlegung zur Metaphysik der Sitten* (1785) (Hamburg: Felix Meiner Verlag, 1999). Also Immanuel Kant: *Kritik der Urteilskraft* (1794), § 40. Suhrkamp Werkausgabe (Frankfurt am Main, 2004). In this book we find an important discussion of the teleology of nature.

53 Gorm Harste, *Kompleksitet og Dømmekraft* (Aalborg: Nordic Summer University, 1994).

54 Peter Kemp, "Bæredygtighedens etik" in *Dansk naturpolitik i bæredygtighedens perspektiv* (Copenhagen: Natur-rådet, 2000). Jacob Dahl Rendtorff and Peter Kemp, *Basic Ethical Principles in European Bioethics and Biolaw* (Barcelona and Copenhagen: Center for Ethics and Law, 2000). Peter Kemp, Mette Lebech and Jacob Rendtorff: *Den bioetiske vending: The bioethical Turn* (Copenhagen: Spektrum, 1997).

55 Peter Singer, *Practical Ethics* (Cambridge: Cambridge University Press, 1993).

56 Hans Otto Apel, *Diskurs und Verantwortung* (Frankfurt am Main: Suhrkamp Verlag, 1988).

57 Tom Regan, *Earthbound: Introductory Essays in Environmental Ethics*, (New York: Random House, 1984).

58 Immanuel Kant, *Kritik der Urteilskraft* (1794) (Frankfurt am Main: Suhrkamp Werkausgabe, 2004), § 40. Dietmar vd. Pforden discusses "Ethik der Andersinteressen" in *Ökologische Ethik* (Hamburg: Rowolt Taschenbuch Verlag, 1996).

59 M. Starik, "Stakeholder Status for Non-Human Nature", *Journal of Business Ethics*, Vol. 14, (1995), 216.

60 *Environmental Challenges to Business* (Bowling Green: The Ruffin Series, No 2., A Publication of the Society for Business Ethics, Philosophy Documentation Center).

61 M. Starik, "Stakeholder Status for Non-Human Nature", *Journal of Business Ethics*, Vol. 14, (1995), 216.

62 This case is selected from Mark A. White, "Effect of the Green Movement on Investors" in *The Greening of American Business. Making Bottom-line Sense of Environmental Responsibility* (Rockville Maryland: Government Institutes Inc., 1992). The case is also a case of environmental crisis management. See Christine M.Person and Mitroff, Ian I., "From crisis prone to crisis prepared: A framework for crisis management, *Academy of Management Executive*, Vol. 7 (1993), Issue 1: 48-59.,

63 Mark H. Allenbaugh, "What's your water worth? Why we need Federal Sentencing Guidelines for corporate environmental crime?", *American University Law Review*, Volume 48, (1999), number 4., 927.

64 John Elkington, *Cannibals with Forks, The Triple Bottom Line of 21st Century Business*, (Oxford: Capstone (1997), 1999), 85.

65 Ibid: 140.

66 Ibid: 234.

67 Ibid: 205.

68 These bear some resemblance to the Sullivan principles, which have been important for respecting human rights in connection with apartheid policies in South Africa.

69 This case is selected from Mark A. White, "Effect of the Green Movement on Investors" in *The Greening of American Business. Making Bottom-line Sense of Environmental Responsibility* (Rockville Maryland: Government Institutes Inc., 1992), 49.

70 Ibid: 49

71 Ibid: 49.

72 Ibid: 49.

73 Ibid: 49.

74 Ibid: 50.

75 Ibid: 50.

76 Ibid: 50.

77 David R. Chittick, "Financial Implications of Environmental Compliance" in *The Greening of American Business. Making Bottom-line Sense of Environmental Responsibility*, (Rockville Maryland: Government Institutes Inc., 1992), 127.

78 Ibid: 146.

79 Ibid: 150.

80 Hans Jonas, *Das Prinzip Verantwortung*, (Frankfurt am Main: Insel Verlag, 1979).

81 Method for discoursive analysis of the text is inspired by Anders Bordum and Jacob Holm Hansen, *Strategisk ledelseskommunikation. Erhvervslivets ledelse med visioner, missioner og værdier* (Copenhagen: Jurist og Økonomforbundets forlag, 2005), 25-63.

82 This case is selected from company website: www.abb.com. ABB is selected as a member of CSR Europe.

83 Ibid.

84 Ibid.

85 Jacob Dahl Rendtorff and Peter Kemp, *Basic Ethical Principles in European Bioethics and Biolaw* (Barcelona and Copenhagen: Center for Ethics and Law, 2000). Peter Kemp, Mette Lebech and Jacob Rendtorff, *Den bioetiske vending: The bioethical Turn* (Copenhagen: Spektrum, 1997).

86 Manuel G. Velasquez, *Business Ethics. Concept and Cases*, fifth Edition, (New Jersey: Prentice Hall, 2002), 310.

87 Peter French, "Terre Gaste" in *The Corporation, Ethics and the Environment* edited by Hoffman, Frederick and Petry (New York, Westport, Conneticut, London: Quorum books, 1991, 4).

88 Ibid: 7.

89 Leo Strauss, *Natural Right and History,* (Chicago: University of Chicago Press, 1953). Leo Strauss, *The City and Man* (Chicago: University of Chicago Press, 1964).

90 Jean-Jacques Rousseau, *Du Contrat social*, (Paris: Flammarion, 2001).

91 John Rawls, *A Theory of Justice* (Boston, Massachusetts: Harvard University Press, 1971).

92 Michel Serres, *Le contrat naturel* (Paris: Flammarion, 1991).

93 W. Michael Hoffman, "Business and Environmental Ethics", *Business Ethics Quarterly*, 1991.

94 Sacha Millstone and Ferris Baker Watts, "Effect on the Green Movement on Business in the 1990s" in *The Greening of American Business. Making Bottom-line Sense of Environmental Responsibility* (Rockville Maryland: Government Institutes Inc., 1992), 12.

95 Mark H. Allenbaugh, "What's your water worth? Why we need Federal Sentencing Guidelines for corporate environmental crime?", *American University Law Review*, Volume 48, (1999) number 4.

96 Because FSGO will be analyzed more deeply in the next chapter, only the aspects of the guidelines relevant to the environment will be discussed here.

97 Mark H. Allenbaugh, "What's your water worth? Why we need Federal Sentencing Guidelines for corporate environmental crime?", *American University Law Review*, Volume 48, (1999) number 4.

98 Ibid: 943.

99 Ibid: 947.

100 Ibid: 959.

5. Towards the good corporate citizen

The previous analysis presupposed the ideal of the good corporate citizen based on the theory of republican business ethics.[1] However, the concept was not sufficiently explained.[2] This chapter will – as a culmination of the previous discussions – look specifically at the concept of the good corporate citizen that follows from the analysis of values-driven management and business ethics. The argument addresses the concepts of moral responsibility, and corporate identity and personhood, in order to define good corporate citizenship as the basis for corporate social responsibility. This analysis aims to clarify whether it is possible to ascribe moral agency to the corporation, or whether the firm should be considered as nothing more than a legal construct and economic device for efficient instrumental action.

The question becomes: To what extent can a firm's social responsibility be formulated in terms of corporate intentionality? To what extent can this agency be conceived as moral? This chapter discusses how we can talk about a firm's corporate social responsibility as a collective agent – an organizational actor to whom we can ascribe intentional action and accountability.

The chapter starts with a discussion of the concept of corporate citizenship and then examines collectivist arguments for corporate moral responsibility. Following a discussion of some possible economic, anti-essentialist, and individualist criticisms of the collectivist concept of corporate social responsibility, a third possible organizational view on corporate group responsibility and the moral agency of the firm is put forward. This view aims to overcome the opposition between collectivist and individualist views on corporate social responsibility.

Accordingly, the chapter is structured in the following parts: 1) republican business ethics as corporate citizenship between responsibility and sustainability; 2) collectivist arguments for corporate moral responsibility; 3) individualist criticism of corporate moral responsibility; and 4) towards an institutional concept of corporate moral and social responsibility of the good citizen corporation.

The corporation as a good corporate citizen
Vision, mission and foundation in republican business ethics

Economic value creation
Stakeholder communication ethics
Virtue ethics and the vision of the good life
Universalism, duties and contract ethics
Republican business ethics
"The good life with and for the other in just institutions"

The ethical strategy of the corporation

Formulation of a vision for good corporate citizenship
Employee involvement in the process of formulating ethics and values
Considering the corporation as a responsible moral agent
Development of high organizational integrity and moral thinking
Trust and accountability of basic principles of corporate ethics

Figure 3.2.

5.1. Republican business ethics as corporate citizenship

The concept of the good corporate citizen is inseparable from the idea of corporate citizenship, which has a long history. The idea of corporate citizenship emerged in the middle of the twentieth century when Peter Drucker, in *The Concept of the Corporation,* conceived of businesses as institutions that integrate human beings in order to develop a free society.[3] Emerging from this context, corporate citizenship was already a holistic concept indicating the active participation of corporations in society.[4] The task is to clarify how the concepts of corporate citizenship and its contemporary offspring, the good corporate citizen, relate to the idea of corporate social responsibility. Because corporate citizenship captures the essence of republican business ethics, it is, therefore, more fundamental and comprehensive than the concepts of values-driven management and corporate social responsibility, which may address aspects of corporate citizenship but fail to address the fundamental concept of the corporation as ethical. In this sense, the concept of the good corporate citizen implies a generalization and development of earlier concepts of corporate social responsibility. Corporate citizenship seems to be the foundation for other concepts like corporate responsiveness, corporate social performance, stakeholder theory, and so forth.[5]

As a refutation of the criticism that corporate citizenship adds nothing new, I want to distinguish my view on corporate citizenship and republican business ethics from some of the most predominant misunderstandings of the concept of the good citizen corporation. First of all, corporate citizenship should not be reduced to a particular concept of corporate social responsibility. For example, to reduce corporate citizenship to charitable giving would fail to understand the scope of the concept. Even though enlightened self-interest may be one of the arguments for corporate citizenship, it is not the only argument. Defending an institutional concept of the good corporate citizen requires going much deeper to understand what corporate citizenship is really about. Moreover, it is important to be aware of the particularity of corporate citizenship in comparison with a conception of corporate social responsibility. As mentioned previously, the idea of the good citizen corporation contains corporate social responsibility but goes beyond it, because it denotes the essential role of corporations in society without restricting institutional responsibility and corporate moral agency to being "socially responsible."

The concept of republican business ethics does not refer exclusively to citizenship, as conceived within the liberal tradition, which confers to citizens certain fundamental social, civil, and political rights.[6] It is a concept of citizenship that refers to the duties of governments towards individual human beings as members of society, though, as Andrew Crane and Dirk Matten have noted, it is hard to apply this concept to corporate citizenship.[7] As discussed in the elaboration of republican citizenship, the idea of the good citizen corporation is, rather, that corporations – like public actors – are in a position in society where they must behave as good citizens, meaning that they act as organizations that contribute to the development of a good and just society. When corporations act as corporate citizens their role in society changes and they cannot be described adequately from the neoliberal or neoclassical perspective – as purely economic agents.

From the point of view of our discussion of different concepts of business ethics, it is arguable that the minimalist, libertarian position posits a very limited role for corporate citizenship: one restricted to following legal rules and standards. The communitarian concept of business ethics can go further, arguing that business citizenship may be possible within the national context of the good society, where individuals and organizations have obligations to contribute to the formation of the common good.[8] At the level of Kantian business ethics, corporate citizenship is considered as an obligation to follow universal principles and to protect rights and liberties, and to contribute with justice to society. As proposed, republican business ethics can be said to regard corporate citizenship on two levels: the level of national community and the level of the international community. At the communitarian level, the corporation participates by substantially contributing to community. At the universal level, the corporation becomes a world citizen defending human rights and universal principles of ethics, while at the same time accepting that there is a free moral space for national standards of business ethics.

We can refer to the tradition of civic republicanism to describe the engagement of the corporation as a good citizen. It is important to note that corporate citizenship is a metaphor for social engagement in society that indicates the fundamental moral responsibility of corporations to engage in particular societal affairs.[9] As Gareth Morgan's work indicates, certain concepts are used as metaphors to characterize different organizations in organizational analysis. In this sense, the concept of corporate citizenship is arguably the best metaphor to describe the stakeholder-oriented socially responsible corporation.[10] The concepts of organizational responsibility, identity, integrity, accountability, and trust are its basis. In refering to the tradition of political philosophy, Jeremy Moon, Crane, and Matten have elaborated on this basis to articulate four models of citizenship: liberalist minimalist, civic republicanism, developmental, and deliberative. These models describe the different forms of participation in society, which could be said to emerge from the idea of corporate citizenship as a metaphor for the relation between business and society.[11] In fact, following our conception of republican business ethics, corporate citizenship can be conceived as containing elements from all four of these ideas, particularly combining civic republicanism (the idea of participation in community), elements of the concept of deliberative democracy, and the idea of open dialogue with stakeholders.

James E. Post defines corporate citizenship as "the process of identifying, analyzing, and responding to the company's social, political, and economic responsibilities as defined through law and public policy, stakeholder expectations, and corporate values and business strategy. . .[it] involves both actual results (*what corporations do*) and the process through which they are achieved (*how they do it*)."[12] This definition of corporate citizenship implies that companies should take responsibility as members of national societies, or as members of the global community.

There is increasing emphasis on the notion of corporate citizenship as a concept for global business ethics. When the Global Economic Forum defines corporate citizenship, it emphasizes that citizenship is not exclusively a question of additional CSR or philanthropy, but rather an integrated part of business strategy and practice. Republican business ethics allows for some free moral space for cultural differences within different societies, which is important because, as indicated by the different ways cultures and countries define the good corporate citizen, there are many local conceptions of corporate citizenship.[13] As argued, to be a good corporate citizen does not exclusively imply following the rules and regulations of the nation-state; rather, corporate citizenship goes beyond the nation-state and requires that the corporation becomes a citizen of the world community – a cosmopolitan. Business ethics should, therefore, address the power of the corporation as a good citizen in the international community. Jeanne M. Logsdon and Donna J. Wood have addressed this notion of global business citizenship, indicating the need for business corporations to be globally engaged.[14] They argue that global business citizenship is linked to efforts to incorporate universal values into a firm's mission and values statements, and to comply with international codes of conduct. Global business citizenship is proposed as a solution for business ethics at the global level in order to ensure social engagement of corporations. Logsdon and Wood define the global business citizen as "a multinational enterprise that responsibly implements its duties to individuals and to societies within and across national and cultural boarders."[15] Global citizenship consists of developing universal standards and at the same time respecting cultural difference, to the extent that firms do not violate minimum international standards. Moreover, it implies the engagement of corporations in a process of learning, developing international norms and values, and respecting human welfare and development.

James E. Post also argues for a concept of global corporate citizenship. According to this approach, corporate citizenship at the global level signifies that the corporation acts as a stakeholder corporation. He argues that global corporate citizenship has to be linked with the issue of values at the international level.[16] Indeed, corporate citizenship is not only about economic value, but also about the public contribution of the corporation to the good of society. It is the commitment to public and civic values that undergirds this concept of corporate citizenship, which implies a close relationship with stakeholder management, including the concepts of sustainability and respect for stakeholders.

A critical reply may be that corporate citizenship is the symptom of a broken contract between society and corporations, where short-term thinking focusing on profits is the rule of the day. This has contributed to the erosion of employee loyalty and it has separated corporations from their stakeholders. Corporate citizenship indicates an effort to bolster the corporation in society as an active, engaged, and constructive citizen. Corporate citizenship implies a shift in focus towards long-term social interests.[17] From this perspective, Moon, Crane, and Matten can be seen as offering a critical evaluation of the approach of Logsdon and Wood.[18] They think that a better conceptual foundation is needed. The starting point of the concept of the corporation as a citizen should be refining the metaphor for citizenship, such that it does not differentiate between liberal and communitarian positions, but instead promotes a continuum between the two positions so that political philosophy can benefit from the insights of communitarianism.[19]

It is important for long-term corporate citizenship that corporations consider themselves as contributors to the common good, or the general interest of society. In this context, the communitarian model of civic participation is very important in order to understand what citizenship really is. Moreover, it is also wrong to restrict corporate citizenship to philanthropy and local participation. As argued, corporate citizenship should not be reduced to philanthropic CSR, but should also be concerned with the application of business ethics to all corporate stakeholders. It is important not to limit the scope of corporate citizenship, but rather to understand corporate citizenship as the most important foundation for corporate social responsibility and business ethics in practice.

This is also the argument of Matten, Crane, and Wendy Chapple, who emphasize that corporations contribute to society by protecting certain rights and duties with the same sense of responsibility as government.[20] They promote corporate citizenship as a very useful concept that goes beyond the concept of corporate social responsibility. Moreover, they think that it also captures elements of social relations of corporations that are not captured by stakeholder management approaches. Therefore, they argue that corporate citizenship is a new and different term that gives us a new and different connotation for the kind of role that we want to give business in society. This extended view of corporate citizenship implies a criticism of a limited liberal concept of citizenship, and opens it to a broader republican concept of the relation between business and society. However this concept of corporate citizenship must go beyond conventional conceptions of citizenship.[21]

In other work, Crane and Matten have also indicated that the concept of corporate citizenship implies that corporations should intervene in areas where governments have ceased to, and where they either do not or cannot administer citizen rights.[22] Corporations are important for protecting and advocating the civil and political rights of citizens, as they play an evermore active role in formulating policies and ideas about social development. As Crane and Matten define it, corporate citizenship (or CC) "describes the role of the corporation in administering citizenship rights for individuals. Such a definition reframes CC away from the notion that the corporation is a citizen in itself (as individuals are) and toward the acknowledgment that the corporation administers certain aspects of citizenship for other constituencies. These include traditional stakeholders, such as employees, customers, or shareholders, but also include wider constituencies with an indirect transactional relationship to the company."[23] This idea is included in the concept of republican business ethics; however, when referring to the idea of the "good life with and for the other in just institutions" it is not sufficient to describe the idea of the good corporate citizen corporation in terms of rights language. Moreover, many issues are left unanswered in this definition, such as in situations where the corporation provides, enables, and challenges social, civil, and political rights.[24]

Crane and Matten are nevertheless aware that there are many problems with the extended concept of citizenship, for example that corporations take over the role of public bodies in formulating political ideas of society. In order to avoid normative criticism, they argue that corporate citizenship is essentially a descriptive concept. Moreover, they state that corporate citizenship is faced with the problem of democracy because, it may be argued, corporations ought to be based on "stakeholder democracy" when they take over the functions and responsibilities of governments.[25] Crane and Matten are arguably too focused on the liberal rights-based concept of citizenship. This preoccupation means that they do not focus on the concept of duty, obligation, and moral responsibility, which – as has been articulated in this chapter – are essential to the concept of the good corporate citizen. Accordingly, in order to really understand the idea of the good corporate citizen, the focus should shift to a presentation of the possible ways that a corporation might be viewed as a morally collective personality.

Simon Zadek has proposed an analysis of corporate citizenship that has been important for the practical realization of the concept through his work as CEO of the British NGO consultancy, Accountability.[26] According to Zadek, the civil corporation is founded on the recognition that "every customer is part of a community and that social responsibility is not an optional area."[27] Zadek subscribes to the idea of sustainability and commitment, to the triple bottom line, as well as the responsibility of corporations to help solve world problems like poverty and environmental damage. Zadek describe these new partnerships arising between business, governments, and NGOs as a *new economy* of corporate citizenship. This concept also includes important considerations of inequality between developed and developing countries, new forms of governance and scope of engagement.[28]

The idea of the new economy of corporate citizenship in times of economic globalization means that the corporations should relate to broader social and environmental issues. Zadek emphasizes that "new civil governance" is essential in the new economy of corporate citizenship. The idea is that rules and norms are constructed within the market, with corporations themselves as key actors.[29] This new form of governance operates through a decentralized network where corporations themselves contribute to forming the social rules and norms. This happens based on willingness to dialogue and share information with stakeholder. Different instruments and standards, like the balanced scorecard or SA8000, are examples of this need for new instruments to regulate corporate activities. The idea of corporate citizenship is, in this context, fundamentally an issue about engaging in community in order to be responsive and accountable, and to make the institutionalization of trust relations among corporations foundational.[30] According to Zadek, good corporate citizenship is about institutionalizing governance frameworks for acting on civil markets in global community. In this context it is important to emphasize that corporate citizenship is more fundamental and more embracing than CSR. Corporate citizenship refers to the most fundamental position of the firm in society, and it deals with all aspects of the firm's activities. It is universal and cosmopolitan in nature because, in that it refers to aspects of world politics and world standards of the UN and other international bodies like the ILO, the Rio Declaration, Global Compact, and so forth.

In this context, corporate citizenship situates the firm in a kind of welfarist economics of the global community in order to deal with problems such as poverty, environmental degradation, and the persistence of undemocratic regimes. Zadek emphasizes that corporations are powerful actors who, despite being a part of a very wealthy community, have not been very able to bring more happiness to the international community. This has created a sense of perplexity that needs to be overcome and has, therefore, become an increasing focus on corporate citizenship. Using the concept of the new economy to define corporate citizenship, Zadek speaks about "speed, knowledge, innovation, and communication" as essential elements of the changed conditions for economic action in modernity.[31] The new economy implies radical changes in organizations, which has resulted in a search for new organizational forms and has centralized the role of ethics and values for corporations. According to Zadek, the idea of corporate citizenship emerged out of the Anglo-American context and many British corporations have been active in developing strategies and policies for corporate citizenship. This does not mean that it is essentially an Anglo-American phenomenon, but international Anglo-American companies have been drivers in developing a culture of corporate citizenship. Corporate citizenship is linked to the idea of doing good and being ethical, and it is supposed that there is an upward spiral between being a good corporate citizen and having success in society. In this sense, corporate citizenship is linked the idea of long-term sustainability of the firm rather than short-term financial gains. At the international level, corporate citizenship is also linked to fair trade and ethical trading initiatives.[32]

Legitimacy is importantly linked with trust as an essential aspect of corporate citizenship, which creates dense networks in the spirit of collaboration and trust in international community. In a sense, the real aim of this new economy of corporate citizenship is to institutionalize the conditions of trust.[33] Unlike NGOs, which are the organizations that traditionally are very close to institutionalized trust, corporations have a long way to go in this regard.

This discussion reinforces the idea that corporate citizenship is more fundamental than corporate social responsibility or corporate social performance. Zadek conceives the idea of the good corporate citizen as closely linked to new forms of "civil regulation."[34] When companies regulate themselves according to corporate governance, they contribute to making themselves more sustainable, which is in their own interests. Moreover, NGOs and critical consumers in society require that corporations act as responsible citizens. People expect corporations to be more responsible and assume certain duties to society. To include society in decision-making is also important for a long-term business strategy. However, it is difficult to define a specific business case of corporate citizenship, because it depends on the context and the specific industry in question. At the same time, in the new economy, corporate citizenship is closely linked to learning and innovation. Moreover, it is possible to develop more sensitive and stakeholder-oriented management systems. "Doing well by doing good"[35] can be done in many different ways.

The demands of corporate citizenship are based on requirements to engage due to public pressure, competency requirements, and demands for legitimacy.[36] Nonprofit organizations such as NGOs play an important role in this regards. The idea of new civil governance is important for business ethics because it indicates the participation of corporations in the governance of society.[37] It is in this context that we can speak of a boom in social partnerships where businesses work with society to create specific alliances. Through partnerships, companies help to build society and to regulate themselves in the social context; therefore, partnerships are essential for corporate self-regulation.

In this context, regulation like the Global Compact emphasizes the voluntary engagement of corporations. This is important, even though critical voices disagree, because it contributes to the self-regulatory behavior of corporations in international business life. We may say that responsible self-regulation can be conceived as an important aspect of good corporate citizenship, which is an important consequence of liberalization and globalization. When corporations have more freedom in the global market, they are also required to be more responsible. Partnerships and self-regulation are essential elements in the contribution of corporations to new forms of civil governance. In this way corporations are integrated in society and they collaborate more actively with NGOs and civil society organizations. Civil governance compels companies to create systems of collaboration and enforcement of regulation, which also implies systems of "penalties and rewards for noncompliance."[38] The concept of civil governance implies, in this context, negotiations and bargaining and mediations between all sorts of organizations in civil society without direct government intervention. In this way, civil governance builds the social relations of society, which are the basis for just institutions.

Civil governance may be defined in relation to values and improvement of learning processes in organizations. The good corporate citizen works with learning processes of communication and engagement in society, adjusting the values and visions of the corporation to the expectations of society. In this way, the corporation takes its role and function as an open system in constant interaction with civil society seriously. Communication and engagement with stakeholders is essential to this process. Values-driven management with visions, missions and goals may be considered as essential in the process of forming good corporate citizenship.[39] Different social and ethical audit measures for alternative reporting and accounting of civil performances also help to develop this role of corporate citizenship. Accountability emerges out of such dialogue with stakeholders and the social environments of corporate activities.

There are different stages of the development of corporate citizenship that are closely related to the development of corporate values and responsibility.[40] These stages can be characterized as different levels of credibility, capacity, coherence, and commitment.[41] The stages of corporate citizenship can go from the elementary level over the engaged level, to the innovative and integrated level and finally to transforming the corporation to be totally open about its financial, social and environmental performance. Such a topology of corporate citizenship may help to clarify the different levels of engagement of different corporations. The final transformative stage is a level where companies really contribute to the transformation of corporations in direction of society in the sense that they engage in civil governance of society.

Thus, from the institutional perspective, corporate citizenship or the idea of the good corporate citizen corporation can be seen as a metaphor for conceiving the corporation as a citizen.[42] To consider a corporation as a citizen is to consider the corporation from an ethical point of view. According to the civic virtues and deliberative politics in republican business ethics, to be a good corporate citizen implies that the corporation takes part of society as a cooperative, responsible, and socially engaged participant. This implies that the corporation adopts the obligations of the social contract of being a member of community.[43] This is what is implied in Rawls's discussion of the "congruence between right and the good"[44] or Ricœur's notion of "the good life with and for the other in just institutions." In particular, the metaphor also suggests that the moral obligations of citizenship also include corporations. The notion of social and political legitimacy, as well as responsibility for the sustainability and future of life on Earth, are elements in this kind of corporate citizenship. In this sense, the concept of corporate citizenship is dependent on a concept of participatory ethics.[45] Corporate citizenship requires institutional responsibility and the engagement of the corporation according to the civic virtues of integrity, accountability, and trust.

Box 12. The ideal of the good corporate citizen corporation: What requirement for ethics statements?

Patrick E. Murphy has collected ethics statements from a variety of American companies, which show how corporations make efforts to appear as good corporate citizens. Since the passing of the United States Foreign Corrupt Practices Act and the FSGO, and also after the enactment of Sarbanes-Oxley, American companies have been formulating ethics statements and codes of conducts.

Murphy emphasizes that written ethics statements serve to build an ethical culture in the firm and documents that ethics has an importance for the firm. Ethics statements in American companies can be classified into three dominating types: "value statements, corporate credo/creed and code of ethics."[46] In 1995, ninety-one percent of large organizations in the United States had a code of ethics, fifty percent had a value statement, and thirty percent had a corporate credo.[47] Value statements are more recent than ethics statements and corporate credos.

This indicates the emergence of values-driven management in American companies. Value statements often combine the description of the mission of the firm with a definition of its ethical values. Value statements describe the most important principles of the firm. They are used in companies to define the culture of the organization and to ensure that employees can cope and live with the common values of the firm.

According to Murphy, a corporate credo is defined more broadly in the sense that it involves describing the ideal responsibility to stakeholders. Corporate credos are ideal and sometimes too imprecise, so that they cannot function as guidance regarding specific ethical issues.[48]

In contrast to statements of values and corporate credos, codes of ethics can be said to include more precise descriptions of ethical policies with regard to different issues, for example bribery, privacy, and so forth. Codes of ethics are close to compliance programs defined as rules for employee behavior and for relations to different kinds of stakeholders.

In corporate practice, however, we find a mixture between value statements, corporate credos, and codes of ethics. Looking at codes of ethics, the step from rules to values also involves formulating these codes so that they include elements of corporate credos and value statements. In this sense, codes of ethics can be used as practical instruments for management.

Murphy describes seven important steps of how to develop an effective ethics statement: 1) write it, 2) tailor it, 3) communicate it, 4) promote it, 5) revise it, 6) live it, 7) enforce it/reinforce it.[49] It is important that the statement is a written draft and that it is compared with other firms and that it is communicated and promoted to employees and stakeholders. Moreover, the corporation should be willing to revise its statement; indeed, the statement should be lived and reinforced as an integrated part of corporate practice.

In addition, we can mention that a good code of conduct should be unique for the firm. It should be based on an open process and it should be consistent and easily understood. It should contribute to the development of the firm and it should be enforced as a part of the culture of the firm.

5.2. An institutional argument for corporate moral agency

This development in the concept of corporate citizenship implies that we need to discuss the foundations of moral responsibility and ethics on the organizational rather than the individual level.[50] To talk about the corporation as a good citizen implies that it is possible to ascribe virtues and responsibilities of citizenship to organizations. Demonstrating that ethics and moral responsibility not only concern individuals but can also be evaluated at the organizational level depends on a number of comprehensive institutional structures like codes and ethical rules of conduct that indicate the degree of a firm's awareness as a corporate citizen and as a moral and legal person with particular accountability, liability, and responsibility. The ethical concepts of integrity, honesty, and responsibility are applied directly at the organizational levels.[51]

In contrast with critical conceptions of the firm as nothing other than a legal construct, the evolving personality of the corporation is from that of a legal construct to a morally responsible agent.[52] Moral agency means that corporations are capable of acting and can be held morally responsible for their actions as institutional forms. Following institutional theory, organizations can be defined as intentional forms based on contracts and interactions among individuals. Organizational agency emerges as the unification of the totality of regulative, normative, and cognitive pillars of organizational behavior of the corporation in a common governance structure, and as an agent that acts with purpose.[53]

Organizations can be held institutionally responsible and evaluated morally at the organizational level. As mentioned previously, this responsibility is dependent on a number of comprehensive institutional structures that indicate the level of institutional awareness of moral agency and accountability as foundations of other ethical, legal, economic, and social responsibility. For notions of organizational culpability and corporate citizenship to really be applicable to corporations, they must be based on the idea that corporate moral agency is the foundation for ethical and social corporate responsibility.

The issue of corporate moral agency can be considered as a general motivation for initiatives of values-driven management in modern corporations. The shift from shareholder to stakeholder values means that the firm is aware of the need to take into account the interests of a wide number of stakeholders, rather than exclusively seeking to maximize profits for the shareholders or owners of the company. Values-driven management should be viewed as a part of this change of values in the corporation. Instead of being based on an amoral concept of a value-neutral market system obeying economic laws, values-driven organizations represent normative values, based on visions and conceptions of corporate social responsibility at the limits of ordinary view of economic markets. It is, therefore, necessary to debate whether the corporation really can be conceived as a moral agent.

The defense of a collectivist concept of corporate moral agency really began with the classical article by Peter French, "The Corporation as a Moral Person." Contrary to the argument that the corporation is nothing more than a sum of individuals and that only individuals can be held morally responsible, Peter French argues that it is possible to consider the corporation as an independent agent with moral responsibility.[54] As showed by institutional theory collective units can have intentions and a common organizational identity, which is more than the sum of individual identities.[55] French states that corporations can be full-fledged moral persons.[56] In doing so he distinguishes between metaphysical, moral and legal concepts of persons. French wants to overcome an anthropocentric understanding of persons and argue for a metaphysical personhood of organizations and see them as members of a moral community.

The argument rests on the presupposition that it is possible to ascribe intentions and purposeful actions to the corporation. French uses Donald Davidson's concept of intentionality as the foundation for his argument for considering the corporation as a moral person. French's argument is a contribution to the debate on collective responsibility, which emerged in 1970s. The problem is whether the corporation could be considered as a moral community with a collective responsibility, being more that the sum of the responsibilities of the individuals implied in particular actions. In considering intentionality not exclusively as an interplay between desire and belief, but rather in redefining intentionality as "planned intentionality", combined with the notion of agency not being restricted to human persons, French was working with the notion of the firm as a moral agent that is attributed liability and responsibility for its actions. The basis of this argument for the firm as an agent of collective responsibility is that corporations as organizational unities of individuals can be morally dangerous agents that are able to do much more harm than individual agents can do. Therefore, it is only natural that corporations are viewed as moral persons that can be held responsible for their actions.

Peter French has developed this theory of collective responsibility, discussing how to conceive the responsibility of individuals as members of collective units, and further how to conceive the responsibility of corporations. French argues that organizations can be held accountable for their actions. Like human beings, organizations make decisions and do things voluntarily, and this has consequences for their character, identity, and culture. This argument implies a criticism of methodological individualism as proposed by Friedrich Hayek and Karl Popper, who argued that collective units are nothing more than an aggregate of individuals and cannot therefore be held responsible.[57] Only individuals can be held responsible for the actions of corporations.

French's counterargument is that groups and collectivities can have intentions and a common identity, which is more than the sum of individuals. For example, the Gulf Oil Corporation is more than the group of individuals who belong to the corporation. It cannot be identified with the aggregation of the persons who are associated with it.[58] Moreover, the capacity of corporations as moral persons and act intentionally poses the difficult question about how to treat corporations as members of a moral and legal community with specific privileges, rights, and duties.

Even though French recognizes an organizational level of intentionality that differs from the aggregate of individuals, he refuses the organic state theory of collectivities, which was proposed by Plato and in F.H. Bradley's conception of ethics.[59] The idea of the corporation as a moral person does not automatically integrate individuals in collectivities; however, Rousseau's distinction between the "will of all" and "the general will" may be mentioned as an example of the distinction between the aggregate of individuals and the idea of the corporation as having a specific kind of intentionality.[60] The medical profession may, for example, be held responsible as a group for the general state of healthcare, even though this does not directly imply the actions and intentions of particular physicians.[61]

This discussion of the status of the corporation as a moral person is based on the philosophical and judicial evaluation of the legal and moral personhood of corporations. Only individuals have traditionally been attributed personhood. Because the notion of personhood was isolated from its biological basis, organizational personhood has been considered to be a legal fiction.[62] According to French, legal personhood cannot, however, be consistent without presupposing more fundamental notions of intentionality and corporate accountability.[63] The predominant legal aggregate theory fails to recognize that there is a difference between a corporation and an aggregate of persons who function as nothing but a crowd of people. In contrast, the concept of corporations as real sociological persons, the so-called "reality theory" of the corporation – as opposed to the "legal fiction" – treats corporations as factual persons without really being aware of their moral status.[64] If corporations satisfy the conditions of being intentional agents, then they must not only be understood as sociological entities but also as responsible moral persons.[65] In order to be able to refer to corporate responsibility, it must be possible to describe corporations as metaphysical persons. The collectivist argument is that a corporation cannot be conceived as a legal person, without also being considered as an independent moral and metaphysical person.[66]

What does it really mean to consider the corporation as a moral person? For most people it would seem rather counterintuitive to describe corporations as persons. They might argue that intentionality is a human notion that can only be meaningfully ascribed to individual human action. French, following John Locke, separates the concept of 'person' from 'human persons.' Donald Davidson argues that there may be intentionality without reference to human consciousness and French is inspired by this point of view.[67] French argues that it makes perfect sense to speak about collective intentionality as something independent and different from individual intentionality.[68] If organizational action is characterized by an intentional unity that cannot be reduced to the sum of individual actions, then it follows that institutional responsibility cannot be shifted to individual actors. It is, therefore, possible and necessary to distinguish between corporate and individual responsibility, when judging the actions of individuals and corporations. This dynamic is also at play in attributing a specific moral identity to a corporation over time, for example, when a corporation attempts to change its identity from that of a firm producing harm to one with bona fide status of a good corporate citizen.

A central dimension of French's notion of corporate responsibility based on corporate personhood and planned intentionality is the concept of the corporate "internal decision-making structure" (CID-structure). French argues that this structure may be understood as the unity of values codes, formulated policy statements, and strategies, and indeed concepts and implied understandings of corporate traditions and cultures. Corporations make many decisions that are based on routines and habits, but this does not mean that they do not originate in the CID-structure. The CID-structure is the totality of meanings and intentions, which illustrates the corporate ethos and culture. It can be seen as an indication of the collective identity of a company. The CID-structure indicates the level of corporate liability and integrity, and is constituted by the identity and history of the organization. The corporation as a collectivity constitutes a community with a certain practice. Individuals are partly responsible for this practice, as they are taking part in the organization, but it is also an independent activity, which determines the purpose and aims of the organization. Indeed, meaningful compliance and ethics programs – as proposed in the different codes of conducts of American corporations – can be viewed as an attempt to objectify CID- structures. They are, therefore, good indications of corporate personality and a firm's level of moral and social responsibility.

At the same time, individuals can be considered responsible for collective actions because of their participation, even though they may not have have been directly and intentionally involved.[69] Regardless of the level of responsibility – whether collective or individual – holding corporations responsible means holding specific entities accountable.[70] This was manifest in the discussion of the Ford Pinto (see case 3), where the company continued to put a car on the market for economic reasons, even though they knew it posed certain unacceptable safety risks.

An alternative example, mentioned by French, is the case of DC-10 airplanes produced by the McDonnell Douglas Corporation, where the company took a calculated risk by producing a product that was prone to accidents.[71] In this case, we may hold the corporation responsible for continuing to produce these airplanes even though it was clear that they constituted a larger risk than other planes. In a theory of individual accountability, it would be difficult to find a particular individual who was directly responsible for this risk-bargaining, while from the perspective of the concept of the corporation as a moral person, McDonnell Douglas would clearly be held responsible for immoral actions.[72]

In addition, French discusses the case of the 1991 Air New Zealand flight that crashed on Mount Erebus. Even though it was a bright day, the pilot of a sightseeing flight trip crashed directly into a mountain. Surprisingly to many, the commission that evaluated the accident argued that it was not only the fault of the pilot but also the airline, because the company should have had organizational rules and adjustment procedures that could have prevented the actions of the pilot. In other words, the CID-structure of the company was insufficiently able to prevent such incidents.

On the basis of this concept of collective responsibility, we may ask how a corporation should be punished. Referring to CID-structures, corporate identities, and cultures may be a way to talk about collective legal liability and responsibility without reducing these factors to the actions of certain individuals. We can attribute fault and culpability to collectives that may be responsible without direct reference to individuals' intentions.[73] However, the problem is how to sentence the corporation when only some of its members are held culpable for criminal actions. Given the concept of the moral personhood of corporations, it would be wrong to state that only individuals can be responsible for the actions of corporations, but punishment of a corporation is not a substitute for individual punishment, because individuals may be viewed as having complicity in the offenses. Instead of a direct retributivism, French proposes a "shame-guilt" model where the corporation in punished by having its reputation tarnished. Indeed, the moral reputation of a company is important, so hurting the image and reputation of a company may be a very strong punishment. An alternative way to punish a corporation would be to submit it to community service, sanction it to pay fines, and – in all possible ways – make it responsible for restitution towards those it has harmed.[74]

Case 25. Novozymes: Sustainability and corporate citizenship

An illustration of an effort to create a reliable CID-structure is the case of the Danish biotechnology firm Novozymes. This company has been selected as a member of CSR Europe and an example of a firm making an *ethical effort*. This case has become nearly classical in the Danish context, and the firm can be considered as a company that contributes to constituting corporate citizenship through developing its policies based on CSR and values-driven management.

This company has set up a Sustainable Development Strategy Group consisting of top-level managers and a Sustainability Development Center that is closely connected to executive management.[75] Novozymes considers sustainable development as central to its strategy: "We imagine a future where our biological solutions create the necessary balance between better business, cleaner environment, and better lives. To get there we will drive a significant expansion of the market for industrial biotechnology with enzymes and micro-organisms as our basis. We will find new and improved solutions to serve the market for biopharmaceuticals. We will achieve double-digit growth with a leadership position in all markets served. Customers and partners throughout the world will seek our collaboration because of what we do and how we do it. People from all over the world will want to work for us because of what we do and how we do it. Society will be inspired by our work to choose biological solutions as a key part of the future."[76]

Novozymes' vision is directed towards defining corporate action and culture as the basis for its institutional responsibility in society. We can say that the values, visions, and stakeholder dialogue are developed to define the firm as a good corporate citizen. In order to conceive its vision of corporate citizenship in a spirit of compliance with international norms and societal expectations, Novozymes has defined its basic commitments in close relation with the declarations and regulations of the United Nations. Novozymes supports the international agreements and conventions that have been mentioned throughout this book, as well as the United Nations Convention on Biological Diversity and the International Chamber of Commerce's Business Charter for Sustainable Development. These norms and guidelines function as the basis for the policy and daily work on sustainability in Novozymes.

Moreover, the company applies the concept of sustainability as expressed in the triple bottom line. The company stresses its financial, environmental, and social commitments and responsibilities in order to ensure economic performance and value-creation, improve environmental performance, and promote respect for biodiversity, dialogue with stakeholders, and respect for fundamental human rights, labor rights, and health and safety issues in the workplace.

In the accordance with its general principles of business, Novozymes has integrated a concern for social responsibility. The approach to corporate social responsibility includes not only risk management and reputation management, but a broader concern for corporate social responsibility as license for the corporation to operate. This is the basis for considering corporate social responsibility as good branding and the foundation of increased corporate competitiveness. As a part of fulfilling its corporate social responsibility, Novozymes has worked to ensure that suppliers respect labor standards and human rights.[77] This effort includes asking suppliers to answer questions about key indicators that reflect compliance with the ethical standards of Novozymes. This evaluation is based on international human rights norms and Novozymes requests that suppliers respect these minimum norms and principles. On the basis of responses from suppliers, the corporation goes into dialogue on problematic issues in order to find convenient measures for compliance.

Novozymes' environment and bioethics policy is founded on the effort to integrate environmental and bioethical considerations in daily business. This means that new technologies and new products, and the use of raw materials, are evaluated according to environmental and bioethical considerations. The corporation works to continually assess its environmental performance in order to follow best practices. The bioethics policy is developed in dialogue with major stakeholders, suppliers, subcontractors, and authorities in order to promote responsible treatment of the issues. In this sense, the corporation expresses its desire to contribute with honest documentation of problems and estimations of its environmental and bioethical performance.

5.4. Individualist criticism of the idea of corporate moral responsibility

It is important to stress that this concept of corporate moral responsibility does not have to rely on essentialist ontology, with the corporate soul as a somewhat strange "ghost in the machine." When we defend the idea of corporate moral responsibility as an institutional concept, it implies the conception of the firm as a social institution. This requires – as previously argued – that we rely on the insights of new sociological institutionalism and its concept of institutionalization as defended by the phenomenological constructivism.[78] This idea of the corporation as an intentional agent combines this institutionalism with concepts from moral philosophy. Viewing the organization as a moral agent means endowing it with moral awareness.[79]

To ascribe personhood to the corporation means that it has the capacity to take a moral point of view and make rational and respectful decisions with honesty, integrity, trustworthiness, reliability, and accountability.[80] From the constructivist and institutionalist sociological and philosophical point of view it makes perfect sense to evaluate the responsibility of corporations in terms of ethical behavior. Some corporations have been establishing systematic features of ethics and compliance programs and internal monitoring systems that help them built their reputations as reliable institutions, and also to distinquish them from less trustworthy corporations.[81]

It is important to say that corporate social responsibility expresses the capacity of the corporation to act as a moral agent regardless of the economic constraints of the market, though this may be a controversial point of tension between sociological, philosophical, and economic institutionalism. It may be argued that economic institutionalism, while recognizing the importance of institutional and organizational economic behavior, does not go so far as to adopt the concept of moral corporate personhood. Economic organization theory cannot overcome the economic concept of self-interested utility maximizing subjects that is assumed in its the analysis of organizations.[82] According to this criticism, economic organization theory conceives the organization in terms of rational choice, principal-agent models, and incentive models that leave no room for defining a particular moral viewpoint of the organization. Organizations are viewed as contract relations between individuals who tend to maximize their own benefit. The argument is that only efficiency and profit maximization are relevant organizational considerations.[83] Consequently, even if economic organization theory recognizes the importance of institutions and institutional agency, it does not have to share the point of view that corporate social responsibility is relevant or possible.

Even though this argument may seem very plausible, I would like to point to some difficulties for such criticism of corporate agency, which count in favor of the conception of the corporation as a moral person. As we have seen, it seems to be embedded in modern economic life that corporations have a specific moral responsibility that transcends the responsibility of its members.

In modern economic life, organizations are supposed to act as independent unities with specific rights and duties. Even strict individualist economic institutionalism operates with the entity of the firm as major point of reference.[84] In addition, it may be argued that in cases where the CEO, or a specific manager, is held responsible it is not done on the basis of her particular personality, but rather because of her position as a representative of the corporation.[85] In this case, the CEO has a function or role as a representative of the corporation as an institution taking part in economic markets and as a social system with specific functions in society.

In order to make this position acceptable for mainstream economics and institutional organization theory, we might propose a strategy of convergence between institutional economics and business ethics as proposed by Boatright (who, as mentioned previously, builds on Coase and Williamson's economics of the governance of contractual relations). The idea is that research in business ethics has been too critical towards the conception of the firm as a "nexus of contracts," based on bounded rationality and a system of more or less formal and informal contracts. Boatright asks: "Should researchers in business ethics adopt the framework provided by the contractual theory of the firm? Certainly, philosophical ethics provides its own perspective and suggests deficiencies in the contractual theory for understanding and addressing business ethics problems; however, the neglect of the contractual theory of the firm deprives business ethics research of a potentially useful framework that could integrate its results with the work in financial economics and corporate law. In addition, the failure of business ethics researchers to work within the contractual theory, or to develop a rival theory with the same intellectual rigor and explanatory power, diminishes the relevance of their work to these other disciplines. Much is to be gained, therefore, by taking seriously the framework provided by the contractual theory. Developing this framework is a necessary step."[86] From this perspective, business ethics and institutional theory should not propose a pluralistic concept of the values and goals of the firm, but rather try to integrate institutional economics and business ethics. Corporate moral responsibility should not be considered as an alternative to contract theory, but instead should integrate business ethics into the already existing legal framework of corporate governance and of the economic market.[87]

In the framework of this theory of the firm as a nexus of contracts, we cannot ignore the economic concerns for efficiency and profit maximization as central goals of the firm and important concerns of organizational governance. However, all goals and values of a firm are ambiguous. The concern for values and stakeholders may be in the interests of owners and shareholders in order to ensure long-term returns. Even though we consider the firm as an instrument for obtaining economic returns, from the perspective of the firm as a system of contracts and negotiations this does not have to exclude ethical concerns and the interests of a broad number of stakeholders. From the perspective of institutional theory, owners and shareholders of the firm have an interest in, and broad concern for, all stakeholders insofar as this helps to increase the firm's competitiveness and sustainability.[88]

This convergence between ethics and economics does not, however, exclude a potential conflict, since transaction cost theory focuses primarily on efficiency and economic return.[89] As a result, institutional economics may sometimes be blind and limited regarding the effort to conceptualize the firm as a moral agent with social and environmental responsibilities. It may not, after all, be so easy to combine institutional economics and the concept of the moral firm.[90] What is needed is a broader concept of the organization, integrating different external and internal value conceptions and views of the goals of the firm. Here we approach the limits of transaction cost economics insofar as this theory does not transcend the neoclassical conception of "economic man" as a self-interested utility and profit maximizer.[91] We must, therefore, move to business ethics and institutional sociology when we want to propose an institutional concept of corporate social responsibility that goes beyond purely economic responsibility.

A defense of the corporation as a moral person could be submitted to criticism from an individualist and nominalist perspective. Manuel Velasquez, among others, challenges this concept of corporate responsibility. He attacks both the idea of the corporation as a moral person and the attribution of responsibility and intentionality to corporations. Velasquez argues that it has not been shown how corporations have intentionality. He argues that intentionality is a psychological notion that presupposes the existence of states of consciousness. From his perspective, French and other collectivists have not delivered anything but a metaphorical attribution of intentions to corporations.[92] Collectivists cannot say that corporations have consciousness in the same sense as human beings. Moreover, in order to talk about intentionality of corporations, we may operate with a functionalist theory of mind, but this does coincide with French's argument for considering the corporation as a moral person. In opposition to the collectivist theory of the corporation as a moral person, Velasquez defends a methodological individualism combined with a constructivist concept of the personhood of the corporation. This means that although we may, in some cases, speak metaphorically of the responsibility and moral personhood of corporations, these concepts cannot be said to have a substantial or ontological content.

In further opposition to French's position, Velasquez argues that, upon deeper reflection, it is not possible to contribute responsibility to corporate groups. According to this position, it is only individuals and not groups who can be responsible.[93] Velasquez differentiates responsibility from liability and causality. He states that compensatory liability is defined for reasons of social efficiency, distributive justice, and relationship to the agent. Indeed, only in cases where it is possible to find a direct relation to agents, is it possible to talk about moral responsibility. According to Velasquez, this kind of responsibility characterized classical criminal law, where an individual was held responsible for an intentional criminal act. In this concept of moral responsibility, it is only human beings who can be blamed and punished for their intentional actions. An individual is morally responsible for her bodily actions. Responsibility originates directly in the intentions of an agent, which are executed through bodily movement. Consequently, Velasquez argues that only individuals can be submitted to blame and punishment.[94] Punishment is only possible from the perspective of classical notions of imputability and responsibility.

On this basis, Velasquez examines French's notion of corporate responsibility (i.e.,that corporations can be held morally responsible for their acts, which they seem to do intentionally).[95] Although he recognizes that organizations may be viewed as fictional legal entities that are conventionally contributed responsibility for their actions, Velasquez refuses to see corporations as the real originators of their acts through their CID-structure.[96] He argues that French has not sufficiently shown how intentions attributed to corporations differ from those of individuals. Following his argument, if corporations have responsibility they must be seen as agents with certain bodily and mental unities that they do not possess.[97] From this perspective, intentionality would be defined as a mental notion that cannot be contributed to corporate entities; however, in developing the concept of the CID-structure, French is close to defining the intentionality of the corporation as a kind of group mind. Still, Velasquez refuses to recognize a specific intentionality in corporate policies and procedures, because they are not the same as the human mind. Corporate policies and procedures are not linked to human bodies and they do not, in themselves, perform intentional actions. The corporation cannot, therefore, be an entity who can be held morally responsible for its actions.[98]

The problem becomes whether Velasquez can contribute responsibility to corporations. He argues that specific persons, not groups, are responsible for specific acts to the degree these acts were intended by these particular persons. When no one intended the act, then no one can be held morally responsible for it. As a group of individuals living in a structured set of relationships, a relationship between human beings or legal entities, the corporation cannot be held directly morally responsible. However, specific members may be held responsible for some of the actions of the corporation to the extent that their intentionality can be determined. The corporation may be held legally responsible as a unity that can have compensatory responsibility towards certain individuals, but this is not the same as moral responsibility. [99]

Velasquez debunks the view that the corporation is a ghostly moral agent: an invisible person that can act on its own, although it is different from an ordinary human person. Velasquez thinks that the capacity of law to construct a number of legal notions in order to make the corporation legally responsible has confused the discussion. Judicial attributions of rights, duties, liabilities, duties, intentions, beliefs, causality, citizenship, and personhood are among the things that have made us forget that corporations are not specific persons, but only artificial collections of human beings acting together.[100] Although Velasquez may be favorable to these legal entities he emphasizes that they are legal constructions, which have nothing to do with how things are in themselves. Consequently, the important debate between collectivist and nominalist conceptions of corporate moral and social responsibility seems to concentrate on the conditions of attributing intentionality to groups, collectivities, or organizations. Because corporations have properties that cannot be attributed to their individual members, they are ontological entities that are distinct from their members, with particular properties like intentionality or responsibility.[101] Velasquez sees this premise as a mistake. The collectivist seems to attribute properties to objects that are not real.

At the same time, it is possible to conceive of a group or an organization as a plurality of individual intentions without seeing them as unity that transcends the level of the individual. There is no specific intentionality of the corporation that is qualitatively different from the aggregate of individual intentions. Velasquez thinks that collectivist accounts of the responsibility of corporations are wrong when they presuppose that responsibility for acts and events may imply a corporate intention. He argues that corporations are not directly causally responsible, but actions are dependent of individual members of the corporation. Velasquez says that when we attribute intentions to groups, we do it in a metaphorical or analogous sense, signifying that corporate intentionality may be determined by an "as if intentionality," a kind of prescriptive intentionality, where intentions ascribed to groups (e.g., their policies and procedures; that is, their CID-structures), are dependent on actions and intentions of individual actors.[102] It is not intrinsic intentionality. It may look like the corporation acts on its own, even though it is dependent on the actions of individuals. To argue that corporations should pay the costs of damages does not imply their moral responsibility, only that they assume legal responsibility for the members of the organization.

Even though this argument may seem plausible, I would like to point to some difficulties for the nominalist debunking of corporate moral responsibility, which may work in favor of conceiving of the corporation as a moral person. As mentioned several times, it seems to be embedded in modern economic life that corporations have a specific moral responsibility, which goes beyond the responsibility of its members.[103] In modern economic life, organizations are supposed to act as independent unities with specific rights and duties. Moreover, these developments imply that vicarious responsibility or *respondeat superior* doctrines are not sufficient in order to capture the specific responsibilities of this new position of the corporation. Significant changes have occurred within the actual development of commercial, welfare, and criminal law. Classical legal doctrines have been opened up in such a way that there is room for group and institutional responsibility. This responsibility does not rely on individual intentionality, but implies compensatory organizational responsibility, even in cases where it is not possible to point to any specific individual fault.[104]

In addition, it may be argued that the CEO or specific managers may be held responsible, not because of their particular personalities, but because of their positions as representatives of the corporation. In these cases, they function as a representative of an institution taking part in economic markets, and as a social system with specific functions in society.

We may also defend the collectivist position against the nominalist criticism by pointing to the fact that the vision of corporate personhood advocated by French does not have to be synonymous with human personhood. The argument for corporations as metaphysical persons does not even have to presuppose an ontological, intrinsic corporate character, which has its own reality independent of human affairs. Indeed, as we have seen, French does not accept the essentialist theories of organic states proposed by Plato, Hegel or Bradley.[105] Instead of being based in a mysterious essentialist world, the idea of corporate responsibility may simply be founded on human collective intentionality.

In connection with this, the CID-structure of corporations may not be based on essentialist ontology; rather it could be viewed as an institution or an institutional fact in John Searle's sense.[106] Even though he is partly inspired by Searle, Velasquez is so eager to debunk the essentialist view of corporate personhood that he does not recognize the implicit ontology of corporate intentionality according to Searle's constructivist position. In fact, Searle distinguished between collective and individual intentionality, agreeing that the latter cannot be reduced to the former, although it is not to be considered as an independent ontological fact at the same level as natural objects. Moreover, when French uses the concept of the general will to describe the CID-structure of corporate decision-making and of collective intentionality as different from a mere aggregate of individual intentional ties, he is not far from Searle's concept of the construction of institutional facts.

Box 13. Imaginary institutionalization of meaning through business ethics

We cannot deny that there seems to be a dream of creating a better world that undergirds the process of institutionalizing values and business ethics. In fact, we can use the work of the Greek and French philosopher and social theorist Cornelius Castoriadis to give a conceptual explanation of this imaginary instutionalization of business ethics. Castoriadis argues that humanity searches to come to autonomic self-expression through imagination as a primary force of history. The social imaginary is a dream of human autonomic emancipation and self-expression. Social institutionalization is a product of this social imaginary.[107]

In contrast to bureaucratic organization of reified institutions, with its strict separation of groups and classes, and with strong hierarchical structures based on instrumental and utility-oriented rationality, the imaginary search for autonomy and emancipation is characterized by strife (similarly to new social groups and their reaction against established social structures). According to Castoriadis, we have to conceive human revolutionary projects as efforts to be emancipated from bureaucratic structures in an imaginary creation of autonomous democratic institutions. The social imaginary is not a picture of anything. It is not predetermined, but expresses a capacity to create from the perspective of hope and desire for a better social reality and new social institutions.[108]

Castoriadis defines this concept of institutionalization as the foundation of a theory of democracy: History is understood as creation (*poiesis*), determined by the human imaginary capacity of creation. Society is created through an imaginary symbolism based on conceptions of meaning and values that are the basis for social existence. We can talk about a social capacity of imagination, which represents a capacity to imagine and thereby contribute to the creation of new social structures and contexts.

Human imaginary capacity can be characterized as a primordial kind of being that contributes to the creation of common imaginary contexts of significance as the basis for community and collective meaning. This horizon of meaning can be based on a greater or lesser degree of autonomy, and is dependant on the form of organization (e.g., democratic or totalitarian).[109]

For Castoriadis, this theory of imaginary institutionalization is the basis for a theory of democracy, because democratic policy is based on an ongoing search for autonomy and critical questioning of existing social institutions. Direct democracy is created in an open process of creation, but also in the capacity of self-limitation and wise and prudent decision-making. The ethos of democracy is an understanding of the limits of human existence and action. It is only by understanding our limitations that we can understand the conditions of human autonomy and democracy.

With this in mind, we can apply Castoriadis's concept of institutionalization to the process of searching for corporate legitimacy. We may say that we experience a process of searching for autonomy and self-limitation within the creations of new meanings of business institutions through programs and policies of values-driven management. This may be the reason why ethics and values are so important for creating new understandings and meanings of business organizations in society. Therefore, business ethics and corporate social responsibility contribute to the institutionalization of democracy in modern society.

5.5. Towards an institutional concept of the good corporate citizen

The following is a defence of viewing corporate agency as a form of moral and social responsibility. This is compatible with a sociological and philosophical institutionalism, based on a constructivist view of institutions and social reality.[110] Patricia Werhane contributes to the development of this collective model of the corporation.[111] She analyzes the collective model of the corporations as a "secondary moral agent" that can be held responsible and accountable for its actions.[112] Although corporations consist of individual persons who, as living human beings, are surely more important than organizations, corporations can still be considered as liable agents who are members of the moral community. The reason is that the corporation is an intentional system that can be considered in terms of intentional predictions.[113] However, as an intentional system, an organization is not merely a functional entity like a machine or a robot. It makes no sense to conceive of organizations as automatic rule-governed machines working for economic ends without any human capacity for responsible decision-making. Although it is often forgotten in the bureaucratization of organizational action, the organization cannot help being a system that displays intentional behavior without directly being an intentional agent, like a human being. An organization's actions are carried out by human persons, and, as such, it can be considered as an organization of individuals.[114] Werhane argues, on the contrary, that the organization is more than merely an association of individuals, because it is a fact of our moral vocabulary that we praise and blame companies for their intentional actions.[115] In this sense, we consider the corporation as a responsible agent with institutionalized moral goals.

The foundation of this idea can be said to be the conception of corporate personhood as a constructed institutional fact, determined by processes and actions. This effort to formulate an anti-essentialist view of corporate moral and social responsibility is partly based on John Searle, who has discussed how institutional reality and constructed social facts are possible.[116] Searle argues that there is a basic difference between natural reality and social reality, which is the result of human symbolic interaction. Social reality, social objects, and institutions are viewed as constituted by a collective intentionality, which cannot be reduced to individual reality.[117] Still, "all institutional facts are ontologically subjective, even though they are epistemically objective."[118] Searle argues that we do not need large essentialist ontology, a mysterious collective consciousness, or a mythical spirit in order to explain social reality.[119] Neither is it necessary to reduce collective intentionality to individual intentionality.

Considering the world of physical objects as independent of social reality, Searle maintains that we can see collective intentionality as a biological fact. Searle's account of social facts and institutions as creations of a specific kind of constructive collective intentionality functions as an important basis for considering the corporation as an independent social actor with specific duties and obligations. From this perspective, corporations and other institutions are the results of collective agreements, or acceptance of them as specific institutional facts that involve rights and responsibilities.[120] We may mention money, marriage, governments, or universities as institutional facts that are resultant of collective intentionality. Even though we have forgotten its original conditions of creation, the institution of money continues to exist as a common social reality.

Searle emphasizes that language is an important constitutive part of institutional reality.[121] There is an ongoing public symbolization of institutional facts, which do not exist outside of language. These facts require the symbolization of language for their existence.[122] This might help us to understand the emergence of the CID-structure of a company as an indication of corporate personhood. In fact, the moral personality of the corporation is not something pre-existing, but as an institutional fact it is constituted as a system of collectively recognized duties and obligations. Searle mentions human rights as an example of the social creation of institutional facts, based on institutional powers and symbolic functions. We might also say that the concept of corporate intentionality and responsibility is the result of such a collective institutional creation, which, once accepted as an institutional fact, becomes an integrated part of what Searle calls the background abilities of rule recognition of actors in social reality.[123]

Patricia Werhane can help us to clarify this concept of the CID-structure. She argues that the moral person theory of corporate intentionality, in opposition to conceptualizing organizations as machines or as simple associations of individuals, emphasizes the importance of the function of corporations as moral agents. Though they cannot ontologically be determined as real moral persons, because only individual human beings can act freely on their own, they can act on behalf of corporations as employees or managers.[124] Therefore, we can describe the moral agency displayed in the CID-structure and the intentional action ascribed to corporations as secondary, or institutional, moral agency. Werhane argues that corporations are not "ontologically real," but exist as kinds of social fictions: collective patterns of behavior that involve intentionality at a secondary level in combination with individual action. Collective secondary action cannot be reduced to individual action because it follows complex patterns of organizational behavior and structures of intentionality at the collective level.[125] Because they are made up of persons with moral responsibility and agency, corporations can act as moral agents at the level of collective action in a way that cannot be reduced to a mere aggregate of individual actions.[126] As secondary moral actors, corporations function as morally responsible although they are not autonomous moral agents in any deep ontological sense.

Peter Pruzan helps to clarify the issue of the relation between the concept of the CID-structure and ideas of organizational identity or organizational personality.[127] He answers the question about organizational consciousness by referring to the values, virtues, and visions of organizations. The argument is that it is possible to define a close relation between strategies, goals, and responsibilities as the basis for defining organizational consciousness. In addition to the theoretical proposals by French, Searle, and Werhane, Pruzan relates not only to deductive reasoning, but also empirical observations, taking into account that ordinary language is characterized by the metaphorical attributions of consciousness and shared values to organizations. When dealing with the concept of organizational consciousness based on corporate moral agency we have to leave the traditional understanding of the relation between individual action and organizational action which says that individuals subordinate their will and action to others higher in the organizational hierarchy. Pruzan emphasises that the relation between company values and individual values is much closer, in the sense that individuals and companies get their work identity from the values of the company. When we talk about values in the organization at the level of the CID-structures, values are not only accepted, but they are shared and communicated among members of the organization as a result of communicative and participatory dialogue.[128]

Accordingly, organizational consciousness is developed out of the construction of shared values of the organization, where individuals together create a CID-structure that makes something common for the organization. Organizational consciousness also means that members of the organization act together and create something together that is related to reflective and purposeful and value-oriented action. This is a definition of the collective community of the organization, which in that sense is not something mysterious beyond the common meaning and values in the corporation, but a mutual horizon and framework of decision-making and action within the organization. Moral agency and moral responsibility within the framework of stakeholder management is a way to explain the function of corporate intentionality in practice. The values, visions, and strategies of the organization together constitute the framework for action and decision-making, which is based on the organizational intentionality as expressed in the culture of the organization.[129]

At another level, legal regulation and argumentation, and judicial doctrine may be considered as important tools for this construction of the social reality of corporate moral agency. The concept of legal subjectivity and ideas of corporate moral agency mutually support the development of the corporation as a moral person. Even though it may seem paradoxical to attribute mental states to organizations, legal theorists like William Laufer and Alan Strudler have argued for the concept of "the criminal state of mind" of the corporation.[130] From the perspective of legal theory, the legal system would function with more fairness and justice if corporations were considered as moral agents with intentionality that can be attributed criminal responsibility. This concept of legal and moral responsibility of the corporation is more comprehensive than the concept of vicarious responsibility because it is based on the idea that it is possible to determine corporate guilt.[131]

Corporations, as legal and moral persons, have specific legal rights and duties.[132] Instead of focusing legal judgment of the company on evaluating the actions of specific persons, it is the totality of the policy, strategy, missions, codes of ethics, and principles of values-driven management – as well as company culture and more or less formal rules and actions – that are judged as expressions of the intentionality of the corporation. It is on this basis, as in corporate law, that the legal determination of culpability, responsibility, and character of punishment (including the size of eventual fines) operates. This legal construction of corporate culpability and responsibility also operates with the criminal identity and history of the corporation as an indication of the level of culpability.[133] Codes of ethics, compliance programs, and other more or less formal and informal structures, are viewed as indications of a firm's structures of intentionality and of the corporation's performance as a responsible social institution.

Even though this concept of legal and moral corporate responsibility should not exclude individual responsibility, it implies that collective corporate intentionality does not necessarily coincide with the intentions of specific employees.[134] Accordingly, corporate intentionality does not reflect the totality of the intentions of individual agents. This third position is the concept of the corporation as a moral and legal person viewed as an independent institutional entity that may be characterized by intentional structures including the following elements: "1) agents whose actions and intentions are related to each other in such a way that they assume the characteristics of a corporate firm; 2) agents whose status in the organization is such that their actions and intentions are those of the organization; and 3) aspects of the organization such as policies, goals, and practices that reflect not merely the sum total of individual agent's intentions, but instead attributes and conditions of the corporation that make it possible for these agents to cooperate and collaborate in legally problematic ways."[135]

This conception of collective agency in the corporation may be viewed as a comprehensive formulation of its CID-structure, including codes of ethics and compliance programs. In the evaluation of corporate legal responsibility these factors are combined with evaluations of purposes of actions, the knowledge of the firm about the illegal action, as well as the seriousness of the offence. It is, indeed, presupposed that individual actions and decisions are framed by the normative structure of the organization. At the same time, the concept of corporate institutional responsibility implies that it is possible to sentence and hold an organization responsible for specific actions without finding a basis for this in the faults and actions of specific individual agents.[136]

On this foundation it may be argued that the legal notion of integrity and the good corporate citizen mediate between the nominalist and collectivist concept of corporate personhood and intentionality. Of course the problem remains of "how to expect a corporation to have a conscience when it has no soul to be dammed, and no body to be kicked."[137] The construction of corporate intentionality and personhood as the basis of corporate integrity cannot totally replace vicarious liability and the doctrine of *respondeat superior*. However, as we shall see, recent legal and ethical developments in both Europe and the United States towards corporate social responsibility and ethics programs have moved towards the concept of corporate integrity as the basis for the idea of the good corporate citizen.[138]

In law, this virtue of corporate integrity can be argued to refer to the standards and duties of professional care that are required by reasonable persons or organizations in specific cases. In this sense it can be said to express a particular legal responsibility of a corporation, as in the FSGO.[139] Here the required standards of professionalism and care can be said to reflect the idea of self-imposed corporate values through compliance and ethics programs.[140] The idea of professional responsibility signifies legal requirements for integrity and virtuous action as the basis of attributing criminal liability. In order to be a responsible and virtuous corporation, it is not sufficient to have beliefs and desires; the corporation must have established compliance and ethics standards to show its good intentions.[141] Based on FSGO (which will be considered in detail in the next chapter), the idea of organizational responsibility goes beyond legal compliance and requires "organizational integrity." This indicates the willingness of the corporation to live up to its moral principles and virtues. Integrity and responsibility are considered important for corporate culpability. In this sense, we have developed a foundation for republican business ethics and good corporate citizenship in the idea of collective moral responsibility.

Endnotes

1 Although the argument that the expectations of society to corporations should be taken seriously by management seems very powerful, it does not directly justify the idea of corporate moral agency. An institutional interpretation of this search for new values to back-up economic markets and business practice is needed, showing how the definition of the corporation as an institutional agent could be integrated into mainstream economics.

2 How should we define corporate agency? It not only refers to the virtue or deontic conceptions of responsibility, but also responsibility understood as a causal link between the corporation and its actions. Moral responsibility is the kind of responsibility that we attribute to intentional agents. An organization can be defined as a distinct group of people who act together. It is this kind of entity to which the law attributes concepts of responsibility, based on ideas of *respondeat superior* and vicarious liability, and which also functions as the basis for corporate citizenship. We can, in fact, emphasize that although there is a difference between moral and legal corporate responsibility, the debate about corporate moral agency influences the legal concept of corporate agency. See Manuel Velasquez, "Debunking corporate moral responsibility", *Business Ethics Quarterly*, Volume 13, Issue 4: 531-562.

3 Peter Drucker, *The concept of the corporation* (New York: John Day and The Mentor Executive Library, (1946) 1964), 23-24 and114.

4 J.A. Butten and D. Birch, "Defining Corporate Citizenship: Evidence from Australia" in Asia Pacific Business Review, Vol. 11: 3, 293-308.

5 Dirk Matten and Andrew Crane, "Note: Corporate Citizenship: Toward an extended theoretical conceptualization" in *Academy of Management Review*, Vol 30, No 1 (2005): 166-179 and 167.

6 Ibid: 170.

7 Ibid: 170.

8 Jeanne M. Logsdon and Donna J. Wood, "Business Citizenship : From domestic to global level of analysis", *Business Ethics Quarterly*, Volume 12, Issue 2: 155-187 and 161.

9 Jeremy Moon, Andrew Crane, and Dirk Matten, "Can Corporations be Citizens? Corporate Citizenship as a Metaphor for Business Participation in Society", *Business Ethics Quarterly*, Volume 15, Issue 3: 433.

10 The concept of citizenship is in itself a metaphor, but it is different from the metaphor of an organization as a political construction because it also focuses on ethical stakeholder relations. May be the metaphor of the web captures the idea of the corporation as a social institution in contact with society. See: Gareth Morgan, *Images of organization* (London: Sage publications, 1997).

11 Ibid: 435.

12 James E: Post, "Global Corporate Citizenship: Principles to live and work by", *Business Ethics Quarterly*, Volume 12, Issue 2, pp. 143-153. See also G.F. Thompson, "Global Corporate Citizenship: What does it mean?", *Competition and Change*, Vol 9., No 2 (2005): 131-152.

13 J.P. Katz, D.L. Swanson and L.K. Nelson, "Culture-based expectations of corporate citizenship. A proposal framework and comparison of four cultures", *The international Journal of Organizational Analysis*, Vol. 9. (2001), No 2., 149-171., p. 149. See also: David Birch and George Littlewood, "Corporate Citizenship. Some Perspectives from Australia", *Journal of Corporate Citizenship*, 16 (2004). In this article they emphasize elements of sustainability, corporate capacity, response to societal expectations and people-oriented economics as essential elements of corporate citizenship.

14 Jeanne M. Logsdon and Donna J. Wood, "Global Business Citizenship and Voluntary Codes of Ethical Conduct", *Journal of Business Ethics* (2005) 59: 55-67.

15 Ibid: 56.

16 James E: Post, "Global Corporate Citizenship: Principles to live and work by", *Business Ethics Quarterly*, Volume 12, Issue 2: 143-153.

17 Sandra Waddock, "Corporate Citizens: Stepping into the breach of society's broken contracts", *Journal of Corporate Citizenship* (2005).

18 Jeremy Moon, Andrew Crane, and Dirk Matten, "Can Corporations be Citizens? Corporate Citizenship as a Metaphor for Business Participation in Society", *Business Ethics Quarterly*, Volume 15, Issue 3: 429-453.

19 Ibid: 431.

20 Dirk Matten, Andrew Crane and Wendy Chapple, "Behind the Mask: Revealing the True Face of Corporate Citizenship", *Journal of Business Ethics* 45 (2003): 109-12.

21 Ibid: 116-117.

22 Dirk Matten and Andrew Crane, "Note: Corporate Citizenship: Toward an extended theoretical conceptualization" in *Academy of Management Review* (2005), Vol 30, No 1. pp 166-179, p. 172.

23 Ibid: 173.

24 Ibid: 174.

25 Ibid: 177.

26 See his 2006 Academy of Management prize-winning book, *The Civil Corporation. The New Economy of Corporate Citizenship* (London: Earthscan 2001), which summarizes and develops his position as it has been formulated since his early work on the concept.

27 Simon Zadek, *The Civil Corporation. The New Economy of Corporate Citizenship* (London: Earthscan 2001)

28 Ibid: 2. Zadek argues that corporate citizenship can be interpreted as in accordance with Friedman's philosophy in the sense that it is in the interest of business to make profits by maximizing financial performance even if it involves engaging more effectively with stakeholders (Ibid:8). According to Zadek the corporate citizenship position is rather a "sophisticated restatement", than a refutation of Friedman's position" (Ibid: 53), because it states that Friedman already was aware that we are in need of businesses that live up to the expectations of society and this is indeed what is expected with the idea of corporate citizenship. Ethics is an economic gain for the corporation from this point of view because it creates trust and long-term sustainability.

29 Ibid: 10.

30 Ibid: 13.

31 Ibid: 27.

32 Ibid: 40.

33 Ibid: 43.

34 Ibid: 51.

35 Ibid: 76.

36 Ibid: 81.

37 Ibid: 90.

38 Ibid: 101.

39 Ibid: 162.

40 Philip Mirvis and Brandley Googins, "Stages of Corporate Citizenship", *California Management Review*, Vol 48 (2006), no 2., Winter.

41 Ibid: 106.

42 Ronald Jeurissen, "Institutional Conditions of Corporate Citizenship" in *Journal of Business Ethics 53*: (2004), 87-96, 87.

43 Ibid: 88. Jeurissen argues: "To be a citizen means to accept the social contract as limitation in everything done. Living under the social contract is a form of rational self-binding. Citizens do this with the reasonable expectation they will benefit in long run. Rawls calls this "congruence of the right and the good" (Rawls, *A Theory of Justice*, 1972): 527. Cited by Jeurissen: 88.

44 As cited by Jeurissen.

45 Ronald Jeurissen, "Institutional Conditions of Corporate Citizenship", *Journal of Business Ethics 53*: 87-96 (2004): 95.

46 Patrick E. Murphy, *Eighthy Exemplary Ethics Statements* (Notre Dame: University of Notre Dame Press, Notre, 1998: 2).

47 Ibid: 3.

48 Ibid: 4

49 Ibid: 5.

50 Lynn Sharp Paine, "Managing for Organizational Integrity", *Harvard Business Review*, 1994.

51 Lynn Sharp Paine, *Cases in Leadership, Ethics and Organizational Integrity. A Strategic Perspective* (Chicago: Irwin, 1997).

52 Lynn Sharp Paine, *Valueshift. Why Companies Must Merge Social and Financial Imperative to Achieve Superior Performance* (New York: McGraw-Hill, 2002).

53 Richard W. Scott, *Institutions and Organizations* (London: Sages Publications Inc, 1995).

54 This concept of the firm can with be said to imply the institutional view of corporations as a blend of regulative, normative and cognitive structures. Institutionalization of common action applies these features as frames for the emergence of a common reality. This level of common action is constituted by the idea of collective intentionality, which is the basis for considering the corporation as a moral person. Therefore we can define corporate social responsibility as group responsibility. See Peter Cane, *Responsibility in Law and Morals* (Oxford and Portland Oregon: Hart Publishing, 2002).

55 Richard W. Scott, *Institutions and Organizations* (London: Sages Publications Inc.,1995), 44-45.

56 Peter French, "The Corporation as a Moral Person" in *Collective Responsibility. Five Decades of Debate in Theoretical and Applied Ethics*, edited by Larry May and Stacey Hoffman (New York: Rowman and Littlefield Publishers, Inc.,199), 133.

57 Karl F. Popper, *The Poverty of Historicism* (London: Routledge and Paul Kegan, 1957). F.A Hayek, *The Road to Serfdom* (1944) (London: Routledge Paperbacks, 1997).

58 Peter French, *Collective and Corporate Responsibility* (New York: Columbia University Press, 1984), 30.

59 F.H. Bradley is believed to have proposed such an essentialist concept in his *Ethical studies*, Oxford 1876 (Oxford: Clarendon Press, 1998).

60 Peter French, *Collective and Corporate Responsibility* (New York: Columbia University Press, 1984), 111. See also Jean-Jacques Rousseau, *Du Contrat social ou Principes du droit politique* (Paris: Union Générale d'Éditions (1762) 1963).

61 Peter French, *Collective and Corporate Responsibility* (New York: Columbia University Press, 1984), 128.

62 Ibid: 35.

63 Ibid: 38.

64 Peter French, "The Corporation as a Moral Person", *American Philosophical Quarterly*, Volume 16 (1979) Number 3, 209.

65 Peter French, *Collective and Corporate Responsibility* (New York: Columbia University Press, 1984), 93.

66 Ibid: 93.

67 See John Locke, *An Essay concerning Human Understanding* (5th Ed.) (Oxford: Clarendon Press (1689), 1975). Donald Davidson, *Essays on Actions and Events*, Second Edition (Oxford: Oxford University Press, 2001).

68 Peter French, "The Corporation as a Moral Person", *American Philosophical Quarterly*, Volume 16 (1979), Number 3, 211.

69 Howard McGary, "Morality and Collective Liability" in *Collective Responsibility. Five Decades of Debate in Theoretical and Applied Ethics*, edited by Larry May and Stacey Hoffman (New York: Rowman and Littlefield Publishers, Inc., 1991), 86.

70 Raymond S. Pfeiffer, *Why Blame the Organization. A Pragmatic Analysis of Collective Moral Responsibility*, (New York: Littlefield Adams Books, 1995).

71 Peter French, *Collective and Corporate Responsibility* (New York: Columbia University Press, 1984), 143.

72 Ibid: 144.

73 Joel Feinberg, "Collective Responsibility (Another Defence)" in *Collective Responsibility. Five Decades of Debate in Theoretical and Applied Ethics*, edited by Larry May and Stacey Hoffman (New York: Rowman and Littlefield Publishers, Inc., 1991), 73.

74 Peter French, *Collective and Corporate Responsibility* (New York: Columbia University Press, 1984), 202.

75 Material for this case is selected from *The Novozymes Report 2004. Novozymes. Unlocking the Magic of nature*. See also the analysis of corporate social responsibility in Novozymes in Helene Tølbøll Djursø and Peter Neergaard, *Social ansvarlighed: Fra idealisme til forretningsprincip* (Copenhagen: Gyldendal Academica, 2006). Theoretical justification of the effort to develop corporate social responsibility is found in Esben Rahbek Pedersen, *Between Hopes and Realities: Reflections on the Promises and Practices of Corporate Social Responsibility (CSR)* (Copenhagen: CBS PhD Series 17, 2006).

76 www.novozymes.com. The analysis of the discoursive elements of this self-representation of Novozymes is based on Anders Bordum and Jacob Holm Hansen, *Strategisk ledelseskommunikation. Erhvervslivets ledelse med visioner, missioner og værdier* (Copenhagn: Jurist og Økonomforbundets forlag, 2005).

77 Helene Tølbøll Djursø and Peter Neergaard, *Social ansvarlighed: Fra idealisme til forretningsprincip* (Copenhagen: Gyldendal, 2006).

78   Peter Berger and Thomas Luckmann, *The Social Construction of Reality. A Treatise in the Sociology of Knowl-egde* (New York: Doubleday, 1966). Richard W. Scott, *Institutions and Organizations* (London: Sages Publications Inc, 1995), 29-30.

79   Kenneth E. Goodpaster and John B. Matthews, Jr., "Can a Corporation have a Conscience", Reprinted in *Harvard Business Review on Corporate Responsibility* (Cambridge Massachusetts: Harvard Business School Press, 2003), 136. When we talk about the corporation as a moral person we go beyond a merely pragmatic legal fiction theory of the firm because the idea of intentionality as purposeful action of the firm is the condition for this kind of corporate personality. See Peter Cane, *Responsibility in Law and Morals* (Oxford and Oregon: Hart Publishing, 2002), 146. The firm is not only a legal subject but in the idea of the firm as a moral person there is a close link between law and morality in the definition of legal subjectivity. Responsibility of groups is based on their ability to act as a unity with a purpose.

80   Kenneth E. Goodpaster and John B. Matthews, Jr.: "Can a Corporation have a Conscience", Reprinted in *Harvard Business Review on Corporate Responsibility* (Cambridge Massachusetts: Harvard Business School Press), 138.

81   Ibid: 140.

82   Francis Fukuyama, *State Building. Governance and World Order in the Twenty-First Century* (London: Profile Books, 2004).

83   Kenneth E. Goodpaster and John B. Matthews, "Can a Corporation have a Conscience", Reprinted in *Harvard Business Review on Corporate Responsibility* (Cambridge Massachusetts: Harvard Business School Press, 2003), 143.

84   Oliver E. Williamson, *Market and Hierarchies: Analysis and Anti-trust Implications* (New York: Free Press, New, 1975). Oliver E. Williamson, "The Economics of Governance: Framework and Implications", *Journal of Institutional and Theoretical Economics* Vol 140 (1984), 195-223. Oliver E. Williamson, *The Economic Institutions of Capitalism* (New York: Free Press, 1985).

85   Kenneth E. Goodpaster and John B. Matthews, Jr., "Can a Corporation have a Conscience", Reprinted in *Harvard Business Review on Corporate Responsibility* (Cambridge Massachusetts: Harvard Business School Press, 2003).

86   John R. Boatright, "Business Ethics and the Theory of the Firm", *American Business Law Journal*, Volume 34/ (1996), 238.

87   Ibid: 218.

88   Ibid.

89   Ibid: 236.

90   Atle Midtun, "Business Ethics and the Logic of Competition: Is There a Scope for the Moral Firm (EBEN: 1999).

91   Ibid: 3.

92   Manuel Velasquez, "Debunking corporate moral responsibility", *Business Ethics Quarterly*, Volume 13, Issue 4, 539.

93   Manuel Velasquez, "Why Corporations are not Responsible for Anything they do" in *Collective Responsibility. Five Decades of Debate in Theoretical and Applied Ethics*, edited by Larry May and Stacey Hoffman (New York: Rowman and Littlefield Publishers, 1991), 112.

94   Ibid: 115.

95   Ibid: 117.

96   Ibid: 118.

97   Ibid: 120.

98   Ibid: 122.

99   Ibid: 128.

100 Manuel Velasquez, "Debunking corporate moral responsibility", *Business Ethics Quarterly*, Volume 13, Issue 4, pp. 531-562, 550.

101 Ibid: 540.

102 Ibid: 546

103 Wim Dubbink, "The fragile structure of free market society. The radical implications of corporate social responsibility", *Business Ethics Quarterly* (2004), Volume 14, Issue 1: 23-46.

104 See for example, François Ewald: *L'Etat Providence* (Paris: Gallimard, 1984). Where it is argued that developments in welfare state law has broken the traditional conceptions of legal responsibility of private firms.

105 We may even insist that some of the traditional criticism of collective action are based on wrong interpretations of Hegelian philosophy. The Hegelian concept of political community as realized through the "Sittlichkeit", the ethical life in community may not imply a kind of supernatural reality that is not a function of human free action. In fact, we can argue that the idea of a collectivity implies a collective action that imply individual freedom and in this sense never goes totally beyond the realm of free individual action, but rather unites different individuals in some kind of collective intentionality.

106 John Searle, *The Construction of Social Reality* (New York: The Free Press, 1995).

107 Cornelius Castoriadis, *L'institution imaginaire de la société* (Paris: Éditions du Seuil (1975) 1999).

108 Ibid.

109 Ibid.

110 In this sense corporate social responsibility is considered as a kind of group responsibility based on the fact that people work together in corporations with common purpose. Together they can do much more harm and good than solitary individuals. This fact of group action is the basis for ascribing responsibility practices to groups in law and morals Peter Cane, *Responsibility in Law and Morals* (Oxford and Portland, Oregon: Hart Publishing. 2002), 146. Concrete practices of purposeful action are the basis for corporate responsibility because we can observe particular actions that corporations are responsible for as groups.

111 Patricia Werhane, *Persons, Rights and Corporations* (New York: Englewood Cliffs), 1985.

112 Ibid: 30.

113 Ibid: 37

114 Ibid: 40.

115 Ibid: 42.

116 John Searle: *The Construction of Social Reality* (New York: The Free Press, 1995), 2.

117 Ibid: 24.

118 Ibid: 63.

119 Ibid: 25

120 Ibid: 36.

121 Ibid: 59.

122 Ibid: 74.

123 Ibid: 126

124 Patricia Werhane, *Persons, Rights and Corporations* (New York: Englewood Cliffs), 1985.

125 Ibid: 57.

126 Ibid: 59.

127 Peter Pruzan, "The Question of Organizational Consciousness: Can Organizations Have Values, Virtues and Visions?", *Journal of Business Ethics*, Vol.29 (2001), 271-284.

128 Ibid.

129 In this context there is a close relation between the ethical formulations of values, visions and virtues on the basis of the idea of corporate moral agency on the one hand the debate about organizational identity on the other hand. In fact we can say that the issue of corporate moral agency shape the issue of corporate identity in the sense the possibility to constitute common values and consciousness on the basis of corporate morality may be considered as the foundation of organizational identity. In fact there are many similarities between our discussions of corporate moral agency and the debate about the problem of organizational identity. See Mary Jo Hatch and Majken Schultz, *Organizational Identity. A Reader* (Oxford University Press: Oxford Management Studies, 2004).

130 William S. Laufer and Alan Strudler, "Corporate Intentionality, Desert, and Variants of Vicarious Liability in *American Criminal Law Review*, Volume 37, (2000), Number 4, 1285.

131 Searles's concept of collective intentionality is based on the view that ideas of the interests, goals, plans and purposes of action together with the policy rules of the firm constitute the actions of the corporation as representative of a group of individuals. This mediation between individualism and collectivism takes collective we-intentionality like the one which is revealed in team spirit and team action as an idea of common sense. It is possible to explain group action out of individual intentionality because individuals would have to presuppose the intentions and beliefs of others as a part of their individual intentions and beliefs. Collective intentionality would have to be explained by individual intentionality, but this would, again, presuppose collective intentionality. Rather we can say that collective intentionality is a part of individual intentionality but not reducible to in-

dividual intentionality. In this sense we cannot ignore the existence of a collective intentionality that is the basis for the firm as a moral agent. This means that individuals as members of organizations are both individually and collectively responsible for the way they take part in and endorse collective action of the group. Individuals can as members of an organization be held resposible for corporate action even though they are not directly responsible for these actions. In this sense the basis for corporate agency is the capacity of common collective action of individuals in groups.

132 William S. Laufer and Alan Strudler, "Corporate Intentionality, Desert, and Variants of Vicarious Liability" in *American Criminal Law Review*, Volume 37, (2000), Number 4, 1295.

133 Ibid: 1305.

134 Ibid: 1308.

135 Ibid: 1309.

136 Ibid: 1311.

137 William S. Laufer cites this old saying used by Peter French, but already said by First Baron Thurlow, Chancellor of England in the early 1600s. See William S. Laufer, "Integrity, Diligence, and the Limits of Good Corporate Citizenship", *American Business Law Journal*, Volume 34/2 (1996), 157.

138 Ibid: 159.

139 It may be argued that the concept of "due diligence" as proposed in tort law or as a requirement of thoroughgoing investigation is not enough for proving that the corporation is established as a moral subject in law. However, such a use of the concept of due diligence can be said to represent a kind of manifestation of a responsibility going beyond mere responsibility to obey the law. The corporation is not only responsible to follow the law, but it should do this without negligence and with due standard of care. Normally, standards of care or due diligence refer to reasonable persons who "proceed with reasonable caution as a prudent man would have exercised under such circumstances" (see for example standard legal definitions of the term in English and American legal dictionaries). It also means that products should be produced with reasonable prudence. We can therefore establish a link between the legal concept of due diligence and the philosophical concept of prudence, judgment or virtue. When the US Federal Sentencing Guidelines in §8B2.1. Effective Compliance and Ethics Program refer to the concept of due diligence in the sense that "Due diligence and the promotion of an organizational culture that encourages ethical conduct and a commitment to compliance with the law", we see how this concept is close to the ethical concept of organizational consciousness. Therefore, we can perceive the emergence in the law of a concept of moral responsibility as an accomplishment to the idea of pure juridical responsibility. Accordingly, we can say that due diligence understood as requirements of reasonable prudence and integrity represents a kind of expression of corporate citizenship in legal terms.

140 William S. Laufer, "Integrity, Diligence, and the Limits of Good Corporate Citizenship", *American Business Law Journal*, Volume 34/2 (1996).

141 Ibid: 160.

Part 4
Legal and political developments: Challenges to global business ethics

1. Values-driven management and ethics programs in the United States

The process of developing organizational integrity through values-driven management in the United States should be considered from the perspective of the country's ethical and legal traditions. In the United States, the description of the free market society, as proposed by Milton Friedman, illustrates the general spirit of business.[1] At the beginning of the eighteenth century, the United States was arguably not at the same level as Britain and continental Europe. After a while, however, the United States became a dominating economic power and also in need of business ethics. This movement and the CSR movement started in the beginning of the twentieth century as a reaction to the laissez-faire situation of the preceeding century. American business ethics were inspired by Calvinism and Protestantism, but also the consumer movement and workers' rights movement. We can say that the general conception of business ethics in the United States has been influenced by the Judeo-Christian tradition of respect for the golden rule (love thy neighbour as thyself) as well as the tradition of Roman law.[2] However, the United States has also encountered great criticism of capitalism. The history of American business is a story of conflict between facilitating capitalism, for example through the doctrine of caveat emptor, and regulation in favor of the common good of society.

Within the framework of a capitalist economy the overall obligations of business in the United States can be said to include, among other things, the maintenance of good quality products, trust, monopoly control, and the recognition of employee rights and consumer needs while still favoring the free market society. Business ethics emerged in this context while never doubting the rules of property and the rights of exchange on the free market.[3] The United States has been characterized by a strong work ethic and belief in the capitalist system, but the development of business ethics was also determined by working class movements and demonstrations. At the same time, the American ethical tradition was rooted in the general Western conception of ethics.

The business ethics of the United States was, therefore, linked to the virtues of the Protestant ethics of honesty, integrity, and trust. An important part of twentieth-century management thought was characterized by the work of Chester Barnard, who focused on moral and ethical management. Barnard was an important initiator of the American tradition of business ethics as central to management, which was developed by later traditions of management thought. This was also related to the development of company policies against employee dishonesty and steeling.[4]

Another striking feature of American management is the concept of corporate philanthropy. As mentioned at the beginning of the chapter, early conceptions of business ethics and CSR were proposed in terms of corporate philanthropy, where corporations were supposed to donate – arguably motivated by the golden rule – an amount of surplus earnings to charity. It is striking that since 1935 American companies have been allowed to use five percent of their income for donations for philanthropy.[5] This was important for developing the American movement of corporate philanthropy, which later became a movement of corporate social responsibility.[6] With the business and society movement in the 1960s and 1970s, which focused on issues like protecting citizen's rights and the environment, American expectations of corporations continued to grow. The enactment of the Foreign Corrupt Practices Act, enacted in the 1970s, indicated this increasing focus on CSR and business ethics. In fact, most corporations do not accept Milton Friedman's criticism of corporate philanthropy and corporate social responsibility.[7] American corporations have been very focused on CSR as a prolongation of the interest in corporate philanthropy, but the United States is also characterized by an approach to business ethics that links business ethics to legal regulation and intervention. Government regulations are needed to eliminate fraud that destroys the free market.[8] Indeed, the protection of the free market was considered as an important task of good government. A close relation is, therefore, perceptible between ethics and law in the efforts of the United States to regulate business. Moreover, there is a tendency to conceive business ethics as the central theme of interest, which effectively subordinates CSR to it.

With regard to government regulation, for many years there was concern to find the best way to sentence organizations and promote the corporation as a good and socially responsible actor in society. A number of practices and rules were developed to be applied in order to sentence organizations prosecuted of a criminal offense. In 1991, the FSGO were decisive for further development of compliance and ethics programs in the United States.[9] The FSGO were innovative because they stated that an organization having established a compliance or ethics program in court could get up to ninety-five percent mitigation of eventual fines. Moreover, corporations without ethics programs could get up to four times stronger punishment.[10]

The FSGO have in recent years been the dominating focus of the American approach to values-driven management and organizational integrity. Even though the FSGO come from criminal law, they have an influence far beyond compliance and have become the major focus of business ethics in the United States. Companies see advantages in creating compliance programs, because they are better off in court, and because there is a chance to generally improve the ethical behavior of employees. Indeed, compliance and ethics programs function as an insurance and legal security, in case the corporation is prosecuted for an illegal action. The FSGO have prompted many companies to use ethics more actively as a major management tool. Moreover, the FSGO imply a reinforcement of the legal subjectivity of corporations. Legal regulation treats the corporation as a collective unit and a form of individual actor or independent entity with its own moral and legal responsibility.

An important culmination of the legal efforts to regulate business ethics and CSR has been the Sarbanes-Oxley Act from 2002, which regulates the corporate governance and transparency of accounting. Sarbanes-Oxley may be considered to be an important supplement to the FSGO because it enforces the requirements of corporations to self-regulatie their corporate activities and helps to make accounting practice more reliable for public authorities.

This chapter discusses the American promotion of organizational integrity through values-driven management with special emphasis on the FSGO. It covers: 1) the background for FSGO, 2) The FSGO requirements for a good and meaningful ethics and compliance program, 3) The FSGO in American business life, 4) The FSGO and the paradox of ethics and compliance programs, and 5) the journey from the FSGO to Sarbanes-Oxley.

Box 14. Need for regulation: The importance of the FSGO and Sarbanes–Oxley

The collapse of companies like Enron, Arthur Andersen, and WorldCom was characterized by a lack of ethical culture among high-level employees and, by extension, the need for ethics and corporate governance in the modern economic system.[11] The firms' executives can be said to have followed the maxims of personal short-term profits over concern for long-term shareholder value and respect for the common ethical norms of society. Good corporate governance involves transparency, accountability, and responsibility. Moreover, it involves openness and fairness with regard to communication with stakeholders.

In these cases, the corporate directors presented a technical and ethical failure to govern their corporations properly. They did not work from the point of view of the concept of the good corporate citizen and they did not try to include the stakeholders in the process of governance. Corporate governance is about ensuring business ethics and that corporate management adopts basic principles of values-driven management. Corporate governance involves respecting duties to shareholders, but also the effort to take into account the legitimate expectations of stakeholders and the community.

The Enron and WorldCom cases are, indeed, based on egoism and the personal search of profit, a behavior that has become a basic half-truth of certain trivial understandings of business life. Greed and self-protection were dominating factors of the case. But we can also mention the case of Arthur Andersen, the accounting firm, which did not think of the public interest, but was concerned with getting more profits. In addition, an important explanatory factor could be the previously discussed idea of the banality of evil, which is arguably the background mentality of American business life, and is one of the reasons for the lack of ethical consciousness of top management of these kinds of firms.[12] Management was lacking any sense of ethical judgment and it was unable to perceive the ethical and legal problems in the practice of hiding controversial accounts. The lack of ethical judgment signifies the inability of management to perceive the ethical and legal problems of a particular situation. Management did not have the capacity of ethical reflection with regard to the ethical problems of the issues of the corporation.

The Enron and WorldCom cases are paradigmatic illustrations of the tensions between ethics and business. The key words of competition, selfishness, and profit contradict the ideals of beneficence and ethical perfection. These cases show how human beings exposed to certain unethical circumstances are likely to have weak ethical judgment. On the other hand, it is necessary to respect the rules of the game (e.g., not to commit fraud, to be honest, etc.) if the economic market is going to function well. Ethics, judgment, and prudence are therefore required for business professions; in these cases, the accounting and corporate management professions. However, we can also perceive the failure of systems and institutions in the WorldCom and Enron cases. The systems for handling such fraud were too weak. The legislation of Sarbanes-Oxley filled the need for better institutional structures. In this sense, the cases of Enron and WorldCom are negative manifestations of the need for ethics in business. These cases show that corporate success implies the need to include ethics in the culture of the organizations. Enron manifested the effort to reach success through unethical behavior and their story is a good example of the consequences: the market loses confidence in the corporation, which can ultimately result in bankruptcy.

The cases of Enron and WorldCom show the importance of good corporate governance. Moreover, corporate governance is not only an issue of legal rules, but also about the need for high integrity management that has an ethical focus on their organizations. The requirements of business ethics as proposed by the FSGO and Sarbanes-Oxley imply, therefore, that limits to self-interest, prudent relations to shareholders, and the ethical principles of fairness, integrity, honesty, and responsibility are very important for the conduct of business corporations. In this context, it is important that business corporations can develop prospects for long-term sustainability and stable relations to communities and stakeholders.

1.1. Background for FSGO

Even though debates about social responsibility and business ethics have been going on for the past twenty to thirty years, they only got a firm legal basis by establishing the FSGO in 1991. In addition to their function as guidelines for sentencing of individuals, the FSGO also contain mandatory guidelines for judges about how to sentence organizations. The FSGO include very detailed descriptions about how to give fines to organizations for specific violations of law and criteria for possible reduction and mitigation of punishment, if organizations have established compliance and ethics programs. Indeed, large organizations with more than fifty employees risk huge fines if they do not comply with the guidelines. The FSGO also encourage collaboration between companies and governments in order to detect violations of the law. Compliance is not only conceived as enforcement, but it should also be understood as an expression of the willingness of the firm to go into a dialogue with the authorities. Cooperation means an effort to improve crime prevention and effectively prevent violations of the law.[13]

In addition to the business and society movement mentioned previously, the historical background of the FSGO can also be found in the development of important American anticorruption legislation. Before the FSGO, society was very critical of the lack of values in business life. Unfair and corrupt business practices were very visible. Compliance programs within organizations were increasingly needed to avoid corporate misconduct. Misconduct and the need for compliance were national problems. Moreover, it was argued, the legal system was not sufficiently efficient at detecting misconduct. New methods of sentencing were needed.

The discussion about corporate codes of conduct has a long history. Legislators in favor of the free market, but skeptical of this development, encourage the self-regulation of business organizations in order to overcome these problems. Others have argued that corporate codes of conduct may minimize corporate criminal liability. The existence of an ethics and compliance program was considered as a possible limitation of the traditional concept of *vicarious liability* and *respondeat superior*, which says that the firm has superior responsibility (it is obliged to give compensation for tort and other violations) for the misconduct of its employees and other actors of the firm, which had governed American corporate liability law.[14] In this context, a corporate compliance and ethics program can help to avoid violations and possibly decrease liability. The need for guidelines was further rooted in arguments for corporate self-regulation, which were initiated with the Foreign Corrupt Practices Act of 1977. This code was made in order to avoid bribery and to recommend that companies develop codes of conduct for international business.

In the 1980s, a number of financial insider trading scandals put pressure on the securities business, and it was discussed how to improve corporate self-government. Among defense industry government contractors, there were also some scandals involving delivery of malfunctioning products for the national defense. As a result, Martin Marietta, a large defense corporation, took initiative to formulate common ethical guidelines.[15] In addition, an enduring concern of American business law has been antitrust regulation, which aims to protect free competition in the market and to avoid unjust market power due to monopolies, mergers, and hostile takeovers. American business law is determined by greater hostility to monopolies and stronger antitrust legislation than Europe and Japan.[16]

The need to establish the FSGO was also motivated by general concerns about internal unfairness, uncertainty, and ineffectiveness in the federal sentencing system. As early as 1975 Senator Edward Kennedy was arguing that it was necessary to establish a system of guidelines for the federal courts in the United States in order to ensure trust in the system, and fairness, generality, and universality in the sentencing of individuals and organizations. The American Law Institute worked on the same issue. It was aware of the importance of legal regulation to improve business practice, preserve values, and guarantee basic freedoms.

Later it was decided that such a system could be most efficiently established by a reform of the sentencing system in order to avoid indeterminate guidelines. The United States Congress set up the Sentencing Commission in 1984. The Commission was charged with investigating the sentencing situation – including examining typical and atypical sentencing procedures – and preparing guidelines. In 1985 the commission came up with its first proposal for guidelines, which were designed to be clear and practical tools for judges to harmonize just sentencing. According to the proposal, the Commission was to produce a manual for sentencing both individuals and organizations in order to improve procedures. In addition, the Commission was to revise, amend, and update the existing sentencing guidelines. It was also to try to develop more efficient systems of sentencing. After many drafts and debates, the Commission formulated a final proposal for the FSGO that was debated and approved by Congress in 1991.

Since that time, the FSGO have had enormous influence on the development of ethics programs in American companies. By formulating requirements for ethics and compliance programs, the FSGO contribute to the definition of a model for objective determination of the ethical profile of corporations.[17] Instead of focusing on individual responsibility and integrity, the FSGO represent an organizational perspective on integrity, as well as legal and moral responsibility.

At the same time, an innovative dimension of the FSGO is their emphasis on self-evaluation. The organizations themselves are responsible to set-up compliance program and other review mechanisms. This is partly due to the lack of resources and capabilities on the part of authorities to undertake this effort. By encouraging organizations to undertake voluntary ethics and compliance programs through mitigating privileges in lawsuits, the FSGO constitute a general basis for the promotion of such programs. Organizations are, therefore, more likely to organize and participate in such compliance programs.

The originality of the FSGO is to ensure just punishment in sentencing individuals and organizations. The Commission wanted to develop concepts of ethics and values that could be applied directly at the organizational level. In the beginning, the Commission worked with a "law and economics approach." This was directed at defining penalties from an economic perspective.

The Commission worked on how to determine fines and culpability scores for companies but also on how to use sentencing systems to improve corporate behavior. An important aim was to convert wrongful harm into financial penalties, in order to account for this harm from an economic perspective.[18] Large fines indicated that it would imply high costs for the firm to act illegally. During its work, the Commission moved from this pragmatic approach, based on cost-benefit calculations, towards the idea of organizational culpability.

Ideas of corporate responsibility and the good citizen corporation were combined with cost-benefit analysis. This involved discussions about how to place responsibility at the institutional level rather than regarding it solely as a matter of liability of employees or executives. In fact, the carrot-and-stick dimension of the FSGO indicates a combination of the pragmatic approach and the idea of an organization's criminal liability, because sentencing can be mitigated if the organization can show that it has done enough to be a good corporate citizen.

The carrot-and-stick metaphor indicates that the commission was interested not only in punishment, but also in having an effective program to detect and prevent legal violations. The principle of mitigation of sentencing in cases of timely self-reporting of offenses also expresses this effort. Voluntary disclosure with no temporal delay helps government institutions to be aware of the seriousness of the offense. Indeed, dialogue and collaboration with authorities is a central part of the self-reporting process. Full disclosure to authorities is considered as a good example of corporate citizenship. If an organization has shown willingness to self-report violations of the law, cooperates, and demonstrates recognition of the law, it may have reduced its culpability scores according to the FSGO.

The good corporate citizen is an organization that sets-up an effective program to prevent and detect legal violations. FSGO gave credit to and encouraged organizations that explicitly show good citizenship. These organizations receive better treatment by the courts because they demonstrate institutional commitment to legal compliance, meaning that they have shown that they are fully concerned with their responsibility for the offenses.[19]

From the perspective of criminal law, the FSGO express a stronger concern for corporations as independent agents in the measurement of punishment. It is not only the management of the corporation, employees, or other individuals, who are responsible for the illegal actions, rather, the corporation, as such, is considered as legal person who can be held responsible independent of employees or management.[20] Courts have moved from vicarious liability to the notion of "corporate ethos" and the "concept of the criminal state of mind," which is determined by evaluating the character and intentions of the corporation, as expressed through its values and strategies.[21] Strategy, purpose, and policy statements play an important role in the legal determination of liability. It is an important part of the FSGO that courts can determine the extent of the intentionality of corporate violations. Criminal law operates by looking at the subjective intentions of companies in order to determine culpability level. This constructed definition of the corporation as a moral actor implies that it is less guilty if it can show that it had good intentions and did not want to commit the offense. Companies are, therefore, considered to be persons with legal responsibility with moral culpability.[22]

In this context, compliance and ethics programs in companies work as an objective instrument to determine the intentions of companies. The strict conditions in the FSGO determining the content of meaningful ethics and compliance programs are the basis for such objective conditions for defining corporate intentions. Lack of compliance programs helps to show the bad intentions of companies, and can be treated as an objective legal fact.[23] Consequently, ethics and compliance program are important indicators of the level of culpability and responsibility of the firm. If it can be proved that ethics and integrity are important parts of the culture and mentality of the firm, the prospects for successful legal defense are much higher.

An example of a practical application of the FSGO is the sentencing of a Japanese company, Daiwa Bank, which was operating in United States. In 1995, Daiwa was sentenced to a fine of 340 million dollars by the Manhattan federal court, because one of its employees was found guilty of illegal transactions totalling more than 1.1 billion dollars. This led to losses for many of the Bank's investors, both small and large. The Bank did not reveal the incident immediately to American authorities because it wanted to wait until after the publication of its audits. Moreover, the Bank did not have any kind of ethics and compliance program that might have prevented this kind of financial crime. Because of the sentencing guidelines, the Bank was convicted and levied one of the biggest fines in American history. In addition, it was barred from doing business on United States territory. The reason for the large penalties was the complete lack of a compliance or ethics program, but also the fact that the company delayed reporting the offense for more than two months, which indicated an unwillingness to cooperate with the authorities.

As can be seen from this example, ethics and compliance programs act as both an insurance and "early warning" system and indicate good business for companies. This explains the growth in ethics and compliance programs in American companies after the introduction of the FSGO. It is an important part of the guidelines that companies are encouraged to cooperate with authorities in detecting and overcoming criminal offenses in the organizations. Because of this, openness and initiative in investigating violations are considered as mitigating factors in legal prosecutions. The FSGO have helped to make values-driven management and concerns for organizational integrity important parts of daily management practices. Good ethics and compliance programs are clearly much more than simply empty credos or mission statements. The FSGO implement very well and clearly defined conditions for a good ethics and compliance program; therefore, companies without such programs are taking high risks and are very vulnerable to criminal behavior and ethical misconduct.

1.2. The FSGO Requirements for a meaningful compliance program

A challenge in formulating the FSGO was the problem of defining the demand of a good compliance and ethics program. The Commission was aware of the need to integrate ethics and compliance programs, in order to develop effective programs to ensure corporate responsibility and avoid illegal actions.[24] It was argued that legal rules and compliance would be more efficient if they were based on ethical values and conceptions of integrity. Legal codes of conduct were to be based on ethical values, meaning that value systems and integrity principles would have a central role in effective compliance programs in order to ensure an important function of ethics in the company.[25] Moreover, it is somewhat implicit in the FSGO that a values-driven model may be more efficient than a compliance-based model. A good compliance program would be founded on ethics and integrity.[26]

This is indicated by the fact that the Commission also stressed that compliance programs did not have to be strictly judicial, but were defined in a much broader way than a traditional legal program. The Commission had a pragmatic approach in stressing that the most important requirement of a compliance program was that it would be effective in preventing offense and help to guarantee an organization's ethical integrity. The Commission wanted, therefore, to integrate ethics and law, compliance and integrity in the efforts to define good programs of values-driven management.[27]

This integrative view on ethics and law did not exclude that the evaluation of companies as good corporate citizens was highly focused on the capacity of the company to take a clear position on criminal offenses and attempts to break the law.[28] By setting up compliance programs, companies are able to distance themselves from the violators of the law and indicate that such actions were not a part of the company's policy and ethical principles. Furthermore, compliance and ethics programs have a preventative function by showing the personnel that eventual illegal behavior is not consistent with the ideas of the company. This message can be reinforced by the information and training about the company's views on compliance and integrity. In case of offense by personnel at any level of the company, well-established compliance programs indicate institutional commitment and the organization may reduce its culpability score.

It should be emphasized that a good compliance program requires recognition by substantial authority in the organization, indicating that there is general support of the program. This means that a program under no conditions can be a set of empty words or a cosmetic "paper program." Compliance programs should involve substantial managerial authority in the organization. Moreover, organizations should avoid giving authority to people who would have a tendency to engage in criminal or illegal activity.[29]

Even though differences in local formulations of compliance programs vary widely according to size, purpose, and structure of specific organizations, programs are supposed to have some mechanisms of monitoring, training, evaluation, and reporting in place as minimal criteria for formalization of compliance. Programs should, indeed, be adjusted to the particularity of specific organizations.

The American Defense Industry Initiative on Business Ethics and Conduct is an example of a compliance programs developed against the background of problems of illegal action in organizations.[30] These guidelines were drafted as an effort to improve ethics standards after the firms in this industry were criticized in the 1986 Packard Commission report.[31] All defense industry contractors with the government agreed to some common principles in order to avoid illegal action. Among others things, it was required in these guidelines that each company should have a written code of business ethics and conduct. These codes should establish high values among the employees in the organization. There should be a free and open atmosphere in each company so that violations could be reported without problems. Each company should take on its responsibility by self-government through appropriate monitoring systems in order to preserve the integrity of the company and the defense industry. Also there should be public accountability of the ethical principles in each company.[32]

These principles, which became standard for the whole defense industry, became important as inspiration for the work of the United States Sentencing Commission. They helped the Commission with its work to define a meaningful ethics and compliance program. A 1990 draft by the Commission's chairman emphasized that the FSGO should provide incentives for organizations to strengthen internal mechanisms for determining and detecting criminal conduct as the basis for adequate punishment of organizations. Moreover, the FSGO should coordinate between organizational and individual sentencing. Indeed, the carrot-and-stick approach was present in this first draft.[33] It mentioned a number of culpability mitigating factors, the most important of which were: non-involvement of top management or leading policy-setting personnel in the offense; maintenance of a efficient compliance program; self-reporting of the illegal actions; cooperation of the organization in order to remedy harm; disciplining of responsible individuals; and action taken in order to stop repetition of criminal offenses.[34]

During a number of meetings between the Commission and different interested parties, it became clear that FSGO should encourage installation of compliance programs in organizations. Moreover, acceptance of responsibility and cooperation with government authorities was considered an essential factor. A working group was started to mete out specific criteria in order to define what the commission would consider an effective and meaningful compliance program. The working group argued that such a compliance program should be present at a daily basis at all levels in the organization. All managers and employees should be concerned about the program. Standards and procedures of compliance should apply everywhere in the organization and include the following procedures: frequent auditing and independent line management; monitoring and inspections by compliance personnel; internal reporting systems with independent procedures for determining the status of specific issues; and frequent evaluation and training of personnel.[35] Indeed, organizations were to establish support and incentives of compliance behavior. In case of prosecution, the defendant should show its willingness and ability to enforce these procedures and achieve excellence. Demonstration of efforts to overcome illegal action in an organization with heavy burdens might make it receive additional mitigation.[36]

On this basis the Commission made seven formal conditions for a good compliance program essential to the FSGO. It is important to stress that the seven steps only function as minimum requirements in order to put into practice an effective ethics or compliance program.[37] The steps should be understood as flexible guidelines and general measures to be applied in small or large companies according to their specific size, structure, and prior history. The seven steps contribute to the determination of dutiful behavior, and the ethical and moral responsibility of an organization. This is based on evaluating the actions of the organization and its employees prior to the illegal action, in order to detect and prevent this action. The seven steps imply that the FSGO operate with the organization as an independent unit with its own integrity and responsibility.

The seven steps defined in the FSGO are the following:[38]

1) *Establish standards and procedures.* The organization must have established compliance standards and procedures to be followed by its employees and other agents that are reasonably capable of reducing the prospect of criminal conduct.[39]

2) *Assign oversight responsibility.* Specific individual(s) within high-level personnel of the organization must have been assigned overall responsibility to oversee compliance with such standards and procedures.[40]

3) *Delegation of discretionary authority.* The organization must have used due care not to delegate substantial discretionary authority to individuals whom the organization knew, or should have known through the exercise of due diligence, had a propensity to engage in illegal activities.[41]

4) *Communication of standards and procedures.* The organization must have taken steps to communicate effectively its standards and procedures to all employees and other agents (e.g., by requiring participation in training programs or by disseminating publications that explain in a practical manner what is required).[42]

5) *Achieving employee compliance.* The organization must have taken reasonable steps to achieve compliance with its standards, for example by utilizing monitoring and auditing systems reasonably designed to detect criminal conduct by its employees and other agents, and by having in place and publicizing a reporting system, whereby employees and other agents could report criminal conduct by others within the organization without fear of retribution.[43]

6) *Enforcement and discipline.* The standards must have been consistently enforced through appropriate disciplinary mechanisms, including, as appropriate, discipline of individuals responsible for the failure to detect an offense. Adequate discipline of individuals responsible for an offense is a necessary component of enforcement; however, the form of discipline that will be appropriate will be case-specific.[44]

7) *Organizational response to ethics violations:* After an offense has been detected the organization must have taken all reasonable steps to respond appropriately to the offense and to prevent further similar offenses, including any necessary modifications to its program to prevent and detect legal violations.[45]

These FSGO requirements for a meaningful compliance program indicate that a company should make standards and procedures that efficiently can prevent and detect criminal offenses. High-level personnel should be involved and assigned responsibility for these programs. A meaningful compliance program should involve that the company has taken reasonable and meaningful measures to enforce compliance with the ethics rules among its employees. This might be done through establishing auditing, evaluation, and monitoring systems, which permit the evaluation of programs and inspection of criminal offenses. Efforts to communicate the contents of the program, and educate and train the employees in the company should be made so that the employees know about the values and ethics program. Moreover, the company should continuously update, enforce, improve, and modify the compliance standards in order to avoid and detect new legal violations.

In this way, the FSGO insist on a change of mentality among high-level managers. They must realize that ethics have to be integrated in the strategy of the company, if it wants to survive and assure long-term sustainability. In addition, ethics and compliance programs must involve employees in a direct and honest way. Compliance rules are most effective when they are formulated in democratic and communicative processes involving all employees and managers at an equal basis. Moreover, programs should focus on real and concrete problems related to the situation of specific companies.

The major issues facing American companies are problems concerning drug and alcohol abuse, employee theft, conflicts of interest, quality control, discrimination, misuse of propriety information, abuse of expense accounts, plant closings and layoffs, misuse of company assets, and problems of environmental pollution.[46] Compliance program may be related to those problems that are most urgent in specific companies. They could be drafted according to these specific needs on the basis of dialogue with the stakeholders of the organization. Moreover, formulating an ethics program must be done in close relation with the different fields in the company: management, marketing, product development, innovation, production, et cetera. Establishing an "ethics task force," including representatives from different parts of the firm, could be an example of a way to ensure this.[47]

The FSGO emphasize the link between ethics and law in the seven steps of a meaningful compliance program. The effort to move beyond compliance towards integrity-based systems of values-driven management is illustrated by their implicit understanding of good codes of conduct. It is important that a given code is written in a language that everybody can understand. Affirmative language is better than negative. Principles might be developed in a separate system of legal rules. The code of conduct is viewed as an element in a dynamic process; it should be flexible and able to be adjusted to new situations and developments where new ideas are integrated into old principles. In this way, programs of compliance can be said to involve the whole organization in a process towards excellence and the common good. Indeed, at any time new issues and themes might emerge, for example problems of environmental responsibilities, which have not been properly addressed.[48]

The importance of such compliance programs for reducing culpability is explicit in the FSGO. The guidelines contain very accurate measures in order to determine the culpability score and fines when sentencing organizations. An illustrative example is a defense industry organization that supplied the United States Government with a product that led to a substantial economic loss. The FSGO says that if the company had had a compliance program, the eventual fine could have been largely reduced. An organization without a program could, in a particular situation, expect fines between ten and twenty million dollars. With a compliance program, the fine could be reduced to between four and eight million dollars.[49] Organizations with more than fifty employees, and that do not have compliance programs, can expect large fines, but smaller organizations would also be better off with a compliance program, even if they are not submitted to the same demands of formally established programs.[50]

Although very few organizations have received direct credit for their compliance programs, they play an increased role in culpability determination both in civil and criminal law. An example is the defense industry company, Lucas Aerospace, which falsified required tests of missile launcher components. The court argued that the company needed a more developed compliance program. The company was requested to engage in independent monitoring of its activities and to establish a business ethics committee in order to be aware of misconduct in the company.[51]

Even though the FSGO leaves open the possibility of a fine being reduced there are still many issues of criminal law that fall at the borderline of the guidelines. Factors that increase the court's evaluation of the seriousness of an offense may be bodily injury, impact on national security, threats to the environment, threats to the market, cases of official corruption, and other instances of exceptional organizational culpability. The FSGO implies that these serious factors may increase the need to introduce stronger punishment, including increasing the size of the fines.

The FSGO make it clear, however, that by having a compliance program an organization's liability can largely be supported, as long as the organization should be able to prove in court that its compliance program has contributed to solving ethical problems. During the legal process, this might involve confidential investigation of the company by the authorities. It is a part of the self-evaluative privilege of organizations in collaboration with governments that full disclosure of information implies confidentiality on the part the authorities. Moreover, it should be emphasized that adversaries cannot use information from voluntary disclosures of information directly in legal proceedings.

Case 26. Ethics in the defense industry:
The controversial case of Lockheed Martin

A controversial example of business ethics in the United States is Lockheed Martin, a company that tries to live up to the FSGO. This is an exmple of a corporation in an *ethical dilemma*: How to develop ethics when you have a product, namely weapons, that few people find ethical. Moreover, it asks the question whether it is really possible to be ethical in the defense industry.

This corporation does a lot for training of its employees and has a developed ethics and compliance program. An illustration of this is Lockheed Martin's use of warning flags to tell people whether an action is ethical and to alert them to ethical dangers. These flags say things like "Well, may be just this once," "No one will ever know," "It doesn't matter how it gets done as long as it gets done," "Everyone does it," "Shred that document," "We can hide it," "No one will get hurt," et cetera. There is also a quick quiz to help employees determine whether an action is ethical. The quiz says, "When in doubt ask yourself" and contains the following questions: "1) Are my actions legal? 2) Am I fair and honest? 3) Will my action stand the test of time? 4) How will I feel about myself afterwards? 5) How will it look in the newspaper? 6) Will I sleep soundly tonight? 7) What would I tell my child to do? 8) How would I feel if my family, friends, and neighbors knew what I was doing?"[52]

The warning flags and the quick quiz indicate that Lockheed Martin is trying to base its ethics program on personal responsibility and employee integrity. Their increased conscientiousness and ability to make sound ethical judgment is the central aim of the ethics program; therefore, the corporation has committed itself to a massive training program with very concrete cases and tests of ethical behavior. Moreover, collaboration with company superiors and managers is important to make the ethics and compliance program work. Lockheed Martin's efforts represent a continuation of the efforts started by Martin Marietta (the company it merged with in 1995) to set-up a good-ethics office, hotline, and system of whistle-blowing.[53] Indeed, the code of ethics and conduct emphasizes that people making a request to the ethics office will be treated with dignity and respect, and that their communications will be kept confidential. People can be anonymous when they talk with the ethics officer. Employees are encouraged to talk with the ethics officer when they meet issues and problems of an ethical nature in their daily work activities.

In his analysis of the Lockheed Martin ethics program, Daniel Terris emphasizes its concrete work-oriented character. After consultation with many of the ethics officers of the corporation – described as a "small army of virtue" – he states that there "is an almost metaphysical infusion of goodness into the company's products: The fighter jets, the space shuttle, the missile and control systems, the hardware and software."[54] The system of ethics training is practical and designed to minimize misconduct among employees, and is characterized by an effective and easygoing, humorous manner.[55] With no formal training in philosophical ethics, the ethics officers are selected from within the organization, typically coming from a background of accounting or human resources.

Terris is ultimately rather pessimistic about Lockheed Martin's efforts in this area, because it looks like the corporation has mostly been focusing on the conception of business ethics as an effort to create virtuous employees. It has been important for Lockheed Martin to encourage the virtue of individual employees in order to ensure the morality of the corporation. In this moral uplift, however, general ethical issues affecting the corporate workforce, as a whole, have not been treated as very important. Moreover, the ethics program does not focus directly on relations to the outside world and on the relation of the corporation to society.[56] This is evidenced by the fact that there is little ethical reflection about the immorality of war profits, which is widely held public view that impacts the defense industry.[57]

Terris argues that the focus on the individual worker in the ethics program leaves many important questions untouched. There are different conceptions of business ethics in the United States that the company has not addressed. There is little focus, for example, on corporate governance and the power, privileges, and responsibilities of corporate leadership. In particular, in the defense industry, the dilemmas of their decision-making must be very complex. Therefore, the ethics program should look more into power and leadership.[58] Indeed, personal morality and integrity are arguably insufficient. It is the involvement of the ethics office in developing structures and procedures for this field that is important. In addition, it is characteristic that the focus on individual responsibility seems to imply a strange kind of "collective innocence."[59] Even though it has a strong ethics program, the corporation is constantly involved in legal and ethical allegations and court cases where it is found guilty and fined millions of dollars. Terris thinks that this is not only a question of size of the organization, but indicates increased focus on the need for treating ethical issues at the collective and institutional level of the firm.

1.3. The FSGO and American business life

The FSGO are strongly reflected in the development of ethics and compliance programs and values-driven management in American companies, and governmental and nonprofit organizations. Even though many organizations already had ethics and compliance programs prior to the enactment of the guidelines, it is evident that the FSGO have had great impact on the development of ethics programs in all areas of business life. A wide range of organization ranging from defense, financial services, health, agriculture, manufacturing, construction, telecommunications, utilities, and energy, to government and nongovernmental organizations follow the FSGO.

Different companies develop different programs according to their particular needs. Programs might include antitrust rules and regulations of fair economic practice. Other programs are focused on bribery, insider trading, or efforts to secure workplace security and safety. There are programs concerning affirmative action, discrimination, and equal opportunity. Other issues are fraud, consumer protection, or protection of the environment. The FSGO have influenced these different programs by giving formal standards for compliance and criteria for how to structure a specific program in a particular organization. The FSGO provide a formal framework for structuring specific ethics and compliance programs in relation to particular problems in specific industries.

In a situation where the FSGO have been functioning for some time, and where many organizations have installed compliance programs, the major challenge is no longer simply to establish such programs, but rather to integrate them into the organizational culture.[60] Successful programs are dependent on integration into organizational structure and policies. The concern for integration of programs and culture reflects a demand of a balance between external requirements (i.e., the FSGO) and internal priorities and strategies. In this context, it can be observed that compliance programs often evolve into more comprehensive programs based on integrity and ethical values.[61] Effective programs also reflect the complexity and multiple priorities of particular organizations. They become a part of a company's informal culture and tradition. Moreover, good ethics and compliance programs are becoming a part of the strategies and policies of the organization.[62]

Despite the fact that this goal may sound relatively straightforward, there is great complexity and variety in implementation and maintenance of ethics programs in different organizations. Empirical studies show that ethics programs cannot be generic, but they have to be shaped according to the industry, size, workforce, leadership style and other particular aspects of an organization's culture.[63] Moreover, the changing structure of modern organizations makes the implementation of ethics programs even more difficult. Transitions, mergers, and acquisitions, internal cultural differences, as well as organizational change have an impact on program integration.

There is widespread agreement that the FSGO, in many cases, were the initial factor for the development of an organization's compliance program. In many cases, the need for ethics also originated in some crisis or public scandal.[64] In these situations, ethical behavior becomes important for the company. Companies start with compliance programs in order to meet the external requirements of the FSGO, focusing on meeting regulatory requirements, minimizing the risks of litigation, and improving the firm's accountability.[65]

After some period of time, most organizations look beyond the initial focus on compliance towards a broader focus on ethics and values. These values-based programs have a wider scope of priorities including maintaining the brand and corporate reputation, retaining good employees, unifying the organization, creating a better work environment, and improving the ethical behavior of the firm. The driving forces for these concerns for ethics and values vary according to specific organizations. They range from economic factors, such as increased competition, and desiring a more competent workforce to organizational issues like desiring a more ethically motivated workforce, and general issues, such as searching for a way to improve stakeholder relationships. In all cases, an organization moves to values-driven management when it wants to integrate ethics programs into the heart of its culture. It is not only pragmatic interest in survival or deontological preoccupations with duty and obeying the law, but also teleological concerns for excellence and integrity that are the basis for the company's focus on ethical values. As Joshua Joseph remarks, companies want to be "doing the right thing in addition to doing things right."[66]

There are many different justifications of ethics and compliance programs in organizations. Improved public relations, avoiding criminal scandals, and higher employee awareness and professional conscientiousness of ethics issues have been mentioned as reasons for successful program evaluation. Moreover, improving management's awareness of ethical issues and the functions of ethics and compliance programs in order to build trust internally and externally among stakeholders of the organization is mentioned as a justification of ethics programs. In addition, general factors, such as the need to comply with regulations, add benefits of the organization, increase the firm's competitive advantage, and reduce its financial and legal risks have also been mentioned. In many organizations, values-driven management is considered as a way to develop new values but also to improve and "honor what is already there in the culture."[67]

On this basis, it is important to emphasize that the structure of ethics and compliance programs vary according to context, culture, and priorities of specific organizations.[68] These differences concern the formulation of codes, the organization of programs, the role of ethics officers and management, evaluation, monitoring, and accounting measures. Organizations define different manners of decision-making, ranging from ethics officers that report directly to chief management, establishing ethics committees, to monitoring the direct involvement of company executives.

Even though most organizations have the same basic features in their programs, including codes of conducts, mission, vision, value statements, and evaluations procedures, concrete formulations are very different. Ethics codes reflect different conceptions about how to draft a code or value statement, and their contents and styles are very diverse. While employees or managers are usually more or less included, very different persons can be involved in the drafting process. Some codes are only short credo statements while others contain many concrete rules and structures; however, most organizations stress the importance of linking ethics and values mechanisms to high-level executives. This ensures credibility, professionalism, and accountability of their ethics programs.

The tension between compliance and values-driven ethics programs means that codes of conduct are roughly separated into two basic kinds: compliance codes and more comprehensive corporate credos or management philosophy statements. In this context, it is important to link the kind of program to the particular context and history of a particular company. Compliance programs make it easier to determine legal liability, while values program are more broadly directed towards social responsibility: however, in general, neither ethics nor compliance program can be solely based on corporate credos. In large organizations, they must imply deeper structures of monitoring, training, and evaluation. In order to emphasize this close relation between law and ethics, and compliance and integrity in the formulation of ethics, it is important that the language used is supportive rather than punitive.[69]

In many cases, compliance and ethics codes include mission statements, defining basic structures of the firm and determining procedures, policies, and practices that constitute the corporate mission and responsibilities. Many companies are today working with international compliance in order to develop the company's global ethics.[70] Frequently, codes address general subjects of equity and human rights, for example relating to human dignity. These issues of rights involve problems of corporate due process, employee health screening, sexual discrimination, affirmative action, shareholder interest, protection of whistle blowers, et cetera. In this context, it may be said that dignity is a subcategory of rights, though there is a tension between an autonomy-based and a community-based vision of dignity.[71] This means that dignity is rooted in the community's sense of decency rather than legal mandates. This concept of dignity is, for example, important in order to ensure the protection of specific employees' privacy. It aims at protecting the respect for the individual in the community.

Many organizations agree about the need to develop their ethics and compliance programs. Better communication, training, and distribution of ethics knowledge are very important for the function of these programs. Precision in monitoring, auditing, and evaluation mechanisms are also recognized as criteria for success. Indeed, good decision-making and higher degrees of employee involvement are criteria for the success of an ethics programs. It is also important to find the right balance between compliance control and monitoring on the one hand, as well as flexibility and excellence in values-driven programs on the other. Hence, trust can be most genuinely ensured through employees feeling a sense of ownership of ethics programs.[72]

Communicating standards and ethics measures to employees is done in many different ways in various ethics programs. Some organizations emphasize formal material codes, while others do it more informally. Internal or external personnel may provide ethics training and education. There are many different levels of involving employees in ethics. Organizations give the following reasons for not involving employees in ethics processes: limited time and resources, fear of adverse consequences for the organization, and belief that employee input is unnecessary because of legal requirements; however, in general, ethics communication and training is considered very important for the success of ethics programs.[73] Having said this, it can be a challenge to encourage employee involvement in these programs. The transition from compliance to values-driven and integrity-based programs may also be difficult, but in values-driven management employee ownership may be even more important than in the case of compliance programs.

The FSGO requirements of ethics officers' compliance responsibility are reflected in the structure of ethics programs in most companies. It is recognized that the working relationship and trust between ethics officers and executive management is very important.[74] Organizations often select a responsible compliance and ethics officer from senior personnel. It is recognized that it should be a generally trusted person who enjoys a high degree of credibility and has sufficient authority to make decisions in the organization. Large organizations may even nominate ethics officers for different areas (e.g., environmental issues, securities, and discrimination) according to particular problems in specific industries. In many organizations, ethics offices have established call-in hotlines to help employees in case they discover ethical problems. The ethics officer's function is to be a neutral ombudsman that employees can talk to without fear of retribution.

Ethics officers should have contact with the company manager, board of directors, or other leading authorities. Ethics officers have general responsibility for developing ethics policies and overseeing the ethics function in the company. They are entitled to carry out internal ethics investigations in the organization, have information about ethics relations, and analyze relevant data. Ethics officers are also in many cases responsible for ethical reporting and evaluations of the company.[75] These audits have important function for securing consistency of ethics programs in organizations. It is important that companies have sufficient resources for ethics offices.[76] It is also important that the ethics officers have the required capacities; therefore, in many cases, it is a person who has been with the company for more than ten years.[77]

Ethics officers are also responsible for program development in times of organizational change. They have to find the right balance between compliance and values-driven programs. In many cases there is employee skepticism and criticism of ethics programs that companies and their ethics officers have to face.[78] Employees say that programs serve to protect management, that they are without substantial purpose, and that they function as monitoring systems. In this context, it is important that an ethics officer find the right balance in achieving their responsibilities for ethics without functioning as a police officer.[79]

There is a particular institutional significance to an ethics officer. This office is often integrated with other departments of the organization, such as human resources and management, and this is essential because it develops the central values of the company. The size, staffing, and structure of ethics offices are dependent on specific organizations.[80] The ethics officer supports the development of the identity of the organization. Compliance should not be reduced to a legal matter, but it is the task of the ethics office to contribute to organizational integrity.

In order to succeed with ethics and compliance programs, the involvement of high-level management and leadership is emphasized. In particular, the ethics function should demonstrate the commitment of the senior management team to ensuring the honesty and integrity of the activities of the organization.[81] It is, indeed, the responsibility of the corporate board to make sure that appropriate compliance functions are set up in the organization. The board is also responsible for making the ethics process work and reviewing whether particular corporate directors and corporate boards are living up to their responsibilities. In practice, ethics programs benefit from active participation of leadership in talking with employees and showing willingness to discuss complicated ethical issues. Moreover, management can improve ethics by modeling ethical behavior in the firm.[82] It is an advantage for leaders to participate actively in ethics programs because they send a dual message of the importance of ethics and their own commitment to the program's success.[83]

Box 15. Important Steps of the FSGO carrot-and-stick approach

It is an ongoing conversation regarding whether the FSGO had worked efficiently to prevent corporate crime. Those who are critical towards the impact of the federal sentencing guidelines point to the scandals of Enron and WorldCom, and the subsequent legislation of accounting practices (e.g., the Sarbanes-Oxley Act) as clear illustrations of the need for stronger action with regard to corporate crime. Looking at the most important events in the history of the FSGO, it is possible, however, to document some important ways that the FSGO have helped to combat corporate crime and misbehavior.

The history of the guidelines illustrates that they have not been ignored by corporations. In the beginning, the guidelines did not contain any incentives for corporations to create ethics and compliance programs. The novelty of the guidelines was, indeed, the concept of self-regulation using the carrot-and-stick.[84] Although as early as 1991, the United States Environmental Protection Agency had referred to the guidelines in a case, many companies did not apply the guidelines because they could only be used for events after their enactment. Still, in 1992, the Ethics Officer Association was formed in order to be proactive regarding compliance and values-driven management. Moreover, state attorneys general began at the same time to suggest that companies were active with regard to implementing compliance programs. [85]

In 1994, Lucas Aerospace, in connection with its sentencing, was required to implement a compliance program. This became the basis for many further cases and started a trend, now followed by many states, requiring reports about environmental audits and compliance programs. In 1995, the important Sentencing Commission conference – Corporate Crime in America: Strengthening the 'Good Citizen' Corporation – was held in Washington D.C., where the importance of companies having compliance or values programs in the case of an offense was emphasized. Moreover, in early 1996, the fining of Daiwa Bank persuaded many corporate directors that their shareholders would hold them responsible for doing nothing to implement compliance programs.[86]

Government agencies working on issues of health or the environment work actively with corporate compliance and different courts have begun using the FSGO more intensively. In 1999, the pharmaceutical company Hoffman-LaRoche was fined 500 million dollars for antitrust conspiracy. BASF AG was ordered to pay 225 million dollars while Rhone Poulenc got off free because it reported the offence according to the guidelines. Moreover, in 2001, TAP Pharmaceuticals was convicted and fined 290 million dollars under the guidelines.[87]

In addition to these sentences, which show the power of the guidelines as a judicial instrument, it is important to emphasize the enormous increase of ethics and compliance programs in the United States after the enactment of the FSGO. Accordingly, it may be emphasized that the American approach to business ethics is not only based on self-regulation, but also on active involvement of authorities. Together with Sarbanes-Oxley, the FSGO are an important instrument to prevent corporate crime.

1.4. FSGO and the paradox of ethics and compliance programs

There are many ways of analyzing the American developments in values-driven management and compliance programs. A remarkable feature is the fact that these guidelines are based on a legal and judicial approach to ethics and values. This legal push to institutionalize ethics has had a major impact on social developments by making ethics more present in corporate life. Moreover, the carrot-and-stick approach of the FSGO constitute a self-regulative and institutional approach to ethics in business life. The programs are institutionalized in such a way that they also have an impact on risk management and reputation management of the organization. It can be argued that public relations are a major component of the reason for viewing values-driven management from an organizational perspective. The programs can be said to increase the security of the organization being confronted with scandals and bad management situations. At the same time, these developments in the United States reflect a highly litigatory society. The FSGO have emerged in the framework of a society, in which corporate law is based on criminal law with a large emphasis on efficient legal compliance. This situation of litigation and legal regulation has been the basis for the tremendous development of values-driven management in American corporations. Moreover, the emphasis on collaboration with authorities and whistle-blowing is important in order to understand the particularity of the FSGO as an American invention. In Europe, there is much more skepticism towards big organizations, which means that individuals are reluctant to recognize whistle-blowing as an acceptable ethical practice. Europeans consider whistle-blowing as an act lacking solidarity with fellow employees. It is also perceived that collaboration with authorities might be less acceptable in particular situations.

Because of these variations, it is important to be aware of the cultural particularity of the carrot-and-stick approach, which can encourage companies to make compliance programs in order to avoid corporate crime while also making firms less vulnerable in case of criminal prosecution. In this context, the guidelines may be considered as an important way of moving beyond the dilemma between law enforcement and deregulation.[88] The FSGO manage, at the same time, to imply increased regulation and deregulation because they are based on the idea of the advantages of self-regulation in compliance and ethics programs prior to the criminal offense. Moreover, they avoid strong sanctions by focusing on self-reporting and collaboration with authorities in case a criminal investigation is conducted in relation to the organization. In addition, it may be argued that the FSGO emphasize organizational integrity in favor of formal compliance. The United States Sentencing Commission stresses that an effective compliance program should be based on a serious effort to comply with laws and ethical standards by the organization.

However, a severe criticism of the FSGO is that they do nothing but institutionalize a heavy ethics bureaucracy in companies. Moreover, it is argued that it is not possible to ensure that companies go beyond utility calculations and establish themselves as good corporate citizens. Critical voices urge that compliance and ethics programs remain cosmetic and that it is impossible for prosecutors and authorities to distinguish clearly between real ethics programs and paper programs. It is stated that the FSGO are able to be manipulate the legal liability of individuals who should be attributed real responsibility for their actions. By establishing ethics programs, managers become able to avoid being prosecuted, because they can point at the firm's ethics programs and ensure good intentions. Indeed, it possible for a firm to show that it is not responsible for illegal actions by individual employees who, after having been made aware of the firm's ethics policies, have acted contrary to the company ethics programs and policies. In addition, many employees consider ethics and compliance programs primarily as an improvement of public relations rather than an indication of genuine ethical intentions.

It may be argued that the continuing scandals in American business life, in particular, show that ethics programs are not working, though they may have been much worse without the growing concern for ethics in business. It is, however, very difficult to formulate precise empirical evidence of the function of codes. It may be argued that their existence has not changed the criminal liability of the firm and the status of responsibility is the same even if corporations have set up ethics and compliance programs. Also, many findings suggest that effective programs contribute to proving that a corporation acted in "good faith."

There are still many other criticisms of the function of ethics programs, including that their focus on morality in the corporation has a negative impact on innovation. Some are concerned that there is little relationship between codes of conduct and the chance of corporate violations.[89] Rather than increasing ethical behavior, the focus on ethics and compliance seems to move the corporation away from solving ethics problems. From this perspective, codes of conduct lead to expensive costs and increased formalism, rather than helping the corporation to develop good ethics. At the same time, vicarious responsibility renders ethics programs useless because the corporation will still be held responsible.[90] Considering the development of the FSGO, it may be maintained that they at least imply a change in the concept of responsibility and that ethical corporations can be rewarded, yet even this situation can be viewed critically from the point of view of the idea of corporate responsibility.

It can be argued that a cynical utility calculation is still the basis of the approach of American corporations to ethics and compliance programs, even if many people sing the gospel of the good corporate citizen.[91] From such a point of view, the FSGO may be viewed as a paradigmatic change of basic structure of corporate criminal law, but this is also the problem, because companies continue to focus on costs and benefits following the FSGO. The FSGO are not, therefore, as efficient as planned, when the concept of the good corporate citizen is introduced. It is true that the FSGO are at the limit of the traditional doctrine of corporate legal liability by focusing on organizational structures and policies. The traditional, and very influential, doctrine of American criminal law was based on the idea of vicarious liability of specific persons in the corporation. The integration of law and economics with conceptions of corporate culpability in the FSGO represent a challenge to usual conceptions of corporate criminal liability, because the FSGO may represent a way for individuals to escape strict vicarious liability.

It is argued that many large corporations, even with the rapid development in corporate ethics programs, still consider corporate ethics first and foremost as a matter of risk management.[92] Companies have been able to shift liability risks from individual top executives to the corporate policies and hierarchies based on the concept of good corporate citizen in the FSGO. It is argued that this represents a paradox of compliance where it has been more difficult to detect liability and to determine the effectiveness of compliance programs.[93] The reason, according to William S. Laufer, is that criminal law, due to the traditional paradigm of vicarious liability, is still reluctant to conceive corporations as moral or legal persons. He quotes the late professor John William Salmond, who once wrote: "Ten men do not become in fact one person because they associate themselves together for one end, any more than two horses become one animal when they draw the same cart."[94]

Traditional criminal law has predominantly considered individual persons liable for the actions of the firm. The *compliance paradox* means that the FSGO has immunized firms from the risk and costs of criminal liability, because they are able to show that the firm had good ethics and compliance programs. Similarly, top management cannot be held responsible because they have contributed to the firm's ethical behavior. As a consequence, liability may be restricted to employees at a lower level of the organization. Since the famous Hudson Supreme Court decision, where managers were found to have responsibility for institutionalizing adequate control systems in organizations, it would be a part of the professional responsibility of the management, if the organization lacked a good compliance program. Accordingly, management would be held legally liable for this lack of compliance. The result of this situation is that it is a strategic advantage for management to institutionalize compliance programs in their organizations, because this would make the organization legally stronger and managers less legally liable in case of criminal prosecution.[95]

Even though he recommends the guidelines, Laufer expresses concerns for the motives of management to comply with the FSGO. Moreover, the FSGO may render criminal law less efficient. This is illustrated by the decrease in legal prosecutions of companies in recent years. It appears that organizations, with help from compliance consultants, manage to avoid prosecutions in formulating compliance programs. In order to avoid paper programs it is a great challenge to companies to use compliance and ethics programs as genuine indicators for corporate integrity and professional responsibility, rather than reducing them to a means to reduce legal risk.[96] Laufer emphasizes the pragmatic dimensions of the FSGO can lead companies to justify compliance as a form of insurance. Compliance programs are conceived as utility investments where cost-benefits are weighed in accordance with a neoclassical theory of the economic costs of moral hazards.[97]

This criticism of the rhetoric of "effective compliance" in favor of an "integrity approach," focusing on direct corporate liability and based on the professional responsibility of management, is a bit too pessimistic with regard to the evaluation of American companys' seriousness regarding compliance. As discussed previously, many companies have moved beyond compliance towards organizational integrity. Indeed, only very few companies have had direct mitigation of punishment because of their compliance programs, but still the development of ethics programs has been very large. The FSGO requirements for effective compliance programs help solve a previous ambiguity regarding how to define compliance. This definition is sufficiently strict in order to avoid situations where compliance is treated solely as a matter of utility. Moreover, the growing emphasis on integrity shows a genuine concern for doing the right thing as opposed to mere public relations concerns. Laufer rightly points to the fact that a growing concern for legal and moral responsibility of firms is necessary in order to do justice to the conception of organizational culpability implicit in the FSGO. These paradigmatic challenges to American law pose the questions about the definition of organizational integrity and the consequences of values-driven management on corporate personality. It may be argued that the FSGO have been very important for raising the consciousness about business ethics, even though they have not been as efficient as expected because of the unavoidable scandals and crimes in American business life.

Case 27. The collapse of Enron and the crisis of American business life

Enron is being discussed, once again, as an illustration of the limits of the FSGO and at same time as a reminder of the need for corporations to work seriously with ethics programs.This is a case of a company that experienced an *ethical crisis*. The scandal of Enron and subsequent bankruptcy and collapse of the firm elucidate the many difficulties of creating any form of corporate integrity.

Enron was an energy trading company that was created in 1985. By 2001, it was listed as the most innovative company in America by Fortune Magazine. The company had become a market maker for gas and other forms energy. The company pursued a strategy of growth and profit with a culture of innovation and competitiveness in the "new economy."[98] In 1990, it had a revenue of 4.6 billion dollars and had reached nearly 101 billion by 2000. When the company was still rising, the CEO and chairman Kenneth Lay, ascribed the success of Enron to its capacity for innovation, and its high quality management, products, and services. Lay was a friend of George W. Bush, whom he supported and from whom he expected favorable legislation in return. Lay was well-respected as a major business leader in the United States and was responsible for the idea of Enron. Because Enron was respected as a very strong company, it came as a total surprise when the company filed for protection from creditors under the United States Securities Act on December 2, 2001.[99] The result was that the market lost confidence in the company and over a few months the company's shares lost most of their value. Many of the small shareholders were taken by surprise. Soon they had lost most of their money when the stock price of the company fell from ninety dollars to thirty-six cents.

The economic consequences of Enron's breakdown were terrible. Nearly 24.000 employees lost their jobs. Many small pensioners and other innocent people lost their savings in stock options. The credibility of the financial market and of the United States stock market, more generally, was fundamentally shaken. The investigation by different authorities and public prosecutors in the months following the firm's collapse tried to create a picture of what had happened. A special Congressional committee held hearings on the issue and subsequently issued a report. It explained the collapse by pointing the finger at key employees who had been enriching themselves with hundreds of thousand of dollars.

One of the main reasons of the failure was the creation of different external entities constructed to hide the financial problems.[100] The company had created a number of partnerships (e.g., Chewco, LJM1, and LJM2), which were designed to make favorable financial accounting statements, but did not follow United States accounting rules. This dubious accounting made it possible to hide problematic economic conditions. There were other transactions that created more than one billion dollars in losses that were not properly reported. The accounting treatments of Chewco and LMJ1, in particular, were full of errors despite the advice and accounting of Enron's accounting firm, Arthur Andersen.[101] The result of the investigation was that much more specific rules for corporate governance and ethical guidelines were needed for the accounting profession.

The ethical problems in the behavior of Enron that were found in the hearings and investigations include: fiduciary failure, high-risk accounting, inappropriate conflicts of interests, extensive undisclosed bookkeeping activity, and excessive compensation to high-level executives.[102] Fiduciary failure means that the company did not do anything to tell shareholders about the collapse of the company, because there was very little transparency in the activities of the firm. High-risk accounting was, indeed, an expression of this lack of responsibility towards shareholders.

Conflicts of interest meant that the directors received personal gain from the different transactions with other companies that they themselves were partners in, thereby allowing them to shirk their fiduciary responsibilities to shareholders. The extensive undisclosed activity implied that the Enron board allowed the company to conduct billions of dollars in off-the-book transactions, and to allow the financial situation to appear better than it was. Finally, the board approved excessive compensation to executives and did not monitor the financial abuses by Lay, who had several billion dollars worth of personal credit financed by the company.[103]

1.5. From the FSGO to Sarbanes-Oxley

Why put so much emphasis on the FSGO when recent legislation – including the Sarbanes-Oxley Act – seems, from the point of view of many observers, to be much more efficient?[104] The Public Company Accounting Reform and Investor Act (SOX) went far beyond the FSGO and was, therefore, was much more important as an instrument to enforce business ethics, CSR, and corporate governance.[105] Moreover, it may be argued to be paradoxical that the FSGO were not able to prevent the business scandals of Enron, World-Com, and Arthur Andersen that shook the financial community of the United States and, indeed, the whole world. These financial breakdowns represented the need for standards of ethical accounting, but also of corporate governance and corporate social responsibility in business organizations. The breakdown of these companies in 2001-2002 led to a serious crisis of credibility, not only of the accounting profession, but of the whole modern business system.[106] The irony is that Enron had a well-written business ethics program on its website and Arthur Andersen was a leading actor in the market of producing and developing ethics programs for organizations. On the other hand, the cases of Enron and WorldCom can be considered of cases illustrating the necessity of corporate governance and corporate social responsibility.

Accordingly, the financial breakdown has been conceived as a crisis of business ethics as a whole, and also as an indication of the lack of efficiency of the FSGO. As mentioned previously, the United States Congress subsequently enacted the Sarbanes-Oxley Act, which, as the most important legislation on corporate ethics since the FSGO, had the task of ensuring transparency and credibility in financial markets. It is a comprehensive legislation addressing issues of financial fraud, corporate responsibility, and business ethics in the financial governance and accounting of the firm. The law also addresses the issue of corporate transparency regarding finance, accounting, and other investment matters of relevance for shareholders and other stakeholders. The Sarbanes-Oxley Act was widely supported in Congress by both Republicans and Democrats that welcomed the increased financial control of the firm and the implied possibility of controlling illegal actions of board members, managers, and employees.

The Sarbanes-Oxley Act can be seen as a continuation of the emphasis on business ethics and corporate responsibility that was initiated with FSGO. It is not so much something radically new as a development of the American tradition of business ethics. On the other hand, when you look at the concrete content of Sarbanes-Oxley, the Act implies a return to sticks rather than a focus on carrots, in the sense that the legal enforcement is much stronger in Sarbanes-Oxley than in FSGO. It is an important intention of the law to re-establish public trust and to ensure reliable corporate reporting mechanisms. One of the most important innovations of the law was to establish the Public Company Accounting Oversight Board (PCAOB) that oversees the accounting and reporting practices of corporations. In addition, the Sarbanes-Oxley Act establishes a link between accounting, financial transparency, and corporate governance.

The content of the law includes the following provisions:

1) The creation of the PCAOB, which is in charge of regulations administered by the Securities and Exchange Commission (SEC).

2) It requires CEOs and CFOs to certify that their companys' financial statements are true and do not include misleading statements.

3) It requires that the corporate board of directors' audit committees consist of independent members who have no material interest in the company.

4) It prohibits corporations from making or offering loans to officers and board members.

5) It requires codes of ethics for senior financial officers; codes must be registered with the SEC.

6) It prohibits accounting firms from providing both auditing and consulting services to the same client without approval of the client firm's audit committee.

7) It requires company attorneys to report wrongdoing to top managers and, if necessary, to the board of directors; if managers and directors fail to respond to reports of wrongdoing, the attorney should stop representing the company.

8) It mandates whistle-blower protection for persons who disclose wrongdoing to authorities.

9) It requires financial securities analysts to certify that their recommendations are based on objective reports.

10) It requires mutual fund managers to disclose how they vote shareholder proxies, giving investors information about how their shares influence decisions.

11) It establishes a ten-year penalty for mail/wire fraud.

12) It prohibits the two senior auditors from working on a corporation's account for more than five years; oher auditors are prohibited from working on an account for more than seven years. (In other words, accounting firms must rotate individual auditors from one account to another from time to time).[107]

When looking closely into the content of the Sarbanes-Oxley Act, it represents a continuation of the focus on the good corporate citizen, which was the focus of the FSGO. Sarbanes-Oxley is a law that seeks to promote the ethical corporation and make the corporation contribute to the common good; however, Sarbanes Oxley is narrower in scope than the FSGO, because it mainly covers issues of financial accounting and professional standards for transparency and public accounting, in particular the regulation of the interactions between public accounting firms and their corporate customers.[108] In this context, the financial fraud of the international accounting firm Arthur Andersen can be seen as one of the reasons why Congress passed the new regulation so quickly and unanimously.

The creation of the PCAOB, which functions as an independent state-sponsored nonprofit organization, indicates an effort to ensure that corporations function as good citizens. This is indicated by the fact that it is the aim of the board to look for quality control and promote good ethics in the corporation.[109] The task of this oversight and control body is to monitor the registered public accounting firms and to enforce compliance with the Sarbanes-Oxley legislation. The board members are required to have high integrity and the function of the organization is to oversee all accounting firms that register with the it. Corporate and professional ethics should play an important role for the board and the oversight board has the duty to monitor professional ethics of accounting.[110] The board should, in collaboration with government agencies, inspect, monitor, and control the audit committees in corporations and in relation to accounting firms.

The Sarbanes-Oxley Act contains an important section on corporate responsibility.[111] It indicates that members of audit committees have direct responsibility for the audits of corporations that they are performing. Both auditing firms and corporate boards have fundamental responsibilities to ensure the adequacy of financial reports. It is part of their professional responsibility that they give coherent representations of the financial situation of the company. Sarbanes-Oxley also requires that senior financial officers should be held to the following standards: honesty and ethical conduct, including ethical handling of actual or apparent conflicts of interests between personal and professional relationships; full, fair, accurate, timely, and understandable disclosure in the periodic reports required to be filed by the issuer; and compliance with applicable governmental rules and regulations. [112]

As an important supplement to the FSGO, Sarbanes-Oxley reinforces ethics and the responsibility of the good corporate citizen within the field of accounting. Sarbanes-Oxley does not replace the FSGO, but is an important reinforcement of aspects of the FSGO that did receive strong legal focus. Together with the FSGO, Sarbanes-Oxley provides important legal and ethical incentives to corporations so that they can behave as good citizens. Sarbanes-Oxley encourages corporations to contribute with a strategy for sustainable compliance that combines ethics and corporate governance in the development of transparent accounting. From the point of view of society and of the legislator, the benefits of Sarbanes-Oxley are linked to the possibility of controlling corporations on the basis of increased documentation and monitoring. Using the law to reinforce business ethics in this way includes more strict public control of businesses leading to better risk management and transparency in corporate governance. From the technical point of view of accountants, the advantages of Sarbanes-Oxley may include much stronger and active participation of the board, more thoughtful analysis and stronger recognition of the role of the auditors. Moreover, from a positive perspective, it is reasonable to expect more structure to the accounting process and stronger efforts to prevent fraud. Indeed, Sarbanes-Oxley may impove the accounts and the relationship between financial risks and decisions across the organization. Financial reports may be more adequate and financial operations may be more consolidated across the organization.[113]

The potential disadvantages of Sarbanes-Oxley, are the dangers of general paranoia of transparency. Sarbanes-Oxley was a result of a strong reaction to very spectacular financial breakdowns and it expresses the outcry of a need for more control, which inevitably leads to more bureaucracy. Critical voices may argue that Sarbanes-Oxley only leads to the production of more paper in an extensive, expensive, and useless documentation process. Learning from the success of the FSGO, it is legitimate to ask whether, because there are poor possibilities for implementation, more legislation – in the form of strict rules – really is the right way to control corporations who have so many ways of escaping government regulation. Another problem is that costs seem to be extremely high and the benefits seem to be low, when there is no efficient implementation of control measures. Contrary to the FSGO, Sarbanes-Oxley arguably focuses too much on outside pressure "sticks" and not so much on inside motivation "carrots," as is the case with the FSGO. From this point of view, it is very important to approach the Sarbanes-Oxley regulation of corporate governance and accounting keeping in mind the general promotion of ethics programs and corporate responsibility as proposed by the FSGO. Without the FSGO, Sarbanes-Oxley risks being understood as a traditional law-enforcement instrument. Seen from the perspective of the the FSGO, however, Sarbanes-Oxley may viewed as a piece of legislation that focuses on compliance in order to make corporations more conscious of their values and efforts to be good citizens.

Endnotes

1   Milton Friedman, *Capitalism and Freedom*, (Chicago: University of Chicago Press, 1962).

2   George C.S. Benson: *Business Ethics in America* (Massachusetts, Toronto Lexington Books, D.C Heath and Company, Lexington, 1982), 1.

3   Ibid: 5. See also Gerald F. Cavanagh, *American Business Values. A Global Perspective* (New Jersey: Prentice Hall, 2006), 177.

4   George C.S Benson, *Business Ethics in America*, Lexington Books (Lexington, Massachusetts, Toronto, D.C Heath and Company, 1982), 58-59.

5   Gerald F. Cavanagh, *American Business Values. A Global Perspective* (New Jersey: Prentice Hall, 2006).

6   See H.R. Bowen, *The Social Responsibilities of Business Men*, 1953.

7   George C.S Benson, *Business Ethics in America*, Lexington Books (Lexington, Massachusetts, Toronto, D.C Heath and Company, 1982), 104.

8   Ibid:147.

9   US Federal Sentencing Commission, "Corporate Crime in America: Strengthening the "Good Citizen Corporation" (Washington: A National Symposium Sponsored by The U.S Sentencing Commission, 1995).

10 Paul E. Fiorelli, "Fine Reductions Through Effective Ethics Programs", *Albany Law Review*, Volume 56, (1992) Number 2, 407. US Federal Sentencing Commission, "Corporate Crime in America: Strengthening the "Good Citizen Corporation" (Washington: A National Symposium Sponsored by The U.S Sentencing Commission, 1995).

11 Leonard J. Brooks, *Business and Professional Ethics for Directors, Executives, and Accountants* (Toronto: Thomson, South-Western, 2003).

12 See Hannah Arendt, *Eichmann in Jerusalem, Essay on the Banality of Evil* (New York: Harcourt and Brace, 1964).

13 US Federal Sentencing Commission, "Corporate Crime in America: Strengthening the "Good Citizen Corporation" (Washington: A National Symposium Sponsored by The U.S Sentencing Commission, 1995).

14 Harvey L. Pitt and Karl A. Groskaumanis, "Minizing Corporate Civil and Criminal Liability: A second Look at Corporate Codes of Conduct" (New York: Fried, Frank, Harrris, Shriver and Jacobsen Law firm, 1989).

15 Lynn Sharp Paine, "Martin Marietta: Managing Corporate Ethics", case prepared by Lynn Sharp Paine with assistance of Albert Choy and Michael Santoro (Cambridge, Massachusetts: Harvard Business School Case 393-016, 1992). Reprinted in *Cases in Leadership, Ethics, and Organizational Integrity. A Strategic Perspective* (New York: Irwin, McGraw-Hill, 1997).

16 Tony McAdams with contributing authors James Freemann and Laura P. Hartman, *Law, Business and Society*, Six Edition (Boston: McGraw-Hill Higher Education, Chapter 10, 2000).

17 Dove Izraeli and Mark S Schwartz, "What Can We Learn From the U.S Federal Sentencing Guidelines for Organizational Ethics" in *Journal of Business Ethics* 17, (1998), 1045. US Federal Sentencing Commission, "Corporate Crime in America: Strengthening the "Good Citizen Corporation" (Washington: A National Symposium Sponsored by The U.S Sentencing Commission, 1995).

18 Jeffrey M. Kaplan, Joseph E. Murphy, Winthrop M. Swenson, *Compliance Programs and the Corporate Sentencing Guidelines. Preventing Criminal and Civil Liability* (New York: West Publishers, 1993), Chapter 2, Corporate Sentencing Guidelines: Drafting History, p. 4. US Federal Sentencing Commission, "Corporate Crime in America: Strengthening the "Good Citizen Corporation" (Washington: A National Symposium Sponsored by The U.S Sentencing Commission, 1995).

19 Jeffrey M. Kaplan, Joseph E. Murphy, Winthrop M. Swenson, *Compliance Programs and the Corporate Sentencing Guidelines, Preventing Criminal and Civil Liability* (New York: West Publishers, 1993 and later), Chapter 4, 4.01, 2.

20 William S. Laufer ,"Corporate Bodies and Guilty Minds", *Emory Law Journal*, Vol 43 (1994): 648-730.

21 Ibid: 667.

22 Ibid: 712.

23 Ibid: 712.

24 Jeffrey M. Kaplan, Joseph E. Murphy, Winthrop M. Swenson, *Compliance Programs and the Corporate Sentencing Guidelines. Preventing Criminal and Civil Liability* (New York: West Publishers, 1993 and later), Chapter 4, 22.

25 Ibid. Chapter 4, 22.
26 See for example Lynn Sharp Paine, "Managing for Organizational Integrity", *Harvard Business Review*, 1994.
27 Jeffrey M. Kaplan, Joseph E. Murphy, Winthrop M. Swenson, *Compliance Programs and the Corporate Sentencing Guidelines. Preventing Criminal and Civil Liability* (New York: West Publishers, 1993 and later), Chapter 4: 24. US Federal Sentencing Commission, "Corporate Crime in America: Strengthening the "Good Citizen Corporation" (Washington: A National Symposium Sponsored by The U.S Sentencing Commission, 1995).
28 Jeffrey M. Kaplan, Joseph E. Murphy, Winthrop M. Swenson, *Compliance Programs and the Corporate Sentencing Guidelines. Preventing Criminal and Civil Liability* (New York: West Publishers, 1993 and later), Chapter 4: 24.
29 Ibid: 34.
30 It was Martin Marietta, which later became a part of Lockheed Martin that took the initiative to establish a common code of conduct for the defense industry. This initiative is remarkable because it was one of the first initatives in the United States to establish such a wide-reaching code of conduct for a whole industry and it later became a model for many ethics and compliance programs.
31 Paul E. Fiorelli, "Fine Reductions Through Effective Ethics Programs", *Albany Law Review*, Volume 56, (1992) Number 2, 411.
32 "Defence Industry Initiative on Business Ethics and Conduct", 1991. *Annual Report on the Public and the Defence Industry* app. A-1 - A-2 (1992).
33 Jeffrey M. Kaplan, Joseph E. Murphy, Winthrop M. Swenson, *Compliance Programs and the Corporate Sentencing Guidelines. Preventing Criminal and Civil Liability* (New York: West Publishers, 1993 and later), 23.
34 Jbid: 23.
35 Jbid: 45.
36 These informations come from Jeffrey M. Kaplan, Joseph E. Murphy, Winthrop M. Swenson, *Compliance Programs and the Corporate Sentencing Guidelines. Preventing Criminal and Civil Liability* (New York: West Publishers, 1993 and later), Chapter 2, Corporate Sentencing Guidelines: Drafting History.
37 Ibid. Chapter 4, 21.
38 USSG Guidelines Manual: Chapter 8, 1995, 1
39 Guidelines, supra note 1, § 8A1.2.
40 Guidelines, supra note 1, § 8A1.2.
41 Guidelines, supra note 1, § 8A1.2.
42 Guidelines, supra note 1, § 8A1.2.
43 Guidelines, supra note 1, § 8A1.2.
44 Guidelines, supra note 1, § 8A1.2.
45 Guidelines, supra note 1, § 8A1.2.
46 Paul E. Fiorelli, "Fine Reductions Through Effective Ethics Programs", *Albany Law Review*, Volume 56, (1992), 415.
47 Ibid: 413.
48 Jeffrey M. Kaplan, Joseph E. Murphy, Winthrop M. Swenson, *Compliance Programs and the Corporate Sentencing Guidelines. Preventing Criminal and Civil Liability* (New York: West Publishers, 1993 and later), Chapter 7, 25. US Federal Sentencing Commission, "Corporate Crime in America: Strengthening the "Good Citizen Corporation" (Washington: A National Symposium Sponsored by The U.S Sentencing Commission, 1995).
49 Jeffrey M. Kaplan, Joseph E. Murphy, Winthrop M. Swenson, *Compliance Programs and the Corporate Sentencing Guidelines. Preventing Criminal and Civil Liability* (New York: West Publishers, 1993 and later), Chapter 4, p. 4.
50 Ibid. Chapter 4, 10.
51 Ibid.
52 Lynn Sharp-Paine, *Cases in Leadership, Ethics and Organizational Integrity. A Strategic Perspective* (Chicago: Irwin 1997).
53 Lockheed Martin, *Ethics and Business Conduct. How the Ethics Process Works at Lockheed Martin.* Updated 2005.
54 Daniel Terris, *Ethics at Work. Creating Virtue at an American Corporation* (Lebanon, US: Brandeis University Press, University Press of New England, 2005), 78.

55 Jim Lyttle, "The effectiveness of humor in persuasion: The case of business ethics training", *Journal of General Psychology*, April 2001.
56 Daniel Terris, *Ethics at Work. Creating Virtue at an American Corporation* (Lebanon, US: Brandeis University Press, University Press of New England, 2005), 40.
57 Ibid: 47.
58 Ibid: 123.
59 Ibid: 130.
60 Joshua Joseph, "Integrating Ethics and Compliance Programs. Next Steps for Successful Implementation and Change" (Washington DC: ERC Fellows Program, Ethics Resource Center, 2001).
61 Ibid: 9.
62 Ibid: 12.
63 Ibid: 18.
64 Ibid: 19.
65 Ibid: 21.
66 Ibid: 23.
67 Ibid: 26.
68 Ibid: 28.
69 Jeffrey M. Kaplan, Joseph E. Murphy, Winthrop M. Swenson, *Compliance Programs and the Corporate Sentencing Guidelines. Preventing Criminal and Civil Liability* (New York: West Publishers, 1993 and later), Chapter 4, 22.
70 Ibid. Chapter 7, 12.
71 Ibid:18.
72 Joshua Joseph, "Integrating Ethics and Compliance Programs. Next Steps for Successful Implementation and Change" (Washington DC: ERC Fellows Program, Ethics Resource Center, 2001), 30.
73 Ibid: 48.
74 Ibid: 29.
75 Jeffrey M. Kaplan, Joseph E. Murphy, Winthrop M. Swenson, *Compliance Programs and the Corporate Sentencing Guidelines. Preventing Criminal and Civil Liability* (New York: West Publishers, 1993 and later), Chapter 7, 5
76 Ibid: 6.
77 Ibid: 6.
78 Joshua Joseph, "Integrating Ethics and Compliance Programs. Next Steps for Successful Implementation and Change" (Washington DC: ERC Fellows Program, Ethics Resource Center, 2001), 45.
79 Ibid: 34. Jeffrey M. Kaplan, Joseph E. Murphy, Winthrop M. Swenson, *Compliance Programs and the Corporate Sentencing Guidelines. Preventing Criminal and Civil Liability* (New York: West Publishers, 1993 and later).
80 Ibid: 40.
81 Jeffrey M. Kaplan, Joseph E. Murphy, Winthrop M. Swenson, *Compliance Programs and the Corporate Sentencing Guidelines. Preventing Criminal and Civil Liability* (New York: West Publishers, 1993 and later), Chapter 7, 27.
82 L. K. Trevinio, L. Hartman L. And M. Brown M., "Moral Person and Moral Manager: How executives develop a reputation for ethical leadership", *California Management Review*, 42 (4).
83 Joshua Joseph, "Integrating Ethics and Compliance Programs. Next Steps for Successful Implementation and Change" (Washington DC: ERC Fellows Program, Ethics Resource Center, 2001), 38.
84 Jeffrey F. Kaplan, "The Sentencing Guidelines: The First Ten Years", *Ethikos*, November/December 2001.
85 Ibid.
86 Ibid.
87 Ibid.
88 US Federal Sentencing Commission, "Corporate Crime in America: Strengthening the "Good Citizen Corporation" (Washington: A National Symposium Sponsored by The U.S Sentencing Commission, 1995).
89 Harvey L. Pitt and Karl A. Groskaumanis, "Minimizing Corporate Civil and Criminal Liability: A second Look at Corporate Codes of Conduct", (New York: Fried, Frank, Harrris, Shriver and Jacobsen Law firm, October 1989), 86.
90 Ibid:108.

91 William S. Laufer: "Corporate Liability, Risk Shifting and the Paradox of Compliance" in *Vanderbilt Law Review, Vanderbilt University School of Law*, Volume 52, (1999), October, 1345.
92 Ibid: 1349.
93 Ibid: 1350.
94 Ibid: 1351.
95 Ibid: 1380.
96 Ibid: 1395.
97 Ibid: 1405.
98 Elements of the case are selected from Loren Fox, *Enron: The Rise and Fall* (New Jersey: John Wiley and Sons, Inc, 2003), Debbie Thorne McAlister, O.C. Ferrell and Linda Ferrell, *Business and Society, A Strategic Approach to corporate social responsibility* (Boston: Houghton Mifflin Company, 2000). Leonard J. Brooks: *Business and Professional Ethics for Directors, Executives, and Accountants* (Toronto: Thomson, South-Western, 2003).
99 Loren Fox, *Enron: The Rise and Fall* (New Jersey: John Wiley and Sons, Inc, 2003), xii.
100 Ibid: 59.
101 Ibid: 126.
102 Leonard J. Brooks: *Business and Professional Ethics for Directors, Executives, and Accountants* (Toronto: Thomson, South-Western, 2003), 60.
103 Ibid: 60.
104 Ibid: 56.
105 O.C. Ferrell, John Fraedrich and Linda Ferrell, *Business Ethics. Ethical Decision Making and Cases* (Boston and New York: Houthton Mifflin Company, 2005), 62.
106 Leonard J. Brooks, *Business and Professional Ethics for Directors, Executives, and Accountants* (Toronto: Thomson, South-Western, 2003), 55.
107 O.C. Ferrell, John Fraedrich and Linda Ferrell, *Business Ethics. Ethical Decision Making and Cases* (Boston and New York: Houthton Mifflin Company, 2005), 63.
108 Sarbanes-Oxley Act, H.R. 3763-4.
109 Sarbanes-Oxley, H.R. 3763-6.
110 Sarbanes-Oxley, H.R. 3763-12.
111 Sarbanes-Oxley, Title III – Corporate Responsibility, H.R. 3763-31.
112 Sarbanes-Oxley, H.R. 3763-45- H.R. 3763-46.
113 Larry E. Rittenberg and Patricia K. Miller, *Sarbanes-Oxley Section 404 Work. Looking at the Benefits* (The ILA Research foundation, January 2005).

2. Business ethics, CSR, and corporate citizenship in Europe

The development of different kinds of values-driven management and corporate social responsibility in Europe has been promoted by the European Commission since the publication of its green paper, *Promoting a European Framework for Corporate Social Responsibility,* in 2001. This document can be interpreted as an effort of the Commission to promote good corporate citizenship, and may be considered as an important political and legal support of business ethics, values-driven management, and corporate social responsibility. The green paper was the foundation of European policies on corporate social responsibility and it was implemented with a communication from the commission in 2002.[1] The green paper represented the culmination of several years of discussion about business ethics and corporate social responsibility; however, the European concern for these issues is still rather recent. It is only during the last twenty years that these problems have reached the level of national government and finally become a concern for the European Commission, and other central political institutions. This process has lagged by the United States where, as mentioned previously, business ethics has been a focus for a longer time. Moreover, the implementation of the FSGO indicates a legal framework for business ethics, which does not exist in Europe.[2]

This lack of direct legal regulation does not imply that European corporations do not have concerns for business ethics and corporate social responsibility; rather, European corporations, due to their cultural and historical legacy, as well of the structure of welfare governments and European economic markets, have traditions of being aware of corporate social responsibility. In this context, the power of trade unions has been important for the availability of employee benefits and expressing the concerns for other stakeholders. The influence of the employees on the decisions of corporations is much more powerful in Europe than in the free market enterprise system of the United States.[3]

The following discussion examines the developments of a legal framework and concern for values-driven management in European economies. The focus is on the European Union and the necessity of corporate social responsibility and business ethics in the open European market. This section begins with a discussion of the historical background for the green paper, *Promoting a European Framework for Corporate Social Responsibility* then moves to an analysis of some of the most important theoretical influences on European concepts of business ethics and values-driven management that are at work in different companies. Looking more closely on the European Commission's proposal for promoting corporate social responsibility, the discussion explores the relationship between corporate social responsibility and corporate governance in Europe. The section ends by looking at the possibilities and particularities of the European approach to business ethics on the internal European market and externally in relation to the global economy.

2.1. European values as the background for corporate social responsibility

Even though the movement of values-driven management and corporate social responsibility started later in Europe than in the United States, some important dimensions of the values of European business culture provide the basis for ethics and responsibility of its corporations. In describing these values, it is important to be aware of the diversity and difference of European business culture compared to the United States and Japan. The Second World War created a sense of responsibility and commitment to community in both southern and northern Europe, although the social structures and economic systems were very different. In general, Europe was characterized by a closer link between markets and governments in the postwar welfare states. This is probably the basis for the many recent initiatives to ensure awareness, transparency, and promotion of corporate social responsibility in Europe.[4]

The history of European business ethics may be described as a combination between Protestant ethics and Catholic social philosophy, which have traditionally been the important ideologies of business leaders. In contrast to management philosophy in the United States, business ethics has not been very predominant in European management thought; rather, it was the figure of the paternalistic capitalist who, as the father of a family, owned the company and felt a natural inclination of social responsibility towards his workers and employees.[5] In the European context, businesses play an integrated role in society. Strong states and governments have been more active in building social relations and welfare states, so that the movement of corporate philanthropy has not been as strong as in the United States. The figure of the Protestant or Catholic paternalistic manager was based less on corporate philanthropy than on mutual relations of obligation between workers and capitalists due to the traditional moral norms of society and a closer relation between management and local community. Moreover, the movement of workers' rights and strong socialist and communist parties and have also played an important role in the institutionalization of values of business ethics and corporate responsibility in Europe. They have also defined the relationship between management, workers, and society as one of conflict, where there is little space for common values to be respected.

As in the United States, in the 1960s and 1970s different more or less radical criticisms of behavior of corporations emerged that influenced future focus on business ethics and social responsibility. Among these criticisms, the environmental movement in Germany and Britain may be mentioned as an important factor of change. In the 1970s, many European countries were marked by economic crisis and as a reaction to this development, countries like Germany, Britain, and Denmark elected conservative or center-right governments that emphasized deregulation and the necessity of free markets.

The result was more focus of economic profit and growth, rather than social responsibility. In the 1990s, the opening of a common and unified economic market through the European Union may have been one of the factors that increased emphasis on social responsibility. Moreover, many European corporations see the common market as a gateway to global markets. In France, Britain, and Germany there was increased interest of the relationship between the corporation and society. In Denmark, the social democratic government of the 1990s created several initiatives to involve corporations in the community. Furthermore, as head of the European Commission Jacques Delors made concern for corporate social responsibility one of the EU's areas of concentration. He contributed to the establishment of the European Business Network for Social Cohesion (EBNSC) in 1995.[6] These initiatives were put forward in a time of transformation and change, when national economic markets were diminished in favor of one unified European economic market.

In addition to these policy developments, there are some aspects of European business culture that explain the charactersistic European focus on corporate social responsibility. Given the diversity of European cultures, the concept of business ethics may not be the same in the different parts of the continent. Indeed, it is necessary to differentiate between, among other divisions, southern and northern countries in the EU, but, as a general commonality, European business leaders consider themselves as managers and their organizations as an integrated part of community.[7] Accordingly, profit maximization is not considered to be the main goal of the company. The company is, in principle, regarded as a participant in society with social obligations. Moreover, European business leaders tend to emphasize long-term strategic thinking rather than short-term deals.[8]

To a larger degree than some American companies, European business organizations are marked by a high number of internal and external negotiations, in which the corporation considers communications and deliberations with employees and external stakeholders to be very important for decision-making. Internal negotiations include dialogue with employees on important decisions in the social market economy, in some instances with employee representation on the corporate board.[9] In contrast to American companies, it is emphasized that decision-making can be a mixture between bottom-up and top-down processes, where management naturally enters into dialogue with stakeholders.[10] In this way, the ideal European management style is considered to be based on responsible concerns for customers and employees. The framework for decision-making in an international environment between European countries requires respect for differences between different members of the organization. The impact of European management on global markets may precisely be this ability to cope with diversity, because this is already a standard operating condition in European markets.[11]

A reason for the absence of formal and systematic programs of values-driven management based on employee compliance to pre-established rules of ethics may be that Europeans tend to be antiauthoritarian and very skeptical towards formal systems of management. Indeed, it is only recently that different strategies of values-driven management have been proposed in European countries, and ethics have in many cases been introduced as an informal basis for decision-making in managerial judgment rather than through formal systems of "ethics bureaucracies." In this context, it is worth noting the elitist conception of good and charismatic leadership, and the high-integrity manager, that have been very popular in southern Europe, for example in France.

The core of the European concept of business ethics and European management could be defined as a humanistic tradition respecting the high value of the individual and concern for the right to privacy. The basic ethical principles of autonomy, dignity, integrity, and vulnerability in the framework of solidarity and responsibility can be seen as an expression of this concern.[12] The concern for humanistic individualism in Europe is also expressed in the concern for the general education of managers, rather than reducing them to mere bureaucrats or technocrats.[13] The humanism of the European tradition is furthermore expressed in a certain respect for the rights of employees to do what they want in their private lives. The corporation cannot be a totalitarian prison demanding total employee commitment.

The social responsibility and the humanism of European business culture may be documented by the strong Socialist and Christian Democratic influence in European countries. This is combined with strong egalitarianism in most Scandinavian countries. In the context of the welfare state, business is marked by a kind of paternalism emphasizing the relation to community rather than the ideal free market; therefore, many European managers stress long-term survival based on concerns for community rather than immediate profit maximization.[14] In this context, it is also important to remember the significance of history and cultural traditions in most European countries. It is arguable that the many wars involving European countries may have led to skepticism towards ideology, authority, and bureaucracies of different kinds. Europeans are, for example, much more critical towards whistle-blowing than Americans, because they do not believe that they can trust authorities enough to tell them about problems with other employees, or ethical dilemmas in relation to other stakeholders.

The spirit of corporate social responsibility in European corporations is based on a substantial recognition of the claims of relevant stakeholders. Accordingly, European companies do not value shareholder interests and the economic bottom line in the same way as many American companies. Placed in the social market economy, European companies are implicitly marked by their concern for their different stakeholders, including employees, clients, creditors, local communities, and so on.[15] Different companies recognize that they have legitimate obligations to different kinds of stakeholders. This may include an obligation to local community, to a particular profession, to the employees, or to the public at large. The spirit is that the company is a part of society and that it should behave as a good corporate citizen. It should comply with government regulations and collaborate with relevant partners in order to secure long-term development and trust among its partners.

Indeed, it could be argued that this description of European corporate social responsibility is rather idealistic. It could be described as a traditional concept that ignores increasing pressure on corporations to demonstrate good economic performance instead of social concerns. Diversity signifies that there are many differences between European countries with regard to organization of economic systems. Accordingly, the cultural and historical context of social responsibility varies in each country.

The United Kingdom has many similarities with the American free market enterprise system. The structure of the business system is based on Anglo-Saxon liberal economics with property rights and common law. Traditionally, in this system, the shareholders' interests were considered to have priority. Though London is one of the financial centers of the world, Britain may still be considered as a part of European culture. An indication of this is its strong cultural skepticism towards business, based on a combination of popular egalitarianism and an aristocratic attitude to concerns about money. Contrary to this, Margaret Thatcher's economic policy in the 1980s involved strong deregulation and incentives to generate profit.[16] The conservatives wanted to promote free market business through tax reform and privatization polity; however, in the 1990s, the movement for socially responsibile business became very strong in Britain. The different consultancy groups on sustainability (with John Elkington as founder) and ethical accounting, Accountability8000 emerged as the result of pioneering activities by different British companies like the Body Shop and the Co-operative Bank.

New partnerships between state and business had high priority for the new Labour government of Tony Blair. In 1998, Blair's government established a unit for global corporate citizenship in the foreign ministry. It also set up a ministerial unit for corporate social responsibility in 2000, which is now a part of the ministry for e-commerce and competition.[17]

In contrast to the United Kingdom, the business culture in the Latin countries (Italy, Spain, and France) are influenced by the Catholic view on the role of business in community. In these countries, business is traditionally closely related to community values. There is some skepticism towards the free market and business is viewed as integrated in the culture of each country. Italy may be characterized by a strong state sector and many family-based small businesses. Northern Italy has heavy industries marked by political confrontation between employers and employees. Traditionally, Italy has been marked by high unemployment, but also a very strong informal, "black" economy. Many parts of financial and economic markets have not been very strongly regulated. Indeed, it is a matter of discussion whether the informal Italian economy is a premodern or a postmodern phenomenon.[18] In this context, the problem of economic efficiency has been highly debated. In general, American principles of scientific management are not used in Italy; however, Italian businesses are undergoing strong change, and there has been great interest in the free European market.[19] In Italy, business ethics has, apart from the workers' movement, been dominated by classical philosophy going back to Aristotle and Thomas Aquinas. Accordingly, there is long tradition of talking about the social responsibility of corporations as integrated in the culture of society. Indeed, this idea is based on the concept of profitability as a combination of economic, social, and environmental concerns.[20]

Spain has many similarities to Italy. Since the death of Franco and the introduction of new democratic principles of government, there has been increased optimism in Spain with strong economic growth and high levels of investment. Along with socialist modernization free trade unions have also emerged.[21] Spain has, indeed, been characterized of concerns for social responsibility, due to different Catholic conceptions of business ethics. There has been a rather strong environmental movement since the 1980s. With the installation of democracy in 1975, Spanish companies have increasingly been focusing on corporate social responsibility.

The influence of Catholic thought and philosophy is also present in France. Traditionally, the French management style has been rather elitist.[22] Moreover, there is also a traditional conception of conflict between employers and employees in industrial relations.[23] Before the socialist government of 1981, and after the Second World War, French politics was dominated by the conservatism of De Gaulle, who focused on the importance of the nation and the values of French culture. Managers were educated at elite schools, such as the grandes écoles (e.g., the École Nationale d'Administration), les polytechniques, or the famous business school INSEAD, which is located just outside Paris. These schools imposed a sense of responsibility for the revolutionary ideals of the French nation on her leaders; however, the French economic system has not been as strong as Germany or the United Kingdom. There are service industries and manufacturing industries, but also industries for luxury goods. Since the 1970s and 1980s, France has been marked by the lack of rich institutional investors and it has faced difficulty dealing with the growing importance of capital markets.[24] After the emergence of the socialist government in the 1980s, there was a sense of revolution in France as the socialists nationalized many companies; however, the management of the new state institutions remains rather elitist. In the 1990s, many companies went back into private hands. France has been marked by a strong legalization of business systems and many people have considered the legal framework of business to be too bureaucratic, but this legal framework has also put strong pressure on the French business system to comply. In general, French business has been positive towards one single European market, although there is some fear that this will have a negative impact on national industries.

German business culture has also been characterized by a strong legalism and regulated economic markets. The rule of law of the "Rechtsstaat" is very important. We may even say "what is not permitted by the law is [forbidden]."[25] This is the background for a rather conservative business culture.[26] The commercial code regulates many aspects of business life. Germany may be characterized as a *soziale Marktwirtschaft* (socialized market economy), where the business culture includes many socially oriented companies. This model can also be called *Rhenish capitalism.*[27] The German concept of capitalism is still very traditional in the sense that network structures with strong unions and professional organizations on the one hand, and industrial hierarchical networks of corporations on the other still dominate the picture. German business culture does not consider shareholders as a primary concern of the firm, but rather a long-term interest. German business culture is also characterized by high wages and strong trade unions. German commercial legislation has tried to introduce social responsibility in the law by securing employee representation in larger companies.

In the beginning of the 1970s Germany started to have its first economic crisis since the Second World War. The phenomenon of *stagflation* was present. Therefore, in the 1980s, the Christian Democratic government tried to deregulate some of the state activities in order to make the market stronger; however, the strong unions and strong representation of employers' organizations was a major factor of power. Moreover, the emergence of a powerful environmental movement in Germany has significantly influenced the perception of social responsibility in European companies. The new Green Party in German politics represented an important challenge to the traditional structure of the economy.[28] Following the Greens, the movement of politically conscious consumers has, indeed, been powerful in Germany; however, in general, due to the need for political reunification and due to the economic advantage of being situated in the middle of Europe, Germany has been rather favorable to the idea of one single market. The German network model of soziale Marktwirtschaft may be somewhat inflexible to new initiatives like CSR, but it may be helped by the tradition of green activism and business ethics. Accordingly, in the German context, CSR cannot really be separated from issues of sustainability and corporate citizenship.[29] This focus on sustainability linked to ecological concerns is even stronger in Austria, which also works with the concept of CSR as a close relationship between business ethics and corporate citizenship.[30]

There are many similarities between Germany, the Scandinavian countries (Denmark, Sweden, Norway, and Finland) and the Netherlands. The concept of a *negotiation economy*, based on communicative rationality, can apply to all these countries. The welfare state conflicts and power struggles are solved in different negotiations among private and public stakeholders. This spirit of the advanced welfare state marks the business culture in the Netherlands. Society is characterized by industrial development and large exports and imports with other European trading partners. The Netherlands experienced deregulation and privatization during the 1980s as a response to the growing welfare state. The country has a large service industry and technology-oriented production.[31] In general, there is a high level of education. The Netherlands is also marked by a strong cooperative movement, which has influenced the perception of corporate social responsibility. Dutch multinational companies, like Royal Dutch Shell, have also worked with ethics and corporate social responsibility. As in Germany, there is a strong environmental movement, which has shaped the demand for corporate social responsibility.

In Scandinavia, the concept of a negotiation economy may be an approach to describe the economic background of the growing emphasis on corporate social responsibility. Norms and the economic distributions of goods are negotiated at different levels of society in tension between conflict and compromise. It is agreed that there are many kinds of preferences and rationality that should be taken into account. Political rationality and economics are mixed in a common agreement about the need to have unified understanding of problems and conflicts.[32] This kind of economic rationality is based on different concerns at many levels of society. Scandinavian countries are characterized by strong welfare states and mixed economies between the public and private sectors.

In this space, economic relations are negotiated at many different levels, between unions and employers, between the state and unions, and between different state authorities. Economic and political power is important in these negotiations, but there are also other kinds of rationality in these games: between parliament, workers, and employers. Different stakeholders and interest groups may have important influences on economic development. A negotiation economy is a situation where many important decisions are made through institutionalized negotiations based on communicative rationality and compromise.[33] The ultimate horizon of these negotiations is the rule of law based on a normative view of the legality of the state. Legislation is characterized by general principles according to the rule of law, which are interpreted locally in different negotiation games and communicative spheres of validity.[34]

On this basis, the Danish Social Democratic government put ethics and corporate social responsibility as a high priority during the 1990s. The Danish

Social Ministry and the Copenhagen Center for Corporate Social Responsibility, which was created by the government in 1998, promoted this.[35] The government also established an informal commission from 2001-2002 of the Ministry of Trade, which was to function as a "think tank" for corporate social responsibility. The initiative has been combined with different initiatives sponsored by private firms for the promotion of corporate social responsibility, including the activities of Novo Nordisk on bioethics, and the development of stakeholder relations and human rights.

The Danish model of corporate social responsibility is very characteristic of the way CSR was reintroduced in Europe after having been on the American agenda for many years. It is striking considering that CSR in Europe, in the beginning, did not refer to a global concept of business ethics, but rather a specific concern about how to change welfare state policy into workfare policy.[36] In 1990, the Danish Social Democratic government was inspired by EU policies to fight social poverty and exclusion by active labor market policies. CSR was, in this context, an important instrument for creating partnerships between private companies and public authorities based on active and flexible social policies. Accordingly, CSR was an instrument to redefine social policy as work activation policy. With the idea of an open and comprehensive work market, the government promoted the idea that corporations should be socially responsible through their treatment of their workers, including providing a comprehensive labor market with work for the elderly, handicapped, partially ill, et cetera. The state gave support to companies so that they could hire such disadvantaged people and to help integrate them into society. Through social work policies, the government had reason to believe that corporations would help to support the development of supportive labor markets. [37]

The Danish government has tried to formulate a closer link between corporate governance and corporate social responsibility. In December 2001, a committee (Nørby-udvalget) was established by the Danish Government in order to propose recommendations for good corporate governance. Its recommendations are important for understanding the interaction between corporate social responsibility and corporate governance. The Danish report on corporate governance can be seen as a development of earlier reports on corporate governance and corporate social responsibility, for example the United Kingdom Cadbury report on the financial aspects of corporate governance from 1992. The Nørby report focuses on operational recommendations in order to ensure good corporate governance. In this sense, the proposals by this committee can be seen as one possible concrete development of a strategy for corporate social responsibility in the European context. Following the OECD guidelines, the report emphasizes that openness, transparency, responsibility, and equal treatment of shareholders should be an important principle for corporate governance.

The shift in November 2001 to a liberal-conservative government presumably would have changed the concerns for corporate social responsibility. In fact, the new government continued the efforts to make corporate social responsibility an important part of Danish policy. In autumn 2002, the government hosted an international conference on the topic of "mainstreaming corporate social responsibility across Europe." It was declared that not only corporate social responsibility, but the wider notion of corporate responsibility, had high priority. In fact, the liberal-conservative government seemed to change the focus from national social issues to corporate social responsibility and globalization.

Case 28. Business excellence and corporate social responsibility: The case of Grundfos

The case of the Danish firm Grundfos has been selected because it is a very good illustration of a corporation searching for business excellence by making an ethical effort. The company represents a classic Danish case of CSR, and of a company operating in an inclusive labor market. In its rhetorical self-representation the firm wants to appear as an organization with strong social values and concern for social cohesion; however, there is also a tension with present efforts to appear as a modern global company. The firm seeks to combine social embeddedness with international ethics.

Grundfos has been one of the pioneers in values-driven management, business ethics, and corporate social responsibility in Denmark. This company is a good example of traditional European business culture. The company was founded by an engineer, Poul Due Jensen, in 1943. The firm mainly produced different kinds of advanced self-regulating electronic pumps that are sold all over the world. Although it started with very few employees, the company has grown to have a worldwide presence. Grundfos has more than 4500 employees globally and an annual production of more than ten million pump units.[38] Grundfos is owned by a foundation that was established in 1975. The foundation owns more than eighty-five percent of the shares of the capital of Grundfos Holding. The rest is owned by family and employees.

Since 1995-1996, the firm has worked with a combination of *business excellence and TQM in its different factories.* This approach to values has a goal to build a new culture that represents all sixty companies that constitute the international corporation. The aim is that the activity and performance of the firm should not only be measured by economic and productive measures, but also by other values. The firm emphasizes the importance of a good working environment and protecting vulnerable and weak employees. Moreover, the company seeks to establish a comfortable workplace based on responsibility for everyone in everyday working life. Some even argue that the social minister, Karen Jespersen, was inspired by Grundfos's idea of an inclusive workplace when she initiated the Danish policy on CSR in the mid-1990s. [39]

Grundfos has tried to develop a culture of "soft values" where issues of ethics, respect for the internal and external environment, and customer and employee satisfaction are included in the measurement of corporate performance. Grundfos works with the social and ethical values, partly inspired by a famous Danish poet and theologian, Nikolaj Frederik Severin Grundtvig. Grundfos emphasizes that economic returns are important but do not have any meaning without ethics. The firm has tried to formulate ethical policies in order to include all stakeholders, not only customers (who are considered as extremely important) and employees. This includes suppliers, who, according the company's values, should not be exposed to high pressure from a large firm just because they are smaller and don't have the same power.

Recently, Grundfos has worked to integrate issues of corporate social responsibility and sustainable development in its policy for a good corporate culture. The company expresses its fundamental values as based on a culture of cooperation and innovation. They express their values as "Be>Think>Innovate," which is central to the exercise of responsibility of the firm. Responsibility is considered as essential for a trustworthy company that also focuses on innovation in a global world. Grundfos links responsibility to sustainability, by connecting the production of pumps with the effort to monitor the production of raw materials and to create durable products.[40]

With this concern for sustainability and responsibility, there has been a change in the firm's branding and marketing strategies. The firm is no longer exclusively a producer of pumps, but rather a contributor to sustainable development and a player in the global effort to solve the problems of water supply. This may be by inventing pumps that can help to supply water resources from deep down in the Earth, pumps that can help to get drinking water from salt water, or recycle already existing water resources. Though these efforts, Grundfos link responsibility with technological innovation.[41]

The case of Grundfos illustrates the close connection between values-driven management and excellence in economic business affairs. Gundfos is interesting as a local family-owned company that has grown to an international firm, and yet still seeks to practice social responsibility towards local community. There is a close relationship between responsibility and the focus on new concepts of management and innovation. The firm does not consider ethics as external to its economic activities, but rather as an internal measure and contribution to good corporate performance. For Grundfos, "good ethics is good business."

2.2. Concepts of corporate social responsibility in Europe

It is difficult to say that there is a unified concept of business ethics in Europe due to the diversity of different practices among national cultures; however, in an overview of the most important approaches in the short history of European business ethics, a general distinction holds between academic business ethics and the movement of corporate social responsibility in different European firms and other organizations.

With regard to academic business ethics, some of the first university chairs in the field were established in the mid-1980s. Some mention Switzerland as the country with the first full chair devoted to the subject, but this is difficult to authoritatively establish.[42] There has, however, been a remarkable increase in the university and business school study of ethics since the 1980s, with more than thirty chairs in the EU today. In opposition to American education and research in business ethics, which focuses on case studies and micro-issues in corporate ethics, European scholars tend to focus on macro-issues: the relation between politics, the market, and the economy. Moreover, European business ethics has, in addition to research in traditional ethical concepts, like utilitarianism, deontology, and teleology, been focused on a grand theory of society, like the approaches found in the philosophy and sociology of Habermas and Luhmann.

Since the foundation of the European Business Ethics Network (EBEN) there has been a growing focus on the integration of different approaches to business ethics. EBEN tries to unite practitioners and academics working simultaneously with macrosystems analysis, mesa-organizational operations, and micro-individual practices.[43] EBEN has established a number of national networks in countries like Spain, the Netherlands, the United Kingdom, and Italy. Representatives from the corporate world also participate in these networks, so there is greater interaction between different groups working with corporate social responsibility.

An example of the macrosystem approach to business ethics is the integrative business ethics of Peter Ulrich.[44] He presents a general theory of society and interaction between different social systems, which argues for a critical analysis of the moral content of economic rationality. Business ethics is considered as a reflective way of dealing with normative questions of a modern market economy in general. Ulrich is inspired by Habermas's concept of communicative rationality, which is applied to problems of business ethics and corporate social responsibility.

In Denmark, the work on values-driven management by Ole Thyssen is another important voice in this tradition. Thyssen formulates a general system theory of organization as the basis for his view on business ethics.[45] Organizations are systems of action and decision-making. Ethics is defined as a second-order cybernetic rationality and self-reflection that helps to make modern organization more efficient and self-perspective. Ethics is viewed as kind of communication that makes the organization more transparent and sensible to the environment. Organizations are systems of communication governed by different media of interaction in systems (e.g., money, power, ethics), or rather rationalities of exchange. Organizations are confronted with inflated demands, and the individualization and victimization of people in organizations.

It is an important dimension of the work of Peter Ulrich and Ole Thyssen that they emphasize the democratic aspects of values-driven management. Ethics is a way to create a broader basis of legitimacy of organizational decisions. This is the sense of Habermas's concept of the "force of the argument" and "domination-free dialogue." Instead of technological solutions based on organizational and bureaucratic power structures, democratic communication and values-driven management improve the sensibility and flexibility of decision-making. This concept of business ethics has been quite popular in the northern European countries. The reason may be that values-driven management fits very well in a society based on a negotiation economy, where rationality emerges from communicative interactions. Thyssen is aware of the constructive aspects of business ethics, in which mutual values in a postconventional society are constructed through compromise and involve communication among people from different life-worlds and parts of society.[46]

In the francophone world, Ricœur has had some impact on theoretical business ethics.[47] As discussed (see chapter 1, section 3), Ricœur defines ethics as the "search for the good life with and for the other in just institutions." The idea of the good life is linked to the development of the individual. Ricœur's philosophy is a reflective hermeneutics trying to bridge the gap between an existentialist, universalistic, and prudential concepts of ethics. From this perspective, ethics is not only an issue about the function of systems in organizations but, indeed, about personal consciousness, self-respect, and responsibility. The role of personal judgment and the search for recognition in ethics cannot be ignored. Ricœur's philosophy proposes a vision of ethics that integrates individuals with "the other" in just institutions.[48]

Emphasizing the role of individuals in decision-making fits with the southern European ethical tradition focusing on personal virtues and responsibilities; however, such views on ethics can be found all over Europe. According to this concept, ethics is based on the capacity of leadership among good managers. The ideal manager has the capacity to engage and communicate with employees in a way that promotes virtue and creativity in a common space.[49] Such a philosophy of leadership is based on the capacity of the leader to communicate and be a virtuous person motivating the community of the firm toward greater and better performance.

Even though these theories of business ethics have had great impact, the European view of corporate social responsibility has, in particular, been influenced by concepts of stakeholder theory based on the idea of the triple bottom line, measuring simultaneously social, environmental, and economic performance. During the 1990s, British consultancy firms had great popularity working with the idea of sustainable development inspired by the report of the Brundtland Commission. As has already been discussed, many firms have been working with concepts from John Elkington, who generalizes the concept of sustainability in accordance with the principles of the triple bottom line, or the "three Ps" of people, planet, and profit.

The idea of sustainability has not only influenced environmental business ethics, but it has become a central concept of European social responsibility. This is combined with an extension of stakeholder theory to consider the interests of employees, customers, clients, suppliers, the public, and the environment as legitimate stakeholders of the firm.[50] It is argued that stakeholder theory based on the triple bottom line ensures long-term performance of the firm. Elkington defines "corporate transparency" to different stakeholders and the public as paramount for a new style of management. Transparency is a basic condition for corporate values-driven management. Moreover, the strategy of sustainable development and triple bottom-line accounting emphasizes the importance of independent auditing and reporting procedures.[51] In the 1990s, there was a dramatic increase in corporate social and environmental reporting due to the perception on the part of European companies of the necessity to protect the environment, and a desire to improve public relations in order to get a competitive advantage. This has been documented in recent studies.[52]

Following the UN definition of sustainability, human rights are also important for the European concept of corporate social responsibility. It is argued that standards of economic, social, and cultural rights are central to the socially responsible company. The many possible human rights include employee rights to proper work conditions, health and safety, and organizational freedom. Moreover, issues of nondiscrimination and equality, rights of privacy, and freedom of expression may be put forward as fundamental rights implied in the concept of social responsibility.[53] In many corporations the focus on human rights from a global perspective has been combined with their work on stakeholder dialogue and stakeholder reporting.

The background for this shift during the 1990s may indeed be found in increased expectations of stakeholders regarding the ethical performance of companies. Political consumers, in relation to issues of food technology or environmental protection, have been very visible during the last twenty years. Moreover, the methods of activists have become more sophisticated and damaging for the public image of corporations. This was the case, for example, with the ATTACK movement, whose approach included actions in public space that brought attention to the "questionable" activities of companies on specific issues. The need for social responsibility is also motivated by the changing role of governments in a global society, where companies act freely across national boarders. Global trade puts more emphasis on the respect for human rights by business-to-business partners and suppliers in third world countries. Public demands for increased disclosure is a fact in many countries where the media are becoming more powerful and sophisticated. Finally, markets are, in general, becoming more competitive, requiring increased performance of companies, which cannot be improved by means of traditional methods of management.

In fact, economic arguments are very visible in the European movement for corporate social responsibility. Ethical values, and respect for people and communities, rather than exclusive focus on shareholder value, have been promoted as bottom-line benefits. It seems to be that companies with an emphasis on stakeholder dialogue and ethics codes have more growth and better financial performance. Moreover, improved work conditions contribute to minimizing operating costs and making employees more motivated to work. It may also attract better employees in a situation of competitive labor markets. It is also argued that concerns for social responsibility may enhance brand reputation.

This is documented by an increased focus on values among costumers who refuse to buy products made by companies who do not respect fundamental human rights, for example by using sweatshops or child labor. Moreover, concerns for animal welfare seem, in some cases, to be as important as product quality. Finally, socially responsible behavior is important for the increased number of institutional investors with strong codes of ethics.

Many European companies have started to work with the implementation of corporate social responsibility. They try to make it a part of their mission, values, or ethics code. Typically, they try to include a broader number of stakeholders in their formulation of strategy and image. Ethics becomes an issue of corporate governance and strategic planning. Moreover, middle managers and employees at other levels of the organization are mobilized in training programs or ethics courses. In some cases, corporations may even put up reward systems in order to promote ethics. Many companies realize that social and environmental auditing and reporting is paramount in order to take ethics codes seriously.

Banks and institutional investors are working consciously with ethical investment policies and developing social auditing practices. They are developing ethical marketing strategies that have well-defined rules for socially responsible investments, excluding for example tobacco, animal testing, and arms production.

On the basis of concrete experiences of European companies, an emerging concept of corporate social responsibility can be defined.[54] In general, corporate social responsibility is about ethics and virtue, and it cannot replace legal regulation. Even though it provides economic benefits, it cannot be solely promoted on instrumental grounds. Priorities include concerns for the wellbeing and creative development of employees, but also a serious and necessary dialogue with other stakeholders. It is very important that the standards of social accounting are externally verified. Corporate social responsibility cannot be exclusively based on the experience of a single company, but implies generally applicable concepts of social capital and the moral market. Sustainability, transparency, and accountability based on the triple bottom line are central notions in the European vision of business ethics.

In addition, European standards should be in accordance with international efforts to achieve global business ethics. European companies seek to comply with international regulations, for example the UN codes for global conduct of business, the ILO standards declarations, and principles and OECD Guidelines for Multinational Enterprises.

Box 16. Integrating ethics in business education:
The case of the European Academy for Business in Society

After debating for many years and as a result of European policies on corporate social responsibility, a number of business people, academics, and politicians took the initiative to establish the European Academy for Business in Society (EABIS), which involves major business schools such as INSEAD, Ashridge in the United Kingdom, and the Copenhagen Business School. [55]

The organization's members also include CSR Europe, a lobby organization of European firms that promotes corporate social responsibility; Accountability, a London-based NGO working for new accounting standards; and the Copenhagen Center, a semi-governmental but independent center working for corporate social responsibility.

The EABIS follows the recommendations of the European Parliament and the European Commission of integrating corporate social responsibility and ethics in corporate practice as supplemental to the legal obligations of the firm. Corporate social responsibility expresses the engagement of the firm with a variety of stakeholders. It is not only considered as a limitation of the activities of the firm, but rather as an integrated part of its business.

From this perspective, ethics and corporate social responsibility represent an investment rather than a cost. The European Parliament emphasizes that the need for corporate social responsibility is driven by business itself, because stakeholder dialogue contributes to a more sustainable business. The goal of corporate social responsibility is, therefore, a better social environment for the firm.

The EABIS promotes these ideas by developing the awareness of corporate social responsibility in business ethics education curricula and by bridging the link between practitioners and academics. To this end, the EABIS initiatied different study groups on corporate social responsibility at its first meeting, held at INSEAD in 2002.

The groups worked on issues such as globalization, innovation, knowledge, strategy, leadership, stakeholder relations, and creating a policy framework. Such discussion groups and the general activities of the Academy were considered as the basis for forming an alliance between the different members of the organization.

The EABIS emphasized that there is a close link between economics and corporate social responsibility. The slogan of the organization, "CSR: It Simply Works Better," emphasizes the internal link between ethics and economics, between social responsibility and economic sustainability. On this basis, the Academy tried to lobby for research money from the European Commission in order to promote the knowledge gain in Europe in the field of corporate social responsibility.

The EABIS constitutes an organization moving corporate social responsibility to the center of the corporate agenda and strategy. This was confirmed at the second international meeting in Copenhagen in 2003 where there was dialogue between representatives from major business schools discussing how to make corporate social responsibility an integrated part of their MBA and other educational programs.

2.3. EU efforts on social responsibility: The EU green paper on social responsibility

The European Community has increasingly worked on social responsibility on the basis of the initiatives of companies that have been very active in the field. The work of the European Commission effectively summarizes the views of many European corporations who have taken initiatives to install different kinds of values-driven management and efforts to improve their social responsibility in relation to different kinds of social, environmental, and economic pressures. Through these actions, companies want to make their stakeholders aware of their good intentions. As discussed, the European approach is based on stakeholder theory, and European company initiatives relate to shareholders, investors, public authorities, consumers, and NGOs. The efforts of the EU to support this development began in 1993 when Jacques Delors, as President of the Commission of the European Community, made an appeal to European businesses to take part in solving the problems of social exclusion, and to establish a European network of companies that could help in this work.

In 2000, an appeal was made by the European Council in Lisbon to the CEOs of European corporations to promote social responsibility and good practices in relation to issues like lifelong learning, better work conditions, the inclusion of socially weak groups, and general efforts to promote sustainable development.[56] At this meeting, it was proposed that European corporations should not undertake commitments that transcend ordinary legal and conventional demands, and that they should improve standards for social development, environmental protection, and social inclusion. On this basis, the Commission proposed to establish a green paper on social responsibility of corporations at its meeting in Stockholm.[57]

The green paper promotes social responsibility and ecological sustainability as basic components of the creation of new partnerships, as well as local and international commitments of companies. Not only multinationals, but all kinds of companies are supposed to be encouraged to be engaged for corporate social responsibility. The green paper on social responsibility should be considered from the perspective of the EU focus on social responsibility, after the meeting in Lisbon, where many social goods were promoted as a part of EU's strategy. This strategy for Europe is defined as a strategy to "become the most competitive and dynamic knowledge economy in the world" that is able to create stable economic growth with more and better jobs and greater social coherence.[58] The European Commission argues for a broad debate, where the actors play a larger role in the creation of a better society with a sustainable relation to nature. The social responsibility of business should be considered from the perspective of increased focus on values and the rights of Europeans. At the meeting in Göteborg in June 2001, it was stated that economic growth, social coherence, and protection of the environment are closely connected.

The globalization process, with its increased emphasis on the environment and transparency due to information technology, is one of the reasons for the need of increased social responsibility. It is argued that emphasizing socially responsible business is necessary to survive in a global economy. Social responsibility is put forward as a part of the economic strategy of the firm. The EU is aware that public policy plays a major role in the development of greater social responsibility in companies; therefore, the European governments wanted to become active in the work for social responsibility. The emerging strategy of the European Community is to establish a general EU framework in order to develop unity in methods, principles, and practice, as well as to develop ideas for social responsibility.[59] This development of methods for good practice and the creation of new ideas are also based on efforts to secure the most effective use of available resources.

The European Commission defines social responsibility as a concept where corporations voluntarily integrate social and environmental concerns into their business activities and interactions with stakeholders. Social responsibility is described as something that goes beyond the legal requirements, so that companies not only act with minimal respect for the law, but also do something more to invest in human capital and the relations to the different stakeholders of the firm. Social responsibility should not, however, only be conceived as an alternative to laws and legal regulation, but rather as means to accomplish social excellence in the corporation.

The green paper focuses on the fact that such an extra effort for social responsibility may increase both a firm's competitive advantage and productivity at the same time. It is argued that there may be many positive effects of a corporation's activities to work for corporate social responsibility. Among the positive effects are the creation of a better working environment and the possibility of getting better and more motivated workers. Moreover, good companies with social responsibility are likely to get increased awareness and attention from consumers and investors. In addition, criticism for lacking social responsibility might be very damaging to a company's good reputation and image. The social index of different stock trading centers shows that investments in social responsibility and sustainability have an impact on the economic status of the company.

Human capital, health, and security are among the important internal dimensions mentioned. It is important for a firm to be aware of the importance of human capital to increase its competitiveness. Social responsibility focuses on the concern for the employees of the corporation. The themes of social responsibility include increased employee influence on decision-making, better information, concern for the well-being of employees, concern for affirmative action and nondiscrimination, and concern for better health benefits. Moreover, general concerns for health and security in the workplace are promoted as important issues in times when many companies struggle with change and structural adjustments.

In particular, integration of the firm into the local community is mentioned as an important goal for the firm. It should deal with the development of local capital for social aims in the community; hence, it is stressed that responsible behavior concerning environmental policies may create win-win situations, where an integration of environmental concerns (e.g., life cycles and company strategy) can improve the firm's economy. Such external concerns for local community and the environment express a social responsibility that goes beyond internal stakeholders, like employees and shareholders towards external stakeholders, such as customers, suppliers, public authorities, and local NGOs.[60]

More broadly, the approach to social responsibility proposed by the European Commission recommends promoting human rights by companies. It argues that European corporations should establish codes of conduct, including respect for human rights. Indeed, values programs in different areas of business ethics are considered important for the establishment of responsible attitudes.[61] It is, however, emphasized that codes of conduct should not be considered as alternatives to binding national, European, or international laws and regulations. These regulations secure minimal standards, while codes of conducts and other regulative programs can help to improve standards beyond existing basic regulations.[62] The codes of conduct that address human rights enacted by the Danish industry organization are put forward as an example.

In general, the green paper of the European Commission proposes a holistic approach to socially responsible business. It is recommended that companies develop general management methods for social responsibility, implying that different kinds of stakeholders, consumers, investors, and other internal and external stakeholders may play an important role for the social responsibility of the firm. Traditional models of management, leadership, organizational behavior, or strategic management may have become inadequate in the present situation. Management should introduce new models for strategy, for example, values-driven management, which can include concerns for social responsibility.

The importance of different kinds of accounting, reporting, auditing, and other evaluations is put forward as a way to encourage socially responsible business. The EU welcomes the many corporations that work with new manners of auditing, which help to account for their social and environmental behavior. The emerging social and environmental indices for investors show the increasing importance of these kinds of auditing procedures. The European Commission mentions the Danish Social Index and Article Sixty-Four of the new French law on new economical rules, which states that companies have to include environmental and social consequences of their behavior in their annual accounts. Social and ethical investing are also mentioned as very important in the development of social responsibility. As discussed previously (see chapter 3, section 2.4), social investments may be made according to negative criteria, excluding firms producing specific products, for example tobacco, alcohol, and weapons, but they may also be made in a positive manner, including companies that have being making progress towards social responsibility. There is still much to be done in order to harmonize the rules and criteria for social and ethical investing.[63]

The proposals of the European Commission promoting the concept of socially responsible business can, indeed, be considered to be an effort to fill of the gap left by increasing globalization and decreasing power of nation-states in modern economies. They can be regarded as a way to make corporations contribute to a European and international civil society; however, the EU's approach seems to focus much more on the economic and strategic consequences of social responsibility, implying a direct clarification of the changed status of the corporation. This includes the ideals of corporate citizenship, which are implied in the movement of corporate social responsibility. Moreover, the European political approach to social responsibility seems to stress the voluntary dimensions of social responsibility without increasing pressure on corporations to act ethically and to demonstrate good social behavior.

Even though ethical problems may be considered to be the immanent background for the concern for socially responsible business, they should have been more directly addressed in the green paper. Ethics should have been more clearly defined. Legal reinforcement of initiatives of social responsibility is needed, perhaps as in the United States. Moreover, the European Commission seems to work with an overly rigid distinction between social and legal responsibility, emphasizing that social responsibility cannot replace legal responsibility and should be considered as a further voluntary requirement. Instead of putting so much emphasis on the voluntary dimensions of responsibility, it may be better to consider social responsibility as a matter of self-regulation and a necessary requirement of good corporate citizenship.

In the communication from the European Commission following the green paper, corporate social responsibility is defined as a "concept whereby companies integrate social and environmental concerns in their business operations and in their interactions with their stakeholders on a voluntary basis"[64] beyond legal requirements, which implies that socially responsible behavior leads to sustainable business success. In particular, it is a part of the EU strategy that companies managing change in a socially responsible way are better off morally and economically, so long as they seek to balance the needs and requirements of various stakeholders into a way that is acceptable to all parties.

But even though the concepts of voluntary corporate social responsibility and stakeholder inclusion have become prevalent in European politics and the regulation of interactions between state and business, the need for research on these concepts is indicated by the fact that there is little agreement about the scope and content of the concepts. The Commission has started a comprehensive process in order to establish and open debate about corporate social responsibility among enterprises, trade unions, civil society, and investor and consumer organizations.[65] The first consultations on the green paper resulted in positive responses from almost all parties, although there were significant differences between the positions expressed. Many European firms stressed the need to avoid strong EU legal regulation, which would be fatal to the flexibility of the market.

They emphasized the importance of the voluntary nature of corporate social responsibility and that there could not be one global solution fitting all companies. Some companies feared that certain visions of corporate social responsibility could even be counterproductive, because they would destroy creativity and innovation. In contrast to this view, trade unions and civil society organizations stated that voluntary initiatives are not sufficient to protect workers and citizens' rights. They argued that a regulatory framework is needed for corporate social responsibility and that all relevant stakeholders should be included in the formulation of activities that are socially responsible. Moreover, they emphasized the need for effective accounting instruments for social and environmental performance. Investors would like to see more transparency with regard to socially responsible practices and consumer organizations have asked for better and more objective information regarding corporate performance related to social responsibility. In addition, there are significant differences in local and national practices within the EU on corporate social responsibility that need to be better explored in order to create common EU policies that respect cultural particularities in coping with both the environmental and human rights dimensions of corporate social responsibility.

These comprehensive disagreements and differences indicate the relevance of a profound theoretical analysis of the possibility and limits of EU strategies for promoting the voluntary nature of CSR. Moreover, the need for further theoretical determination of the concept of 'stakeholder,' and its role in a democratic network society and knowledge economy, is evidenced by the extensive use of this concept in EU policy initiatives and in the formation of the European framework for CSR.

Box 17. European Union: Resolution of the Employment and Social Policy Council on CSR

In December 2002, the Employment and Social Policy Council of the European Union made an important resolution on the policy of corporate social responsibility. Corporate social responsibility was, forthwith, to be considered central to the economic process of the EU's sustainable development. The resolution was a follow-up to the green paper and to the Commission's communication on corporate social responsibility. Corporate social responsibility is regarded as an accomplishment of UN processes of sustainability and the protection of human rights.[66]

In the resolution, corporate social responsibility is defined as based on voluntary action. It is closely linked to credibility and transparency, and it is argued that corporate social responsibility practices add value when they are based on a balanced account of the relation between "economic, social, and environmental issues, as well as consumer interests." Corporate social responsibility concerns not only large corporations, but also small- and medium-sized enterprises (SME's). Moreover, it is important to respect and use existing instruments.[67]

It is typical of the approach of the European Union that corporate social responsibility should be considered as "over and above legal requirements." Moreover, corporate social responsibility should be viewed from the perspective of globalization, involving suppliers and taking into account organizational complexity, as well as issues of corporate governance and dialogue with national communities. Corporate social responsibility implies both external and internal aspects of the corporation.[68]

The European Commission should, in particular, have a global attitude toward corporate social responsibility by promoting it in good practice and management, facilitating the development of CSR tools, and integrating them in member state policies. Indeed, the Council welcomed the establishment of the European Multi-Stakeholder Forum on Corporate Social Responsibility. This Forum is considered central to furthering the process of developing instruments and ideas in Europe. Moreover, member states in Europe are encouraged to develop policies and strategies of corporate social responsibility with public-private partnerships, civil dialogue, to promote excellent management standards, and to exchange information.

2.4. From CSR to corporate governance

The area of corporate governance also seems to be a field of development within the framework of corporate social responsibility. Corporate governance is increasingly proposed as a legal provision of corporate social responsibility and business ethics. In this regard, early British initiatives on corporate governance preceded the American discussions and the European debates on corporate social responsibility. The United Kingdom concept of corporate governance has been quite influential in the European debates that developed quite independently of the discussion of corporate social responsibility, even though today the two fields of discussion are converging. In the United Kingdom, corporate governance was dominated by the Cadbury report from 1992, which was important for further development of the debate about corporate governance.[69] As in the United States, the background for the Cadbury report was also a crisis in business life. The Cadbury report was proposed as a way to make boards more professional in order to restore confidence in the stock market. The result of the Cadbury report was a proposal for a code of best practices for British business life.[70] After the Cadbury report, a number of recommendations and reports followed that addressed specific issues of corporate practice. These reports concerned the size of a director's remuneration, implementation of committee recommendations, the protection of long-term shareholder value, concern for stakeholders, internal control and accounting, the financial responsibility of board directors, the responsibilities of institutional investors, and the modernization of a company's legal and financial institutions.[71]

The Cadbury report still remains the most influential proposal for good corporate governance in Britain, and has become the model for most of the European debates on corporate governance. As compared to the previous discussions of business ethics and corporate governance, the Cadbury report may still be considered as a code of best practice that is primarily focused on concrete legal principles of governance of the board. These principles include proposals: 1) for the board of directors, 2) nonexecutive directors, 3) executive directors, and 4) for reporting and control.[72] It is emphasized that the board of directors should meet regularly, have a clear division of labor, include nonexecutive directors, have a formal schedule and an agreed procedure for taking independent professional advice. In addition, all should have access to the service of the company secretary. Nonexecutive directors should have the ability to make independent judgments. The majority should be independent of the company, appointed for specific terms and selected through formal processes.[73] Executive directors should not exceed three years without shareholder approval and their salaries should be clearly explained. They should be subject to the recommendations of a remuneration committee. With regard to reporting and control, the Cadbury report emphasizes that it is the obligation of the board to present a balanced assessment of the company's position. There should be an objective relation with the auditors and an audit committee with independent membership. Moreover, directors should be aware of their responsibilities and ongoing concern about the company's business.[74]

From the point of view of the general theory of corporate citizenship, linking corporate social responsibility with business ethics and corporate governance, the Cadbury report both represents progress and a limitation. As was argued in the presentation of the situation of the FSGO and Sarbanes-Oxley Act, efforts to regulate corporate governance should be considered from the broader perspective of good governance and business ethics. The Cadbury report should play a role in integrating them into the broader framework of creating good corporate citizenship. In this sense, the proposals of the report must be linked to a general theory of governance and business ethics in order to be efficient. In fact, this is precisely the closer link that should exist between corporate social responsibility and corporate governance.

The proposals of the Cadbury report are very important and many of them have been implemented in the American context through Sarbanes-Oxley. A number of international organizations, like the OECD, have also been inspired by the Cadbury report in their recommendations for corporate governance. Moreover, a year after Sarbanes-Oxley, in 2003, the recommendations of the Cadbury report became a part of the United Kingdom's combined code.[75]

The efforts of the European Union to develop policies on corporate governance have, indeed, been inspired by the work of the Cadbury committee. The EU corporate legal experts were convened to begin this discussion in 2002, independently of the EU work on corporate social responsibility. In addition to its connection with Sarbanes-Oxley Act, the European focus on corporate governance can also be seen as a continuation of local initiatives like the Danish Nørby report on corporate governance from 2001.[76] On May 21, 2003, the European Commission developed some plans for action to modernize corporate law, corporate governance, and rules for accounting. The initiatives of the European Commission were presented in a report that focused on a better use of resources in order to strengthen the competitive capacity of corporations. It was emphasized that good corporate governance is in the interest of both shareholders and stakeholders. The report emphasized that corporate governance should not only be considered as an American problem, but principles of corporate governance are a universal issue, even though they should be related to local developments in each country.

The themes of the Commission's report are that efficiency and competition are important. Moreover, the role of the shareholders in corporate governance should be reinforced. Openness, transparency, and information are central aspects of regulation that should be included in decision-making. Corporate governance should not only be based on developing new legal frameworks in the overall EU context, but each country should work proactively to develop its own guidelines. The principle of "comply or explain" is very important in this context. The reports of the Commission on corporate governance indicate that companies should include a statement on corporate governance in their annual reports. It also recommended that companies should start to use new information technology (i.e., electronic communications) in order to develop their relations to shareholders and democratic decision-making during corporate general assemblies. It implies, for example, that shareholders can participate in general assemblies without being directly physically present in the corporation.

Companies should enforce the nomination of new corporate board members who are independent of the management of the corporation. Moreover, companies should ensure that decisions about corporate salaries and accounting are made by persons, the majority of whom are independent. In this context, it is also a requirement that institutional investors are explicit about their policy for investing in companies and their policies on giving pension fund customers access to voting. Thus, it should be emphasized that the board is, in its totality, responsible for giving correct financial information. This is also the case when there may be suspicion of insider trading or wrongful trading. In its recommendations for good corporate governance, the Commission emphasizes the importance of independent members of the board. The commission has also been formulating recommendations about the rights of shareholders and the salary of corporate management. In addition, there have been initiatives formulated regarding responsibilities for untrue or misleading information, for example in connection with new proposals for rules of corporate accounting. Transparency with regard to salaries should be ensured. Companies on the stock market should make their politics on salaries for the board public on an annual basis. Policies on this issue should be debated and decided in the general assemblies of the corporation. With this in mind, the Commission hopes to stimulate confidence in global economic markets.

Other countries in Europe have also been working with principles for corporate governance. These countries have been inspired by the Cadbury principles and by different international codes about corporate governance.[77] The issues in continental Europe include the protection of shareholders and investors, but they also seem to take into account broader relations to stakeholders, even including issues of corporate social responsibility. The reports and recommendations of the different countries tend to mirror the different national ownership structures.

The result of the work of the Danish Nørby committee from 2001 was seven recommendations, which were considered very important for good corporate governance. The principles include the following areas of focus: 1) the role of the shareholders and interaction with the board; 2) the role of stakeholders and significance of the company; 3) openness and transparency; 4) tasks and responsibility of the board; 5) responsible selections of members of the board; 6) salary of the board and of management; and 7) risk management. Throughout the recommendations of the Nørby committee good communication and dialogue with shareholders is emphasized, for example through the use of information technology. Moreover, it is recommended that corporations formulate a communication policy and procedures for public information about important decisions in the corporation. In addition, the report emphasizes the need for responsible decision-making of the board. It is important that the members of the board are independent. The report specifically proposes that only six members of the board can be elected at the general assembly of the corporation. Furthermore, the board and management should be attributed a fair salary. There should be transparency about how, and according to which criteria, the salary is given to the board and management. Finally, it is important that the corporation establishes and introduces good and coherent risk management systems.

It is important to be aware of the differences in business culture when dealing with issues of corporate governance.[78] Comparing Denmark to other countries it can be observe that Danish business culture is characterized by relatively few companies on the stock market, a number of family and other foundations, and a great number of SMEs. In addition, because of a historical interest in protection from hostile takeovers by family-owned companies and foundations, Danish corporate law distinguishes between A and B shares in a company, where only owners of A shares have voting rights in the corporation. In contrast to other countries, Denmark has, since 1972, had employee representatives in the corporate board. Some conside this to be a hindrance to international investors, because it is perceived as a limitation that employees have influence on board decisions.

The growing focus on corporate governance and the recommendations of the Nørby committee have been met with different opinions in Danish business life.[79] Business managers normally emphasize the necessity of good morality in management. Too many rules and bureaucratic procedures pose a danger of rendering management much less efficient. The organization of Danish industrialists (Dansk Industri) has been very sceptical towards more regulation of the management of companies, and they have also been worried about European standardization. They are afraid that strong rules take responsibility away from the owners. They have argued that it is important to remember that regulation is not enough to ensure good management.[80] Critical voices have also argued that the report from the Nørby committee is too rigid. Because it contains so many bureaucratic requirements, it is not considered to be very efficient. Legislative initiatives on corporate governance, like Sarbanes-Oxley, are considered as ideological legislations that do not contribute to better management.

Such concerns are not shared by all commentators. Others emphasize that internationalization and professionalization of the boards and top management is needed. They understand that there is a close relation between good ethics, CSR, and corporate governance. It is wrong to limit corporate governance to a relation between owners and management, because in the future, there will be much more connection between corporate governance and social responsibility. In addition, the development of new external and internal communication and management forms will reinforce the competitive ability of corporations. Good ownership is important and it can be reinforced with the rules for corporate governance. Moreover, it should not be considered as a hindrance, but as a resource to have employee representatives in the corporate boards. Danish legislators should be more aware of the problems with the distinction between A and B shares. From this perspective, the debate about corporate governance represents a necessary step to globalize Danish companies.

We may acknowledge that the values of openness, transparency, integrity, and fairness are central in the debate about good corporate governance in SMEs.[81] Eva Parum emphasizes that corporations have been very efficient in communicating their work with corporate governance. The response of Danish companies can be defined as the "attentive and arrogant response, the selectively communicating response and the holistic response."[82] Communication of corporate governance aims to create trust and necessary accountability in the annual report of the company. Considered from the perspective of communication and public relations this also concerns the effort to go from one-way communication or press releases to a two-way symmetrical form of communication that is based on dialogue and comprehension rather than manipulation and uniform messages.[83]

With regard to the general emphasis on the relation between business ethics, corporate social responsibility, and corporate governance, it can be argued that the debate on corporate governance is important because it concerns the heart of corporate ownership, though there are still many things to do in order to link the somewhat legalistic debate on corporate governance with broader issues of business ethics and corporate citizenship. In order to be really efficient, corporate governance should be considered – from the point of view of business ethics – as fundamentally integrated in the business strategy of the firm. Many corporations make this link in practice, but it still needs to be made more clearly present in codes of corporate governance.

Case 29. Novo Nordisk:
Corporate governance, CSR, and stakeholder management

The case of Novo Nordisk has been selected as an illustration of a company making an *ethical effort*. This Danish pharmaceutical industry and healthcare corporation had, in 2004, over 20,250 full-time employees in more than 78 countries and sales in 179 countries. Novo Nordisk is a company that arguably tries to work with a broader definition of corporate governance as stakeholder management, which is a good example of the European approach to corporate citizenship. The company considers itself as a healthcare company and a world leader in diabetes care. The main product of Novo Nordisk is insulin, which is used to treat diabetes, but the corporation also works with researchers trying to cure the disease and to created new medicines and treatments (e.g., research in genetic manipulation, use of genetically modified organisms [GMOs], stem cell research for treatment, etc.). In addition, the company works in such areas as homeostasis management, growth hormone therapy, and hormone replacement therapy.[84]

In its 2004 annual report, Novo Nordisk tried to place itself in the center of the effort to improve global health policy. The report addresses the issue of whether diabetes be defeated. In this regard, it is important that the corporation appear not only as a producer of diabetes medicine, but as a contributor to education about and treatment of the disease. The aim is, simply put, to save the world from diabetes. In the report, the corporation emphasizes its effort to have an integrated view on corporate social responsibility: "Novo Nordisk is a biotech-based healthcare company that strives to conduct its activities in a financially, environmentally, and socially responsible way."

The corporation represents itself as a global company engaged in global health policy according to UN goals and the Oxford 2020 vision about global healthcare. In 2004 alone, it provided insulin to between eleven and thirteen million people worldwide. This is considered as an important contribution to increased social responsibility. The strategy of the company is a global contribution to the combat of type one and type two diabetes in the Western world, but also in developing countries, where these problems are becoming even more important. The corporation wants to stress its involvement in concrete projects with local stakeholders aimed at improving health, human rights, and environmental issues in the developing world. In the 2004 annnual report, Novo Nordisk stressed that its reporting goes beyond global standards, such as AA1000AS, ISAE 3000, and the Global Compact principles of the UN. Reporting in line with these standards is an indication of the effort to satisfy the expectations of society.

In connection with Sarbanes-Oxley, Novo Nordisk has also contributed with improved structures of corporate governance. The firm also follows the recommendations of the Nørby report.[85] Corporate governance includes measures of transparency and openness of corporate management and corporate accounting. Novo Nordisk cites the Nørby definition of corporate governance on their website: "The goals, according to which a company is managed, and the major principles and frameworks that regulate the interaction between the company's managerial bodies, the owners, as well as other parties, who are directly influenced by the company's dispositions and business (in this context jointly referred to as the company's stakeholders). Stakeholders include employees, creditors, suppliers, customers, and the local community." In connection with corporate governance improvements, the corporation has also established a whistle-blower system, although this does not play such great role in the firm's use of values-driven management.[86]

The firm's rhetoric puts stakeholder management in the center of their conception of corporate governance. In fact, in conceiving their place in the world as a participant of the stakeholder diagram, Novo Nordisk presents itself as a part of monocyclic diagram, where all links are closely connected. What is particularly interesting about this stakeholder diagram is that the organization is pictured – not in the center – but at some other place. We can talk about a stakeholder web and the idea of the web becomes the new metaphor of stakeholder management. The corporation is there to serve society. The mission of Novo Nordisk is first and foremost to cure diseases, in particular diabetes. This symbolizes the role of Novo Nordisk as a contributor to society rather that as at the center of society.[87] Stakeholder management is about listening and contributing, not only about instrumental strategies for survival and collecting economic returns.

2.5. The future of the European approach

How should we judge the European developments in business ethics, values-driven management, and corporate social responsibility? Compared with the United States, Europeans tend to be antiauthoritarian and skeptical towards formal bureaucratic systems. Also, they dislike systems of formal ethics without real content. At the same time, the movement of social responsibility and business ethics is very strong. As in the United States, the business ethics movement in Europe emerged after the breakthrough of bioethics and environmental ethics in many countries. Moreover, European corporations have, in the last twenty-five years, increasingly combined the language of efficiency and profitability with a concern for social responsibility.

As in the United States, many consultancy firms or idealistic institutions have emerged to help firms set-up programs of business ethics. But while this process in the United States has been based on the establishment of codes of ethics and compliance on the basis of the legal requirements of the FSGO and other legal procedures, European firms have worked with ethics on a less formal basis. This does not, however, mean that business ethics is absent from European corporations. On the contrary, ethics has become an integrated part of human resources, marketing, and public relations. Moreover, an increased number of companies work with ethics programs, auditing and accounting, procedures. In addition, as we have seen, many business schools and research institutions are setting-up programs of education in business ethics and corporate social responsibility.

The European approach to corporate citizenship, in contrast to the United States, arguably focuses on business ethics and compliance rather than sustainability and corporate social responsibility. When they want to be good corporate citizens, European corporations, such as Novo Nordisk and Shell, start by making the triple bottom line a central part of their corporate strategies. In addition, these corporations try to integrate values and values-driven management in the heart of corporate culture. In this context, the instruments of values-driven management and sustainability are promoted in order to ensure integrity and good corporate governance in corporations. Hence, the European approach implies that values are considered as more important than rules. Values, rather than rules, are used to integrate the corporation and to formulate its vision and strategy. Corporations use values-driven management and the management of stakeholder relations to create a strong strategy.

European business ethics – faithful to the idea of the triple bottom line – is arguably dominated by a reaction to the neoclassical view that economic behavior has a cultural basis. Gilles Lipovetsky has characterized these developments as "the corporation in search of a soul."[88] Even though they do not have formalized ethics programs, as in the United States, many European corporations are realizing that economic growth is based on values-driven management. Lipovetsky emphasizes that the new conception of ethics is not primarily idealistic, but rather based on the pragmatic conception that ethics pays. This utilitarian conception of ethics is also found in the European business ethics movements and the green paper of the Commission. In addition to being a political issue of macro-economic politics, ethics is increasingly considered as a matter of *bonne conduite* of corporations. We may say that ethics is considered as an integrated part of the "project of the firm."[89] While companies in the United States are developing a kind of moral contract with the employees in the set-up of written ethics and compliance programs, European companies are working with a more open and less formal agreement with employees about company ethics. Even though the two models may, in practice, be very different, in both cases an increased sensibility for ethics is inculcated.

As discussed, this implies that the European view on corporate social responsibility considers the firm to have multiple stakeholders, who are taken into account in the formulation of the corporate credo. Lipovetsky considers this view of the corporation as an expression of a posttechnocratic and post-hierarchical historical period, where business ethics is a very good example of the "secularization of morality in postmodernity."[90] In Western society, the legitimacy of the corporation is neither traditional, nor charismatic or rational-technological. What is happening is that "consensual demands of legitimacy" have replaced the great conflicts of modernity between employers and employees. Democratic legitimacy of the corporation implies that an organization should find a harmony between individual and collective interests. The combination of ethics and business is a good example of this search for harmony. Accordingly, the idea that "good ethics is good business" expresses a postmodern instrumental view on virtue.[91]

In this context, European efforts toward corporate social responsibility illustrate the emergence of a new discourse of management, one based on respect integrity, loyalty, and a humanistic concern for the vulnerability of the employee. This is partly a response to new conditions of action in a multidimensional and unstable economic environment. At the same time, it is argued that holistic intelligence and multiple managerial skills based on ethical behavior will, on a long-term basis, will lead to high growth. Even if the idea of corporate social responsibility emerged out of radical environmental and social criticism of economic activities, it has now been integrated as a major management concern for the community of the firm. As is evidenced in the European Commission's green paper, social responsibility is considered as a moral obligation, which is qualitatively different from compliance with legal rules. The company is required to have values and ideals that go beyond positive legal norms.[92] This is the proper place of the idea of corporate citizenship, where the firm is considered as a mature, responsible, and reflexive organization.

Lipovetsky borrows the expression, *auto-institution* (i.e., self-governance and self-institutionalization) from Castoriadis to express the constructive aspects of the idea of the moral personality of the corporation.[93] Business values may be seen as the result of a rational deliberative process within the firm. In this context, the ideal of corporate social responsibility in Europe, as in the United States, is based on a belief in the self-regulatory capacity of the corporation without direct state intervention in their process of value formulation. Based on the ideal of sustainable development, business ethics has changed the economic conception of the future. The concept of sustainable development implies that the corporation finds the right balance between profit maximization and the prudent use of resources. Lipovetsky sees this as an indication of an ethics of compromise and an Aristotelian "just mean" between extremes.[94]

The essence of this reasoning is the negotiated economy and the effort to find a balance between the individual concerns of different stakeholders.

An important aspect of European business ethics is the conception of ethics as an integrated part of public relations. Ethics programs, audits, and social responsibility reports are viewed as of communicative strategies to improve the corporate image and institutional legitimacy. Lipovetsky is aware of the fact that changing conditions for economic activity imply that the open system of communicative legitimacy has replaced the invisible hand of Adam Smith.[95] Companies like Shell, Novo Nordisk, or the Body Shop use ethics as conscious strategies in order to improve public relations. Concerns for social responsibility emerge as strategic tools in situations of organizational crisis – where corporations have to protect their image. It is in these situations that corporations can take advantage by using good public relations methods to present themselves as good corporate citizens, because honesty and responsibility about bad products may change public judgment and criticism.[96] In the modern climate of competition, firms use ethics and values as a marketing and branding device to improve their reputation among consumers.

Lipovetsky seems to argue that we cannot exclude these strategic dimensions from European business ethics. Moreover, such a combination between strategy and values seems to be a constitutive dimension of the morality of corporate social responsibility. From the postmodern perspective, we live in a postmoralistic time in which morality functions as a tool for differentiation and personalization of the firm.[97] The ideas of integrity and excellence should, from this perspective, not be exclusively viewed as moral ideals, but also as ways to integrate the firm in community. Marketing and public relations based on corporate social responsibility no longer consider consumers as blind and stupid machines of desire, but rather as responsible individuals, who want to make good moral choices. Moreover, control and power of the firm on the market have become more sophisticated. The corporation has to respond to democratic human beings in an open structure of communication. According to this view, marketing products based on values is very efficient in a society with a highly individualistic culture, where citizens are highly conscious of their consumer choices and personal style.

Accordingly, Lipovetsky can argue that management and ethics do not exclude each other. The replacement of Tayloristic scientific management with a more soft values-driven management is nothing but the logical development of management strategies in order to make them fit with a posttotalitarian society. Values-driven management emphasizes commitment, personal responsibility, dialogue and communication, sharing profits, and continuous training and education of employees. But according to Lipovetsky this cultivation of employee creativity and human resources in a project-oriented organization – justified on criticism of hierarchical and bureaucratic organizations – is necessary to increase managerial efficiency.[98] Emphasizing personal responsibility and creativity is the most functional method to make modern radically individualized human beings take part in the community of the firm. Soft and communicative values integrate individuals into the organization in the context of a highly competitive environment. Put differently, values are efficient ways to manipulate the individual to feel that she belongs to the firm.

Agreeing with Lipovetsky, the view that "ethics is good business" seems to be paradoxical, because the firm has to hide that the concern for ethics is based on strategic calculation in order to receive acceptance. This is also the case with public relations, as well as values-driven management and firms promoting themselves as socially responsible. Moreover, it is also a sad paradox, the true *ruse de la raison entrepreneuriale* (the genius of entrepreneurial reason) that values-driven management, rather than promoting the ideal of individual autonomy, in many cases seems to be primarily an advantage for the corporation. Promoting the value of personal responsibility seems to be extremely efficient way to encourage individual work performance. [99]

In this case, the paradox is that values-driven management is the most efficient strategy to cope with modern individualism, but at the same time it may be counterproductive to positive aspects of the culture of individualism, because it seeks to adapt the individual to the performance pressure of corporations. From this perspective, moralizing work may imply that individuals will be continuously asked to be creative and self-realizing on the job. Replacing discipline and duty with responsibility and virtue can lead to increased pressure on individuals because values are determined by internal conscience rather than external sanctions.

The danger of an ethics of responsibility trying to overcome the opposition between private life and work may be a *hyper-absorption* of the individual in the firm, rather than personal liberation. New imperatives of creativity, virtue, and innovation are replacing old totalitarian views on the workforce. Accordingly, personal development, teambuilding, trust, solidarity, and responsibility take over the function of Tayloristic management tools in order to motivate postmodern individuals. The result is not freedom and social responsibility but increased stress and incidences of psychological breakdown among workers pressed to perform up to their ultimate potential. Accordingly, the emphasis on values-driven management in corporations may lead to greater existential instability.[100]

The function of corporate social responsibility and business ethics needs to be critically evaluated; however, these possible paradoxes in the links between managerial technology and ethics do not sufficiently support an argument for abandoning business ethics and corporate social responsibility as an important aspect of European business culture. Even Lipovetsky seems to be aware of that. After denouncing the Tayloristic use of the ideal of individual responsibility, he emphasizes the need for an ethics of respect for human rights. Moreover, it is important to be aware of the human demand for recognition in social relationships. Instead of exclusively using business ethics as a new management tool, we should work for an authentic integration of individuals in community. [101]

Management should not reduce ethics to a mere tool of the corporation. Even Lipovetsky, who fears that values-driven management may become the new "opium of the people," defends the dignity of human beings.[102] What is important is to respect the autonomy, dignity, integrity, and vulnerability of people working in corporations. With this in mind, there is no reason to be pessimistic with regard to the potentialities of business ethics. From the perspective of a modern postconventional society, the importance of equality and personal rights, in which there is a general concern for community, cannot be ignored; yet, this also signifies that social responsibility cannot be considered exclusively at the level of the firm. In order to succeed, strategies of social responsibility should also have an impact on the economic structure of markets and economic systems. An ethics of social responsibility should work at the macrolevel; therefore, it is very important that the European community assumes efforts to implement social responsibility simultaneously on the levels of both the corporation and community activity.

Endnotes

1   European Commission, Directorate-General for Employment and Social Affairs, Industrial Relations and Industrial Change, Unit EMPL/D.1: *Promoting a European Framework for Corporate Social Responsibility, Green Paper*, July, 2001, Office for Official Publication of the European Communities, Luxembourg, 2001/*Corporate Social Responsibility. A Contribution to Sustainable development*, Office for official publications of the European communities, Luxemburg 2002/*EU Multi-stakeholder Forum on Corporate Social Responsibility*, Office for official publications of the European communities, Luxemburg 2003/Mapping instruments for CSR, Office for official publications of the European communities, Luxemburg 2004/*ABC of main instruments of corporate social responsibility*, Office for official publications of the European communities, Luxemburg 2004/Corporate Social Responsibility: *National public policies in the European Union*, Office for official publications of the European communities, Luxemburg 2004/*European Multistakeholder Forum.Final results and recommendations*, Office for official publications of the European communities, Luxemburg 2004.

2   There is great difference between the United States and Europe with regard to the choices made for finding ways to institutionalize good corporate citizenship. In Europe, the focus is on corporate social responsibility while American developments have been related to business ethics and promoting self-regulation through the legal system. Because of the differences in political systems and culture, the two regions have approached the issue of promotion of ethics and responsibility in different ways.

3   The most striking difference between the development of business ethics and corporate social responsibility in Europe and the United States is that the United States began the debate and legal regulation of business ethics and corporate social responsibility much earlier than Europe. The focus in the United States has been on developing business ethics in terms of legal regulation, while the European Union has been more interested in conceiving business ethics in terms of voluntary social responsibility. Today, this difference is present in the fact that the United States has used legal regulation of business ethics to promote good corporate citizenship, while European countries have been more focused on using instruments to foster CSR as an expression of good corporate citizenship. Moreover, responding to the criticism that I compare two things that cannot be compared, namely business ethics in the United States with CSR in Europe, I would answer that this comparison is justified due to the very different social and political cultures in the different regions. In fact, even though CSR and business ethics may sometimes be considered to be different, it follows from my view on corporate citizenship that it is possible to find a link between the two approaches. The development of the legal regulations and institutionalization of business ethics and CSR in the regions represents a convergence towards a global concept of responsibility and ethics that is expressed in my concept of corporate citizenship based on the idea of the responsibility, integrity, and accountability of the corporation. So I argue that corporate social responsibility and business ethics are two sides of the same coin and that the differences between Europe and the United States lie in this use of two different, but somewhat interlinked, vocabularies to express a common concern for good corporate citizenship.

4   European Commission, *National public policies in the European Union* (Luxemburg: Office for official publications of the European communities, 2004).

5   Jerôme Ballet and Françoise de Bry, *L'éthique de l'entreprise* (Paris: Éditions du Seuil, 2001).

6   European Commission, *Corporate Social Responsibility. A Contribution to Sustainable development* (Luxemburg Office for official publications of the European communities, 2002).

7   Helen Bloom, Roland Calori, Philippe de Woot, *Euromanagement. A New Style for the Global Market. Insights from Europe's Business Leaders*, The European Round Table for Industrialist and Groupe ESC Lyon (London: Kogan Page Limited, 1994).

8   Ibid: 18.

9   Ibid: 61.

10   Ibid: 19.

11   Ibid: 53.

12   Jacob Dahl Rendtorff and Peter Kemp, *Basic Ethical Principles in European Bioethics and Biolaw* (Copenhagen and Barcelona: Center for Ethics and Law, 2000).

13   Helen Bloom, Roland Calori and Philippe de Woot, *Euromanagement. A New Style for the Global Market. Insights from Europe's Business Leaders*, The European Round Table for Industrialist and Groupe ESC Lyon (London: Kogan Page Limited, 1994), 27.

14   Ibid: 35.

15   European Commission, Corporate Social Responsibility: *National public policies in the European Union*, (Luxembourg: Office for official publications of the European communities, 2004)/*European Multistakeholder Forum. Final results and recommendations*, (Luxembourg: Office for official publications of the European communities, 2004).

16   Collin Randlesome and William Brierly, Kevin Bruton, Colin Gordon, Peter King, *Business Cultures in Europe*, 2nd Edition (Oxford: Butterworth-Heinemann Ltd, 1993), 206.

17   Michel Capron and Françoise Quairel-Lanoizeelée, *Mythes et réalités de l'entreprise responsable. Acteurs, Enjeux, Stratégies* (Paris: La Decouverte, 2004), 36.

18   Collin Randlesome and William Brierly, Kevin Bruton, Colin Gordon, Peter King, *Business Cultures in Europe*, 2nd Edition (Oxford: Butterworth-Heinemann Ltd, 1993), 178.

19   Ibid: 193.

20 André Habisch, Jan Jonker, Martina Wegner and René Schmidpeter, *Corporate social responsibility across Europe*, (Berlin: Springer Verlag, 2005), 275.

21 Collin Randlesome and William Brierly, Kevin Bruton, Colin Gordon, Peter King, *Business Cultures in Europe*, 2nd Edition (Oxford: Butterworth-Heinemann Ltd, 1993), 295.

22 Ibid: 130.

23 André Habisch, Jan Jonker, Martina Wegner and René Schmidpeter, *Corporate social responsibility across Europe*, (Berlin: Springer Verlag, 2005), 98.

24 Collin Randlesome and William Brierly, Kevin Bruton, Colin Gordon, Peter King, *Business Cultures in Europe*, 2nd Edition (Oxford: Butterworth-Heinemann Ltd, 1993).

25 Ibid: 18.

26 Ibid: 23.

27 André Habisch, Jan Jonker, Martina Wegner and René Schmidpeter, *Corporate social responsibility across Europe*, (Berlin: Springer Verlag, 2005), 112.

28 Collin Randlesome and William Brierly, Kevin Bruton, Colin Gordon, Peter King, *Business Cultures in Europe*, 2nd Edition (Oxford: Butterworth-Heinemann Ltd, 1993), 52.

29 André Habisch, Jan Jonker, Martina Wegner and René Schmidpeter, *Corporate social responsibility across Europe*, (Berlin: Springer Verlag, 2005), 121.

30 Ibid: 126.

31 Collin Randlesome and William Brierly, Kevin Bruton, Colin Gordon, Peter King, *Business Cultures in Europe*, 2nd Edition (Oxford: Butterworth-Heinemann Ltd, 1993), 323 ff.

32 Klaus Nielsen and Ove K. Pedersen (eds.): *Forhandlingsøkonomi i norden* (Copenhagen: Jurist og Økonomforbundets Forlag, 1989), 11.

33 Ibid: 20.

34 Ibid: 38.

35 From the outset, the Copenhagen Center represented a very interesting and innovative creation as a government funded independent organization for corporate social responsibility in Europe searching for new partnerships between business and local community. When the center changed to become a think tank focused on globalization in 2003, it lost much of its political importance as a key player in establishing a European culture of corporate social responsibility. In spring 2007 the Center was finally closed, perhaps because it had fulfilled its mission of setting CSR on the European agenda.

36 Jacob Torfing, "Velfærdsstatens institutionelle forandring" in Klaus Nielsen (ed.): *Institutionel teori. En tværfaglig introduction* (Roskilde: Roskilde Universitetsforlag, 2005).

37 Mølvadgaard og Nielsen, "Det sociale ansvar og det rummelige arbejdsmarked" in *Social ansvarlighed. Fra idealisme til forretningsprincip* edited by Helene Tølbøll Djursø og Peter Neergaard (Copenhagen: Gyldendal, Academica, 2006).

38 Material for the case about Grundfos has been selected from Anders Bordum and Jacob Holm Hansen, *Strategisk ledelseskommunikation. Erhvervslivets ledelse med visioner, missioner og værdier* (Copenhagen: Jurist og Økonomforbundets forlag, 136-142). Moreover, elements from the case have been selected from the company website: Be>think>innovate>Grundfos – In Brief. Grundfos Management A/S. www.grundfos.com. Method for discoursive analysis of the text is inspired by Anders Bordum and Jacob Holm Hansen, *Strategisk ledelseskommunikation. Erhvervslivets ledelse med visioner, missioner og værdier* (Copenhagen: Jurist og Økonomforbundets forlag, 2005), 25-63.

39 André Habisch, Jan Jonker, Martina Wegner and René Schmidpeter, *Corporate social responsibility across Europe*, (Berlin: Springer Verlag, 2005), 29.

40 Be>think>innovate>Grundfos – In Brief. Grundfos Management A/S. www.grundfos.com

41 Ibid.

42 Larry Gilbert, "International Business Ethics in Western Europe", Paper presented at the 1999 International Conference of Academy of Business Administrative Science (Spain; Barcelona, 1999).

43 Laura Spence, "Building a Focus for Business Ethics in Europe" (EBEN, 1999).

44 Peter Ulrich, *Integrative Wirtschaftsethik. Grundlagen einer lebensdienlichen Ökonomie*, 2 Auflage (Stuttgart, Wien: Haupt 1998). Also Peter Ulrich and Thomas Maak: "Integrative Business Ethics – A Critical Approach", *CEMS Business Review* 2 (1997): 27-36.

45 Ole Thyssen, *Værdiledelse. Om organisationer og etik*, 2. reviderede udgave (Copenhagen: Gyldendal, 1999).

46 Ibid : 135 ff.

47 Paul Ricœur, *Soi-même comme un Autre*, (Paris: Le Seuil, 1990). Marc Maesschalck. L'éthique professionnelle et
som champ de compétence " in R. Cobbeaut and M. Maesschalck, "Ethique des affaires et finalité de l'entreprise",
Faculté des sciences économics, sociales et politiques (Louvain: Université catholique de Louvain, 2000).

48 Jacob Dahl Rendtorff, "Critical Hermeneutics in Law and Politics" in *Paul Ricœur in the Conflict of Interpretations*, edited by Lars Henrik Smith (Århus: Århus Universitetsforlag, 1996).

49 Ole Fogh Kirkeby, *Ledelsesfilosofi, et radikalt normativt perspektiv* (Copenhagen: HandelsHøjskolens forlag,
1997, 103.

50 Ibid: 20.

51 Ibid: 164.

52 Evans, Pruzan and Zadek, *Building Corporate Accountability* (London: EarthScan, 1997).

53 Sune Skadegaard Thorsen, *Konsulentopgave vedr. Forbrugerinformations arbejde m. den røde prik, nu Etikdata-
basen, Erhvervsministeriet and Corporate Social Responsibility* (Copenhagen: Forbrugerinformation, 2001).

54 European Commission, Corporate Social Responsibility, Meeting of High Level Group of National Representatives, March 2001: *Draft Discussion and Issues Paper on CSR* (Brussels 2001).

55 www.eabis.org

56 European Commission. Directorate-General for Employment and Social Affairs, Industrial Relations and Industrial Change, Unit EMPL/D.1, *Promoting a European Framework for Corporate Social Responsibility, Green Paper,*
July, 2001 (Luxembourg: Office for Official Publication of the European Communities, 2001), 3

57 Ibid.

58 Ibid: 3.

59 Ibid: 6.

60 Ibid.

61 Ibid.

62 Ibid.

63 Ibid: 22.

64 *Corporate Social Responsibility. A Contribution to Sustainable development* (Luxemburg: Office for official
publications of the European communities, 2002). See also *EU Multi-stakeholder Forum on Corporate Social
Responsibility* (Luxemburg: Office for official publications of the European communities, 2003).

65 *Corporate Social Responsibility. A Contribution to Sustainable development* (Luxemburg: Office for official
publications of the European communities, 2002).

66 Council Resolution on CSR (3/12/2002)

67 Ibid.

68 Ibid.

69 Christine A. Mallin, *Corporate Governance* (Oxford: Oxford University Press 2004), 20.

70 Ibid: 22.

71 Ibid: 23-26.

72 Sir Adrian Cadbury, *Report of the Committee on the Financial Aspects of Corporate Governance* (London: Gee
and Co, Ltd, 1992).

73 Ibid.

74 Ibid.

75 Christine A. Mallin, *Corporate Governance* (Oxford: Oxford University Press, 2004), 27.

76 Erhvervs- og selskabsstyrelsen, *Nørby udvalgets rapport om Corporate Governance. God selskabsledelse i Danmark*, (Copenhagen: Erhvervs- og selskabsstyrelsen, 2001).

77 Christine A. Mallin, *Corporate Governance* (Oxford: Oxford University Press, 2004), 124.

78 Jens Valdemar Krenchel og Steen Thomsen, *Corporate governance i Danmark. Om god selskabsledelse i et dansk
og internationalt perspektiv* (København: Dansk Industri, 2004).

79 Ibid: 81.

80 Ibid: 4.

81 Eva Parum, *Strategisk kommunikation om ledelse. Et corporate og public governance perspektiv* (København:
Handelshøjskolens forlag, 2006), 14.

82 Ibid, 34.

83 Ibid, 44.

84 Elements for this case have been selected from Marianne Gramstrup, "Novo og Miljøet", *Ledelse og erhvervs-økonomi*, Årgang 59 (1995); Anders Bordum and Jacob Holm Hansen, *Strategisk ledelseskommunikation. Erhvervslivets ledelse med visioner, missioner og værdier* (Copenhagen: Jurist og Økonomforbundets forlag, 2005), 144-148. See also Helene Tølbøll Djursø and Peter Neergaard, *Social ansvarlighed: Fra idealisme til forretningsprincip* (Copenhagen: Gyldendal Academica, 2006), 283-291. See also Debra M. Amidon: *The Innovation Superhighway*, (Elsvier: Butterworth Heinemann, 2003). Furthermore, I have consulted the company website: www.novonordisk.com. Method for discoursive analysis of the text is inspired by Anders Bordum and Jacob Holm Hansen, *Strategisk ledelseskommunikation. Erhvervslivets ledelse med visioner, missioner og værdier* (Copenhagen: Jurist og Økonomforbundets forlag, 2005), 25-63.

85 www.novonordisk.com/about us/corporate_governance/nn_approach.asp

86 Novo Nordisk, *Annual Report 2004. Can Diabetes be defeated?* Financial, Social and Environmental Performance,

87 Novo Nordisk, *Triple Bottom Line Report 2001. Dialogue about Dilemmas.* (Rapportering på den tredobbelte bundlinie. Dialog om dilemmaer), 17.

88 Gilles Lipovetsky, " Les noces de l'éthique et du business ", *Le Débat* (1991), numéro 67, (1991), 145-167. See also Gilles Lipovetsky, *Le Crepuscule du devoir. L'éthique indolores des nouveaux temps démocratiques* (Paris: Gallimard, 1992). In the book the argument is extended to the totality of the sphere of ethics in (post) modern society.

89 Gilles Lipovetsky, " Les noces de l'éthique et du business " in *Le Débat* (1991), numéro 67, (1991), 147.

90 Ibid: 148.

91 Ibid: 149.

92 Ibid: 149.

93 In the discussion of legitimacy, it was demonstrated how Castoriadis's theory of institutions is rather convenient for understanding the imaginary game, which is present in the visions and proposals for business ethics by modern corporations. See chapter 4.

94 Gilles Lipovetsky, " Les noces de l'éthique et du business " in *Le Débat* (1991), numéro 67, (1991), 152.

95 Ibid: 155.

96 Ibid: 154.

97 Ibid: 156.

98 Ibid: 159.

99 Ibid: 161.

100 Ibid: 164.

101 Ibid: 164.

102 Ibid: 165.

3. Towards ethical guidelines for international business corporations

The discussion so far has considered different elements of international business ethics. The globalization and liberalization of business markets have been analyzed as reasons for the increased focus on ethics. This included a discussion of the legal and political aspects of business ethics and corporate social responsibility in the United States and Europe.

The problem now is how to formulate universal ethical norms and guidelines for international and transnational corporations who operate all over the world. This issue can be related to the problem of governance at the level of the international community. At the level of the EU and United States, there are strong institutions of governance, but this is not the case at the level of the United Nations. At the same time, an increasing number of global problems pose the question of how to deal with international decision-making, and also what the role of nonstate actors, like corporations, are in this context.

The philosopher and political theorist Michael Walzer has presented a framework for understanding the future constitutional structures of world society. He draws a line of continuum from total anarchy to a global state.[1] The issue is: What kind of constitutional structure would be most suitable for world society, and what would be the role of corporations in this context? From the left side, called *unity*, Walzer discusses the global state, multinational empire, and federation. From the right side, called *division,* he defines three degrees of global pluralism and finally world anarchy. In contrast to the government of strong empire and close to a weak federation, the third degree of pluralism is a condition of the international community, where states build-up international institutions without creating a supranational government.

From the left side: Unity
global state, multinational empire, federation
→→→→→→→→→→→→→→→→→→→→

←←←←←←←←←←←←←←←←←←←←
From the right side: Division
3rd degree, 2nd degree 1st degree of global pluralism, anarchy

Figure. 4.1. Walzer's Contiuum

Walzer's model is useful for understanding the framework of corporate activities in the world community. The problem is how to determine the right conditions of government for the world community and how government will relate with nonstate actors like corporations. In fact, the business ethics of corporations may be said to contribute to the formation of cosmopolitan political structures based on interactions between sovereign states and strong civil society actors like corporations and other organizations. This is a situation that implies a position somewhere in the middle of Walzer's model: between federation and the third degree of pluralism. Corporations function as nonstate actors in the international community by contributing to the formation of global structures of decision-making that are built on a variety of social and political institutions.

Business ethics functions as a foundation of corporate citizenship in the international community. It is based on the principle of the sovereign equality of states, which would, in fact, be very close to the idea of global pluralism and an anarchy of states. The advantages of a global federation would be combined with the advantages of international pluralism. It is in this context that republican business ethics and the cosmopolitan citizenship of corporations can be situated as contributions to the creation of the international norms of civil society.

The UN Global Compact principles can be considered as powerful expressions of such a development.[2] There are strong economic arguments for firms to seek countries with the lowest production and transaction costs and this has spurred international trade and business. Moreover, global investment in foreign countries is growing. There is much more focus on business possibilities in foreign countries. At the same time, economic globalization has raised difficult ethical questions. What standards should be valid for corporations who don't belong to particular cultures and have activities in many different countries? What about Western companies with activities in the developing world? Should these corporations follow the norms of their home country? Should they accept all the standards of the country in which they are operating, even if there are far fewer legal and ethical requirements than in their home country?

The challenge of international business ethics is the requirement to develop ethical norms and institutional foundations for these norms that can help and guide companies in international business. The construction of a regime of basic ethical principles (i.e., autonomy, dignity, integrity, and vulnerability), human rights, and republican business ethics can be conceived as the normative basis for international business conduct.[3] This chapter will investigate this hypothesis more closely by looking at the development of particular norms and guidelines of values-driven management for multinational business practice.

The discussion covers the following themes: 1) problems facing international business organizations; 2) the integrity and responsibility of cosmopolitan business ethics; 3) ethical guidelines for international business; and 4) values-driven management in multinational corporations.

Case 30. Nestlé and marketing baby milk products in developing countries

One of the famous examples of the need for international business ethics is the case of Nestlé. Nestlé Corporation has, since the 1970s, suffered a terrible decline in its reputation for the role its products have played in increased infant mortality rates. This case is selected as an example of a corporation in *ethical crisis* in the international community. It is a classic case of the problems of marketing in developing countries. In the 1970s, the corporation had started an extensive program of marketing and promoting infant formula in developing countries.[4] The infant formula is a product consisting of powder that, when mixed with water, can be used to replace breast milk. In the Western world this product has been widely accepted and used without major controversy. Like Nescafe, and other products of this kind, infant formula is considered as a practical and useful product that makes life easier.

When Nestlé started to market the product in developing countries, the company was heavily criticized. In the first years of promoting the product, there were many damaging unforeseen consequences, such as the role the formula was found to play in leading to children's malnutrition. The dangerous consequences of the product arose from the fact that it must be mixed with water, which in many developing countries is unsafe for human consumption. In these cases, pure milk from the mother is much safer. Many of the mothers in these countries are also illiterate and unable to understand the use of the product, which raised the risk of improper use and damaging consequences. In addition, when used regularly, women stopped being able to breastfeed. When used continuously, the infant formula made the mother totally dependent on this kind of milk for feeding her child. In countries with severe poverty it was often untenable to pay for a constant supply, meaning that babies went hungry.

Much of the criticism of Nestlé was due to very extensive marketing of the product in African countries.[5] The Nestlé Corporation simply used some of the same marketing techniques it used in Western countries. This included free samples, advertisements, and encouraging hospital personnel to promote the products. This resulted in the unforeseen consequence that women gave up natural breastfeeding because they thought the infant formula was better. Because of this and the very different overall health conditions in developing countries, the product proved fatal for many newborns.

Since the 1970s, Nestlé has been connected with these events and the corporation has been described as cynical and irresponsible. Although it has tried to argue that it has become much wiser and responsible with its marketing practices, many NGOs still use Nestlé as an example of irresponsible capitalism. The corporation is still exposed to the risk of boycotts and severe damage to its reputation. In this way, the Nestlé case is a classical manifestation of the need for business ethics, and to be aware of the cultural differences between countries and their importance for strategies of marketing. Moreover, the case illustrates how business ethics is very important and how corporate social responsibility has profoundly impacted the success or decline of business strategies in developing countries.

3.1. The problems facing international business organizations

The need for values-driven management in international business is marked by the increased difficulties of international relations. Historically, the problem of corruption and bribery was one of the most difficult ethical issues of international business. Large corporations were giving presidents and politicians of developing countries, but also highly placed persons in Western institutions, large gifts in order to secure lucrative business deals. With the intention of dealing with these problems, the United States and other Western countries began, in the 1970s, to enact legislation against national companies using bribery in international business.[6]

Today it is not only bribery and corruption that are mentioned as pressing problems. One of the most general and controversial issues is the extent to which multinational corporations and international business have an obligation to help developing countries overcome problems of famine or poverty. Globalization of the economy has created a need to harmonize values and to find a universally respected normative framework for business.[7] Since the 1960s, multinational corporations have been considered, by left-wing critics of capitalism, as instruments of neocolonialism and the prolongation of state exploitation of the developing world. International public debates are characterized by skeptical attitudes towards the willingness of international corporations to contribute to world development. Voices of the antiglobalization movement express critical outcries about the cynical practices of international corporations.[8] According to the desperate protestors, ongoing liberalization of the world economy will not be an advantage to developing countries, but rather increase corporate greed and exploitation of the developing world.

This skepticism may be an indication of the need for corporations to have reflective attitudes towards their contributions to development policy. At the international level, social responsibilities include helping local communities and contributing to the welfare of the developing world. The global economy needs an ethic of gift-based generosity to supplement the neoclassic paradigm of self-interest.[9] Debates about free access to vital medicines illustrate this point. In 2002, the international pharmaceutical industry was exposed to strong criticism in the international media because they wanted to protect their patents and fight copies of their products, which were being sold at much lower prices in developing countries.

The pluralistic context of international business, where many different norms are at stake, adds to the complexity of issues such as corporate social responsibility for development policy. It is unclear to what extent it is morally justifiable to trade with people and countries who do not share the same moral principles and worldview. International business ethics is constantly confronted by cultures with different moral viewpoints and conceptions of the good life.

This issue is becoming even more pressing when companies include people from different parts of the world in their workforce, which means that the company has to deal internally with diversity and cultural difference. Even though diversity management may prove to be good business for corporations, it is still a challenge to find common values for multicultural corporations.

The debate about international business ethics is clearly linked to managing diversity, especially when dealing with problems such as "culture clash" between different religious and cultural understandings.[10] When people from different cultural backgrounds (e.g., Mulims and Jews, or Protestants and Catholics) have to work together, their different understandings of moral obligation, and fundamentally divergent worldviews, may create great ambiguity and confusion. Corporations must think about the ambiguity of moral principles in international environments in order to cope with the stress of multicultural confrontation.[11]

These issues of diversity as a cause of stress and clash between moral principles may lead to the more fundamental problem for creating common values in the international business system as a whole. Strangely enough, common structures and values are needed in order to have good business relations. The liberalization and globalization of free markets requires some conception of basic business norms like trust, sincerity, telling the truth, abiding by contracts, and so on. At the same time, the international system is marked by the lack of strong institutions. Having discussed previously how values-driven management contributes to more powerful international institutions with regard to international cooperation, business ethics, in an international context, aims at this reinforcement of the institutional framework for economic interactions. The most important task of international business may be to help reinforce international background institutions that can support the development of ethical principles on a global scale.

International justice is also important at many levels of society. It is important that corporations contribute to global justice through their activities in the international community. Respect for human rights is an important way for the corporation to promote international justice and to implement the basic principles of respect for autonomy, dignity, integrity, and vulnerability in international business ethics. The Global Compact principles, among other initiatives, have led corporations and businesses to create international regimes of cooperation (informal norms of interaction) based on the effort to formulate soft law codes of conduct as the foundation for common values and ethical norms for business relations.[12] The international norms of business interaction are shaped by these regimes, but they may also be creating them by formulating norms and codes of values-driven management.

As previously discussed, the problems of international business ethics cannot be separated from issues of allocation of goods and resources. International business ethics should be viewed from the perspective of global economic justice.[13] An important debate in this context has been the distribution of risk and the damaging effects on the environment. As Ulrich Beck has convincingly argued, there is a tendency toward unequal risk distribution in the international community.[14] Different heavy industries are responsible for serious pollution in connection with their operations in the developing countries. For example, international agricultural firms sell crops and GMOs that have the potential to pollute local production. The hazardous business of natural resource (e.g., minerals and metals) extraction is another good example of inequitable risk distribution.

In addition to questioning the record of multinational corporations regarding the environment, the problem of human rights violations in developing countries also needs to be addressed.[15] Multinational corporations have been particularly attacked as being incapable of respecting basic human rights. This may be directly related to the production facilities of companies who do not give their workers the same salary or rights to medical care as in most Western countries. As already discussed (see chapter 2, section 1.5), the manufacturing industries have come under heavy fire for providing very low wages in sweatshop condition, and in some cases also for using child labor. In the case of Nike, the problem of labor rights does not exclusively concern the facilities that are owned by the companies, but also the suppliers and sub-suppliers of goods and services. This situation has led Nike, among others, to disavow responsibility by arguing that the company was not responsible for the activities of the factories that were producing their products because the corporation did not own these firms and their factories. They argued that they are only responsible for economic gain and that they cannot be held morally responsibility at the international level.[16] Such arguments have not been well-received by the international community, who are likely to promote companies, such as Max Havelaar, whose image is built on selling products exlusively from sub-suppliers who respect human rights and environmental sustainability.

Environmental issues and issues related to employees are not the only ethical concerns that may arise in global business. Buyers of products and services are also important stakeholders to take into account as relations to consumers are becoming more difficult in situations of cultural difference and diversity. Products that are sold with one purpose will have another effect on the market, as in the Nestlé case. Moreover, there are issues of corporate responsibilities to consumers when selling in countries with a more relaxed regulatory environment. Philip Morris, for example, has focused its sales in overseas markets because they can sell more cigarettes in countries with less awareness of the danger of smoking. There are also pressing issues of how companies acting abroad should deal with states who violate human rights. A predominant attitude has been to argue that companies should stay neutral and stick to their own business, but there have been many incidents that have challenged this view. When companies have acted at the limits of state policies of boycotting human rights violators, for example in Apartheid-era South Africa or under the totalitarian regime of Saddam Hussein in Iraq, it has been difficult for companies to be neutral with regard to national policies.

An additional problem of corporate neutrality arises around the problem of corporations selling weapons to these governments. If weapons sales can even be accepted as an ethical practice in principle, it is necessity to clarify who could qualify as an acceptable buyer. The weapon producer seems to come into serious troubles when arguing that the corporation has the right to be neutral with regard to moral conceptions of the buyer. As discussed around the case of Lockheed Martin (see case 24), the United States Government, as its main contractor, has been pushing the American defense industry to formulate codes of ethics that also include restrictions of possible buyers of the weapons they produce.

The complexity of business ethics is substantially increased when dealing with issues of international business ethics. The aforementioned examples might seem clear examples of situations where business should work with values and improve their ethics profiles; however, in some cases ethical action is characterized by a confrontation between between high ethical standards and utilitarian economic arguments, which seem to challenge the business ethics strategy of a triple double line respect for the environment and human rights as central to sustainable development.

Cynical economists argue that it in some cases where governments are violating human rights, companies may do more damage to the local stakeholders by leaving the country rather than staying and supplying services and goods, or, in cases where businesses have production facilities and factories, that the violations are outweighted by support to local economies. Basically, from an economic perspective, companies provide needed institutional support to these countries. This kind of argument presupposes that developing countries would be much worse off if the international corporations did not operate in the countries. In this context, a defender of a less severe commitment to business ethics might argue that corporations are required to comply with local and norms and values. They state that in cases where environmental damage and lack of concern for human rights are tolerated, corporations are simply following local law and custom. Others argue that we should also be critically aware of the economic advantages of multinationals operating in the developing world. Lower standards regarding human rights and the environment translate into lower operating costs for firms in these countries in comparison with their home countries.

Case 31. Responsibilities of multinational corporations: Levi-Strauss in China

To what extent does a multinational corporation have to impose minimum standards of human rights and social responsibility in developing countries, and when should it be required to abandon these countries because of political and social problems? These issues are at stake regarding the activities of Levi-Straus in China. This case was selected as an illustration of how to deal positively with an *ethical dilemma,* in this case, whether to stay or to withdraw from a country operating under an authoritarian regime.

In the early 1990s, after violent political confrontations with the totalitarian Chinese government, Levi-Strauss was requested by stakeholders to evaluate whether the firm still would continue to operate in China. At that time, Levi-Strauss used factories in China as sub-suppliers for a number of products. The corporation had, therefore, to evaluate whether it wanted to continue with this practice in a situation where Chinese authorities were not respecting the ethical values of Levi-Strauss and violating international norms of human rights.

The firm's values were developed as a result of its history. The company was founded in San Francisco in the 1850s, when a German immigrant named Loeb Levi-Strauss came to the United States and started to sell trousers. Soon after, the firm invented the original cowboy jeans, which became an iconic symbol of the twentieth century representing American values of freedom, youth, and originality.[17] The Levi-Strauss Corporation was family owned and today the successors of Levi-Strauss still own 95% of the shares of the company. In 1984, one of the family members, Robert Hass, was elected as chairman of the board.

During the 1980s, there was a decrease in the national demand for jeans. As a result, Levi-Strauss had to close many factories and release many employees. Moreover, restructuring was necessary in order to give better service to customers. At the same time there was growth in international sales and customers were willing to pay higher prices for a quality product like Levi's jeans. In the beginning of the 1990s, Levi-Strauss products were made and distributed in more than twenty countries and marketed in more than sixty countries, based on different agreements with local distributors and producers. [18] During this time, the company employed roughly 25,000 people in the United States and 34,000 elsewhere in the world. Levi-Strauss started to outsource much more of its production overseas because it was less expensive than in the United States. This outsourcing resulted in establishment of factories in China, among other places.

The firm has a well-developed code of ethics and mission statement emphasizing human rights and corporate social responsibility with regard to outsourcing and selection of countries. These principles were communicated in ethics programs and training sessions for employees. Levi-Strauss stresses the need for ethical business and personal accountability, as well as the need for trust in their ethics statements. Moreover, the firm has developed principles of environmental management.

The policy developments in China became an issue for the corporation because of their violation of human rights, including freedom of religion and speech, and because of the general political situation of the country, but it was also difficult to find alternative suppliers. After some reflection, and even though there was criticism of the human rights situation in China, Levi-Strauss decided to stay in the country (though, at the same time, they left Burma [now known as Myanmar], where the human rights situation was even worse). The question remains whether the decision to stay after the human rights violations of 1992 was really in accordance with the firm's code of conduct.

3.2. Towards cosmopolitan business ethics: Responsibility, integrity, and trust

As a response to all these problems and dilemmas of ethics in international business the positive significance of global trade and international interaction of business life should be emphasized. From the perspective of the international institutional theory of regime-building[19] we can see a way to overcome the concept of international relations as a power game of actors who are in a quasi-state of nature. With international regime theory we can point to the potential possibilities of business to build and maintain international institutional bonds.[20] Recent studies in international regime theory point to the fact that international interaction not only takes place on the level of high politics among states, but also at the level of commerce among members of civil society.

If one views international relations from the perspective of republican business ethics, the emphasis of the positive impact of international business relations on the integration of world affairs is good news. The Kantian enlightened cosmopolitanism, which was discussed earlier, argues for world peace and international cooperation as the aim of world history.[21] As Francis Fukuyama has emphasized, liberal society at the end of history is about business relations and cooperative recognition among civil societies.[22] Capitalist economies have had tremendous influence on world modernization and democratization. In the universalistic perspective of republican business ethics, such international cooperation should not transcend national differences, but leave a local space of development for local communities. The level of common norms and values for the international community can be defined on the basis of the categorical imperative, which has the kingdom of ends-in-themselves as the regulative ideal for human action. Kant thought that it was possible to formulate a minimum morality for international affairs, which could be used to outlaw unethical practices that cannot be submitted to the test of universal validity of the categorical imperative.

According to republican business ethics, the close interaction among people from different cultures based on open-minded and trustful relations to strangers – who are necessary for successful business – can help to integrate the world community.[23] Many authors argue that one of the reasons of the collapse of the former Soviet Union and the decline of the communist world was the advent of increased international trade. Following this interpretation, the ethical values of international business may be central to formulating an international civil society, which can create a spirit of solidarity and mutual understanding. Business people engage in commitments and exchange views within the civil life of international networks and other interactions. Conscious engagement for universalistic values and common understandings about shared problems and ideals can make business a decisive actor in stabilizing international institutional bonds and can, thereby, contribute to perpetual world peace (in the Kantian sense).

The philosopher Richard T. de George is one of the pioneers developing the concept of integrity as foundational for international business ethics. He defines integrity as a commitment to values and principles, and as the capacity to act consistently according to their values and principles.[24] Thus, not only action with consistency, but commitment to moral principles is essential for international business. What are the moral principles that would be appropriate for multinational business corporations? To answer this question about international corporate social responsibility, De George focuses on the relations between integrity and autonomy. In an international business environment where corporations have increased power of self-determination what is important in the concept of integrity is the ability of the corporation to set limits to its own activities. With increased autonomy and power follows increased responsibility and moral commitment. The concept of the integrity of multinational corporations should, therefore, be defined as the capacity to self-impose moral norms and comply with international standards and codes of conduct.

Naturally, this definition of integrity implies that these norms should be made in accordance with general moral principles.[25]

It is important to reinforce and develop solid background institutions in order to create fair markets in international business. Multinational corporations can contribute to such fairness by trying to avoid exploitation of less developed countries and cultures in the international community. In particular, multinational corporations need to develop policies on issues like unfair competition, lack of tax payment, the creation of starvation, the abuse of power for oppression of employees and other stakeholders, and the transfer of dangerous industries to underdeveloped countries. In order to deal with such issues, from the point of view of integrity, de George states that the first moral norm of business is not to do any intentional harm.[26] But this is not enough. There should also be moral justification for the activities of multinationals in particular countries, and they should always protect human rights, which should be an important part of codes of conduct of multinational corporations.[27]

In an effort to elaborate on the moral principles from the perspective of republican business ethics as an indication of good corporate citizenship, we can discuss some common conceptions of the morality of international business, which are mentioned by Richard de George.

The first attitude may be called the "Myth of Amoral Business."[28] This view is sometimes promoted by orthodox economists, and it is a version of the "business of business is business" argument with regard to international relations. This view maintains that the major concern of business corporations in international relations is economic efficiency and earning money without attention to moral affairs or issues of development politics. What is important for international business is to be able to operate unhindered on the free market. Although issues of efficiency in international economics cannot be forgotten, commerce and trade in a multicultural context cannot be abstracted from the impact of social norms on business. Western capitalism is not easily integrated in the traditional values of many developing countries and without concern for the impact of these values on business multinational corporations. In these countries, a strict separation between markets and social values is not maintained. It is even more difficult to maintain the strict separation between economics, ethics, and politics that is found in Western countries.

The second view differs from the conception of business ethics and morals as important for good business, but only so in a pragmatic sense: as something you cannot avoid taking into account. This view is called "When in Rome Do as the Romans Do."[29] It states that business corporations should work according to the ideals of the country in which they operate. If these countries require expensive gifts for business transactions, tolerate strong discrimination of employees, and accept racism then you have to accept their view even though you would not do the same thing in your own country. This view is based on a kind of ethical relativism, with different standards for the country you visit and your home.[30] This concept implies that the multinational corporation acts according to the norms of the country where it has business interactions. This might imply that the corporation changes behavior when it leaves the country and that it has different strategies in different countries.

Republican business ethics agrees with the implications of this view. Such a hermeneutic attitude of getting to know the other from the inside is very important for open and tolerant business corporation; however, republican business ethics would not stop with this uncritical acceptance of the values of the other, because culturally determined moral convictions have to be tested according to universal standards. There are limits to the acceptance of local custom, and corporations have a moral obligation to refuse practices that they find incompatible with universal standards of human rights. This would be the case even in circumstances where this would not have a pleasing effect on business partners. This represents a potential conflict between partners and it is, therefore, a critical point of the business transaction where business partners search for common values in their relations.

There is a delicate balance between criticism based on universal convictions and a converse ethnocentrism based on the universalization of doubtful values from one's own culture. With De George, this opposite position of ethnocentrism may be called "Act in the American Way," implying that American or European corporations should follow strictly their own local European traditions as they act in other countries. The idea is that Western corporations should follow their own ethical values and norms when they deal with local trade partners and workers.[31] This idea of following your own values without hermeneutic openness to the customs of other traditions risks a sort of cultural imperialism, which is ignorant of the local values of other cultures.

Sometimes such an unreflective universalization of Western values ends up in a kind of a naive moralist thinking, believing in the possibility of a universal morality for corporations acting in different countries. This point of view quickly meets the reality of a global and multicultural way of life in many different countries, which have very different concept of ethics and morals. What is important for the idea of republican business ethics is a situated view of the possibility of universalization as a critical hermeneutics that takes the integrity and particularity of national culture into account.[32]

An ethics of integrity and responsibility in international business means searching for the right balance between cultural relativism and naive universalism. When appealing to the idea of integrity as the ability of the corporation to govern according to self-imposed norms, it is necessary that the corporation formulate minimum universal norms for values-driven management at the international level. These norms should, however, also leave space for situated judgment to reflect on cultural particularities and formulate solutions according to specific situations. Such a strategy implies recognizing the values of particular stakeholders of the corporation. Furthermore, it seeks to establish a certain universality of norms regarding the actions of the corporation.

The idea of organizational integrity based on self-imposed norms may not be very simple. What is important in De George's analysis is that integrity really matters and makes a difference. To act with integrity means that you cannot compromise on your fundamental principles and values.[33] If the firm is committed to human rights, it cannot do business with countries or partners who violate fundamental human rights, because this would be incoherent with regard to basic ethical principles. From the point of view of republican business ethics, the self-imposed norms of the firm include respecting people's autonomy, dignity, integrity, and vulnerability. Moreover, the ethics of self-imposed norms requires constant and independent exercise of judgment in order to establish basic values of interaction in international business. Thus, corporations need to formulate guidelines and ethical codes of conduct to compete with integrity in international business.

Case 32. Between universalism and cultural relativism: The case of Arla Foods

The case of Arla Foods is an example of a corporation in an *ethical crisis*, which it seeks to overcome.

In 1999, MD Foods Amba (Denmark) and Arla Foods (Sweden) initiated a merger resulting in the largest milk product distributor in Scandinavia. Arla Foods had a strong strategy of growth, which later led to a merger with Express Dairies in Britain. The new firm was quite aggressive with regard to maintaining a monopoly in relation to suppliers. This led to the danger of not fully respecting different stakeholders. The internal organizations in Denmark and other countries were searching for values and ethics that were also needed regarding external relations. Danish consumers have been reacting against the monopoly and sales methods of Arla Foods, which seem to be without ethical values or values of good corporate citizenship.

Arla Foods reacted to this skepticism by emphasizing their profile and image as ecologically responsible. The firm has stressed the importance of ecological food and milk products, which has become a part of their marketing. Moreover, the company developed a policy on responsibility with regard to environmental and social issues. It is the company's mission to develop healthy products that give consumers wellbeing, a feeling of security, and a balanced diet. Arla Foods has developed guidelines based on respect for food safety, health, and the environment. In its discusive self-representation, the firm has emphasized that respect for internationally recognized human rights is a part of its policy and strategy, for example regarding requirements of suppliers.[34]

With the so-called cartoon crisis, where the Muslim world reacted with great disgust towards the fact that a Danish newspaper had published cartoons pictures of the prophet Muhammad, Arla Foods suddenly became a part of international politics. For consumers in Saudi Arabia, Kuwait, Iran, and other countries in the Middle East the products of Arla became symbols of the Danish state and angry consumers boycotted their milk, butter, and cheese products. Moreover, in order to show their sympathy, shops in the Middle East removed Arla products from the shelves. Angry Muslims proved to be very active political consumers, reacting strongly towards what they thought were disrespectful policies of the Danish state.

As a result of the cartoon crisis, the Arla Corporation suffered economic deficits and losses in the Middle East. Before the boycott, 50,000 shops and supermarkets in the region sold the products of Arla. Afterwards, the refusal of Arla products was nearly total. This required that the corporation act immediately. Instead of following the official policy of the Danish state by refusing to condemn the publication of the cartoons (citing due to respect of the right to free expression as a fundamental right in a democracy) Arla Foods started to act proactively in order to get their products back in Arab shops and supermarkets. The corporation produced statements, advertisements, and marketing messages and published them in major Arab newspapers. In these advertisements the corporation stated that it respected the values, culture, and religion of Arab countries, and that it did not agree with the publication of the cartoons.[35]

In order to change its marketing policies, Arla decided to emphasize its understanding of the need to respect the religions and cultures of the world. This effort included collaboration with the International Red Cross in establishing humanitarian projects supporting handicapped children, cancer patients, and starving people in Arab countries.[36] In order to further reestablish its image as a trusted business organization, Arla Food announced that it wanted to sponsor an international conference of trust and respect between the cultures and religions of the world. With this search for a new policy of respect and tolerance, Arla Foods enters into the dilemma between universalism and cultural relativism. Can this new image of tolerance be combined with the policies of respect for human rights in developing countries?

3.3. Ethical guidelines for multinational corporations

An element of strong regime-building in international relations can be analyzed as the basis for promoting ethical guidelines for multinational corporations. In some cases, it may even be argued that the process of formulating guidelines and codes of conduct for business goes beyond, or is at the forefront of, what has been possible to achieve at the level of national regulations, because they are still very dependant on the cultural frameworks of tradition and culture of the nation-states. Applying Richard W. Scott's definition, we may conceive these guidelines as something that contributes to the shaping of international institutions insofar as an institution is conceived as a set of "cognitive, normative, and regulative structures and activities that provide stability and meaning of social behavior."[37] The emergence of international regimes may even have economic interpretations, because they may contribute to reducing transaction costs regarding public criticism of dubious ethical behavior by international corporations.

In this context, the emergence of an international human rights regime should be the foundation of the minimum norms to guide the action of multinational corporations. This human rights regime can be said to have emerged out of the international declarations and conventions on human rights.[38] The 1948 Universal Declaration of Human Rights laid the basis for the later conventions on political and social rights. Declarations on cultural rights and on the protection of the human genome in technological development have also been made and adopted by most countries in the world. Human rights functions as a point of reference for discussion and improvement even for states that do not fulfill their international obligations regarding the protection of human rights.[39]

Some of these international conventions and declarations have a direct impact on corporations, for example when they concern working conditions, protecting children, or the freedom of assembly. There are also specific codes of conducts and regulations of soft law directly concerning multinational corporations. The ILO has worked with formulating a number of codes of conduct for workplaces all over the globe. The World Health Organization (WHO) has formulated similar recommendations around controversial health issues, such as the distribution of drugs or the marketing of controversial products by the pharmaceuticals industry.[40] Moreover, there are the guidelines and regulations that have been mentioned throughout this book, from the World Trade Organization (WTO), from the World Bank, the

OECD Guidelines for Multinational Enterprises, and the Global Compact principles. All these organizations and guidelines contribute to the creation of a soft law regime of common values and norms of cooperation for international business organizations.

In this context, there are also global reporting initiatives to create accounting and certification instruments to ensure sustainability on the basis of UN standards. Moreover, SA8000 is also directed towards documenting whether a corporation complies with international norms for the protection of human rights. On several occasions since April 2004, the United Nation's Human Rights Commission has discussed a proposal for principles for the responsibility of corporations for human rights.[41] The proposed principles for human rights and corporate social responsibility are called UN Norms on the Responsibility of Transnational Corporations and Other Business Enterprises with Regard to Human Rights. These principles represent an important initiative to formulate internationally binding norms for corporate social responsibility. They have to go through the system of negotiation of the UN and all stakeholders, investors, public authorities, unions, and NGOs will be included in the debate on these norms before they are adopted.

These norms represent an important break with the conventional dogmatism of human rights, which argues that states, first and foremost, have the responsibility to protect the human rights of individual citizens. The decision to formulate principles for human rights and corporate social responsibility for corporations indicate an initiative to contribute to the formulation of international civil law norms and to motivate corporate actors to contribute to the strengthening of those norms. Corporations have an obligation to contribute to supporting and developing the protection of fundamental human rights in international relations. By formulating such an obligation, the international norms of the Human Rights Commission are challenging the prevailing idea that human rights protections are the sole obligation of states.

These principles contribute to this new formulation of human rights by arguing that corporations in the realm of their power have both negative and positive obligations to protect and promote human rights. Accordingly, it can be argued that the norms of the Human Rights Commission go beyond the UN Global Compact principles, which are restricted to more negative formulations of the obligations of companies to participate in the violation of human rights.[42] Because the norms are a development of already-existing UN law, international declarations, and codes of conduct they can be interpreted as a contribution to the emergence of the corporation as a subject of international law. This may be said to reinforce American legislation that makes it possible to make corporations legally responsible for their international actions.

In this context, the important notion in the principles of the UN Human Rights Commission is the concept of the sphere of activity and influence of the corporation. The norms proposed by the Human Rights Commission represent a development of the work of the ILO and other international organizations regarding human rights on the labor market.[43] Corporations are said to be responsible for workers' rights like nondiscrimination, workplace conditions, fair wages, workplace safety, noncorruption, consumer protection, and environmental protection. These norms and principles reinforce the protection of the international covenants of civil and political rights, as well as social and cultural rights.

A pressing issue of definition is the scope of the sphere of activity and influence of corporations. Companies should not contribute to violations of human rights, and they should protect the rule of law and human rights where states are irresponsible and weak. Corporations should be responsible for the activities of their suppliers and ensure that they maintain the international norms. If corporations do not live up to their responsibilities, the principles of the Human Rights Commission predict that the corporations will be submitted to the criticism of the international media and lose legitimacy.[44]

Even though the presence of such an international human rights regime of corporate social responsibility is plausible, it may be objected that the moral obligations of multinational firms to "promote the common good" cannot be conceived as a universal duty for corporations. Manuel Velasquez presents this realist argument against the proponents of universal cooperation in the international community. The realist objection is first of all an objection to the idea of an international community. It follows the Hobbsian argument that morality has no place in international affairs.[45] Moreover, international relations are characterized as a state of nature, where there is no sovereign or government to aim at the common good and enforce the law, and where everyone follows their own interests. In this situation the multinational corporation seems to be in a prisoner's dilemma, where it can choose either to cooperate or not to cooperate with other firms. Because of the lack of third-party enforcement there is no rational motivation for cooperating and complying with morality, because there is no insurance that others will also cooperate. Corporations or states can gain a strong competitive advantage by not cooperating.[46]

This provocative argument is incorrect for several reasons. First, it is based on a purely instrumental concept of rationality. The only ethical element in the concept of rationality is concern for self-preservation. Moreover, Velasquez does not take into account the reality of international regimes, where expectations of cooperation among nations and companies have been established. Becoming a free rider is not normally justified simply because they may possibly gain a competitive advantage; however, this argument may help explain how corporations who are trying to be free riders might reason about ethical issues. It is important to remember that this strategy of being a free rider is a limited endeavor, given that other companies will exclude those who choose this strategy repeatedly in games of cooperation.

In opposition to this view, Norman Bowie argues that moral obligations of multinational corporations in the international community can be justified. Indeed, multinationals can help to promote democracy and freedom when they follow the morality of Kantian capitalism, which implies a universalistic morality of the market.[47] Bowie argues that cultural relativism, as implied in by Velasquez, is incoherent. The cultural relativist who argues that multinational corporations should follow foreign morality abroad and their own morality at home is stuck between individualism and universalism. It is not possible to maintain a culturally relativistic stance because this position is confronted with the individualist who does not even want to follow cultural norms. So there is not even a justification for following specific norms abroad, or at home, and it will be impossible for multinational corporations to have any stable values if they maintain cultural relativism.

Cultural relativism ends in individual relativism, with no argument against realism and free rider opportunism in international relations. Hence, the universalist position seems preferable, because it helps to formulate stable norms to guide multinational corporations. This position is, furthermore, more closely connected to the reality of international relations, in which countries are boycotted and banned by corporations because of human rights violations or racist policies.

Even accepting the validity of the universalist position, multinational corporations still have obligations in international politics. These obligations imply that they should respect the minimal moral rules of the countries in which they operate.[48] In cases where there may be rules that can be justified universally but which are not practiced internationally, a corporation would still have to promote and respect such rules where they are practiced. Moreover, when foreign countries follow moral principles that cannot be universally justified, multinational corporations keep their integrity and refuse to apply these rules.

Insofar as they accept the market morality of capitalist society, multinational corporations may even have an active role to play in promoting universal norms for the international community. Corporations already contribute to building this morality by following the good customs and the laws of healthy markets, including respecting contracts, promise-keeping, truth-telling, and the establishment of reciprocal and mutual trust relations among business partners. When multinationals follow and promote such market rules and when they keep the norms of local cultures, which are universally justified, they are helping to construct international regimes of economic behavior that may help to promote democratic attitudes in different parts of the world.

From the perspective of Kantian morality, systematic free-rider opportunism would be contrary to this morality of the market, which is implied in the capitalist economic attitude that considers market freedom as essential for economic prosperity.[49] The full consequence of this approach would necessarily be respect for human rights as a precondition for economic freedom, because racism, discrimination, or depravation of liberty are simply inefficient and represent a hindrance to the development of free economic markets.

Codes of conduct and values-driven management for multinationals in the international community may, therefore, help to stabilize, shape, and form the activities of the corporation, while at the same representing active contributing to the promotion of democratic values in the cultures of the countries in which they operate. The problem still remains of defining exactly which norms and values are truly universal, and not simply mistaken reflections of Western ethnocentrism.

For these reasons, the task of developing codes and norms of conduct at the international level is a very subtle and time-consuming process. The process of determing global values has to carefully account for the plurality of values in the international community. John Rawls has discussed the possibility of agreements in international relations as a reply to international regime theory. Rawls's theory of the *laws of peoples* can be considered as an effort to find a common point of view outside of comprehensive doctrines, which characterize different local cultures in the international community.[50] Rawls interprets the laws of peoples as a result of a double process of constituting a social contract. Ideally, a democratic republic is the result of rational deliberation among free individuals who choose to live in a democracy. Rawls conceptualizes a hypothetical situation of interpretation of a social contract. Ideally, after a democratic regime is constituted with the social contract it chooses to form an international community with others. This would create a second, or similar, social contract, which becomes the foundation of the laws of peoples between states. The laws of people are founded on an original contract between states and the use of free public reason.[51] The idea of a universal law between states and of protecting the humanity of world citizenry is realistic because it is built on democratic principles, and because it recognizes pluralism and the impossibility of a world state. The idea of laws of peoples is built on agreements between different states with democratic constitutions and overlapping consensus. The principle of toleration of difference and pluralism seems to be important in such a "realistic utopia."

International corporations arguably contribute to the formation of the foundations of the laws of people, when they formulate their values and codes of conduct. A classic set of ethical principles for multinationals, which have been very influential for shaping the values and ethical consciousness of international corporations, are the Sullivan Principles, which were proposed by Gilbert Sullivan, who in the 1970s and 1980s was a very active spokesman against apartheid in South Africa. He later became a member of the board of General Motors corporation, and in this capacity he took the initiative to formulate principles that would function as common standards for the action for multinational corporations.

The Sullivan Principles are basically a code conduct for combating racism. They promote desegregation in work facilities, equal and fair employment practices regardless of race or color, equal or comparable salaries, training and management programs for nonwhites, and improving the quality of employees' lives outside the work environment.[52] The Principles represented a breakthrough in international guidelines for corporations, and they express an important manifestation of dialogue between the developing world and Western corporations, even though they were primarily developed in the United States. In the 1980s, many American corporations used the Sullivan Principles to stop trading with South Africa. This may be considered as an expression of uncompromising integrity in business.[53]

The Caux Round Table for business leaders, which from 1985 took place in Caux in Switzerland, can be analyzed as another very important effort to create international principles of business ethics. This Roundtable discussion was established at the initiative of the former president of the Philips Corporation, in collaboration with prominent business leaders and business ethicists from different parts of the world, among others representatives from large Japanese corporations.[54] The outcome of the Caux Round Table discussion was very important, because it led to the formulation of the 1994 Caux Round Table

Principles for Business Conduct.[55] The content of the code of conduct are seven principles, which are followed by a list of stakeholder principles. These principles combine and integrate the Japanese idea of *kyosei*, which means "living and working together," with the Western emphasis on the sacredness of human beings expressed in the principles of respect for human dignity, but they also contribute with an extended ambitious program for business ethics for the common good of humanity.

The Caux Principles reflect an interesting and challenging paradox: the politics of liberalization of world trade has opened a dynamic debate on ethical principles. The preamble of the Principles promotes the responsibility of the corporation to respect the dignity and interests of its stakeholders. The Principles include:

1) Responsibilities of the corporation: Beyond shareholders towards stakeholders

2) Economic and social impact of corporations: Toward innovation, justice, and world community

3) Corporate behavior: Beyond the letter of law toward a spirit of trust

4) Respect for rules: Beyond trade fiction toward cooperation

5) Support for multilateral trade: Beyond isolation toward world community

6) Respect for the environment: Beyond protection toward enhancement

7) Avoidance of illicit operations: Beyond profit towards peace.[56]

These principles can be conceived as proposals for self-imposed norms of high integrity corporations with power and autonomy. Although the principles may be conceived as very general, it is important to note that they do not only reflect Western norms, but they try to be an intercultural expression of ethical values. In this context, the Japanese idea of *kyosei* expresses the perspective of the basic ethical principles of autonomy, dignity, integrity, and vulnerability and in the framework of the concepts of trust, justice, and global sustainability. This idea of living together not only includes labor and management, but goes beyond local culture to include other countries, the environment, and future generations.[57]

In addition, the principles promote peace, stakeholder dialogue, transparency, and the need to comply with UN and other international soft-law regulations as central to the principles of international business. The principles are, however, also expressions of the need to recognize the morality of the free market, because they are good for the importance of a free global market.[58]

The Caux Round Table Principles were important predecessors of Kofi Annan's UN Global Compact principles, which today have become essential for defining the values of international business ethics. On the foundation of the principles of cosmopolitanism that emerge out of John Rawls's laws of peoples, we can argue that multinational corporations have positive obligation that are outlined in the theory of international law. These obligations involve the minimal duties of assistance of the kind that applies to a "society of well-ordered peoples."[59] The Global Compact principles arguably contain a defense of a workplace republicanism that should be applied in international corporations.[60] Moreover, corporations can be seen as morally obliged to fulfill the duties of assistance following from Rawls's concept of the laws of peoples. Accordingly, the Global Compact can be conceived as an "important umbrella" where companies, states, and other organizations can come together with visibility and global reach to develop global values.[61] The Global Compact helps to establish a platform for global cosmopolitan citizenship and helps companies to focus on global inequalities and their responsibility towards the poor, to enhance the acceptability of human rights, and to focus on the legitimacy of corporate performance so that companies are responsible, in practice as well as theory, to their principles.[62] Against critics who argue that the Compact principles are too weak, and that they support free market economics at the global level, it may be emphasized that the principles are directed towards enforcing virtues of corporate citizenship in the international community by enforcing the moral underpinnings of the economy.[63] Moreover, compared to other codes and principles, it is important to emphasize that the Global Compact represents a collective initiative of large corporations that is supported by the United Nations. Accordingly, the Global Compact principles have created an international network that discusses emergent global values. As such, they contribute to the formation of corporate citizenship in the international community.[64]

Box 18. International norms: Kofi Annan's UN Global Compact principles

The UN Global Compact principles, as proposed by Kofi Annan, former Secretary-General of the UN, may be considered as the most important principles for an international code of conduct on international business ethics. They were formulated in an address to the World Economic Forum in 1999 and later developed in 2000. The Global Compact principles are foundational for an international code of conduct of corporate citizenship in the world economy, based on fundamental respect for human rights, labor rights, protection of the environment, and anticorruption.[65] The Global Compact is a voluntary international network that encourages corporate citizenship. Every corporation that supports the principles can be a member. The principles are very simple, but they also express clear commitments to the principles of the triple bottom line and sustainable development.

Human rights
Principle 1: Businesses should support and respect the protection of internationally proclaimed human rights within their sphere of influence.

Principle 2: Businesses should make sure their own corporations are not complicit in human rights abuses.

Labor
Principle 3: Businesses should uphold the freedom of association and the effective recognition of the right to collective bargaining

Principle 4: Businesses should uphold the elimination of all forms of forced and compulsory labor.

Principle 5: Businesses should uphold the effective abolition of child labor.

Principle 6: Business should uphold the elimination of discrimination in respect of employment and occupation.

Environment
Principle 7: Businesses should support a precautionary approach to environmental challenges.

Principle 8: Businesses should undertake initiatives to promote greater environmental responsibility.

Principle 9: Businesses should encourage the development and diffusion of environmentally friendly technologies.

Anticorruption
Principle 10: Businesses should work against corruption in all its forms, including extortion and bribery.[66]

3.4. Corporate citizenship as global cosmopolitan citizenship

All of these important international guidelines help to create the framework for the concept of global corporate citizenship in international relations. When the term can be applied to nonstate organizational actors, such as corporations, it refers to their ability to promote citizenship in the international community and enhance their legitimacy worldwide. The new term of global corporate citizenship is necessary in order to capture the fundamental aspects of corporate engagement in the international community. It is closely linked to the respect and development of the international declarations, norms, and codes of conduct discussed previously. With this concept of global business citizenship, corporate citizenship can be considered as an attempt to capture the universal values that unite human cultures, ethics, and religions. Global corporate citizenship is directed towards ensuring corporate accountability in international society. Efforts by corporations to include universal values in their business mission and values statements can be considered as a necessary contribution to this development of global business citizenship. Moreover, engagement and communication with stakeholders is considered to be an important part of this process of forming global corporate citizenship.

Logsdon and Wood argue that global business citizenship implies that libertarian free market thinking has been replaced by a sort of communitarian approach based on the promotion of citizenship in different countries; however, with the concept of global citizenship they also emphasize that the nation-state must be transcended in order to establish a firm basis for global business ethics.[67] Lodsdon and Wood want to redefine CSR and values-driven management in terms of corporate citizenship. Further, they have considered whether the rights and duties of individual citizens is a useful concept for understanding the role of corporations in society. While the corporation at the national level emerges as a responsible actor that is committed and engaged in community, corporate citizenship at the international level means that the organization is committed to hyper-norms, while at the same recognizing the free moral space of specific cultures.[68] When the the corporation is considered as a universal citizen, a member of the international community, it is entitled to work for its stakeholders and contribute to the positive development of international community.

This concept of global business citizenship arguably encloses the concept of corporate social responsibility. The idea of citizenship at the international level is based on the morally responsible corporation, which is the foundation for policies on corporate social responsibility. To argue for good corporate citizenship at the international level is to focus the notion of CSR on a specific conception of the corporation and its obligations towards the international community. In international business, corporate self-regulation from the point of view of corporate citizenship is the solution to the definition of the corporation in society. It is important to notice that the obligations of business to society are based on this adaptation of the concept of global corporate citizenship.

In their argument for global business citizenship, Logsdon and Wood argue that defending human rights is very important for developing citizenship at the international level. Human rights may be considered as a foundational level of universal ethical principles. Focus on human rights implies that the good society protects basic individual rights and that it finds the right balance between protecting those rights and developing welfare policies for the community. As good corporate citizens, corporations comply with the Universal Declaration of Human Rights and they work to promote business ethics on that foundation. Logsdon and Wood accept the argument of Donaldson and Dunfee that the corporation takes part of in macrosocial contract where it follows universal ethical principles.[69] It is, however, also important to recognize the crosscultural variations that are permitted within consistent local norms and a free moral space, as long as they do not violate the hyper-norms of macrosocial contracts. From the strategic perspective this means that corporations should actively engage in protecting the norms of macrosocial contracts, though at the same time moral free space gives allows corporations to respect local cultural values, as long as they are consistent with hyper-norms.

The basic ethics principles are the foundation for the required protection of human beings in international business. The principles of respect for human autonomy, dignity, integrity, and vulnerability constitute what Klaus M. Leisinger calls a required *minima moralia* for multinational corporations. From this point of view, respect for human dignity is the fundamental responsibility of business when it operates on the global scale.[70] This respect for human dignity is expressed in the concern for fundamental human needs as the foundation for universal human rights. Respect for the golden rule expresses this concern for a fundamental ethics of the international community. Hans Küng has taken the initiative to formulate an ethics for the world community that he calls *Projekt Weltethos*, or an ethos of the world where universal moral norms are expressed as the foundation of international transactions.[71] In this ethos of the world, it is essential to protect the basic ethical principles of autonomy, dignity, integrity and vulnerability within the framework of the vision of the good life with and for the other in just institutions.

In terms of the political philosophy of the international community this vision of corporations as good citizens of the international peace can be understood in light of Immanuel Kant's search for perpetual peace in the international community. In contrast to the argument that it is impossible to find good ways of handling the anonymous structures of power in globalization, the vision of global corporate citizenship imagines the corporation as a contributor to the support of democracy and global sovereign states. Kant conceived the teleology of perpetual peace as a development towards a global *Rechtsstaat* (legal order) in international relation with respect for the rational interdependence of states.[72] The Kantian concept of republicanism implies protection of democratic representative government of sovereign states in the international community. We may argue that corporations contribute to this vision of a cosmopolitan condition by the development of codes of conduct for business ethics and values-driven management of good citizenship in the international community. The individual citizen, but also the corporation, must be world citizens and the state must, in order to establish a universal legal community, go into collaboration with other states and create international and cosmopolitan institutions. This is the final aim of the law of cosmopolitan citizenship, which is the peaceful enlightenment and development of culture and the art of humanity by the universalization of particular principles of people's sovereignty.

3.5. Values-driven management for the corporate citizenship of multinational corporations

With this concept of global corporate citizenship, we are now able to make a more concrete formulation of elements of codes of values-driven management and corporate social responsibility for multinational corporations. Logsdon and Wood refer to the Clarkson Principles of Stakeholder Management to describe the strategic engagement of corporations for international business citizenship.[73] These principles provide a framework for developing an international ethics of corporate citizenship. The Clarkson Principles are also proposed by James Post as particularly apt for conceptualizing global corporate citizenship.[74]

Box 19: Stakeholder management in the international community: The Clarkson Principles:

"[A]s multinational corporations expand their activities and linkages, both corporate managers and their critics search for principles for action that transcend national borders and cultural values, and modes of operation that will achieve the broad purposes of the corporation on a long term and sustainable basis, without undue conflict with diverse human and social norms."[75]

Principle 1. Managers should *acknowledge* and actively *monitor* the concerns of all legitimate stakeholders, and should take their interests appropriately into account in decision-making and operations.

Principle 2. Managers should *listen* and openly *communicate* with stakeholders about their respective concerns and contributions, and about the risks that they assume because of their involvement with the corporation.

Principle 3. Managers should *adopt* processes and modes of behaviour that are sensitive to the concerns and capabilities of each stakeholder constituency

Principle 4. Managers should *recognize the interdependence* of efforts and rewards among stakeholders, and should attempt to achieve a fair distribution of the benefits and burdens of corporate activity among them, taking into account their respective risks and vulnerabilities.

Principle 5. Managers should *work cooperatively* with other entities, both public and private, to insure risks and harms arising from corporate activities are minimized and, where they cannot be avoided, appropriately compensated.

Principle 6. Managers should *avoid altogether* activities that might jeopardize inalienable human right (e.g., the right to life) or give rise to risks which, if clearly understood, would be patently unacceptable to relevant stakeholders.

Principle 7. Managers should *acknowledge the potential conflicts* between (a) their own role as corporate stakeholders, and (b) their legal and moral responsibilities for the interests of stakeholders, and should address such conflicts through open communication, appropriate reporting and incentive systems, and where necessary third party review.

Global corporate citizenship can be defined as a sort of cosmopolitan international citizenship where corporations, following their definition as corporate citizens, continue their efforts to work engaged at the level of the international community. Cosmopolitan business citizenship means that the corporation is not only engaged in local affairs, but that it contributes to the formation of the international community through respecting human rights and the basic rules of conduct at the level of the international community. Corporations have, however, to give meaning to such universal principles when they meet concrete local conditions of business. International business ethics opens the way for a kind of values-driven management that is founded on universal ethical principles, but also marked by the necessary tolerance that is important for working with cultural differences with an open and constructive attitude, so that diversity is an asset for the social and economic development of the firm. Accordingly, strategic values-driven management for international corporations can try to combine the search for profits with respect for social values.

In this context, three levels of policies of multinational corporations can be discerned: 1) the level of providing a moral minimum of respect for basic human rights from multinational corporations in international politics; 2) the level of creating proactive policies for promoting corporate social responsibilities in international trade; and 3) the level of formulating norms respecting the delicate balance between minimal universal norms and concrete application of these norms and values.

Concerning the first level, Thomas Donaldson has argued that it the task of business ethics to specify the obligations required on the basis of the international declarations, conventions, and guidelines on human rights.[76] If the language of international human rights instruments is binding, the corresponding duties to these rights must be acknowledged. According to this perspective, human rights can be understood expressing substantial elements of human being and personality that should not be violated. Human rights are the bottom line of ethics in the community and rotecting them concludes the concern for the inviolability of the autonomy, dignity, integrity, and vulnerability of human persons. Following Henry Shue, basic rights are those that are needed in order to have other rights.[77] It is meaningless to consider certain rights as basic if their depravation will lead to the depravation of other fundamental rights.

Because of this, corporations should respect all the basic political and social rights, including the right to: subsistence, political participation, freedom of physical movement, ownership of property, freedom from torture, fair trial, nondiscriminatory treatment, physical security, freedom of speech and association, and education.[78] Such rights may require correlative duties and protection by corporations and should, therefore, be important elements in formulation of their codes of conduct. Following Nickel and Donaldson, granting these rights could be seen as dependant on fair distribution, which implies that corporations have the means to afford them.[79] This means that corporations have an absolute negative duty to refrain from depriving persons of having these rights, but that their positive duty to promote these rights is dependent on their concrete situation and economic resources. Thus, the basic rights approach is essentially a deontological approach of minimum international standards to be respected.

Concerning the second level, taking into account the Caux Principles and the work of de George, the following principles can be proposed as basic guidelines for organizational justice and integrity in international business:

1) Multinationals should do no intentional direct harm.

2) Multinationals should produce more good than harm for the host country.

3) Multinationals should contribute, through their activities, to the host country's development.

4) Multinationals should respect the human rights of their employees.

5) To the extent that local culture does not violate ethical norms, multinationals should respect the local culture and work with and not against it.[80]

6) Multinationals should pay their fair share of taxes.[81]

7) Multinationals should cooperate with local government in developing and enforcing just background institutions.[82]

8) Multinationals are responsible for making due compensation for any harm they do, directly or indirectly, intentionally, or unintentionally.[83]

9) The majority control of a firm carries with it ethical responsibility for actions and failures of the firm.[84]

10) If a multinational builds a hazardous plant, it has the obligation to make sure that it is safe and that it runs safely.[85]

11) In transferring hazardous technology to developing countries, multinationals are responsible for appropriately redesigning such technology so that it can be safely administered in the host country.[86]

These principles can be clarified by looking at the stakeholder principles from the Caux Round Table. These stakeholders include: customers, employees, owners/investors, suppliers, competitors, and communities. The Caux Principles can be paraphrased in the following way as the basis for values-driven management of multinational corporations.

The Principles start with respect for *customer dignity*, fairness, and a high quality of goods and services, as well as in marketing and advertising, and when handling customer satisfaction. High levels of health and safety, environmental quality, and respect for the integrity of the cultures of customers are also promoted.[87]

A high level of responsibility should guide the *treatment of employees.* Applications of the concept of dignity include concern for the social welfare of workers, such as improving their general life conditions and their specific work conditions materially, and protecting them from illness, but also psychologically regarding honest information sharing and negotiation in conflict. Moreover, respect for human dignity implies avoiding discriminatory practices and concern for handicapped and disadvantaged people.

Regarding *owners and investors,* the Principles do not refrain from stressing the importance of returns and profits, and they emphasize the duty of corporate governance based on trust and responsibility with competent and fair treatment of assets from investors. They also include respect for suggestions, proposals, and formal resolutions from investors.

Suppliers are also important stakeholders. The relation with subcontractors should be based on freedom, mutual respect, and fairness. The Principles emphasize long-term relationships with suppliers that are based on value, quality, and reliability, and that the suppliers have employment practices that respect human dignity.[88]

The Caux Principles mention *competitors* as stakeholders. The increasing wealth of nations relies on respecting open markets. Competitive behavior fosters social development and does not damage the environment. Moreover, competitors should be treated with mutual respect for intellectual property rights and the ethics of competition.

Stressing *community* as a stakeholder, the Caux Principles promote the corporation as a world citizen who should respect and promote human rights and democratic institutions by recognizing the legitimate obligations of governments.[89] Corporate citizenship at the international level implies contributing to sustainable development and to promoting the health and social well-being of the citizens, as well as respecting the integrity of local cultures.

The third level concerns the necessity of reflective judgment in formulating values of multinational corporations. The Caux Principles are very elaborate guidelines for values-driven management that would properly express international regimes of business ethics. Even though the perspective of republican business ethics emphasizes the cosmopolitan approach to international business ethics, it is true that corporations face many difficult problems and seemingly impossible dilemmas when applying these norms in relation to concrete problems. As mentioned, the naive moralist position in international relations is unjustifiable. Issues of child labor and corruption, but also differences in salaries and maybe even environmental protection, may have some cultural aspects that should be investigated very closely, even from the cosmopolitan perspective. Acknowledging Tom Dunfee and Thomas Donaldson, there is a free moral space for each culture in which there is room for difference and national integrity even though a minimal morality may be said to exist, which is valid for all cultures.[90]

Donaldson analyzes this relationship between this moral minimum and differences that are acceptable. In addition to formulating a list of rights that corporations should respect, he has proposed to distinguish between norms that are based on economic poverty and norms that have their roots in cultural diversity and national tradition. Questionable situations are cases where corporations do nothing to change local norms, and rather than being justified in cultural traditions, are based on social poverty and inequality. On the other hand, situations may be justified when it is not possible to consider a local norm as based on bad economic conditions and when there is not a clear case of serious human rights violations.[91] What is important for reflective judgment is a consistent and coherent application of general principles of business ethics in concrete situations without contradicting the concern of the principles or violating the nature of the situation, which may represent complicated challenges to basic moral principles.

Business ethics functions as a foundation for corporate citizenship in the international community based on the principle of sovereign equality of states. Remembering Walzer (see chapter 4, section 3), this condition would, in fact, be very close to the idea of degrees of global pluralism in an anarchy of states.[92] In this sense, cosmopolitan business ethics can be considered as part of a global pluralism of decision-making and norm-creating policymaking institutions (e.g., UN military forces capable of peace keeping, the UN Security Council, World Bank and IMF, the WTO, and a World Court), which implies creating a number of alternative centers in the world, while at the same time building on existing constitutional structures. This should be supported by a great number of civic organizations and corporations that operate internationally and create international structures and ethical norms and values that contribute as sources of international politics and law. It is in this context that republican business ethics is situated as a contribution to the creation of structures of international norms of civil society.

In this sense, the corporation can contribute as a world citizen to solving the important problems of modernity. As actors at the global level, in a time of interstate interdependence with regard to world ecological, economical, and political problems, it is a challenge of the corporation to contribute to build-ing-up an international community of virtue that can protect basic rights. This vision of universal corporate citizenship could be described as the *world ethos* of business ethics. Under this ethos, corporations should not only protect universal human rights, but also give those rights meaning in relation to the particular cultures in the countries where they operate. By protecting universal rights that are dependent on the charter and declarations of the United Na-tions, corporations can act for good international relations that go beyond the interests of particular communities of republics and nations. By doing this, corporations can, when they really want to appear as good citizens, help to build a world community that implies the universalization of procedural virtues of liberal society. Corporations can, at the same time, be cosmopolitan and situated in particular societies, in the sense that they foster universal prin-ciples while making those principles work in concrete practice.

Endnotes

1   Michael Walzer, "Governing the Globe" in Michael Walzer, *Arguing about War*, (New Haven and London Yale University Press, 2004), 186.

2   www.unglobalcompact.org.

3   In this way we can perceive an empirical expression of the basic ethical principles of republican business ethics, which is manifested in the international institutional norms of business ethics.

4   Andrew Crane and Dirk Matten, *Business Ethics. A European Perspective* (Oxford: Oxford University Press, 2004), 300.

5   This case is selected from Andrew Crane and Dirk Matten, *Business Ethics. A European Perspective* (Oxford: Oxford University Press, 2004) and from Laura Pincus Hartman, *Perspectives in business ethics* (Chicago: Irwin McGraw-Hill, 1998), 507-515. See also Chris Megone and Simon J. Robinson (eds.), *Case Histories in Business Ethics* (London: Routledge, 2002), 141-159 where the case is discussed in a narrative perspective as an illustra-tion of the importance of case studies for understanding business ethics dilemmas in practice. Moreover, the case was very important for turning international focus on the global responsibility of corporations. This policy of social responsibility was initiated by the WHO.

6   The Foreign Corrupt Practices Act is considered as a one of the first legislative initiatives to formulate interna-tional rules for business ethics. This act forbids American corporations from bribing government officials in any country of the world. See Richard De George, "International Business Ethics" in *A Companion to Business Ethics* edited by Robert E. Frederick (Oxford: Blackwell Companions to Philosophy, Blackwell Publishing, 1999), 235.

7   G. R. S. Rao, "The Ethics Agenda Facing the International Community" in *International Business Ethics. Chal-lenges and Approaches* edited by Georges Enderle (London: Notre Dame University Press) 1999, 37-38.

8   For example Naomi Klein, *No Logo. Taking Aim at the Brand Bullies*, (New York: Picador, Saint Martins Press, 2000) and Serge Latouche, *Justice sans limites: Le défi éthique dans une économie mondialisée* (Paris: Fayard, 2003)

9   Serge Latouche, *Justice sans limites: Le défi éthique dans une économie mondialisée*, (Paris: Fayard, 2003), 78-79.

10   André Rae, "Diversity Stress as Morality Stress" in *Journal of Business Ethics* 14 (1995): 489-496, 490.

11   Ibid: 492.

12   Walter W. Powell and Paul J. DiMaggio, *The New Institutionalism in Organizational Analysis* (Chicago and London: The University of Chicago Press, 1991), 7.

13   Serge Latouche, *Justice sans limites: Le défi éthique dans une économie mondialisée* (Paris: Fayard), 2003, 7.

14   Ulrich Beck, *Risikogesellschaft* (Frankfurt: Suhrkamp Verlag, 1986).

15   The story of an American mining company, Freeport-McMoRan Copper and Gold, Inc., in West Paqua, Indonesia might ilustrates this point. The mining company operated on some remote island where they employed the indigenous population, who had no previous work experience and who were educated by the firm to work in the mines. In order to help the local people, the firm created housing and hospitals; however, this was after a protest action by the locals had been violently suppressed by the Indonesian army. The firm was in a dilemma of increasing pressure by the Indonesian government for income and knowledge that they would not be able to leave the mining field because so much money was invested in the place. In the meantime, their strategy was to increase human rights and the social protection of the workers in order to avoid another riot requiring military intervention by the government, but also to take the social responsibility of the firm seriously and do some good for the local community.

16   Patricia H. Werhane, "The moral responsibility of multinational corporations to be socially responsible" in Michael Hoffman et al. (eds.): *Emerging Global Business Ethics*, Quarum Books, Greenwood Publishing Group Inc., Westpoint 1994, 136-142.

17   This is a Harvard Business School case 395-127. Lynn Sharp Paine, *Cases in Leadership, Ethics and Organizational Integrity. A Strategic Perspective* (Chicago: Irwin, 1997), 349. The case is also selected from Laura Pincus Hartman: *Perspectives in business ethics* (Chicago: Irwin McGraw-Hill, 1998).

18   Ibid: 753-759.

19   Walter W. Powell and Paul J. DiMaggio, *The New Institutionalism in Organizational Analysis* (Chicago and London: The University of Chicago Press, 1991).

20   The work of Keohane and Nye about regime theory in international politics overcomes the contrast between realism and idealism in the theory of international relations and argues that investigation into different regimes of cooperation shows increased interaction among states and people from civil societies to nations.

21   Norman Bowie, "A Kantian Approach to Business Ethics" in *A Companion to Business Ethics* edited by Robert E. Frederick (Oxford: Blackwell Companions to Philosophy, Blackwell Publishing, 1999), 14.

22   Francis Fukuyama, *The End of History and the Last Man* (New York: The Free Press, 1990).

23   Norman Bowie, "A Kantian Approach to Business Ethics" in *A Companion to Business Ethics* edited by Robert E. Frederick (Oxford: Blackwell Companions to Philosophy, Blackwell Publishing, 1999), 15.

24   Richard De George, *Competing with Integrity in International Business* (New York and Oxford: Oxford University Press, 1993). See also Richard De George: "International Business Ethics" in *A Companion to Business Ethics* edited by Robert E. Frederick (Oxford: Blackwell Companions to Philosophy, Blackwell Publishing, 1999), 234.

25   Richard De George, *Competing with Integrity in International Business* (New York and Oxford: Oxford University Press, 1993), 5-6.

26   Richard de George, *Business Ethics*, Fifth edition, (New Jersey: Prentice Hall, Upper Saddle River), 522.

27   Ibid: 529.

28   Richard De George, *Competing with Integrity in International Business* (New York and Oxford: Oxford University Press, 1993).

29   Ibid.

30   See Richard De George, "International Business Ethics" in *A Companion to Business Ethics* edited by Robert E. Frederick (Oxford: Blackwell Companions to Philosophy, Blackwell Publishing, 1999), 235.

31   Richard De George, *Competing with Integrity in International Business* (New York and Oxford: Oxford University Press, 1993).

32   Jacob Dahl Rendtorff, "Critical hermeneutics in law and politics" in Lars Henrik Schmidt: *Paul Ricœur in the Conflict of Interpretations* (Aarhus: Aarhus University Press, 1996).

33   Joseph R. Desjardins and John J. McCall, *Contemporary Issues in Business Ethics*, Fourth Edition (Belmont, California: Wadsworth, Thomason Learning, 2000), 495.

34   This case about Arla is selected from www.arlafoods.dk *Our Responsibility. Arla Food Guidelines*, Arla 2005.

35   www.arlafoods.dk. The method of discursive analysis of the text is inspired by Anders Bordum and Jacob Holm Hansen, *Strategisk ledelseskommunikation. Erhvervslivets ledelse med visioner, missioner og værdier* (Copenhagen: Jurist og Økonomforbundets forlag, 2005), 25-63.

www.arlafoods.dk.

Richard W. Scott, *Institutions and Organizations* (London: Sage Publications, 1995), 33.

James W. Nickel, *Making Sense of Human Rights* (Berkeley: University of California Press, 1987).

An important actual process is the work of the Human Rights Commission of the United Nations in order to formulate an international policy on the "Social Responsibility of Business Corporations".

Thomas Donaldson, "Moral Minimum for Multinationals" in *Ethics and International Affairs*, 1989, Volume 3.,164.

Peter Pruzan Jørgensen, "FN ønsker erhvervsliv med samfundsansvar", Kronik, *Berlingske Tidende*, 2004. See also *Business and Human Rights. Dilemmas and solutions*, edited by Rory Sullivan (London: Greenleaf Publishing, 2003).

Peter Pruzan Jørgensen, "FN ønsker erhvervsliv med samfundsansvar", Kronik, *Berlingske Tidende*, Marts 2004.

Ibid.

Business and Human Rights. Dilemmas and solutions, edited by Rory Sullivan (London: Greenleaf Publishing, 2003).

Manuel Velasquez, "International business, morality and the common good" in *Business Ethics Quarterly*, vol. 2, (July 1992) issue 1. Reprinted in Joseph R. Desjardins and John J. McCall, *Contemporary Issues in Business Ethics* (Belmont California: Fourth Edition, Wadsworth, Thomason Learning), 2000, 515.

Ibid: 515.

Norman Bowie, "The Moral Obligations of Multinational Corporations" in Steven Luper-Foy: *Problems of International Justice* (Boulder Colerado: Westview Press), 1988.

Ibid: 528.

Ibid.

John Rawls, *The Law of Peoples* (New York: Oxford University Press, 1999).

Ibid: 56.

Norman Bowie, "The Moral Obligations of Multinational Corporations" in Steven Luper-Foy: *Problems of International Justice* (Boulder Colerado: Westview Press, 1988), 531.

Joseph R. Desjardins and John J. McCall, *Contemporary Issues in Business Ethics*, Fourth Edition (Belmont California: Wadsworth, Thomason Learning, US 2000), 495.

Georges Enderle, *International Business Ethics. Challenges and Approaches* (London: Notre Dame University Press, 1999), 131-132.

Principles for Business, Caux-Roundtable, Haque, 1994. Reprinted in *International Business Ethics. Challenges and Approaches* edited by Georges Enderle (London: Notre Dame University Press, 1999), 143-150.

Ibid: 143-150.

Toshio Matsuoka argues this in the article "The Caux Roundtable Principles for Business: Presentation and Discussion" by Henri Claude de Bettignies, Kenneth E. Goodpaster, and Toshio Matsuoka in *International Business Ethics. Challenges and Approaches* edited by Georges Enderle (London: Notre Dame University Press, 1999), 134.

Henri Claude de Bettignies argues this in the article "The Caux Roundtable Principles for Business: Presentation and Discussion" by Henri Claude de Bettignies, Kenneth E. Goodpaster, and Toshio Matsuoka in *International Business Ethics. Challenges and Approaches* edited by Georges Enderle (London: Notre Dame University Press, 1999), 137.

Nien-hê Hsieh, "The obligations of transnational corporations: Rawlsian justice and the duty of assistance", *Business ethics Quarterly*, Volume 14, Issue 4, 643-661.

Ibid: 652.

Oliver F. Williams, "The UN Global Compact: The challenge and the promise", *Business Ethics Quarterly, Volume 14*, Issue 4, 2004, 171.

Ibid: 755.

Ibid: 760.

Ibid: 768.

www.unglobalcompact.org

Ibid.67 Jeanne M. Logsdon and Donna J. Wood, "Business Citizenship: From domestic to global level of analysis", *Business Ethics Quarterly*, Volume 12, Issue 2: 155-187.

68   Ibid: 156.
69   Ibid: 170.
70   Klaus M. Leisinger, „Globalisering, Minima Moralia und die Verantwortung multinationer Unternehmen"in *Unternehmensethik und die Transformation des Wettbewerbs*, edited by Brij Nino Kumar, Margit Osterloh und Georg Schreyögg., Schaffer/Poeschel 1999, 330
71   Hans Küng, *Projekt Weltethos* (München/Zürick, 1990). Hans Küng, *Weltethos für Weltpolitik und Weltwirtschaft* (München/Zürick 1995).
72   Immanuel Kant, "Zum Ewigen Frieden" in *Werke in Sech Bänden* (Darmstad: Wissenschaftliche Buchgesellschaft, 1983).
73   Jeanne M. Logsdon and Donna J. Wood, "Business Citizenship: From domestic to global level of analysis", *Business Ethics Quarterly*, Volume 12, Issue 2, (155-187), 178.
74   James E. Post, "Global Corporate Citizenship: Principles to live and work by", *Business Ethics Quarterly*, Volume 12, Issue 2, (143-153), 151.
75   James E. Post, "Global Corporate Citizenship: Principles to live and work by", *Business Ethics Quarterly*, Volume 12, Issue 2, (143-153), 151.
76   Thomas Donaldson, "Moral Minimum for Multinationals", *Ethics and International Affairs* (1989), Volume 3., 170.
77   Henry Shue, *Basic Rights* (Princeton: Princeton University Press, 1982). See also Thomas Donaldson, "Rights in the Global Market" in *Business Ethics: The State of the Art*, edited by R. Edward Freeman (Oxford: Oxford University Press, 1989). Reprinted in Joseph R. Desjardins and John J. McCall, *Contemporary Issues in Business Ethics*, Fourth Edition (Belmont California: Wadsworth, Thomason Learning, 2000), 501.
78   Thomas Donaldson, "Rights in the Global Market" in *Business Ethics: The State of the Art*, edited by R. Edward Freeman (Oxford: Oxford University Press, 1989). Reprinted in Joseph R. Desjardins and John J. McCall, *Contemporary Issues in Business Ethics*, Fourth Edition (Belmont California: Wadsworth, Thomason Learning, 2000), 501. Thomas Donaldson, "Moral Minimum for Multinationals" in *Ethics and International Affairs*, Volume 3 (1989), 173.
79   James W. Nickel, *Making Sense of Human Rights* (Berkeley: University of California Press, 1987). See also Thomas Donaldson, "Rights in the Global Market" in *Business Ethics: The State of the Art*, edited by R. Edward Freeman (Oxford: Oxford University Press, 1989). Reprinted in Joseph R. Desjardins and John J. McCall, *Contemporary Issues in Business Ethics*, Fourth Edition (Belmont California: Wadsworth, Thomason Learning, 2000), 503.
80   Richard De George, *Competing with Integrity in International Business* (New York Oxford: Oxford University Press, 1993), 52.
81   Ibid: 53.
82   Ibid: 54.
83   Ibid: 90.
84   Ibid: 91.
85   Ibid: 92.
86   Ibid: 93.
87   Principles for Business, Caux-Roundtable, Haque, 1994. Reprinted in *International Business Ethics. Challenges and Approaches* edited by Georges Enderle (London: Notre Dame University Press, 1999), 146-147.
88   Ibid: 148.
89   Ibid: 148-149.
90   Tom Dunfee and Thomas Donaldson, *Ties that bind*, (Cambridge Massachusetts: Harvard Business School Press, 1999).
91   Thomas Donaldson, "Moral Minimum for Multinationals" in *Ethics and International Affairs*, 1989, Volume 3, 178.
92   Walzer, Michael, "Governing the Globe" in Michael Walzer, *Arguing about War*, (New Haven and London: Yale University Press, 2004), 186.

Part 5
Policy proposals for corporate strategy: Basic ethical principles for business ethics and corporate citizenship

1. Strategizing Global Business Ethics

The next chapter puts forward some policy proposals as practical consequences of the theoretical discussion of the ethics, responsibility, and legitimacy of corporations. This general discussion can be viewed as the basis for strategizing global business ethics. The discussion so far has put forward a relatively comprehensive view on corporate strategy, covering major areas of application of business ethics, including the power and responsibility of large corporations, business conduct in specific industries and markets, relations to employees and other stakeholders, social responsibility and relations to the environment, and the issue of legitimacy of profits and of specific economic activities.[1] The proposed corporate strategy of business ethics covers mainly the issue of values-driven management, but it may also be considered as a proposal for corporate governance. To put it bluntly, there is no corporate governance without business ethics and values-driven management.

From the point of view of corporate strategy, it has been an important point to show that business is an ethical practice, and that ethics should, therefore, be conceived as the heart of the science of corporate strategy. Corporate strategies and management policies become illustrations of ethics as an "already through and through" business practice, and as an aspect of human existence.[2] Accordingly, strategy is arguably fundamentally about responsible behaviour and includes stakeholder management as an accomplishment of corporate strategy.[3] This new formulation of strategy must imply that ethics and responsibility move into the heart of management education and management practice. This approach agrees with Henry Mintzberg that business ethics and responsibility should play a much stronger role in management.[4] The essence of this criticism is that we have to rethink management science, practice, and themes because ethics and responsibility are not only there to improve efficiency and shareholder value, but to make managers responsible persons who make good decisions with integrity and concern for stakeholders.[5] Accordingly, the close relation between ethics, responsibility, and corporate citizenship needs to be considered when formulating long-term strategies for corporations. This implies a new conceptualization of the science of strategy that conceives ethics as closely related to strategy.[6] As has been demonstrated, good and efficient economic and organizational management depends on the values and ethics of the corporation and on its capacity to behave responsibly in society. It is not meaningful to conceive of management and strategy without ethics, responsibility, and legitimacy. Strategic management is not possible without technical and economic knowledge, but it is ethical reflection about possible choices of actions that creates and develops a sustainable corporation.

Accordingly, the following strategic policy proposals conceive ethics and values as strategic instruments for good management that develops the strategic coherence of the corporation. The strategic management of ethics and responsibility combines values-driven management with concerns for business and economic development of the corporation. In contrast to economic or bureaucratic conceptions of strategic planning, values-driven management and business ethics may be defined as a holistic form of management, which surpasses traditional disciplines and combines elements from different conceptions of strategic planning.[7] This is why the thematic of strategy in the following policy proposals may be broader than traditional concepts of business strategy. All policy proposals are considered as relevant to what could be called a really virtuous organization, which means they must be rather comprehensive. This does not mean that the policy proposals are unfocused, but that they constitute together the totally of a strategy to be implemented in order to work for corporate citizenship. It is, however, important to acknowledge that corporations operate under varying conditions. Consequently, it is the task of managerial judgment to apply the proposed management principles with care to concrete business practice.

The following figure shows the focus and structure of strategy in relation to a process of implementation in particular corporations. The idea is that the corporation begins by formulating its strategy and vision for corporate citizenship. With this figure in mind, the strategy for corporate citizenship may include: formulations of strategic foundations, the realization of corporate governance as stakeholder management, and implementation of business ethics through values-driven management.

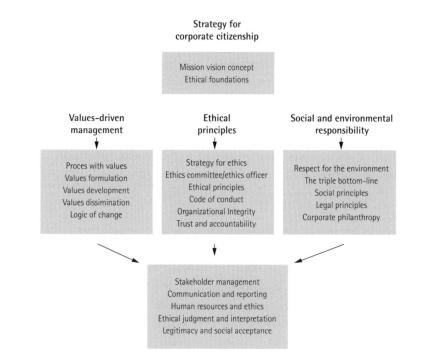

1.1. Strategic foundations of policy proposals

1. The focus of the strategy. Applying the basic ethical principles in values-driven management clarifies the concepts of responsibility, ethics, and values of corporations as core to the strategy of the firm. The focus of such a strategy for action, culture, and identity of the firm should be corporate governance, business ethics, corporate social responsibility, values-driven management, stakeholder management, and sensitivity to the values of culture and identity of the firm.

2. Need for a new strategy. There is a need for a new strategy that combines the theory and practice of values in organizations, corporate social responsibility and business ethics. We may call this the basic ethical principle in values-driven management and business ethics. This should be considered as an institutional approach to corporate social responsibility. The need for strategy is reflected in empirical developments in corporate ethics and policy making in the United States and Europe.

3. Close relation between values, organizations, and management. A sustainable strategy of business ethics should focus on the close relation between values, organizations, and management. Strategy should explore the significance of values in the organization, because values are important in order to understand the function, meaning, and goals of the organization. We need to acknowledge that organizations are characterized by many different kinds of values with different meanings: economic values, social values, and environmental values. It is therefore important to clarify and distinguish carefully between different kinds of values. The aim is to expose clearly what kinds of values determine the business activities of the firm.

4. A strategy for integrative business ethics. It is important that a strategy for business ethics and values-driven management try to integrate the insights of different theories of organizations and business ethics. Values-driven management should be based on mediation and differentiation between the cognitive and practical potentialities and limits of different theories of business ethics. The most important theories to use for practical application are: rational choice theory and utilitarian concepts of profit maximization; stakeholder theory, including strategic stakeholder communication and stakeholder management; communitarian concepts of business that see the firm as a community and a common life form; Kantian and universalistic conception of firms that defends human dignity and rights in the workplace; and integrated social contract theory that proposes a tentative mediation between the life form in a particular culture and universal norms in the international society. It is the aim of judgment to find the right balance between opposing views, as this is the foundation of a republican and critical democratic approach to the theory of the firm, where the firm is searching for good corporate citizenship.

5. Enforcement of ethical principles in organizational ethics. On the basis of the integrative approach to business ethics, it is important to apply concrete ethical principles. In particular, it is necessary to be concerned with ethical principles that are defined as respect for autonomy, dignity, integrity, and vulnerability. These ideas are conceived as middle-level principles concerned with the person as the turning point. They should be considered within the framework of principles of solidarity and justice. Within a strategy for business ethics, these principles constitute the framework for stakeholder dialogue in a democratic conception of business ethics. As such, they function as critical measures for organizational ethics. Autonomy expresses the concern for self-regulation of the firm in a liberal market economy. Dignity expresses respect for human beings in the workplace and in organizations. Integrity expresses the unity and wholeness of the organization with regard to trust, honesty, and moral identity. Vulnerability expresses the condition of the firm in a strongly competitive market economy.

6. Development of the idea of institutional responsibility. The concept of social responsibility should be paramount in the strategy of business ethics. It is important that management strategies accept the shift from shareholder to stakeholder value – with appropriate fiduciary duty to shareholders. Social responsibility strategies recognize the fact that economic action is embedded. Institutions have ethical and social responsibilities, because it is possible to identify values in their internal decision-making structure (CID). Managers are not only responsible for profit maximization and shareholder value, but should include all relevant stakeholders. Firms are political actors. To be neutral in ethical matters is in itself a political attitude. Social responsibility as institutional responsibility goes beyond long-term shareholder value. The firm should be conceived as a moral person with responsibility, integrity, liability, and accountability. This is the institutional conception of good corporate citizenship.

7. Proactive strategy for compliance with legal regulations. A major purpose of business ethics is to contribute to a strategy of compliance. Corporations should, to the extent it is appropriate, develop a strategy of self-regulation like the one proposed in the FSGO. A business ethics strategy should recognize the organization's responsibility and culpability. An important element of corporate strategy is that self-regulation should occur throughout the firm based on the dynamic interplay between carrots and sticks. Strategy should build on ethical and legal concepts of institutional responsibility, which imply a legal dimension of ethics as more than cosmetics and corporate image.

8. Dynamic tension between compliance and values in management. Corporate social responsibility, values, and business ethics should not only be based on the interest in obeying the law, but they should also imply voluntary efforts to pursue the good and strive to achieve excellence. Strategy should follow the recommendations of the European Union for corporate social responsibility. Values, ethics, and responsibility are internal efforts to be just and benevolent rather than only to obey the law. Corporations should combine these external and internal aspects of corporate ethics and responsibility.

9. Ethics the heart of corporate culture. When beginning ethics and programs of values-driven management, corporations should focus on ethical value propositions in the daily practices of the firm. Management should go beyond practical and instrumental issues of production, service delivery, and finance, and ask fundamental questions about the role of ethics in the activities of the company in order to examine possible scenarios of best practice. This implies that: 1) basic ethical dilemmas are recognized; 2) ethics is viewed as the core value of the enterprise; 3) management works to realize their ethical visions and anticipates ethical tensions in daily decision-making; 4) debates about all ethical issues and questions are considered important, and that the firm is aware of ethical values and possible conflicts of interests; 5) management seeks to engage employees in its ethical values, and seeks a role to play in local community; 6) there is continuant evaluation and a renewal of the ethical commitments of the corporation.

10. Integrity as the basis for the firm's ethics strategy. The focus of corporate strategy should be corporate integrity, both at the organizational level, but also as a virtue of individual behavior. Integrity is a virtue of excellent moral behaviour and of uncorrupted character. It implies value coherence of organizations, accountability, and transparency. Integrity expresses the unity and wholeness of the organization with regard to trust, honesty, and moral identity. Business ethics shifts the focus from individual to organizational integrity to the history, culture, and values of the organization. It is important to acknowledge that corporate social responsibility and corporate values define integrity. Moreover, corporate intentionality (i.e., CID) is the basis for institutional responsibility and integrity in which stakeholder dialogue defines good corporate citizenship.

11. Awareness of pitfalls and problems of values-driven management. Strategy of business ethics should be critical towards the possible alienation and instrumentalization of ethics in business corporations. The danger is creating a Weberian "iron cage of rationality" with professionals without spirit and hedonist consumers without heart. Values-driven management should not be reduced to a new kind of disciplinary tool. Soft values should not become new hard values, where ethics and values in management lead to stress and personal breakdowns. Business should not be reduced to a new kind of power instrument. The virtues of values-driven management are not pragmatic, but also concern real ethical substance in dilemmas facing an organization.

12. Institutional business ethics should not forget the importance of individuals. Strategy must be aware of the limits of ethics. Theories, credos, and mission statements in ethics programs may not overcome power relations or ethical dilemmas. Moreover, individual judgment is always necessary in concrete situations. Ethics program should not exclude self-defining activities of individuals who contribute with important ethical decisions, sometimes confronting individual and personal norms with the norms of the organization. Values and ethics programs, as the basis for institutional responsibility, cannot be anything more than a frame for individual decisions and interpretations. Moreover, values and ethics cannot exclude motivations of power and success as the basis for individual action; therefore, individual responsibility and personal values are also important in "right versus right" dilemmas, and defining moments.[8] Managers and workers are constantly confronted with the tension between personal values and organizational demands. The problem is whether you can keep your integrity and dignity when making hard decisions involving other human beings. Perhaps it is exactly such decisions that illustrate the necessity of ethics. They shape moral identity, show which values constitute moral identity, which values have been introduced in the organization, and they challenge our theories of organizational ethics.

Organizational development can be viewed as a multilevel structure of different aspects of an ethics strategy for a corporation to develop full corporate citizenship:

Level	Strategy focus	Activity focus	Implementation focus
1	corporate citizenship strategy formulation	refinancing ethical foundations and the mission, vision, and concept	judgment as conflict mediator between different ethical theories and principles
2	development of the concept of institutional responsibility	integration of individual and collective responsibility; constitution of CID ethics decision-making structure	formulation of programs of values-driven management, ethics, and compliance; development of a policy for corporate social responsibility
3	development of a strategy for sustainable development (triple bottom line)	stakeholder engagement and stakeholder dialogue; development of balanced scorecard or other instruments for sustainability management	communication with stakeholders about implementation of good corporate citizenship with focus on triple bottom-line management, reporting, and auditing
4	corporate governance based on stakeholder management	integration of CSR, business ethics, and values-driven management in a holistic concept of corporate governance	communicating with stakeholders about principles of stakeholder management and the "good life with and for the other in just institutions"
5	stakeholder management as sustainability management	sustainability and stakeholder management from the perspective of purpose, principle, and people	integrating citizenship and CSR as a result of values-driven management; develop procedures for reporting of CSR and corporate citizenship
6	values-driven management as organizational democracy	developing collective identity with respect for individual rights	application of principles of corporate citizenship as the basis for organizational identity

Figure 5.2. Levels of focus of organizational development towards corporate citizenship

1.2. Corporate Governance and stakeholder management

13. Corporate governance strategy as sustainability management. In corporate governance a strategy for sustainability management must be based on the triple bottom line. The organization should be committed to economic and financial responsibility, constantly improving financial performance with high objectives for growth, value creation, and competitive performance. Environmental responsibility implies efforts to improve environmental performance and integrate considerations about the environment and the biosphere in the daily activities of the firm. Social responsibility means that the firm works to improve its social performance with objectives for integrating environmental, social, and human rights, as well as health and safety concerns, in the business of the firm. In corporate governance, sustainability management for the triple bottom line should be based on open dialogue with stakeholders as well as compliance with, and development of, international reporting standards for reporting financial, environmental, and social performance. This involves support for international conventions, declarations, and codes of conduct related to triple bottom-line management.

14. Corporate governance as explicit compliance with international standards. This means that firms should actively subscribe to international agreements. It should be explicit in corporate governance standards and initiatives that this compliance to social expectations expresses the fundamental commitments of the organization. Commitments may be linked to international agreements, conventions, and codes of conduct, for example the recommendations of the United Nations Commission on the Environment, the Brundtland Commission, the Nations Universal Declaration of Human Rights, the United Nations Global Compact, the United Nations Convention on Biological Diversity, the International Chamber of Commerce's Business Charter for Sustainable Development, the Sullivan Principles, Caux Roundtable Principles, et cetera.

15. Transparent framework for corporate governance. Strategy should be based on an ethical framework for corporate governance. This involves high integrity of the board and management with a high level of transparency. The division of responsibilities of the board and of management should be transparent. There should be procedures for control of the board and of management. Corporate governance should be based on clear rules and codes of conduct.

In this context, values-driven management is important for ethical corporate governance. In order to protect shareholders corporate governance should be aware of fiduciary duties to shareholders, but corporate governance must also go beyond that to a broader inclusion of stakeholders; therefore, there is a close relationship between corporate governance and corporate social responsibility (as stakeholder responsibility) in order to develop well-functioning and transparent economic markets.

16. Vision of good corporate governance. It is important to develop a vision about where the organization is heading. This vision can indeed be very ambitious, for example, addressing how the corporation contributes to creating a better world. It may be a clear description of what the organization does to achieve its fundamental aims. There should be a connection between aims and vision. It is important to include relations to stakeholders in this description of the fundamental aims of the corporation. The vision helps the organization to formulate its values and self-conceptions. Values of integrity, accountability, responsibility, engagement with stakeholders, commitment, teamwork, and citizenship can help to clarify the relationship between a fundamental vision of the corporation and its strategy for corporate governance.

17. Corporate social responsibility and corporate governance. Social responsibility as stakeholder responsibility should be conceived as an integrated part of corporate governance.[9] The corporation should work for better social performance at the organizational, regional, and global levels. It should try to identify areas of social responsibility and be open to the opinions of stakeholders, for example by respecting human rights and international labor standards, or by being responsible for the content of products and their consequences for customers. Moreover, social responsibility in corporate governance not only includes employees and customers, but other stakeholders, such as suppliers. Important standards of social responsibility are freedom of association, non-discrimination, respectable working hours, wages, and benefits, the prohibition of child labor and forced labor, and high standards for employee health and safety.

18. Environmental responsibility and corporate governance. Environmental responsibility includes a sustainable business strategy integrating economics and ecology with the social context of operations. Technology should be sustainable with ecologically efficient life cycles. Life-cycle analysis and long-term duration should be central elements in environmental strategies. Bioethical and ethical principles of respect for autonomy, dignity, integrity, and vulnerability from the perspective of solidarity and justice should be extended as principles for protecting the whole living world. The corporation should be aware of global problems of sustainability, as well as growth and development. Environmental responsibility implies respect for the integrity of ecosystems and a wider conception of ethics, including animals and nature. To the extent it is relevant, the firm should propose bioethics and environmental ethics in how it handles issues such as genetic modification and biotechnology, and the use of animals in research and production or in agriculture and food production.

19. Corporate governance as stakeholder management. Stakeholder management should be promoted as a general framework for good corporate governance. Stakeholder management is based on communicative action. Stakeholder judgment includes the search for legitimacy and leads to a conversations about corporate stakeholder responsibility. Stakeholder management includes many different kinds of stakeholders (e.g., power, urgency, and legitimacy) and is also open to nonstakeholders.[10] Business ethics and values are central in stakeholder management. In corporate governance, stakeholder management can be used descriptively, normatively, and prescriptively. Stakeholder management integrates ethics and economics. Stakeholder management implies a broad view of stakeholders as those who affect or are affected by the organization. Stakeholder management concerns the common good (including civil society as a stakeholder).

20. Stakeholder management as an open-ended vision of governance. Stakeholder management is about being open to the world and surrounding community of the firm. Stakeholder management should be used to increase corporate self-reflection in the process of decision-making and corporate governance. This implies panoramization (broader perspective), prioritization (conscience of complexity), politicization (inclusion in decision-making), and particularization (reflective self-awareness). Stakeholder management is also risk management, but it is important to move beyond strategic management to ethical stakeholder reflection. Civil society should be conceived as a stakeholder (i.e., the firm is not the center of the universe). Companies should no longer place themselves in the center of the stakeholder framework, but rather consider themselves as servants of society as a whole. This is the essence of the idea of good corporate citizenship.

21. Fundamental principles of stakeholder management. Stakeholder management could advantageously adopt Freeman's ten stakeholder principles (see chapter 3, section 1.4, box 11).

1) Stakeholder interests go together over time.

2) Stakeholder consists of real people with names and faces and children. People are complex.

3) We need solutions to issues that satisfy multiple stakeholders simultaneously.

4) We need intensive communication and dialogue with stakeholders, not just those who are friendly.

5) We need to have a philosophy of voluntarism; to manage stakeholder relationships ourselves rather than third parties such as governments.

6) We need to generalize the marketing approach.

7) Everything that we do serves stakeholders. We never trade off the interests of one versus the other continuously over time.

8) We negotiate with primary and secondary stakeholders.

9) We constantly monitor and redesign processes to make them better serve our stakeholders.

10) We act with purpose that fulfills our commitment to stakeholders. We act with aspiration towards fulfilling our dreams.[11]

22. Corporate stakeholder responsibilities and the common good. Stakeholder responsibility in corporate governance can be summarized as aiming for the "good life with and for the other in just institutions."[12] What is important is integrating different approaches to stakeholder management and business ethics. Business is not only about survival, self-reliance, and self-interest, but also a contribution to the common good. Even though it is difficult, and it should not override respect for rights and protections of persons, stakeholder management should search for solutions for the benefit of all. This involves pragmatic integration and differentiation between different concepts of business ethics.

23. Values-driven management, corporate governance, and justice. Our Kantian and universalistic approach to principles of justice in organizations implies organizational fairness as a principle of justice in a stakeholder economy. In this sense, fairness in stakeholder management includes application of Rawls's principles of justice to organizational behavior and values-driven management, in particular the principles of respect for political freedom and the principle of difference.[13] Good values-driven management should be based on the principle of fairness as a fundamental principle in a just stakeholder model (i.e., fairness goes beyond contracts).

24. Corporate governance, stakeholder management, and judgment. Judgment should be recognized as a basic principle of corporate governance and stakeholder management. Ideas of sustainability, justice, and ethics are abstract principles that only reach real significance in concrete situations. Values are realized concretely as a part of corporate culture. Integrity should be realized as a result of reflective judgment on the part of managers who go beyond mere compliance with legal rules to realize values in daily practice. Judgment contributes to the realization of corporate social responsibility and corporate governance through strategies for sustainable development and stakeholder dialogue integrating economic, social, and environmental concerns in the strategy of the firm.

Box 20. "Walk the talk!": Corporate citizenship and CSR as a practical strategy

The Danish Commerce and Companies Agency (Erhvervs- og Selskabsstyrelsen), the European Social Foundation, the Danish Labor Market Board, and the Ministry of Employment have collaborated on practical information and teaching materials about CSR. In the publication stemming from this collaborative effort, a number of practical and strategic proposals for companies that work with CSR are put forward. Their work has informed the policy proposals in this section.

They emphasize that CSR should be used to improve the bottom line and competive advantage of corporations, in the sense that CSR is concretely related to the management, mission, and values of the firm. We may add the vision of business ethics of the firm to this list. This should be done on the basis of extended communication with the stakeholders of the firm.[14] The proposals also point to the idea that it is possible to refer to CSR innovation, which is an integration of CSR in relation to the innovative processes of the corporation. In addition to those general activities, activities in relation to employees, customers, the environment, society, and suppliers could also act as focal points for internal and external strategic CSR.

They also emphasize that stakeholder activities are based on dialogue between stakeholders, which includes active selection and proactive contact with stakeholders. In this context, employees are important stakeholders and strategic CSR activities imply striving to improve health in the work environment, physical and psychic work conditions, job possibilities for senior employees, diversity in the corporation, and other issues on their behalf. [15]

Strategic customer activities are defined as a dialogue with the customers about their expectations, but also as concern for consciousness about product responsibility, for example through using the EU environmental labels (i.e., using the symbol of the swan) or the Nordic environmental label (i.e., using the symbol for a flower) in product packaging.[16] By complying with the demands of these environmental labels, corporations can express integrity and accountability. They can express a social responsibility in relation to the customers that, in the end, can increase their own sustainability.

Activities in relation to suppliers primarily imply intensive communication about CSR with suppliers involving clarification of how they deal with forced work, child labor, discrimination, freedom of expression, work environment, conditions of employment, health and disease, product development, corruption, and bribery, and so on.[17] Suppliers may also be informed about international rules and codes of conduct, such as the Global Compact principles.

Social activities include corporate engagement in the local community. This can happen by sponsoring cultural or sporting events, support for charity and education in the form of internships, student jobs, et cetera.[18]

Strategic environmental activities include the work with environmental governance and environmental management as integrated elements of company products and service deliverables. Examples of such strategic environmental activities include good use of energy and water use, requirements to suppliers regarding raw materials, the use of cleaner technologies, or using ecological materials in the design of products.[19]

Their practical guidance about how to implement CSR is a very good example of the possible concrete realization of the proposals for corporate strategy put forward in this book. The guidance presents CSR as an instrument and a tool that is closely integrated with other management instruments to ensure corporate sustainability with efficiency. In companies that pursue a concrete focus on social responsibility, it is no longer an expression of abstract strategic and philosophical discussion (i.e., talking the talk), but has become integrated in the practical life of the corporation (i.e., walking the talk!).

1.3. Basic Principles of values–driven management

25. Stakeholder management as values-driven management. Creating an ethical strategy of corporate governance and stakeholder management leads to values-driven management. Basic ethical principles include: respect for people; autonomy and respect for rights; the principle of dignity; the principle of integrity and respect for the coherence of life; the principle of vulnerability and respect for human fragility; justice and fairness; and reflective judgment to mediate between values. Compliance with these principles in concrete situations should be the foundation for developing codes of conduct and ethical rules in different business organizations and corporations. Moreover, they are foundational for developing and improving organizational culture.

26. Values-driven management and integrity strategy. Values-driven management should involve an integrity strategy, including attention to the three Ps: purpose, principle and people.[20] *Purpose* refers to the mission and value of the organization. *Principle* refers to the obligations and ideals that are central to the ethical behavior of the organization. *People* refers to the required respect for different stakeholders and constituencies of the organization. High integrity strategies involve fair treatment of these different stakeholders in specific situations. Integrity-based strategies use frameworks of values and mission statements to achieve organizational wholeness and unity. Integrity strategies search to build organizational structures and systems that develop and maintain integrity values and ideals of the organization.

27. Values-driven management. Organizational development should be committed to foundational values. Important norms and foundational values include integrity, trust, accountability, responsibility, fairness, transparency, citizenship, compliance, and honesty. Such values could constitute a code of conduct: however, honest and profound interpretation of values of the firm is necessary. Values should be more than clichés and they should have real importance for employees and other stakeholders. Values-driven management should be closely linked to CSR in relation to the different stakeholders of the firm. CSR activities include environmental, social, and economic activities to improve the relation of corporations with their social environments.

28. Combination of compliance and values in values-driven management. A good program of values-driven management recognizes the difference between compliance and values. While compliance programs should ensure obedience to the law, values should appeal to inner motivation. The contrast between compliance and ethics programs is important for integrating ethics into organizational culture. Compliance programs are based on institutional authority rather than individual autonomy. Value-based programs focus on promoting individual autonomy and responsibility in order to evoke individual engagement and motivation, as well as a larger space for personal decision-making by employees and other stakeholders. Even though the difference between values-driven programs and compliance programs should be clear for decision-makers, a good program of values-driven management may, indeed, be a program that preserves the tension between rules and values, allowing for individual autonomy and responsibility while keeping the advantages of institutional authority.

29. Important steps of values-driven management. A good program of values-driven management should have an impact of the institutional structure of the organization. In order to achieve values-driven management, Michael Hoffman and others have identified ten steps that are create the conditions for an effective ethics and compliance program:

1) *Self-assessment.* Evaluation and examination of ethics and values in the organization.

2) *Commitment from the top.* Board and management support the program.

3) *Codes of business conduct.* There should be a written code of ethics and values of the organization.

4) *Communication vehicle.* There should be an ethics communication policy.

5) *Training.* Critical and constructive training in ethical values of the organization is important to communicate and create an ethical culture.

6) *Resources for assistance.* The organization should set-up hotlines or helplines, and offices where employees can get help and protection.

7) *Organizational ownership.* Ethics must be integrated at all levels of the organization.

8) *Consistent response and enforcement.* This involves systems of incentives, evaluations, and measures for improvement.

9) *Audits and measurements.* Ethics and compliance programs should be continuously evaluated and audited.

10) *Revision and refinements.* Ethics and compliance programs should be continuously revised and refined from the perspective of new ethical experiences, corporate policies and strategies.[21]

All of these steps include development of special strategies for implementing an organizational values program according to the specific context of the firm, which implies specific legal, values, or virtue-oriented codes according to the specific identity and history of the firm.

30. Application of the seven steps of the FSGO.[22]

1) Establish standards and procedures. There should be established structures of compliance.

2) Assign oversight responsibility. Specific individual(s) within high-level personnel of the organization must be assigned responsibility.

3) Delegation of discretionary authority. Persons that have the tendency to exercise illegal activities must not have great responsibility.

4) Communication of standards and procedures. The organization must have taken steps to effectively communicate its standards and procedures (e.g., by requiring participation in training programs or by disseminating publications that explain in a practical manner what is required).

5) Achieving employee compliance. The organization must have taken reasonable steps to achieve compliance with its standards (e.g., by utilizing monitoring and auditing systems).

6) Enforcement and discipline. The standards must have been consistently enforced through appropriate disciplinary mechanisms.

7) Organizational response to ethics violations. After an offense has been detected, the organization must have taken all reasonable steps to respond appropriately and to prevent further similar offenses, including any necessary modifications to its program to prevent and detect legal violations.

31. Use of values to create a collective identity and mission with respect for individual rights and values.
Values and ethics are important for the common good of the organization. Values and values-driven management are paramount in order to create a collective identity and institutional consciousness of the organization. The initiative of values-driven management can be said to create a consciousness and self-reflection at all levels of the organization. This is the foundation of corporate culture. The program of ethics or compliance contributes to an ethical learning process of the organization. This is a possible result of values-driven management and it is the condition for avoiding ideological dimensions of values-driven management, making values function as the integrating force of the organization. In this sense, the organization moves from being an insensitive and bureaucratic monster towards greater economic, social, and environmental principles according the international concern for sustainability of corporations in a free world market.

32. Justification of values according to their field of application in different business practices. It should be evident that principles of values apply differently in different fields of business. There are specific issues and concerns in different industries, countries, and with regard to different stakeholders. It is, however, also important to follow general principles of good business conduct as the foundation of application, such as the Global Compact principles and the Caux Principles. Such principles cover: 1) the responsibilities of the corporation: beyond shareholders towards stakeholders; 2) the economic and social impact of corporations: toward innovation, justice, and world community; 3) corporate behavior: beyond the letter of law toward a spirit of trust; 4) respect for rules: beyond trade fiction toward cooperation; 5) support for multilateral trade: beyond isolation toward world community; 6) respect for the environment: beyond protection toward enhancement; and 7) avoidance of illicit operations: beyond profit towards peace. Such principles are important for specific application in particular fields of business.[23]

33. Values-driven management should be used in the interests of the employees. Because employees are major stakeholders of the organization, it is important that values-driven management is used to mediate between employer and employee in order to ensure rights and increase competition. It is important to emphasize that value and ethics function as a tool for democratizing the firm. Values contribute to strengthening employee inner motivation and effort to do something more at work Values ensure loyalty and trust at the work place. Employees should be included in management of the firm in order to reduce conflicts between employees and management; however, the tension between values-driven management and the conception of the workplace as open to employee efforts to work for a more democratic work market is unavoidable.

34. Judgment and values-driven management. Strategy formulation should account for the creative function of moral thinking in management. Values-driven management is not only an issue of applying rules, but about understanding context and concrete decision-making; therefore, managers and employees should be educated in the art of personal judgment. Ethical judgment in stakeholder management seeks to integrate ethical principles in relation to stakeholders in connection with a global theory of organizational justice. Ethical judgment as reflective and determinant works with dilemmas and problems of values-driven management. Judgment provides interpretations, arguments, and proposals for decisions and action regarding problems such as the question of whether integrity management is moral. What about values compromise? Can collective values and principles determine individual decisions? Is corporate social responsibility really a win-win situation? Judgment and moral thinking contribute to a management structure where values and ethics are frames for decision-making.

35. Judgment as a decision-making model for values-driven management.

Management should use ethical judgment and moral thinking as frameworks for decision-making. This implies reflecting on the ethical value proposition of the firm and integrating different ethical frameworks in the firm's conception of values. More or less important frames of reference are business ethics, professional ethics, research ethics, environmental ethics, the ethics of public relations, and the ethics of innovation. In all fields of the firm's operation ethical issues may emerge, so it is important that they are integrated in all processes of the firm. Important questions to ask in innovation, technology, and research are: What is the potential social utility? Are the environmental risks too high? What are the risks for human research subjects and animals? Is informed consent respected? Is animal welfare respected? Important questions to ask in production are: Is the product useful for society? What are the environmental consequences of the product? What is the risk for employees? Does the product violate or hurt specific groups in society? Does the product respect basic ethical principles? Important questions to ask different stakeholders are: Are suppliers treated with fairness? What is customer satisfaction? What is employee risk? Can we identify other relevant stakeholders who are affected by, or affect the production? With such questions, decision-making utilizes the interplay between technological innovations, ethical analysis, and policy decision-making.

36. Approach concrete issues of ethics from the point of view of critical judgment.

Concrete decision-making in values-driven management is contextual and should focus on many concrete issues, including bribery and corruption, conflicts of interest, safety and the environment, insider trade and personal gain, discrimination and harassment, professionalism, social responsibility, and respect for the rules of the market (e.g., antitrust). In all such cases the function of critical decision-making, the following procedure is implied: 1) information is evaluated; 2) it must be considered how the decision might affect all involved; 3) it must be decided what company values and ethics principles are relevant; and 4) the best course of action is determined.[24]

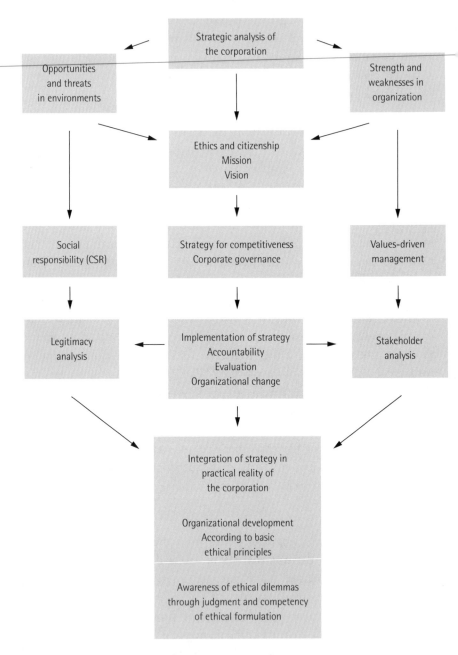

Figure 5.3 Strategic management for corporate citizenship
The figure illustrates the close relation between values, ethics and social responsibility in the strategic development of corporate citizenship.

Endnotes

1   Daniel Terris, *Ethics at Work. Creating Virtue at an American Corporation* (Waltham Massachusetts Brandeis University Press, 2005).

2   Daniel R. Gilbert Jr., *Ethics through Corporate Strategy* (Oxford: The Ruffin Series of Business Ethics, Oxford University Press, 1996), 7.

3   Ibid: 84 and 104.

4   Henry Mintzberg, *Managers not MBAs. A Hard Look on the Soft Practice of managing and management development*, (San Francisco: Prentice Hall, 2004).

5   Ibid: 42.

6   Lynn Sharp Paine, *Cases in Leadership, Ethics and Organizational Integrity. A Strategic Perspective* (Chicago: Irwin, 1997), viii.

7   Henry Mintzberg, *The Rise and Fall of Strategic Planning*, Pitman Publishing, London 1994, 3. We can argue that with my approach to strategy we move strategy development away from the predominant use of military metaphors towards a use of ethical metaphors. This does not take away the practical side of strategy as a science of action, but it links strategy with the ethical aim of "the good life with and for the other in just institutions."

8   Joseph Jr Badaracco, *Defining Moments* (Cambridge, Massachusetts: Harvard Business School Press, 1998).

9   R. Edward Freeman develops the term, "Stakeholder Responsibility". See R. Edward Freeman, "Managing For Stakeholders: An Argument, Ten Principles, and Eight Techniques", Lecture Copenhagen Business School, November 2004. Also printed in R. Edward and S. R. Velamuri, "A New Approach to CSR: Company Stakeholder Responsibility" in A. Kakabadse and M. Morsing *Corporate Social Responsibility: Reconciling Managerial Strategies Towards the 21st Century* (London: Palgrave MacMillan 2006).

10 See Ronald K. Mittchell, Bradley R. Agle and Donna S. Wood, "Toward a Theory of Stakeholder Identification and Salience: Defining the Principle of Who and What really counts", *Academy of Management Review* 1997, Vol 22, No 4, 853–886.

11 R. Edward Freeman, "Managing For Stakeholders: An Argument, Ten Principles, and Eight Techniques", Lecture Copenhagen Business School, November 2004. Also printed in R. Edward Freeman and S. R. Velamuri, "A New Approach to CSR: Company Stakeholder Responsibility" in A. Kakabadse and M. Morsing *Corporate Social Responsibility: Reconciling Managerial Strategies Towards the 21st Century* (London: Palgrave MacMillan 2006).

12 Paul Ricœur, *Soi-même comme un autre* (Paris: Le Seuil, 1990), 202.

13 Robert Philips, *Stakeholder Theory and Organizational Ethics* (San Francisco: Berrett-Koehler, Inc, 2003).

14 Erhvervs- og Selskabsstyrelsen, *Overskud med omtanke. Praktisk guide til virksomheders samfundsengagement*, (Copenhagen: Erhvervs- og Selskabsstyrelsen, 2006), 11.

15 Ibid: 37f.

16 Ibid: 79f.

17 Ibid: 99.

18 Ibid: 113.

19 Ibid: 125.

20 Lynn Sharp-Paine, *Cases in Leadership, Ethics and Organizational Integrity. A Strategic Perspective* (Chicago: Irwin,, 1997).

21 Michael Hoffman, Dawn-Marie Driscoll and Mollie Painter-Morland, "Integrating ethics into organizational cultures" in *Business ethics. Facing up to the issues* (London: The Economist Books, 2001).

22 Guidelines, supra note 1, § 8A1.2.

23 Principles for Business, Caux-Roundtable, Haque, 1994. Reprinted in *International Business Ethics. Challenges and Approaches*, edited by Georges Enderle (London: Notre Dame University Press, 1999), 143-150.

25 A critical reply to this very comprehensive strategy for integrating business ethics, corporate governance, corporate social responsibility, and values-driven management for corporate citizenship may be that this seems to be some kind of monstrous "ethics bureaucracy" and that it is not really possible to implement in practice in organizations. To this argument, I would first refer to the importance of judgment. It is, indeed, the work of ethical judgment to find the right applications of ethical principles and values-driven management to particular organizations. As we have discussed, there may be many possible applications of ethical values in specific contexts, and it is important to be aware of the specific challenges of specific contexts of particular organizations. Secondly, I would like to reply that ethics in practice should not be interpreted as some kind of new bureaucratic legal structure of organizations. Ethics is related to values and ethics in organization should, therefore, be founded on personal capacities of judgment and evaluations of specific alternatives of action. This is what is described with my model of ethical formulation and competency within the framework for ethical judgment in organizations. In addition, what is is a framework that is applicable in concrete reality of organizational decision-making and strategic management.

References

Abdolmohammadi, Mohammad J. and Mark R. Nixon, "Ethics in the Public Accounting Profession" in *A Companion to Business Ethics* edited by Robert E. Frederick (Oxford: Blackwell Publishing (1999), 2002)

Allenbaugh, Mark H., "What's your water worth? Why we need Federal Sentencing Guidelines for corporate environmental crime?", *American University Law Review*, Volume 48, (1999), number 4., 927

Almond, Brenda and Bryan Wilson, *Values. A Symposium* (Atlantic Highlands, Humanities Press International, 1988)

Amidon, Debra M., *The Innovation Superhighway*, (Elsvier: Butterworth Heinemann, 2003)

Apel, Hans Otto, *Diskurs und Verantwortung* (Frankfurt am Main: Suhrkamp Verlag, 1988)

Arendt, Hannah, *Eichmann in Jerusalem - A Report on the Banality of Evil* (New York: Penguin Books, 1964)

Argandona, Antonio, "The Stakeholder Theory and the Common Good", *Journal of Business Ethics*, (1998), Vol. 17

Armstrong, Mary Beth, "Ethical Issues in Accounting" in Norman E. Bowie (ed.), *The Blackwell Guide to Business Ethics*, Basil Blackwell, Oxford 2002

Aristotle, *Ethics* in *The Complete Works of Aristotle*, edited by W.D. Ross in The Revised Oxford Translation, vol. 2, revised by J.O. Urmson and edited by Jonathan Barnes (Princeton: Princeton University Press, 1984)

Arrington, Robert L., "Advertising and Behavior Control", *Journal of Business Ethics 1* (1982): 3-12, reprinted in William H. Shaw & Vincent Barry: *Moral Issues in Business*, 7th edition (Belmont California: Wadsworth Publishing Company, 1998)

Badaracco Joseph Jr. and Richard F. Ellsworth, *Leadership and the Quest for Integrity* (Cambridge, Massachusetts: Harvard Business School Press, 1991)

Badaracco, Joseph Jr., *Defining Moments* (Cambridge, Massachusetts: Harvard Business School Press, 1998)

Bak, Christian, *Det etiske regnskab: Introduktion, erfaringer, praksis* (Copenhagen: Handelshøjskolens forlag, 1996)

Bakan, Joel, *The Corporation: The Pathological Pursuit of Profit and Power* (London: Constable, 2004)

Ballet, Jerôme and Françoise de Bry, *L'éthique de l'entreprise* (Paris: Éditions du Seuil, 2001)

Balzer, Philipp, Klaus Peter Rippe, Peter Schaber, *Experten Bericht, "Was heisst Würde der Kreatur?"* (Bern: Bundesamt für Umwelt, Wald und Landwirtschaft (BUWAL), 1997)

Bauman, Zygmunt, *Globalization: The Human Consequences*, (New York: Columbia University Press, 1999)

Bauman, Zygmunt, *Liquid Modernity, The Individualized Society* (London: Polity Press, 2000)

Beck, Ulrich, *Risikogesellschaft* (Frankfurt: Suhrkamp Verlag, 1986)

Beck, Ulrich: "Living Your Own Life in a Runaway World: Individualism, Globalisation and Politics" in *Global Capitalism*, edited by Will Hutton and Anthony Giddens, (New York: New Press, 2000)

Beck, Ulrich, *Power in the Global Age: A new political economy* (London: Polity Press, 2006)

Benson, George C.S., *Business Ethics in America* (Lexington, Massachusetts, Toronto Lexington Books, D.C Heath and Company, 1982)

Berger, Peter and Thomas Luckmann, *The Social Construction of Reality. A Treatise in the Sociology of Knowlegde* (New York: Doubleday, 1966)

Berman, Harold, "World Law", *Fordham International Law Journal*, Vol 18, No 5: 1619

Beyer, Peter, *Værdibaseret ledelse. Den ældste vin på nye flasker*, 2 udgave (Copenhagen: Forlaget Thomson, 2006)

Bloom, Helen, Roland Calori, Philippe de Woot, *Euromanagement. A New Style for the Global Market. Insights from Europe's Business Leaders*, The European Round Table for Industrialist and Groupe ESC Lyon (London: Kogan Page Limited, 1994)

Blowfield, Michael and Allan Murray, *Corporate Responsibility. A Critical Introduction* (Oxford: Oxford University Press, 2008)

Birch, David and George Littlewood, "Corporate Citizenship. Some Perspectives from Australia", *Journal of Corporate Citizenship*, 16 (2004)

Boardman, Calvin M. and Hideaki Kiyoshi Kato, "The Confucian Roots of Business Kyosei", *Journal of Business Ethics*, Volume 48, (2003), Number 4, 317-333

Boatright, John R., "Business Ethics and the Theory of the Firm", *American Business Law Journal*, Volume 34/2, (1996), Winter.

Boatright, John R., "Does Business Ethics Rests on a Mistake", Presidential Address to the Society of Business Ethics, 1998, reprinted in *Business Ethics Quarterly*, 1999

Boatright, John, "Globalization and the Ethics of Business", *Business Ethics Quarterly*, January 2000, Vol 10, no. 1.

Boatright, John R., *Ethics in Finance (Foundations of Business Ethics)* (Oxford: Basil Blackwell Publishers, 1999)

Boatright, John, "Justifying the role of the Shareholder" in *The Blackwell Guide to Business Ethics* edited by Norman Bowie (Oxford: Basil Blackwell, 2002)

Boatright, John R., *Ethics and the Conduct of Business*, Third Edition (New Jersey: Prentice Hall, 2003)

Bonnafous-Boucher, Maria, "Quelques enjeux philosophiques de la corporate governance: Le propriétisme et la théorie des parties prenantes" (Paris 2004)

Boltanski, Luc and Eve Chapello, *Le nouvel esprit du capitalisme* (Paris: Gallimard, 1995)

Bordum, Anders, *Det Etiske Regnskab - principper for ledelse mellem magt og konsensus* (Copenhagen: CBS-Ph.D. series: 1998-4; Copenhagen: Samfundslitteratur, 1998)

Bordum, Anders and Jacob Holm Hansen: *Strategisk ledelseskommunikation. Erhvervslivets ledelse med visioner, missioner og værdier* (Copenhagen: Jurist og Økonomforbundets forlag, 2005)

Boyer, André, editor, *L'impossible éthique des entreprises* (Paris: Éditions d'organisations, 2001)

Bowen, H.R., *The Social Responsibilities of Business Men* (1953)

Bowie, Norman, "The Moral Obligations of Multinational Corporations" in Steven Luper-Foy: *Problems of International Justice* (Boulder Colerado: Westview Press, 1988)

Bowie, Norman E., *Business Ethics. A Kantian Perspective* (Cambridge, Massachusetts: Basil Blackwell Publishers, 1999)

Bowie, Norman E., "A Kantian Approach to Business Ethics" in *A Companion to Business Ethics*, edited by Robert E. Frederick (Oxford: Blackwell Publishing (1999) 2002)

Bradley, F.H., *Ethical studies*, Oxford 1876 (Oxford: Clarendon Press, 1998)

Brenkert, Georges, "Marketing for the vulnerable" in *Perspectives in business ethics*, edited by Laura Pincus Hartman (Chicago: Irwin McGraw-Hill, 1998)

Brenkert, Georges, "Marketing Ethics" in *A Companion to Business Ethics* edited by Robert E. Frederick (Oxford: Blackwell Publishing (1999), 2002), 178-194

Brooks, Leonard J., *Business and Professional Ethics for Directors, Executives, and Accountants* (Toronto: Thomson, South-Western, 2003)

Buchanan, James, "The domain of constitutional economics" in *Constitutional Political Economy*, Vol 1.

Buchholz, Rogene A. and Sandra B. Rosenthal, "Social Responsibility and Business Ethics" in *A Companion to Business Ethics*, edited by Robert E. Frederick (Oxford: Blackwell publishing (1999), 2002)

Butten, J.A. and D. Birch, "Defining Corporate Citizenship: Evidence from Australia" in *Asia Pacific Business Review*, Vol. 11: 3, 293-308

Cadbury, Sir Adrian, *Report of the Committee on the Financial Aspects of Corporate Governance* (London: Gee & Co, Ltd, 1992)

Cane, Peter, *Responsibility in Law and Morals* (Oxford and Oregon: Hart Publishing, 2002)

Capron, Michel and Françoise Quairel-Lanoizeelée, *Mythes et réalités de l'entreprise responsable. Acteurs, Enjeux, Stratégies* (Paris: La Decouverte, 2004)

Carr, Albert, "Is Business Bluffing Ethical?", *Harvard Business Review*, 1968

Caroll, Archie B., "A Three Dimensional Conceptual Model of Corporate Performance", *Academy of Management Review*, Vol 4, (1979), no. 4.

Carroll, Archie B., "The pyramid of corporate social responsibility. Toward the moral management of organizational stakeholders", *Business Horizons* (July-August 1991), 39-48

Carroll, Archie B and Ann K. Buchholtz, *Business and Society. Ethics and Stakeholder Management* (Canada: South Western, 2002)

Carroll, Archie B. "Ethics in Management" in *A Companion to Business Ethics, Blackwell Publishing*, edited by Robert E. Frederick (Oxford: Blackwell Publishing (1999), 2002)

Carson, Thomas, "Friedman's theory of Corporate Social Responsibility", *Business and Professional Ethics Journal*, Vol 12 (1993), no 1.

Carson, Thomas L., "Ethical Issues in Selling and Advertising" in *The Blackwell Guide to Business Ethics* edited by Norman E. Bowie (Oxford: Basil Blackwell, 2002)

Castells, Manuel, *The Rise of Network Society, The Information Age, Economics, Society and Culture*, Volume I. (Oxford: Blackwell Publishers, 2000)

Castells, Manuel, "Information Technology and Global Capitalism" in *Global Capitalism*, edited by Will Hutton and Anthony Giddens (New York: New Press, 2000)

Castoriadis, Cornelius, *L'institution imaginaire de la société* (Paris: Éditions du Seuil (1975) 1999)

Caux Principles in *International Business Ethics*, edited by Georges Enderle (Notre Dame: Notre Dame University Press, 1999)

Cavanagh, S.J., Gerald F., "Political Counterbalance and Personal Values: Ethics and Responsibility in a Global Economy", *Business Ethics Quarterly*, January 2000, Vol. 10, no. 1: 43-51

Cavanagh, Gerald F., *American Business Values. A Global Perspective* (New Jersey: Prentice Hall, 2006)

Chauvenau, Alain and Jean-Jacques Rosé, *L'entreprise responsabile, Développement durable, responsabilité sociale de l'entreprise, éthique* (Paris: Editions Organisations, 2003)

Chittick, David R., "Financial Implications of Environmental Compliance" in *The Greening of American Business. Making Bottom-line Sense of Environmental Responsibility* (Rockville Maryland: Government Institutes Inc., 1992)

Clarkson, M.B.E., "Defining, Evaluating, and Managing Corporate Social Performance: The Stakeholder Management Model" in *Research in Corporate Social Performance and Policy,* edited by W.F. Frederich (Greenwich, Conn.: JAI Press, 1995), 331-358

Coase, Ronald, "The Nature of the Firm" (1937) in *The Nature of the Firm: Origins, Evolution and Development* edited by Oliver E. Williamson and Sidney G. Winter (Oxford: Oxford University Press, 1991)

Coff, Christian, Lise Christiansen Walbom and Eva Mikkelsen, "Forbrugere, etik og sporbarhed: om forbrugernes holdninger og handlinger på fødevareområdet" (Copenhagen: Center for ethics and law: 2005)

Comte-Sponville, André, *Le Capitalisme est-il moral? Sur Quelques ridicules et tyrannies de notre temps* (Paris: Albin Michel, 2004)

Cowton, Christopher J., "The Use of Secondary data in business ethics", *Journal of Business Ethics* 17 (1998): 423-434

Crane, Andrew and Dirk Matten*, Business Ethics. A European Perspective* (Oxford: Oxford University Press, 2004)

Ciulla, Joanne B., *The Working Life, The Promise and Betrayal of Modern Work* (New York: Three Rivers Press, 2000)

Danish Government, *The Globalization of Denmark*, Report (Copenhagen 2003)

Daly, Herman, *Beyond Growth* (Boston: Beacon Press, 1996)

Davidson, Donald, *Essays on Actions and Events*, Second Edition (Oxford: Oxford University Press, 2001)

Davies, Keith, "Can business afford to ignore its social responsibilities" (1960)

Davis, Keith, "What does a businessman owe society?" (1967)

De George, Richard, *Competing with Integrity in International Business* (New York and Oxford: Oxford University Press, 1993)

De George, Richard, *Business Ethics* (Upper Saddle River, New Jersey: Prentice Hall, 1999)

De George, Richard, "International Business Ethics" in *A Companion to Business Ethics* edited by Robert E. Frederick (Oxford: Blackwell Companions to Philosophy, Blackwell Publishing, 1999)

Desjardins, Joseph R. and Ronald Duska: "Drug Testing in Employment in *Contemporary Issues in Business Ethics*, 3ed, Belmont, Calif, Wadsworth 1996, reprinted in William H. Shaw and Vincent Barry, *Moral Issues in Business*, 7th edition (Belmont, California: Wadsworth Publishing Company, 1998)

DesJardins, Joseph R. and John J. McCall, *Contemporary Issues in Business Ethics*, Fourth Edition (California: Wadsworth, Thomson Learning, 2000)

Desjardins, Joseph R., "Business' Environmental Responsibility" in *A Companion to Business Ethics*, Blackwell Companions to Philosophy edited Robert E. Frederick (Oxford: Blackwell Publishers (1999), 2002)

Desjardins, Joseph R., "Environmental Responsibility" in Norman E. Bowie: *The Blackwell Guide to Business Ethics* (Oxford: Blackwell Publishers, 2002)

Dienhart, John W., *Business, Institutions and Ethics. A Text with Cases and Readings* (Oxford: Oxford University Press, 2000)

Djursø, Helene Tølbøll and Peter Neergaard, *Social ansvarlighed: Fra idealisme til forretningsprincip* (Copenhagen: Gyldendal Academica, 2006)

Dobson, John, *Finance Ethics* (New York: Rowman & Littlefield Publishers, 1997)

Donaldson, Thomas, "Rights in the Global Market" in *Business Ethics: The State of the Art*, edited by R. Edward Freeman (Oxford: Oxford University Press, 1989). Reprinted in Joseph R. Desjardins and John J. McCall, *Contemporary Issues in Business Ethics*, Fourth Edition (Belmont California: Wadsworth, Thomason Learning, 2000)

Donaldson, Thomas, "Moral Minimum for Multinationals" in *Ethics and International Affairs*, 1989, Volume 3.

Donaldson, Thomas, *The Ethics of International Business* (Oxford: Oxford University Press, 1991)

Donaldson, Thomas and Lee E. Preston, "The Stakeholder Theory of the Corporation: Concepts, Evidence and Implications", *Academy of Management Review*, Vol. 20, (1995)

Donaldson, Thomas and Thomas W. Dunfee: "Towards a Unified Conception of Business Ethics: Integrative Social Contract Theory in *Academy of Management Review*, Vol. 19 (1994), no 2.

Donaldson, Thomas and Thomas W. Dunfee, *Ties that Bind. A Social Contracts Approach to Business Ethics* (Boston Massachusetts, Harvard Business School Press, 1999)

Donaldson, Thomas, Patricia H. Werhane and Margaret Cording: *Ethical Issues in Business. A philosophical Approach* (Upper Saddle River, New Jersey: Prentice Hall, 2002)

Driscoll, Dawn-Marie and W. Michael Hoffman: *Ethics Matters. How to Implement Values-Driven Management* (Waltham Massachusetts: Center for Business Ethics, Bentley College, 2000)

Drucker, Peter, *The concept of the corporation* (New York: John Day and The Mentor Executive Library, (1946) 1964)

Drucker, Peter, *Management. Tasks, Responsibilities, Practices* (Oxford: Butterworth, Heinemann, 1974)

Dubbink, Wim, "The fragile structure of free market society. The radical implications of corporate social responsibility", *Business Ethics Quarterly*, Volume 14, (2004), Issue 1: 23-46

Dunfee, Thomas W. and Thomas Donaldson, "Social Contract Approaches to Business Ethics: Bridging the "is-ought" gap" in *A Companion to Business Ethics*, edited by Robert E. Frederick (Oxford: Blackwell Publishing (1999) 2002), 38-56

Dworkin, Ronald: *Law's Empire* (Cambridge MA: Harvard University Press, 1986)

Dworkin, Ronald "Intrinsic Value. A false Foundation" in Tara Smith, *Viable Values, A Study of Life as the Root and Reward of Vitality* (New York: Rowman & Littlefield Publishers, 2000)

Dworkin, Ronald *Sovereign Virtue: The Theory and Practice of Equality* (Cambridge Massachusetts: Harvard University Press, 2000)

Dyhr, Villy, "De nye regnskaber", *Tidsskrift for arbejdsliv*, nr. 2 (1999):73-93

Elkington, John and Julia Hailes, *The green consumer guide: From shampoo to champagne: high-street shopping for a better environment* (London: Gollancz paperback, 1989)

Elkington, John, *Cannibals with Forks. The Triple Bottom Line of 21st Century Business* (Oxford: Capstone (1997), 1999)

Enderle, George, *International Business Ethics, Challenges and Approaches* (Notre Dame: University of Notre Dame Press, 1999)

Enderle, Georges, "Global competition and corporate responsibilities of small and medium-sized enterprises", *Business Ethics. A European Review*, 2004

Environmental Challenges to Business (Bowling Green: The Ruffin Series, No 2., A Publication of the Society for Business Ethics, Philosophy Documentation Center)

Erhvervs- og selskabsstyrelsen, *Nørby udvalgets rapport om Corporate Governance. God selskabsledelse i Danmark* (Copenhagen, 2001)

Erhvervs- og Selskabsstyrelsen, *Overskud med omtanke. Praktisk guide til virksomheders samfundsengagement*, (Copenhagen: Erhvervs- og Selskabsstyrelsen, 2006)

Etchegoyen, Alain, *La valse des ethiques* (Paris : Le Seuil, 1991)

Etizioni, Amartya, *The Moral Dimension. Towards a New Economics* (New York: Collier Macmillan, 1988)

European Commission, *Green Book: A European Framework for Corporate Social Responsibility* (Bruxelles, 2001)

European Commission. Directorate-General for Employment and Social Affairs, Industrial Relations and Industrial Change, Unit EMPL/D.1, *Promoting a European Framework for Corporate Social Responsibility, Green Paper* (Luxembourg: Office for Official Publication of the European Communities, 2001)

European Commission, *National public policies in the European Union* (Luxemburg: Office for official publications of the European communities, 2004)

Ewald, François, *L'Etat Providence* (Paris: Gallimard, 1984)

Falk, Richard, "The Making of Global Citizenship" in *Global Visions. Beyond the New World Order*, edited by Brecher et al. (Boston 1993)

Feinberg, Joel "Collective Responsibility (Another Defence)" in *Collective Responsibility. Five Decades of Debate in Theoretical and Applied Ethics*, edited by Larry May & Stacey Hoffman (New York: Rowman & Littlefield Publishers, Inc., 1991)

Ferrell, O.C., John Fraedrich and Linda Ferrell, *Business Ethics. Ethical Decision Making and Cases* (Boston and New York: Houthton Mifflin Company, 2005)

Fiorelli, Paul E., "Fine Reductions Through Effective Ethics Programs", *Albany Law Review*, Volume 56, (1992) Number 2

Fisher, Colin and Alan Lovell, *Business ethics and Values* (London: Prentice Hall, 2003)

Fisher, Colin and Allan Lovell, *Business Ethics and Values. Individual, Corporate and International Perspectives* (Pearson Education, Essex, UK: Prentice Hall, Financial Times, 2006)

Foucault, Michel, *Surveiller et punir* (Paris: Gallimard, 1973)

Foucault, Michel, *Naissance de la biopolitique* (Paris, Gallimard-Seuil, 2004)

Fox, Loren, *Enron: The Rise and Fall* (New Jersey: John Wiley & Sons, Inc, 2003)

Frederick, William C., "Anchoring Values in Nature: Towards a Theory of Business Values", *Business Ethics Quarterly*, Volume 2, 1992

Frederick, William C., "From CSR1 to CSR2: The Maturing of Business and Society Thought", *Business and Society, Vol. 33*, August 1994

Frederick, William C., *Values, Nature and Culture in the American Corporation* (New York: Oxford University Press, 1995)

Freeman, Edward R., *Strategic Management, A Stakeholder Theory of the Modern Corporation* (Boston Massachusetts Pitman Publishing Inc., 1984)

Freeman, R. Edward and W. Evan, "A stakeholder theory of the Modern corporation: Kantian Capitalism" in *Ethical Theory and Business*, edited by Thomas L. Beauchamp and Norman Bowie, 5th Edition (Englewood Cliffs, N.J., Prentice Hall, 1993), 75-84

Freeman, R. Edward, "The Politics of Stakeholder Theory: Some Future Directions" in *Business Ethics Quarterly*, (4) 4, 1994, 409-422

Freeman, Edward R., "The Stakeholder Corporation" in Laura Pincus Hartman: *Perspectives in business ethics*, (Chicago: Irwin McGraw-Hill, 1998)

Freeman, R. Edward and John McVea, "A stakeholder approach to strategic management" in *The Blackwell Handbook of Strategic Management*, edited by Michael A. Hitt, R. Edward Freeman and Jeffrey S. Harrison (New York: Blackwell Business, 2004)

Freeman, R. Edward and S. R. Velamuri, "A New Approach to CSR: Company Stakeholder Responsibility" in A. Kakabadse and M. Morsing *Corporate Social Responsibility: Reconciling Managerial Strategies Towards the 21st Century* (London: Palgrave MacMillan 2006)

French, Peter, *Collective and Corporate Responsibility* (New York: Columbia University Press, 1984)

French, Peter, "The Corporation as a Moral Person", *American Philosophical Quarterly*, Volume 16 (1979) Number 3

French, Peter, "Terre Gaste" in *The Corporation, Ethics and the Environment* edited by Hoffman, Frederick and Petry (New York, Westport, Conneticut, London: Quorum books, 1991)

Friedman, Milton, *Capitalism and Freedom* (Chicago: University of Chicago Press, 1962)

Friedman, Milton, "The Social Responsibility of Business is to increase its profits", *New York Times Magazine,* September 3, 1970. Reprinted in Scott B. Rae and Kenman, L Wong, *Beyond Integrity. A Judeo-Christian Approach to Business Ethics* (Grand Rapids Michigan: Zondervan Publishing House, 1996), 241-246

Friedman, Thomas L., *The Lexus and the Olive Tree* (New York: Ferrar, Straus, Giroux, 1999)

Frey, Donald E., "Individual Economic Values and Self-Interest: The Problem in Puritan Ethics", *Journal of Business Ethics*, Oct. 1998

Fukuyama, Francis, *The End of History and the Last Man* (New York: The Free Press, 1992)

Fukuyama, Francis, *Trust, The Social Virtues and the Creation of Prosperity* (New York: The Free Press, 1995)

Fukuyama, Francis, *State Building. Governance and World Order in the Twenty-First Century* (London: Profile Books, 2004)

Garriga, Elisabeth and Domènec Melé, "Social Responsibility: Mapping the Territory", *Journal of Business Ethics*, 53 (2004), 51-71

Gauthier, David, *Morals by Agreement* (Oxford: Clarendon Press and University Press, 1986)

Giddens, Anthony, *Runaway World. How Globalization is reshaping our lives* (London: Routledge, 1999)

Gilbert, Daniel R., Jr., *Ethics through Corporate Strategy* (Oxford: The Ruffin Series of Business Ethics, Oxford University Press, 1996)

Gilbert, Larry, "International Business Ethics in Western Europe", Paper presented at the 1999 International Conference of Academy of Business Administrative Science (Spain; Barcelona, 1999)

Gilligan, Carol, *In a Different Voice* (Cambridge Massachusetts: Harvard University Press, 1982)

Gini, Al., *My Job, My Self, Work and the Creation of the Modern Individual* (Chicago: Routledge, 2000)

Goodpaster, Kenneth, "Business ethics and Stakeholder Analysis", *Business Ethics Quarterly*, Number 1: 53-73

Goodpaster, Kenneth and T. Holloran, "In defense of a Paradox", *Business Ethics Quarterly*, Number 4: 423-30

Goodpaster, Kenneth E. and John B. Matthews, Jr., "Can a Corporation have a Conscience" Reprinted in *Harvard Business Review on Corporate Responsibility* (Cambridge Massachusetts: Harvard Business School Press, 2003)

Goldberg, Ray A. and James M Beagle, "Royal Ahold NV: A Global Food Provider", Harvard Business School Case 902-416

Gramstrup, Marianne, "Novo og Miljøet", *Ledelse og erhvervsøkonomi*, Årgang 59 (1995)

Green, Ronald M., *The Ethical Manager: A new Method for Business Ethics* (New York: Macmillan, 1994)

Grey, R and D. Owen, *Accounting and Accountability Changes and Challenges in Corporate Social and Environmental Reporting* (London: Prentice Hall, Europe, 1996)

Grey, Christopher and Hugh Willmott, *Critical Management Studies* (Oxford: Oxford University Press, 2005)

Griffin, J.J and J.F. Mahon: "The Corporate Social Performance and Corporate Financial Performance Debate: Twenty Five Years of Incomparable Research", *Business and Society*, Vol. 36. n. 1. 1997, 1-31

Grunig, James E. and Todd Hunt, *Managing Public Relations* (Orlando: Harcourt Brace Janovich College Publishers, 1984)

Habermas, Jürgen, *Strukturwandel der Öffent-lichkeit* (Frankfurt am Main: Suhrkamp Verlag, 1990)

Habermas, Jürgen (ed.), *Hermeneutik und Ideologiekritik*, edited by (Frankfurt am Main:Suhrkamp Verlag, 1971)

Habermas, Jürgen, *Theorie des kommunikativen Handelns I-II* (Frankfurt: Suhrkamp Verlag, 1981)

Habermas, Jürgen, "Die Postnationale Konstellation und die Zukunft der Demokratie, in Jürgen Habermas, *Die Postnationale Konstellation* (Frankfurt am Main: Suhrkamp Verlag: 1998, 91-169)

Habisch, André, Jan Jonker, Martina Wegner and René Schmidpeter, *Corporate social responsibility across Europe*,(Berlin: Springer Verlag, 2005)

Hagedorn-Rasmussen, Peter, Søren Jagd and Jacob Dahl Rendtorff, *Fra værdiledelse til værdier i arbejdslivet*. (From values-driven management to values in the worklife). Rapport til LO projekt støttet af EUs Socialfond, Institut for samfundsvidenskab og erhvervsøkonomi (RUC 2006)

Hansen, Jørgen Valter, Thomas Riise Johansen and Teddy Wivel, *Corporate Governance- Et bud på danske bestyrelsers rolle* (Copenhagen: Forlaget Thomson)

Hardt, Michael and Antonio Negri, *Empire* (Cambridge Massachusetts: Harvard University Press, 2001)

Harste, Gorm, *Kompleksitet og Dømmekraft* (Aalborg: Nordic Summer University, 1994)

Hartman, Erwin M., *Organizational ethics and the good life* (Oxford: Oxford University Press, 1995)

Hartman, Laura Pincus, *Perspectives in business ethics* (Chicago: Irwin McGraw-Hill, 1998)

Harvard Business Review on Corporate Governance (Cambridge, Massachusetts: Harvard Business School Press, 2000)

Hatch, Mary Jo and Majken Schultz, *Organizational Identity. A Reader* (Oxford University Press: Oxford Management Studies, 2004)

Hayek, F.A., *The Road to Serfdom* (1944) (London: Routledge Paperbacks, 1997)

Hayek, F.A., "The Corporation in a Democratic Society: In Whose Interest Ought It and Will It Be Run" (1960), Reprinted in H. Igor Ansoff (ed.): *Business Strategy* (London: Penquin Modern Management Readings, 1969

Hayek, F.A., *Law, legislation and liberty. A new statement of the liberal principles of justice and political economy*, including Vol 1: *Rules and order*, Vol 2: *The mirage of social justice*, Vol 3: *The political order of a free people*, (London: Routledge, (1983), 1998)

Held, David and Anthony McGrew, *The Global Transformation Reader. An introduction to the globalization debate* (London: Polity Press, 2002)

Hendry, John, *Between Enterprise and Ethics. Business and Management in a Bimoral Society*, (Oxford: Oxford University Press, Oxford 2003)

Hofstede, Geert, *Cultures and Organizations: Software of the Mind* (New York: McGraw-Hill, 1997)

Hoffman, W. Michael "Business and Environmental Ethics", *Business Ethics Quarterly* 1991

Hoffman, W. Michael, Robert Frederick and Edward S. Petry (editors), *The Corporation, Ethics and the Environment* (Westpoint, Connecticut, London: Quorum Books, New Port, 1990)

Hoffman, Michael, Dawn-Marie Driscoll and Mollie Painter-Morland, "Integrating ethics into organizational cultures" in *Business ethics. Facing up to the issues* (London: The Economist Books, 2001)

Holley, David M., "A Moral Evaluation of Sales Practices", *Business Ethics and Professional Ethics Journal 5* (1987), reprinted in William H. Shaw & Vincent Barry, *Moral Issues in Business*, 7th edition (Belmont, California: Wadsworth Publishing Company, 1998)

Holmström, Susanne, *Grænser for ansvar - Den sensitive virksomhed i det refleksive samfund* (Roskilde: Center for værdier i virksomheder, Skriftserie, RUC 5/2004)

Hsieh, Nien-hê, "The obligations of transnational corporations: Rawlsian justice and the duty of assistance", *Business ethics Quarterly*, Volume 14, Issue 4, 643-661.

Huntington, Samuel P., *The Clash of Civilizations and the Remaking of the World Order* (New York: Touchstone Book (1996), 1998)

Hutton, Will and Anthony Giddens, *Global Capitalism* (New York: New Press, 2000)

International Labour Organization, *A Guide to Tripartite Declaration of Principles Concerning Multinational Entreprises programme* (Geneva: ILO, 2002)

Izraeli, Dove and Mark S Schwartz, "What Can We Learn From the U.S. Federal Sentencing Guidelines for Organizational Ethics" in *Journal of Business Ethics* 17, (1998)

Jensen Michael, "A Theory of the Firm, governance, residual claims and organizational forms", *The Journal of Financial Economics,* 1976

Jensen, Michael C., "Value Maximization, stakeholder theory and the corporate objective function", *Business Ethics Quarterly*, Volume 12, (2002), Issue 2.

Jensen, Michael C., "Value Maximization, stakeholder theory and the corporate objective function" in *Unfolding Stakeholder Thinking*, edited by J. Andriof (New York: Greenleaf Publishing, 2002)

Jeurissen, Ronald, "Institutional Conditions of Corporate Citizenship" in *Journal of Business Ethics 53*: (2004), 87-96

Joas, Hans, *The Gensis of Values* (Chicago University of Chicago Press, 2000)

Jonas, Hans, *Das Prinzip Verantwortung* (Frankfurt am Main: Insel Verlag, 1979)

Jones, Thomas M., "Instrumental Stakeholder Theory: A Synthesis of Ethics and Economics", *Academy of Management Review*, Vol. 20, (1995), No 2.

Jones, Thomas M., Andrew C. Wicks and R. Edward Freeman, "Stakeholder Theory: The State of the Art" in *The Blackwell Guide to Business Ethics*, edited by Norman Bowie, (Oxford: Blackwell Publishers, 2002), 19-38

Joseph, Joshua, "Integrating Ethics and Compliance Programs. Next Steps for Successful Implementation and Change" (Washington DC: ERC Fellows Program, Ethics Resource Center, 2001)

Kant, Immanuel, *Kritik der praktischen Vernuft* (1784) (Hamburg: Felix Meiner Verlag, 1985)

Kant, Immanuel, *Grundlegung zur Metaphysik der Sitten* (1785) (Hamburg: Felix Meiner Verlag, 1999)

Kant, Immanuel, *Metaphysik der Sitten* (1797) in Immanuel Kant, *Werke*, Band IV (Darmstadt, 1983)

Kant, Immanuel, *Kritik der Urteilskraft* (1794) (Frankfurt: Suhrkamp Werkausgabe, 2004)

Kant, Immanuel, *Gesammelte Werke* (Frankfurt: Suhrkamp Verlag, 1972)

Kant, Immanuel, "Zum Ewigen Frieden" in *Werke in Sech Bänden* (Darmstad: Wissenschaftliche Buchgesellschaft, 1983)

Kaplan, Jeffrey M., Joseph E. Murphy and Winthrop M. Swenson, *Compliance Programs and the Corporate Sentencing Guidelines, Legal Manual* (New York, 1994-2002)

Kaplan, Jeffrey F., "The Sentencing Guidelines: The First Ten Years", *Ethikos*, November/December 2001

Katz, J.P., D.L. Swanson and L.K. Nelson and Diana Swanson, "Toward an Integrative Theory of Business and Society: A Research Strategy for Corporate Social Performance", *Academy of Management Review* 24 (3) (1999): 521-596

Katz, J.P., D.L. Swanson and L.K. Nelson, "Culture-based expectations of corporate citizenship. A proposal framework and comparison of four cultures", *The international Journal of Organizational Analysis*, Vol. 9. (2001), No 2., 149-171.

Kemp, Peter Mette Lebech & Jacob Rendtorff, *Den bioetiske vending* (Copenhagen: Spektrum, 1997)

Kemp, Peter, "Bæredygtighedens etik" in *Dansk naturpolitik i bæredygtighedens perspektiv* (Copenhagen: Naturrådet, 2000)

Kemp, Peter, *Genteknologi og etik: konventioner ved Peter Kemp og Kjersti Lunde,* Biotik-litteratur (Copenhagen: 2001)

Kirkeby, Ole Fogh, *Ledelsesfilosofi, et radikalt normativt perspektiv* (Copenhagen: samfundslitteratur, 1997)

Kjonstad, B. and H. Willmott, "Business Ethics: Restrictive or Empowering", *Journal of Business Ethics*, 1995, Vol 14.

Klein, Hans (ed.): *Case Method. Research and Application, Selected Papers of the Sixth International Conference on Case Method and Case Method Application,* (Waltham, MA: Bentley College, 1989)

Klein, Naomi, *No Logo. Taking Aim at the Brand Bullies* (New York: Picador, Saint Martins Press, 2000)

Knudsen, Hanne, "Licens til kritik – og andre måder at bruge værdier på i organisationer" in *Offentlig ledelse i managementstaten,* edited by D. Pedersen (Copenhagen: Samfundslitteratur, 2004)

Kohlberg, Lawrence, *Stages in the Development of Moral Thought and Action* (New York Holt Rinehart and Winston, 1969)

Kohlberg, Lawrence, *Essays in Moral Development, Volume 2, The Psychology of Moral Action,* (New York: Free Press, 1994)

Korton, David C., *When Corporations rule the World* (San Francisco: Kumarian Press, Berrett-Koehler Publishers, 1995)

Kunde, Jesper, *Corporate Religion. Building a strong company through personality and corporate soul,* Prentice Hall (London: Pearson Education, 2000)

Küng, Hans, *Projekt Weltethos* (München/Zürick, 1990).

Küng, Hans, *Weltethos für Weltpolitik und Weltwirtschaft* (München/Zürick 1995)

Krenchel, Jens Valdemar and Steen Thomsen, *Corporate governance i Danmark. Om god selskabsledelse i et dansk og internationalt perspektiv* (København: Dansk Industri, 2004)

Larsen, Øjvind, *Den samfundsetiske udfordring* (Copenhagen: Hans Reitzels forlag, 2005)

Laufer, William S.,"Corporate Bodies and Guilty Minds", *Emory Law Journal,* Vol 43 (1994): 648-730

Laufer, William S., "Integrity, Diligence, and the Limits of Good Corporate Citizenship", *American Business Law Journal,* Volume 34/2 (1996)

Laufer, William S., "Corporate Liability, Risk Shifting and the Paradox of Compliance" in *Vanderbilt Law Review, Vanderbilt University School of Law,* Volume 52, (1999), October.

Laufer, William S. and Alan Strudler, "Corporate Intentionality, Desert, and Variants of Vicarious Liability in *American Criminal Law Review,* Volume 37, (2000), Number 4.

Latouche, Serge, *Justice sans limites: Le défi éthique dans une économie mondialisée* (Paris: Fayard, 2003)

Laustsen, Carsten Bagge and Jacob Dahl Rendtorff, *Ondskabens banalitet. Om Hannah Arendts Eichmann i Jerusalem* (Copenhagen: Museum Tusculanums Forlag, 2002)

Le Goff, Jean-Pierre, *Le mythe de l'entreprise* (Paris: La Decouverte, 1995)

Le Roy, Fréderic and Michel Marchesnay, editors, *La responsabilité sociale de l'entreprise. Mélanges en l'honneur du professeur Roland Pérez* (Paris : Management et société, éditions EMS, 2005)

Leisinger, Klaus M., „Globalisering, Minima Moralia und die Verantwortung multinationer Unternehmen"in *Unternehmensethik und die Transformation des Wettbewerbs,* edited by Brij Nino Kumar, Margit Osterloh und Georg Schreyögg., Schaffer/Poeschel 1999

Lévinas, Emmanuel, *Totalité et infini, Essai sur l'extéorité* (La Haye: M. Nijhoff, 1961)

Levy, David L. and Peter J. Newell, *The Business of Global Environmental Governance* (Cambridge MA: MIT Press, 2005)

Levitt, Theodore, "Marketing Myopia", reprinted in Ben M. Enis and Keith K. Cox, *Marketing Classics. A selection of influential articles* (Boston: Allyn and Bacon, 1991)

Levitt, Theodor, "The Morality of Advertising", *Harvard Business Review 48* (1970) July-August,84-92) reprinted in William H. Shaw and Vincent Barry, *Moral Issues in Business*, 7th edition (Belmont, California: Wadsworth Publishing Company, 1998).

Lipovetsky, Gilles, "Les noces de l'éthique et du business", *Le Débat*, numéro 67, (1991), novembre-decembre, 145-167

Lipovetsky, Gilles, *Le Crepuscule du devoir. L'éthique indolores des nouveaux temps démocratiques* (Paris: Gallimard, 1992)

Lipovetsky, Gilles, *Le bonheur paradoxal. Essai sur la société d'hyperconsommation* (Paris: Gallimard, 2005)

Lippke, Richard L., "Work, Privacy and Autonomy", *Public Affairs Quarterly 3* (April 1989) reprinted in William H. Shaw and Vincent Barry, *Moral Issues in Business*, 7th edition, (Belmont, California: Wadsworth Publishing Company, 1998)

Lippke, Richard L., "Advertising and the Social Conditions of Autonomy", *Business and Professional Ethics Journal* 8 (1989), reprinted in William H. Shaw & Vincent Barry: *Moral Issues in Business*, 7th edition (Belmont, California Wadsworth Publishing Company, 1998)

Lyttle, Jim, "The effectiveness of humor in persuasion: The case of business ethics training", *Journal of General Psychology*, April 2001.

Locke, John, *An Essay concerning Human Understanding* (5th Ed.) (Oxford: Clarendon Press (1689), 1975)

Logsdon, Jeanne M. and Donna J. Wood, "Business Citizenship: From domestic to global level of analysis", *Business Ethics Quarterly*, Volume 12, Issue 2

Logsdon, Jeanne M. and Donna J. Wood, "Global Business Citizenship and Voluntary Codes of Ethical Conduct", *Journal of Business Ethics* (2005) 59: 55-67.

Lomborg, Bjørn, *The Skeptical Environmentalist* (Cambridge: Cambridge University Press, 2001)

Lorsch, Jay W., "Empowering the Board", *Harvard Business Review on Corporate Governance*, 2000

Maccio, Charles, *Exercer une responsabilité* (Lyon: Savoir communiquer, Chronique sociale, 2001)

Machan, Tibor R., "Business Ethics in a Free Society" in *A Companion to Business Ethics* edited by Robert E. Frederick (Oxford: Blackwell Publishing (1999), 2002)

Maesschalck, Marc, L'éthique professionnelle et som champ de compétence " in R. Cobbeaut & M. Maesschalck, "Ethique des affaires et finalité de l'entreprise", Faculté des sciences économics, sociales et politiques (Louvain: Université catholique de Louvain, 2000)

Maggio, P. J. Di and W.W. Powell: "The Iron Cage Revisited: Functional Isomorphism and Collective Rationality in Organizational Fields", *American Journal of Sociology*, no. 48, (1983), 147-160

Mallin, Christina A., *Corporate Governance* (Oxford: Oxford University Press, 2004)

Margolis, Joshua D., "Toward an Ethics of Organizations", *Business Ethics Quarterly* 9: 619-638

Martin, Hans-Peter and Harald Schumann, *Die Globalisierungsfälle. Der Aufgriff auf Demokratie und Wohlstand* (Hamburg Rowolt Taschenbuch Verlag, 1998)

Martin, Mike W. "Whistleblowing: "Professionalism and Personal Life", *Business and Professional Ethics Journal vol 11*, no. 2 (1992) reprinted in William H. Shaw and Vincent Barry, *Moral Issues in Business*, 7th edition, (Belmont, California: Wadsworth Publishing Company, 1998), 401-402.

Matsuoka, Toshio, "The Caux Roundtable Principles for Business: Presentation and Discussion" by Henri Claude de Bettignies, Kenneth E. Goodpaster, and Toshio Matsuoka in *International Business Ethics. Challenges and Approaches* edited by Georges Enderle (London: Notre Dame University Press, 1999)

Matten, Dirk, Andrew Crane and Wendy Chapple, "Behind the Mask: Revealing the True Face og Corporate Citizenship", *Journal of Business Ethics* 45 (2003): 109-12

Matten, Dirk and Andrew Crane, "What is stakeholder democracy? Perspectives and Issues", *European Journal of Business Ethics*, Volume 14, (2005), Number 1, 6-13

Matten, Dirk and Andrew Crane, "Note: Corporate Citizenship: Toward an extended theoretical conceptualization" in *Academy of Management Review* (2005), Vol 30, No 1: 166-179

Maurice, Jack, *Accounting Ethics* (London Pearson, Professional Limited, Pitman Publishing, 1996)

McAdams, Tony with contributing authors James Freemann and Laura P. Hartman, *Law, Business and Society*, Six Edition (Boston: McGraw-Hill Higher Education, Chapter 10, 2000)

McAlister, Debbie Thorne, O.C. Ferrell and Linda Ferrell, *Business and Society, A Strategic Approach to corporate social responsibility* (Boston: Houghton Mifflin Company, Boston 2005)

McCall, John J., "Participation in Employment" in Joseph R. Desjardins and John J. McCall: *Contemporary Issues in Business Ethics*, 3ed, Belmont, Calif, Wadsworth 1996, reprinted in William H. Shaw and Vincent Barry, *Moral Issues in Business*, 7th edition, (Belmont, California: Wadsworth Publishing Company, 1998)

McIntosh, Malcolm, Deborah Leipziger, Keith Jones, Gill Coleman, *Corporate Citizenship, Successful Strategies for responsible companies* (London: Financial Times, Pitman Publishing, 1998)

Megone, Chris and Simon J. Robinson (eds.): *Case Histories in Business Ethics* (London: Routledge, 2002)

Meyer, J. W. and B. Rowan: "Institutionalized Organizations: Formal Structure as Myth and Ceremony", *American Journal of Sociology*, Vol. 83, (1997), no. 2, 340-363

Midttum, Atle, "Business Ethics and the Logic of Competition: Is there a Scope for the Moral Firm". Unpublished Paper (EBEN conference, 1999)

Milgram, Stanley, *Obedience to Authority: An Experimental View*, (New York: Harpercollins, 1974)

Millstone, Sacha and Ferris Baker Watts, "Effect on the Green Movement on Business in the 1990s" in *The Greening of American Business. Making Bottom-line Sense of Environmental Responsibility* (Rockville Maryland: Government Institutes Inc., 1992)

Mintzberg, Henry, *The Rise and Fall of Strategic Planning* (London: Pitman Publishing, 1994)

Mintzberg, Henry, *Managers not MBAs. A Hard Look on the Soft Practice of managing and management development*, (San Francisco: Prentice Hall, 2004)

Mintzberg, Henry, Robert Simons and Kunal Basu, "Beyond Selfishness", *Sloan Management Review*, Vol 44 (2002), No. 1: 67–74

Mirvis, Philip and Brandley Googins, "Stages of Corporate Citizenship", *California Management Review*, Vol 48 (2006), no 2., Winter

Mittchell, Ronald K., Bradley R. Agle and Donna S. Wood, "Toward a Theory of Stakeholder Identification and Salience: Defining the Principle of Who and What really counts", *Academy of Management Review*, Vol 22, (1997), No 4, 853–886

Monks, Robert A. G. and Nell Minow, *Corporate Governance*, Third Edition (Oxford: Blackwell Publishing, 2004)

Moon, Jeremy Andrew Crane, and Dirk Matten, "Can Corporations be Citizens? Corporate Citizenship as a Metaphor for Business Participation in Society", *Business Ethics Quarterly*, Volume 15, Issue 3: 429-453

Morgan, Gareth, *Images of organization* (London: Sage publications, 1997)

Moriarty, Jeffrey, "On the Relevance of Political Philosophy to Business Ethics", *Business Ethics Quarterly* Volume 15, Issue 3.

Morsing, Mette, *Den etiske praksis – En introduktion til det etiske regnskab* (Copenhagen: HandelsHøjskolens forlag, 1991)

Morsing, Mette and Peter Pruzan, "Values-based Leadership" in *Ethics in the Economy. Handbook of business ethics* edited by L. Zsolnai, (Oxford: Peter Lang, 2002), 253-293

Morsing, Mette, "Værdier i danske virksomheder – skitse af et fænomen", Copenhagen Business School, 2003

Morsing, Mette and Christina Thyssen (editors), *Corporate Values and Responsibility. The Case of Denmark* (Copenhagen: Samfundslitteratur, 2003)

Murphy, Patrick E., *Eighthy Exemplary Ethics Statements* (Notre Dame: University of Notre Dame Press, 1998)

Murphy, Patrick E., "Ethics in Advertising" (University of Santa: Unpublished paper, 2001)

Murphy, Patrick E., "Marketing Ethics at the Millenium: Review, Reflections, and Recommendations" in *The Blackwell Guide to Business Ethics,* edited by Norman E. Bowie (Oxford: Basil Blackwell, 2002)

Mølvadgaard, Kjeld and Ove Nielson, "Social ansvarlighed i danske virksomheder" in *Social ansvarlighed. Fra idealisme til forretningsprincip* edited by Helene Tølbøll Djursø og Peter Neergaard (Copenhagen: Academica, 2006)

Mølvadgaard, Kjeld and Ove Nielsen, "Det sociale ansvar og det rummelige arbejdsmarked" in *Social ansvarlighed. Fra idealisme til forretningsprincip* edited by Helene Tølbøll Djursø og Peter Neergaard (Copenhagen: Academica, 2006)

Neuman, W. Lawrence: *Social Science Research Methods. Qualitative and Quantitative Approaches.* Fifth Edition (Boston and New York: Pearson Education, 2003)

Nickel, James W., *Making Sense of Human Rights* (Berkeley: University of California Press, 1987)

Nielsen, Klaus and Ove K. Pedersen (eds.): *Forhandlingsøkonomi i norden* (Copenhagen: Jurist og Økonomforbundets Forlag, 1989)

Nielsen, Mie Femø, *Profil i offentligheden. En introduktion til Public Relations* (Copenhagen: Samfundslitteratur, 2001)

Nozick, Robert, *Anarchy, State and Utopia*, (New York: Basic Books, Incs Publishers, 1974)

Nygaard, Claus, *A Reader on Strategizing* (Copenhagen: Samfundslitteratur, 2001)

OECD, Les *Principes Directeurs à l'intention des entreprises multinationals* (Paris : OECD, Rapport Annuel, 2002)

Oliver, C., "Strategic Response to Institutional Processes", *Academy of Management Review*, Vol 16. (1991), no. 1., 145-179

Paine, Lynn Sharp, "Law, Ethics and Managerial Judgment", *The Journal of Legal Studies Education*, vol. 12, (1994) no 2.

Paine, Lynn Sharp, "Managing for Organizational Integrity", *Harvard Business Review*, 1994

Paine, Lynn Sharp, *Cases in Leadership, Ethics and Organizational Integrity. A Strategic Perspective* (Chicago: Irwin, 1997)

Paine, Lynn Sharp, *Valueshift. Why Companies Must Merge Social and Financial Imperative to Achieve Superior Performance* (New York: Mc-Graw-Hill, 2003)

Parum, Eva, *Strategisk kommunikation om ledelse. Et corporate og public governance perspektiv* (København: Handelshøjskolens forlag, 2006)

Pedersen, Esben Rahbek, *Between Hopes and Realities: Reflections on the Promises and Practices of Corporate Social Responsibility (CSR)* (Copenhagen: Copenhagen Business School PhD Series 17 2006)

Person, Christine M. and Mitroff, Ian I., "From crisis prone to crisis prepared: A framework for crisis management", *Academy of Management Executive*, Vol. 7 (1993), Issue 1: 48-59

Pfordten, Dietmar vd., *Ökologische Ethik* (Hamburg: Rowolt Taschenbuch Verlag, 1986)

Pfeiffer, Raymond S., *Why Blame the Organization. A Pragmatic Analysis of Collective Moral Responsibility*, (New York: Littlefield Adams Books, 1995)

Philips, Robert, "Stakeholder Legitimacy", *Business Ethics Quarterly*, Volume 13, (2003), Issue 1.

Philips, Robert, R. Edward Freeman and Andrew C. Wicks, "What stakeholder theory is not", *Business Ethics Quarterly*, Volume 13, 2003, Issue 4: 479-502

Philips, Robert *Stakeholder Theory and Organizational Ethics* (San Francisco: Berrett-Koehler, Inc., 2003)

Pine, Joseph B. and James H. Gilmore, *The Experience Economy. Work is Theatre and every Business is a Stage*. (Boston, Massachusetts: Harvard Business School Press 2005)

Popper, Karl F., *The Poverty of Historicism* (London: Routledge & Paul Kegan, 1957)

Pitt, Harvey L. and Karl A. Groskaumanis, "Minizing Corporate Civil and Criminal Liability: A second Look at Corporate Codes of Conduct" (New York: Fried, Frank, Harrris, Shriver & Jacobsen Law firm, 1989)

Porter, Michael E. and Mark R. Kramer, "The Competitive Advantage of Corporate Philanthropy" in *Harvard Business Review on Corporate Responsibility* (Harvard, Cambridge, Massachusetts: Harvard Business School Press, 2003)

Porter, Michael E. and Mark R. Kramer: "Strategy and Society. The Link between Competitive Advantage and Corporate Social Responsibility", *Harvard Business Review*, December 2006

Post, James E., Anne T. Lawrence and James Weber, *Business and Society, Corporate Strategy, Public Policy, Ethics* (New York: McGraw-Hill, Irwin, 2002)

Post, James E., "Global Corporate Citizenship: Principles to live and work by", *Business Ethics Quarterly*, Volume 12, Issue 2, pp. 143-153

Powell, Walter W. and Paul J. DiMaggio, *The New Institutionalism in Organizational Analysis* (Chicago: The University of Chicago Press, 1991)

Pruzan, Peter, "The Question of Organizational Consciousness: Can Organizations Have Values, Virtues and Visions?", *Journal of Business Ethics*, Vol.29 (2001), 271-284

Putnam, Robert B., *Bowling Alone. The Collapse and Revival of American Community* (New York: Touchstone, 2000)

O'Dwyer, Brenda, "Stakeholder Democracy: Challenges from social accounting", *European Journal of Business Ethics*, Volume 14, (2005), Number 1, January, 28-38

Rae, Scott B. and Kenman L. Wrong: *Beyond Integrity: A Judeo-Christian Approach to Business Ethics* (Michigan: Zondervan Publishing House, 1996)

Rae, André, "Diversity Stress as Morality Stress" in *Journal of Business Ethics* 14 (1995): 489-496

Rafalko, Robert J."Remaking the Corporation: The 1991 US Sentencing Guidelines" *Journal of Business Ethics*, 13 (1994): 625-636

Randlesome, Collin and William Brierly, Kevin Bruton, Colin Gordon, Peter King, *Business Cultures in Europe*, 2nd Edition (Oxford: Butterworth-Heinemann Ltd, 1993)

Rao, G. R. S., "The Ethics Agenda Facing the International Community" in *International Business Ethics. Challenges and Approaches* edited by Georges Enderle (London: Notre Dame University Press) 1999, 37-38.

Rawls, John, *A Theory of Justice* (Cambridge Massachusetts: Harvard University Press 1971)

Rawls, John, *Political Liberalism* (Cambridge Massachusetts: Harvard University Press 1992)

Rawls, John, *The Law of Peoples* (New York: Oxford University Press, 1999)

Rawls, John, *Justice as fairness. A Restatement* (Cambridge Massachusetts: Harvard University Press, 2001)

Regan, Tom, *Earthbound: Introductory Essays in Environmental Ethics*, (New York: Random House, 1984)

Rendtorff, Jacob Dahl, "Critical Hermeneutics in Law and Politics" in *Paul Ricœur in the Conflict of Interpretations*, edited by Lars Henrik Smith (Århus: Århus Universitetsforlag, 1996)

Rendtorff, Jacob Dahl, *Bioetik og Ret, Kroppen mellem person og ting* (Copenhagen: Gyldendal, 1999)

Rendtorff, Jacob Dahl and Peter Kemp, *Basic Ethical Principles in European Bioethics and Biolaw, Vol I-II* (Barcelona & Copenhagen: Center for Ethics and Law, 2000)

Ricœur, Paul, *Le conflit des interpretations* (Paris: Le Seuil, 1969)

Ricœur, Paul, *Du texte à l'action. Essais d'herméneutique II* (Paris: Le Seuil, 1986)

Ricœur, Paul, "La function herméneutique de la distanciation" in Paul Ricœur, *Du texte à l'action. Essais d'herméneutique II* (Paris: Le Seuil, 1986)

Ricœur, Paul, *Soi-même comme un Autre* (Katheleen Blamey, trans., *One Self as Another* (Chicago: University of Chicago Press, 1992)

Rittenberg, Larry E. and Patricia K. Miller, *How Sarbanes-Oxley Section 404 Works. Looking at the Benefits* (The ILA Research foundation, January 2005)

Rousseau, Jean-Jacques, *Du Contrat social ou Principes du droit politique* (Paris: Union Générale d'Éditions (1762) 1963)

Rosenau, J. and E-O Net Czempiel, *Governance without government, Order and change in world politics* (Cambrigde: Cambridge University Press, 1992)

Sandel, Michael, *Liberalism and the Limits of Justice*, (Cambridge: Cambridge University Press, 1982)

Sartre, Jean-Paul, *L'existentialisme est un humanisme* (Paris: Nagel, 1946)

Sartre, Jean-Paul, *L'Être et le Néant* (Paris: Gallimard, 1943)

Schwartz, Mark S. and Archie B. Carroll, "Corporate social responsibility: A Three domain approach", *Business Ethics Quarterly*, Volume 13, (2003), 503-530

Schein, Edgar H., *Organizational culture and leadership*, Second Edition (San Francisco Jossey-Bass Publishers, 1992)

Scherer, Andreas G. and Albert Löhr, "Verantwortungsvolle Unternemensführung im Zeitalter der Globalisierung – Einige kritische Bemerkungen zu den Perspektiven einer liberalen Weltwirtschaft" in *Unternehmensethik und die Transformation des Wettbewerbs*, edited by Brij Nino Kumar, Margit Osterloh and Georg Schreyögg., (Schaffer/Poeschel, 1999)

Schumpeter, Joseph, *Capitalism, Socialism and Democracy*, 3rd edition (London and New York: Routlegde, (1950) 1994)

Scott and Hart, *Organizational America* (Boston: Houghton, Mifflin Company Paper Back, 1979)

Scott, Richard W. *Institutions and Organizations* (London: Sage Publications, 1995)

Searle, John, *The Construction of Social Reality* (New York: The Free Press, 1995)

Sen, Amartya, *Development as Freedom* (New York: First Anchor Books Edition, 2000)

Serres, Michel, *Le contrat naturel* (Paris: Flammarion, 1991)

Shaw, William H. and Vincent Barry, *Moral Issues in Business*, 7th edition, (Belmont, California: Wadsworth Publishing Company, 1998)

Shiva, Vandana, "The World on the Edge" in Will Hutton and Anthony Giddens, *Global Capitalism* (New York: New Press, 2000)

Shue, Henry, *Basic Rights* (Princeton: Princeton University Press, 1982)

Singer, Peter, *Practical Ethics* (Cambridge: Cambridge University Press, 1993)

Smith, Tara, *Viable Values, A Study of Life as the Root and Reward of Vitality* (New York: Rowman & Littlefield Publishers, 2000)

Smith, Adam, *The Theory of the Moral Sentiments*, Cambridge: Cambridge Texts in the History of Philosophy, Cambridge University Press, (1759), 2002)

Smith, Adam, *An In Inquiry into the Nature and Causes of The Wealth of Nations* (New York: The Modern Library (1776), 2000)

Soles, David E., "Four Concepts of Loyalty", *The International Journal of Applied Philosophy 8* (Summer 1993) reprinted in William H. Shaw and Vincent Barry, *Moral Issues in Business*, 7th edition (Belmont, California: Wadsworth Publishing Company, 1998)

Solomon, Robert C.,*Ethics and Excellence, Cooperation and Integrity in Business* (New York: Oxford University Press, 1992)

Solomon, Robert C., "Business Ethics and Virtue" *A Companion to Business Ethics*, edited by Robert E. Frederick (Oxford: Blackwell Publishing, (1999), 2002)

Sparkes, Russell, *Socially Responsible Investments. A Global Revolution* (London: John Wiley & Sons, 2002)

Spence, Laura "Building a Focus for Business Ethics in Europe" (EBEN, 1999)

Starik, M., "Stakeholder Status for Non-Human Nature", *Journal of Business Ethics*, Vol. 14, (1995)

Strauss, Leo, *Natural Right and History*, (Chicago: University of Chicago Press, 1953). Leo Strauss, *The City and Man* (Chicago: University of Chicago Press, 1964)

Strong, Maurice, *Where on Earth are We going?* (New York and London: Texere, 2000)

Suchman, M.C., "Managing Legitimacy: Strategic and Institutional Approaches", *Academy of Management Review*, Vol. 20. (1995), no. 3.

Sullivan, Rory, (ed.) *Business and Human Rights. Dilemmas and solutions*, (London: Greenleaf Publishing, 2003)

Swanson, Diana, "Addressing a Theoretical Problem by Reorienting the Corporate Social Performance Model", *Academy of Management Review*, 20 (1) (1995): 43-64

Swanson, Diane L., "Toward an integrative theory of business and society: A research strategy for corporate social performance", *Academy of Management Review* Vol 24 (1999), No 3, 506-521

Sørensen, Mads P., *Den Politiske forbruger* (Copenhagen: Hans Reitzels Forlag, 2004)

Terris, Daniel, *Ethics at Work. Creating Virtue at an American Corporation* (Lebanon, US: Brandeis University Press, University Press of New England, 2005)

Thomsen, Steen, "Holdninger til corporate governance i dansk erhvervsliv", in *Corporate Governance i Danmark. Om god selskabsledelse i dansk og internationalt perspektiv*, edited by Jens Valdemar Krenchel and Steen Thomsen (Copenhagen: Dansk Industri, 2004)

Thompson, G.F., "Global Corporate Citizenship: What does it mean?", *Competition and Change*, Vol 9., No 2 (2005): 131-152

Thyssen, Ole, *Værdiledelse, Om organisationer og etik*, 2. reviderede udgave (Copenhagen: Gyldendal, 1999)

Torfing, Jacob, "Velfærdsstatens institutionelle forandring" in Klaus Nielsen (ed.): *Institutionel teori. En tværfaglig introduction* (Roskilde: Roskilde Universitetsforlag, 2005)

Toynbee, Polly, "Who's afraid of Global Culture" in *Global Capitalism*, edited by Will Hutton and Anthony Giddens, (New York: New Press, 2000)

Treviño, L. K., L. Hartman L. And M. Brown M., "Moral Person and Moral Manager: How executives develop a reputation for ethical leadership", *California Management Review*, 42 (4)

Ulrich, Peter and Thomas Maak: "Integrative Business Ethics – A Critical Approach", *CEMS Business Review* 2 (1997): 27-36

Ulrich, Peter, *Integrative Wirtschaftsethik. Grundlagen einer lebensdienlichen Ökonomie*, 2 Auflage (Stuttgart, Wien: Haupt, 1998)

United Nations, *The Global Compact. Report in Progress and Activities. July 2002-July 2003*, (New York: United Nations Global Compact Office, June 2003)

US Sentencing Commission, *Proceedings of the Second Symposium on Crime and Punishment in the United States: Corporate Crime in America. Strengthening the "Good Citizen Corporation"* (Washington D.C.: US Sentencing Commission, September 7-8, 1995)

Velasquez, Manuel, "Why Corporations are not Responsible for Anything they do" in *Collective Responsibility. Five Decades of Debate in Theoretical and Applied Ethics*, edited by Larry May and Stacey Hoffman (New York: Rowman & Littlefield Publishers, 1991)

Velasquez, Manuel, "International business, morality and the common good" in *Business Ethics Quarterly*, vol. 2, (July 1992) issue 1. Reprinted in Joseph R. Desjardins and John J. McCall, *Contemporary Issues in Business Ethics* (Belmont California: Fourth Edition, Wadsworth, Thompson Learning), 2000

Velasquez, Manuel G., *Business Ethics. Concept and Cases*, 5th edition (New Jersey: Prentice Hall, 2002)

Velasquez, Manuel,"Debunking corporate moral responsibility", *Business Ethics Quarterly*, Volume 13, Issue 4: 531-562.

Virilio, Paul, *Vitessse et politique* (Paris : Éditions Galilée, 1977)

Vallentin, Steen,"Socially responsible investing: Approaches and Perspectives" in *Værdier, etik og socialt ansvar i virksomheder. Brudflader og konvergens*, edited by Jacob Dahl Rendtorff (RUC: Center for Værdier i virksomheder, 2003)

Walzer, Michael, "Governing the Globe" in Michael Walzer, *Arguing about War* (New Haven & London Yale University Press, 2004)

Van de Ben, Bert and Ronald Jeurissen, "Competing Responsibly", *Business Ethics Quarterly*, Volume 15, Issue 2: 299-317

Waddock, Sandra,"Corporate Citizens: Stepping into the breach of society's broken contracts", *Journal of Corporate Citizenship* (2005)

Wayne, Norman and Chris MacDonald: "Getting to the bottom of the triple bottom line!", *Business Ethics Quarterly*, Volume 14, Issue 2, (2004), 243-262

Weber, Max, *The Protestant Ethics and the Spirit of Capitalism*, translated by Talcott Parsons from: Max Weber: *Die Protestantische Ethik und der Geist des Kapitalismus* (Allan & Unwin 1930). Reprinted with an introduction by Anthony Giddens (London: Unwin Paperbacks, 1987)

Weber, Max, (1903), *Wirtschaft und Gesellschaft. Grundriss einer verstehende Soziologie*, Mohr 5 auflage, Edition 1972, Tübingen 1976. English translation: *Economy and Society* (Berkeley: University of California Press, 1978)

Welford, Richard, *Environmental Strategy and Sustainable Development. The Corporate Strategy for the 21st Century* (London: Routledge, 1995)

Werhane, Patricia, *Persons, Rights and Corporations* (New York: Englewood Cliffs, 1985)

Werhane, Patricia, *Adam Smith and his legacy for modern capitalism* Oxford: Oxford University Press, 1991)

Werhane, Patricia H., "The moral responsibility of multinational corporations to be socially responsible" in Michael Hoffman et al. (eds.): *Emerging Global Business Ethics*, Quarum Books, Greenwood Publishing Group Inc., Westpoint 1994, 136-142.

Weiss, Joseph W., *Business Ethics. A Stakeholder and Issues Management Approach*, Third Edition (Canada: Thompson, SouthWestern, 2003)

Wheeler, David & Maria Sillanpää, *The Stakeholder Corporation. The Body Shop Blue Print for Maximizing Stakeholder Value* (London: Pitman Publishing, 1997)

White, Mark A., "Effect of the Green Movement on Investors" in *The Greening of American Business. Making Bottom-line Sense of Environmental Responsibility* (Rockville Maryland: Government Institutes Inc., 1992)

Willmott, Hugh, "Towards a New Ethics? The contributions of Poststructuralism and Posthumanism" and Hugo Letiche: "Business Ethics: (In) Justice and Anti-Law – Reflections on Derrida, Bauman and Lipovetsky" in *Ethics in Organizations*, edited by Martin Parker (London: Sage Publications, 1998)

Williams, Oliver F., "The UN Global Compact: The challenge and the promise", *Business Ethics Quarterly, Volume 14*, Issue 4, 2004

Williamson, Oliver E., *Market and Hierarchies: Analysis and Anti-trust Implications* (New York: Free Press, New, 1975)

Williamson, Oliver E., "The Economics of Governance: Framework and Implications", *Journal of Institutional and Theoretical Economics* Vol 140 (1984), 195-223

Williamson, Oliver, *The Economic Institutions of Capitalism* (New York: The Free Press, 1984)

Wolfensohn, James D., "Foreword" In *Perspectives on the New Economy of Corporate Citizenship*, edited by Simon Zadek, Niels Hojensgard and Peter Paynard (Copenhagen: The Copenhagen Centre, 2001)

World Commission on Environment and Development, *Our Common Future* (New York: Oxford University Press, 1987)

Wood, Donna, "Corporate social performance revisited", *Academy of Management Review* 16 (4) (1991): 691-718

Wood, Donna and R.E. Jones, "Research in Corporate Social Performance: What have we learned?", in *Corporate Philanthropy at the Crossroads*, edited by D.R Burlinggame and D.R. Young (Bloomington, Indiana: Indiana University Press, 1995), 41-85

Write, Jr., William H., *The Organization Man* (New York: A Clarion Book (1956), 1972)

Zadek, Simon, Peter Pruzan and Richard Evans, *Building Corporate Accountability* (London Earthscan, 1997)

Zadek, Simon, Niels Hojensgard and Peter Paynard, *Perspectives on the New Economy of Corporate Citizenship* (Copenhagen: The Copenhagen Centre, 2001)

Zadek, Simon, *The Civil Corporation. The New Economy of Corporate Citizenship* (London: Earthscan, 2001)

Zahle, Henrik, *Praktisk retsfilosofi* (Copenhagen: Carl Ejlers forlag, 2005)

Subject index

503

Name index